SLANDER
and
Sweet Judgment

The Memoir of
an Indiana Congressman

Andy Jacobs, Jr.
U.S. Representative, Retired

Guild Press of Indiana, Inc.

© 2000 by Andy Jacobs, Jr.

All rights reserved. No part of this book may be reproduced in any form without express permission from the publisher. For further information, contact

GUILD PRESS OF INDIANA, INC.
10665 Andrade Drive
Zionsville, Indiana 46077
(317) 733-4175

ISBN 1-57860-086-3
Library of Congress Catalog Card Number 00-110211

Also by Andy Jacobs, Jr.:

The 1600 Killers: A Wake-up Call for Congress
(Alistair Press, 1999)

The Powell Affair: Freedom Minus One
(Bobbs-Merrill, 1972)

For Kim, Andy, and Steve —

my greatest loves.

Contents

Acknowledgments vii
Preface x
Introduction: Tactics xii

chapter 1
Getting Started 1

chapter 2
"A" for Effort 53

chapter 3
Never Again is Always a Guess 74

chapter 4
The Sure Bet 114

chapter 5
Disturbance 133

chapter 6
Four More Years — of War 152

chapter 7
From Glass, a Stone's Throw to the Senate 163

chapter 8
Mapped Out 175

chapter 9
Interlude 191

chapter 10
The Second Time: A Long Way Around 201

chapter 11
Double De-fault 222

chapter 12
The Moral Equivalent 228

Contents (continued)

chapter 13
Rabbit Punch 250

chapter 14
Landslide 264

chapter 15
"Enter, Stage Right" 288

chapter 16
Hard Times 301

chapter 17
Reform 330

chapter 18
Big Money — Ask Not to do Much
    for Your Country 352

chapter 19
State of Vice Presidents 378

chapter 20
The Six-pack 401

chapter 21
The Governors 414

chapter 22
The Mirror 425

Epilogue: Knowing What I Knew Then 442

Acknowledgments

When I announced my retirement from Congress, I thanked all my constituents in general and several of them in particular. Those specified included my mother, Joyce Welborn Jacobs; my father, Andrew Jacobs, Sr.; my "best gal, real pal" who is my wife, Kim Hood Jacobs; my little sister, Marjorie Jacobs Landwerlen; my big sister, Wanda Jacobs Strange; and my super brother (-in-law), Tom Landwerlen.

Also of great help were Bob and Judy Aitken; Mary Kay and Mark Anderson; Mary Atwell; Sandy Augliere; Dr. Gary Ayres; Hoover Baker; Taylor Baker; Liz Bankowski; Steve and Sue Barnett; John Bartlett; Birch, Evan, and Susan Bayh; Jim Beatty; philologist Phyllis Beatty; Judy Barrett; Walter Bell; Jerry Bepko; Mary Berry; Bill Blomquist; Ken Bourke; Dr. Otis Bowen; Rozelle Boyd; Shel and Barbara Breskow; Jim Brower; Andrew and Rosa Lee Brown; Billi Breaux; Don and Ginny Burkert; Dr. Mary Busch; Catherine Butler; Max Brydenthal; Dan Carpenter; Shirley Chater; Pat Chavis; John and Eileen Christ; Cathy Clark; Tony and Phyllis Coelho; Ben Cole; Jim Corman; Bill Crawford; Grace Curry; John Day; Joe Deitz; Jack Dillon; Knute Dobkins; Winnie Donaldson; Keith Dooley; and Paul Duke.

Also, Don and Edie Edwards; Frank Edwards; Dehaviland Elder; Bob Elliott; Pat and Eleanor Endsley; Nancy Endsley; Chris Fager; Carolyn Fay; Will Fay; brainy *Indianapolis Business Journal* editor Ann Finch; Bessie Gasaway; Elton Geshwiler; Mart Gibson; Henri and Riley Gibson; Eugene Glick; John Godich; Charlotte Goode; Dr. Mason Goodman; Charlie and Margaret Gray; Pat Grant; Stan Gregg; Theresa Guise; David and Elizabeth Haas; Jud Haggerty; Jay Haggerty; Dick Hahn; M. C. Hansburough; Neal, Wanda, and Priscilla Holder; Buford Holt; Glen Howard; Dorothy Huffman; Mark Hulbert; Jed and Sidney Johnson; Mable Johnson; Frank Jose; Bob Kaiser; Bob and Kay Kelly; Margaret, Colleen, and Rob King; David and Maryann Kozak; John Krull; John Kyle; Nancy and Trixie Land; Dan Landwerlen; Greg Landwerlen; man-mountain Marty Landwerlen,

Tom Landwerlen; Aurelia Little; Dr. Frank Lloyd; Tom and Maryann Logue; Miles Loyd; Cynthia Lyons; Florence Mahoney; Louie Mahern; Lou Maiden; Charlie and Gwen Mains; Joe Mansini; Louise Marr; Arlene Martin; Dave Mason; Bill and Marc Matheny; Elsie Mason; Jack McCann; Coleman McCarthy; Virginia McCarty; Pat and Rachel McGeever; Doug McDaniel; Dan and Deb McGinn; Bob, Skip, Kevin, and Marni McKinney; Howard and Gussie Mills; Jeff and Jennifer Modisett; Owen Mullin; Marcia Munshower; and Bud Myers.

And finally, Helen Niehaus; Cathy Noe; Betty Nolan; Al Nolan; Jim and Helen Noland; Art Owens; Paul Page; Judy Pennington; Vic Pfau; Greg Porter; Max and Charlotte Potter; Francis and Ellen Quigley; Milana Riggs; Trisha Roberson; Joe and Theresa Romer; Liz Roslewicz; Dulcy Russell; Dick Sallee; Bill Schreiber; Luther and Rosie Searfoss; Betty Selden; Dal Sells; Jim and Sylvia Shannon; Phil Sharp; Sue Shively; Herb Shockney; Charlie Siegel; Greg Silver; Pete and Libby Singleton; Marie Smith; Jim Snyder; Andy Steffen; George Stuteville; Markey Sullivan; Owen Sweeney; Joe Summers; Steve Talley; Gary Taylor; Grace Thompson; Bob Traugot; Pat Ulen; Sargent Visher; John Preston Ward; Wilma Warren; Jim Warrum; Charlie Walton; Mary Ellen Weiland; Don and Liz Weiss; Patty Welch; Matt Welsh; David Wildes; Merle and Regina Wilgus; John V. Wilson; Ed Yates; and George and Sylvia Zazas.

But in the beginning there was James Porter Seidensticker, Jr., whose sobriquets were "Sei" and "Sidewinder." He was the first person, with the clear exception of myself, to broach the subject of my running for Congress. Having seen it all, Sei was the first to read it all in the manuscript, and made some much-needed corrections. I am indebted to the practiced eye of my friend.

Wonderfully talented fine-line editors Ann Finch and Megan McKee provided the finishing and right touches for this work.

Though I typed each word of this book, I had indispensable help from others, including this Toshiba laptop. I had never touched such technology before September 3, 1997. That was eight months after my departure from the United States House of Representatives where I had served Indianapolis for thirty years. Before that September, I had used the Smith Corona Sky Writer manual typewriter given to me by my father and taught to me by my mother when I was in high school. I used it for forty years for such tasks as taking the Indiana Bar Exam, letters in my law practice, and answering congressional mail.

The difference between this lap top and my old manual is like the difference between cutting our six-acre yard with the five-foot-swath Dixie

Acknowledgments ix

Chopper my wife and I bought from the Carmel Welding Company and cutting it with a nail clipper. After wearing out the letters of eight of these keys, I remain awed by this proof that "big things come in small packages."

I made about twelve calls to the information section of the Indianapolis Central Library and each time, with efficiency and, more important to me, with warm friendliness, the scholars there found a dozen obscure facts for me. I think they could find a red needle in a haystack on Mars.

Shelly Wells applied her considerable talent to the task of making excellent graphic art of my idea for the dust jacket.

My friend Andy Murphy, whose maiden name was Anderson and whose husband was Jim Murphy, was my literary agent. A well-received author in her own right, Andy played a significant role in getting this book into your hands.

Kim Hood Jacobs, popular Indianapolis television feature journalist, cartoonist, master seamstress, and epicurean wizard, made invaluable suggestions as she was kind and patient enough to read the manuscript. She was also kind and patient enough to marry me and share the joy of rearing our two sons, Andy and "Bronco" (Steven) Jacobs. I asked for and received much good advice from my very literary sister Marjorie Landwerlen, whose sons, my nephews, Tom, Marty, Dan, and Greg were willing to read or listen to passages of this work and tell me what was wrong. My sister Wanda Strange, an English teacher, was also helpful. *Indianapolis Star* feature writer Bill Shaw helped steer me away from some pitfalls of boredom. Another Shaw—Mark—legal scholar, author, and radio talk show host, did much the same for me. Indianapolis WTHR Channel 13's innovative television producer Kevin Finch enriched my understanding of historic events. James P. Maley made many useful suggestions, as did Loretta Raikes, the Honorable Julia M. Carson, Patty Welch, *Washington Post* columnist Coleman McCarthy, author and financial whiz Mark Hulbert, Gary Taylor, Louis Mahern, Jr., and James Ward Beatty.

One of the principal and principled inspirations for this work was the Honorable Frank O'Bannon, forty-seventh governor of Indiana. He, his wife, Judy, and his lieutenant governor, war-hero Joe Kernan, brought a refreshing wholesomeness and down-to-earth wisdom to the people of Indiana, of whom I am privileged to be one. The headline of the *Indianapolis Star/News* story that reported Frank's 1996 election was "NICE GUY FINISHES FIRST."

Amen.

PREFACE

If a feller has any flair for writin', there's nothin' like being fired off a big government job ta bring it out.

— Kin Hubbard's Abe Martin

Doesn't quite fit; when I retired from Congress in 1977 after serving Indianapolis there for thirty years, I wasn't fired. Moreover I have my doubts about any connection between a "flair" and my writing. But obviously I'm willing to give it a try. In fact, I tried twice before, the results being *The Powell Affair—Freedom Minus One,* and the first volume of this memoir, *The 1600 Killers* (Alistair Press, 217 pages).

This is a stories book, a book of stories, all true to the best of my knowledge. But the best of my knowledge is not good enough to guarantee absolute accuracy. "Tell it like it is." That was the slogan of the sixties—as well as of bad grammar—when people who are in *their* sixties at this writing were admonished not to "trust anyone over thirty."

But in the best reality we can perceive, no one can tell it the way it was, because it *wasn't* the way it was. It was the way each honest witness saw it. As one of those witnesses, one who had the privilege of seeing and hearing nearly forty years of significant American history up close, I have tried in this volume to tell it as I believe it was. And what I saw and heard from my privileged position is what I tell you in the following chapters. Most of the stories are in chronological order and the ones that flash forward or backward are, I think, in logical order. Much of the material is controversial and you will inevitably find some of it at variance with your own view. Where that occurs, I ask that you credit me with an honest difference of opinion. If you are primarily interested in the dramatic sweep of, and funny stories from my experiences in Congress, you might want to skip over a few paragraphs now and then because they are slightly technical. They are included in this work because I think they are of some importance to the historic record.

Slander and Sweet Judgment xi

The title of this book, *Slander and Sweet Judgment,* refers to dirty political campaigning and to money used by lobbyist, in the words of Robert Bolt, "to sweeten the judgment" of the United States Congress.

I think the title I wrote for this volume best describes its contents. If you disagree, please feel free to choose one of the following which also occurred to me:

> The Fall of the Chips in May
>
> Downloading the Cup
>
> Knowing What I Knew Then
>
> The Great American Novelty

I grew tired of repeatedly finishing this work "once and for all." So I clicked "Exit" on the laptop and breathed the sweet sigh that comes with closure. In a volume this size, it is probably inevitable that a story which could have been told is not told, and that a person who should have been mentioned was not. But, since I have mentioned my mother, oversights in this book, though regrettable, can't be too serious.

My mother says that if you can't say something nice about someone, you shouldn't say anything at all. And my country cousin Delmer Claise says he hates "to put a name on a bad story." So, except for cases of low-road campaigning and dastardly official deeds so prominent as to make the offender obvious, instead of naming names, I simply tell the tactics.

Introduction

TACTICS

You can't throw dirt without losing ground.
— Adlai Ewing Stevenson

"You take the high road, and I'll take the low road. And I'll get to Scotland before ye." To which might be added, "Nice guys always finish last." Always? Here's another: "Show me a good loser and I'll show you a real loser." The other side was probably written by Ted Sorenson: "Civility should not be confused for weakness."

Most of us exalt the term *gentleman*. But how often are we conscious of what it means? A gentleman is a man who is gentle. When a man began telling a vulgar, as distinguished from risque, story at a White House party, the president demurred only to be reminded by one of his aides that "there are no ladies present." To which the president replied, "There are gentlemen present." It was Ulysses Simpson Grant; you might say an officer *and a gentleman.*

I entered politics at age six when my father and some of his friends challenged the official Democratic organization in Indianapolis by filing for public offices in the spring primary. But my dad's group had another name for the organization. The challengers called themselves the Machine Busters.

For the good of the community, my father ran for prosecuting attorney. If he became prosecutor, he said, the political bosses would not chomp their cigars and make him look the other way on crimes that lined their pockets. In short, he would clean up the wide-open city and establish the decency that citizens say they savor. The nice guys versus the bad guys. Dad was one of the nice guys; he finished last.

During his primary campaign, he asked me if I'd like to pass out his brochures door-to-door around our block. For my super dad? Of course. I didn't run into any of the Democratic "machine" supporters on my appointed round, but I did run into a couple of ten-year-olds whose parents were strong Republicans. My brochures were expropriated and I went home with torn clothing and a black eye. It wouldn't be the last time I sustained physical injury in the civic arena, but I'm happy to report that the early encounter was the worst. Actually I never was quite sure whether my offense was being a Democrat or being six—or being on the wrong side of the block. I certainly don't mean to suggest in the slightest that all Democrats are nice and nonviolent.

For instance, in 1962 when the public opinion polls showed him enormously popular, President Kennedy came to Indianapolis to campaign for Birch Bayh, the Democratic challenger to veteran Hoosier Senator Homer Earl Capehart. Kennedy's disastrous support of the ill-fated Bay of Pigs invasion was behind him, but Senator Capehart was leading the congressional chant for direct U.S. military action against Cuba because, he said, Castro was harboring Russian intermediate-range nuclear missiles. Though quite aware of the missiles, Kennedy was not very interested in another invasion attempt. He had decided on a nuclear confrontation with the Soviets instead. But neither Senator Capehart nor the Young Americans For Freedom knew about that at the time.

The Young Americans For Freedom organization was, in essence, the farm league equivalent of *The* John Birch Society. They insisted that the commies be wiped out, but seldom, if ever, volunteered to help do the wiping. This fearless group—their personal plans included very little for them to fear—announced that they would picket Kennedy's visit at the Indianapolis Airport with placards declaring him to be a coward.

The announcement inspired two countermeasures from two different groups of Democrats, with neither aware of the other's planned approach to defending the president's honor.

My group consisted of Marine Corps infantry combat veterans. As lawyer for the group, I went to the Indiana Secretary of State and filed a not-for-profit corporation whose name was "Young American *Combat Veterans* For Freedom." Our group—corporation—made a huge sign designed for display in front of the ones held by our *war wimp* counterparts. Ours read: YOUNG AMERICAN COMBAT VETERANS FOR FREEDOM SUPPORT OUR PRESIDENT WHO ALSO FOUGHT FOR FREEDOM. If nothing else, we figured, it would be good for a laugh.

The other group of Democrats who sought to defend the President at the airport, mostly labor union members, was thinking more along the lines of the action taken by those ten-year-olds who had been displeased with the campaigning I did for my dad. I'm told that the young vocal chord freedom "fighters" were roughed up physically.

I leave it to you which approach was more effective. This much is unarguable: my buddies and I broke no law or anything else. Offhand, I'd say that the ten-year-old Republicans could be forgiven for acting like two-year-olds more easily than the grown men who acted that way. Labor has, with few exceptions, long since grown up. And even then, most union members were quite civilized. That is true of most Republicans and Democrats, too.

There are many stories about nice guys who finished first in politics and many about nice guys who finished last. An example of both is Senator Richard Lugar of Indiana. He ran for president in the Republican primaries of 1996 and was nearly alone in his refreshing civility. He lost. But he displayed that same civility throughout his time in Hoosier politics and usually finished first.

In 1996 I addressed the local Democratic slating convention of several hundred delegates and specifically commended Senator Lugar for bringing honor to our state by setting the refreshing example of courteous campaigning for the presidency. The entire convention of *Democrats* gave the senator a standing ovation, a real-life man-bites-dog event completely missed by the media.

I ran seventeen times for the United States House of Representatives and lost twice. Four of my opponents were sterling examples of candidates who chose the high road of campaigning. They included the former U.S. Attorney for the Southern District of Indiana, Don Tabbert; the sixteen-year mayor of Indianapolis, Bill Hudnut; and the kindly community activist, Mike Carroll, who lost his life in a plane crash while in the service of our community. The fourth was the courtly and wise economics professor Janos Horvath. With scant exception, my other opponents were a long way this side of primitive.

My fall opponent in 1970 was State Senator Dan Burton. Twelve years later when he finally achieved his dream of serving in Congress, having run this time in another district, Dan introduced me to his freshman Republican friends with these words, "This is Andy Jacobs. I ran a dirty campaign against him in 1970 and he beat the hell out of me—and I deserved it." How could you dislike a person who could say a thing like that? Besides, he didn't run a dirty campaign against me, anyway. It was aggressive and he was young, even, you might say, callow. But even then, he rejected an offer of substantial campaign money to join in a slander against me then being carried on by some elements of his party. And he has long since slipped into the Pantheon of highroad campaigners, who only in rare moments of petulance, utter ill-considered epithets. Beyond that he is a kind and caring person, sensitive to the suffering of others and tenderhearted about pets. He is utterly intellectually honest. If he says it, whether you agree with it or not, you can rest assured that he sincerely believes it. He is my friend.

The list of wonderfully civilized campaigners I have known is too long for this volume. It includes U.S. Representatives Jim Corman, Phil Sharp, Ralph Regula, Bill Bray, Bill Nature, Charles Bennett, Lane Evans, Jim Traficant, Glenn Poshard, Frank McCloskey, John Myers, Pete Visclosky, Pete McCloskey, Ed Roush, Lee Hamilton, Tim Roemer, Jill Long, Bud Hillis, John Brademas, Neal Smith, and Indianapolis city councilman Beurt SerVaas. There are many more.

People in politics will not soon forget the Willie Horton TV ad aired during the presidential campaign of 1988. The facts aren't much in dispute. Horton was given furlough from a Massachusetts prison and, while out, committed the heinous crimes of rape and murder. The Democratic candidate for president in the fall election was Massachusetts Governor Michael Dukakis. The ad implied that Dukakis was partly responsible for the crimes. Good or bad, the prison furlough program was not a uniquely Massachusetts phenomenon.

When the 1988 incumbent President, Ronald Reagan, was governor of California, a mass murderer was given prison furlough there and, while out, did some more mass murdering. It obviously was a terrible mistake to give either of these felons a furlough. Equally obvious is the fact that neither governor made either of the mistaken judgments. Obvious, too, is a reasonable assumption that the people who ran the Horton ad would not have made the same absurd attack against President Reagan. Indeed, it was essentially the same people who in 1998 conducted a snarling chorus of cat calls, chanting "liar, liar" at President Clinton after he publicly confessed to having lied about his sex life. And, true to their right-wing extremist character, they never spewed such intense and protracted hatred when, in the 1980s, President Reagan lied about sending lethal and sophisticated weapons at taxpayer's expense to terrorists.

During the 1988 campaign, when I was running for re-election myself, I was asked at a high school convocation what I thought about the Willie Horton ad. I said it was wrong. A hand flew up and I called on its owner who said, "Well, it's working." To which I replied, "I don't say that if you robbed a bank, you wouldn't have more money; I say it is *wrong*."

In his 1956 try for the White House, with McCarthyism rampant, Adlai Stevenson addressed, or tried to address, an outdoor rally of students at an Ivy League university. The preponderance of the crowd shouted insults at Stevenson for several minutes, all the louder each time he attempted to speak. As the rudeness continued, Stevenson suddenly said, "Will you please be quiet?" And for some reason the crowd stopped its bellicosity. Stevenson said the following and no more:

"My strongest memory of my visit to the Soviet Union thirty years ago is that the opposition to the incumbent government was not allowed to speak. Good night."

A refreshing example of civilized campaign conduct happened when Dan Quayle ran for U.S. senator in 1980 and the "religious wrong" ran a scurrilous and therefore un-Christian TV ad against Quayle's incumbent opponent, then-Senator Birch E. Bayh. Quayle publicly denounced the tawdry deed. And when, in 1992, it was Dan Quayle's turn to lose in his bid for re-election as vice president, he made his TV concession before a partisan crowd in Indianapolis. As some of them roared their disdain for the winners, Quayle quieted them with these *extemporaneous* words about Clinton and Gore: "If they run the country as well as they ran their campaign, we'll be alright." *Elevated* high road.

So what do we have? There are the high road (Quayle, Lugar, Sharp, Corman, etc.), the low road (the Young Americans for Freedom and their physical counterattackers), the gutter (the Willie Horton ad) and the sewer (examples coming up). One candidate known for his vicious political attacks responded to a fairly mild and not personal criticism by saying he wouldn't get in the gutter with the critic. This moved my friend Jud Haggerty to say, "To get in the gutter, he'd have to come up some." Hence the fourth category: that which flows beneath the street. In the following pages I shall undertake to rate various political practices according to these categories.

"Sticks and stones will break my bones, but words will never hurt me." Put that in the same rubbish bin as "Spare the rod, spoil the child" and "Them as can, do; them as can't, teach." Remember Kipling's words, "They only said intimidate and talked and went their way. By God, the boys who did the work were braver men than they." Violent words can inspire violent deeds.

The Reagan administration's Federal Communications Commission repealed the Fairness Doctrine regulation which, for fifty years, as a condition for licensing, had required wireless broadcasters to provide time for discussion of important community issues with fair representation of various sides. Sounds pretty American to me. But with the repeal came the kind of phenomenon which bedeviled Bosnia. There, the dominant politicians in each of the three sections monopolized television and used it to spew hatred for the people of the other two sections. Never mind that the Croats, Muslims, and Serbs had been getting along pretty well before the tirades. The daily unchallenged doses of hatred inspired the spiral of horrible violence which followed.

Despite repeal of the Fairness Doctrine, American broadcasters continued to enjoy the federal license which prohibited other citizens from buying transmitters and broadcasting on the respectively assigned frequencies. And some broadcasters began hurling one-sided hatred at the same federal government which regulated the rest of us to the broadcasters' benefit. In essence, they angrily insisted that the American government was un-American. In time, the purveyors of broadcast hatred fell all over each other denying that their venomous words had anything to do with hateful deeds such as the bombing atrocity at the federal building in Oklahoma City. "They only said intimidate." In his zeal to be a heel, one of them referred the President's little girl as "a dog" (sewer).

According to Will Rogers, politics and humor are usually propinquities. And Steinbeck wrote that, in the grand march of the circus, "The parodies of kings and heroes are designed to say, 'Don't get too big, because you're very close to funny.'" Superlative cartoonist Bill Mauldin said of his work, "If it's big, hit it. You can't be far wrong." Remember Abe Martin: "Nothin' will take the starch out of a great man like meetin' a feller who don't think much of it." In one of his presidential campaigns, Adlai Stevenson said, "First they accuse us of being too humorous; next they accuse us of being too somber. I leave it to you whether I am more prone to invite people to laugh or to weep. Both, in my judgement, are good for the spirit." Let us then proceed with some nonfiction about seeking political office and see which you consider laughable and which you see as *weepable*. My guess is that you will find a mixed bag.

It was Senator Everett McKinley Dirksen of Illinois who said, "Money is the mother's milk of politics." Communication, honest and intelligent or otherwise, is the ultimate mother's milk of politics. Therefore, print and broadcast journalism are of paramount importance to the process. It is not unusual for candidates to court good relations with the news media. But some do not bother to do the buttering up. One of the best examples of the latter would be my father, Andrew Jacobs. His relationship with Eugene C. Pulliam, publisher of the *Indianapolis Star* and the *Indianapolis News* can be described as stormy. It began happily enough when Dad went to Congress at the beginning of Truman's elected presidency in 1949. Mr. Pulliam and my dad were both strong-willed individuals and at first they were very fond of each other. They fell out over belittling attacks against Truman by the *Star*. Years later, my father explained the riff thus:

I told Gene that if he didn't stop his vicious attacks on the President, I was going to unlimber Big Bertha (an awesome World War I artillery piece). In retrospect, I realize I had no Big Bertha, just a big mouth.

Dad said the extremists "thought they had Truman in 1948 and ever since, they've been going around like a mad dog whose victim escaped."

The attacks against Truman were mean and vicious. And the daily doses of venom took a toll. A friend's mother told me Truman was "a gutter snipe." He fell to 24 percent in the polls. The same shame applies to vicious attacks against Lincoln and John Adams. Lincoln almost lost his bid for re-election in 1864. The verbal attacks against Adams were so effective that he was scarcely welcome at his successor's inaugural. The attacks against President Clinton included charges of murder spread by two prominent right-wing spokesmen, assertions that Mr. and Mrs. Clinton somehow committed crimes in the Whitewater land deal in which they *lost* money, and charges of criminal activities in something called Filegate and something else called Travelgate.

A right-wing judge appointed by a right-wing senator managed to bring about the appointment of a right-wing special prosecutor to investigate the vague charges. After spending forty million tax dollars trying to develop actual criminal charges against Clinton and his wife, the prosecutor came up with nothing except an extramarital affair of the President and the fact that Clinton had lied to the public about his private life. The special prosecutor also alleged that Clinton had lied about his sex life under oath in a sham sexual harassment lawsuit and therefore had committed perjury. Both Republican Lawrence Walsh, the special prosecutor in the Iran/Contra investigation, and Republican John Dean, the star witness in the Watergate investigation, said Clinton had not committed perjury. Some, including me, say the political enemy prosecutor "labored mightily and brought forth a mouse." But as I read history so far, Clinton has been maligned in the same manner as Adams, Lincoln, and Truman, mostly by innuendo. Clinton's adultery was bad and violated his wife's trust. Reagan's use of tax dollars to send arms to terrorists was much worse and violated the *public* trust. But I would not have impeached either one of them.

My father's fuss with Gene Pulliam "Senior" began in the late 1940s. Pulliam was from the old school which held that if you owned a newspaper, it was yours to do with as you wished. And there is a ring of logic in that. But, of course, if a publisher follows that course and uses a paper simply to advance his opinions as news, his paper is quickly dismissed as a source of factual news. Joseph Pulitzer had said, "Accuracy to a newspaper is like virtue to a woman." To which the proverbial wag added, "However a newspaper *can* print a retraction."

Under the leadership of the elder Pulliam, there were few retractions. And he was not the only pupil enrolled in the old school of journalism. His classmates included such prominent names as Robert Rutherford McCormick, owner of the *Chicago Tribune*; Harry Chandler, who owned the *Los Angeles Times;* and Henry Robinson Luce, owner of *Time* magazine. Eventually, *Time,* the *Chicago Tribune,* the *Los Angeles Times,* and the *Indianapolis Star* all turned into fine and accurate sources of news and information. Even when Pulliam Sr. was at the helm and praising Senator Joseph McCarthy of Wisconsin, his son Eugene S. Pulliam signed a Newspaper Editors' Alliance denunciation of the same senator's tactics. The *Indianapolis Star* entered the world of trusted journalism when Gene Pulliam "Junior" took the helm.

It is a fair assumption that Pulliam, Jr. was a conservative Republican. But when it came to the news sections of his papers, it is more than an assumption that he was a journalist first.

In 1975, the older Pulliam died and the *Star*'s Washington correspondent, kindly and brilliant Ben Cole, asked members of the Indiana congressional delegation for comments. Mine was:

> It's hardly a secret that Mr. Pulliam and I had our differences. In a sense, though, that makes his passing all the more personal to me. He was a man of strong convictions who was gentle with his employees. That alone is admirable.

I am told that because of my father's unexpected courtesy toward Gene S. Pulliam, who was a witness in a libel suit my dad handled against the *Star,* the two men eventually became friends. Dad had filed the case on behalf of Republican Sheriff Fields of Marion County. And the sheriff's case was successful. The jury found that the *Star* series which accused Sheriff Fields of the murder of a jail prisoner were libelously false. That didn't seem to diminish the mutually high regard Dad and Gene Jr., as he was often and almost accurately called, had for one another. In fact, it is a pleasure for me to say that I liked and respected Gene Jr. very much, and I sorrowed at his death in 1999.

"Corruption of Blood" seemed to be the rule applied to me by the Pulliam Sr. press when I entered politics. The papers printed my name but usually with the philosophy that if you can't say something *bad* about someone, don't say anything at all. In the Indianapolis Congressional election of 1962, I competed with the incumbent Donald Bruce. By chance, he worked at a radio station owned by the senior Pulliam.

Beginning with that election and up to the time the younger Pulliam took over, the *Star* was virtually a campaign brochure for each of my congressional opponents. My dad said that the news media are like a telescope. If the little end is pointed toward the public, the candidate will look very large. And if the big end is pointed toward the public, the candidate will look very small. In my case, during those early years in politics, my six-foot-three inch frame looked several feet shorter to newspaper readers.

Bright and early one morning during one of my early campaigns for re-election to the U.S. House, my friend Jim Beatty called to tell me I must have a news conference immediately. I summarily replied, "No way." I was just leaving my parents' house to drive to Washington with friend Mike Scanlon, TV reporter for Channel Six in Indianapolis. He was on assignment to Washington and you might say I was, too. It was going to be a pleasant drive with much good talk. And I was already in the uniform of the travel day, grubs. Too grubby for a news conference. But I did ask Jim why. "Obviously," he said, "you haven't seen the *Star* this morning. Your opponent is on the front page accusing you of every evil short of murder which I'm not sure he doesn't imply." "What's new about a lopsided story on me in the *Star*?" I pointed out with a question mark.

"Andy, it's the first salvo for this year and I think you should respond."

"Jim, this is my day to relax on a driving trip to Washington with Mike Scanlon. A lot of people understand about the *Star* and my dad and therefore me. I doubt that they take this stuff seriously. Besides, I'm in old clothes and want to get going; it's a twelve-hour drive."

Beatty tried once more: "Look at it this way: It's absurd enough that you just might have some fun with it. Come on down the way you are and I'll lend you my tie. The cameras don't go below the waist." Fun. That made me think about the libel case Dad had won against the *Star*. The jury found that the *Star* had not told the truth. "Well," said I, "maybe you're right. I could catch [Highway] Forty (the old National Road) downtown and go from there. I'll do it."

The attack on the front page had been unusually virulent and the news conference was unusually well-covered—by broadcast journalists. When the conference began, there I was, wearing Jim Beatty's favorite tie.

"No doubt, a large number of people read the front page story about me this morning," I said. "And, of course, you would expect me to say the charges are demonstratively false. But I am here mainly to underscore a point which can easily be seen in the article's own words. Traditionally when the newspaper gives a slanted report about me, it goes to the trouble to camouflage its calumny by adding at the end, 'Jacobs could not be reached for comment,' which I always can be. But, as you can plainly see in the story this morning, some people at the paper have become so callous as not even to bother with that claim of attempted effort to give both sides. Campaign attacks, while usually unattractive are sometimes not untrue. As JFK said, 'Sincerity is always subject to proof,' and I am perfectly willing to discuss and provide proof of the falsity of these specific attacks. But just in case you are wondering whom to believe generally between the *Star* and me, let me point out that while the *Star* and I have many differences, perhaps the most fundamental difference between us is that *no jury ever found me guilty of lying*."

The cameras and recorders were packed up, Jim got his tie back, and Mike and I were on our way to Washington. With apologies to Glenn Campbell, I said to Mike, "By the time we get to Wheeling, the news will be airing." And indeed it was. Did it make much difference? Beats me. As Gloria Steinem said, "Saying things on TV is like putting messages in bottles. It's usually difficult to know whether they arrive."

The 1964 presidential election proved immensely frustrating for the editor of the *Indianapolis Star*, Jamison Campaign. As befitted a *Star* editor in those early times, it was said that his politics were somewhere to the right of Charlemagne's. He had suffered along with such Republican apostates as Dewey and Eisenhower, both products of the "eastern liberal establishment." Even Nixon was far too pragmatic for the righteous right side of the body politic. But suddenly it was 1964 and St. Swithims had stepped out of the woods in the form of the honorable Barry Goldwater. Here at last was "a choice, not an echo."

Campaign had waited and his turn at bat had come. Just watch the *Star's* smoke on this election. But there was a fly in the smoky ointment. Let's call the fly Clint Merchenson, tycoon of Texas and part owner of Lyndon Baines Johnson's political career. Merchenson was also a corporate board colleague of Eugene Pulliam, the elder. Merchenson had brought Pulliam and LBJ together and LBJ had cultivated the friendship to the best of his considerable ability. And now, in 1964, Pulliam was friends with both the inevitable presidential winner, Johnson, and the inevitable looser, Goldwater. What to do? Neutrality. Neutrality between a certified conservative Republican and an FDR Democrat!? Yep. Editor Campaign had climbed all the way to the ideological mountain top only to be ordered by his employer to make a molehill of it. For the presidential election of

1964 the *Star* was to apply actual journalism. Apply it, that is, to the *presidential* election, not to the Indianapolis congressional contest.

There was one more shock in store for Campaign. Though bulging with a carte blanche blessing to do all that could be done with the mighty pen to defeat my bid for Congress, he couldn't use my opponent Don Tabbert to make personal attacks against me. Don wouldn't do it. Too much of a gentleman. Don Tabbert was a heavy-duty conservative who preferred civil discussion of the issues to false, angry and personal slurs against his opponent. On top of that, he was my friend. He had been my counselor at Indiana University.

How maddening it must have been for Campaign. He had orders to play down Goldwater's criticism of Johnson, of which there was much, and orders to play up Don Tabbert's criticism of me, of which there was none.

By 1964 the elder Pulliam was spending most of the falls and winters in sunny Arizona where he owned the Phoenix newspapers. And, as we all know, when the cat's away, the mice will play. Campaign brought his fertile intellect to bear on the opportunity and came up with this: He couldn't print Goldwater's sharper attacks against Johnson, but he had blanket authority to print whatever Don Tabbert had to say. And, truth be known, Don did not have the respect and affectionate regard for Johnson that he had for me. Bingo! Just get Don to express his heartfelt feelings about LBJ's policies and print them on fireproof paper. Don couched his criticism of LBJ through me, in essence praising me with faint damn: "Andy is a good and honest person, but he does support Lyndon Johnson who does the following things wrong . . ."

For several consecutive days, the front page of the *Star* was like this: "GOP Eleventh District congressional candidate Don Tabbert accused his Democrat [sic] opponent of supporting Lyndon Johnson for president." True. I believed Johnson when he said there would be no escalation in Vietnam. The banner headline was always something in the passive like, "Johnson accused of icky policies."

My resourceful friend Jim Beatty had an idea. LBJ was scheduled to be in Evansville, Indiana, a few days after the *Star* series against him began. One of the Democratic bigwigs assigned to greet the president was the brilliant and scintillating candidate for state attorney general, Jack Dillon. Dillon went to Evansville armed with three or four editions of the *Star*'s criticism of Johnson. By Dillon's account, when he handed the papers to the great man, LBJ looked silently at the first, then the second, and, without looking at the third, he dropped all of them on the a table and mumbled, "That son-of-a-bitch. Get Clint Merchenson on the phone." The

Indianapolis Star's attacks against LBJ vanished for the rest of the campaign. But for the editor of the *Star*, it must have been a few delightful days of furious fun—until he got that likely call from the boss.

As long as we're on the subject of the *Indianapolis Star* during its earlier and less-journalistic incarnation, let's do four more stories.

In the 1964 Democratic congressional primary, despite the fact that I was competing with a candidate who was the former mayor, former county chairman and former prosecutor, all but a few of the forty or so Democratic ward chairmen and chairwomen had agreed to serve on my campaign committee. Since building momentum is exalted in politics, my friends and I decided to announce the names on our very impressive committee a few at a time. But the late cartoonist for the *Indianapolis News* misunderstood. He thought that since we had only announced five ward chairpeople as members of the committee that day, five ward chairpeople were all we had. So the very next day, before we had announced any more of the thirty-eight who were supporting me, a cartoon about me was published in the afternoon paper. It depicted my friend, County Chairman Jud Haggerty using me as a battering ram against a solid stone wall marked "Democrat (sic) Ward Chairmen." The caption had Jud saying, "Have patience, Andy, I'll get you in." The next day, we announced the other thirty-three, bringing the total to almost all the chairpeople. "He who laughs last, laughs (with zest)."

Over time, Gene Pulliam Sr. was deprived of an opportunity to fire his real *Big Bertha* and shower me with the shrapnel of public embarrassment. The deprivation occurred by chance at a New York congressional campaign fund-raiser for my friend Al Lowenstein where I acted as master of ceremonies. It was a pleasure for me to do so because of the radiant roster of his famous supporters, including some of the prettiest ladies in films and modeling and an impressive array of prominent actors and various celebrated people in the arts. The procedure was in keeping with the poorly organized, yet somehow very effective, world of Allard K. Lowenstein.

The elder Pulliam surely would have coveted a camera shot of what happened just before the meeting began. Al was introducing me to some of those famous and beautiful. I assumed he was joking when he said, "Andy, have you met Alger Hiss?"

"No," I joked back, "but I always suspected he was the one who was stealing our pumpkins." Ha, ha—except that Al was not kidding. Shakespeare tells us, "Absence, like death, sets a seal on the image of those we have loved." Along with those who knew about the likes of Benedict Arnold, I had no love whatsoever for the Alger Hiss who, I'm convinced, committed treason against our country. But as I turned, there stood the latter-day caricature of the despicable face that betrayed both America and President Harry Truman. Reflexively, I shook hands with him. What a shot for the front page of the paper whose publisher did not care for my dad. But unfortunately for Pulliam Sr. and very fortunately for me, there was no camera to catch the innocent, but what could have been embarrassing, handshake. The incident took place when it was stylish in New York liberal circles to suppose that Hiss was, after all, innocent. One sympathetic writer set out to clear Hiss and halfway through the project became absolutely certain that the FBI had, indeed, got its man. I recovered my hand with disdain.

One day the *Star* saw a cute article in one of the Washington, D.C., gossip magazines. The piece undertook to name the *Ten Craziest Members of Congress,* most of whom were exponents of the extreme right edge of the flat Earth. But one of those named was I, partly because I was odd enough not to accept money from lobbyists.

When the magazine got to me they were kind enough to say, "Andy Jacobs is a nice crazy . . ." and went on to cite a couple of funny stories I had told during official debate which, they were also kind enough to say, were effective in advancing my side of the issue. But the headline was enough. I figured it would take the *Star* about an hour to call me about the ambiguous appellation. I had to think fast. When the inevitable call came from one of their hapless reporters, my answer was, "If you're sane in Indianapolis, you gotta be crazy in Washington." No *Star* story.

More than a decade later, my propensity to structure some arguments to humor was mentioned in another publication, a book titled *Will the Gentleman Yield.* It was a survey of congressional humor which named Senator Howard Baker of Tennessee and me the funniest senator and representative in Congress. The book was very well received. But, while I had and have much admiration for Senator Baker, I sent a cogent letter to Senator Bob Dole of Kansas: "Dear Bob: If I were you, I'd demand a recount." Bob Dole had one of the driest and best wits I ever encountered anywhere. I told his bright and lovely wife, Liddy, that were it not for him and Senator Bill Hathaway of Maine, I would no longer be alive. In those House-Senate conferences between the Ways and Means and Finance Committees on highly technical tax language, I would have died of boredom without their wit.

In the summer of my first year in the U.S. House, Lenny Bruce the comedian died from an overdose of proscribed drugs—which I think is any dose at all. To put it mildly, Bruce's humor was topical. Whether the topic was the Vietnam War or idiotic racial injustice, he held up the proverbial mirror to the silly hypocrisies of society. Most people laughed—and thought about reform. Some did not.

The *Indianapolis Star* ran a hot editorial almost before the brilliant comedian's body was cold. The title was crude:

Death of a Clown
Lenny Bruce was a minor tin god to a widespread revolution of dissatisfied who are still trying to make a religion of sex, drugs, four-letter words and pacifism . . .

That first sentence reminded me of a college exam question: "What word does not belong in this series?" So I placed the whole editorial in the *Congressional Record* with the following preface of my own:

Mr. Speaker, it might be pointed out that two thousand years ago there was a widespread revolution that tried to make a religion out of pacifism and some of the dissatisfied are still trying.

Referring to my effrontery in the *Congressional Record*, one of my father's close friends sadly informed me that my first term in Congress would now be my last. He might have been right. But he wasn't.

Because he wasn't, several years later I was able to place another *Star* editorial in the *Congressional Record*. One of the most respected U.S. senators ever was the quiet, brilliant and modest Phil Hart of Michigan, widely dubbed the "conscience of the Senate." Both he and his wife took exception to the United States policy in Vietnam, she more demonstrably. She withheld the part of her income tax which she figured was her required share of the U.S. cost of Vietnam. The latter inspired another Star editorial, entitled "The Liberal Death Wish." The gravamen of the *Star*'s message was that Jane Hart opposed having any military defense for our country. That was obviously untrue.

My father, who was a walking treasure house of information—*Oh, my Papa*—told me about a similar editorial in the same paper several years before. It was about Utah Governor J. Bracken Lee. He, too, had withheld a part of his income tax, not to protest a U.S. policy of killing people in poor countries, but a policy of feeding them. The editorial, published in the *Star* on May 28, 1952, under the title, "Challenging Federal Colossus," included these words:

J. Bracken Lee has announced that he will not pay his income taxes. . . . Perhaps he merely wants to stir up protest among Americans against being the milch cows for people in scores of nations most of us have never heard of. If that is his purpose, we're all for him.

I placed the editorial praising Governor Lee and then the editorial criticizing Ms. Hart in the *Congressional Record*. This time my preface read:

A City of Two Tales
Mr. Speaker, it was the best of ideas; it was the worst of ideas.

In his youth, my nephew Marty Landwerlen carried an *Indianapolis Star* paper route with occasional help from members of our family. At four-thirty one winter morn when, to paraphrase the immortal words of W. C. Fields, it was not a fit morning out for man nor beast, it was my turn. Under the circumstance it was not a pleasant task. It became even less pleasant when we got home and I sat down to read words I had helped deliver. For on that day's editorial page appeared a declaration of my *horribleness*. It's one thing to smile at such an insult, but it's quite another to help deliver it. All in a day's love for a nephew.

The funniest example of biased news coverage I ever saw in the old Pulliam press, appeared on the front page of the May 17, 1973, edition of the *Indianapolis News*. It did not say, "Nixon Denies Knowing about Watergate Extent, Coverup." It did not say, "White House Aides Say Nixon Unaware of Watergate Extent, Coverup." It said, "Nixon Unaware Of Watergate Extent, Coverup." In fairness to what was then an unfair newspaper, I must add that the story itself quoted White House aides as denying what turned out to be the facts. But, in essence, the headline said that what *they said,* was true.

In 1968 the *Star* actually explained how to get away with perjury. Governor George Wallace of Alabama was running for President in the Democratic primaries. Since his platform was essentially racism, the less Lincolnesque wing of the Republican party smiled on his candidacy. Many Hoosier Republicans wished to cross over and vote for Wallace in the Indiana Democratic Primary. But there was a hitch. Under Indiana law, if a party official suspects such shenanigans, she or he can block the interloper's scheme unless the crossover voter signs an affidavit that he or she intends to vote for a majority of the invaded party's candidates in the fall election. This is where the front page of the *Star* came in. On that page an editorial in the guise of a story explained how a crossover Republican could sign the false affidavit with impunity. After all, the pitch/story said, since the fall vote would be secret, no one would ever *know*. In other words, the crime would be okay if the criminal couldn't get caught. In its worst nightmare, the *Indianapolis Star* of the last quarter of the twentieth century would never even have dreamed of running such a piece. By then it had become an actual newspaper.

Perhaps *Time* magazine gave the all-time best example of news bias. I am at a loss to identify and give well-deserved credit to the university professor who did the research, but following is part of the historic record she or he dug out to show how the earlier, Harry Luce incarnation of *Time* treated President Truman, and later President Eisenhower, on the *same* subjects. Get ready, this is really funny:

> *Time*, 1950
> About May 1, after a month back at his desk, President Truman will begin a slow trip westward... Officially, the trip will be billed as nonpolitical, an ancient device whereby a president can pay his expenses from his $40,000 travel allowance instead of from the party treasure.
>
> *Time*, 1955
> From time to time, the president of the United States must travel around the country... Last week President Eisenhower announced one of the most intensive tours since he assumed office.
>
> *Time*, 1952
> The subject of Harry Truman's 1952 intentions came up again in his weekly press conference. The president wasn't saying, just acting deliberately mysterious. It has become an unprofitable inquiry and a stale joke.
>
> *Time*, 1955
> Eisenhower has skillfully refused to commit himself on 1956.

And:

> Adroitly, [Eisenhower] fielded questions about a second term.

And now, the best of three:

> *Time*, 1946
> Last week... President (Truman) eased his croniest crony,

George E. Allen, into the board of directors of the Reconstruction Finance Corporation . . . George is all the more remarkable because, to the naked eye, he is a clown.

Time, 1954

Last week, the President [Eisenhower] chatted quietly with . . . golfing companion George E. Allen, Washington lawyer and friend of Presidents.

The *Indianapolis Star* in its earlier, or let's say *primitive* years rivaled the old *Time* magazine in one case.

Our friend Indianapolis lawyer Owen Mullin was a budding Democratic politician in the 1950s, and because of his connection with the *Indianapolis Star* faction of his party, he was praised by the paper. Then he fell out with the *Star* Democrats and consequently fell from grace at the *Star*. Here's how he described his journalistic transmogrification:

"For a time I was a young man who was witty and articulate. Then I became a pol who was wisecracking and glib."

During the nineties, as was the case with the *Wall Street Journal*, the *Indianapolis Star* editorial page was a study in daily, unwavering and vitriolic attacks against President Clinton. But, also like the *Wall Street Journal*, the *Star*'s news pages were a study in excellent and fair journalism. By then I would trust no other paper more than I would trust the *Star*'s news section.

Let's move now to the tactics of less than scrupulous politicians.

The nature of smear tactics has remained essentially the same over the centuries, always violating God's Commandment, "Thou shalt not bear false witness against thy neighbor." But, as with antibiotics, in time a particular smear will lose its nefarious potency only to be replaced by another. As history unfolds, there always seems to be a new poison for the smearsmith's pen and tongue.

In the slimy Spanish Inquisition, it was the witch. And no one, according to author Samuel Shellabarger, "was too innocent to be proved guilty." Of course, at the Inquisition *everyone* was, in fact, innocent for the simple reason that there was and is no such thing as a witch. In Salem, the weapon of choice for character assassination—and murder—was once more the witch. The weapon grew strong in the mucky soil of ignorance until the daughter of one of the judges was accused and the smear disappeared—quickly.

In Jefferson's time, it was the Bible. The smear alleged that he was going to confiscate every copy of the Good Book in America. Ignorance worked again. Historians tell us that good women hid their Bibles in wells against the onslaught of that *atheist monster*. That nonsense lingered in some pockets of our population for two centuries. In the late seventies, when I was a guest on a religious radio call-in program, a woman at the other end of the line began rattling off one issue after another on which she and I disagreed. But she didn't know about our disagreement because she never asked and almost never paused to draw a breath. She finished her exposition with this: "And they're even trying to pass a law in Washington now to where (sic) you can't own a Bible." As God's nature forced her to break for oxygen, I seized my chance. Borrowing shamelessly from one of actor Burt Lancaster's lines in the film *Elmer Gantry*, I waded in:

"Ma'am, I am not a violent person. But if anyone tries to take my mother's Bible away from her, well, I'll scratch him and I'll kick him and I'll punch him."

The woman was pleased with, what I suppose to her was my gentle, *Christian-like* answer. Having not the slightest idea that we disagreed on several of the *real* issues, she cooed, "Well, we need more men like you in Washington." I suppose I should have been ashamed; instead, I confess I was amused.

The outrage of official racism wasn't the only government stupidity of the fifties. The main smear was the red one. It was my privilege to teach a course in political science at Indiana University-Purdue University Indianapolis after I left Congress on January 3, 1997. One day I asked the twenty-eight students what came to mind at the mention of the word "red." I got many different answers; not one was "communism." In the 1950s all the answers would have been "communism." It was the devastating smear of those years.

In the late 1960s a new smear emerged. Some of my critics settled upon what one of my friends crudely called the "queer smear" against me. The purveyors of that smear were roughly, so to speak, the same folks who had suggested earlier that I was "soft on communism." But the red smear was beginning to lose steam. McCarthyism had been so thoroughly discredited that those who traveled the political gutter moved to this new strain of slander.

The false accusation of homosexuality, then libel per se, was particularly insidious because it was usually anonymously whispered or, in a word, cowardly.

As was the case with the 1950 "communist smear" against Helen Gahagan Douglas in California, the smear against me was not Republican in origin. Congresswoman Douglas' Democratic senate primary opposition began whispering the smear, "pink lady," meaning a communist sympathizer. Richard Nixon's Republican campaign picked it up for the fall election and retailed it. And so it was with the latter-day smear against me.

In the spring of 1968 I received a call in Washington from my father in Indianapolis. He said he'd like to pick me up at the airport when I flew home for the weekend. That was somewhat unusual and naturally made me curious. As we drove from the terminal, he told me that a vicious whispering campaign of origin unknown to him was being conducted against me as a part of the primary contest I faced. The anonymous fabrication claimed that my sex instincts were not normal (sewer). My first reaction was to laugh. It was hard to imagine any man more fascinated with or romantically interested in women than myself. "Women" became woman when my wife, Kim, and I met. I can't think of a better sex of which to be opposite.

When I started my journey through politics, my father lamented my inattention to the law practice, saying to his friends, "My son practices politics, chases girls (Dad used the designation of the old school when it came to women) and dabbles in law." But none of that mattered to the smearsmiths. They figured most people wouldn't know one way or another, so truth be damned.

At first, it did seem funny to me. But when scurrilous and anonymous phone calls were made to my distraught mother, the humor waned.

Nineteen sixty-eight was the most virulent year of the smear. By then, some elements of the Republican Party were spreading it systematically. At a suburban Indianapolis patio party in 1972, a Republican city official uttered the smear straight out. A woman had taken exception to my putative Republican opponent, William H. Hudnut III, on the ground that he was an ordained minister and ought not be in politics—an assertion with which I completely and publicly disagreed. The city official demanded of the Hudnut critic, "Well, would you rather have a queer?" I'm told she answered in the affirmative.

By chance, a friend of mine heard the remark and told the public official that he had committed a slander and she would be my witness. At that traditional neighborhood party the following year, my friend asked the official if he planned to repeat the slander and he said he'd found out it wasn't true. Obviously he had not bothered to find that out in the first place, which is called "reckless disregard" in the landmark libel case, *New York Times v. Sullivan*.

Despite the protracted efforts of its perpetrators, I don't think the smear ever harmed me politically. Apparently voters either knew better or if they did believe the farfetched attack, didn't care.

When I publicly took strong exception to the Reagan administration's unconstitutional invasion of Grenada, I received a lot of angry criticism, including a call from an irate constituent who said he thought I favored communism. I assured him I did not, but that I did favor common sense and gave my reasons for judging the invasion not to be in the best interests of our country. At that, he became all the more irate and told me that no country in the world had ever gone communist when a Republican president was in office. When I suggested he had overlooked Cuba, he paused for a moment and shouted through the phone, "You're the dumbest homo I know!" and hung or, actually, slammed up. He was mistaken on two points. I was not a "homo" and he did not know me. Just how many "homos" he did know and what their intelligence levels were, he did not stay on the phone long enough to say.

Then there was the time a friend told me she'd had an argument with someone who insisted the smear against me was true. Later, that same friend asked me if I knew a certain woman. "Yes," I said, "she was a grade school classmate, easily one of the two prettiest girls in the group. I imagine she turned out to be a beautiful woman."

"You haven't seen her since grade school?" my friend asked. "Not to the best of my knowledge," I replied. "Then," said my friend, "you'd better be glad because there's a rumor going around that you've been seeing her and you've broken up her marriage."

"Well," said I, "you'll have to confess the rumors are getting better."

If it is true that "imitation is the sincerest form of flattery," the Watergate miscreants should feel flattered by my hometown. While the big 1972 Watergate was going on in Washington, a little one, replete with a political break-in, was going down in Indianapolis. Three years later, the *Indianapolis Star* reported a criminal investigation which revealed that, as a part of the Indianapolis *little Watergate operation,* a "redheaded" woman had been recruited to go to Washington in 1972 and "seduce" me in the manner of a scene from the film, *From Russia With Love.* In that scene, our friend James Bond is lured into a hotel room by a pretty Russian woman and a secret movie camera records their dalliance.

For reasons not reported in the story, the caper was called off. We can speculate, however, that the right hand did not know what the Far Right hand was trying to do by way of the gay smear. I can just hear the more vicious ones saying to the more traditional smearsmiths, "Are you crazy? We're trying to get people to believe he's queer!" The redhead tactic wouldn't have worked anyway. At the time I was dating the pretty blond and pretty bright secretary of one of our senators.

When the 1975 story appeared, the Indianapolis Republican county chairman was suffering bad publicity generally. His law partner was under federal indictment—later found not guilty—and for various reasons the chairman had fallen from grace with much of his own party. The chairman, Keith Bulen, was a fellow lawyer and I liked his keen mind and sharp sense of humor. He played rough in politics but probably was surprised when people took his tactics personally. In any case, it occurred to me at the time that Keith was probably like the storied Maytag repairman, "the loneliest man in town." So I gave Keith a call to cheer him up.

Right off the bat, Keith said to me, "I had nothing to do with that redhead." Which prompted me to say, "Keith, through the years, you've tried a lot of tactics on me. One of your candidates suggested I was soft on communism; you gerrymandered me a couple of times; you stood by while some of your operatives spread vicious rumors about my sexual instincts. Then you come up with something that might be of interest to me and you scotch it. I'm beginning to wonder if you're my friend."

Just as violence was not the exclusive province of Republicans, the homosexual smear has also been hurled by some Democrats. It happened in an Indiana fall election for a U.S. Senate seat. The Democratic incumbent was in a tight contest with the Republican opponent and one of the incumbent's operatives thought he could narrow the gap by a campaign of innuendo that the perfectly straight Republican was gay (sewer). The public suggestions included such phrases as, "he lives in a fairy land." And of course the whispering campaign said the smear plainly. The Republican won. Under the circumstances, it was the correct result.

The most stunning case of a gay smear happened on television secondhand. NBC hired a journalist to profile the Republican presidential primary candidates of 1980. One of them was Jack Kemp, then a U.S. representative from New York. On the *Today* show, the journalist asserted that Jack would have "one obstacle, the old gay rumors" (sewer). I had a letter in the mail to NBC within the hour:

> Dear NBC:
>
> I have known Jack Kemp for more than a decade. It is obvious that he is not gay. More than that, before your broadcast this morning, I never heard so much as the slightest hint otherwise.
>
> In the words of Joseph Welch, "At long last, sir, have you no decency . . . ?"

There are two kinds of losers in politics and three kinds of winners. Just as there are good and sore losers, there are good and sore winners. The third category of winners is the most obnoxious, those who gloat.

An example of a sore loser was the congressman who lost his bid for re-election and said on TV, "If that's what the G__ d__ people of this district want, they can have it!" Those would be the same people who had earlier given him the gift of their public trust and the privilege of serving in that historic institution of freedom. My father said you should never hold against a person what he or she says about you during one twenty-four-hour period. All the same, the TV concession speech was not gracious and betrayed poor breeding. As we shall see, my 1964 Republican opponent, Don Tabbert, was an example of a *good* loser. Actually he didn't so much lose to me as to a Democratic landslide.

Bill Hudnut was a good example of a good winner. When he won and I lost the Indianapolis House seat in 1972, he said that I was "a good man who deserves respect." And he said it to an audience of his fellow Republicans.

On the subject of sore winners, a few days after I was elected to my first term in Congress, I received a delightful letter from my father's good friend Judge Herb Spencer. The judge gave me some advice about entering upon my public duties. He said I should read more than ever before. I should keep my work current, especially the official correspondence with constituents and so on. Then he wrote this: "You're not mad at anyone; why should you be? You won." He was right. I was not mad at anyone, only grateful. Wouldn't anybody be? Not quite.

An example of a sore winner was Speaker of the House John W. McCormack of Massachusetts. In the late 1960s, U.S. Representative Morris K. Udall of Arizona was a candidate to compete with McCormack for the speakership. I was one of Mo's supporters. When Mo lost in the Democratic caucus, he was very pleasant about it, joking to the assemblage, "I've asked my supporters to turn my campaign buttons upside-down." That way they read "OW." Speaker McCormack, on the other hand, was not pleasant at all in his remarks to the caucus. He was angry, a sore winner. By chance, my sister Wanda was visiting at the Capitol that day. She was a Catholic nun in full harness. By even more chance, Speaker McCormack ran into her as he left the caucus meeting. Being an Irish Catholic from Boston, he gave my sister a courtly bow and asked, "Who are you, Sister?" To which she replied, "I'm Andy Jacobs' sister." To which the Speaker replied, "Your father is one of the finest men I ever knew, but your brother is a bad boy."

Bad as a sore winner is, the one who gloats is worse by quanta. The sore winner is acting from the emotion of anger and, while failure to control that emotion is repugnant, it is not cold-blooded. Gloating *is,* and betrays a stunning lack of character.

On my first day in Congress I was present when a re-elected House member referred to his defeated opponent as, "that jerk I clobbered" (gloat). The opponent was certainly not a "jerk." I knew him to be one of God's noblemen. At least the incumbent didn't gloat publicly. Neither did the incumbent I challenged and lost to in 1962. But, that year, some of my opponent's supporters did some gloating shortly after the polls closed and they did so directly to me. As an elected precinct committeeman, I had just finished performing my duties at the polling place when four young men drove up and alighted from their automobile. Knowing as I did that key precincts had already projected their candidate to have won, they proceeded to jeer at me. But they did so in the presence of my friends, some of whom were the Republican officials in the precinct. The latter told the visitors to "grow up." A generation later the gloaters' spiritual heirs did the same primitive jeering at Bill Hudnut in the Indianapolis Republican organization endorsement convention as he narrowly lost the party endorsement for Congress (gutter). This after his bringing repeated success to his party by being elected Republican mayor of Indianapolis four times in a row.

In 1972 when the gerrymandered handwriting of defeat was on the wall for me, renegades of the opposition held a fund-raiser dinner/dance. The advertised name of the band was "Andy Jacobs and the Has-Beens." (Somewhere between gloating and sophomoric—mild gloating).

Probably the most gaudy case of gloating came on the heels of the 1994 election. Following four lean decades, the Republican Party had won control of the U.S. House. Bumper stickers blossomed or, you might say, *thorned* all over Washington saying, "Speaker Gingerich. Get used to it." It wasn't very long before the drivers of some of those cars, themselves, were having trouble getting "used to it."

In 1992 two of my super-colorful friends in the U.S. House came up with one of the more bizarre tactics in the politics of personal attack. In an absurd McCarthyism atavism, they charged that while a student at Oxford, Bill Clinton was working for Soviet secret police when he went on a field trip to Moscow (gutter). Ridiculous as the assertion was, the congressmen actually talked President Bush into publicly wondering if it might be true. I am very fond of George Bush and he is by nature a much nicer person than this tactic would indicate. But he wanted to win and he failed to resist the temptation subtlety to sully Clinton's loyalty to our country. The ploy, of course, was unsuccessful.

I liked *New York Times* editor James "Scotty" Reston's *Memoir* for several reasons, two in particular. First, it was laced with love and respect for his wife and children. Second, it informed me about an incident concerning Senator William Proxmire of Wisconsin. The incident was stunningly coincidental with another one involving me. Reston reported that just before one of Proxmire's re-election campaigns, a publication in Washington undertook to rate members of the Congress. Out of the clear blue sky, it rated Proxmire "least effective." Something was weirdly wrong about that assessment. Proxmire was generally considered to be among the most effective in Congress, a model of rectitude and efficiency. Knowing this to be true, Reston ran down the source and debunked the attack.

I had been the target of the same kind of attack from another Washington publication. In my case, the late *Indianapolis Star* columnist Thomas R. Keating played the roll of Reston. He telephoned the Washington periodical to inquire the basis of the assertion, only to be told the publication did not know. The spokeswoman said that an outside reporter had been hired to do the rating and she could not reveal the reporter's identity. In his column, Keating wrote that the rating was false on its face inasmuch as there were a couple of falling-down drunks in the Congress at the time. A *Washington Post* reporter told me the identity of the reporter who had done the dirty work and, yes, it turned out to be someone who had a personal animus toward me.

A year later the Washington publication repeated its rating feature, preceded by a flattering retraction which ended with these words:

"Andy Jacobs is one of the more intelligent, honorable people in Congress and last year's rating was off-target."

This time the message was carried home by *Indianapolis News* columnist David Mannweiler who wrote critically, "Jacobs only had to wait a year to get his name cleared." So that was the end to it, right? Not quite.

For people in Indianapolis politics, the Mannweiler column was a must. Though the retraction was well known to them, for several elections the opposition cited the original attack as if it had not been retracted. (Not sewer, not gutter, but very definitely low-road.)

Tom Keating and David Mannweiler pioneered the transition from rag to newspaper when Eugene S. Pulliam, the son, took over the *Star/News* with his steadfast devotion to genuine journalism.

In another campaign, another opponent said that my voting record, cited by various rating groups as frugal, was not frugal at all. The assertion was that I only talked that way and was in reality a big spender. A few years later, my Hoosier friend, then-Congresswoman Jill Long, asked if I would come to her district for a joint news conference. She told me that her opponent's campaign manager was the same man who had been my opponent's campaign manager when I was accused of being a big spender. Only now his pitch against Jill went this way: "Andy Jacobs is a genuine conservative ("parsimonious progressive," if you please), but Jill Long is a big spender," which, with her Ph.D. in business, she certainly was not.

Asked by Jill to do so, my family and I journeyed to Ft. Wayne for her news conference on the subject. Upon our arrival at Jill's headquarters, I was shown a headline in the *Fort Wayne Journal-Gazette*. It named a Hoosier GOP congressman and Jill as the biggest frankers (users of congressional mail in the form of newsletters) in the state. Jill said a question about the mailings might come up at the news conference, to which I said, "That'd be my guess." We laughed and went into the room with the reporters.

When the anticipated question was asked of me, I said the following:

"A few years ago when I ran for re-election, the opposition said I had 'perpetuated (myself) in office by use of the frank.' When the opposition found out that I did not waste the taxpayers' money on such self-promotion, the opposition didn't miss a beat; they put out brochures saying, 'Most congressmen keep in touch with their constituents by sending newsletters, but not Jacobs.'

"So I have concluded that the most difficult thing in politics is to please your opponent."

I don't think the big-spender attacks in Indianapolis and later in Fort Wayne were as low as "low-road." Let's just say a bumpy road of medium elevation. The rule my mother often cited would be a good one for politics: "If you can't say something nice about someone, say nothing at all."

Margaret Chase Smith was a U.S. Senator from Maine and something of an American heroine. Very small in physical stature, she stood tall as she became the first senator to challenge the gutter tactics of her fellow Republican, Joseph McCarthy of Wisconsin. The big tough guys in the Senate at the time who found McCarthy's slanderous conduct obnoxious lacked her courage. By 1972, however, when she ran for re-election, she had become very frail with the afflictions of age. Her Democratic opponent was U.S. Representative Bill Hathaway, a good friend of mine who had been taken prisoner by the Nazis when his bomber was shot down during World War II. He was one of the most pleasant people I ever knew.

One day in October, Bill sat down beside me in the House chamber and asked my opinion about advice a few of his supporters were giving him.

They thought he should start campaigning about Senator Smith's shortcomings. I told him I didn't think much of the idea. In the first place, it would be unkind and disrespectful of one of the world's most wonderful women. In the second place, the voters of Maine probably knew that it was time for her to go into retirement, anyway. Therefore, I suggested a third alternative, *praise her*. Not only did she deserve it, but it would show the voters that if they chose to retire her, the replacement would be a kind and decent person. He said that idea made sense, did it, and won—in a Republican landslide year. Nice guy with nice approach finished first.

One of my dearest friends, more like a sister really, Julia M. Carson, was the nominated Democratic candidate to replace me when I chose not to run for Congress again. She became my coworker in the Indianapolis Congressional office when I was first sworn-in thirty-two years before. When I was defeated by Bill Hudnut in the Nixon landslide of 1972 in a newly gerrymandered district, she was elected to the Indiana State House of Representatives.

Later, having made her mark so wonderfully in Indianapolis politics (the only woman ever to have been twice chosen "Woman of the Year" by readers of the *Indianapolis Star*), she was elected to the Indiana State Senate. Next, she was elected Indianapolis Center Township Trustee, where the challenge was daunting. Her predecessors had run up a huge debt pursuing the principal responsibility of the office, poor relief. In short order, she reversed the business-as-usual and paid off the debt, moving the Republican county auditor to say of the Democratic officeholder, "Julia Carson wrestled the monster to the ground."

She led the country not in cold, histrionic welfare-reform speeches, but in sensible welfare reform. Long before the idea went national, she changed the policy toward welfare beneficiaries' unwed teenaged daughters who became mothers themselves. Before Carson took office, such girls became additional welfare accounts with additional apartments. She changed that. The young and unwed mom would stay with her welfare-client mom, same account. Good idea for the girl and baby; good idea for the taxpayers. Julia didn't just cut off welfare payments erroneously paid to people who cheated the system; she also took legal action to recover the taxpayers' money. And the budget surgery was done with knowledgeable precision which harmed no child in need.

During the fall congressional campaign when Julia and her opponent made a joint appearance before the Indianapolis Bar Association, they took questions written on index cards from unidentified members of the audience. One of the questions directed to Julia read, "Do you give bottles of whiskey to your voters?" Julia was of African descent and the question was clearly meant to be an ethnic slur from a partisan participant. (Sewer at the concentrated confluence of effluvium.) With remarkable composure and the beauty of quiet dignity, Julia went to the microphone and softly said, "No."

To illustrate the crackpot and primitive ignorance of the questioner, the majority of "(her) voters," both in the primary and later in the fall election, were not of African descent, most being of European origin. Later, in a rare disclosure of her innermost self and deepest hurt, she glanced away and barely audibly said to me, "I never felt so alone." She was not alone; decent people were with her.

Julia won that 1996 election with 53 percent of the vote, despite the mean and sarcastic distortion in television ads against her. The ads were crafted by conscienceless Washington *insultants*. The same Washington character assassins returned to Indianapolis two years later and resumed their primitive handiwork. And, with the able help of her campaign chairman, Bart Peterson, who was destined to become the Indianapolis mayor in 2000, Julia won again, this time with 58 percent of the vote.

There are hundreds of historical examples of highroad, low-road, gutter and sewer politics as well as good and sore losers, and winners. Fortunately, the gloating winners are not so numerous. When our election campaigns lack civility, no matter which candidates win, America loses.

The map for low-road, gutter, and sewer politics is not arcane. Simply find out what people don't like, better yet what they fear, and accuse your opponent of it; find out what people do like, such as protection against what they fear, and accuse yourself of it. And don't be squeamish about doing violence to the truth.

I gave a facetious example of the mindless low road to my twelve-year-old nephew when he asked me, "What is your opponent like this time?" My tongue-in-cheek reply: "He's a dirty, rotten so-and-so, Tommy. And I'll tell you more about him as soon as they choose him." In the politics of personal attack, the same fault that shows friends are only human, will show adversaries are horribly inhuman. It's not what is wrong, but *who* is wrong. Faults describe friends and disqualify adversaries.

The map for the high road is not obscure, either. Simply and sincerely be yourself. Know that neither the world nor you will perish if you lose an American election and that, therefore, you can easily afford to do what, in decency, you should do; treat your opponent as though you were sitting across the table from her or him as a dinner guest in his or her home.

Back when Hoosiers had to jump through hoops to register to vote, on the last night of registration at the courthouse, it was like the income tax lineup at the post office on April 15. The double line of citizens trying to register sometimes stretched for more than a tenth of a mile. It was a traditional occasion for campaigning. Candidates would work the lines, passing out cards to potential voters who usually discarded the cards as quickly as they received them. The scene was always festive and gaudy. Refreshment vendors set up stands. It was one big two-party party.

The main event consisted of a shouting match between one champion from each party. This spectacle evoked either disgust or hilarious laughter, depending on one's taste in high camp. One year, I took a seat on one of the courthouse steps next to sweet Betty Peak, a hardworking precinct official. The steps under those circumstances were more like bleachers for spectators of the spectacle in the open arena below. For this occasion, the Republican stalwart was a giant of a man, probably six feet, seven inches tall. He had a foghorn voice and was using it at top decibel. The Democratic antagonist was a small woman who couldn't have been more than five feet tall. If anything, though, the Democrat's Klaxon was even more nerve-shattering than that of her counterpart. Big things, or at least noises, come in small packages. It was David and Goliath. But taking into account the natural capabilities of each, it was hard to tell which was which.

The two citizens sitting directly in front of Betty and me on the next step down happened to be drunk. In fact, they looked as if they happened to be drunk often. The word "derelicts" comes to mind. And as the verbal battle raged below in its less than edifying fashion—"You're the war party!" "Oh yeah? Well, you're the depression party"—one of the low-end citizens in front of us rolled his bloodshot eyes and said to the other, "I'd get out of this country if God would only let me."

During the 1970 Indianapolis congressional campaign, Channel 6 TV staged "an old-fashioned political rally" at the Indiana State Fair. Each candidate was invited to say whatever he or she thought appropriate for the occasion. This, in part, was how I said my piece:

"Labor Day is here. And so we begin again that act of freedom we Americans call an election campaign. Our campaigns are the civilized substitute for war. And the less angry, the less accusatory, the less warlike, the more civilized they are and the prouder we Americans can be of them..."

Of course, Abraham Lincoln said it best:

"I shall do nothing out of malice; what I deal in is too *vast* for malice."

chapter 1

GETTING STARTED

THE VENERABLE EMANUEL CELLER told me this story about Abraham Lincoln: The future president was attending church where he promptly fell asleep. While he slumbered, the preacher said to the congregation, "All those who want to go to heaven, please stand." Everyone but our superlative sleepyhead stood. Among the chuckles, the preacher added, "All those who do not want to go to heaven, please stand." No one stood. As Lincoln was nudged back to consciousness, the preacher addressed him directly, "Mr. Lincoln, where *do* you want to go?" Lincoln replied, "I just want to go to Congress."

My father did not want to go to Congress even when he went. He had to be talked into it. And though he ran for re-election, after serving one term, he really didn't want to go back. He didn't like it and seemed elated when he lost. He was fond of saying that his re-election campaign cost the price of the one postage stamp he used to mail his declaration of candidacy to the Indiana Secretary of State.

I was more Lincolnesque in one way *only*—Dad was the most Lincoln-like person I ever knew—I *wanted* to go to Congress. Lincoln had also said, "I shall prepare myself and when the time comes, I shall be ready." I was a police officer working my way through the last year of night law school when I told my father I wanted to run for Congress. Dismissing the idea of a sanity inquest for me, he said, "If that's what you really want to do, then you should start by running for the state legislature. If you shine there," he paused and continued, "and it's so easy to shine there (at the time, not later)—people may begin thinking of you as a serious candidate for Congress."

2 ⛪ Slander and Sweet Judgment

Four years later, having served one two-year term in the Indiana House of Representatives, I filed for the U.S. House. Speaking of preparing, I must have spent forever writing and rewriting my announcement speech. In fact, the effort was probably begun in my mind as soon as a government contractor maximized his profits by not feeding us Marines aboard his private ship on which he contracted with the government to take Marines to the Korean slaughterhouse—there were plenty of U.S. Navy transport ships available at the time, but, no doubt, the contractor had put a few campaign contributions in helpful (to him) places. Phrases like this came to mind:

> They fatten up most animals before the slaughter. Condemned felons get sumptuous last meals. Why not the Marines? Because some bozo who calls himself a patriot wants to make more than his share from the taxpayers.

And during those civilian years leading up to my 1962 political effort, lofty paraphrases came to mind. "Education 'bends the twig so the tree grows straight.'" And, "The public servant is supposed to serve the public." If ever a speech was polished, mine certainly was. Sanded, finished, practiced, and ready to go. Trite perhaps, but ready to go. Sounded good to me each time I rehearsed in front of the dresser mirror. "Work, for the day is coming."

And it finally did, that day in November, a year before the 1962 congressional elections.

The stage was set, an announcement lunch in a downtown hotel with several of my supporters in attendance. TV, too. One of the three Indianapolis newspapers sent a reporter. Which one? Well, not the *Indianapolis Star* or *News*, not in those days. It was the Scripps-Howard *Indianapolis Times* which by the summer of 1965 was gone. There were several radio microphones at the ready.

I didn't eat; too nervous. I pored over my masterpiece, every word, every inflection. This was about to be recorded for history. As lunch was being served, a distinguished citizen entered the dining room. It was my father. My campaign manager, James Porter Seidensticker, Jr., was on his feet to insist that Dad be seated at the head table and that he make remarks. My father had left public office twelve years before and the congressional seat had been held all but two of those years by a Republican, but Dad was colorful and his law practice continued to bring him local fame despite orders at the *Star/News* that he, like Red China, did not exist and was not to be recognized in print.

Getting Started   3

That night, my lady friend and several other supporters came to my apartment for cold cuts, coffee, and chips and some dip. We settled in to see how the speech of the century came across on TV. It didn't.

The only thing on TV concerning my candidacy was a bite from my father's remarks:

"If my son wants to go to Congress, I want him to go to Congress. *He'll learn.*"

A third of a century later, which was two years after tobacco killed my father, I announced at an Indianapolis news conference that I would run for Congress no more. I recalled for the reporters my father's admonition of long before and, casting my eyes Heavenward said, "It's taken me quite a while, Dad, but I think I've finally learned."

There was a long political and nonpolitical journey to that moment of television glory in 1961 when I choked on a chip. As mentioned in the introduction of this book, my first brush with politics at age six was physical. Ten years later, the difference between Democrats and Republicans was still unclear to me—still is. At sixteen, though, I knew we had a President and a Congress and that the President's name was Truman.

A few years before, my dad had told me that my Uncle Karl Jacobs had a friend who was an Illinois Congressman and I was amazed. Uncle Karl knew a congressman? In high school civics we were shown a magazine picture of a group of congress*men* and federal judges. In their spiffy dark suits they looked awesome. On my sixteenth birthday Dad came home to tell us that the Mayor of Indianapolis, Al Feeney, had asked him to switch his candidacy from county prosecutor to Congress. Knowing his chances to become prosecutor were only a little better than they had been ten years before, he reluctantly agreed.

President Truman was running for election in his own right that year and somehow I began to understand that both he and my dad were Democrats. I also understood that Truman, according to the polls, was going to be swamped by New York GOP Governor Thomas E. Dewey. With a straight-party lever in Indianapolis and a Republican tradition there as well, my dad's chances of election were roughly those of a kerosene cat's in Hell. That's how Dad explained it to my mom, my sisters, and me. But he told us we shouldn't feel bad about it. He had some ideas he wanted Hoosiers to hear and, he said, he'd have fun expressing them. By then, I was playing tackle in high school football and, though having broken a leg on the gridiron, I did not get beaten-up when I proceeded around many blocks passing out my dad's literature. I didn't get a very warm reception, though. In 1948 Hoosier Democratic candidates were tripping over each other

4 🏛 SLANDER AND SWEET JUDGMENT

trying to get away from association with the badly slandered and therefore apparently unpopular Harry Truman. But not my dad; he campaigned for Truman and did so in no uncertain terms.

On election eve at our house, we listened to Governor Dewey and then-President Truman sum up their campaigns. Dewey sounded as though he had already won and was telling us what he was going to do "come January twenty." (He didn't say *twentieth*.) Then we heard Truman. At the end of his talk, in a flat tone, he simply said, "I have told you the truth." My mother switched stations in time to hear the only Hollywood movie star who campaigned for Truman. His name was Ronald Reagan. Sounded pretty good.

When the polls closed on election day, Dad came home for dinner and asked me if I'd like to go to the county headquarters with him to learn the returns, adding in his rural southern Indiana and Lincolnesque-relaxed grammar, "It don't look too good." Certain defeat never does.

As the precincts began reporting, though, something strange seemed to be happening. They obviously were not coming in accurately. My dad was ahead. And he won. It was a school night and I left my dad at headquarters to enjoy the congratulations. The bus was my transportation home and when I arrived, the ladies of our house were listening to WIBC radio, where "showman-newscaster" Frank Edwards was interviewing my dad. "I guess we can call you, Congressman-elect now, can't we?" said Edwards. "Okay by me," my father replied in a not-unhappy voice. Now Uncle Karl knew another congressman, an Indiana one at that.

Frank Edwards was one of my father's close friends and he was a delight. He certainly earned his sobriquet, *showman newscaster*. He had been a comedy writer for Bob Hope and when he went on to be one of the original anchors at Indianapolis Channel 13 (the same station where Kim Hood, who would become my wife, became an anchor much later) the news was absolutely never dull. Seated right there on the desk in front of Frank every night was Candy, his little Boston bull dog. On hot summer days he would give about as much weather as we would hear later on the same NBC station from Willard Scott. One of Frank's predictions for a next day was, "High in the low nineties, low in the high nineties."

Before Frank landed at Channel 13, he was a national radio news commentator whose sponsor was the huge American Federation of Labor. Each weekday evening one could hear the enthusiastic voice of announcer Joe McCaffrey say, "Ladies and gentlemen, ten million Americans bring you Frank Edwards and the news. Mr. Edwards has more sponsors than any other commentator in radio, because he is sponsored by the men and women who make up the American Federation Of Labor." Eventually Frank was fired by AFL president—and plumber—George Meany because Frank refused to put a labor spin on the news. Frank wrote a book about the ordeal titled *My First Ten Million Sponsors.* The book told the story of his refusal to compromise and how the union president was "an old meany." A couple of decades later, Frank finally hit it rich. He made a fortune from *UFOs.* One of his best-selling books, *Flying Saucers: Serious Business,* had a special message on the dust jacket: "WARNING! IF YOU SEE A FLYING SAUCER, DO NOT APPROACH IT. NOTIFY THE AUTHORITIES." Somehow I was reminded of the old-time carnival barkers who sold bottles of stuff which would cure anything and admonished, "Don't get too close with that ice cream cone, little boy; it's mighty hot up here."

I knew Frank must be doing well when I saw a full-page ad for his book in the weekly TV magazine of the *Washington Post.* The blurb was hilarious:

Frank Edwards got so close to the truth about flying saucers that high officials in the Pentagon had him fired from a network commentator job.

Enclosing the ad that proclaimed a brand-new reason for Frank's dismissal by the AFL, I wrote this simple letter to him:

Dear Frank:
    Does this mean Meany's forgiven?
                                          Congratulations,

Frank died on a summer's Saturday afternoon just after showering for an evening out with his wife. He had lain down to rest for a few minutes and never got up. Moments before his great heart stopped, his wife heard him say, "I feel funny;" exactly how he felt all his life. Those last words would make a dandy title for a book about Frank. When I called my father to express sympathy about his loss of a dear friend, my father wistfully mused an affectionate tribute, "Frank never grew up." Dad meant that Frank never lost the enthusiasm and imagination of youth. Just so.

By midnight, November 2, 1948, we still did not know who would be president after noon on January 20, 1949. Nor did the country know even early the next morning. Wednesday, November 3, was a high school day for me. When I reported for my morning class in civics, I was elated about my father's election to Congress, although it was difficult for me to imagine him there; he didn't own a spiffy suit. As for President Truman, Ronald Reagan's

6 🏛 SLANDER AND SWEET JUDGMENT

closing campaign speech was heartwarming, but there was no doubt in my mind that Governor Dewey would win. He didn't.

My civics teacher at Indianapolis Shortridge High School was a Dewey person. To say she didn't like Harry Truman would be putting it mildly. She explained his *badness* to us every class day. She was a Republican precinct committeewoman. As our civics class was dismissed on that November day, several of us were still within the sight and hearing of Mrs. Temporley as a schoolmate burst into the room shouting the news to me: The impossible had happened. The pundits and even the polls were wrong—Harry Truman had won.

Suppressing the second of two elations in twelve hours came easily to a student who wanted a good grade from Mrs. Temporley. If she was not happy with the news, I must not be so myself. I somberly nodded my acknowledgment of the news. I got a B.

In January 1949, much to the dismay of the children, the Jacobs family packed up and moved to the nation's capital.

The driving trip from Indianapolis to Washington, D.C., took seventeen hours. There were no interstates. A small part of the trip was on the legendary four-lane Pennsylvania Turnpike which tunnels through the Appalachian mountains. Otherwise in Pennsylvania and Maryland, it was up the mountains in one-lane single file behind endless processions of eighteen-wheelers at a top speed of zilch.

We arrived later than the wee hours of a morning, but we still beat the moving van to the house Dad had rented. The van arrived the next day and the two-man crew walked into our empty living room to look the job over. One of them, who could have passed for the Jackie Gleason character, "Loudmouth Charley Bratton," officiously demanded of my dad, "How much help do we have here?" Dad promptly replied, "Looks to me like there're two of you," whereupon the two men proceeded to the task quietly. When Dad went to the office, I did pitch in and help and the guys actually thanked me. At one point I offered the leader a stick of chewing gum. He studied the pack for a moment and said, "Yeah, I'll chew one with ya." To which I replied, "Er, could I go first?"

Perhaps one of the most famous photographs ever was the one of Truman holding up the old *Chicago Tribune* headline: DEWEY DEFEATS TRUMAN. A week or so later the newsreels showed Truman riding through a gate at the White House in my dream car, a pea green 1949 Cadillac convertible. That car is on display at the Truman Library to this day. Truman was Cinderella. The shoe had fit and the marriage was made. The honeymoon, however, was short-lived.

The angry and persistent vilification of Truman by his most extreme adversaries, including Senator Joseph McCarthy of Wisconsin, placed the President in a special pantheon of mine, occupied then by only two other U.S. presidents: Adams, the elder, and Lincoln. I saw those three as the most maligned while they served.

Declaring some of the Truman haters hoggish for federal policies which would enrich them, my dad said that the good name of anyone who dared to oppose them would "be dashed with foul slander." He also said that getting into a fuss with a slanderer is "like wrestling with a hog; you both get dirty, but he's more used to it." He also said, "they thought they had Truman in '48 and ever since, they've been going around like a mad dog whose victim escaped."

The smearing of Truman was efficient. By 1952, when he declined to run again, his popularity in the polls was 24 percent. History disagrees. So did a college professor whose name I have been unable to find in the historic record. He wrote an article during Truman's crucible which was published either in the *Washington Star* or the *Washington Post*, titled "A Few Kind Words For Harry Truman." And the good Lord knows there were very few at the time. The only thing I remember about the article was an incident at Washington National airport. The United Kingdom's Elizabeth II had just arrived in the United States for the first time since she had ascended the throne. President Truman stood a few feet from her as he read the message of welcome. After the first couple of sentences, he glanced up to see a queen who was also a visibly nervous young woman. As though he had read all there was to read, he folded the pages, placed them in the breast pocket of his double-breasted suit, walked over to the royal visitor, and extended his hand, saying, "Welcome to America." In time, the clear and unbiased vision of history made Truman himself, and his memory, enormously welcome in America.

Dan Quayle did something similarly noble during his televised debate with Jill Long, his Democratic opponent the second time he ran for the U.S. Senate. (We shall read more about that contest later.) In order for Dan and Jill to be the same physical height for the appearance, they each stood behind podiums, he with his feet on the floor and she standing on a stool. When the debate was over, Dan stepped to the space between them to shake hands; the studio microphones were off and a booth announcer was saying the final words about the civic sponsor and the station's public service. Jill was in stocking feet and if she stepped down, it would have been Mutt and Jeff. She told Dan her dilemma and without hesitation, while their images were still being telecast, he walked the rest of the way to her podium and shook hands. They smiled warmly and sincerely. It was a decent deed done by Dan.

In 1998 Bill Clinton made a similar and unsolicited gesture when he and Chinese Premier Jiang Zemin stood together before television cameras, moving the Premier later to say to colleagues, "From such small gestures, you can discern the character of a politician." In the same vein, during the early days of U.S. occupation of defeated Japan, an enraged former Japanese soldier is said to have been en route to Allied Headquarters with a concealed bomb. But, on the way, he saw an American soldier help an elderly Japanese lady onto a street car. The story goes that the would-be terrorist *wouldn't be* after all. He went home. "No act of kindness, no matter how small, is ever wasted." (Aesop)

My father's short tenure in Congress was nothing if not distinguished and memorable—enormously honorable, too. When I entered the House fourteen years later, most of the old timers who knew him thought he had served for ten years. Though he was retired after his freshman year, he was not a retiring freshman. For example, when he was the lawyer for some rank-and-file members of the International Carpenters Union, he brought suit and recovered for their union an enormous amount of money and property which their rajah president William L. "Big Bill" Hutchinson had converted to his personal use.

In those days, the trade unions, with exceptions, tended to be ruled autocratically, whereas the industrial unions, whose members were not out on scattered job sites and attended union meetings in huge numbers, tended to be honest and democratic. Dad thought there ought to be federal law to ensure regular and fair elections as well as periodic accounting of funds in all unions. He managed to be assigned to the Education and Labor Committee. There, by sheer force of personality—of which he had an abundance—he prevailed upon the full committee chairman, John Lesinski of Michigan, to name a select subcommittee on union democracy and name the brash freshman from Indiana as its chairman. This was most unusual, considering that he *was* a freshman and some of the members, including one from Massachusetts named John F. Kennedy, were senior to Dad.

As soon as the subcommittee was established, the greatly politically feared columnist Westbrook Pegler published a piece which included these words:

> If Mr. Jacobs of Indiana wants to know about the lack of democracy in labor unions, he need not waste one penny of the taxpayers' money. The whole evil story is in my files.

Dad issued a subpoena for Pegler to appear before the newly minted subcommittee. That action was seen by some as audacious, so much so that a Fort Wayne newspaper editorialized:

> For Westbrook Pegler it will be just a boring afternoon before amateurs. But for Rep. Jacobs, it will be the most withering experience a rookie congressman ever had.

Naturally I am biased, so I'll let the same Fort Wayne paper tell you how the whole thing came out. The paper ran another editorial after the hearing, complaining that my dad had been too rough with Pegler.

Rough? Well, here are a couple of examples. Pegler takes the oath and Dad reads the above quoted words from Pegler's column and asks Pegler:

"Do you acknowledge authorship of those words?"

"Yes, I do," Pegler replies.

Dad says: "You have the undivided attention of this committee. You may proceed."

Problem. Pegler had nothing with which to proceed: His claim was bluster. It is not an exaggeration to say that this lion of letters fumbled around before the subcommittee inarticulately. At one point Pegler, who had once written nice things about a snake named Hitler, said, "Not to mince words or fence, I take it that by 'democracy,' which I don't admire, you mean protection of the individual from the organization."

"That's right, Mr. Pegler," Dad intoned. "But we're not here to write a dictionary. Now, you said you have facts about the lack of democracy in unions, and we'd like to hear them."

Still no facts.

My father was the first ever to offer federal legislation which would facilitate enforcement of child support orders in cases where the delinquent parent removed to another state and thumbed his nose at the original court. Dad called his legislation the "Runaway Pappy Bill." His proposal was uncomplicated and far more effective than the maze-like legislation that found its way into law in later years. His proposal would have simply declared that every dependent child had a federal right to adequate support from her or his parents. Under the First Judiciary Act, which dates back to the beginning of our republic, state courts are delegated authority to enforce not federal criminal laws, but federal civil rights. His proposal would lengthen the arm of state laws far enough to reach the havens of Runaway Pappies. Without going around the Robin Hood's barn of the full faith and credit clause, a custodial parent could apply to the haven state court, which then could conduct a hearing and directly enforce the original order.

Simple. But too complicated for Congress to this day. I introduced Dad's bill in each of the fifteen Congresses in which I served. Again, to no avail. Something has to be complicated to attract congressional attention.

One of my dad's Congressional colleagues had the distinct reputation of being a ladies' man. In fact he was suing a newspaper at the time for libel because the paper had said the he was having an affair with the wife of a prominent businessman. One day the congressman in question took up the subject of Congresswoman Helen Gahagan Douglas of California: "She claims to be a person of the people. If that's true, then why did she tell a tourist that a Capitol ladies' rest room was for Congresswomen only?"

Dad stepped up to the plate: "I have some legal advice for the gentleman."

"How much will you charge?" inquired the other.

"Nothing," said Dad, "I pledged not to accept legal fees while serving in Congress. Here's my legal advice: I understand the gentleman is suing a newspaper in his district for libel. The gentleman should understand that when you sue someone for libel, the same someone is liable to prove it." The other congressman laughed at this statement, but not at the next one. "Now," said Dad, "I have some practical advice for the gentleman: Libel cases can be volatile. They bear watching. So I advise the gentleman to keep his eye on that libel case and off the door to the ladies' rest room." The congressman never spoke to my father again. I would have; I thought it was pretty funny. So did every one else in the Chamber at the time.

My dad worked too hard in Congress. Like Lincoln, my dad was a master at humor and was conscientious beyond the call of duty, so far beyond, in fact, that he came down with pneumonia his first winter in Washington. When he went by the Capitol physician's office, a young Navy doctor gave him the usual couple of aspirins and sent him back to his office where Dad promptly collapsed. The same doctor rushed from the physician's office to my dad, took one look and said, "Why didn't you tell me you're a Congressman?" To which my dad painfully replied, "Did you think I would have been any less sick if I'd been the janitor?"

Federal aid to parochial schools was a big issue in Congress when Dad was there. In those days, "parochial" in essence meant Catholic, which my father was. He opposed the proposal. That got him into some hot water with some Catholics back home. At mass one Sunday, I heard a priest named Hoover preach a sermon instructing the parishioners to get after my father with letters and straighten him out. As a teenager, I imagined every eye in church, especially God's, was on me. It was not pleasant. Looking back now, it seems funny; but not then. As a fourth degree white-tie-and-tails, sword-toting member the Knights of Columbus, Dad was invited before the lodge to engage in a debate about federal school aid with another Catholic layman. The moderator was a priest.

As the discussion progressed, it was clear that Dad was getting the upper hand with the huge audience, so much so that his opponent said in frustration, "Well, Andy, you'll have to admit that the Lord wants his children educated in the right way." At that point, Dad stood, put on his coat, and made as if to leave. The moderator said to Dad, "Where are you going?" Dad replied, to the great humor of the crowd, "Home. If you have Him on your side, I can't win." The fact that the debate continued indicated that the Lord hadn't taken a position on this Congressional issue after all.

An Indianapolis citizen who was pleased to be known as a "silk stocking" lawyer wrote my dad a letter one day insisting that federal judges be voted a pay raise. But instead of sending it to the Washington Congressional office, he sent it to the editor of the *Indianapolis Star*, who subsequently published it:

> An open letter to Congressman Andrew Jacobs:
> A pay increase for federal judges is long overdue. They are insufficiently compensated to maintain the social positions they have achieved. You should correct this shameful situation immediately.
> Sincerely,

Dad answered by the same route, and the *Star* also published his letter:

> An open letter to _____:
> The federal judges to whom you refer have not achieved the social positions you suggest. Those positions were conferred upon them. Your letter is quite understandable, though. A lawyer with as many cases as you have before the federal courts would naturally be tempted to use taxpayers' money to curry favor with the judges.
> Sincerely,

During the second of my father's two years in Washington, I went to the war in Korea as a Marine combat infantryman. President Harry S Truman had sent airmen, soldiers, sailors, and marines there for a military engagement which violated the U.S. Constitution. That, however, takes nothing away from the sacrifice of those who did the fighting. The war was illegal; their valor was valid.

When somehow I came back home in 1952, it was Ike's year. Bill Mauldin, the immortal World War II cartoonist, came to Indianapolis that year to campaign for Ike's opponent, Adlai Stevenson. The Democrats were looking for a combat veteran of the Korean war to introduce Mauldin to the rally. Freshly minted, I was chosen to do the honors. And what an honor! When I was a little boy I would join my father on the sofa, laughing at the collection of Mauldin's masterful work.

In my fifteen seconds or so of fame, I acknowledged Ike—who, not counting the giants, turned out to be one of my three favorite presidents ever—as "the soldiers' general," but declared Mauldin "the soldiers' soldier . . . and we Marines liked him, too."

Following the rally, as autograph-seekers mobbed the poor cartoonist, I was given one of my most prized possessions. He glanced over at me and said, "I have one for you, Chief." The look in his eyes was the scintillating and celebrated twinkle of the latter-day actor Jack Nicholson. And with that, he drew a personalized cartoon for me on the back of a program. Willie and Joe were his two dog-face infantrymen. Faster than I could sign my name, he drew Joe in a Marine Corps helmet with the caption, *I musta got mixed up wid da Marines.* And he autographed it. Then he went back to the line of people with programs clutched in their hands.

Home from the war, I had returned to my school-days job of delivering concrete blocks to construction sites and going to undergraduate night school at Indiana University in Indianapolis. One day I heard my name mentioned by a city police officer who was working part-time on a building project. He saw me unloading and thought I couldn't hear him. But I could; the damage done to my left ear by a Chinese mortar round had not yet taken its progressive toll. The policeman was telling workers that he had stopped me for speeding about a year before and that I had threatened to use my father's congressional influence to get the officer into trouble. I walked over and asked him where the arrest was supposed to have taken place and when. "West Sixteenth Street," he replied, "and it was a year ago last July."

"Interesting," I said. "I was about ten thousand miles west of West Sixteenth a year ago last July. And I wasn't speeding in a car; I was crawling in mud, which was my personal preference to being shot."

The other hard hats gave my slanderer the fish eye. The best he could do was to say, "Well, he said he was you."

"Oh?" I responded. "You mean you didn't even look at his driver's license and certificate of registration?" He apologized and acknowledged he was trying to sound important by telling the whopper. I forgave him. Why not? It was a rather mild slander compared to the one aimed at me eighteen years later, the one we read about in the Introduction. In politics, one never knows what falsehood will be said next about her or him. If I had a quarter for everyone who went to Indianapolis Cathedral High School with me, despite the fact that I never went to Cathedral, I'd have a lot more spending money.

Richard Nixon made his famous Checkers Speech that year. In his campaign to become Ike's vice president, he had declared himself to be "clean as a hound's tooth." But as my dad put it, "The hound's tooth developed a cavity." Turned out that Nixon had something called a special (*and secret*) campaign fund consisting of gifts from people having business interests in Congressional decisions in which Nixon participated.

Well, guess who had a similar fund? The Democratic candidate for president, Adlai Ewing Stevenson. But his fund was not for himself; it was for the purpose of helping state legislators meet expenses while in Springfield. That still didn't make it right, but there was one other difference between Nixon's and Stevenson's situations. Stevenson had not pontificated on the subject. One day at lunch with his cronies at the Indianapolis Bar Association, my dad was asked what he thought about Nixon's special fund. Dad said, "It's like a preacher's being caught in a whorehouse."

"Well, what about Stevenson's fund?" demanded a Nixon loyalist. "He's not a preacher," replied my pop.

Some of Ike's detractors said that, having been a general, he would get us into war. Another piece of logic along the lines of "all cottage cheese is made in cottages." Ike did no such thing. Unlike his vocal counterparts, Ike knew the horrific costs of war.

The 1952 national nominating conventions were the first to be covered "gavel to gavel" by TV. And they commanded an enormous audience, including all of us in my parents' home. Edward R. Murrow made many interesting observations, including this:

> At the Democratic Convention this year, The Reverend _____ blessed the cheering delegates and assured them that God would surely reward their efforts with victory in the fall. At the Republican Convention, the Reverend _____ blessed the cheering delegates and told *them* God would surely grant their wish in the fall.
>
> I doubt that God is either a Democrat or a Republican. In fact, I doubt that God is only just an American.

My dad had phrased it a bit differently: "Both political parties try to make a precinct committeeman out of God." The preacher who gave the invocation at one of the convention night sessions indicated his approval of the Bible quotation, "and the lion shall lie down with the lamb." I could barely hear my dad mutter with reference to the preacher, "He probably just polished off a big steak for dinner." That made me consider becoming a vegetarian.

During Ike's first term, he suffered severe health setbacks including a major heart attack. Senator William E. Jenner of Indiana was one American who did *not* like Ike—at all. The feeling was mutual inasmuch as Jenner had called Ike's mentor, General George Catlett Marshall, "a living lie." When asked if he would be willing to sit on the platform with Jenner during a 1952 campaign visit to Indianapolis, Ike was reported to have said, "I'd like to punch him in the nose." But Jenner was up for re-election that year and Ike was up—way up in the polls—for election on the same ticket. If not "bedfellows," at least they were strange chair fellows. They sat together on the platform at Butler University's field house. Later, as the presidential election year of 1956 approached, Jenner was asked at an Indianapolis news conference if he thought the ailing Eisenhower would be a candidate for re-election. In his usual pithy and earthy way, Jenner said, "We'll run 'im if we have to stuff 'im."

Those were the improbable years of McCarthyism, when, by golly, you'd better be prepared, in the parlance of the period, to prove you were *100 percent American!* And the malignant ministers of that self-styled litmus for *Americanism* managed to ruin the lives of many loyal and decent citizens. But sometimes the scam was so ridiculous as to be funny.

Take the case of the new mural in the Indiana State Senate Chamber. To one high state official, it was suspicious. Who was this artist anyway? And why did he lace the picture with *red* birds? Red meant communism, didn't it? And what about that pig in the farm scene, why did it have *two* tails? Did a Russian pig have two tails? No, it didn't, and neither did the one in the mural. On closer investigation, the *tails* turned out to be one tail, a curly one. Okay, but what about all those red birds? Not really too sinister; they were cardinals, the Indiana state bird. Well, you couldn't be too careful. They'd let the artist go, *this* time.

Then there was the Indiana State Text Book Commission. They'd ferret out subtle, insidious, and surreptitious commie infiltration into the minds of our children. Ah, ha! They found it. A full-blown communist plot right there on the shelves of school libraries all over the state. Commies were everywhere, else how did they manage this epidemic of encrypted communist inculcation? Er, what book was it? Robin Hood. That rotten red commie, dressed in deceitful green, stole from the rich and gave to the poor.

He must not be allowed to mangle the minds of our minors. My dad pointed out that the courageous text book commission had no objection at all to Ali Baba and the Forty Thieves who stole from everyone and kept it for themselves.

Let's not overlook Dr. Fred Schwarz and his Christian Anti-Communist Crusade. Fred was an Australian national who worked various U.S. cities for contributions from businesspeople who would try anything to stop what they imagined to be the spread of communism in the central nervous system of our body politic. From all accounts Schwarz made pretty good money at it. He didn't have much competition. *The Exorcist* hadn't been written yet and *Ghost Busters* wasn't even a gleam in Bill Murray's eye. Fred easily got the use of the Indiana World War Memorial to hold school on the dangers of communism; maybe it was your neighbor and almost certainly it was the family in the next block.

When Fred was a guest on a radio call-in program one evening, I called, using a voice that sounded like an anti-red redneck. "Dr. Schwarz," I said. "Don't you think we should bomb them Russians before they get a chance to bomb us?"

"No," came the Australian-accented reply. "The people who advocated that several years ago might have had a point. But now with all those thermonuclear devices in the atmosphere, it just wouldn't be feasible." Injecting a tone of excitement to my voice, I plodded on, "Well, yer against communism aren't you?"

"Well, yes I am—"

I interrupted to seek solace and safety from the host: "Joe!"

"Yes?"

"Joe?" I said again in an even more exited tone

"Yes?"

With panic in my voice, "Joe, are you there?"

"Yes, I'm here."

My tone became hysterical: "Do you think we can trust these things to anyone who isn't 100 percent American?"

All this moved me to take pen in hand to write this letter to the *Indianapolis Times*:

> Dear Editor:
>
> What with Robin Hood textbook reform and the temporary one room school house at the World War Memorial, perhaps Santa's give-away program should be expurgated. To wit:

16 ⚛ Slander and Sweet Judgment

You'd better watch out,
  You'd better not buy
Polish ham; I'm telling you why.
  Dr. Schwarz is coming to town.

With local tin horns and lunches of crumbs,
  He'll prove that it's red to aid kids in slums.

He sticks pins in Mao's picture
  Why bother with the draft
To be a home-front hero
  Simply fight Reds with witchcraft.

He sees things in White River; he knows where they've been
  What might just look like logs to you, really are Russian frogmen.

He has a surprise; the Reds are absurd.
  What do you mean, you already heard?
Doc Schwarz is just getting the word.

Joseph McCarthy, of course, was finally revealed to the public for what he was and censured by the U.S. Senate. But even then, some senators were still afraid of McCarthy and either voted against censure or managed to duck the vote altogether. When a certain senator visited my mother and dad in Indianapolis shortly after the censure vote, my mother asked how he had voted. "Well, Mrs. Jacobs," the senator said, "I was on the high seas when that vote was taken." An hour later the same senator was explaining to my parents that there was a "controversial gubernatorial primary coming up in (my state) next spring and I'm afraid I'm going to be right in the middle of it." Dad grinned at the senator and said, "The high seas will still be available."

Dad had a very good way with words. When I was in my sixth U.S. House term, the *Washington Post* asked me to comment about crooks in Congress. I said that if there are crooks in the society generally, they will be represented proportionately in the Congress. My father, I said, told me about a quotation from Lincoln on the point: "You can't dip clear water from a muddy stream." When I showed Dad the *Post* article, he smiled and said it was not Lincoln who coined that metaphor. It was my own papa. That, of course, was not the only time a real author was slighted by not being cited.

While Ike was serving his first six years as president, I graduated from Indiana University undergraduate school and IU School of Law. At the same time, I graduated from my old job of delivering concrete blocks and joined the Marion County Sheriff's Department as a police officer.

I began my law enforcement career as a jail deputy. The duties included checking prisoners in and sending those whose trials were pending to the respective courts. One of the experienced deputies warned me about "mean" Maude Smith, the bailiff at Criminal Court. Expect a tongue lashing, I was told, whenever she calls. And, sure enough, the first time I heard her voice on the phone, it was an angry one. "Deputy, you said you'd have prisoner number 33363 here five minutes ago. Where is he? Can't you ever get anything straight? How did you ever get your job? You're incompetent! We have a long docket in this court and we have better things to do than deal with your inefficiency!"

The lady had a pair of lungs. She continued reading my pedigree interminably. My immediate thought was to point out to her in stern terms that I had never had a conversation with her before in my life, let alone promised her that I would send the prisoner to her court. But as I waited for her to draw a breath, I began to look at the matter philosophically.

When she finally did take on oxygen, I said, "Mrs. Smith, I don't blame you for being upset. I was wrong and I only hope that somehow you can find it in your heart to forgive me." The silence seemed to last as long as her diatribe had. Then, in a refreshingly soft tone, she said, "Well, I think I was too harsh. We all make mistakes." It didn't end there. Maude Smith was a Republican precinct committeewoman. And a few years later when I was a Democratic candidate for the Indiana Legislature, she was heard to ask the Republicans in her precinct to vote for me. At heart, she was a nice lady who hungered for punctuality. And in that cause she came to be at war with the sheriff's department. It was a privilege and a pleasure for me to negotiate the peace treaty and learn a lot about psychology in the process.

It seemed to me that there was something profoundly wrong with the sheriff's department in Indianapolis. The posse had always been picked by political patronage. It was a two-platoon system. Each time a new sheriff was elected, he had appointed an entirely new enforcement team, all members of his political party. But this was police work. Could there be two ways to make an arrest, one Democratic and the other Republican? Obviously not. Law enforcement should follow only one philosophy, firm and fair enforcement of the law.

The new sheriff didn't think much of the existing system either. And he set about changing it. He was Robert A. O'Neal, former superintendent of the Indiana State Police, most prestigious of departments, replete with a long-standing merit system—no politics. Sheriff O'Neal modeled his administration after the State Police. He was a Democrat and his predecessor was a Republican who had chosen his deputies politically. Nevertheless, O'Neal kept all those Republican officers on the job and, what seemed even more odd to old political hands, he kept them in grade. If you were a captain before O'Neal arrived, you remained a captain. But wasn't this just patronage all over again even though, in effect, it was a Democratic sheriff who picked an all-Republican force which had been recruited through politics? In a way, but there was a larger logic in what he did.

If the Democratic sheriff was to persuade the partly Republican state legislature to pass a sheriff merit law, how effective would his arguments be if he had done the very thing he advocated against? He could have fired all the Republican patronage officers and hired new people on the basis of merit, but he still would have been seen as a Democrat firing Republicans wholesale and deciding for himself what merit was. In effect, he bent over backward to set a nonpartisan example. He had to fill the vacancies in the ranks when he arrived, but he filled them according to experience, and other elements of merit. My Marine combat record was taken into account, and the fact that I had finished my undergraduate work and was embarking on my night law school studies helped. College-educated police were pretty few and far between in those days. The fact that my education was rare in that work gave me hope for advancement in the department.

The salary was not handsome, but then neither was I. Probably because the county paid so poorly and our police cars were so flimsy, I thought of the county as being poor itself. In time, when I was promoted from patrol duty to head the traffic safety division, the department gave me an office in a remote part of the building. There was no furniture and I didn't have the heart to burden the county with the purchase of a desk and chairs. Instead, I bought my own at a used furniture store. When I mentioned the purchase to my father, he smiled and said, "That's a lot of overhead for the salary they're paying you. I think Marion County can afford to buy the furniture it needs." Of course, he was right. Everyone who owned property paid taxes on it. Though I'm still not sure why officers were paid slave wages, I did find out why officers had to get along with such awful autos. And it wasn't because Marion County, with its lavish property tax base, was poverty-stricken.

The county commissioners were charged with the responsibility of procuring police cruisers for our department and the cruisers they procured had straight-six engines so weak that, in a chase, a kid with good legs could get away on a bike. These cars were for public safety work by police officers. Why the substandard quality? One of my superior officers, Captain Bob Elliot—later Sheriff Bob Elliott—told me why.

Somehow, each year, the most influential county commissioner wound up with a brand-new, top-of-the-line car of his own from the dealer to whom the police car contract was awarded. The procurement was done by bidding, but not competitive bidding. Year after year, no other dealer had noticed the published legal notices which were made as obscure as possible. And the commissioners did nothing more than the law required to attract competitive bids. Moreover, a lot more over, the commissioners agreed to pay the favored dealer an astronomical price per unit, considering the fact that the annual purchases amounted to fleet proportions. Captain Elliott was distraught when he said to me, "You're a law student. What can we do?"

"Bob," I answered. "We can straighten this out a lot more easily than by going to court. All we have to do is drum up some business." I picked up the phone and called the zone office of one of the competing automobile manufacturers and asked a direct question: "Do you fellows have authority to sell at fleet prices?"

"Well," said the company official, "that depends on what you call a fleet."

"How about eight to ten units?" I asked. The executive's answer: "That's a fleet."

So we concocted a plan. I told the zone executive that it would be unwise to submit his bid early. He should wait until a few minutes before the noon deadline on the appointed day for bids (theretofore "bid"). Then he should enter the commissioners' office quietly and submit a sealed bid according to the published specifications.

It would be too late for the commissioners to pull strings; the news media would be present for the opening of the envelopes. It's a pleasure to report that our plan came off beautifully.

Maybe you had to be there—Captain Bob Elliott and I were—to appreciate it fully. But imagine this: The influential commissioner was shocked when a second bid turned up. But when it was opened, the old bull was devastated. His unusually large jaw didn't just go slack—it collapsed. I don't imagine he was ever much good at poker. But this was worse than a bad poker hand; this cunning commissioner was going to have to make other personal transportation arrangements from then on.

The traditional bid had come before the commission in the traditional way, a rip-off. Barely meeting the specifications, the price per unit was sky-high. The new bid exceeded specifications substantially. A bicycle with jet engines wouldn't outrun these cars with powerful V-8 engines. And the price? Not 10 percent less, nor 20 nor 30 nor even 40. The new bid came in at *one-half* the price of the perennial one.

From then on, the sheriff's department was riding high, or at least at high enough speeds when necessary to carry out its duties.

Juggling law school and full-time police work meant shortchanging one of three things: law school, police work, or sleep. Since neglect of either of the first two was unacceptable, I tended to burn the candle at both ends which tended to shortchange both the police work and law school to a degree.

Law school has been described as a series of crises. Exam week was more like a series of tortures. And during that painful period, the three factors of law school, law enforcement, and fatigue combined to produce some pretty unusual and funny things. There will never be anything funny about sweating out exams. But police work is not always drudge and danger.

One exam week I was working the third, or graveyard shift from eleven at night to seven in the morning. On average, of course, this is the quietest period. There can be reports of prowlers or break-ins, but the typical offense is a traffic one. And that's just what I observed, or thought I observed, at a four-way-stop intersection during the exam week. It was in the wee hours of a Wednesday morning and for me it was two exams down and two to go. In terms of fatigue, I was pretty much gone myself as I pulled a motorist over and approached his car. Suddenly I was seized with doubt and said to the citizen, "Sir, I can't remember. Did you run that stop sign?" He replied, "Officer, I'm afraid I did."

"Well," said I, "would you not do that anymore?" And he said, "I'll sincerely try not to." My parting words were, "Have a nice morning." I couldn't have sworn in court that I'd observed an offense. Besides, I suspect the exchange between us was far more likely to improve his driving than an expensive ticket would have. Did I pass the final two finals? Yes, but in the case of one, only by the proverbial skin of my teeth. A long time later when I was serving in Congress, I was given the privilege of speaking at the commencement of my law school alma mater. And I began with this:

> We tend to think of natural immutable laws as negative—Murphy's Law, Parkinson's Law, the Peter Principle, etc. But there is one natural law that is very much positive. That one says the longer you're out of law school, the less likely they are to look up your grades and the more likely they are to let you be the commencement speaker.

From there I suspect my talk was downhill, but I began on such a lofty plane.

When I went to work at the sheriff's department, about forty people were being killed annually at railroad crossings in our county. The reason was no mystery. At the crossings on back roads there were no automatic flashing signals to warn motorists of approaching trains. There were stationary wooden signs, but to drivers unfamiliar with the route, the non-blinking cross-buck signs were like green lights. And carnage was common. Here's the solution that occurred to me: regular red octagonal street-intersection stop signs at all railroad crossings where there were no automatic blinkers. I went to the county commissioners—who still didn't have a clue that I had sabotaged the cozy deal they had with the car dealer—and asked for an ordinance requiring the signs.

The commissioners passed the ordinance and the following year there was a grand total of zero railroad crossing fatalities in our jurisdiction. Ironically, one of those signs saved my life one night. During a patrol, as I approached one of them on a lonely road, I saw two men seemingly suspiciously beside a car on the other side of the track. There was a possibility of contraband and it was my duty to check it out, quickly. Should I stop for the sign I had caused to be installed or, since this might be an emergency, should I keep going across the track? I decided that the situation called for me to rush through the crossing without stopping. *I* decided that, but my right foot didn't; it automatically slammed on the brake. Just as the police cruiser jerked to a halt, tons of steel streaked through the crossing just a few feet beyond the front bumper of the cruiser, rocking me from side to side. After the freight train passed, I proceeded to find two perfectly decent citizens with a flat tire. The main lesson here is the slogan we've heard from childhood: *Safety First.* If one makes no exception to fastening the seat belt and obeying stop signs and red lights, he or she forms the safety habit. And no matter where the conscious mind is—a shocking news report on the radio or a cell phone—the trained subconscious will apply the brake and save that person's life.

I was twenty-two years old when I became a police officer and although I had been through a war as a Marine infantryman, I came from a family where both mother and father were pretty straitlaced. Therefore, the first arrest I ever made, which involved drunk driving, embarrassed me. The offender was a woman seated at the wheel of a car stopped in one of the driving lanes at Twenty-second and Meridian streets in Indianapolis. A crowd was trying to persuade her to get out of the car. When I approached, the subject took one look at me, took her foot off the brake, and jammed it heavily onto the accelerator. She and the car lurched forward. I followed and it was anything but a merry chase; it was harrowing. Between Twenty-second and Thirty-fourth streets, she charged through three red lights. At Thirty-fourth, the green light suddenly turned yellow and then red and she slammed on the brake. I ran to the car, pulled open her door, grabbed the keys from the ignition and breathed a sigh of relief. She breathed a sigh of alcohol. Let me be candid: Yuck!

I called for the paddy wagon and began to look for the bottle or bottles in the car, whereupon she began some unladylike talk. It started out almost conversational, "I know Sergeant So-and-so on the vice squad." I replied, "Somehow that doesn't surprise me." She continued, "I know you police. You pull a woman over just for sex." That did surprise me and I chose not to dignify it with a reply. That did not stop her. Next she said, "If I thought you were man enough, I'd let you make love to me." I ignored that, too. Then I guess you might say she insulted me. She said, "You're not man enough for me." Here's where I may not have measured up to *Dragnet*'s Sergeant Friday. I looked at the subject and said, "You're wrong." This time it was her turn to be surprised, until I added, "You're not woman enough for me."

The wagon arrived with a matron, I finished and signed a preliminary report, and radioed out of service. It was two hours beyond my three to eleven o'clock shift and I went home to bed. In those days information did not pour forth from computers. Therefore the stolen-car check I had requested from the desk lieutenant was not immediately available. I figured it would be the next day. At about three A.M., I was awakened by a call from the department; the car *was* reported stolen. That just didn't quite sound right to me. So then and there I called the citizen who had phoned in the complaint about his car. It was my turn to wake someone up. When he answered and acknowledged making the report, I told him it sounded fishy and asked if he knew the penalty for filing a false report. He wondered if he could call me back in ten minutes. Now confident that I had the real story, I knew why he wanted to call back. About ten minutes later he did. And confessed. No, the car had not been stolen, but he didn't want to talk in front of his wife. I told him that if he went to headquarters and withdrew the report within the next hour, we could talk further. Both happened.

The man had taken the woman I arrested to a bar. She had drunk too much, wandered out into the parking lot, and got into his car, finding the keys in the ignition. She had no driver's license when I arrested her because she had never applied for one and essentially had never driven before. In other words, she knew what she was doing when she got drunk, but she did not know she would be driving. Although I had placed a charge of driving under the influence of alcohol, I was beginning to think more along the lines of public intoxication. She had done a dangerous thing, but fate had spared harm. It seemed to me she did not have the same culpability as would have been the case if she had been accustomed to driving when she undertook her inebriation.

The next day in court, I decided that I could not properly withdraw the charge, but when I testified, I did explain the unusual circumstances, assuming the defendant would receive a light penalty. She had no lawyer, but even the prosecutor seemed to agree with leniency. It didn't happen. The judge threw the book at her: three months in the Indiana Women's State Prison. Out of line. At the time, under the drunk driving law, even first-time offenders who knew they would be driving when they began drinking their "demon rum" were not incarcerated. The law should have been more stringent, but as applied it wasn't. So this was a curiously harsh result. After some checking, I knew what had happened. It was a reverse fix. Ordinarily a fix meant the judge had agreed to let a defendant go. The reverse fix meant outside influence for greater punishment.

The defendant was the sweetheart of more than one married man— three more, in fact, two of whom were good friends of the judge. These pillars in the community wanted to quit the extramarital affairs without trouble from the paramour. The judge was all too happy to help, which is to say he abused his authority. The same judge issued a search warrant for us to make a gambling raid one night and somehow the gamblers found out we were coming. They seemed downright saintly when we entered the premises. Sad way to learn about crooked judges. The sheriff gave us a list of the honest ones which, I'm happy to say, was almost all of the local judiciary. The exceptions belonged in jail ahead of regular criminals.

There is another and shorter story about the education of a young police officer. It happened at the scene of an accident in an upscale neighborhood. A car with two occupants veered off a street and crashed into a utility post. The driver was not badly hurt, but the lady in the passenger seat was. Her injuries were mostly internal. Under the circumstances, regulations required that I give first aid but await the arrival of a paramedic to move her. The arrival of the paramedic was inordinately delayed for an inexcusable reason. On the day before, the police had given a traffic ticket to an ambulance driver who was not on an emergency run. And now the ambulance drivers were paying the police back—at the expense of injured citizens. Our ambulance had driven exactly thirty miles per hour even though it was using its red lights and siren.

As the victims and I waited, about ten women from the neighborhood gathered around us. When at last the injured people were on their way to the hospital, the ladies asked to speak to me. "Officer, we were just discussing this situation and wondering: If one of us should be injured in an accident, would it be wiser to call a private ambulance?"

"No," I said and told them the problem, adding that I was sure it was only temporary, very temporary, once I reported the outrage to the proper authorities. "Besides," I said, "private companies are not usually prepared for emergency runs." Another lady asked, "Can't you do anything in a situation like this?"

"Well," I replied, "there are strict rules against our moving an accident victim who has internal injuries. It would be enormously dangerous. Now, in a case, say, of a child who has a serious laceration that requires stitches, I'll apply a pressure bandage, lay the child in the back seat of the police car, and do a run to the emergency room."

All the women seemed pleasant and reasonable, except one. Now she chimed in caustically, "Did you do that this time?" Here's where an unintended double entendre can mortify a young police officer. Without thinking the sentence through before saying it, I did say, "Well, ma'am, I can't lay a woman in the back seat of a car." Halfway through I realized where the sentence was going, but I decided it might be even worse if I stopped. The ladies were all much older than I and, in retrospect, I suspect they might have been suppressing giggles. I was just trying to suppress perspiration as I saluted and "marked back" into service. If you happen to be one of those ladies, rest assured that in time I began to think it pretty funny, too. Not that day, though, nor that year, or even decade.

Another neighborhood situation was illustrative of the less-attractive aspects of human nature. My dad liked to tell the story of a church board that met to condemn *others* for drinking. You may recall that Mark Twain said something like, "To do good is noble; to advise others to do good is also noble—and much less trouble." A man phoned the sheriff's department one day to report his outrage at the people who were speeding on his street. My assignment was to visit the man and promise that we would set up a speed checkpoint in three days, which was as soon as we could get to it. By chance, as I approached his street, a speeder whizzed by. When I stopped the offender and was handed his driver's license and certificate of registration, there was the color of the familiar. I carried the documents back to the cruiser to check on the car and driver and it dawned on me. Glancing at my clipboard, I confirmed it. As I handed the documents back to the citizen at his car, I politely inquired, "Did you call the sheriff today?"

"Yeah I did, officer. I'm the one who called to complain about speeding right where I was speeding. I guess I know what you're going to say." To which I replied, "I was just going to ask what your house is built of. Glass by any chance?" He got a warning ticket, which is what we would do the following week when we set up the checkpoint. I think he got the point, too.

There are, of course, endless stories about my three-and-a-half year police career. Big Don Burkert was one of my fellow officers, a lifelong friend, and one of the funniest people God ever thought up. One night he had a run described as "domestic trouble." The trouble was a spoiled grown son who was still living at home. Like most spoiled kids—I call it "the gentle brutality"—he had no respect for his parents; he was reported to be physically beating his father. When Don and his partner, Walt Thickston, arrived, the son turned, grabbed Don's winter uniform coat and tore off a button. The son was arrested and taken to jail. But there was a delay in his departure from home; Big Don made him sew the button back.

Then there was the lament of the Ravenswood Town Marshall. Ravenswood is a small community situated on the banks of White River within Indianapolis. Except for investigating vandalism and perhaps catching a speeder now and then, there wasn't really much for the town marshal to do until that fateful night when murder came to his town. Most murders are domestic, spouse vs. spouse, and this one was no exception. I don't think the marshal had much of a problem with the sheriff's participation in the investigation. I had worked with him before and I was on the run this time. But he was nervous; nothing like this, he said, had ever before happened in his jurisdiction. He seemed embarrassed and was perspiring profusely. The shock of the investigation was bad enough, but when a television crew asked him to do an interview on the spot, well, he was overwhelmed. After he stumbled through the questions and answers on camera, he was wiped out, a nervous wreck. As he ranted and raved about his professional misfortune and how he'd never, ever give a TV interview again, I couldn't resist. So I said, "Quoth the Ravenswood Marshall, 'Nevermore.' "

Now that I was a police officer, I told my sister, Marge, I was thinking of getting an *AR* license plate for my personal car. For some reason beyond me such a license plate was supposed to designate importance at the time. Marge is the wit of our family. And she spared me not. She replied, "*AR* plate; big deal." It was foolish of me to press the matter by saying, "Well it isn't just anybody who can get one."

"No," Marge agreed. "You have to a have a car." Thank God it happened before I went to the Legislature and to Congress. I never picked up the special license plates available to officials in those offices, not as long as Marge was around. As time went by I began to consider such plumage pretty silly. As we shall see, a good friend of mine in the Indiana Legislature saw the matter differently.

When I commanded the safety division, I discovered that, in an eight hour period, officers in my division had issued twenty-three speeding tickets as a result of defective timing devices. So I canceled them, considering my decision no more than fair, an act of simple justice. My action drew banner headlines and I was amazed. Should it be news when one remembers why we find erasers on pencils?

I confess I was not surprised when another idea of mine wound up in the newspapers. It was Indianapolis 500 race time and I asked my officers at the ticketing end of speed check courses to use the checkered flags I had bought to signal offenders to stop. The same kind of flag at the track did not mean a speeding ticket even though the speeds there were considerably higher.

One of my new officers was James Wells, who showed considerable promise. He was constantly friendly and efficient and years later he was elected sheriff.

When he ran the first time in 1978, he asked me to do a broadcast endorsement, which I agreed to on the condition that I could write it. I did so in the manner of a commercial then being run by a credit card company. A well-known person off camera would say some nice things about how the credit card helped her or him in a tight spot. At the end of the spot, that person would be identified. My ad for Jim went this way:

> As is the case with others, my family and my property are important to me. Therefore, sound law enforcement is important to me. Jim Wells can provide that; he is a well-trained professional. I know; I trained him.

Then I identified myself. What can I tell you? He was elected. Of course, since he was one of the best police officers in town and had an unusually pleasing personality, I guess he just might have got there without my help. But my foray into advertising was fun.

After a few years of police work, I finished my part-time law studies and, with bloodless knuckles, passed the bar exam. My occupation was changed. No longer a policeman, I began the practice of law. And, in a sense, one of my first clients was a lawyer and later a judge—my father. In this case, my work was a result of cross-training, police officer and lawyer.

One afternoon, I received a call from one of my former fellow officers; could I go to headquarters and meet with him? It was, he said, urgent. When I arrived, the detective came slowly to the point. He wanted to know if my father had any unusual habits. "Well," I said, "he's honest without exception. Sad to say, I guess that's somewhat unusual."

"I mean," continued the detective, "do you know if he has any unusual sex problems?" That floored me. My dad was from the very old school when it came to that subject. "Straitlaced" would only begin to describe his social rectitude. As was the case with President Grant, my dad would not even so much as tolerate an off-color joke—even a very good and funny one. (I would, though.) "Unusual," I repeated. "Well, he's what you would call pure as the driven snow. I suppose you'd say that's unusual, too. It seems to me that we've come to the point where you ought to tell me what you're getting at." He agreed and did.

"We just received a complaint from the father of a six-year-old girl that the male driver of a Karmann Ghia drove slowly by the citizen's home two times and exposed himself to the girl." That raised hackles somewhere around the back of my neck. My dad drove a Karmann Ghia. And sure enough, the detective said the car was registered to my dad. I told the detective, "This won't compute." My police training went into, you might say, high gear.

At my suggestion, the officer and I went to Dad's parking garage, checked out the little car and drove to the complaining citizen's home. We were told that the family had just taught the little girl to tell them immediately if any man made what they explained were improper gestures to her. And she had told them that the man driving the car was unzipped as he sat behind the wheel while passing in front of her. She added that she saw "his weenie."

"Okay," I said to the little girl, "where were you standing?" She showed us a place on the steps of the front porch. Now I suggested that I drive the car to the position where she said it was before. The father, mother, and detective stood on the designated step and looked at me in the car.

Karmann Ghias had very low bucket seats. The case was solved. Even though the adults were much taller than the girl, they simply could not even come close to seeing my lap. My father was six feet tall, I am six feet, three.

Obviously I wanted to do what I could to straighten the absurd matter out before my father was subjected to any anxiety of the sort Henry Fonda portrayed in the film *The Wrong Man*. Now I suggested the child's father, the detective, and I go to my father and tell him what had transpired.

Explanation? Couldn't have been simpler. My dad invested in nothing but multifamily real estate. The apartment building across the street was for sale. He had rounded the block to get another look before calling the real estate agent. Case not only solved, but closed before it was ever opened. But what happened next shot up the hackles below my rear hairline again.

The little girl's father who had phoned in the mistaken report began to take a high moral tone with my dad. Offended, I interrupted. "Just a minute, *pardner* (police parlance at that time and place), you're overlooking who turned out to be the victim in this situation. The power of suggestion was obviously working overtime with your little girl. The police have many cases of this kind. And both you and she made a perfectly understandable mistake. But don't come in here and take out your frustration on the people you not only have inconvenienced, but also caused some anxiety." He turned out to be a nice guy and apologized. Accepted. That kind of incident represented a serious dilemma for law enforcement. Where young children with big imaginations are involved, the authorities normally look for corroboration. The problem there is that sometimes there is no additional evidence, one way or the other. Many times the child is right, but often it is extremely difficult to tell whether the crime has been committed. DNA won't do much good in alleged exposure cases.

The same kind of mistaken accusation that fate brought to my father, later visited one of the most decent political leaders I have known in Indianapolis. He was John Sweezy, Marion County Republican Chairman for nearly a third of a century. And, unfortunately, the farfetched matter reached the news media and was published as was his subsequent exoneration. Many of his friends failed to be at his side to presume the truth, that he was completely innocent and falsely accused.

Dad's best friend was Asa J. Smith, who remains an enormous icon of Hoosier history. And he was a character. He was gassed at Belleau Wood as a Marine Corps enlisted man in World War I, a casualty that cost him fatherhood later in life and eventually took his sight. Following the first worldwide war he became a lawyer and served in the Indiana Legislature. He became a colonel in World War II. When he was a provost martial, the base chaplain reported mistreatment of Marine brig prisoners, Marines accused of crimes. The first thing Asa said to the chaplain betrayed one of the contradictions about him. "What branch of the superstition do you belong to?" he demanded of the junior officer. Asa was a practicing agnostic. He also billed himself as a right-wing Republican who hated the word "conservative" because it sounded too liberal. Yet, as a follower of Alexander Hamilton, he believed strongly in federalism—no state lines and all governmental authority at the federal level. There was one exception to his agnosticism; he adored Alexander Hamilton.

Asa sent me a book about Hamilton when I was in college and I did not have time to read it. A few weeks later, a letter arrived from him: "Sir: Return my book. I have friends who can read." I hesitated to write letters to Asa; they always came back corrected. "Animals are *raised,* children are *reared.*"

The Jesuits had a discussion group that met each week in Indianapolis and Asa was their devil's advocate. Being a practicing agnostic, he knew as much about the Catholic religion as the Catholics did; and he did not hold back. One evening he asserted, "Nothing will be discussed here tonight that was not written about by William Shakespeare." One of the participants tried to nail the crusty war veteran on that statement: "At our table, we were discussing artificial insemination. Would you be good enough to tell us in what instance the bard wrote about that?"

"Simple," said Asa, "he wrote a whole play about it: *Love's Labour's Lost.*"

Asa's claim to permanent fame was his role in the 1920s murder conviction of the Indiana Ku Klux Klan panjandrum D. C. Stephenson. Asa was the family lawyer of the victim and took her dying declaration which held up in court. In the 1960s, Asa and my dad met every workday afternoon for coffee. One day my dad arrived first and discovered a new waitress as well as a section of the restaurant velvet-corded off. Stepping over the cord, Dad sat down at a table in the closed section. When the new waitress explained that the section was closed to Dad, who already knew it perfectly well, he told her a made-up story: "I understand, ma'am, but I'm a parole officer and one of my ex-cons is reporting to me here for the first time. He just got out of prison where he served for forty years. I want to keep him away from normal people as much as possible, especially women."

When the waitress returned with coffee for my dad, she asked what the crime was. "Well," Dad said. "It was a sex crime and he hasn't been around women for a very long time." She understood. At that moment, Colonel Smith arrived, hopped over the velvet cord and joined Dad. (You need to know that Asa was a benign but persistent flirt.)

The new waitress brought a cup of coffee to the "ex-con." She did so with logical trepidation, whereupon she heard from the unwitting butt of Dad's joke. "Well, come over here, you sweet thing," Asa effused. I would not be surprised if some coffee was spilled, by startled accident or on purpose.

Years before the restaurant incident, when air-conditioned buildings were yet to happen, Asa was sitting in his office one afternoon when he noticed that his tilt-out window formed a perfect periscope with the one in the office immediately above him. And in that accidental periscope were the images of a man and a woman making love. Asa raced to the lobby of the building, consulted the directory, identified the man on the next floor and found a phone. When the sex participant answered the phone, breathing heavily, he heard Asa's booming and apocalyptic voice say, "This is God; I disapprove."

It was partly under Asa's tutelage that I became a candidate for the Indiana State House of Representatives the same year I passed the bar exam. One of my pledges was to introduce legislation to make mandatory the police merit system Sheriff O'Neal had voluntarily established.

Following my filing for the office, the first order of political business for me was to report to the Marion County Democratic Party treasurer with a *slating fee*. That meant my name would go before the party precinct workers who would vote by secret ballot in convention to choose candidates for party endorsement for the primary.

Party treasurer Larry Sexton was kindly, dapper, and courtly, a perfect gentleman on the edge of being the caricature of one. In other words, the word, "courtly" doesn't quite catch it.

My friend Jack Dillon, future Indiana Attorney General and commander of the Indiana National Guard, told me that on one occasion Larry had fallen from favor with the real party chief, Indianapolis Mayor Phil Bayt. Phil had called Larry to demand resignation from the party post and did so in strident tones. After a couple of minutes of Phil's excited recitation of the treasurer's supposed sins and after a moment of piercing silence, Larry is said to have said with the friendliest of inflections, "Well, Mayor, other than that, how've you been?"

Larry was also the president of the Indiana Democratic Club and he was among the few to call it by its correct name, *Democratic*. Most others, Democrats and Republicans alike used the word chosen by former Republican National Chairman Leonard Hall as a slur against the opposition, "Democrat Party." Need one add that Joseph McCarthy was the first to take it on the road? The correct name appears on the ballot and most of the people who use the incorrect one don't even know that the origin of their error was an insult. My friend Jim Beatty once said to our friend, Tom Titsworth, "People who say, 'Democrat Party' should be hung." To which Tom quietly corrected, "Hanged." And my dad, who had toiled in the political vineyards during the days of McCarthyism, occasionally fired back with "Publican Party." You will recall that biblically "publicans" were tax collectors, a sin done excessively in different forms—pursuant to different forms of excessive spending—by both major political parties.

Larry was the party treasurer I approached with trepidation and a certified check to file for the party slating convention. He accepted the check, entered my name as one more hopeful, and in a prophetic purr, predicted, "You'll run for the State House of Representatives this time, the State Senate next time, and in 1962 you'll run for the U.S. House of Representatives." As he tucked the check neatly into a drawer, he concluded, "Good luck."

In those days, the campaign gimmicks knew no bounds, except for decency in most cases. My friend Patrick J. Barton was a candidate for Congress in the slating convention the year I ran for the Indiana Legislature. His gimmick was a group of weightlifters doing their thing under a huge sign which read, "BARTON IS THE STRONG CANDIDATE." Wonderful Walter Bell stood next to an old dinner bell, kicking the lanyard occasionally while passing out cards reading, "RING THE BELL (on the convention voting machine) FOR BELL."

One of the perennial candidates for public office in Marion County was Percy Hardin. And he put his name to good use with the campaign slogan, "You could do worse than vote for Perse." The convention did worse; didn't vote for Perse.

When the convention votes were counted, I was endorsed along with ten other Democratic candidates for the eleven at-large Indiana State House seats of Marion County. Only one of those endorsed lost the primary. I was not he.

Was my Marine combat record a political asset? I doubt it. As was the case with Ike, it may have been something of a shield when I stood up against using our military personnel as campaign cannon fodder for unworthy politicians. But after all, I *was* defeated for Congress in 1962 by a candidate whose exemption from the draft in World War II looked suspicious. He lost his vocation to be a preacher at about the time they repealed the draft.

Churchill certainly believed that a combat record would advance his political career and went out of his way to establish such a record. But historians discount its effect in his campaigns. Erroneously believing a military record to be of political importance, more than one member of the Congress has shot himself in the political foot faking it.

There was a representative from New York who made the fraudulent claim of a combat record. When the lie was exposed, his days in politics were done. What a shame. He was one of the handsomest men ever to serve in Congress, with charm to match. And before the lie left him in the dust of discredit, his political future seemed unlimited. He would have done fine in politics without a military record, but with so many Rambo-like movies assaulting public taste, he probably believed it necessary either to be a combat veteran or *seem* to be one. So friendly, so likable. So sad.

Not so sad was the case of the pugnacious Representative Wester Cooley from Alfalfa, Oregon, a state where they actually have a law against lying in politics. When a citizen files for Congress there, she or he is required to file a biography, *under oath*. In Oregon politics, fibbing is a felony. Cooley falsely claimed he had fought in the Korean War. When an enterprising newspaper reporter unearthed the truth which had been "crushed to Earth," the paper reported that the congressman had never left Fort Bragg. Cooley's initial response to the exposure was that there was no official record of his fighting in Korea because he was a perdu, with classified orders which were later lost, not because his dog ate them, but because of a house fire. Of course, the house fire story didn't hold water, either.

Cooley was *not* a likeable man. At one point, he approached the reporter who unearthed his lie. She was pregnant and sitting down when he doubled up his fist and thundered, "If I wouldn't be charged with assault, I'd punch you in the nose." Big Wes the commie killer, who also specialized in terrorizing pregnant women.

I was nominated for the state legislature in 1958, which turned out to be a landslide Democratic year. It was the second off-year election of the Eisenhower tenure and, more significant, it was a year of deep recession. But none of this dissuaded the yet-to-be-reformed *Indianapolis Star*.

It took action reminiscent of the attacks against Al Smith and John Kennedy, attacks that claimed the Pope would take over America if either of those Catholics would be elected president—The joke at the time was that when Smith lost, he sent a one-word cable to the Pope: "Unpack." The *Star* ran not headlines but *footlines* the size of banner headlines at the bottom of the front page day after day, telling the voters, "Don't Vote Indiana Over to Reuther," referring to Walter Reuther, president of the United Auto Workers. The right wing was particularly unhappy with Reuther because a congressional investigation of dishonesty among labor union officials had turned up some crooks like Hutchinson of the Carpenters Union and Beck and Hoffa of the Teamsters, but they were Republicans.

When the committee had turned its attention to Democrat Reuther, some of the members were sorely disappointed to learn he was honest. They cringed when credible evidence showed that his official union car was a modest model and that he dug into his wallet to use his personally purchased stamps on letters that were borderline between business and personal. As was the case with the joke about the unsuccessful police raid on the burlesque house, the investigators found they had nothing on Reuther. Most frustrating. Even worse, he didn't double-cross his members by selling out at the bargaining table for his own personal gain.

In the eyes of the far right, Reuther was a full-fledged villain. Since they genuinely believed it themselves, they figured he was the best one they could use to scare Hoosiers. To paraphrase the words of Hoosier poet James Whitcomb Riley, the footlines in essence said, "Reuther'll getcha if you don't watch out."

I didn't have two nickels to rub together so far as my campaign was concerned. Friends often asked me for my "cards," which they offered to pass out. When I explained that I couldn't afford cards, supporters sometimes seemed disappointed. So I went by the dime store and bought two decks of playing cards and tendered that kind of card when asked. And, of course, I couldn't begin to think about paid radio or TV time. One piece of good fortune did come my way, though.

The League of Women Voters sponsored a television discussion among three Democrats and three Republicans running for the legislature. And I was one of the Democrats chosen. Need I say that when the camera was pointed at me and the red light came on, I was more than a tad tense? My dad said that in public speaking, debate or otherwise, how well you do depends less on how much you know than on how well you feel. Richard Nixon wouldn't have disagreed with that after his first 1960 debate with John F. Kennedy. And the immortal comedian Jackie Gleason opened his TV variety show each time by shouting, "I feel great tonight!" In the first Kennedy-Nixon debate, the latter did not feel well at all and it cost him dearly. I felt fine physically except for those insects with beautiful wings who were fluttering inside my stomach.

The presentations before mine that night had been bland, the best way to build storm sewers, what to do about stray dogs, and whether snow removal from sidewalks should await snow. But now it was my turn and what I said was anything but docile. I took a very deep breath and plunged into a recitation of the lines I'd composed for the program. The moderator posed the question: "What is your favorite issue?" I somehow managed to get through the following:

Truth. For the past ten days, we have been treated to front-page editorials in the form of banner footlines that say, 'Don't Vote Indiana Over to Reuther,' as though Walter Reuther were the boss of the Democratic Party. He is not.

Ten years ago, Thomas E. Dewey said in Pittsburgh that "these misnamed Democrats ask for the power to put labor into chains." Now suddenly his party says labor is going to put Democrats into chains. Nobody is ever going to put my Party into chains. And nobody but the far right ever tried to.

The morning paper suggests Democrats consort with labor crooks, which Reuther has been conclusively proved not to be. David Beck is a Republican. James Hoffa is a Republican. Indianapolis labor racketeer Maurice Hutchinson is not only a Republican, but up to a few months ago he was a member of the Republican National Committee. Therefore, *somebody* is consorting with labor crooks.

I whispered under my breath, "Wow, I got through it. Thank you, Lord." There were three more candidates to be heard from, two of whom were Republicans. But there was no response to my words. All three of the Republican participants were of the moderate variety and, if anything, were embarrassed by the savagery of the *Star*.

One of the issues the Indianapolis Democrats stressed that year was malapportionment of the legislature. Americans had been on the move for decades from farms to cities, but they had not taken their representatives and senators with them. Those officials were left behind to represent rocks, streams and the relatively small populations who had not left. This meant that rural residents had greater influence per capita on making laws and appropriations than urban residents. We were still about six years away from the U.S. Supreme Court decision in *Baker v. Carr* which interpreted the Constitution as requiring "one person/one vote," meaning legislative districts of populations equal to one another.

In 1964 Lee Hamilton was elected to cast one congressional vote for the 250,000 citizens of the rural Ninth District of Indiana. At the same time I was elected to cast one vote for the 750,000 people of the Indianapolis Eleventh District. Thus, people in the Eleventh District had only one third the congressional vote of those in the Ninth.

The same phenomenon applied to state legislative districts. That malapportionment is all history now. But it was rampant then. So my fellow legislative candidates and I cooked up a public demonstration to illustrate our point, which was also the American founders' point: taxation without representation. We conducted a "Boston Tea Party" around Monument

Circle in downtown Indianapolis, replete with some of our number who, dressed as early native Americans, passed out tea bags. Correct apportionment would not only be logical, but also would have improved urban standing in the legislative halls. That would tend to mean an improvement in the Democratic Party in the legislative process. So our position, while constitutionally correct, was not self-sacrificial.

To complete the picture of a Boston Tea Party, we towed a sailboat around the Monument. Each time we arrived at the Columbia Club, a watering hole for prominent Republicans, we paused and, on a public address system, played the popular Tennessee Ernie Ford recording, *Sixteen Tons*. At first, our Republican friends were having almost as much fun as we were. But when we advanced the audio for the line, "I owe my soul to the company store," they closed the windows and drew the curtains. At that point, super wit Jud Haggerty turned on the microphone and, in the police-siege style of grade B movies, intoned, "We know you're in there. We can hear you breathing." This time it was lots of laughs *and* lots of votes.

The inevitable happened; Democrats were swept into office by the tide of the year. I was a state representative.

Before the 1959 session of the Indiana House of Representatives convened in January, a conference was held at the Union Building on the Bloomington campus of Indiana University. All members-elect were invited and given parking passes for the lot forbidden to students, one of whom I had been just a few months before. My favorite campus cop was a sourpuss we called "Smiley." He roamed the campus on his three-wheeler avidly seeking university rule violators. He specialized in parking tickets and almost got me a couple of times. He knew my ancient Chevy well and, I am sure, he did not know that I had advanced from the Indiana University to the Indiana Legislature. God's humorous side was at work that day. As I pulled my seasoned car into the rarified lot, there was Smiley, smiling less than ever, with pencil and ticket poised. As he approached the seeming parking violation, I tried to look as guilty as possible. Three steps from his objective he saw the parking pass hanging from my rearview mirror. He didn't even say, "Hi." I looked at him and shrugged, hoping I had spoiled at least part of his day. The incident came close to making mine.

Once sworn in by Speaker Birch Bayh, I introduced the bill for a merit system in the sheriff's department. After I rounded up a surprisingly large number of supporters, the bill easily passed the House and was sent to the State Senate where it languished until nearly the end of the session. In the meantime, God dealt me a delightfully good hand: my seat mate, Lealand Buxton. He was assigned to seat thirty-four, and I drew seat thirty-three.

Lealand fits nicely in the pantheon of unforgettable characters. He represented Blotcher, Indiana, a name one would not likely forget, either. He had played semipro baseball, was a lay Baptist preacher, and he very definitely was a character. To the best of my knowledge, I was the only one in Indianapolis he addressed by name. Everyone else was simply "sir" or "lady." And he didn't shake hands. If one were extended to him, he would step back one pace, bend down and wave his arms over one another in the manner of a baseball umpire ruling a runner safe at third. That was his concept of shaking hands. It was noticeable. He was noticeable, even, you might say, notorious.

Lealand went to the legislature to pass one bill. It was a wonderful idea except for one thing; it would have bankrupted the State of Indiana. The proposal would allow a farmer to notify the county commissioners that the weeds along the road by his farm needed cutting. If the commissioners didn't take care of the problem within ten days, the farmer could do the cutting himself and deduct from his property tax what *he* thought his services were worth. The House leaders did not favor the legislation. In particular, the chairman of the agriculture committee looked ill every time Lealand brought up the subject.

Perhaps needless to say, the chairman of the agriculture committee bottled up Lealand's bill. But there is a method for a representative to bring her or his bill to the floor for a vote, regardless of a committee's refusal to report it. The motion to discharge was known as a bill to blast. And Lealand made the motion repeatedly, each time, as his popularity grew, with more support. By the time he had the whole House in daily stitches, things looked pretty promising for Lealand's motion to discharge. So promising that Speaker Bayh asked for my promise not to tell Lealand he was entitled to a roll call vote on the issue. In a moment of monumental weakness, I promised. I didn't think any harm would come from passage of the proposal in the house. The senate clearly would have killed it.

When the fateful day arrived, the ambient feeling was festive. I had put up a large sign in the lobby, "DON'T BUCK BUCKY BUXTON'S BILL TO BLAST." The house was hushed as Lealand stepped to the microphone, Bible in hand, to deliver the great oration. He took as his text the scriptural *good shepherd*. "'What good shepherd would not leave his flock to find the one lost sheep?'" he paraphrased. "My little bill is the lost sheep of this session. Help me restore it to the flock." The speech lasted for several minutes. And when it was finished, the bipartisan laughter was vibrant. It seemed as if the Capitol dome had raised a few inches and settled in a cloud of dust.

Lealand returned to his seat beside me. The speaker put the question,

"All in favor, say 'Aye.'" The affirmative vote was deafening. Lealand looked at me and smiled. Then the Speaker said, "All opposed, say 'No.'" One voice, that of the agriculture committee chairman, said, "No."

Lealand was still smiling when the speaker declared, "The no's have it." Bad grammar. It should have been, "The no has it." Lealand never cussed. The strongest expletive I had heard from him up to then was, "By golly." But this time, this time! It was different. The dike burst. Lealand turned to me, his features contorted, and vehemently intoned, "Andy, by golly—gee whiz!"

Our friend Frank Edwards had a local TV variety show at the time and, as agent without portfolio, I had no trouble scheduling Lealand for guest appearances. At the time there had been a rash of horrible Electra airline crashes, one at Tell City, Indiana, on the banks of the Ohio. Flying on an Electra was beginning to look dicey. So one evening Frank asked Lealand, "Do you travel by air, Representative Buxton?"

"No, sir, I don't."

"Why?"

"Well, I'll tell you, sir. There's too many a-goin' that's not a-comin' back." Lealand Buxton, best thing since Abe Martin. And on one occasion very useful to my pet cause.

On the night the state senate took up the sheriff merit bill, languidness was the rule there. The senators were out of sorts. The huge tote boards, the ones that showed the electronically recorded votes, were a sea of red negatives, bill after bill. And my poor little Tess Trueheart of a merit bill was on the conveyor headed for the sawmill. What to do? This bill was essentially my *raison d'être*, if you don't count that distant dream I shared with Abraham Lincoln, to go to Congress.

I had to think fast. The Honorable Lealand Buxton, state representative from Blotcher, just might be the answer. Republican Lieutenant Governor Crawford Parker was a good friend of mine. We shared an insatiable appetite for humor and he agreed that it would be fun to present Lealand to the senate for a speech. My plan was gelling.

At about 9:15 P.M., the Honorable Crawford Parker introduced to the senate the man they had all heard about, the Honorable Lealand Buxton. He began his address with his baseball umpire signal and said:

"Honorable Senators, this is an honor I never thought would come to a weed-and-bush man from Blotcher . . ."

When he finished five minutes later, the entire body of each member of that body was weak from laughter, some clutching their stomachs in pleasant pain. It is no overstatement to say that the mood of the Senate had changed. When the voting resumed, the tote boards looked like Ireland, verdant. Nothing but "Aye's" as far as the eye could see. The suddenly positive dispositions helped produce the Indiana Sheriff Merit Law, which, in turn, helped produce some of the finest police officers in the nation. One of them was Neil Holder who, years later, along with his teacher wife Wanda and daughters Priscilla and Jessica, became my wife Kim's and my close friends and neighbors. Neil was my kind of cop, kind, soft-spoken—tough as nails.

In the remaining days of the session, Lieutenant Governor Parker would put questions to the senate by saying, "All senators in favor will indicate so by the usual sign." Thirty-eight senators would rise, stretch their arms outward and give the umpire's safe sign. I saw it happen.

In 1959, the sheriff's department was not the only aspect of Marion County government stunningly behind the times. There was no plumbing code beyond the old city borders.

After farmers had moved to the cities and had taken on the ways of the slickers for a while, many of them prospered and moved to the suburbs. And they left something behind again, the plumbing codes. Septic tanks and finger systems got a detrimental grip on suburban Indianapolis. It got so bad that something which didn't smell so good began percolating through the well-manicured lawns surrounding stylish homes. I even made up a bumper sticker on the subject: "Shit Happens, But Fecal Matters." And an enormously talented *Indianapolis Star* writer, Bill Brooks, did an editorial entitled "The Evolution of the Ranch-style Outhouse." I was told that he didn't press for its publication in what was considered to be a family newspaper—if you didn't count the picture ads for the local burlesque theaters.

Early in the session, I was approached by a lobbyist for plumbing contractors. He asked me to sponsor legislation which would extend the city plumbing code into the rest of Marion County. Made sense to me, so I did. Made sense to everyone else, too. It passed and was signed into law by Governor Harold W. Handley in record time. This is where the plot sickens a bit.

Shortly after enactment of the plumbing law, the plumbing lobbyist threw a celebration bash one evening at the Iron Skillet Restaurant. It was a family-style place with large bowls of potatoes and other delights on the tables to be drawn from at will. And I was hungry, very hungry.

Former Indiana Governor Henry Schricker had said of politics, "It's a poor day in this business when you can't pick up a free meal." The plumbers' dinner party was not held on a poor day, but it was a day when I was poor indeed.

Some say you should never serve in a legislative body if you've never met a payroll. As a brand-new lawyer on his own, I not only had to meet a payroll, but had a hard time doing it. There is a story about the new lawyer who had just moved into a small office and wasn't being inundated by clients. He was like the Maytag repairman. After days of rearranging his office furniture and filing his fingernails, a man entered his office. It seemed wise to show the visitor that the young professional was competent and successful. So he picked up his phone and with raised voice, said, "No, we will not take five hundred thousand. When we say a million, that's what we mean. Pay it or we'll see you in court." Hanging up, he turned to his guest and said, "Now, what can I do for you?" To which the other replied, "Not much; I'm here to connect your phone."

Though I never tried such a ploy, my embryonic law practice was not producing a lot of net income after I paid my secretary, Phyllis Butler, the law book company, the landlord, and, yes, the phone company. On that hungry evening, I was just this side of broke. But I was the proud owner of that old Chevy. At least that was a plus. But it was a plus with a minus. I was out of gas, which in those days could be had for around nineteen cents per gallon. The price was a plus, but the fact that I didn't have the nineteen cents as ready cash was another minus. Another young state representative who was destined for great things in the Mead-Johnson Corporation was *almost* as I that evening, but he did have nearly a dollar. We coalesced. I provided the car, he provided the gas and, at the Iron Skillet, the plumbing contractors provided as much as we could eat.

When we arrived, I was not filled with self-confidence. But as the epicurean delights began to work their wonders, I felt a rising euphoria. So much so, that when the lobbyist arose to say a few words to his thirty guests, I arose, too, and asked if I might say a few words first. With part of my tongue planted firmly in my cheek, I said to the group, "As the sponsor of the new plumbing code, I am pleased to welcome all of you to *our* dinner. If there's anything you wish by way of additional dessert, please do not hesitate to ask. And please drive safely." Of course the one who understood my facetiousness best was the future executive of the Metrical company which encouraged dieting.

Fun as it was to eat a good meal and then make inside jokes about my meager means, that evening had a troubling aspect for me. Should a lobbyist ever be in a position to give a legislator something the latter desperately wanted, even, you might say, to have a legislator eating out of the lobbyist's hand? That night I lay awake thinking about it and decided that, in public office, I would never again accept so much as a morsel from anyone advocating legislation. The pledge was tough to keep for a while, but by and by my business took hold and the resolve became a piece of cake. In a third of a century in public office, I never broke that pledge.

I can't say as much for myself concerning indirect gifts in the form of PAC (political action committee) campaign contributions from lobbyists. It would be several years before I would come to my senses about this other kind of "gratuity."

In the legislature, I introduced a bill which some people called, but was not, anti-labor. It mirrored my Dad's earlier effort to ensure democracy in labor unions. The proposal would require regular and fair elections and accounting of funds. Generally, the industrial unions, such as Reuther's UAW, were quite honest and democratic. Some of the trade unions, however, presented problems. In addition to the autocratic and thieving ways of the Hutchinson dynasty in the Carpenters Union, the rajahs of the Stone Cutters Union in Southern Indiana had not bothered to hold an election for decades. The bill had nothing at all to do with the contests between labor and management, except to the extent that union leaders who never faced their members on secret ballots were more likely to betray their members' interests with so-called sweetheart labor/management contracts.

The bill attracted a great deal of support, including that of State Representative Henry J. "Bud" Kintzele, Jr., a union official elected on a democratic ballot and a man of stunning courage. But there was opposition—mostly, of course, from unions where the autocratic leaders were less than keen about letting their membership have any say about who did what with their destinies. The American Federation of Labor comprised most of the trade unions, and the Congress of Industrial Organizations was the national umbrella for the industrial unions. The two giant entities wed in the mid-fifties, becoming known as the AFL-CIO. For their Hoosier leader, they made a splendid choice. He was Dallas Sells, head of the United Auto Workers region which included Indiana. Dallas Sells was one of God's noblemen. Deeply and quietly religious, Dal was also brilliant. He understood and believed in the importance of democracy and fair play. But when it came to my bill, he had a constituent problem, not with his industrial unions who generally already practiced democracy. His problem was with the likes of the Stone Cutters Union, and I understood and accepted his silence on the issue; he never denounced me over what he obviously agreed with personally.

As my effort gathered steam, one of the leaders of my party asked me if I would agree to some modifications in the proposal and suggested I sit down with a veteran state legislator from eastern Indiana to learn the details.

Of course. Well, when I sat down, the first thing I noticed was the inscription at the top of his yellow legal pad: AFL. It took no genius to guess what was on that pad. It was a combination of amendments that would kill the bill. Naturally they were unacceptable and a committee hearing on the legislation was set. I couldn't wait to hear public statements in America against the American principle of democracy. And listen is all I did because of a foolish Faustian bargain, foolish on my part.

The same official of my party who had proffered the lethal amendments told me that if I would agree to say nothing at the hearing—he said he wanted to avoid confrontation—he would see to it that my bill passed. I was young; I believed him. (Make your own jokes.) The bill, of course, was killed in committee. Sadder and wiser, I don't believe I ever fell for that pigeon drop again. That same year, I met Senator John F. Kennedy at the Indianapolis home of my good friends, Pat and Marian Barton. He told me he was working on a bill in Congress to ensure union democracy. It was far more stringent than my proposal and, unlike mine, it had labor/management overtones. It became the landmark Landrum-Griffin Law.

In addition to the decadent political system in the sheriff's office and the bad plumbing in suburbia, there was one more thing in Marion County which I thought anachronistic: the county commission. It was the county's governing body with three executive heads. There were too many cooks, one of whom, Dutch Ayres, was a delightfully colorful politician of my party. He was the Thirtieth Ward Democratic Chairman and had a lot of influence. Not a man to cross. So before I introduced the bill to establish a single county executive, I called him with enough political sense to say that I would support him for that post. I made the argument to him that I planned to make to members of the legislature, sans some of the public speaking poetry.

County commissions would do for a sleepy pastoral community, but Marion County had become a metropolitan area. Some executive decisions had to be made quickly in order to be made efficiently.

Should Dutch have to wait around for two redundant executives in order to make simple common sense decisions? Why was there only one mayor, one governor, and, in deed, one president at a time? The county of the state capitol already had a legislative body, the county council. A single executive was overdue. But none of this would persuade Dutch. He said, "I wish I could change your mind." And I said the same to him, adding that, as a matter of conscience, I had to introduce the proposal. The conversation ended cordially; he even thanked me for the "courtesy" of my call. I proceeded to inflict on myself not political suicide, but a few political wounds, by filing the bill. It didn't fare so well as the plumbing one; it was voted down at the behest of politicians who had appointed themselves to protect the no longer useful past. But before it failed, I did manage to wedge in that public speaking poetry I had in mind:

"Mr. Speaker, no three mortals can act in concert as one. The only supernatural aspect to such an arrangement is the eternal triangle, around which the buck forever orbits."

That was the end of the effort, but it is not the end of the story.

In the following election I was a candidate for one of the at-large state senate seats from Marion County, and the crowded primary field of candidates meant tough sledding for each of us. Respectively, we needed all the help we could get from people like the Thirtieth Ward Chairman, yes, Dutch Ayres. At his ward's candidates night, we competitors were looking for slating convention votes. When it was my turn to speak, I shelled out the kind of campaign oratory corn that might be expected from a young and callow candidate, things like this reference to Richard Nixon's big poker winnings in the Navy:

"We've gone from the New Deal to a fast shuffle in one generation."

One of my fellow state representatives was also my fellow candidate for the state senate and he was there that night. What is more, he had voted with Ward Chairman Dutch against my county executive reform proposal. Dutch would, of course, be for my colleague; I was off sides. But, lo and behold, Dutch was for me. Since my colleague and I were running for more than one at-large seat, we were competing only indirectly. Therefore, Dutch could have been for both of us, but he wasn't. He was *against* my colleague despite the fact that he had voted Dutch's way. Why?

The explanation could constitute an entire psychology course. True, my colleague had been on Dutch's side and I had not. But, according to Dutch, I had been courteous to him and the other fellow had not. When my colleague approached the chairman that night, Dutch asked emphatically, "Do you know me?" Later I learned that when the legislative vote on my proposal was pending, Dutch had tried to speak to my colleague about it and the colleague told Dutch he didn't have time for him. My having called him trumped my colleague's vote for him. "No act of kindness, no matter how small, is ever wasted." (Aesop)

Pinball machines. Big controversy in Indianapolis during my legislature days. *Indianapolis Star* publisher Eugene Pulliam the elder had decided they were evil and had to go and he conducted a protracted editorial effort to bring that about. The editorial effort was not confined to the editorial page or even the op-ed one. Indianapolis Mayor Phil Bayt was a Democrat who went to lengths to please Mr. Pulliam. I'm afraid my otherwise straight-as-a-string Sheriff Bob O'Neal hankered for the affection of the publisher, also. So much so that when the *Star* thundered its demand that the police confiscate those machines of sin and banish them from the realm, both of these Democratic officials hopped to it. But before they did, they asked legal advice from the sheriff's lawyer, my dad. His advice: "Don't do it." Sinful or not, pinballs were not illegal. And the owners who had invested fortunes in them, might just call upon the courts to replevin what was theirs. "Well, no," the officials told Dad, "this is an emergency." In essence, there was "trouble in River City." Pinballs had to go. The *Star* was anti-Communist, but in this case there were to be no legal niceties about private property and due process.

The cops got their orders and they began summarily expropriating the property. And—surprise, surprise—my father turned out to be right. The owners didn't like it. So they took the mayor and the sheriff to court. Winners in the quest for Mr. Pulliam's affection, the officials were losers before the bar of justice. Dad was pressed into service to represent in court the officials who would not take his advice.

It turned out to be a very short trial, following which my father stepped out into the courthouse hall and encountered a television reporter with crew at the ready. The reporter said, "Could we ask you some questions? To which Dad replied, "Make it snappy." No publicity hound, he. Lights, camera, question: "Mr. Jacobs, do you think the public is opposed to pinballs?" Answer: "When it comes to pinballs, the public is divided into two categories, those who play them and those who don't give a damn." That probably did nothing to patch up his former friendship with Mr. Pulliam.

While the legislature was in session, a newspaper reporter friend of mine, John V. Wilson, fixed me up with a lady he described as the perfect date. And he wasn't far off. She was pretty and pretty witty. But she had a litmus test for legislators, pinballs. Actually, Dad was not quite right. When it came to pinballs, there was a third category: those who were secretaries at companies that were in the pinball business. She was one of them. When I called for her with a little more gas in my car, she, well, demanded, "How do you stand on pinballs?" As I stood on the porch on that cold February night, I said, "Not very well; I'm not much on ice skates, either." It appealed to her witty side—even after I confessed that I belonged to Dad's second category. Nice evening.

At their meeting on the lofty subject of pinballs, the mayor wondered aloud what my dad thought of a public statement the mayor had made in criticism of the Supreme Court. It involved a decision that upheld the U.S. Status of Forces Treaty with Japan. The agreement provided that U.S. military personnel stationed in Japan and charged with crimes against Japanese citizens would be tried in Japanese courts rather than U.S. military courts. Despite the obvious fact that the U.S. citizens who objected to the treaty would never have put up with anything but U.S. courts if the situation were the other way around, they took the question all the way to our highest court. The far right was up in arms about the controversy and the Democratic mayor who fawned on the far right publisher was shooting for brownie points. Dad said he didn't like the mayor's jingoism and the mayor said, "But the Supreme Court was wrong, Andy." Then Dad asked the mayor, "Have you read the opinion?" The mayor replied that he had not. "Then," said Dad, "that makes you an expert. I'm handicapped by the fact that I have read and studied the opinion." The sheriff joined the discussion, "Andy, the people (meaning the loudest people) are against that decision." Dad's reply was memorable: "For God's sake, with civilization tottering on the brink, some people must think their political careers are pretty important."

"But for a nail, a kingdom." But for a postcard, a car deal. On the issue of buying sheriff cars, only one car dealer had a disagreeable encounter with me. *All* Hoosier car dealers had an expensive encounter with my dad a few years later.

Before I went to the legislature, Indiana personal property taxes on automobiles were paid directly to the various county treasurers. The law provided that a citizen could not buy a license plate without showing proof that the property tax on the car to be licensed had been paid. "Many a slip twixt the cup and the lip." The tax was easily evaded. There was no cross-reference system and often a friendly smile at the license branch counter would allow a person to buy a plate without having paid the tax; friendly smile or bribe; there were some indictments.

The remarkable Walter Maehling, a state representative from southwest Indiana, had an idea and it was a good one: Pay the property tax on the car along with the license fee when the plate is purchased. That has been the law in Indiana ever since 1959 when he proposed it. But the new law raised a question. Since the property tax was to be paid as one bought a plate, what about the case of an automobile dealer plate? One plate, one tax? Or, since the dealer plate represented many cars in inventory, would it be one tax for each *car* represented by the one dealer plate? If it was the former, the dealers would enjoy a walloping and unintended tax cut. They made it their business to make sure the former was the interpretation by filing a case in the Marion County Superior Court. They sued for a declaratory judgment that each dealer plate represented only one car. And to make sure the judgment would be binding, they sued every public official they could think of. The sheriff was included as a defendant.

As lawyer for the sheriff, my dad appeared in court at the appointed time and moved to dismiss the suit against the sheriff on the ground that he was not a relevant defendant. Motion denied. Before the hearing was over, the judge wished he had granted the motion.

Dad argued that the dealers' deal would be unconstitutional because the charge was a tax on an automobile, not a license plate fee. Under the Indiana Constitution, the tax had to be equally applied to all cars according to the value of each. The judge called a recess and one of the lawyers for the dealers said to Dad, "Andy, what's your interest in this matter?" To which Dad replied, "You fellows are the ones who sued my client; ask yourselves. But, of course, what you really mean is why should I care about the public interest? And the answer is that in this case I'm being paid by the public. Don't bother to tell me that most of the public would never know about your little game nor thank me for doing my duty to break it up. I'm well aware of that. But I still owe something to the public that pays me and *I owe something to myself.*" He meant self-respect. By then it was clear that the Indiana judge was not altogether enamored with the Indiana Constitution, so when the hearing resumed, Dad moved again for dismissal of the case against the sheriff. Motion granted—gladly.

Several months later, on a pleasant summer day, my dad began to leave his office for lunch when he ran into the letter carrier. By chance, the delivery amounted to one post card which Dad put into his pocket, intending to read it at the table. When he had ordered lunch, he glanced at the card and discovered it was from the Indiana Supreme Court. Somehow, the sheriff had not been dismissed from the license plate case after all. That meant Dad had standing to present an argument before the Supreme Court where a friendly appeal was pending. Moreover, the argument was set for that very day at two P.M.

Dad finished a leisurely lunch with friends and strolled over to the Statehouse for the hearing. The dealers' lawyers made out just fine, thank you, in the trial court with strangely friendly opposition from the public officials named in the suit. And the plaintiffs obviously were expecting clear sailing again in the Supreme Court where no opposing argument was anticipated. Clearly they were less than overjoyed to see my dad sitting there, less joy yet when they learned that their friendly trial judge had fouled up the dismissal of the Sheriff as a defendant. There was no way around it, though. Although he was sitting when the other lawyers walked in, Dad had standing in the case.

The plaintiffs would not win the appeal by default. In fact, the plaintiffs would not win the appeal. A few well-chosen words from my dad and the apple cart went belly-up. The dealers lost the appeal and therefore their case. They probably also lost a lot of money on lawyers' fees. "But for a postcard" and a Lincolnesque lawyer who liked justice and knew what he owed to the public and to himself . . .

It seems to me I should acknowledge that there are many reputable automobile dealers, jokes on the subject to the contrary not withstanding. In fact, my nephew Greg Landwerlen is one of them. Back when the Automobile Dealers Association was trying to hit the jackpot with the new license law, most of the members were probably good citizens as well, willing to meet their civic obligations including fair taxes. Many of those dealers quite likely didn't even know what the association was doing. Besides, the failure of the lawsuit preserved one of the dealers' favorite advertising gimmicks, the pre-spring "tax sale."

During this period, the Indianapolis Junior Chamber of Commerce sponsored a weekly debate among two young Republicans and two young Democrats. It was broadcast by radio station WIBC and I was a frequent participant, as was my friend and partial mentor Jim Seidensticker. The debate was meant to mirror the politics of our respective parties' real politicians. One of the young Republicans was Columbus, Indiana, lawyer Bob Dalmbert. And it was he who delivered one of the best debate squelches I ever heard. It was at my expense.

There was some talk at the time about possible purchase of the Indianapolis Water Company by the City of Indianapolis. This to Bob was out-and-out world Socialism. I didn't like the idea, either, but after all this was a debate. The day before the debate, I had seen a headline to the effect that the water company had made an embarrassing mistake. But as we sat there speaking into the microphones, I couldn't say what the mistake was alleged to have been. I just figured everybody else would know. So in answering Bob, I said, "Well apparently the city couldn't do much worse than the Water Company is doing now." Bob Dalmbert shot back, "What's the matter with the Water Company?" I didn't have a clue; I had stepped onto thin frozen water and it was cracking fast. As I groped for some face- or voice-saving response, Bob delivered the knockout: "The last time you turned on the faucet, the water came out, didn't it?" Now I couldn't give any response; I was laughing too hard. I conceded.

Decades later, Bob took a seat immediately in front of me on a flight to

Washington. Before we took off, he turned and asked, "Did anyone ever say that you look like Andy Jacobs?" Now it was my turn; I replied, "Did anyone ever say you look like Bob Dalmbert?" Bob exclaimed, "Is that you, Andy?"

"Yup," I said, "I'm right here in this skin."

In time, my dad became a Marion County Criminal Court Judge. He was considered a veritable hanging judge by defense attorneys because he wouldn't give exemption to first-time convicted felons. If a first-time offender were convicted of a felony in Dad's court, the felon would serve some time in prison. It might not be a very long time, depending on the offense, but the Judge said that to spare the first-time felon from prison made the felon a "walking billboard proclaiming that the first one is free." Quite often, "first-time" is actually the first-time caught. Defense lawyers stayed away from Dad's court in droves—except in cases where they really believed their clients to be innocent. In those cases, the lawyers pushed to *get into* his court because they knew their clients, no matter how unpopular, would get a fair decision from a justice-loving judge.

Indiana was the only jurisdiction in the United States where a defense lawyer in a criminal trial could get a change of judge without even alleging bias on the part of the judge. Dad petitioned the Indiana Supreme Court to change the rule and relieve Indiana from being the sore thumb of the nation's judicial system. To no avail.

Defense lawyers took so many cases out of his court that there was less and less for him to do. So he tendered his resignation to Governor Otis Bowen. Governor Bowen was a Republican and my Democratic dad's resignation meant a juicy political plum for the governor. He could appoint a Republican to fill the vacancy. But he didn't, because he didn't accept the resignation. Instead, he phoned my father and persuaded him to stay on. Doc Bowen said the community couldn't afford to lose such a good judge.

When Governor Bowen's second term was over, President Reagan appointed him U.S. Secretary of Health and Human Services. I was serving on the U.S. House Ways and Means Committee where HHS Secretaries spend a lot of time testifying. And when Doc Bowen made his maiden appearance before the Committee, some of the younger and, therefore, more partisan Democratic members had their forensic long knives out for him. They never used them. As his fellow Hoosier, I was, by tradition, given the privilege of introducing the secretary to the committee. In doing so, I told the story of his sacrificing political patronage by persuading my father to stay on as judge. Doc sailed through that first appearance with nothing but smiles from all of the panel.

Dad was the only trial judge ever to be commended in an official Indiana Supreme Court opinion for extraordinarily excellent performance on the bench. The opinion mentioned the fact that dad, by cutting useless legalistic red tape, had actually tried *two* jury trials in *one* day.

Sad to say, I was able to visit my father's court only once, but I didn't come away empty-handed. During the trial, one lawyer objected to another's question "on the ground that it (called) for a conclusion by the witness." That is boilerplate legal language. My dad ruled, "I believe the question does call for a conclusion by the witness, but it is a conclusion that even a fool could reach. Overruled."

Then there was the case of the gambling arrest at a below-poverty-line American Legion Post. The police had caught the legionnaires playing poker for quarters in their tarpaper shack headquarters. After my hanging-judge father heard the evidence, he said he had a question for the post commander, a man in ragged pants and an un-ironed Legion shirt. "What," Dad said evenly, "do you suppose I would do if the State Legion Commander, a lawyer, a businessman and a doctor were playing poker for money at the Indianapolis Athletic Club?" In the eyes of the post commander there was searching optimism as he cautiously said, "Well, Judge, I expect you'd let them go."

"Wrong," said the judge, bursting the balloon of hope. The post leader looked crestfallen until the judge added, "I wouldn't let them go because they'd never be brought in here in the first place. Case dismissed." Even the deputy prosecutor had to smile at that one. The defendants certainly did.

My dad was good at most things. He played down-home fiddle fit for a hoe down. He was a self-described "hatchet and saw carpenter" and "coal oil blacksmith." He built a thirty-by-sixty-foot workshop at his home and installed three-phase factory electricity. It was equipped with industrial drill presses, lathes, saws, and heavy-duty welding devices. He said all the lawyers thought he was a great carpenter and all the carpenters thought he was a great lawyer. The carpenters were absolutely right and the lawyers weren't far from it. One day at the Indianapolis Bar Association lunchroom, one of his friends playfully threatened to have him cited for a zoning violation—operating a factory in a residential neighborhood. "I have the perfect defense." said my dad, "I've never produced anything useful." Not true. But it was an example of his deft self-deprecating humor. He told about the man who was caught in a rural district driving a tractor out of someone else's barn, the sheriff asking the suspect, "What are you doing?" The furtive fellow on the tractor said, "I'm waiting for a streetcar."

"Do you think anybody is going to believe that?" asked the sheriff as he clamped on the cuffs. "Some fool will," replied the prisoner, "and that fool just might turn out to be the judge."

"Oh, my papa, so funny, so adorable . . ."

My dad never went to college, but he was far better educated than most who did. I do not believe Shakespeare (or Roger Bacon) ever wrote a word my father didn't read. That was true of most serious literature, including especially what Lincoln and Lincoln scholars wrote. When, on his death from tobacco, we followed his request by burying him in a plain box at that small family cemetery on that southern Indiana farm from whence he came, we buried a library.

He did go to the small Benjamin Harrison night law school in Indianapolis, handling baggage at the interurban train station by day and eating stale crackers and dry cheese. But before he graduated, he was admitted to the Indiana Bar under the same kind of relaxed rules which allowed Lincoln to become a lawyer with no law school at all. As the years went by, he continued to read and apply law to the point where he was one of the most respected lawyers and jurists in Indiana history. He was widely recognized as one of the best libel lawyers in the country, a fact expensively overlooked by the once Reverend (he shed his cloth and denied ever having been an evangelist when he wanted to run for President) Pat Robertson.

The Indianapolis Democratic Slating Convention was once again kind to me in 1960. I received the nod of endorsement for the state senate. And the convention's nod was echoed in the actual primary election in May. One of my best friends and one of the world's best raconteurs, James Porter Seidensticker, Jr., was endorsed and nominated to be a Democratic candidate for the State House of Representatives that year. And we campaigned together throughout that dreary and, for the Democrats, hopeless year.

It was hopeless, of course, because of Kennedy's Catholicism and the Ku Klux Klan tradition in Indiana. Beyond that, though, there was something new, something of a departure that characterized the 1960 presidential campaign and election. As Kennedy was to point out, this was the presidential year of strictly twentieth century candidates. Kennedy or Nixon would be the first president of the United States to have been born after the nineteenth century. And they seemed to be of a new breed. It would also be the first television campaign which, in turn, would usher in the era of political consultants and make-up artists. Kennedy called his platform The New Frontier. But this frontier was to be pushed back, not with covered wagons, but with Cadillacs. Not much hardship in the offing or the offering. The ringing Kennedy phrase was, "ask what you can do for your country." And John Kennedy described the concept as "not a set of promises," while both candidates made grand promises all the same, just as in the past.

One thing was certain. Nixon was far happier to be equated with Kennedy than the other way around. In fact Kennedy deeply resented a widely published newspaper article of eloquence written by the TV sage Eric Severeid. In that 1960 article, entitled "The Button-Down Candidates," Severeid did indeed equate the two:

> Kennedy and Nixon are neither princes of blood nor sons of the soil ... they are junior executives trained in the home office with an unerring eye on the big chance. These Brooks Brothers wrinkle-proof suits—how much is real, how much synthetic?

In 1962 after Kennedy had been a popular President for a full year and I was pleasing my father by buckling down to my law practice, I presumed to write a letter to Severeid suggesting a Button-Down Candidate Revisited piece. He favored me with the reply that my suggestion was an interesting idea and that he would "kick it around," a journalistic phrase of the time. The President was killed the next year with no Severeid sequel having been published. By then no sequel was gracefully possible. I sent the correspondence to the Kennedy Library but saw no sign of it when Kim and I visited there many years later.

My dad and Kennedy didn't get along, whereas my dad and Nixon became friends. Dad let it be known at the Liars Table in the Indianapolis Bar Association dining room that, though a Democrat, he was having a hard time deciding between Kennedy and Nixon, declaring that he was thinking of taking "a stiff drink of whiskey and voting the Prohibitionist ticket." My dad didn't drink and did end up voting for Kennedy because of Nixon's seeming pledge of American military action to defend the Chinese orbit islands of Quemoy and Matsu. But he voted for Kennedy without affection which made all the more interesting an exchange between one of the other lawyers at that fun table and my dad. The other had just said. "Well, I see Rose Kennedy is out campaigning for her little boy." To which my dad looked up from his soup and snapped, "I think we can get through this campaign without slurs on the families. I imagine a mother would be for her son." He didn't like Kennedy, but he liked injustice and the politics of personal attack even less.

Back in what he enjoyed calling "the microcosm," Jim Seidensticker and

I were hard at work at our law profession. Therefore, our campaigning was confined to the evenings. And that campaigning essentially consisted of passing out party brochures door-to-door. Our final foray came on an evening just two days before the fall election. As we respectively proceeded down opposite sides of a street and night was falling along with freezing light rain, we found ourselves at a dead end, in more ways than one.

The cold rain may have been light, but the Democrats were about to be swamped. Anything but buoyant, with water streaming down our faces and clothes, we began the halfhearted half-mile trek back to the car. After a few steps, my friend stopped, you might say, cold. In that bleak moment he turned and, in the manner of *Damn Yankees,* said to me, "Your next shot is going to be Congress." The message was unmistakable; "Ya gotta have hope." He didn't mean, "Wait'll next year," he meant wait 'til the year after next, the election year of 1962.

Despite the 1960 Republican landslide in Indiana, Democrat Matthew E. Welsh was elected Governor and served with enormous distinction. But his election was unacceptable to the *Indianapolis Star.* So the paper undertook to prove that Matt wasn't elected after all. A headline proclaimed, "Welsh May Not Take Office." I told friends that a subsequent headline might read, "And Then Again, He Just Might." As proof of Democratic fraud, a *Star* headline said, "Lake County Voters Gave Church As Their Address." That looked pretty damning—until the *Indianapolis Times* ran this headline the next day: "Lake County Voters Gave Church As Their Address," the sub-headline adding, "They Live There." And so they did. The church was a storefront on the first floor of an apartment building. Still, the *Star* thought there ought be a recount.

The whole series in the *Star* was ludicrous to the point that Democrats and Republicans alike were laughing about it. My dad said that the *Star* was remarkable in that "they have never lost an election; they've had a few stolen from them, but they've never lost one." As they frequently did, my dad's words inspired me. I got Jim Seidensticker and my Franklin friend Bill Jones, fellow losers in the same election, to join me in filing another not-for-profit corporation with the Indiana Secretary of State. We named it *The United States Recount Corporation, Incorporated.* In our little news release we confessed that the name "is redundant, but then so is a recount." In the purpose section we wrote:

> To provide towels, mops and buckets for the tears of losing candidates. Having managed to kick the crying habit ourselves, we shall provide

coins to losing candidates to call us when they feel crying jags coming on. The slogan of our corporation shall be, "The reason we sobbed was we was robbed."

I still had the ambition Lincoln expressed in church. In 1962 Jim Seidensticker and I were going to put on a dazzling campaign for Congress, the likes of which had never been seen before. "For we were young and sure to have our way."

chapter 2

"A" for Effort

JAMES PORTER "SEI" SEIDENSTICKER was a scholar, dapper gentleman, Army veteran, lawyer, amateur historian, and a superlative storyteller. His knowledge of Franklin Roosevelt's career was encyclopedic. And in those early days of our professional lives, he was pleased to think of himself as my Louie Howe. Howe was devoted to Roosevelt's political career earlier and more enthusiastically than any other friend. He was certain Roosevelt would go all the way to the White House and toiled day and night toward that end.

Sei's ambition for me was not quite so lofty. The U.S. House would be enough and, he said, somehow we were going to do it. But how? This was the Eleventh Congressional District of Indiana which, at the time, comprised all of Republican Marion County.

Before we worried much about that, however, we had a roll reversal to tend to. Sei was a convention candidate to become Indiana National Committeeman for the Young Democrats. And he needed a speech for the convention of budding politicians. My roll was to help write it. Our friend Mary Ellen Weiland suggested a slogan for Jim Seidensticker's elaborate campaign (campaign expenditures: zero):

HIS NAME IS JIM. VOTE FOR HIM.

The speech, of course, was for a partisan convention, and seated at my little Smith Corona Skywriter manual typewriter, partisan pitches came to mind. As my dad had said, both parties tried their best to make a precinct committeeperson out of God. So I tapped out an oration for Sei to tell the partisan delegates, which included:

I realize our Republican friends think of Jesus as a Republican. But I know of no instance in which He rode into Jerusalem on an elephant.

Corn well shelled, I thought. I had occasion to use the line myself during an appearance on C-Span two decades later and after that I read that Reverend Jesse Jackson had used it. I have no idea whether he heard me say it, picked it up from the wine vine, or thought of it independently.

Sei won hands down and it was time to turn once again to my campaign for Congress. Running in Republican Marion County wasn't my only problem. At twenty-nine I was considered by some to be too young. That's hard to believe now, but it wasn't then.

One of my father's best friends, a man who had sent me letters of encouragement when I was in combat, told Dad that one term in the legislature was not enough. I should "earn my political spurs" before presuming to run for Congress. Dad asked the friend if he knew how old Alexander Hamilton was when he began shaping the destiny of our republic. The friend granted that Hamilton might have been as young as thirty-two. My dad broke the news that Hamilton was seventeen when he began playing that fateful role. Surely, in the manner of Senator Lloyd Bentsen's unfair retort to Dan Quayle, my dad's friend must have said, "Andy's no Alexander Hamilton."

It would be uphill, but we were determined to climb that hill, especially because it was *Capitol Hill.* Then it was that our hearts soared above and sailed beyond the harsh restraints of reality. We foolishly believed we'd win.

The incumbent United States Representative had been present at the creation of the John Birch Society on Washington Boulevard right there in Indianapolis. He hadn't quite joined, but did espouse many of the society's more ridiculous assertions, which amounted to flat-Earth politics. He was a war hawk without the portfolio of participation in war. We foolishly fancied that his extremism would tame the strong Republican tide which was certain to wash our way.

But that was months away. Our first hurtle was the Democratic primary. My competition consisted of two very high-grade candidates, Jack Bradshaw and George Zazas. We all campaigned to the Democratic precinct committeepeople who would vote on the question of whom the Democratic organization would endorse. Our campaigns consisted of direct mail, joint appearances before small meetings of the committeepeople, and such news coverage as we could muster. There wasn't much of that from the *Indianapolis Star* and *News* since none of the three of us was in the party faction of the mayor and prosecutor who were generally thought of as *Indianapolis Star* Democrats.

When it came to publicity in the old *Star*, though, I did have one ace up my sleeve, and that was Lester Hunt, the facile writer who had been the publicist for the Teamsters Union. In 1948 he was fired by union president Dan Tobin. Tobin was a supporter of Harry Truman until the closing days of the presidential campaign when opinion polls made clear that Truman didn't have "a kerosene cat's chance in Hell," at which point Tobin announced that he would vote for Truman's opponent, Thomas E. Dewey. When Truman won and the union leader was caught offsides, Hunt sent a thoughtful telegram to him saying, "Congratulations on your strategic change of parties."

Eventually, Hunt went to work for the *Indianapolis Star* where he rapidly rose to the status of fair-haired, the political champion of rightward-leaning Republicans. Other Republicans weren't too crazy about him. But my dad was. Hunt and he were warm friends; Dad was his lawyer. These were facts which Hunt did not stress in the presence of his new employer, Eugene Pulliam, the elder. Les Hunt helped me in the Democratic Primary, but he did it so artfully that Mr. Pulliam, Sr., surely saw it as just the opposite. This is what Les included in his column:

> In the Democrat [sic], [but Les knew what he was doing at the then-biased Republican paper] Primary, most voters are opposed to Jacobs because they consider him too much of a *New Frontiersman*.

Beautiful! *New Frontiersman* meant a supporter of President Kennedy's domestic policy—aid to education, Medicare, etc.. That policy was an anathema to the *Star*, but not less than heartwarming to Democratic voters. They were more than thrilled with their young president; he was enjoying astronomical poll numbers at the time. So my dad's clever pal, Les Hunt, had scored points with Mr. Pulliam, Sr. by seeming to attack me while actually throwing me into a remarkably bountiful *briar patch.*

Les Hunt's counterpart at the Scripps-Howard *Indianapolis Times*, Irving Leibowitz, perhaps unwittingly, gave me a boost as well. Here's what he wrote in his column:

> In the race for the Democratic nomination for Congress, Zazas seems to have the intellectual vote; Jacobs seems to have most of the precinct committeemen.

The day after that appeared, I was in the courthouse on business and our old friend, county commissioner and ward chairman Dutch Ayres shouted to me through a large crowd, "Hey, I seen in Leibowitz where the intellectuals are for Zazas and the committeemen are for you. Hell, that's what you want." Indeed. During a speech given by Adlai Stevenson at Oxford, he was interrupted by a friendly shout from the audience, "Every thinking person will vote for Governor Stevenson." Stevenson paused long enough to say, "Thank you very much, but I would prefer to have the majority." That was what I appeared to have in the upcoming convention.

Brilliant, civilized, and handsome George Zazas suffered a grinding car crash during that primary. It snatched him from the contest and snatched his wife from this life.

When my other friend in the race, Jack Bradshaw, switched his candidacy from the U.S. House to the State Senate, it became likely that I would be successful in the slating convention and I was. My friend, Jud Haggerty, "beat city hall" by defeating its candidate in the endorsement convention for county prosecutor. That did not please the *Star* or its Democratic friend, the mayor of Indianapolis, Charles Boswell, who in reference to the endorsement decision of the elected precinct workers, issued a statement of Freudian magnitude:

> We've had an experiment in democracy; Now we (the *Star* and himself) must decide what's best for the community.

The statement was about as far he went. The mayor didn't have much political time to bother with arraying his city hall minions against us. He, himself, was a candidate for Congress, the United States Senate.

The mayor's preoccupation with his own campaign was a windfall for me. I had many friends who were precinct committeepeople and worked at city hall. But they could be fired whenever the mayor chose and therefore were likely to do his bidding had he had the time to express it to them. He didn't.

The mayor's opponent for the U.S. Senate nomination was one Birch E. Bayh who, you will recall, had been Speaker of the Indiana House when I served there. He was young, handsome and contemporary. Since the mayor was none of these things, he had his hands full. It was the propitious time for Sei and me to do some political tiptoeing as we courted city hall workers. We did not make a lot of noise about the mayor's reactionary campaign and our discreet help for Birch.

And the city hall workers heard nothing from their boss with regard to my candidacy. My dad sat Sei and me down one day to express his disappointment over our lack of aggressiveness toward the mayor whom he considered to be an apostate. Referring to his long ago primary battle with another city hall, he told us, "In those days we stood toe to toe against the organization. We usually didn't win, but they respected us." To which I responded, "Well, Dad, they may not respect us, but I think we're going to win." And we did—in the primary.

Mayor Boswell's campaign was geared to the flat-earth philosophy of the old *Star*. A large number of Democratic leaders were imbued with the absurd notion that if the mayor were our nominee, the Star would support the entire Democratic ticket in the fall. The Democratic governor, Matt Welsh, stayed neutral as the mayor's campaign statements drifted further and further to the right. At one point, the mayor even suggested that child labor laws, as written, may not have been a very good idea. Somewhere in the progression, or rather retrogression, of the mayor's positions, it was said that the governor could take no more. He endorsed Birch Bayh and Indiana learned how to pronounce the latter's last name (prounounced "By").

In 1962 Indiana was still nominating U.S. Senate candidates by conventions which took place after the direct primary nominations for the U.S. House. Therefore I became the nominee for the U.S. House a few weeks before a nominee was to be chosen for the Senate. And on primary night, a bizarre incident occurred, featuring the mayor and me.

As was the custom for candidates after the votes were in, I went to party headquarters for fellowship with fellow Democrats. But as I entered the building, I was met by an *Indianapolis Star* reporter who said she had a message for me from the mayor. Since the mayor himself was standing only about thirty feet across the crowded room, the reporter's mission seemed odd. "The mayor," she said, "has a proposition for you." Things were going from bizarre to odd to weird. In the first place, it was paradoxical that the *Star* would be delivering a message from the mayor; it was usually the other way around. In the second place, a message delivered so ominously was bound to be a little out of sync with celebration of my success in the primary. So, cocking my head slightly, I said to the reporter, "Yes?" And she said, rather authoritatively, I thought, "The mayor says he will drop out of the race for the Senate if you will resign from the ticket for the House."

Remarkably ridiculous. The voters had just given me the nomination for the U.S. House and the mayor's campaign for the Senate was clearly dead in the water. It occurred to me that the offer wasn't much of an offer, so I replied, "Isn't that like offering 'a cracker for a ham?'" She did not smile and I continued, "There's no reason for the mayor and me to be contentious. I'll go over and speak to him."

When I reached the mayor, I extended my hand to shake his, saying, "Mayor, let's show our friends that our disagreement on issues is not personal." He jerked his hand away, angrily saying, "Not with you, Andy."

I could not, of course, be watching my reaction, but the *Louisville Courier Journal* subsequently described it:

> Stunned, Jacobs said to the mayor, "Mayor, the issue between us as Democrats is that I am a Kennedy Democrat and you are a Goldwater Republican."

To which the mayor shot back, "The issue is whether the people of Marion County want Boswell or Jacobs."

Standing at the front of the crowd was Jud Haggerty, who had just won the primary for county prosecutor. With lightning speed he began clapping his hands and shouting, "Hooray! We'll take Jacobs!"

With that, the crowd, including me, began to leave. Driving home, I listened to the WIBC radio report of the incident. When it got to its recording of Jud's performance, the echo of his words and applause in the huge uncarpeted room sounded as if everyone in there were giving me an ovation. Let's hear it for electronic sound effects.

All this was on Tuesday night. The following Saturday, by law, both parties held their conventions for the precinct workers to choose the respective county chairpeople. The incumbent Democratic Chairman had been handpicked by the mayor two years earlier. He, of course, would run for re-election—until Jud Haggerty announced his candidacy for the position. The mayor and his supporters weren't so sure their chairman could win a contest with our attractive candidate.

So the county chairman was ordered to drop out of the contest and, yes, the mayor, himself, dropped in. The oft-repeated political maxim was, "You can't beat city hall." Jud had just done so in the contest for the prosecutor nomination. His second tilt with the temple of politics was destined to be different.

The mayor's decision to run for county chairman made it easier for him to ease out of his already moribund campaign for U.S. Senator. At a preconvention rally for Jud, Charlie Maines, chairman of the Wayne Township Democrats, badly wounded World War II veteran, and lawyer of stunning eloquence, went to the podium and discussed the mayor's subtle withdrawal from the Senate race:

"It's like the Irish general who said, 'Alright men, we're going to stay on this line and fire up all our ammunition; then it's every man for himself. And since I have a bad leg, I'm leaving now.'"

Lots of laughs—which did not translate into enough votes.

The mayor's campaign was strident, if not pugnacious. So much so that his campaign buttons bore the image of boxing gloves and he dubbed himself, "The Fighting Mayor." The mayor's stratified radio ad invited the general public to come to a rally and watch the mayor "fight for his political life." The contest for county chairman had become a life-or-death matter. And the Republican *Indianapolis Star* became the political brochure for the mayor's campaign to become Democratic Chairman. The mayor won.

As Jud and I left the state fairgrounds convention hall, we proceeded through a gauntlet of the mayor's supporters who were celebrating with picnic fare from the trunks of automobiles. There were catcalls, the funniest of which was, "Guess us old frontiersmen showed you new frontiersmen." Jud and I didn't have to "guess." We knew it. As we braved their bragging, Jud quietly said to me, "We left a chunk of our asses on that convention floor, Andy." But it didn't involve actual weight loss; we survived. Fewer than four months later, not two years, Jud was the county chairman. How could that be?

The end of the mayor's tenure in city hall was at hand when U.S. Senator Vance Hartke offered him the post of Indianapolis Postmaster, "political Heaven," as my dad described it. But there was a condition. The senator wanted Jud Haggerty to be the mayor's successor as county chairman and the mayor must do a "one eighty" and tell the convention voters who had just made him county chairman to make Jud county chairman instead. Strange bedfellows? Let's just say "flexibility."

As we entered the 1962 fall campaign, Mayor Boswell was Postmaster Boswell, Jud Haggerty was both the Democratic nominee for prosecutor and Democratic County Chairman, Birch Bayh was the Democratic nominee for U.S. Senator, and I was the nominee for the U.S. House. None of the three of us had a chance in the election. It was the off-year in JFK's administration and Indiana and Marion County generally went Republican anyway. The Republican congressional candidates, Homer E. Capehart and Donald C. Bruce, were respectively the incumbent Senator and the incumbent Representative. My campaign was fathoms below the poverty line. But the campaigns were not boring.

In my contest, the "eternal" spring of hope was sorely tested. The regular polls published by the *Indianapolis Times* consistently showed Congressman Bruce ten points ahead of me. Still, drawing on my view of war, which was actual, I dared to hope the voters would reject Congressman Bruce's hawkish foreign policy.

The congressman was pleased to stress the "Victory Resolution" he had introduced in Congress. He described it one night at a broadcasted rally of what my dad called "witches and goblins." This is some of what he said:

My resolution calls for *total* victory over Communism! The first step is to declare that as our purpose. Now this next step, they say you just don't dare do. Oh no? What's the next step? (pause for effect) *Break relations with every communist country!*

The place went wild. As Dad would say, there wasn't a dry pair of pants in the hall. In those Birch Society days, it wasn't crime, it wasn't welfare, it wasn't drugs, it wasn't junkets, not even gays: it was *communism* that stamped the passport to public office for politicians who would stoop to use it against their opponents.

According to the Birch Society, the domestic commies, who actually were very few in number and mostly crackpots, closely monitored by the FBI, were under every bed and out to get you. The Russian commies, who throughout the Cold War remained light years behind us in military capability, would have attacked us at any moment were it not for the courageous vocal cords of the Birchers and their friends. In the sense of badly needed villains, the commies were manna from Heaven for demagogic domestic politicians. And, by golly, those politicians hated the evil of Communism much, much more than their despicable opponents who, said the demagogues, traitorously and implausibly—wanted to give up the joys of freedom for subjugation by a foreign slave state way out on the edge of the flat Earth.

The few advertising dollars we had in my campaign were spent on a radio ad produced in my basement apartment with an old tape recorder and some excerpts from an Edward R. Murrow history record called *Hear It Now,* together with a tape we made of the wild rally at which Congressman Bruce had spoken. From those recordings, we were able to cobble a professional-sounding ad:

Voiceover: Listen. These are the sounds of war:
[*Sound effects: Bombs exploding, reciprocating Spitfire aircraft engines roaring.*]

Voiceover: These are the sounds that cause war:
[*Sound effects: The recording of Congressman Bruce's excited tones at the rally, "Break relations with every Communist country!"*]

Voiceover: If you believe the Cold War should be won with heartfelt common sense and not hysteria, please choose Andy Jacobs to be your representative in Congress.

The announcer doing the voiceover was my friend Gary Tyler, who was then and remained an officer in the Chamber of Commerce.

At that fun rally for the right, Congressman Bruce also had exhorted the faithful by saying, "The communist can be counted on to dodge and maneuver and to make outrageous demands. And we must say 'no' with a resounding roar."

That also served as an inspiration. Using my little manual Smith-Corona Skywriter again, I tapped out a news release which included the following:

> Patriotism is not a roaring matter. It is an abiding thing, strong and steady on stormy seas as well as in the safety of the harbor.
>
> To roar hatred for our country's adversaries may fire the passions of some Americans. But, as with marriage, passion isn't much on which to build a lifetime of loyalty.

The far right didn't care much for the federal government, which was "infested with traitors," mostly Democrats, and salted with a few wayward, Ivy League Republicans. Congressman Bruce had a couple of favorite examples of how the un-American American government wasted tax dollars. God knows there's a seemingly endless list of genuinely wasteful expenditures by the government. But Congressman Bruce's two favorites were off the mark.

They both sounded ridiculous, especially if mentioned in mirth. Speaking to a group of medical students, who should have known better, the congressman got big laughs by saying, "The government spent three hundred thousand of your tax dollars to study why monkeys love their mothers. I'll tell you why; because that's where they get their milk."

The congressman was referring to the Harlow project at the University of Florida, one of the most efficacious mental health developments ever. That study alone has to its credit more human well-being and happiness as well as enhanced business profits than almost any other in the twentieth century. It was a national bargain.

The second had to do with government stockpiling: "They have squandered another three hundred thousand dollars on goose feathers."

The students roared. We have no way of knowing whether the medical students had yet taken up the subject of severe frostbite, but that was what the feathers were about. By some good fortune, I didn't get into Korean combat until the early days of that first winter of war had passed. I suffered some frostbite with permanent distortion of my body thermostat and wintertime pain in my fingers. But that is minor compared to the icy brutality inflicted on the Marines I helped replace. During those early days, the preponderance of U.S. combat casualties were from frostbite. Hands and feet were lost to amputation. They were *chilled* in action. In the first year of that Hell-frozen-over, there were no goose down mountain sleeping bags to protect our forces; they had only the old brown blanket bags left from World War II. It took many weeks of crash effort in the United States to gather the feathers and make the goose down bags to rush to the front. The congressman's joke to the med students wasn't really so funny after all.

My answers to these charges met the fate of the tree that falls in the forest, except for the relatively few voters I could reach in person. There was no money for an additional radio ad. Later the U.S. Supreme Court ruled that, in addition to the freedom to say what you want to say, the right to buy enough air time to drown out what your opponent has to say was also a matter of free speech. Call it the right to buy (the election) decision. "'Money talks,' so it's entitled to be speech under the First Amendment." If you're a lobbyist with tons of money from government favors, under *Buckley v. Valejo*, you can spend all you wish to get rid of a member of Congress who has the effrontery to represent the public interest instead of your private interest in hitting the jackpot at the U.S. Treasury.

I should and do say here that I never met a more sincere group than most of the John Birch Society people. They seemed to be true believers, albeit believers in some cases in foreign policies that were gravely—"Where have all the flowers gone?"—mistaken.

Donald Bruce ran unsuccessfully for the U.S. Senate two years after he defeated me in 1962. And as in the case with so many former members of Congress, he chose to stay in Washington, eventually moving south into Virginia. He was most gracious when he helped me set up the Eleventh District office in 1965. We had lunch together and he gave me a great deal of useful information about the nuts and bolts of the place. And he laughed when I joked about one of the staff positions he had established during his two terms. He told me the full-time assignment for the very well-paid staffer was to study communism. Twinkling as best I could, I said, "Well, I think I can save the taxpayers some money on that one; I've already made up my mind about communism."

Don Bruce died a year or so later and I assumed I would see all of my Hoosier Congressional colleagues at the funeral. But as it turned out, I was the only member of the Indiana Congressional delegation to attend. The *Indianapolis Star* Washington correspondent, brilliant and gentle Ben Cole, was there, too. In his published story he mentioned the absence of the others and the mail poured into our office from John Birch members. The letters I got were warm and appreciative. It was a time for time-out from politics.

A similar phenomenon happened when U.S. Representative Larry McDonald perished in the stupid Russian attack on Korean airliner flight 007. At the time he was the president of the Birch Society. I knew and personally liked Larry. He, like my friend John Rousselot, was a Bircher with a delightful sense of humor. When the Indiana John Birch Society held a service for Larry at the World War Memorial in Indianapolis, it sent invitations to Republican and Democratic officeholders. Again, I was the only one of us to attend. And I did so without fanfare. I simply and quietly took a seat at the rear of the nearly filled auditorium. After a few minutes, the nicely dressed woman sitting, yes, to my right, turned and softly said, "We're very grateful to you for attending." A few minutes after that, a young man entered from the rear and told me that the chairman for the occasion would like for me to come forward and speak. I did and never regretted it.

I'd like to tell you a story about one more John Birch Society member. He was U.S. Representative John Rarick (R–Louisiana). The "R" did not stand for Republican; he was a Democrat. The "R," impure and simple, stood for *racist*. He placed in the *Congressional Record* some of the most God-awful, primitive, and crackpot material ever found under any rock. He was a study in rattlesnake racial arrogance. Because of the "ick" in his attitude as well as in his name, I was happy to keep some distance between us. But one day he approached me from the *right* and, before I saw him, began to speak to me. "How's Andy?" What in the—? We'd never met. He was referring to my dad whose origins were in southern Indiana along the Ohio River. Turned out that's where Rarick was reared and he knew my dad. He was a Hoosier who moved to New Orleans, married a wealthy woman, became a hanging judge, and then went to Congress.

One day Rarick approached me as I stood among six or eight other representatives in the cloakroom and asked in his acquired southern drawl, "Andy, can you co-sponsor my bill?" Without hesitation I said, "Certainly, Judge; what is it?" Said he, "It's to send our undesirables up north."

"Sounds fair enough to me, Judge," I said. "We sent one of ours down South."

I was involved in two other incidents with the "Bull Conner" of Congress. During consideration of an education appropriation, the judge offered an amendment which provided that none of the funds could be used in the "futile" attempt to educate children of African descent. The judge droned out a litany of what were essentially non sequiturs. As soon as Rarick finished his ornery oratory, I was on my feet and the first to be recognized by the chair for a five-minute response. That was more than enough, to wit:

"Mr. Chairman, members of the Committee of the Whole House on the State of the Union, *Ho and Hum*. I yield back the balance of my time."

The next member recognized was Ron Dellems from California. Dellems was of African descent, himself, and one of the brightest intellects in the House; Rarick obviously was not. There was no indignation in Dellems's tone nor his words, words well chosen and laced with grammar that was flawless. When he finished and had time remaining, I asked him to yield and he did long enough for me to say, "Mr. Chairman, let the record show that the gentleman from California has just spoken completely extemporaneously, whereas the sponsor of the amendment has read his remarks from a text."

Of less significance, but quite funny, was a chance meeting I had with Rarick in the Longworth House Office Building. As an impromptu metaphor of our respective congressional activities, we were headed in opposite directions as we met in a hallway. I thought I was better armed than he because my Great Dane was at my side. Wrong. Mostly in jest—oh, alright—completely in jest, I thrust a finger toward Rarick and directed the Dane to "kill!" The huge beast jumped up and grabbed *my* arm. As he walked on by, Judge Rarick shook his finger at me and said, "You ain't never gonna beat us." I had a strange, perhaps even eerie feeling as I recalled the movie in which aliens took command of people's pets. I couldn't help wondering what had possessed that dog to do such a thing. But I didn't ask and the Dane never muttered a word about it.

Now let's return to 1962. My father said Senator Homer Capehart had a political gift: he was an essentially intelligent man who appeared to be a buffoon. Not much argument about the second part, and I saw flashes of the first part now and then. But his campaign for re-election in 1962 betrayed very little brilliance on the part of his so-called consultants.

The beautiful, bright and true-blue balladeer Mary Lou Conrad wrote a parody of a popular song for Birch Bayh's radio and television ads. It was scintillatingly catchy:

Hey, look him over; my kind of guy.
  First name is Birch, the last name is Bayh.

The image on the screen was a lively orchestra with a pretty blond young woman belting out the verse.

The Capehart ad people tried to match the jingle. Didn't make it. Their lyrics, set to shopworn music, included:

He'll work for you; he'll fight for you.

Worse, the image on the screen was a rotund Senator Capehart down on the farm. By then, most Hoosiers did not live on farms.

Time had passed the senator's campaign managers by, and so had Birch Bayh, at least in campaign pitches. After what must be called a dismal beginning, America's space program was beginning to succeed and excite the nation and Birch declared, "Space-age problems cannot be solved with stone-age thinking."

Good stuff; bad year though for Hoosier Democrats. All his friends were delighted with his dazzling performance, but they knew poor Birch didn't have a chance.

Birch Bayh is one of my favorite people. Like his eventual opponent, Dan Quayle, he didn't have a naturally mean bone in his body. Birch was warm and generous, and in 1962, I wanted to help him.

A good friend of mine who was the son of a prominent Republican had told me that Senator Capehart was enthusiastic about private investments in Latin America. From that I erroneously concluded that Capehart, a wealthy man, had made such investments himself. When Capehart started saber-rattling toward Cuba, I said publicly that his investments were motive enough to send other peoples' sons to die on the beaches. Rough charge and, as the senator pointed out with celerity, an incorrect one. I believed what I said, but I was blameworthy because I had not checked it thoroughly. And I apologized publicly. It was a stern lesson for a starry-eyed young stumper.

There was some comic relief for me, though. My good friend John V. Wilson, the newspaper reporter's newspaper reporter, accompanied Senator Capehart on the campaign trail one day and was with the senator when the solon stopped at his Washington, D.C., (Washington, Indiana, is in Daviess County) home to dress for an evening banquet. The home was not run-of-the-mill. It was five rectangle prefab houses arranged in the shape of an "H." As my friend John waited in a living room, he was startled to hear my voice emanating from the private quarters. As he listened, he realized it was a tape recording of the news conference in which I had apologized for mistakenly suggesting a possible motive for the senator's martial advocacy in the Caribbean. Presently Senator Capehart appeared in the doorway and in stern soliloquy, intoned, "I don't mind when they call me fat and I don't mind when they call me stupid. But when they lie about me . . ."

This would not be the last time John V. Wilson was a "mole" for me. Two decades later sheer fate would give him that roll again.

During the campaign, the senator claimed that Soviet nuclear missiles were in Cuba. When that claim was validated by events, Birch's up-to-date campaigning appeared to be overshadowed and to no avail. It was hard to argue with the *Indianapolis Star* editorial that joyously declared that the senator's prescience had assured him another term; the election was already over, the editorial said—in October.

I sat four down from President Kennedy when he spoke for Birch Bayh at the Indianapolis Airport in 1962. In those pre-Vietnam and pre-Watergate times when presidents were still awesome, I was thrilled. All the more so because I had thought up the Young American *Combat Veterans* for Freedom who defended the President's honor on that day and in that place.

President Kennedy and my dad had served together with Richard Nixon on the same committee during those two years of my dad's congressional service fourteen years earlier. And I had found myself face-to-face with Kennedy as he jogged in shorts around a corner in a hall of the Longworth House Office Building one day. And, of course, I had seen him as a senator at the reception in the Barton home in 1959. But on that fall day in 1962 on that platform in Indianapolis, it was different; he was the President. I knew that Kennedy and my dad didn't get along very well when they worked together on the House Education and Labor Committee. You might even say there was bad blood partly because of Dad's hostile encounter with the far right columnist, Westbrook Pegler, a friend of JFK's father. This unpleasant fact crossed my mind when the President finished his speech and proceeded down the line of Hoosier Democratic candidates, shaking hands. When he got to me he was charming without a hint of his difficulties with Dad. In his clipped Boston accent, he said, "Good luck, Andy. I knew your fathah." Couldn't help liking him.

I had another surprisingly pleasant encounter that year with someone I assumed to be an unfriendly intramural adversary. He was James Ward Beatty, proconsul of those young intellectual political activists in the yuppie Twenty-seventh Ward. They were the "intellectuals" columnist Leibowitz said were supporting my Democratic Primary competitor George Zazas. I think they saw me as something of a clod, the ex-Marine who wasn't an officer, the ex-police officer who was a law student, but not the pipe-smoking full-time scholar sort. And, perhaps a little too plain-spoken.

Because they were fair-minded, they had invited me to one of their coffees probably to confirm their image of me and maybe snicker a bit as I split my infinitives. I think they were genuinely surprised when I didn't. I don't think they were disappointed so much as relieved. They were, quite rightly, still for George Zazas, but they and I did find rapport. By 8:30, though, I said to my new friends, "Now, if you will excuse me, I must go to the south side rally where I think I can get some votes." Leibo was right in his *Indianapolis Times* item; at the rally it was clear that I was favored by most of my fellow precinct committeepeople.

Jim Beatty not only was working to nominate George Zazas for Congress, he was also a candidate, himself, for the state legislature. He lost. When he spoke at the pre-slating convention meetings of precinct officials, I was usually present. And it seemed to me he was unusual, unusually wholesome. He was an idealist who later told me, "I never regretted doing what I thought was right." The thing he had done right on the occasion of that utterance was reject an opportunity to make a lot of money the bad old-fashion way, dishonestly. And he was enthusiastic about bettering the world through his church and his civics. He had a rare gift; he could think brilliantly on two important levels in politics. Most people in politics are good either at nuts-and-bolts organization or at public policy issues. He was superlative at both and, in time, acquired multitudes of radiant admirers.

I was already an admirer of Jim Beatty when he worked for my opponent, but not quite a radiant one yet. My admiration for him was strengthened after he had lost the primary and, without missing a beat, went to work campaigning in the fall for his successful primary opponents.

Beatty reported to the Democratic headquarters each day, taking time off from his law practice. County chairman Jud Haggerty soon came to value highly Beatty's good counsel and hard work. Eventually Beatty, with Haggerty's support, became the Democratic county chairman.

One day in mid-October, as I was driving home from work, I saw Jim Beatty waiting for a city bus. I still scarcely knew him except as an unusually decent fellow who supported my opponent. But an incident in the Marine Corps and maybe a little bit of common courtesy compelled me to offer him a ride. When our Marine reserve unit arrived in California, we were taken by bus from Camp Pendleton to the Marine Corps Recruit Depot in San Diego by diesel buses. Halfway down the coast, the fifteen buses in the convoy formed a circle in an ocean-view parking area. We sat for thirty minutes with the engines running. That meant all the Marines were treated to heavy doses of diesel exhaust. As we became painfully nauseous, I vowed that if, by some miracle, I ever got home alive, I'd never pass a person at a bus stop if it was safe to offer a ride.

Beatty was a person at a bus stop. But I didn't realize that the bus he awaited was headed in a direction quite different from mine. And his route followed a traffic-jammed street. It was an hour out of my way. Time well spent, though, because it produced a close, lifelong friendship. We discovered that the same things that mattered to the one, mattered to the other; and most of the things that did not matter to the one, did not matter to the other. More than any other, my three wise men Jim Seidensticker, Jud Haggerty and Jim Beatty—and my four wise women, Kim Hood Jacobs, Marjorie Jacobs Landwerlen, Julia Carson, and Loretta Raikes, eased my way through public life. My nephews Tom, Marty, Dan, and Greg Landwerlen, contributed mightily in the same direction.

Vice president Lyndon Johnson came to town that fall of 1962 to be the main speaker at the annual Indianapolis JFK dinner. In his warm-up remarks he said, "I realize now that I will never achieve my highest ambition," Everybody knew what he was talking about. He had always hankered to be another Franklin D. Roosevelt in the White House and had given it such a good try in 1960 that he ended up being vice president. But there wouldn't be another opening for a Democrat until 1968. And there were already rumors that President Kennedy might drop him from the ticket in 1964. Besides, the presidency was beginning to look like a young man's game and Johnson would not be young by 1968. So we sympathized—until the vice president went on to specify the ambition he had in mind, "to be a Hoosier." He knew what we were thinking and turned it into some pretty tricky humor. The audience response was genuine laughter. No one then could possibly have imagined how ironic that joke turned out to be—barely a year later.

When the polls closed on that brisk November evening of 1962, it was clear that the Marion County Democrats had suffered our usual fate; we lost. And, of course, we had it on the authority of the old *Indianapolis Star* that Birch Bayh had lost back in October. *Of course*; *to be sure*. Except that something strange was beginning to happen as dawn broke on that Wednesday morning after the election night before. Something like what had happened on that Wednesday morning of Harry Truman fourteen years before.

The statewide totals were tipping toward Birch Bayh. In the November *recount* of the *Indianapolis Star*'s October "result," there was a reversal. And the whole country would soon know how to pronounce "Bayh" (by).

Birch went to Washington and I went back to work at my one-person law practice. The dream I shared with young Abe Lincoln had, in my case, not come true. So there would be no more politics for me except as a civic-minded precinct committeeman. It was time to start earning a good living.

My dad was pleased; my secretary, too. Sister-like Phyllis Butler plainly told me, "You're a nicer person when you're not running for public office." I felt nicer. Besides, why run again anyway? It was Republican Marion County and I was a Democrat.

In 1963 Indianapolis held its quadrennial election for mayor. The Democrats always elected a city party chairman for the odd-year event and they usually went on to elect a mayor. Most of my friends, including County Chairman Jud Haggerty and his close ally Jim Beatty, supported Center Township Assessor James Francis Cunningham to be city chairman. But not I.

George "Dutch" Ayres was Cunningham's opponent, the same Dutch Ayres who had so kindly supported me in the primary of 1960. I endorsed and cast my vote as a precinct committeeman for Dutch. That put me offsides with my friends and, as it turned out, offsides with the winner, Cunningham.

That night in my inner-city basement apartment, I watched the jubilant winners on the evening news and concluded that my decision to go to work seriously on my law practice was opportune. I would continue serving as precinct committeeman—that was up to my neighbors who almost certainly would continue to elect me—but clearly I was washed up in politics so far as the downtown party officials were concerned. I was on the losing side. Twenty-four hours later, City Chairman Jim Cunningham appointed me chairman of my Fourth Ward. And seventy-two hours after that, the city chairman and the county chairman announced that I was their candidate for mayor. As Jim Beatty said more than once, "You never know on a given day whether you've won or lost in this life."

Serving in Congress had been my goal, but I was tempted by this new opportunity. The first thing that came to mind was my assurance to my father that I would eschew politics and get to work on my profession. That was not a problem, though; he thought I should run. But I didn't. A day or two after Cunningham and Haggerty announced their support for me, one of their key allies cut a deal with the Democratic Governor of Indiana to support his Superintendent of State Police for the mayoral nomination. That split the regular organization, making my nomination improbable. The defecting ally was quoted in the *Indianapolis Star* as saying that, yes, he had told Cunningham and Haggerty he would support anyone on whom they could agree, but that he "had no idea they would pick Jacobs." Of course, the slur was calculated to delight the newspaper publisher who loathed my dad. So, on that "given day," I hadn't won after all. Or had I?

Circumstances were such that had I become mayor, I would never have gone to Congress, my strongest ambition. Jim Beatty was right. You never know.

I went back to work on my law practice. But my friend Patty Welch, a lady of letters with an exquisite intellect, said I should not dismiss the possibility of public service just because I had been dismissed by it in my first try for Congress. That remained somewhere toward the back of my mind, but not all the way there.

(*Left*) My dad as a teenager on the farm, with (*from left*) his mother, Maud, brother Karl, sisters Elizabeth and Katherine, and father, Mike.

(*Below*) By the age of two I had already learned that among the best friends a guy could have were his sister (Wanda Jacobs Strange) and a couple of pups.

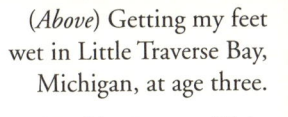

(*Above*) Getting my feet wet in Little Traverse Bay, Michigan, at age three.

(*Right*) My stage fright wasn't showing when I posed in my George Washington costume for a school play when I was six.

Hamming it up for the camera during reserve (a few days out of combat).

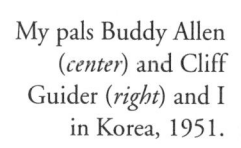

My pals Buddy Allen (*center*) and Cliff Guider (*right*) and I in Korea, 1951.

A couple of comarades and I (*at right*) enjoyed a welcome lull on line in the Korean mountains in 1951.

My dad (*standing at left, with pipe*) in 1948 with (*standing, from left*) his Republican congressional opponent, former Indianapolis mayor George Denny, Progressive candidate William Ransom, (*seated, from left*) Frank Fairchild, the Republican candidate for Marion County prosecutor, and George Daly, the Democratic candidate. (*Indianapolis News* staff photo)

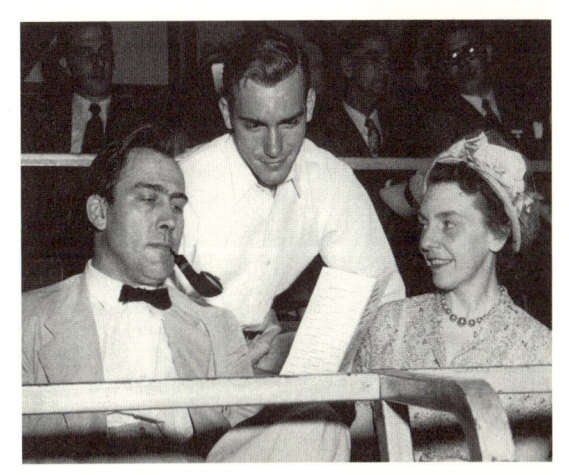

At the 1950 Democratic State Convention with my parents, Andy, Sr., and Joyce Jacobs. A year later, at age nineteen, I headed for Korea, and combat. (*Indianapolis Star* staff photo)

As a Marion County Sheriff's deputy in 1955, I often had the unpopular task of writing tickets to lead-footed—and less than pleased to see me—drivers. (Palmer collection)

chapter 3

NEVER AGAIN IS ALWAYS A GUESS

ON NOVEMBER 22, 1963, the United States President was killed and the United States was badly wounded by gunfire. In that monstrous moment, there were no Democrats or Republicans, just Americans; a man was murdered, but the Presidency was assassinated. If you were then older than seven, you now know and always will know where you were when you learned that Lincolnesque history had come back and killed again. When England lost its last foothold on the European Continent, "Bloody" Queen Mary said, "When I die, Calais will be written on my heart."

A paraphrase of those words echoed often in my mind during that forlorn and hopeless weekend, "When I die, *Kennedy* will be written on my heart." It was as if every police officer in America were shot dead on that same dastardly day. One was. He was Dallas Officer J. D. Tippit.

In mid-December, the *Pogo* comic strip showed Pogo and his little buddy in a rowboat. One said to the other, "It just doesn't seem like Christmas; it's been a year when we've lost so much," the other replying, "We didn't lose it; we just gave it back after using it awhile."

In his inaugural, Kennedy had said of his program:

> All this will not be accomplished in the first one hundred days. Nor will it be finished in the first one thousand days, nor in the life of this administration, nor even perhaps in our lifetime on this planet.

Ironically, the second, third, and fourth phrases turned out to be essentially the same length of time; So poetic, so prophetic, so pathetic.

The dead President and the new President flew back from Dallas to Washington on Air Force One. When the plane landed, the former emerged from a cargo door and the latter from the regular one. The thirty-sixth president of the United States Lyndon Baines Johnson stepped onto the tarmac and spoke through a welter of microphones as the planet listened:

"This is a sad time for all people . . . I ask for your help and God's."

Johnson said a questionable thing when he addressed Congress for the first time as president. Years, nay, decades later, when for the first time I was a father and one of Kim's and my sons lost part of a finger in a kitchen accident, I wrote this letter for him to read later in life:

Dear Andy:
   When Lyndon Johnson became President because of the assassination of President Kennedy, he appeared before Congress and said, "All that I have, I would have given gladly not to be standing here today."
   I did not believe him, which is not to say that he did not believe himself. He may not have thought of it literally—all his worldly possessions.
   Sacrifice in the abstract comes easily, not so much so in the actual doing of it.
   The one time when a person can know for certain that he or she would give up much for another is when the other is his or her child.
   So it is that I am certain I would *gladly* give up mine if only that would only restore that part of your finger.

A tragically misguided instance of that unlimited love granted by nature to parents occurred in Indianapolis when I was still a police officer. On a terrifying Tuesday a little girl drowned in Fall Creek on the east side of town. On Thursday, we found her father drowned in the same spot. He had tied his neck to debris anchored in the creek bed.

Even though the hand specialist had said that Andy "wasn't going to be a pianist anyway," Kim and I knew otherwise when Andy won a statewide contest to play the piano at the Indiana State Fair. Praise the Lord and pray for all the other parents whose hearts were broken not just temporarily, but permanently.

By Christmas 1963 I was settled comfortably into what was becoming a successful law practice. And I think my secretary Phyllis Butler, whose nickname was Muffet, was at least somewhat right about my being more pleasant in the quiet life of private citizenship. I tried to take only those cases in which I believed and thus suffered very little anxiety about how they would come out with a jury. No more politics for me. Public office was for masochists, people who enjoyed being jabbed and maligned. My lady friend and I would be going to dinner. It would not be political meetings with their long lines waiting to make short campaign pitches. But there *was* that matter of the government contractor who nearly starved the Marines on their way to war. And how many members of Congress would stand up to a president who might sacrifice on the altar of politics the lives and dreams of hapless young Americans? Such thoughts did not keep me from tending to my rewarding business nor us from going to dinner, but they nagged.

My comfortable life was beginning to itch. In addition to my second thoughts over the dearth of congressional objectors to presidential wars, there had been outside stimulus. My dad's TV news friend Frank Edwards had told us that the well of emotions about the tragedy of the century would mean a landslide for the Democrats in 1964. Super pals Sei and Jim Beatty thought I should try again. The itch intensified and the moth flitted into the flame. I once again entered the heat of Harry Truman's kitchen. The comfortable and quiet life was drifting away.

This time it would be different; it would be easier—or at least possible—in the fall. But, precisely because it would be easier in the fall, it would be harder in the spring. The nomination might be worth something—and attract strong competition. It did.

Phil Bayt was tall, friendly and courteous. In 1964 he was also the former Mayor of Indianapolis, the former Prosecutor of Marion County, and the former Marion County Democratic Chairman. And he had an expensive campaign brochure which cost him nothing, well nothing in terms of money. It was the same *Indianapolis Star* that he had wanted to sue for libel when he was defeated in his bid in 1951 to remain mayor and the same *Indianapolis Star* with which he decided to curry favor in order to win for mayor in 1955.

By 1958 he was rightly known as an *Indianapolis Star* Democrat. The formula worked very well. Phil would say the things Mr. Pulliam, Sr., liked to hear, and Mr. Pulliam would publish the things that signaled his Republican readers to vote for Phil. Since he was on the Democratic ticket, most Democrats would automatically vote for him and, in his case, many Republicans crossed over and did the same. So, in the manner of the mayor who competed with Birch Bayh to run for U.S. Senator two years before, Phil was a great fall election vote getter, for himself. The same Democrats who foolishly thought Mayor Boswell's favored status at the *Star* would mean *Star* support for all the Democrats in 1962 entertained that pipe dream again in 1964, this time about Phil Bayt.

What did all this have to do with me? Phil was the one who made my second path to the congressional nomination formidable. He was my Democratic competitor. And the *Star* was his campaign brochure, beginning with his announcement. Technically it was a news story, but it read more like an editorial. The *Star* "story" celebrated Phil as a born winner. He had lost the mayor's race in 1951, but that was before he became cozy with *Star* publisher Gene Pulliam, Sr. The newspaper "story" was all the more significant because the same writer lengthened my name during that campaign. In a subliminal suggestion that had the sound of criminality, in every critical story he wrote about me—which was every story he wrote about me—I was identified as, "Jacobs, a *two-time loser* in Marion County politics." Considering the ethical *Indianapolis Star* which emerged in the 1970s, the old paper's contrived coverage of that 1964 primary contest now seems comical.

The 1964 Marion County Democratic Slating Convention did not feature a two-way contest for Congress. It was three-way. Besides Phil and me, there was a spoiler. And the spoiler's campaign threatened to spoil mine because with only two exceptions, the relatively few committeepeople who voted for him would have voted for me in the absence of his candidacy.

As previously mentioned, most of the ward chairpeople supported me, if for no other reason than the fact that the *Star* supported Phil. But Phil still had many friends among the committeepeople. Through the years, he was in a position to do many favors and did so for party workers who were more interested in jobs at city hall than political philosophy. And Phil was a likable personality. I was fond of him. All in all, the outcome of our contest was not predictable, although those who tried to predict, predicted Phil.

There was no cognizance of the Indianapolis political realities at the Washington-based *Congressional Quarterly*, the private periodical about congressional work and congressional politics. It flatly predicted that I would be signally defeated.

February, March, and April of 1964 did not pass quickly for me; I was not having a good time. The campaign effort was grueling even though I did my best to keep in shape for it. I worked out with weights, calisthenics and did run each morning before going to work. And after work, I took a thirty-minute nap before heading out on the campaign trail. One Sunday at my parents' home, my dad walked into the living room and found me using a coffee table to write personal messages on postcards to each of the fourteen hundred precinct workers who would vote in the convention. When he asked and I told him what I was doing, he said, "It's a hell of a way to make a living." You will recall that two years before, my dad had said, "If my son wants to go to Congress, I want him to go to Congress; he'll learn." As I applied myself to the law practice during 1963 and appeared happy doing so, Dad may have begun to believe that I had *learned.* But here was his *politiholic son* again, off of the profession wagon and back on the bandwagon. For the record, because of my father's example, I did not then and do not now imbibe. Dad said his thinking was "muddled enough without it."

Most of the old-time pols in both parties tended to agree with *Congressional Quarterly.* At a Wayne Township Democratic organization meeting on the far-west side of Indianapolis, I overheard a discussion about my chances to win the slating convention endorsement. At one point, Criminal Court Judge Richard Salb gave his opinion. It came from one corner of his mouth—the other corner held a cigarette—with the look of a knowing smile: "What difference does it make? Either way, Bayt will clobber him in the primary." That meant the rank-and-file Democratic voters were less likely than precinct committeepeople to understand Phil's relationship with the *Star*. That was one more uncertainty in my attempted climb up Capitol Hill.

But there were uplifting evenings as well. One occurred at the home of Marie Smith, one of the most intelligent, civilized, and pleasant women I ever met. Indiana's beloved Abe Martin, the mythical philosopher invented by Indianapolis-based national columnist Kin Hubbard, said, "I never could remember whether a pleasant woman was pretty." Well I can remember about Marie. She was beautiful and most wise as well as radiantly pleasant.

The crowd of committee workers at Marie's home that night was enormous. And they favored my candidacy enthusiastically. For me it was a tonic. My first and worst Marine infantry battle was on a murderous Korean mountain called Hill 902. Marie Smith's street address was 902 and the street was Congress! It looked like an omen. Two decades later, I accidentally discovered the politically useful intersection of Indianapolis and Congress. From then on, my campaign posters bore a picture of me (on an unseen stepladder) next to the street intersection sign.

There was another very special lady in my political life. She stood about four feet, eight inches and she was a powerhouse, a mighty Ms. I met her at an east-side ward meeting where most of the precinct officials favored my opponent Phil. And many of them were downright hostile to me that night. When I addressed the crowd, there were silent catcalls in facial expressions. And there were unfriendly tones in the questions directed at me. Then the short arm of a very short woman went up. She stood and, in the midst of the fray, said, "Well, Andrew Jacobs, Jr., I hope you keep on refusing to bow down to Mr. Pulliam [Sr.]." The next day I asked if she would be an officer in my campaign committee and she agreed. Her name was as delightful as she, Bessie Gasaway.

Many campaigns later, Bessie was in a nursing home dying of cancer and probably weighed no more than forty-five pounds. When I visited her one day, she was utterly alert and, in reference to the political opposition, raised that tiny and wasted arm from the sheets, shook a clinched fist, and declared in an outdoor rally pitch, "We're not afraid of 'em!" Some of Bessie's political cronies included Chet Shonaker, Jimmy Slinger, and Sei's former Marine Corps drill instructor dad, Port Seidensticker, who once had served as an Indianapolis city councilman. When Port made a stem-winding speech in protest against the "downtown politicians," it usually went like this, "Are we going to take this? Nooooo! We're the little people, but they're going to learn that we add up." They added up to delightful characters of the Damon Runyon variety. I always needed and had their support. It was a joy.

When the day of the convention finally arrived, my stomach was host to the butterflies of anxious youth. All three of us candidates shook every delegate's hand. The session took forever and when the votes on the backs of the machines were at last counted, I had won by eighteen out of several hundred cast. Had the spoiler candidate received ninety-eight instead of the seventy-nine he did receive, Phil would have won by one.

The *Indianapolis Star* was not pleased with the result and pushed all the harder for Phil's nomination in the actual primary. Phil said he would likely distribute his own slate of candidates in opposition to the official Democratic organization slate; his was to be called the Bayt Slate.

The official party slate included a large number of Democratic candidates for various offices. And they were nervous.

Phil was perceived as formidable and his slate might mean defeat for those official organization candidates. Which slate should these hopefuls throw in with? Was a young and poorly financed candidate for Congress, who had the dedicated opposition of the largest newspaper in Indiana, worth ruining their own chances? Was the fact that I was moderate and Phil far to the right worth risking their political ambitions?

The ideal solution was for other Democratic candidates to be on *both* slates, official and Bayt. One of those candidates was the distinguished, principled, and erudite Democratic governor of Indiana, Matthew E. Welsh. He wasn't running for re-election, but he was running as a stand-in or surrogate for Lyndon Johnson in the Indiana presidential primary. It was not necessarily going to be a snap. George Wallace of Alabama was the other candidate. And nobody was sure just how well the race card would play among Democratic voters in this traditional northern Klan state.

County Chairman Jud Haggerty announced that candidates could not be on both of the opposing slates. *Consternation.* Just back in Indianapolis from a campaign swing through northern Indiana, the governor telephoned the county chairman: " Jud, what's this business about my not being allowed to be on the Bayt Slate?" Said Jud, "Well, Governor, you can be on the Bayt Slate if you want to."

"Well, good," said the relieved governor. But Jud added, "Now of course, you can't be on the official party slate, too." Matt Welsh was not given to cussing, but on this occasion he made an exception, "[Expletive deleted], Jud, I'm on seventeen different slates in Lake County alone. This is a moral matter." At the time, Phil was one of Matt's appointees in state government. And this is where Jud applied the Haggerty magic: "Governor, have you considered that if you're not on the Bayt Slate, there won't be a Bayt Slate?" There was no Bayt Slate. There was, however, a strong Bayt campaign in the primary.

On the eve of the primary, Jim Beatty and Jim Seidensticker stood on the sidewalk outside Phil's storefront campaign headquarters where a protracted rally was in progress. They were there to see how many people Phil had to work the precincts the next day. Quite a few. A pleasant young Democrat named Bob Staten was Phil's campaign manager and when he saw my supporters, he stepped outside to invite them inside, saying, "We're all friends, come on in." Phil probably felt the same way until he saw Sei.

Sei came from a long line of Hoosier Democrats. His grandfather had been the Indianapolis postmaster for sixteen years. And for reasons never explained to me, there had been bad blood between Phil and Sei's progenitors. Phil was addressing the large crowd as Jim Beatty and Sei entered the hall. As Phil glanced from face to face, his eyes met Sei's. The dike burst. The subject changed. With vehemence, Phil declared, "The Seidenstickers have been cutting me up as long as I can remember and—" A sudden shriek. Phil looked startled as the shrill words shot across the chamber in high-pitched dudgeon, "Throw that scum outta here!" It was our old friend Dutch Ayres, county commissioner and ward chairman, this time on the other side. The *scum,* my supporters, James Ward Beatty and James Porter Seidensticker, Jr., thought it best to throw themselves out, and withdrew.

I received 57 percent of the primary vote in the contest with Phil, and I expressed my best wishes and friendship for him election night. He was most gracious. The next day when I went to the courthouse on business, I was greeted by *Indianapolis Star* reporter, and later Editorial Editor, Jerry

Lyst. His friendly words remain firmly and fondly in my memory: "You really slammed one home yesterday." By a happy coincidence, years and years later when I got around to being a father, Jerry's wife, Sharon, was a volunteer at the Indianapolis Second Presbyterian Church's Mother's Day Out program. Kim's and my younger son, Steven, a.k.a. Bronco, participated in the program. We shall always be grateful to Sharon and Jerry. Wonderful people.

Dutch Ayres's ill-considered outburst on primary eve led to a very funny incident barely a week later. On the Saturday following the primary, in the regular convention to elect a county chairman, Jud Haggerty stepped aside in favor of Jim Beatty. And the following Tuesday, Jim and I dropped in on a meeting of Larry Sexton's beloved Indiana "Democrat" Club. Dutch Ayres was there and approached the new county chairman to apologize for being carried away by the emotions of primary eve. Jim Beatty is one of the kindest people I ever knew. He would not intentionally hurt good old Dutch's feelings. But his response inadvertently cut Dutch to the quick. Jim had so many things on his mind, he honestly did not remember the incident.

The Indiana "Democrat" Club meetings were held in a part of town frequented by, well, bums. And many of them crashed the proceedings because of what Larry dubbed, the "famed smorgasbord," which usually consisted of cold cuts and loaves of bread broken open in the middles. The participation of the derelicts made the meetings seem like religious mission services, where the down-and-out's must listen to the sermons before meals are served. Only, in the case of the club, the sermons were political speeches—some sounding like sermons. When I was called upon for a speech, I looked into the bloodshot eyes of the hungry faithful and made the national news. In fact, my friend Ginny Welch, who had preceded me to Washington and worked at the Democratic National Committee, sent me a copy of the daily news summary prepared by the Committee for President Lyndon Baines Johnson. The last item to come before the great man was a quotation from a wire service story:

> In what promises to be the shortest political speech of the campaign season, Andrew Jacobs, Jr., a candidate for Congress, said to the assembled crowd at the Indiana Democratic Club, "Fellow Democrats, let's eat."

In a way, the results of the primary were mixed; I had won the nomination, but lost my voice. It was laryngitis. The latter was put to the test several days later when I stood before a Clowes Memorial Hall theater audience on the occasion of the Indianapolis premiere of the musical *Camelot*. I had been asked to precede the performance with a memorial statement about the slain president. I must confess that my bachelor blood began to stir when I was escorted through the curtains of the backstage toward the microphone above the orchestra. Beautiful young women from Broadway, in what seemed an endless sea of fishnet stockings, were scurrying about in preparation for their cues. Most distracting. My performance was problematic. With a whiff of nasal spray, I could speak for about sixty seconds. Therefore my memorial service could not exceed a minute. Thus began my endless effort to avoid making endless speeches. This one came in at thirty-three seconds:

> I have been asked to explain the connection between this play and President Kennedy. It's just this: It was his favorite. And when he was gone, Mrs. Kennedy said the phrase that echoed in her mind was, "Don't let it be forgot, that once there was a spot, for one, brief shining moment, that was known as Camelot."
>
> But perhaps the shining moment is not so brief at all. It occurs to one how difficult it would be to imagine President Kennedy's ever growing old in any way.
>
> He might have been President for only eight years. But now, he will be President forever.

My wise, witty and judicious friend—who later did become a judge—Vic Pfau was seated in the audience next to one of my critics. He later told me that as I walked on stage, the detractor made a disparaging remark. When I finished, he turned to Vic and apologized. "A soft word turneth away wrath."

On the night of the primary, I knew I had been successful by eight o'clock. But six months later, when election day had come and gone, I still did not know whether I would be going to Washington.

My Republican opponent had been my dorm counselor during the year I was required to spend on the Bloomington campus of Indiana University in order to receive my undergraduate degree at IU in Indianapolis. Don Tabbert was tall, bright, friendly, and eternally young—probably personally acquainted with Ponce De Leon. He was strongly for his party's presidential nominee, Barry Goldwater, so we were at odds in our young political views. But we were very much *not* at odds in terms of our friendship. To the surprise, shock, and maybe dismay of our respective supporters, we made clear throughout the election that we were warm friends. It remained that way.

In mid-summer Sei and I had been naive enough to attend a Democratic "how-to-get-elected" course in Washington. While there, I went through what dad called the *sheep-dip* with President Johnson—picture and all. Once back home we turned the picture into a campaign postcard. There we were, the odds-on favorite to win the presidential election and the one grabbing for his coattails in Marion County, Indiana. That year, the President's anti-war coattails were the "how-to-get-elected" so far as I was concerned. And it was by no means certain that the fabric would be long and strong enough to drag me through the Indianapolis GOP obstacle course. Indeed, James Reston had written in the *New York Times* the year before:

> If the Republicans think they have something with Goldwater, then they should nominate him. Of course he probably wouldn't carry a state outside the South except Arizona and Indiana.

As the fall campaign got under way, Don Tabbert and I made a joint appearance before the Junior League of Indianapolis, a group of mostly Republican and very civic-minded young women, who I later learned were not so Republican when it came to Don; he had defeated their candidate in the Republican primary. At one point, Don produced one of the pictures of the President and me and said, "There is entirely too much secrecy in government and, Andy, I challenge you to state exactly what you and the President were saying to each other when this picture was taken."

I thought to myself, *Don, you really are a good friend*. I loved it. First I feigned a furtive, almost guilty look. Then I got a big laugh from everyone else in the room, especially Don when I replied:

"Well, er, ah, I was ushered into the Oval Office and seated at the desk there (I pointed to the picture in Don's hand). The President smiled and I said, 'Mr. President, I have some ideas about Vietnam—'

"'Next!' came a deep voice from somewhere. And the 'next' thing I knew, I was standing in the Rose Garden where a guy was pointing me toward the bus that would take me back to How-To school."

My next sheep-dip was an elaborate one. It happened in mid-October when I flew with the governor to Gary, Indiana. LBJ was to arrive the next morning for a rally before flying on to Indianapolis at noon. I would have the honor of emerging from Air Force One in my hometown with my *peace* President. Heady stuff.

At the Gary rally, LBJ told the enormous crowd that there would be a

Great Society for "Dad, Molly, and the kids. And they will live as citizens of our prosperous America, not just with food in the refrigerator, but with a rug on the floor and pictures on the wall." The crowd loved it. He then undertook to explain the difference between the Republican and Democratic parties. Referring mainly, I think, to his well-known cooperation with the Eisenhower administration and the GOP's vilification of Truman, he said the difference was "we don't hate their Presidents." The crowd roared.

Three decades later, when Kim and I had driven to Gary to speak my sincere and heartfelt praise for Frank O'Bannon, the Democratic nominee for governor, I made a comment that referred to the contemporary vilification of Mrs. Hillary Clinton:

> A third of a century ago, I stood here in Gary and heard the Democratic President explain the difference between Democrats and Republicans. He said "We don't hate their presidents." It is a sad commentary on civility in American politics that a third of a century later it is relevant to say, "We don't hate their president's *wives*."

Of course it was a political rally and I was not referring to the vast majority of both rank-and-file and office-holding Republicans who did not approve of such conduct by certain national GOP leaders. For my part, I liked every one of the seven first ladies who occupied the White House while I served in Congress.

When LBJ finished his speech, we followers climbed aboard buses and went to the airport where we boarded the great silver bird of the United States. At the time it was a Boeing 707 with slightly floppy wings. And there I was, seated in something like a side sofa next to the President, who radiated a huge smile and extended a notably scratched and swollen hand. He had been to a lot of places and there was no telling how many hands he had shaken in each of them, nor how many times fingernails slipped across his epidermis.

As we flew south, the President extended his hand again and I reciprocated—erroneously. He said, "Would you move over?" He was preparing for a hand massage and I was in the way of the therapist. Did nothing to calm my youthful nervousness.

Air Force One docked at Indianapolis International Airport at about one in the afternoon. And after a long delay that was just as inexplicable for the people inside the craft as it always is for those greeting the arrival, the great man and the awed congressional candidate stepped out and waved to the cheering throng.

My joint appearance with the President in the doorway was as short-lived as our airborne handshake. I followed from a distance of several line jumpers as the President worked the crowd along the snow fence. Then I was comported by someone to a limousine and I got in. It was not the presidential one; it was the next one back. Engines were started, police motorcycles revved, and we began to roll. But not very far. Suddenly the motorcade stopped; the right rear door of the President's car flew open. And now you get a glimpse at the kindly thoughtfulness and generosity of then-Senator Birch Bayh. The senator sprinted from the lead limo to me, grabbed my arm, and pulled me toward the President. As he did so he said to me, "I'm not running this year; you are." And the next thing I knew I was on a jump seat immediately in front of the thirty-sixth President of the United States.

The trip into town took about twenty minutes. Our route was along Washington Street in Indianapolis and there were cheering citizens on the sidewalks all the way. After a minute or so of presidential waving to the crowd, the leader made a discovery and blurted it out: "They don't know which car Ah'm in." He turned to his assistant, Jack Valente, and said, "In the next town Ah want a flat-bed truck in front of ma car with a band playin' 'Hello, Lyndon.'" That was his campaign song to the tune of "Hello, Dolly." You don't want to know what my campaign song was or at least I don't want to tell you.

The President then asked of the local folks in his car, "What are they saying about Bobby Baker here?" By whom he meant his former assistant who had got into some kind of fast-deal hot water, an embarrassment to the President. Baker was the President's former assistant, whereas the President's opponent, Barry Goldwater, had some bad luck in picking his running mate, New York Congressman Bill Miller. It turned out that Congressman Miller had a problem somewhat like Bobby Baker's. As the Democratic nominee for governor, Roger Branigan, rolled his eyes and smiled and another passenger assured the President that Baker shouldn't be a problem, I took a deep breath and once again offered a suggestion to the U.S. President. Only this time nobody said "*Next!*" before I could get it out. Here's what I said:

"I tell people that when we find a bad apple, we get rid of him. But when they find one, they run him for vice president of the United States."

Had I impressed the President? Maybe. LBJ more or less mumbled, "We didn't run him for vice president."

Good. My "peace" president was taking me seriously. When he later revealed that he was not my "peace" president and I took strong exception to his perfidy, he took me seriously in a much less favorable way.

The President drew a crowd of about seventy thousand in Republican Marion County, whereas when Barry Goldwater came to town, his crowd was substantially smaller. The coattails were flapping in my direction.

In the closing weeks of the campaign, a crowned beauty queen at Indiana University made news by switching her support from Goldwater to Johnson. Why the switch? Was it the Medicare issue? Was it Vietnam, where her boyfriend might be sent? Aid to higher education? Well, no. Let's just listen to the actual words she used to disclose the important issue that moved her: "It's always good to be for a winner." You'd have to give her this: She was certainly more candid than that Teamster Union president who switched sides back in the closing days of the Truman election—probably prettier, too.

Peter, Paul, and Mary came to Indianapolis and campaigned for Lyndon Johnson. It was a warm fall day and the leaves were an exquisite oil painting. As they sang, I saw blue and peaceful skies ahead for my country. Win or lose, I felt good about the future.

On November 3, 1964, the polls opened in Indianapolis at six in the morning and closed twelve hours later. Most candidates for Congress have little to do on election day, but I had civic duties in another capacity. I was still the precinct committeeman for the Eleventh Precinct of the Fourth Ward, much to the consternation of Jim Seidensticker. Back in the spring my primary opponent's supporters had filed the wife of a city fireman to compete with me for the post I held as precinct committeeperson. Sei decided I was working harder on my committeeperson campaign than on my congressional one. And he may have been right. If I lost for Congress, it would not be embarrassing because a lot of people expected that I would lose. But if I lost among my neighbors for precinct committeeperson, that would be humiliating. In a moment of frustration, Sei had said to me, "Damn it, Jacobs, you can't be running for Congress and putting it together in the Fourth." The Lord smiled; I was simultaneously successful in both of those spring contests.

The fourth precinct had gone Republican every year I'd lived there. But when the voting was finished on that November 3, I was amazed to discover that the Democrats, including me, had carried the day strongly. Having finished my committeeman's duties, I repaired to my apartment, which was located in *my* apartment building—I owned it and had, with my own hands, remodeled it. It was directly across the street from the polling station. Alone, I felt the exhilaration of success.

Carrying that precinct surely meant I had won the election.

But as I awaited what later became the traditional call from my friend Jim Beatty to let me know the actual outcome, I began to have my doubts. An hour went by and there was no call. That would mean no known results and that would indicate a close call. It was.

Late on election night, neither Don Tabbert nor I yet knew who had won. I was ahead, but the absentee votes would not be counted until the next morning. And absentee ballots usually were mostly Republican. The outcome was very much in doubt when one of my fellow candidates, Daisy Lloyd, slipped a good luck metal into my hand and assured me it always worked. Another friend, Bud Myers, who eventually became my top coworker in Washington, joined a Republican counterpart in literally sleeping with the ballots that night for security.

I spent part of the evening at the Democratic County Headquarters where one of the television reporters asked if I'd like to speak to my opponent, Don, through the station's connection between the Democratic and Republican gatherings. Don and I spoke at length, reminiscing about our days together at Indiana University. I recalled and thanked him again for all those Sunday mornings when breakfast was not available at the dorm dinning room and Don and his wife hosted me for the meal in their campus apartment. This election night was the first time Don and I had experienced a closed-circuit television conversation. Correction: it wasn't closed circuit. The next morning, everywhere each one of us went, it was the same thing. Over and over people told us how nice it was to see political opponents speaking so warmly to one another. Without our realizing it, the whole conversation had been on the air.

At eleven o'clock on that Wednesday morning, I was at the City-County Building where the vote count was finished. The Democratic member of the Marion County election board, "North-Side" Charlie Johnson, emerged from the counting inner sanctum to inquire jubilantly, "Where's my Congressman?" Obviously, the count had fallen my way. Don and I had tied among the absentees, thanks in no small manner to Jim Beatty's foresight. As county chairman, he had set up for the first time an absentee ballot committee to take applications to shut-in Democrats.

The headline in the noon edition of the *Indianapolis Times* was, "JACOBS WINS BY 3,300." Don came to the City-County Building to shake hands with me and wish me well. Later in the day, I happened to drive past his downtown campaign headquarters and there it was, that huge sign in the window, "Congratulations, Andy." Having done so myself two years before, I knew it was no fun for him to loose. What a prince.

Had it been two years before or two years after among the same voting population, Don Tabbert surely would have won. But '64 was a Democratic landslide year of such immense proportions that traditional voting patterns didn't count.

Radio reporter Bob Mead was the first to interview me after the results became known on November 4. "Andy, the Democrats have had a smashing victory. The Republicans have been repudiated. How do you feel about it?"

"Well, first, I would not use the word, 'victory'; it sounds too warlike. Second, I really wouldn't say the Republicans were repudiated. Elections are snapshots. They reflect the majority view at the moment. That view can change and probably will as time consumes the present. It helps to remember Kipling's words, "triumph and disaster . . . two imposters." The interview went on, but looking back, I take some pride in what I said and realize that it may have been partly inspired by Don Tabbert's splendid civility. And, of course, the snapshots have changed back and forth many times over the years. Larry O'Brien wrote a book about politics, *No Final Victories*. You can learn a lot from that book, even before you open the cover.

I doubt that any Republican would have been elected President in 1964. It seems to me that the Frank Edwards theory was valid. Perhaps some Republican other than Barry Goldwater might have done better. In any case, most Republican candidates that year thought Goldwater was their problem. A long time later, when I was a member of the House Ways and Means Committee, Senator Goldwater wrote me a letter asking for help on a tax measure. I'm happy to say that I agreed with him and was able to help. But when I sent my affirmative reply I touched on another matter:

> Dear Senator Goldwater:
> I agree with you and shall be happy to help.
> I'd like you to know that I am disposed to like you. First of all, you along with Harry Truman are like Popeye, "I yam what I yam."
> Second, your son and I are friends.
> And third, you elected me to Congress in 1964.

He liked it. Barry Jr. was one of my colleagues in the U.S. House. At the time I wrote the letter, I had completely forgotten another connection I had with the senator. When I was a deputy sheriff and going to night law school, one of my dreariest annual assignments was the Indianapolis Five Hundred Mile Race. My job each year had been to help gather up the drunks from the infield. But in my last year as a police officer, I got a break.

My assignment that year was to be the bodyguard for a VIP who was a close friend of Eugene C. Pulliam himself. I understood that the VIP was a state senator from some other part of the country, but I couldn't understand why he had an assistant with him. In those days state legislators simply didn't have staffs. His assistant emerged often from the Pagoda guest suite that overlooked the track. As he stretched his legs he talked my right arm off about my service firearm. I was beginning to wonder if the drunk detail was so bad after all.

The VIP, on the other hand, was very quiet and at the end of the day thanked me in a most courtly manner. I later learned he was not a state senator; he was a *United States* one. And this time I caught the name: Barry Goldwater, a name that didn't ring a bell at the time. But, in 1964, the name became a carillon that rang in a new year and a new career for me. Perhaps I had more reason than I might have thought, on that warm day in May, *to protect, preserve, and defend* that nice man's life.

Judge M. Walter Bell was our Hoosier poet-jurist. He stopped me on the street the day after the election and said he was sure I would serve in the Congress for twenty years, the record held at the time by my dad's predecessor, U.S. Representative Louis Ludlow. Walter was known for being overly optimistic. This time, though, he was underly so. I served in Congress for thirty years.

Judge Bell was one of the most delightful people I ever knew, always there with the light touch. The judge presided over a civil court with no criminal jurisdiction. But one fine spring day he came to lunch at the St. Moritz restaurant, sat-down with several of us and announced, "Boys, I just sent a man to the penitentiary." How puzzling. A civil court judge sent someone to the penitentiary? While we were scratching our heads, Judge Bell added, "I filled out my income tax." Being as honest as a summer day is long, he could afford to joke about it.

Sandburg tells us that in 1863, Abraham Lincoln "told close friends that he expected to loose the next election." In 1964 that's how I saw my chances for re-election in 1966. As we have seen, Democrats in Marion County had traditionally won only once per decade, going back to before my dad's election in 1948. But in my pessimism, I was overlooking a new factor. It involved two of my fellow citizens, one named Baker and the other Carr. In *Baker v. Carr*, the U.S. Supreme Court, so far as I was concerned, had ruled it wrong for the Eleventh District of Indiana, which I was elected to represent, to have three times the population of the Ninth District of Indiana, which Lee Hamilton had just been elected to represent. They called it "One Man, One Vote," but that was a male chauvinist concept. The actual holding was "One *Person,* One Vote."

Specifically, *Baker v. Carr* meant that the Indiana Legislature elected in

1964 would draw a new Congressional map for Indiana. And that Legislature was heavily Democratic. A district favorable to my re-election two years hence seemed a cinch. And that's the way it was. But there was a fly in the ointment. The Democrats thought they had complied with the Supreme Court ruling perfectly. There was only a 10 percent disparity between the most populous district and the least. Compared with the previous 200 percent disparity between the Ninth and the Eleventh, the new map seemed a political purist's dream come true. It didn't seem that way to the Indiana Republicans. They filed suit to have the map declared un-Constitutional on the ground that a ten percent disparity was too great. And they won. But the new map did hold for the next election of 1966. Had it not, I surely would have served the single term normally allotted the Marion County Democrats each decade.

Following the election of 1964, my first order of business was to wind up my business. At the time and for a long time thereafter, there was no rule prohibiting the practice of law by a member of Congress. But there should have been.

When my dad went to Congress, he gave up his law practice and badly suffered financially when he came home two years later. His clients had gone elsewhere, and he had to start all over again. He regretted going to Congress, but he did not regret obeying his conscience while he was there. His point: A law practice is the perfect place to disguise a bribe to a member of Congress. My dad would *not* be the last person in the world to take a bribe; he wouldn't take one even then. He rightly judged that continuing his law practice would have amounted to a conflict of interests. The public is entitled to be assured that a law practice does not influence a representative's official policies. And the only way the public *and the representative,* himself or herself, can be absolutely sure that it doesn't, is for the representative not to have a law practice. Besides, the job of a member of Congress is not a full-time one; it is an overtime one. And if a member is moonlighting—in the case of a law practice, more likely *sunlighting*—she or he is cheating the employers out of time for which they pay. Call it double billing.

A university sent me free season tickets to its football games, obviously to "sweeten my judgment," as Thomas More would put it. I returned them with a cover letter which said in part:

> Returned herewith are the $400 (adjusted to the mid-1990s) worth of saleable season football tickets you sent me.
>
> The number of officials each year given free tickets to your games is unknown to me. My guess would be about one hundred seventy-six.

This would mean a university expenditure of about seventy thousand four hundred dollars (adjusted to the mid-1990s) or almost enough to pay two university instructors or, say, one coach.

If the purpose of the present is persuasion, why not pay the coach and give logical explanation of your needs to legislators?

When I found the letter while researching for this work, it was marked "pending," which means I never got an answer; never got any more tickets, either.

There were other matters that came under the often unctuously misused title of ethics. What about investment in capital stock if one is serving in Congress? Can anyone imagine how many cases of conflicts that might bring? Better skip it, I thought and *pledged.* Government bonds seemed relatively safe from conflict; hometown real estate, too. Then there was WTLC.

Well known years later in Indianapolis as a radio station of African American programming, in 1965 it was merely a gleam in the ears of a few of my friends. It was an FM classical music station. And at the time hardly anyone had an FM receiver. The owners of the station had the receivers and they enjoyed the music in their respective homes. When it became less expensive and less inconvenient to have classical music libraries in those homes, the owners put the station up for sale. The price was eighty-five thousand dollars. A decade later it was worth millions. My friends decided to buy it and invited me to participate in the investment. They said a rhythm and blues radio station was overdue in Indianapolis and the return on the investment would be handsome. Of course, it turned out to be better looking than that. And it would have been legal for me to participate, but it didn't seem right.

I had read about Lyndon Johnson's broadcast holdings and saw them as a major conflict of interests for a member of Congress. Senators and representatives repeatedly cast votes on laws governing the Federal Communications Commission. So I declined, not having the slightest doubt that the venture would be the prodigious success it became. At the close of my thirty years of congressional service, I realized my family and I would have been substantially better off financially, had I chosen to accept the attractive deal. But I had no regret about the matter. As my friend Jim Beatty said, I never regretted doing what I thought was right. My wife, our children and I eat every day and have a very nice roof over our heads. That puts us so far ahead of most people on Earth that we are profoundly grateful for God's merciful generosity.

Going to Congress was thrilling. I'm not quite sure, though, which brought the greater euphoria, entering Congress or retiring from Congress after all that time. The answer, I suppose, is "each to its own season."

When I did go to Washington initially, there were two considerations in hiring a staff. Did the person know the ropes on Capitol Hill and did the person "know the territory" in Indianapolis? Few who applied knew both.

So which consideration should take precedence? Simple. It's easier to learn the procedures in Congress than to learn about the people back home. The new staff went with me from Indianapolis to D.C. The administrative assistant was Paul Cantwell, who had been elected county commissioner at the same time I was elected to Congress. But under the staggered terms then in place for the commissioners, he would not take office until a year later. During that year he did his best to disturb the pseudo-dignity of the U.S. Capitol. In doing so, he followed the formula of mythical Hoosier philosopher Abe Martin, who opined: "Nothin'll take the starch out of a great man like meetin' a feller who don't think much of it."

Paul was in Washington for just a year, but a lot of great men there would probably never again be as starched as before Paul's arrival. He had been in town only three days when he wound up on the front page of the *Washington Post*. Here's how it happened. Paul and I attended a banquet at which the President was due to speak. Since the President was late, the Speaker of the House spoke—at length—to kill time until the President arrived. Speaker McCormack was from the very old school. Modern subtleties and humor tended to escape him. He began his oration where the twentieth century began. By the time he had praised President Franklin Roosevelt through the Great Depression of the 1930s, he plunged into World War II where Franklin Roosevelt "smote down the unholy forces of *Hitler!*" Those in the audience who had not fallen asleep rolled their eyes. But not Paul; he seized the moment by jumping to his feet and shouting maniacally, "*Boooooo, Hitler!*" It brought down the house. I thought I even saw a self-deprecating smile creep across the House Speaker's lips. The *Post* reported that "someone in the audience showed that he really carried a grudge." Of course, so few deserved to have a grudge carried against them as that Nazi degenerate.

It was Paul who, weary from the mountains of mail I received, suggested we rubber-stamp every reply we mailed out with the words, "WRITE YOUR SENATOR." His friend, my sister Marge, suggested a boilerplate answer to every opinion letter regardless of subject: "Dear _____: You may be right."

My apartment in Washington was not in Washington; it was across the river just above the Iwo Jima monument in Arlington. The brand-new building gave tenants a commanding view right down the mall on which is situated the Lincoln Memorial, the Washington Monument, and finally the U.S. Capitol. When I went to the office of the huge complex to sign the lease, I encountered one of my dad's old congressional friends. We did not get off on the right foot. Just as I was about to identify myself, the elder man snapped at me, "Where's my carpet? You said it would be delivered three days ago!" He obviously took me to be his carpet salesman and I thought it was funny. So I played the part: "Oh, I'm sorry, Congressman. Now, what color did you say you wanted?" Believing now that his carpet had yet even to be ordered, he did a fast burn on the rear of an ascending Roman candle. The jest was done; I said, "No, Congressman, just kidding. I'm not your carpet man; I'm Andy Jacobs' son." Didn't help. I'm actually convinced that he remained angry about my impertinence all the years we served in Congress together. Sometimes when you pull a rope, it turns out to be a snake tail. He was the one who gave me the devil for trying to get rid of the tax-paid limousines on Capitol Hill. Oh, well.

On the following Fourth of July, Paul and my other coworkers came to my apartment to watch the vaunted Washington fireworks on the Mall. Occupying the hillside below our balcony were literally hundreds of people with picnic baskets. When the last flash of fire faded into the night air, our friend Paul stepped to the rail to make his parting announcement. He shouted to the multitude, "Ladies and Gentlemen, our next attraction! The biggest traffic jam in Washington history." These examples scarcely scratch the surface. Paul thrived delightfully on the bizarre.

Sisters-like Phyllis "Muffet" Butler (later Coelho) and Julia Carson worked with me in Washington from the start. So did former *Indianapolis News* reporter Dick Franzene and Bud Myers, the one whose strange bedfellows on election night had been absentee ballots. Loretta Raikes would join Wilma Warren and Jud Haggerty in the Indianapolis congressional office where Julia thought we could best do casework, checking on veterans benefits, Social Security, passports, etc. Because of Julia's suggestion, we were among the first congressional offices in the nation to take advantage of the Executive Departments' regional cabinet offices.

During summers, interns would join us and were almost always very helpful if not altogether experienced. On one occasion, I was rushing to make a vote on the House floor when a mini-emergency arose. One of my coworkers asked me to dictate a quick note of reassurance to the mayor of Indianapolis on a problem we thought we'd be able to solve. One of the interns was seated at a typewriter and agreed to type the note. I said something to the effect that we could probably "redress the problem." When I said the verb, she looked puzzled and I asked if she knew what "redress" meant. She paused and said, "To put your clothes back on?" Now I had another reason to rush; I wanted to get out of the door before I started laughing.

Hear comes Paul again. I was in Indianapolis one day when a letter arrived in Washington asking me to sign a full-page ad for the *New York Times*. Muffet asked Paul about it. He took one look, saw that it was a pledge to oppose China's admission to the United Nations and, since it was against the Commies, told her to sign my name and send it in. I knew nothing about it before the ad was published and my friends began asking why I had decided the earth was flat and that its population was only three fourths what scholars supposed.

I might as well confess that while I abhor stealing and all its cousins including gambling, I did snatch one item shortly after I arrived on Capitol Hill. Perhaps I'm being too hard on myself; the thing I swiped was in a trash can just outside a committee room which was catercorner across from the office in which I worked. Maybe we could say I just retrieved some abandoned property. It was a mostly used-up memo pad with a few sheets left, and I wanted it for the souvenir it was destined to become. The title on the pad read:

CONGRESS OF THE UNITED STATES
HOUSE OF REPRESENTATIVES
COMMITTEE ON UN-AMERICAN ACTIVITIES
WASHINGTON, D.C.

Naturally I would have preferred a memo pad from the Spanish Inquisition. I still have a few sheets of the un-American paper and once in a while send one to a friend on Halloween.

If you spend a third of a century in an institution, you will inevitably be asked whether it has changed. And in the case of my long congressional tenure, the answer is clearly yes. But some of the changes were for the better.

In 1965 when I arrived in Washington, blatant racism was everywhere, especially on the part of many members from the old South. The House District of Columbia Committee was chaired by a mossback from South Carolina who regarded the District of Columbia as his plantation. Hiring policies for blue-collar workers at the capital of the Land of the Free were without decent standards. Males of European descent were hired first and given the promotions, next came women of European descent, generally according to how physically attractive they were. Then it was females of African descent, again according to good looks. Last and very definitely least were men of African descent. I was astonished. And I set about being a "troublemaker" scarcely before I found a place to hang my coat.

I gathered ten or so like-minded members of the House, and we began to push—maybe agitate—for compliance with the laws on fair labor standards, which Congress had passed for everyone else but itself. The effort went on for several years before it began to bear fruit.

The congressional pay raise of 1969 was stunningly out of line. Cumulative inflation since the next previous adjustment was about 14 percent. The raise in 1969 came to 41 percent. Senator Everett Dirksen of Illinois undertook to justify the grab. He said, "Senators have to eat, too."

The best-paid food workers at the Capitol weren't paid much; the worst-paid got even less. It was a disgrace. In the words of old Hoosier friend Abe Martin, if these workers "were paid in iron, they could carry it alright." So one morning during the one-minute speech period, about ten of us lined up to throw light on the outrage. Alluding to Senator Dirksen's declaration, I gave a little speech which consumed about one twelfth of my allotted time: "Mr. Speaker, people who serve food to Senators who have to eat, too, have to eat, too, also."

H. R. Gross of Iowa was the member of the House who argued most vociferously against the 1969 Congressional pay hike. And then he took the money. The unofficial description of such a shenanigan was, "Vote no and take the dough." I did no grandstanding on the issue, but the grab was so bad that I was bothered about taking the money myself. It was attractive, even tempting until I thought it through.

I called the appropriate official to arrange for my pay not to be raised. But it wasn't that simple. He told me that the law required him to send the full amount. So I figured the take-home part of the raise for each month and sent that amount by personal check to the U.S. Treasury and said nothing about it publicly. Several months after I began sending the money back, a wire service reporter called to say someone at the Treasury Department told him that "a nut in Congress is sending back part of his pay each month." And he asked me, "Is that true?" I said, "Are you asking if I'm that 'nut?'"

"Well," he said, "I wouldn't put it that way. But are you sending back the pay raise?" The correct answer was yes and I gave it, adding, "Unlike H. R. Gross, I'm willing to put the money where my mouth is. And, I might add, a considerably smaller mouth." In time I learned to like H. R. Gross, but I would have to say that occasionally his name seemed generic. For example, *during* the mourning period for JFK, H. R. demanded to know how much the Eternal Flame cost the taxpayers. The answer was, nothing. It was privately funded. At the time, the question was indeed gross.

Before deciding not to accept the pay raise, I had phoned my wisest counselor on public policy, my dad. He had said succinctly, "Son, if you think it's wrong, don't take it. But don't expect any appreciation from the public." And I didn't expect any; but this time, Dad was mistaken. Things had changed since he was in Washington and even since I had arrived four years before. Vietnam was already shaking citizens' blind faith in government.

Even after the reporter called me about my sending the raise back, I doubted he would write a story. But he did and I was stunned by what happened. The story went through the country like wildfire. The mail, letters of praise, poured in from everywhere. The *Indianapolis Star*, which had not yet undergone redemption, even ran an editorial that praised me with faint damn: "We're glad *somebody* [turned it down]."

Through the years as I judged congressional pay too high, I was asked by reporters why and generally answered this way:

> When I was in combat I was paid sixty-five dollars a day—once a month. I would rather do this federal government job at that salary than that federal government job at this salary, speaking of relative worth.

At the Indianapolis Press Gridiron, one of the roaster-jokesters mentioned my accepting less than the full pay and said, "It's okay by me; he knows what he's worth." My reply: "Yes, I do know what I'm worth, the same as any other law-abiding child of God. The point is what the *job* is worth."

The Architect of the Capitol who, in fact, was not an architect, ran the restaurants on Capitol Hill. He was a former congressman who didn't know a speed square from a protractor. Because of this anomaly, I introduced a resolution that said:

> The Architect of the Capitol shall be an Architect or, in the alternative, the Capitol Physician shall not be a doctor.

Of course everybody could see the merit of having a real M.D. writing prescriptions; a mistake there could result in death. But, I argued, you would have the same kind of result if one of the buildings on Capitol Hill caved in.

It was one thing to ignore people-made laws such as fair hiring practice requirements, but you could get into some big trouble by skirting a people-made law which happened also to be one of *God's* laws of nature. That's just what happened toward the end of the 1960s on Capitol Hill. Being antinomians, the "Architect's" people had blithely skipped legal requirements for health inspections of Capitol Hill kitchens and kitchen workers. Tuberculosis broke out among those workers and the people, including tourists, who ate on Capitol Hill were placed in maximum peril.

Singer Roger Miller had a hit record at the time whose lyrics, in part, were:

> *Got a letter just this mornin'*
> *It was postmarked Omaha.*
> *It was typed and neatly written,*
> *Offering me this better job,*
> *Better job, at higher wages, expenses and a car.*
> *But I'm on TV here locally,*
> *I can't quit; I'm a star.*

To prod the Architect, I wrote this parody for the *Congressional Record*. Vice President Spiro Agnew had just denounced his adversaries as "intellectual snobs." This is what I read into the Record:

> *Mr. Speaker: With apologies to Roger Miller:*
> *Got a letter just this mornin'*
> *From an intellecshul snob.*
> *It was typed and neatly written,*
> *Askin' me to quit my job.*
> *Quit my job of playin' architect,*
> *With restaurants as a ploy.*
> *But we got TB here locally,*
> *I can't give up my toy.*

Shortly afterward, we got a real architect—and kept the doctor.

When I arrived in Congress, the female staff assistants, to a person, looked like *Vogue* ads, dressed to the nines—usually size six. The male staffers were pretty spiffy, too. That made our crew stand out and—in the obvious condescension of the establishment—*down*. There are bulletin boards at every turn in the congressional office buildings. And a good share of the personal notices were quests for roommates to share rents. The one that my friends and I found the most amusing said: "WANTED: ROOMMATE FOR BEAUTIFUL CAPITOL HILL APARTMENT. MUST BE HILL-TYPE LOOKING PERSON."

Imagine. One need not even be a "Hill type," just Hill-type *looking*.

Our happy little band didn't go to Washington to be looked at, however; we went there to work. When I asked the architect's office to send us a door sign that simply read "11TH DISTRICT, INDIANA," I was told such a sign would not be printed because all the door signs had to be the same, by which was meant the representative's name, i.e., *John J. Jones, Ohio*. "They all have to be the same?" I inquired. "Well what name must they all be? Tell you what—forget about the sign; I'll make my own; it will read "CONTRARY TO THE OPINION OF THE ARCHITECT OF THE CAPITOL, THIS OFFICE BELONGS TO THE HALF MILLION AMERICANS WHO LIVE IN INDIANA'S 11TH DISTRICT OF WHOM JACOBS IS JUST ONE AND A SERVANT TO THE OTHERS AT THAT." The official on the other end of the line said, "We'll have your 'Eleventh District' sign there in the morning."

There were sideshows such as the proposals severely to punish those who physically desecrated the flag of the United States. Whether the proposals were wise or not, the target was conduct and not speech and, in terms of logic, not unconstitutional. But the distinction between conduct and speech was consistently lost on the U.S. Supreme Court. Was the prohibition wise? Maybe, but it should be borne in mind that the purpose of such protest was to get attention. Nothing like going to jail as a demonstrator to get widespread attention. If that is the object, perhaps a *yawn* would be the greater punishment. In any case, the members of Congress who took up the valiant battle enjoyed the attention they got.

The hearing on the anti-flag-burning bill was held at the House Judiciary Committee to which I had been assigned. The night before the great event, I happened to be standing in a group which included the sponsor of the bill. Someone said to him, "You're going to get some publicity tomorrow." In phony modesty, the sponsor furled his brow and said, "I don't care about the publicity. I just want to protect our flag." I couldn't suppress the urge to ask, "You didn't call up the newspapers and ask them not to use your name, did you?"

When he appeared before the Judiciary Committee the next morning, he proposed an amendment to his own bill. The amendment would outlaw beach towels that bore the image of the U.S. flag. When it was my turn to ask questions, I said the usual welcome from the committee, to which he responded, "And I want to compliment you on your outstanding war record." That caught me by surprise. I said, "Well, thank you, but lately I've been working on my *peace* record. I must ask if you have carefully considered this amendment you propose for your bill."

"Yes," he said. "It's just terrible the way those towels that look like the flag are ground down into the sand." I said, "I mean, do you really want to make it a crime to wrap yourself in the flag?" Lots of laughs from everyone but the sponsor. He wasn't angry about my joke; he just didn't get it.

Aside from seeking out the contractor who made extra money by starving Marines, I looked forward to supporting legislation for civil rights, a good and honest national defense, health care, adequate education, and fair taxation. On the subject of formal education, I realized most thought of it as beginning in kindergarten or first grade. But in the cases of children whose parents were below normal in terms of education, kindergarten was way too late to begin the formal process. "As the twig is bent, so grows th tree." That was a phrase familiar to most Americans who seldom stopped to think what it meant concerning these educationally disadvantaged kids.

About a year before I went to Congress, I read a book written by *Fortune* magazine editor Charles Silberman titled *Crisis in Black and White*. It was a brilliant analysis of social misbehavior. But unlike much of the literature on the subject, it went beyond analysis to the solution which was the kind of cognitive preschool training for educationally disadvantaged children which Israel had successfully operated for decades. It was a deliverance of children whose mothers often were children themselves in families with generations of undisturbed ignorance. Despite the title of the book, the majority of such children are of European descent. Such children simply do not acquire in their homes the basic linguistics which are indispensable to gaining the skills necessary for self- propelled citizenship.

A tiny part of President Johnson's anti-poverty program touched on this solution, but it was inadequate to the purpose. Operation Head Start was like a light dust job during the summer before first grade. A Westinghouse study found it too little and too late in a child's life. In terms of cognitive development, we are old men and women by the time we reach age three. During the *first* year of life we have the greatest capacity to acquire linguistics. Lose that year to ignorance, and the damage is horrendous, but lose five more, letting the child grow like a weed until the summer before first grade, and that life is essentially ruined. In turn a life so ruined could easily ruin or even end other lives and destroy property, too.

For my first four years in Washington, I tried to get the attention of Congress to explain why Head Start meant attacking the fire when not much was left but the basement. But once the inadequate Head Start program was started, the problem of educationally disadvantaged children met with Congressional and local governmental neglect. Other matters mattered more to most members of Congress. Slaughtering young American lives to straighten out or kill Commies in Vietnam was believed to be more important than straightening little American human twigs that were not being bent toward civilization in their early years. These little ticking time bombs were the real threat to our national security.

By 1968, great strides forward had been taken in civil rights, Medicare and education from kindergarten up. And great strides backward had been taken in our foolish Vietnam involvement.

For reasons to be discussed in the next chapter, my 1968 re-election was cast in substantial doubt. It seemed odd, therefore, to some people, including some of my strong supporters, that I would choose to use scant campaign funds my committee had to make a short video on the enormous national benefit I saw in a cognitive preschool program for educationally disadvantaged children. I wrote the script, narrated it, and even wrote the words and music for the theme and closing song. My music was beautifully sung by dear friend Arlene Martel, one of the towering talents of national television commercials. In those days, TV time was less expensive and my committee was able to air the thirteen-minute tape several times during October 1968. The video did relate to the 1968 campaign in one respect: President Nixon's PR people decided on crime as their big issue. The political attack, of course, was that Democrats were fond of felonies. This, in part, is what was said and sang in my video which I titled, *I Walked With a Child*:

> "All that I am or ever hope to be, I owe to my angel mother." That was fine for Abraham Lincoln, but what if, in the educational sense, one's mother were not an angel? What would he be or ever hope to be?
>
> That question is not before the American people. But it *should* be, because it is a subtle question which almost completely encompasses the more obvious questions about crime and violence and overburdened welfare rolls.
>
> Back in law school, I was strongly concerned about the rise of violence on our streets. I wanted to learn more about it. So I became a police officer and worked on the streets of our community to find out how human beings could bring themselves to do violence to others. If I learned no other lesson from my four years of police work, I did learn this: At times, violence is a natural temptation to anyone. And rather than bring oneself *to* violence, it is the function of self-control to bring oneself *away* from violence when the temptation occurs.

The people I was obliged to arrest in such cases just didn't have that self-control. Why? A few were mentally ill, but only a few. Most of these violence doers were sane. Most of them were unemployed. Most of them were either grade or high school dropouts. Most of them hardly knew how to read. And, indeed, most of them hardly knew how properly to hear and understand linguistics.

And, indeed, too, most of them came from homes where the same catastrophe of ignorance plagued their parents and grandparents before them for generations.

So I have long since concluded that if we really want to do more than just listen to politicians complain about crime; if we really want to prevent crime as well as punish criminals; if we really want to make our streets safe for decent living, rather than just close the cell door after violence is done to loved ones—if this is what we really want, then we must cut short the chain of ignorance that runs through generations in some homes and produces the educationally disadvantaged children of today. If we fail to take sensible action, the embellished ranks of these educationally deprived children will descend with predictable violence upon the society of our children's generation. And because of the higher birth rate among the uneducated, the next generation could be swamped by an ocean of ignorance, an ocean of ignorance in which it might truly be folly to be wise.

Once a little boy was given a newspaper map of the Earth. The map had been cut into a puzzle which he was asked to put together. In less that a minute he had assembled the pieces correctly—every country, every ocean in its proper place. His elders were astonished until he explained that he had merely turned the over the pieces and reassembled them into the picture on the other side of the page, a picture of a little boy. And the moral: If you put the child together right, the world will take care of itself.

No one of us is born with the kind of kindness which the safety of civilization requires. For the first two thousand days of our lives we tend to become what we will be or can "ever hope to be."

Opportunity in terms of formal education or even remedial linguistic training tends to be lost on deaf ears if the twig-like child cannot distinguish among the subtle sounds of his language, indeed his mother tongue.

If his mother's tongue and ear and eye cannot speak and understand and read the language, from whence will he acquire the linguistic key to the door of education? And if he and his early adult associates live in an atmosphere of that hopeless ignorance which begets truculence, how shall he learn of the beauty of gentleness which he will never have touched during the first six years of his life?

Psychologists tell us that if a child has not acquired proper auditory skills before he enters kindergarten, he will find it nearly impossible to acquire reading skills in *any* school. And he will be the school dropout, the unemployed and likely as not, the criminal of violence.

The program is not complicated. It supplies the early-life basic education which simply is not there in the disadvantaged homes of millions of American children.

In Israel, they know all about the problem and with what in essence is an effective cognitive preschool program, they are solving it. Along with the academic aspect, little children are shown how to reason out their conflicts with others, rather than strike them.

The Indianapolis Junior League has such a program, although its size is necessarily small. Young educationally disadvantaged mothers participate in the program with their children. And even though these mothers may not grasp all that their children are learning, they show an interest and thereby encourage their children to achieve. Though lacking in educational skills, in most cases these mothers prove to be angel mothers in the sense of child development, once they are motivated to participate in breaking the chain of poverty and ignorance between their generation and the next.

Studies of the effect of this program have proved just what you would hope. The participating children enter the first grade with sufficient momentum to keep pace with the majority of children who've had educational advantage in their homes.

This fantastic potential, to shape the twig so the tree grows straight, to install a guidance system for civilized conduct—all this is there, lying in the litter of poverty like some wondrous genie in the bottle. If we as a nation could summon the common sense to release that genie in its full potential, a safe and decent future for all of us could be assured.

But it is clear that they "have to be taught before it is too late, before they are six or seven or eight." And unless we do this with America's educationally disadvantaged children, we will not even begin to solve the problem of impersonal street crime in our country.

As a former police officer, I know well the need for sound and just law enforcement. But I know also that this can never be enough alone to cure the disease of crime which is moving toward epidemic proportions in our country.

In our quest for a solution to such crime in the coming decade, let others speak of colder and harsher philosophy and nothing more than the brute force to beat back the savage element amongst us. But let *us* speak of building decent citizens, who won't commit crime in the first place.

As the credits were crawling, Arlene began singing my song also titled "I Walked With a Child":

> *I walked with a child and talked with a child*
>   *But only in the night*
> *Yet, out of that child, came thoughts so mild*
>   *That hardened eyes found sight.*
> *I found in this child no crux reconciled*
>   *No words that sang with rhyme*
> *But things that seemed wild, when seen by the child*
>   *Seemed good and clean and kind.*
> *Through eyes of a child, I see naught that's riled*
>   *No fears with which to cope*
> *And in this child whose thoughts are mild*
>   *A troubled world finds hope.*

It was not until Ronald Reagan's last year in office that I was able to persuade the Congress to pass my specific proposal for preschool. It came in the form of an amendment I offered to the 1988 Welfare Reform legislation. It required the U.S. Government to conduct ten pilot projects around the country to solicit *unpaid* volunteers to help in cognitive preschool programs. But its principal provision required the Department of Health and Human Services to call on universities to give academic credit to students for going into educationally deprived homes of children, age zero to three, to help the haggard moms, and simply speak the correct English which we know will be automatically stored in those little human tape recorders.

I was confident that the results of the effort would be the same here as in Israel. President Reagan signed the bill into law before he flew west for retirement. And in the following eight years, the law was honored in the breach by two national administrations, one Republican and the other Democratic.

Thirty-three years after the inadequate Head Start program was given birth, there was a feature about it on NBC's *Today* show. The reporter said that, "because of *recent* research" (italics added), the program was being expanded to include infants and toddlers. "Recent research." One wonders who did the research for the ancient verity, "As the twig is bent, so grows the tree."

During my first year in Congress, an incident occurred that inspired me to go momentarily into show biz. Actually I made the front page of *Variety*.

The inspiration was my then eight-year-old nephew, Daniel Anthony Landwerlen. He and two of his brothers, Andrew Martin Landwerlen and Thomas Leo Landwerlen, Jr., had just got into my car for an avuncular trip to the movies when I reminded them to "buckle up for safety." The two brothers did so without comment. But Dan balked, "Batman doesn't buckle up in the Batmobile."

"Well, he should," I weakly replied. An idea came to mind. The following Monday I sent a letter to William Dozier, producer of the spoof *Batman* series on ABC. Robin was given to saying things like, "Holy Dirty Crooks, Batman, we have to stop the Joker and his gang." So the punchline of my letter read, "Holy belt buckle, think how many lives might be saved if Batman would set a good example by buckling up."

A few weeks later, the ABC affiliate in Indianapolis, WTHR Channel 13, sent a car for the nephews and on the next day's news there they were in the station's studio watching the following scene from *Batman*: As the crusaders jumped into the Batmobile, Robin exhorted, "Let's go, Batman; let's get those dirty crooks."

"Just a minute, Robin," said the batperson, "safety first." And with that, our hero clicked his seatbelt into place." For a several days afterward, Channel 13's outside marquee bore these words, "Holy Belt Buckle." *Variety* was kind enough to say I was high camp. That was about the extent of my theatrical career.

Aid to education and the Medicare program passed into law during my first, the Eighty-ninth Congress. Medicare was bitterly opposed by the American Medical Association which, decades earlier, had also opposed the emerging idea of *private* health insurance. Medicare, the AMA said, was socialized medicine which had ruined the United Kingdom. A long time later, witty pundit George Will *un*wittingly helped give a clean bill of health to the British health system. It happened on the television program, *This Week with David Brinkley*. In an effort to discredit the Clinton administration health proposal, Mr. Will pointedly asked British Prime Minister Margaret Thatcher, icon of the American Right, if her country mandated employers to provide health insurance for employees. Certainly not, she said, "We're quite happy with the system we have." No one on the set seemed to realize she, the Conservative's Conservative, had just praised the ogre of American politics, socialized medicine! It was pretty funny.

Shortly before Medicare passed Congress, the very talented and personable television journalist Douglas Kiker interviewed freshman Republican Representative Bo Calloway and freshman Democrat me on the subject. Mr. Kiker asked me how I responded to charges that I was a rubber stamp for Lyndon Johnson when it came to Medicare. My answer was uncomplicated: I was for Medicare before Johnson was. When I was in college it made sense to me. If either Johnson or I were a rubber stamp for the other, it would have to be Johnson who was a rubber stamp for me.

ON MARCH 25, 1965, A WOMAN NAMED Viola Liuzzo died, not just for her country, but for her country's soul as well. Remember the words of Solon: "Civilization is impossible until the unconcerned are as outraged as the victim."

At home in Michigan, Viola Liuzzo was not a victim. But she was outraged. The victim was a group of American citizens around Selma, Alabama, who were, under unconstitutional color of local law, denied the most fundamental of American rights, the right to vote and thus participate in "the consent of the governed." So Ms. Liuzzo traveled to Selma to see if she could help in the righteous effort to eradicate the outrage. And there, fate and a demon racist used a firearm to hurl this wonderful woman into the whirlwind and forever into the pantheon of murdered martyrs to the cause of justice. Blessed are they who thirst for justice. Blessed was she.

She was taken from us as she was driving citizens to Selma to register to vote. As she drove those qualified but denied voters along the road of redneck resistance she was shot to death from the window of another car. The legendary John Lewis was nearly killed in the same peaceful and constitutional effort when a Georgia "peace officer" deliberately, hatefully, and wantonly crashed a truncheon onto John's skull. Those civil rights workers were martyrs and they were proof of those sage words of Hoosier broadcaster Elmer Davis:

"This country was not created by cowards and it will not be maintained by them, either."

The shock of the Selma nightmare electrified America. In short order, President Johnson stood before Congress to propose a new and toothful law. If enacted, it would ensure, once and for all, that when it came to voting in

America, there would be liberty and justice for all. Until then we said it, but we were not "one nation, under God." We were two nations in contempt of God.

The President's prepared speech was pretty pedestrian except for when it borrowed from a contemporary civil rights song. He paused and intoned, "And we shall overcome." But at the very end and apparently extemporaneously, his words came alive and betrayed a sincerity about civil rights that few could doubt. I don't quote precisely, but in so many words he said:

> When I was a young teacher, my students were poor and rejected. I couldn't give them much except what little I knew. And I vowed at the time that if I were ever in a position to help them in ways I couldn't then, I would do it. Well, I'm in that position now.

It was warm and human and inspirational. And the positive response from his congressional audience, minus the racists in our midst, was thunderous and sustained.

It was my historic privilege to participate in the production of that pivotal law known as The 1965 Voting Rights Act. I was one of the two freshmen Democrats on the House Judiciary Committee that year. The other was the soft-spoken and powerfully effective John Conyers, Jr., of Michigan. He and I later double-dated roommates. I married mine; his married an Indiana State Trooper.

When the bill was presented to the House for amendment and certain passage, several southern members had their knives out to pare the effective provisions into platitudes. A few of the amendments they offered were sensible, but often redundant.

Picture Bill Tuck, former governor of and by then U.S. Representative from Virginia. He was a tad rotund, as befitted a politician of the old school. With white flowing mane, sartorial splendor replete with a fresh red rose in his lapel each day, and a rich and resonate voice that spoke the smooth honey of a magnolia accent, Bill Tuck was every inch a southern *gentleman* who didn't think much of civil rights legislation.

When Congressman Tuck, usually called Governor Tuck, offered an amendment so acceptable to everyone that it was already in the bill, the venerable chairman of the Judiciary Committee, Emanuel Celler of New York, explained why the amendment was unnecessary. Governor Tuck had an answer:

"Well, it's like the fella who got a telegram from California sayin' that his mother-in-law had died there. The message he received asked for instructions about disposal of the body. 'Should we bury her, cremate her, or put her in a vault?' The son-in-law fired back, 'Take no chances; do all three.'"

His amendment was voted down, but not his performance. Of course, we heard the threadbare argument that "you can't pass laws to make people like each other." And I had an answer:

"It is precisely because you can't pass laws to make people like each other that I know why we need laws to protect people who are not liked."

In the final moments of the floor debate, the governor rendered an oration that was awesome. The rafters rang, as he invoked almost every generally accepted icon from mother, home and hearth to God and apple pie. He missed one.

Bill Tuck and I were the only members of Congress at the time who were Marine combat veterans, discharged with the lofty rank of private, he from World War I and I from the Korean War. And as soon as the governor finished his platitudinous speech, I approached him and said, "Governor, I was deeply offended by that speech,"

"Well," said the still perspiring orator, with more than a hint of irritation, "you fellas are wrong about this."

"Governor, I'm not talking about the bill. I just want you to know that if you ever list all the wonderful things about America again and leave out the Marine Corps, I'll have to drum you out of it."

"My God," said the governor, "did I leave that out?"

The bill became law and it worked. As mentioned before, southern white racist Congressmen were suddenly—and often—seen entertaining constituents, *voting* constituents, that is, of African descent at lunch in the elegant House Dining Room. In essence, those Congressmen were eating crow, *Jim Crow*. Strom Thurmond enrolled his children at an integrated public school. "There will be more rejoicing in Heaven if one sinner repenteth." Praise the Lord.

Sometime in 1965 I composed a logo for our congressional office stationery. Thinking specifically about both the unconstitutional presidential war in Vietnam and the wholesale unconstitutional violation of some citizens' constitutional rights in America, this is what I had printed at the bottom of that stationery:

THE ROAD TO PEACE IS PAVED WITH JUSTICE.

The Judiciary Committee took up another significant proposal during my first year there. It was offered by my friend and senator, Birch Bayh.

When Congress and the several states were finished, it became the Twenty-fifth Amendment to the United States Constitution. It provided a sensible system of presidential succession in the sort of case that swept Jerry Ford from Congress to the White House in 1974. When the Committee reported the bill, it was not controversial. But floor amendments were offered.

One of the proposed amendments would have required ratification by state conventions rather than by state legislatures. The constitution allows either method. The sponsor of the unusual method argued that it had been used to repeal Prohibition. This time Emanuel Celler had the answer:

"I know why they used the convention method. It was because of the publicity. Franklin Roosevelt wanted to get as much credit as possible for giving people back their beer. I was in on it!"

Quite true. Emanuel Celler was first elected to Congress in 1922 when the decade roared with Prohibition, bootlegging, and Al Capone. The chairman continued:

"Back then a man was traveling across Kansas on a train that stopped in a small town. The passenger stepped onto the platform and sheepishly said to the stationmaster, 'Sir, I don't mean to offend, but I simply cannot get all the way across your state without a libation. Is there anywhere in town where I can get a drink?'

"The stationmaster gave the visitor a stern look and said, 'Go two blocks down that street and turn right. You'll see a little red schoolhouse. That's the only place in town where you can't get a drink.'"

In that, my freshman year on the Judiciary Committee, I was assigned the pleasant task of sitting next to the chairman at the floor manager's table and helping however I could. When he returned from the House well (where most House speeches are made) to his seat at the table, I told him I thought the laughter in the chamber was much more than politeness. They liked the joke. The two sides in the controversy over Prohibition were known as "the Wets" and "the Drys." Referring to those monikers, Mr. Celler quietly said this to me:

"Andy, there was another joke I couldn't tell in the well. When I ran for Congress the first time in '22, my platform included repeal of Prohibition. There was a speakeasy on every corner of the district. And some of the young men in my campaign passed out cards that read, 'Vote for Celler and your wet dreams will come true.'"

During my first year in the Congress. Representative Michael Joseph Kirwan of Ohio was chosen to give the orientation lecture to us freshmen and women. He had the shortest biography in the Congressional Directory. It was a line and a half—including his full name. One reason for this might have been that he had almost no formal education. But his informal one was prodigious. Like Lincoln, he had enough of a start to have learned to read and what he read produced an encyclopedic knowledge of U.S. history. He told funny stories, two of which follow.

In 1934 when Kirwan first ran for Congress, FDR had been in office for almost two years and was popular times beloved. The chances of Republican Congressional candidates were slim that year and the GOP primary in Mike's district was not crowded. The Democratic one was—very. Mike told about the most important rally of the primary campaign. Thousands of voters attended—not much else to do in those depression days. There certainly was no TV.

Each of the numerous candidates was given a few minutes at the public address system; Mike was last. All his competitors had the same message, practically word for word. "I want to go to Washington and help Franklin Roosevelt." Mike disappeared from the rally until just before his turn. He had gone across the street to make a purchase from the dime store. When introduced to the acres of humanity, he tore the paper wrapping from his purchase and held high the content for everyone to see. It was a large picture of the thirty-second president of the United States, FDR. With that, Mike shouted to the throng, "Look at this man. Does he look like he needs any help from me?" The voters loved it—and him. They sent him to Congress and kept him there 'til he died.

Much more off-the-wall was his story about being indicted. One night during his trial, he was dining at a restaurant in his district. The waiter, obviously a fan, asked the congressman how things were going. Mike Kirwan said they could be better. "Why?" asked the black-tied server. "Well I'm being tried on criminal charges," replied the worried representative. Said the waiter, "You don't have anything to worry about."

"Well, I'm afraid I do," Mike explained, "This is pretty serious business."

"You're not going to be convicted," the waiter said with conviction. Mike posed a relevant question: "How do you know that?" The fan gave a relevant answer: "Because I'm on the jury." Kirwan was acquitted and served in the U.S. House a couple more decades.

I know nothing about the case brought against him and I have no idea about whether justice was done. But I do know about the indictments of two other members of Congress in the 1980s where justice was done, but also partly denied because it was long delayed. And, for that matter, a measure of justice was denied simply because the indictments were brought in the first place. The malicious prosecutions were bipartisan, one of the victims was a Democrat, and the other a Republican. In both cases, the United States Attorneys who obtained the indictments were respectively long-standing political enemies of the defendants. In both cases, when the long awaited trials were held, acquittals snapped back from the juries like rubber bands.

My dad used to say that a prosecutor had no power over a citizen unless the citizen had done something criminally wrong. That may have been nearly true at one time. But in the latter part of the twentieth century, with most legal fees in outer orbit, prosecutors could do enormous damage to innocent citizens. And in the case of members of Congress, indictments in and of themselves constituted severe punishment. Both Democrat Harold Ford of Tennessee and Republican Joe McDade of Pennsylvania were indicted by political enemies. And under House rules, both victims were required to give up positions of high honor pending the outcomes of the trials. In both cases, the *pending* went on for years. God knows the astronomical legal fees the victims *and* the taxpayers had to pay. Donald Smaltz, the special prosecutor who obtained the 1990s indictment of Secretary of Agriculture Mike Espy, gave a good example of what damage could be done by a prosecutor. When the case fell flat on its face with the swift acquittal of Espy, Smaltz bragged that he had already punished Espy anyway just by indicting him. Swell. Thanks for proving my point, Don.

No thoughtful citizen should rest easy, knowing that the criminal justice system can be so transmogrified as to serve as a political weapon. It is a deadly menace to democracy.

Appropriate reform of the existing rule would be simple: Prosecutors who can effectively punish before trials should be held to the same standard of disinterest as judges. They should not be allowed to participate in investigations of political enemies. In plain English, prosecutors, and that includes special or "Independent" prosecutors, should be biased *after* examining evidence, not before.

During my first year in Congress, a controversy arose over the design of the federal interstate inner-loop highway in Indianapolis. One leg of it was designed to cut a diagonal swath two hundred feet wide through the northwest part of the city. Seventeen hundred property-taxpaying housing units along the way were scheduled to be demolished. A very slight alteration in the route would have obviated 90 percent of the housing and property tax base loss. But highway departments at that point had little experience with urban road construction. Most of the interstate system had gone through open farm fields. It seemed that having these fellows build interstate links in cities was roughly the equivalent of having butchers do brain surgery.

Never Again is Always a Guess

The route chosen in Indianapolis was bad enough, but the design evaded any semblance of logic. The highway was scheduled to be elevated on a dirt embankment which would sever forever a great number of city streets, thus disrupting traditional neighborhood activities. Indianapolis was a poor place to build several miles of dirt embankment anyway. With scant exception, the city is as flat as a tabletop: glaciated.

Trying to persuade the highway people to see the enormous dividends from a slight route change proved futile. The view through the transit is not panoramic. The elevated design, however, should have been something altogether else. Surely they would come to their senses on that one. Inner-loops all over the country were below grade, out of the way. The reasons were obvious. Severed city streets could gradually be reconnected by bridges, whereas burrowing through a couple of hundred feet of dirt wall and shoring up tunnels was prohibitive. Then there was the question of traffic safety and wear on break pads. Entering a freeway downhill meant gravity's help in acceleration. Entering a city uphill meant gravity's help in deceleration. The larger the vehicle the larger the problem if a freeway emptied downward into a city street. The plan seemed Kafkaesque. Surely there must be some explanation beyond just "dumb." There was. It was found in the transcribed record of a legally required but little-noticed public hearing held a few years before.

Lo and behold and eureka, the original design drawn by the consulting engineer *did* call for the same below-grade method used in the rest of the country. Why, then, the sudden change? The answer was clear and right there in the record. The phone company had testified that it did not want to suffer the expense of moving its underground trunk lines to make way for the below-grade highway and, therefore, argued that the throughway should be elevated. And, indeed, it would have been grossly unfair to force the phone company to bear the cost of relocation after already having paid its share of gasoline taxes to pay for the highway. At the time the eminent domain law did not provide for compensation of costs to the company. Justice demanded one of two things. The title to a Jerry Lewis film was, *Don't Raise the Bridge, Lower the Water.* The phone company asked that the highway be raised, but common sense and the rest of America said pay the phone company to lower its trunk lines. And the latter was precisely what the next session of the State Legislature authorized the State Highway Department to do.

Once the law was changed to reimburse the phone company for moving those underground trunk lines, the company, in essence, became the title of another old movie, *Rebel Without a Cause.* And that should have been that.

But it wasn't. The phone company was on record as having said the design should be changed. One would expect that when the reason for its request to change the design was removed, the company would remove its request. But unfortunately the president of the phone company at the time, Texan by birth and rearing, had an ego. When President Johnson was still popular, it was fun listening to the phone boss trying to sound like LBJ. The company president had a chauffeur-driven corporate car, too. I'd seen him use it to ride for just a couple of downtown blocks.

Having once argued for the elevated design, the phone president couldn't back up even though the expense of moving the trunk lines was no longer a factor. His fragile ego forced him to stick by his gripe. And in doing so he served both his adopted city and his company not well. The expense of moving the cables was minuscule compared to that of finding and hauling those millions of yards of dirt. But our Texas transplant managed to do that dirt to the city. How did he get his absurd way?

Well, he used phone company ads to sponsor local TV news programs. That made one station manager very happy—and grateful. The sensible side of the controversy did not fare well on that channel. At a dinner I attended in an official capacity, the station manager sarcastically announced from the head table, "I see Congressman Jacobs is in town (where I lived and from which I commuted to D.C.) to help us build our new highway." My response: "I'm here to help build it *right*."

The *Indianapolis News* ran a Robinson editorial cartoon depicting me in overalls with a team of mules plowing for votes in the neighborhoods to be savaged by the right-of-way. I was waving off a bulldozer operated by one of the most neighborly Hoosiers imaginable, replete with an old slouch hat. He looked so bewildered. The caption had me saying, "Go bulldoze somewhere else." Quite apart from the unflattering suggestion about my motive, the people to be displaced weren't likely to be moving out of the Congressional District anyway.

The thing that evoked a chuckle from those who noticed was that not long after the cartoon appeared, a similar one, drawn by the same cartoonist, was published. Once again a bulldozer was featured. The subject was another federal project, which my election opponent and I both opposed. Only this time the images were different. Gone was that lovable Hoosier operator. Gone were the overalls. And gone was I. This time all that was seen of the bulldozer was its enormous blade, no operator, just huge letters across the imposing colossus, "FEDERAL BULLDOZER." (The earlier cartoon's bulldozer was just as federal) And there, in remarkably neat attire, was my opponent, holding his hand high, palm out, and saying, "In the name of the people, halt."

For fun, and it was that, I photocopied the two cartoons together and personally mailed them to a large list of public-spirited citizens. My caption under the graphically slanted cartoons was, "STRAIGHT SCOOP."

My allies, who were therefore the public's allies in this case, included, but were not limited to, labor union leader and city councilman Max Brydenthal, brainy book editor Patty Welch, county chairman Jim Beatty, attorney Kurt Pantzer, Dr. Frank Lloyd, environmentalist Greg Silver, political scientist Pat McGeever, future attorney Rachel McGeever, and Sylvia Zazas. The phone president and the TV manager won. The public lost, in this case, forever.

We took our case to the federal highway administrator, a man named Boyd. His agency was paying 90 percent of the project cost, but he told us straight away that design and route were in the complete discretion of state authorities. So much for the overreaching federal government. In this case, it didn't reach even far enough to protect the interstate highway gas taxpayers from an eccentric abuse of their trust and trust fund. The outrage would never have happened under the phone company and that TV station management teams of the 1980s and 1990s. As in the case of the *Indianapolis Star*—and *Merry Olde England*, for that matter—those companies improved with age.

chapter 4

THE SURE BET

UNITED STATES REPRESENTATIVE DANIEL J. FLOOD of Pennsylvania was the proverbial *institution*. They loved him in Wilkes-Barre. He was clearly an unforgettable character. Among many other occupations, he had been a Shakespearean actor before 1944 when he was elected to Congress. In fact, he was pretty much an actor throughout his congressional service. He was tall and slender with jet black hair and he sported a Snidely Whiplash moustache. He was poetry both in motion and in discourse.

In 1965, when John Kennedy's long-promised Appalachian relief legislation came up for a vote in the House, it was Flood who made the towering oration, replete with references to the classic novel *How Green Was My Valley*. His peroration was his own classic:

> Now, Mr. Speaker, you might approach one of our unemployed rawboned miners and tell him that this legislation is Socialism. But if you do, duck!

By chance I was present when Flood walked off the floor into the speaker's lobby and encountered Speaker of the House of Representatives John McCormack. The latter gushed, "Magnificent! I never heard a better speech." It couldn't have been too bad; the bill passed overwhelmingly.

Then there was the time when Representative Sid Yates of Chicago offered an amendment to an appropriation bill. The purpose of the amendment was to increase funds for Chicago. Poor Sid ran into a brick wall in the person of Dan Flood who chaired the subcommittee that reported the bill. It was Flood's job to steer the legislation through the

House without amendment. Flood responded to Yates's arguments for the amendment. Once again it was showtime in the U.S. House. They didn't quite lower the lights, but, as always, there was both a stir and a hush as Dan Flood gracefully glided to the well of the House. Pages and other floor personnel emerged from the cloak room and members suspended their private conversations. "The chair recognizes the gentleman from Pennsylvania." Sounded more like, "Ladies and gentlemen, *The Old Vic* proudly presents Sir Daniel Flood":

> Mistah Speakah, I don't blame the gentleman from Chicago for wanting more than its share for Chicago. It's a matter of loyalty and affection for his constituents. Of course, if each of us got more than his or her district's share, this would be the Big Rock Candy Mountain. And it isn't. I have the greatest affection for the gentleman from Illinois. He comes from a wonderful town. I never was in musical comedy, but I'll give it a try.

And with that, the Honorable Daniel J. Flood of Pennsylvania successfully performed a soft shoe dance right there in the well of the United States House of Representatives, and sang, *a cappella*, Frank Sinatra's rendition of "Chicago." It brought down the House. Forget it, Sid, Chicago would have to settle for what Dan thought best. Amendment defeated.

When the Dan Flood show was booked again the following year, I couldn't resist. A conspiracy was formed among two pages and me to cap Dan's performance with the traditional gesture following Broadway plays. I bought a box of long-stemmed American Beauty roses and as Dan returned to the manager's table following his formidable feature, the pages turned into ushers, rushed down the aisle, and presented the open box to the virtuoso as he basked in the usual standing ovation from his colleagues. Dan called me later that day and I was prepared for a laugh from him or even anger. But I did not anticipate his actual reaction: he was touched.

It will not surprise you to learn that Dan Flood and his wife owned a snow-white Cadillac convertible. They rode in it each weekend to Pennsylvania and always took two friends with them, their French poodle and their goldfish, in the bowl—on Dan's lap.

Dan was involved in a spoof milking contest in downtown Washington one evening between the "city slickers" and "hayseeds" in Congress. Referring to the cow he milked, he was quoted in the *Washington Post* the next day thus: "She asked for my phone number." I think it's not unreasonable to assume that Dan got a lot of fun-loving fan mail on that one.

Nineteen sixty-six was the year of Abner Mikva and Barratt O'Hara. Ab Mikva was one of the best and, yes, brightest people ever to serve in Congress. But 1966 was not his year to be sent there. With a little, well, a lot of help from the Daley machine in Chicago, O'Hara repulsed the first Democratic primary challenge from Ab, who was nominated and elected two years later. O'Hara didn't run again. Small wonder. He was born April 28, 1882. Unlike Mike Kirwan's, Barratt O'Hara's congressional directory biography was extensive. He had done everything. When he was a sophomore in high school, he enlisted in the Thirty-third Michigan Volunteer Infantry and, led by Teddy Roosevelt, participated in Cuban combat. Yes, he was a Spanish-American War veteran and still in Congress two-thirds of the way through the twentieth century with two more years to go. At the age of thirty, he had been elected lieutenant governor of Illinois. He had been a newspaper editor, a radio commentator and a practicing lawyer. He also served as an infantryman, or doughboy, in World War One.

During the primary contest, O'Hara produced an authentic quotation from the great and celebrated lawyer Clarence Darrow: "I wish I had the courage of Barratt O'Hara."

"The past came alive on that primary night of 1966. The octogenarian Congressman was asked in a news conference how it felt to win. Thrusting his fist skyward, he declared in his mellifluous tones, "Like charging up San Juan Hill!" Bully for Barratt.

As already indicated, the 1965 Indiana Legislature was under court order to draw a new congressional map. Because of the Democratic landslide of 1964, the Democrats were the majority in both Houses of that legislature. They drew a map favorable to *all* the Hoosier incumbent Congressmen except one. He was Winfield K. Denton who had entered Congress with my dad in 1949. But the Democratic governor in 1965, Roger Branigan, elected, in effect, to sabotage Democrat Denton's 1966 re-election effort.

Denton was perplexed. In his rich southern Indiana parlance, he said to me, "I never heard of a party's cold-decking its own man." He called the governor to see if there was some misunderstanding. There wasn't. Governor Branigan made fun of Denton on the phone. Winfield called my dad for advice, or perhaps just comfort. "Winfield," my dad said, "you don't have to take that abuse from Branigan. He's a very small and petty man. Why don't you just retire? You surely have an adequate pension by now."

"Andy," Winfield replied, "there are just a few things I'd like to finish before I leave." And Dad gently pointed out, "Winfield, that would be true seventy-five years from now." The governor's practical joke had its impractical effect; Winfield lost the fall election after an Evansville, Indiana, television station gave credence to the absurd assertion by his opponent that, despite enormous farm surpluses, "food rationing" was on the Democratic administration's agenda for implementation after the election.

Nineteen sixty-six was the only year of my congressional experience when I did not have a Democratic primary opponent—no thanks to Governor Branigan who did his best to recruit an opponent for me. My friends and I learned about it a few days after the primary. County Chairman Jim Beatty and I decided on what the phrase-mongers at the Pentagon called a limited response. We conspicuously failed to attend the governor's statewide Jackson Day Democratic dinner shortly after the primary.

Not long after that, while attending the Indianapolis Press Club Gridiron dinner, I was accosted by Governor Branigan who sternly scolded, "We *missed* you the other day." Amused, I said, "I heard you took a shot at me, Governor." Then his excellency, the governor of Indiana, said something quaint and scatological: "Oh, piss on you guys in Marion County. All you want to do is fight the *Star*." To which I replied, "We have better things to do than that, Governor. We just don't take orders from them." It was widely thought that he had just done that. Branigan, a lawyer, had spent decades voicing his opposition to the death penalty. The repeal had just passed the Legislature and awaited his signature. The *Star* editorialized that he should veto the repeal; he did.

Roger Branigan did have one redeeming quality; he was funny, genuinely. While he was governor, President Johnson got into a fuss with the aluminum companies because he thought their price increases were so high as to exacerbate the inflation his credit card war had ignited. The President ordered the U.S. government stockpile of aluminum to be dumped on the market to force the price down. By chance, just a day or so later, the Indiana State Chamber of Commerce held its annual lunch. And who was the guest speaker? Who else? The president of Alcoa Aluminum. The tables were laced with Hoosier Alcoa management personnel. I was there and I can report that everyone was walking on eggshells in the manner of *don't-say-divorce*-at-the-dinner-party.

When I spoke, I managed to skirt the subject. And so did all the others. All except one. Governor Roger Branigan broke the ice. Right off the bat, he said, "I understand Alcoa is sponsoring a new television show, *The Price Is Not Right*." What a relief; the crowd roared. Roger wasn't finished, "And so far as I can tell, there's no truth to the rumor that Alcoa has adopted a new corporate slogan, 'We Meet Any and All Competition.'" He was funny. Here's another one:

Birch Bayh held a Hoosier art show at the U.S. Capitol in 1965. Many members of Congress and other officials, including Governor Branigan, attended. The guest of honor, the Hoosier art display, was not present, however; it had been delayed en route from Indiana. It was my understanding that, rather than disappoint the guests, curators hastily found replacement, well, substitute art. The guests were not impressed. Congressman—later Senator—John Tunney was the Ivy League son of the great boxer. Polite and soft-spoken, John was the essence of diplomatic civility. And there he was at the D.C. Hoosier art show. Rubbing my hands together in the manner of a Rolls Royce salesman, I feigned exuberance: "John, what do you think of our Indiana art?"

"Well, I tell you, Andy, it's really incredibly bad." Branigan did even better. He said, "In case of theft, the police have been instructed to arrest anyone who interferes." Roger Branigan was funny. He should have been in the theater, not the governor's office.

A few weeks after the primary, when I was a guest on a small Indianapolis radio station call-in show, a woman called about Jack O'Brien. Jack was a Democratic nominee for county office and a delightful wit. His campaign consisted of passing out boxes of Cracker Jack. That earned him a nickname that stuck. From then on he was known as "Cracker Jack" O'Brien. The caller read aloud from an Indiana election law that prohibited candidates from giving anything of value to citizens to buy their votes. When she had set out the law, she said, "Jack O'Brien has been passing out boxes of Cracker Jack to children in grade schools. Why isn't that a law violation?"

"Simple," I said. "Children don't vote." It was a glib answer, but obviously the Cracker Jacks were in the nature of campaign cards, nothing that could be seriously considered in the nature of vote buying.

As for the fall election in the Indianapolis congressional district, a Democrat would have to work hard to lose. Which is to say I did not have to work very hard to win, despite the fact that my opponent seriously and publicly—in the *Indianapolis Star*—suggested that I was "soft on communism." No telling what he might have said had he known about an incident in the Korean War when a couple of commie gunners were soft on me and my buddies by holding their fire as we carried our dying lieutenant on a litter toward his early trip to eternity.

So it was back to Washington for me in 1967, but before I left home I received a long distance call from Speaker John McCormack. Would I be willing to serve on a select (temporary) committee to study and make recommendations concerning the case of Adam Clayton Powell? Powell had been overwhelmingly re-elected to the House in 1966, but his seating was being challenged on the ground that he had engaged in "official misconduct." I had the same feeling about serving on that committee that most of us have about jury duty. But duty it was and I did it.

The bipartisan panel, with only one dissenting vote, recommended that Powell be seated as a member. He met the three Article One qualifications for membership in the U.S. House, seven years a U.S. citizen, at least twenty-five years of age and *inhabitancy* of the state—not necessarily the district, from which he had been elected. We, the jury-like select committee, were out for several weeks. As we wrote our report, there was a disagreement over which word to use to make one of our points. The discussion was protracted and I was reminded of the all-lawyer jury that was out for three weeks when the judge sent the bailiff to see how things were going. The bailiff reported that, "They're still making nominating speeches for foreman." So I suggested we flip a coin to resolve the impasse over which word to use. Chairman Emanuel Celler thought not and told this story:

> A man went to the hospital and asked to be castrated. "Surely not," said the surgeon. "I'm paying for it," said the man, "and I know what I want."
>
> "Well, okay," said the incredulous doctor. After the operation, the patient was wheeled to the recovery room where he asked the patient in the next bed what procedure he had undergone. "Oh, just a circumcision," the other replied. Snapping his finger in realization, the first patient said, "That's the word!"

Chairman Celler continued, "Words are important, gentlemen. Let's find the right one."

The committee's recommendation was rejected by a margin of twenty-two votes on the House floor. Powell was not seated. He took the constitutional question to the Supreme Court and won.

The landmark case was *Powell v. McCormack*. Powell had swiped some airline tickets from the public and converted to his private use other things that belonged to the taxpayers, but that was misconduct. And, under specific provision of the Constitution, it was not a factor in seating a member-elect. Misconduct, if judged serious enough, could be a cause for expulsion *after* the elected Representative is seated. And the difference between a seating decision and an expulsion decision is not a mere technicality. A decision on seating is essentially a ministerial matter. Was Powell over twenty-five? Yes, way over. Had he been a citizen of the U.S. for at least seven years? Definitely. Was he an inhabitant of New York, the state from which he was elected? Clearly.

The decision to seat a Member-elect is made by simple majority. Expulsion for misconduct requires a two-thirds majority vote. The founders wanted some serious thought and wide concurrence on the question of misconduct, before the people's choice in one district could be overruled by members of Congress from other districts. Congressman Chuck Wiggins of California underscored this point with stunning eloquence in arguing that the Constitution required the seating of the nationally unpopular Powell. Chuck was a Republican and therefore at the time, a minority member of the House. He spoke libraries in these few words:

"As a minority member of this House, I take a dim view of the notion that my seat in Congress is at the whim of the majority."

Chuck later served as a United States Circuit of Appeals Judge in Las Vegas. But there was never a gamble when it came to his decisions; each litigant got justice. They couldn't have picked a better judge.

I wrote a book on the unconstitutional refusal to seat Adam Powell. The text was easier for me than the title. The one I composed was *Freedom Minus One*, but the publisher wanted something else. Powell was nothing if not a ladies' man. He made fooling around seem like sending a Valentine card in the sixth grade. So the publisher's choice was the double-entendre, *The Powell Affair*. I thought mine said more in terms of the Constitutional gravamen of the matter. So we arm-wrestled to a draw. The title is Victorian, *The Powell Affair: Freedom Minus One*. My brother-like friend Shell Breskow suggested another double-entendre title, *No Sit*.

Richard Hatcher is a significant part of United States history. And that's not because he was my law school classmate at Indiana University. He was elected mayor of Gary, Indiana, in 1967. Ordinarily, being elected mayor of Gary wouldn't be historically significant. But Dick Hatcher was a Gary mayor of African descent. And he was the first U.S. citizen of that descent to be elected mayor of a big city. Later it became a yawn. Just as was the case of an Irish-Catholic President Kennedy, an African American president, possibly named Powell, seemed perfectly plausible as the twenty-first century drew near.

But, as was the presidential case prior to 1960, before 1967 hardly anyone thought in terms of an African American mayor for a big city. When Dick Hatcher was nominated for the office, his opposition came just as strongly from his East European American Democratic county chairman as from any Republican in Gary, maybe even more strongly. Shortly after Dick was nominated, Attorney General Jack Dillon, Marion County Democratic

Chairman Jim Beatty, Jim Seidensticker, and I drove in my car from Indianapolis to Gary. I was guest speaker at the Lake County Young Democrats annual banquet. As I sat at the head table awaiting my turn, the Lake County Democratic Chairman arrived unexpectedly. The dinner chairman called on the late arrival to speak and speak he did. Right there in public, not in a party meeting of closed-door candor, the Democratic chairman proceeded to trash his party's nominee for mayor who was seated six feet away. And I mean *to trash*, phrases such as, "I'll support any Democrat for mayor, black or white, but not *red*!" As tirade turned to smear a young lawyer from Indianapolis, Vic Stivers, arose, walked to the head table and shook hands with Dick Hatcher. When the county chairman finished, he walked from the hall and I was introduced to speak and said:

> I came here tonight to talk about the issues before Congress. But I see that my duty lies elsewhere. The proudest boast of Democrats who were active then was "I helped Harry Truman when other Democrats were abandoning and even denouncing him." Those Democrats in Gary who help elect Dick Hatcher Mayor will take pride in their loyalty as time goes by. Dick Hatcher is a good and decent person. I know; he was my law school classmate.

Considering the fact that several shouting matches and one fist fight had broken out among the dinner participants, it was difficult for me to continue. So, half in jest I said the words of old-time live television, "We're running a little late, folks, (it was probably about eight) so good-night." After shaking hands with Dick Hatcher ourselves, Jack, Jim, Jim and I walked in a straight line out of the building into the parking lot. There, with flashlight in hand, I raised the hood of my car, which was one year old, and, I'm happy to say, lived for another thirteen years and 240,000 miles. At this precaution, Attorney General Jack Dillon bent over backward in unrestrained laughter. After checking for newly added wires, I gave an opinion to the Attorney General of Indiana: "Jack, I've just made up a brand new old political saying: It's better to be laughed at than cried over."

We got home that night in four pieces, one each. Dick was politically controversial throughout his long tenure as mayor and we remained warm friends even as I found friendship in some of his non-racist adversaries.

A few weeks after the Gary experience, I attended a political dinner in Indianapolis. Robert Vaughn, better known in those days as the star of the TV series *Man From Uncle*, was the guest speaker. I was pleased to learn that he shared my view in opposition to the Johnson administration's unconstitutional war in Vietnam. Three of my sister Marge's sons attended the event with me. They were, respectively, ten, eleven, and twelve years old—and active. In twenty-five minutes they and other kids had established an economy of their own in that large meeting room. The medium of exchange was the autograph. Just as my nephews traded baseball cards, they were now trading autographs collected at the dinner. As I was about to go to the podium and introduce Mr. Vaughn, one of the boys rushed up to me and instructed, "Here, sign this ten times."

"Why ten times?" I asked. "Because," said the entrepreneur, "I can get one Vaughn for ten Jacobses." I introduced the speaker of the evening with great humility.

Martha Griffiths of Michigan was one of the brightest and most intellectually honest people ever to serve in Congress. She had been a judge and would become the lieutenant governor of her state. She loved her husband, Hicks, so much that when he became seriously ill she left Congress despite the fact that she was about to become chairwoman of the U.S. House Ways and Means Committee.

There was another man in her life, but not romantically. Hardly; he was Emanuel Celler who had spent decades working against congressional passage of a resolution to amend the Constitution specifically to include women within its protections. The Equal Rights Amendment was an anathema to Manny Celler. It was a cause celebre to Martha. And the latter undertook to do something about it. She filed a discharge petition to take the amendment away from the House Judiciary Committee, of which Manny was chairman and I was a member. I committed the congressional sacrilege of signing the petition. So did more than 217 other members. The Committee was ordered by the petition to report the resolution for a floor vote.

As the fateful committee session began, one could hear the proverbial pin drop. Here was the very elderly chairman who was bitterly opposed, conducting the proceeding which was the first step toward enactment.

Probably as evidence of Manny's male chauvinism, there was no female member of the committee. And on this occasion, every female staffer discreetly—or to keep from throwing-up—had left the room. Except for one. She was Manny's very long time staff assistant, brilliant lawyer, Bess Dick. She sat in stony-faced silence during the hour-long session, which is to say I never knew which side she was on.

The most memorable part of the meeting was Emanuel Celler's last stand. When he spoke, he quoted the biblical absurdity: "Wives, obey your husbands." And—I don't know—I began to laugh out loud, involuntarily.

I tried to suppress it; I just couldn't. The member who sat directly in front of me turned and angrily ordered me to "shut up!" I managed to compose myself. But it was like a cough you just can't hold back. If the Bible quotation had ended with those words, I would have been OK. But it didn't. And as Manny plodded on down that ancient and dusty road to unreason, the involuntary cough of my laughter broke out again. Each time the impertinent mirth slipped from my grip, my colleague blurted again, "Shut up!" In retrospect it's funny, but not then. Everyone in the room, except Manny who was concentrating on the quotation, was embarrassed, none so more than I.

The amendment passed the House and Senate and, requiring no presidential signature, was referred to the several states for ratification. But that never happened; probably didn't have to at that point in history. Most of its purpose has been produced either by changed custom or specific statute. Shortly after the resolution cleared Congress, I was asked why, not being a woman, I was so devoted to the amendment. Following Manny Celler's example, I chose a Biblical quotation for response. Mine was from The Sermon on the Mount, "Blessed are they who thirst for justice."

Following a congressional career that a half century, Manny was defeated in his 1972 Democratic Primary. The winner? Of course. Elizabeth Holtzman, every bit a woman except for the second syllable of her last name. Emanuel Celler lives through history as one of the legislative giants in the civil rights arena, if you don't count the ERA.

A huge Great Dane named C-Five was my constant companion even at work. Each morning as he and I stepped off the elevator, I removed his lead and he bounded into Congresswoman Griffiths's office a few doors from the one I used. He was most welcome. Martha not only missed her husband during week days she was in D.C., but also their beautiful standard poodle, Yuki. C-Five cheered her up during the week.

Martha had a constituent who was summarily fired from her job as an airline flight attendant because some vice president at the airline decided that, at thirty-five, she was losing her looks. The congresswoman intervened with a letter to the vice president. He answered that it was imperative that the "cabin girls be young, attractive and appealing." Martha's next letter was short and very much to the point:

Dear Vice-President:
    What are you running, an airline or a whore house?

In a House debate on a bill to provide funds for rat extermination in poor neighborhoods, some of the white-collar redneck members undertook to "laugh it out of court." One representative got big laughs with this line: "I think it would be a 'raat' good idea to kill this rat bill 'raat' now."

It was Martha Griffiths whose disturbing eloquence paved the way for the bill's success a few days later. She said that before the Committee of the Whole got too carried away with its condescending fun, a few facts should be part of the record. Among those facts, she said, was the reality that rats and the disease they often carry have been responsible for more human death than all the military action ever. Some of the members were laughing at her, too. But "he (or she) who laughs last, laughs best." Within the week, Martha was in the position to laugh last.

The ones who made fun of the rat extermination legislation had built careers by ridiculing proposals, some of which were actually zany and some of which made good sense but sounded funny. The bill to get rid of rats belonged to the latter category, but these fellows hardly ever bothered to study the bills past their titles. Usually it didn't make any political difference because, at a distance, they all looked needless to the public. But public reaction to this bill was different. When the mail from suburbia began to pour in to their offices, the flat-Earth fellows expected pats on the back. That is not what they got. Instead, they read outrage from affluent mothers who empathized with their impoverished counterparts in tenements. "What do you mean voting to let rats bite babies?" they demanded. Public opinion was overwhelming: the fun guys had goofed. The politicians became desperate to mend their ways on the matter.

Almost before you knew it, the defeated bill had found its way through the red tape and back onto the floor for another vote. This time there wasn't much debate—no jokes at all. It is standard operating procedure for some member, usually the bill's manager, to rise at the conclusion of floor consideration of a bill and ask "unanimous consent that all members have five legislative days to revise and extend their remarks on the bill just passed." During the short floor discussion—you'd hardly call it a debate this time—I obtained time and said:

> Mr. Speaker: A strange change has come over this chamber. Diction has improved over that of last week on this legislation. Members are saying, "right now" instead of "rat now."
>
> "Where are the clowns?" I wonder if the lack of humor on the bill this time is a consequence of the short notice we received about its consideration the "second time around." Members just haven't had time to make up new jokes about rats that bite babies.

So I ask unanimous consent that all members have five legislative days in which to extend and perhaps *revise* their jokes on this bill.

One of the House humorists of a few days before didn't get this joke. He objected. Unanimous consent denied. Gee.

In addition to my assignment on the House Judiciary Committee, beginning with my second term I was also placed on the House District of Columbia Committee. The controversy there was over home rule for the District of Columbia, which had always been governed by three presidentially appointed commissioners. For the first century of our Republic there wasn't much problem with the arrangement because not much of a city was involved. D.C. was mostly the federal government. But by the mid-twentieth century, D.C. was definitely one of America's thriving cities, with businesses, local parks, people, and politics. The local government, however, was not local and did not have the "consent of the governed." The issue, then, was whether the Congress would allow the Capitol of a free nation to be free, itself. Would colonialism continue—government by someone from somewhere else—or would the people of the city elect their own city government? Each side on the House D.C. Committee was made up of both Republicans and Democrats. Anti-home-rulers were Southern Democrats and Republicans; pro's were Northern Democrats and Northeastern Republicans.

From my prospective, Shakespeare's words applied to pro-home-rule Republicans like Gilbert Gude of Maryland and Frank Horton of New York: "'Tis but thy name that is my enemy." On the other hand, I was compelled by logic to apply the precise reverse of that romantic exchange between Romeo and Juliet to the Committee's Southern Democrats: "'Tis but thy name that is my *friend.*"

Eventually, democracy did come to the Capitol of our democracy. But no thanks to the Democratic/Republican plantation coalition on the District of Columbia Committee. It wasn't easy. The chairman, John L. McMillan of South Carolina, was a Democratic member of the anti-home rule coalition as was the very bright Thomas G. Abernethy of Mississippi.

Hearings were held on the controversy at the subcommittee chaired by Abernethy and Mr. McMillan participated. Mr. McMillan had a bad habit. He interrupted when other members had the floor. As he did so he tapped the gavel. Chairman or not, he had no right to do it. But if another member were saying something with which he disagreed, "Johnny Mac" would tap and tiptoe into the other's time without bothering to ask his colleague to yield. *Rude!* So rude, in fact, that I went out one evening and bought my own gavel. And every time the chairman pulled that trick on me, I rapped back thunderously and asked, "Did the gentleman, by any chance, wish me to yield?" When he said yes, I always did.

Gilbert Gude of Maryland was a freshman Republican on the committee at the time of the hearing. And he was on our home-rule side. As Mr. Gude politely propounded a question to one of the witnesses, the spirit moved Chairman McMillan. And, true to form, Mr. McMillan interrupted to ask, "Well, if you're so all-fired interested in givin' the vote to folks in the District of Columbia, what would you think about giving Maryland's part of D.C. back to Maryland?"

A trick question because such a move would be a big financial loss to Maryland. On the other hand, a substantial part of the original Virginia grant for the District had already been given back to Virginia, notably Arlington. That area was then represented in the U.S. House by one of the plantation coalition, Joel T. Broyhill. Of course, if that territory had not been ceded back to Virginia or if it were reclaimed by the U.S. Government once again to be part of D.C., Mr. Broyhill would be without a seat in Congress and Mr. McMillan would be short one ally.

Sensing that Gil Gude was hesitant to answer McMillan's question, I asked Gil to yield to me. He did and I said:

"Well, let's just turn that coin over to the other side. Since our colonial friends on the Committee think the federal government is so 'all-fired' fragile that it cannot survive the alien soil of local democracy, and considering that the sensitive Pentagon and CIA are located in the district of the gentleman from Virginia, Mr. Broyhill, what would the gentleman from Maryland think about putting that former part of the District of Columbia back into the District of Columbia where it can be safe from those dangerous local voters?"

With that, Mr. Abernethy, the one with the official gavel, rapped it and said, "Let's get on with the hearing." To which I said to Abernethy, "Does the chairman mind if the gentleman from Maryland uses his own time to answer my question?" To which the chairman said, "Well, we have a lot of witnesses waiting." To which *I* said, "Would those be the same witnesses who were waiting when the gentleman from South Carolina butted in without the courtesy of asking that the floor be yielded?" No love lost between our two opposing bipartisan camps in those days.

In fact when a reporter for the old *Washington Star* did a story about my Great Dane, he asked me if I had considered taking my *King Kong* to a D.C. committee meeting to meet Chairman McMillan. My reply: "Wouldn't work. C-Five is too gentle." In time I came to like Tom Abernethy personally, but it was hard to get to know Johnny Mac. Had I done so, I expect I would have found something to like in him—following a diligent search.

Back when the Home Rule hearing was announced by Sub-Committee Chairman Abernethy, a young man, a very young man came to see me about a problem he had with regard to Home Rule. As a citizen of the District of Columbia, he had been denied a request to testify. Charley Seigel was thirteen, far too young and far, far too idealistic for the plantation coalition. He gave me a copy of his proposed testimony and I suggested he attend the first day of the hearing. When it was my turn to question one of the coalition's witnesses, I used my five minutes to read Charlie's testimony into the record. Then I asked him—and answered for him—some questions. Charlie sat in the audience and beamed, having more or less testified.

Then there was the time when it was my seniority turn to be chairman of a subcommittee. Johnny Mac passed over me and appointed the next Democrat in line. Since Mr. McMillan gained his position as Chairman of the Full Committee by the *seniority* rule, I pointed out that he was trying to have his cake and *cheat* it, too. I offered the Democratic leadership a deal. Forget about me, but recognize that the only human on earth who had the *consent of the governed* in the District of Columbia was its nonvoting delegate to the U.S. House, Walter Fontroy. Let him be the subcommittee chairman. Let my turn be home rule's turn. Well, no, they wouldn't do that either. In time, the Democratic leadership was shamed into my appointment as chairman of the subcommittee in question. After all, punishing me because I favored Home Rule was a tad embarrassing to them. Home Rule was in the Democratic National Platform. Mr. Fontroy was a member of the subcommittee. So each time we had a meeting, I mysteriously developed a terrible cough and, greatly distressed, handed the gavel to Walter, who then presided until my ailment passed. And it always did—right after a meeting was adjourned. It must have been the Luden's.

Now let's take a look at J. Edgar Hoover, who was the dictator of the Federal Bureau of Investigation for a half century, each successive president declining to replace him for fear of what damaging information might be in the autocrat's files.

The only time I was near him was during the initial phase of the Civil Rights struggle. I, along with about twenty others, was a guest of Lyndon Johnson in the basement of the White House. Hoover was a very old and old-looking man by then. Mean-looking, too, I thought, something like a hostile English bull dog. The great man was introduced by the President, and Hoover spoke. Among his remarks he said, "It's getting so that there is no respect for law enforcement officers. A few days ago in New York, a police officer was being beaten in front of a hundred people and none of them stepped forward to help him."

"The FBI has important business," Hoover continued, "and we're not going to be drawn into the problems of troublemakers in the South."

By whom he meant civil rights volunteers like the lady from Michigan who lost her life at Selma in the struggle to make real our national boast of freedom. As we walked away from the White House that night, my friend and colleague Jim Corman said to me: "Let me see if I have this right. If a police officer is in danger, a citizen should go to his aid; but if a citizen is in danger, a police officer should not go to *his* aid."

Then there was the occasion shortly after LBJ's friend Abe Fortas resigned from the Supreme Court. Birch Bayh's late wife, Marvella, had asked me to dinner at the home of a single friend of hers. Marvella liked me, I think, because when she invited me to Birch's and her home to be the "extra man," she could count on me not to bring a date. That could not be said of one of my bachelor colleagues who kept Marvella's party numerically off-balance one evening by bringing a date when she expected him to be the extra man.

This occasion was in the hunt country of Maryland. I was to play extra man opposite the wealthy and single hostess. And there, seated at the table in the wake of something akin to public humiliation was the fallen Supreme Court Justice Abe Fortas—and his wife. She was said to be one of Washington's hot-shot tax lawyers. Thank God I was not yet on the Ways and Means Committee. It was bad enough that I was then serving on the Judiciary Committee. The tax lawyer could be classified somewhere between my seatmate and my tormentor. As soon as someone mentioned my membership on the Judiciary Committee, she gave me a piercing stare and demanded that I explain why I had ruined "domestic help in this country." I told her that I didn't realize I had. It turned out to have something to do with the new immigration law. It was long overdue.

The purpose of the act was to remove racism from immigration quotas. I thought that was good. The tax lawyer, in no uncertain terms, did not. Next she took up the subject of J. Edgar Hoover: "You know, he's homosexual," she said to me.

"No," I said, "I don't believe I've heard that. And I certainly don't know, you might say, one way or another about him."

"Well, he is," she said. "It's okay, but it's true."

Now the justice had something to say. He said he wouldn't be surprised if the day would come when taxes would allow no citizen an annual after-tax disposable income exceeding what in 1999 dollars would be about two hundred thousand dollars. That really animated his wifely tax lawyer. Picking on me once more, she snapped, "Nobody can live on (two hundred thousand dollars) a year!" This time I counterattacked, "Well there's a whole bunch of us who'd like to try."

J. Edgar Hoover's 1960s FBI—and it pretty much was *his* FBI—was often contorted into a small-minded snoop rather than a high minded-sleuth. He sought and—humans being what we are—got embarrassing gossip on those he chose to be his political enemies, as well as the presidents he wanted to keep in line in order to keep his job. And he especially tried to besmirch the good citizenship of those who were wise enough to see through the fatally foolish Vietnam War policy.

In 1964 the landlocked state of Tennessee had ironically sent two former U.S. Navy submarine commanders to the U.S. House of Representatives. George W. Grider commanded the first U.S. sub to enter Tokyo Harbor during World War II and William R. Anderson commanded the *Nautilus* on its historic voyage under the polar ice cap. Both men were authentic American heroes.

It was Bill Anderson who, on a tour of a prison operated by our client government in the south of Vietnam, had the gumption to look farther than the guide intended. Bill discovered the infamous *Tiger Cages* where military and political prisoners were tortured by lime which was poured onto their perspiring bodies from grids above.

Later, Anderson took up the cause of the Barrigan Brothers, a pair of priest-protesters against U.S. policy in Vietnam. One or both of them had broken into a military draft board and poured blood on files. This brought prison time for the priest or priests. One day Bill Anderson secured floor time at the end of regular House business—so-called special orders—to talk about the case and, God forbid, criticize J. Edgar Hoover. During the *Special Order,* Congressman Larry Hogan from Maryland, a former FBI agent himself, asked Anderson to yield the floor so that Hogan could comment on some of Anderson's assertions. It would be difficult to imagine a more polite person than Bill Anderson. Humble would not be an excessive description of his personality. His reply to Hogan was that Anderson would yield some of his time to Hogan as soon as Anderson completed his initial and prepared statement, whereupon Hogan demanded a quorum call which, in those days, took up about forty minutes. It was obviously meant to punish Anderson, who had done what most members would do in the same situation.

When the roll call was finished and Anderson was finished too, Hogan embarked upon his own *Special Order,* having elected not to ask again for some of Anderson's time. Somewhat amused by the foregoing, I decided to see if Hogan would respond any differently from Anderson if asked to yield during his initial statement. So I rose and asked Hogan to yield. He, as Anderson, declined to yield, saying he would after he completed his prepared statement. I followed suit by demanding a quorum call. Hogan repeated that he would yield after he finished his prepared statement. And I asked if this weren't the same situation which had just happened between Anderson and him. No, he said, this was quite different. At which point I withdrew my demand for the forty-minute quorum call. I wasn't interested in punishing Larry. I just wanted to illustrate how funny a double standard could be.

This is where J. Edgar comes in once more. Some years later, I was curious enough to obtain my FBI file under the Freedom of Information Act. The file was really funny. From time to time I had visited the FBI, usually accompanying constituents on tours. In my FBI file I was surprised to find entries for each of those occasions, each entry being laudatory and containing these words, "Congressman Jacobs is a former police officer and understands the problems of the FBI. *He was most cordial.*" That last part of the entry was boilerplate. I assume "cordial" was a favorite word of Hoover's. But suddenly I came upon an entry that surprised me even more. It stated that special agents were in the visitors gallery of the U.S. House for the Anderson and Hogan *Special Orders.* And there I was in living black and white:

> Congressman Hogan asked Congressman Anderson to yield the floor, but Anderson stubbornly refused . . . Congressman Jacobs badgered Congressman Hogan while Mr. Hogan was trying to speak.

Of course, Congressman Hogan was *most cordial*; not I, anymore. So much for J. Edgar Hoover, who clearly was entirely *too* much for America.

In 1964, thirty days before I was first elected to Congress, I was one of the speakers at a JFK memorial dinner for Marion County Democrats. (Erich N. Bretzman photo)

Two "Young Turks"—my good friend Jud Haggerty and I in 1964. (*Indianapolis Star* staff photo)

Disembarking from a plane at Indianapolis in the fall of 1964: (*from rear*) Marion County Democratic Chairman Jim Beatty, Senators Birch Bayh, I, John Barton, and Hubert Humphrey. (*Indianapolis Star* staff photo)

Congressman Bill Bray of Martinsville and I at a 1966 American Legion gathering.

Shortly after *The Smothers Brothers Comedy Hour* was cancelled for being too "controversial," Tommy Smothers (*seated*) met with (*from left*) Congressman Lionel Van Deering (California), yours truly, and Tom Reese (also California).

Freshman Reps Brock Adams (Washington), Lee Hamilton (Indiana), Jed Johnson, Jr. (Oklahoma), and I. (Dev O'Neill photo)

Taking a break from politics for the favorite Hoosier pastime with my nephews, Tommy, Martin, and Dan Landwerlen in 1964.

chapter 5

DISTURBANCE

I HEARD ABOUT THE MURDER of Martin Luther King, Jr., on the car radio as I drove to my apartment on Capitol Hill. Because of those violent years that had preceded, I was too numb to be stunned. It fell in place with the murder of Medgar Wiley Evers and John Fitzgerald Kennedy. Firebrand H. Rap Brown had said that violence was "as American as cherry pie," an assertion with which it was hard to quarrel in those surrealistic times. Arriving at the apartment, I switched on the television and stark details spewed out. It was a motel balcony in Memphis. Presently the image of King was shown by tape recording from the night before. Speaking to a rally on behalf of striking sanitation workers, Dr. King was saying that "we've come a long way toward the Promised Land," adding ominously, "I may not get there with you. But that doesn't matter anymore."

But that doesn't matter anymore. Those five words brought back feeling to my benumbed being and I lost it. In my God-awful grief, I felt the dusty orange clay of Korea rush up to engulf the eighteen-year-old Marine I had been in the early fifties—the one who, exhausted, had allowed himself to fall into the thick dust of that desolate killing hill, sobbing at the sight of an "ugly American" slapping a hapless and elderly Korean man at the end of a battle, when it was safe for that disgraceful interrogator do his interrogating. This time, though, I was alone. And I was grateful, remembering the admonition Grace Kelly's father wrote in his holographic will: "Thoroughbreds don't cry in public."

Bobby Kennedy was told about the tragedy en route by air to Indianapolis only weeks before the same insanity was to engulf him. Upon his arrival, the Indianapolis police authorities asked that he not go to the

133

planned rally of mostly people of African descent at Seventeenth and Broadway. They anticipated the violence that was erupting throughout most of the rest of the nation. No, he said, he would keep the appointment and be the first to announce there what had befallen the soul of America. He had something to say, and at the appointed place, say it he did. He recalled for the audience the murder of his brother, suggesting that a violent reaction made grieving people not much better than the villain. Grieving there was, dignified and painful, but expressed in prayer rather than anger—*rendering not violence for violence done.*

The riots were mostly in the mega-cities, including Washington, where not only the famous Fourteenth Street corridor was burned and looted, but also a neighborhood just to the northeast of Capitol Hill where palls of smoke were easily seen rising like a surrealistic Shakespearean play within a movie. The National Guard patrolled the streets of D.C. and enforced a strict curfew.

In warped response to the Washington riots, the plantation politicians on the District of Columbia Committee rammed through the committee a three-percentage-point increase in the sales tax on groceries. Under then existing House rules, it was not possible for those of us who opposed the mean-spirited bill to get a recorded floor vote and bring the haters out in the open. That usually meant the Neanderthals would win.

"For what purpose does the gentleman from Indiana rise?" asked the Speaker. "In opposition to the bill," I responded. "The gentleman is recognized for five minutes." This is what I said:

"Mr. Speaker, this is a proposal conceived in frustration and its consequent superficial logic. In the first place, a tax is a poor substitute for criminal prosecution. In the second place, even if it were appropriate, it would miss the mark in this situation. Bulletin: Looters don't pay sales tax; law-abiding citizens do. This measure would punish the poor, but honest. Moreover, when a food tax is raised 3 percent, the poor do not pay three percent more; they eat three percent less."

The unexpected happened; our side won. The bill was defeated even though there was no recorded vote. It was a voice vote. A couple of days later, the *Washington Post* ran an editorial which began with these words:

"An entire economics course could be summed up by a few words spoken by Representative Andrew Jacobs during debate on the ill-considered proposal for a D.C. tax hike on groceries."

In the summer of 1968, those of us who opposed the Vietnam policy were still trying to get our say on the House floor. About the only way we could do it was before or after regular House business. Usually our attempts occurred before the regular business during the free-for-all one-minute morning speeches. One morning as I attempted to speak on the war, I ran out of time before finishing my point. The next member to be recognized was Dick Fulton of Tennessee. Dick looked like a matinee idol and, in fact, was a professional song writer and singer. He was a quiet man, never having said much in my presence about his position on the war. To the consternation of the House chicken hawks, Dick courageously stuck his neck out by yielding his time to me to finish my statement. I shall never forget it or him. He looms large among my former colleagues whom I admire most.

In the long struggle toward civilization for the United States, 1968 was a very rough spot in the road. Seven years earlier, John F. Kennedy had said, "The world is very different now. . . ." He was talking about the dramatic changes during that "century and three-quarters" between the beginning of our Republic and the 1961 Kennedy Inaugural. But as he stood there coatless at the east entrance to the U.S. Capitol facing an adoring crowd and a bitterly cold breeze, neither he nor anyone else could have suspected what would take place during the next seven bad-luck years.

Shortly after the Democrats' landslide success of 1964, the vice president-elect, Hubert H. Humphrey, said in all sincerity, "We [the Democrats] just might be the dominant party for the rest of this century. And we must learn to walk humbly with our God." As it turned out, learning to walk humbly came easily for the Democrats in the very next election. The party was humbled by mammoth losses in the House.

And now in the year 1968, the Democrats were about to be humbled some more. While the Democrats retained nominal control of the House after both the '66 and '68 elections, the old Dixiecrat-Repubcan coalition would control the outcome on most controversial votes. It was this phenomenon in the 1950s that validated the claim by Indiana's Charles Abraham Halleck that in the U.S. House, he was "the Minority Leader and the leader of the majority."

Larry O'Brien wrote the book *No Final Victories*. The title of that volume spoke volumes about the two party system of politics in America. In 1956 Ike led a landslide for the Republicans. The Democrats would never recover from this mauling. Never, that is, until two years later when the Democrats swept the boards. Then it was in 1964 that Hubert Humphrey figured the Republican elephant had become essentially extinct. To paraphrase the words of Churchill, *some extinction*. Two years later, in 1966, the pachyderms stampeded over the donkeys. In 1972, the Nixon landslide was prodigious. McGovern and the Democrats were ground to pieces. How could the Democrats *ever* recover from that? How? How 'bout Watergate. In 1974, nine of the eleven congressional districts in Indiana went Democratic. After a twelve-year dry spell, the Democrats won the White House in 1992. The Republicans were at last out of business. How could they possibly come back? How? How about the House Bank and Post Office scandals? In '94, after forty years of nominal political minority, the Republicans won both Houses of the U.S. Congress.

In U.S. politics, 1974 and 1994 were mirror images of each other. The Democrats did not receive many more votes than usual in their 1974 landslide. It was just that the Republicans received substantially fewer because many of their voters, either embarrassed or disgusted—or both—over Watergate, stayed home. The Republicans did not receive many more votes than usual in their '94 landslide; it was just that the Democrats received substantially fewer because many of their voters, either embarrassed or disgusted—or both—over the House Bank and Post Office scandal, stayed home.

It seems reasonable to assume that the American public will continue to flit back and forth between the two parties, whatever those parties may call themselves as time unfolds. I think there are two reasons for this. First, the party in office is perfectly capable of getting into trouble sooner or later and the public tends to forget that the other party has the same sad capability. Second, both parties promise the impossible, *the repeal of reality*. And both will always fail to deliver such nonsense.

The first jolt for Hoosier Democrats—and good news for Republicans—in the bumpy political road of 1968 was called the Saint Valentine's Day Massacre. The refreshing 1965 Democratic correction of the Hoosier congressional malapportionment was declared not refreshing enough by the Supreme Court. The Democratic legislature had whittled the disparity in population among districts from 200 percent down to ten percent, but the Supreme Court said it had to be *zero* percent. And, by the time the decision was handed down, the Democrats no longer controlled the legislature. In fact, when it came to reapportionment, no one controlled the Legislature; no map had a enough votes to pass. There was a consequence. For the first time ever, the federal courts actually *drew* the congressional districts in Indiana.

The map was announced by a three-judge panel on February 14, 1968. That was Valentine's Day and for Indiana Democrats, it *was* a massacre. The lethal stroke of the politically poisoned pen was made by the former chairman of the Indiana Republican State Committee. A Republican state chairman drawing a congressional map? How? Very simple; the pen was held by the Honorable Cale Holder, chief judge of the federal court panel that drew the map.

The new map of the Indianapolis congressional district came in the form of a gas chamber for me. So much so that an *Indianapolis News* cartoon showed me in a swim suit walking into the new district across elephants whose heads and trunks looked like crocodiles.

As the spring primary came and went, my chances for re-election in 1968 seemed slim. On the Saturday following the primary, there were the usual county conventions at which the respective parties chose their chairpeople. As I stood with about thirty other people outside the Democratic convention hall, waiting for the equivalent of three puffs of white smoke in the Vatican, a woman burst from the proceedings and walked briskly toward me. She was wearing heavy shoes and carrying a huge purse. When she reached me she demanded, "Do you know what they did to me in there?" I pled innocence. "Well," said she, "they kicked me!" And with that, she kicked *me* with one of those heavy shoes right on the shin, to the amusement of my fellow loiterers. There was more: "And they hit me!" You guessed it; she whirled her purse around and crashed it against my stomach. To all of which I said, "Well, Mary, I . . . I think I know just how you feel." My attempt to remain above the fray had been in vain. It occurred to me that this was only a precursor of the figurative beating likely to come my way a few months hence on election day.

The beatings at the Democratic National Convention in Chicago that year were not figurative; they were disfiguring. And the national events leading up to that pandemonium made nightmares seem nice.

By April, Lyndon Johnson was out of the race for the White House; Gene McCarthy and Bobby Kennedy were in. Kennedy's first major presidential primary was in Indiana, bringing swarms of national news organizations to the state. Indiana is pleased to call itself the Crossroads Of America and because Bobby began his campaigning there, the Crossroads were suddenly on the American map.

There are a slew of war memorials and parks in downtown Indianapolis. The national headquarters for the American Legion is nestled among them. When national columnist Joseph Craft filed his first report on the Hoosier presidential primary in 1968, he began with, "Downtown Indianapolis is like a salute to Mars."

The merely slightly Democratic governor of Indiana, Roger Branigan, was the stand-in presidential candidate, first for Lyndon Johnson and then for Hubert Humphrey. And, like the predictable sunrise in the east, the old *Indianapolis Star* became a campaign brochure for Branigan. One of the funniest headlines was something like this:

> BRANIGAN ACCUSES KENNEDY OF INJECTING NATIONAL ISSUES IN INDIANA PRIMARY

Make that, Indiana *Presidential* Primary. How dare Bobby talk about the job the Indiana presidential primary was about. He had the contemporary haircut worn in various degrees of long by Vietnam war critics. A *Star* editorial called the junior senator from New York, "Unshorn and un-American." Haircuts were a big issue between the pro- and anti-war citizens at the time. Just as many fathers were disgusted with sons who did *not* wear beards and long hair during the American Civil War, many fathers were disgusted with sons who *did* wear beards and long hair during the American Vietnam War. One way or another, sons had to be different from their fathers who, as Mark Twain pointed out, had a lot to learn by the time the sons reached twenty-two or so.

Following Sunday service at an Evansville church in the late sixties, a young minister who wore his hair long stood with his little boy to greet the congregation as it left. When a particularly boorish man in his chicken-hawk fifties approached, he loudly directed a sarcastic question to the little boy: "And how do you like your father with that haircut?" Little kids don't understand sarcasm and the son spoke from the heart. He replied, "I think he's wonderful. He looks just like Jesus."

The *Star* and its candidate in the presidential primary adopted the theme that Kennedy and Eugene McCarthy were unwanted interlopers in the close-knit family of five million Hoosiers. The paper ran a front-page editorial cartoon showing Branigan and his Hoosier wife—she was all the voters in Indiana—at their modest dinner table. Kennedy and Gene McCarthy were at the table, too. They were romancing the shapely personification of the electorate, with flowers and candy. When I saw the cartoon in the paper, I gave it the slight attention it merited. But later, the *Columbia Journalism Review* published a study on the bizarre *Star* tactics in the 1968 Indiana Presidential Primary. The *Review* included the suitor cartoon and called attention to the fact that in the farce, one of Kennedy's hands was drawn firmly on one of the breasts of the mythical Hoosier housewife. This was in addition to the burlesque theater ads farther back in the paper. The stars of those vaudeville exposures included Evelyn West "and her fifty thousand dollar [Lloyd's of London insured] treasure chest," a six-foot, four-inch lady known as the "Eye-full Tower," and a native American woman whose moniker was "Running Bare." Perhaps by now they are heavenly bodies of the celestial sort.

The Indiana presidential primary produced some interesting social life. My two very good friends and coworkers in the congressional office, Bud Myers and Louie Mahern, were strong supporters of Bobby Kennedy. But the Kennedy people lacked something the Gene McCarthy people had plenty of: upscale supporters. McCarthy was the darling of the Adlai Stevenson folks, generally well-to-do Democrats. They were patrons of the arts. And they threw magnificent parties for Gene's *supporters,* which Louie and Bud were not. But my friends liked fancy parties. Without Bud's knowing it, Louie went to one of those glittering affairs in a north side Indianapolis mansion. When asked his name for a lapel tag, Louie, the Kennedy supporter who wanted his attendance to go undetected, promptly said, "Bud Myers," and walked toward the champagne, only to encounter Bud Myers—wearing a name tag reading "LOUIE MAHERN." Have fun, guys.

Bobby Kennedy won the Indiana presidential primary handily and in California he won the primary and lost his life. Memorial services were everywhere. I attended the one at St. Patrick's in New York, but returned to Indianapolis in time for the one held there. Asked to speak, I did:

> Especially no one here bought the bullet or tripped the trigger. But before we dismiss ourselves too lightly, perhaps we should reflect on what we as a people have come to accept and even want on the on the part of those who speak publicly to us and those who entertain us. What sort of social environment have all of us helped to maintain? How much does it encourage violence in the least stable among us?
>
> Every time we fail to carry out God's mandate to control the temptation, born of fear or misunderstanding, to speak or print harsh words, we burn so much incense to the god of violence.
>
> Social mores tend to influence various members of a society in varying degrees. If an unstable person lives life surrounded by an atmosphere of hostility and hate, he is more likely to become a part of it and think that violence is the thing to do in order to earn respect from those who have expressed hatred for the victim. Violent words are akin to violent deeds. A suspect in the murder of Martin Luther King is said to have said, "I'm going to kill Martin King and get a bounty."

A casual accounting of American habits with television and movies reveals a taste for violence which is incompatible with safety, which is the hallmark of true civilization.

While one channel shows *The Dirty Dozen,* another runs news pictures of Vietnam; and somehow the fiction and the reality merge and we begin to have difficulty distinguishing one from the other. A newspaper finds it possible to refer to the killing of enemy soldiers as a "turkey shoot."

We give lip service to the term *gentleman.* But how many remember what the word means? A gentleman is a man who is gentle. Yet harsh words are heaped upon a young Senator because he has the temerity to take seriously the commandment of Christ to "love thy enemy" as well as friends.

It is possible to oppose without hating. And neither a nation nor a person can hate adversaries without developing the habit and having it spill over onto friends. Gentleness is not a weakness; there is a difference between strength and brutality.

It is a shameful commentary on the American volume of violence that in this century a third of our Presidents have been targets for the assassin's bullet.

So what shall we do, we who are sick in our hearts from the grief that violence brings?

Improvement in our methods of apprehension and punishment for violence already done is a necessity, but not enough if we continue to accept for ourselves and our children the words and ways of violence as an index to patriotism and respectability.

Instead, we could begin to teach our little children what is really represented when they play with toy guns and use harsh words and watch television and movies that do the same.

We, ourselves could begin to reject hateful and violent words spoken and printed about others and perhaps even come to the defense of those who are the targets of such abuse, even those who in some way are our adversaries. Then we could claim not only our beloved American society, but our beloved and majestic American Civilization where citizenship would mean civility.

The 1968 Democratic field for president had narrowed once more. Then-Senator George McGovern entered much too late to be seen as a viable candidate. And a Georgia governor named Lester Maddox was in for the racist vote. But the real contenders were Hubert Humphrey who had essentially skipped the primary contests, being the pick of the people who controlled the convention, and Eugene McCarthy who had been in it from the start when he dared to challenge the "unbeatable" Lyndon Johnson in the New Hampshire primary.

Humphrey was nominated.

Hubert Humphrey was a smart man and, despite his mock hawk position throughout the previous three years, he knew that he must distance himself from his mentor, Lyndon Johnson, before the fall election. But he didn't think he could be the out and out peace candidate that he had sincerely been in 1964 when it was easy. He had a lot of supporters who remained hawkish, including organized labor, except for the United Auto Workers. They, like Bobby Kennedy, switched in 1968 to be against the Vietnam War policy. But those supporters were not enough to win in the fall. He needed the help of the labor hawks who, by God, wanted to win the war. But he also badly needed the Democratic doves who were betrayed by the 1964 Johnson/Humphrey ticket. Humphrey was between a rock-concert dove and a hawk place as he arrived in Chicago to find those two birds in a cockfight.

After the Chicago Democratic Convention, when the broken bones and lacerated human flesh had been set and stitched, Gloria Steinem appeared on the *Tonight Show* with a middle-age Caucasian male. The subject of Chicago came up with Steinem as critic and the other guest as defender of the Police. The man explained how awful the hippies were, no soap, no barbers and no respect for their wiser elders who knew from World War II that you couldn't afford to let aggression go unchecked. Ms. Steinem pointed out that what the man said about aggression obviously had been so in the case of Nazi Germany, but that Vietnam was different in that the two "sides" of that contrived war were both Vietnamese. The vaunted 17th Parallel was not an international border. As for the Chicago police, she said, after everything was said that could be said, "there was no excuse for a paramilitary organization to *break ranks.*" Which gave rise to the term *police riot.*

The literally unwashed Yippies called themselves the Yippie Party with their own candidate for president who happened to have been born a pig. The candidate's name was Pigasus. One day early in 1968 before the Yippies picked the pig, two of their number were seated immediately in front of my friend Louie Mahern in the House gallery. Indiana octogenarian congressman Ray Madden was delivering his annual oration against *Big Oil!* Big Oil had once made the big mistake of contributing a few dollars to Ray's election opponent. As the rafters vibrated, one of the hippies said to the other, "That cat's my man for president." Ray would not have been flattered.

In Chicago, there could be no doubt about who the Democratic nominee would be; McCarthy would be counted out by the so-called power brokers. But there just might be a chance for one late entry—if he would enter. He was the slender and handsome surviving brother of Joe, Jack and Bobby Kennedy. Teddy Kennedy's national popularity then could not be overstated. *Star Quality* would be an understatement. Some friends suggested I attend a rump meeting on the subject in a remote room of the Chicago Stockyards where the convention was held.

At that meeting I was introduced to Allard K. Lowenstein, who as leader of the Dump Johnson Movement, had tried first and unsuccessfully to persuade Bobby Kennedy to oppose President Johnson in New Hampshire. Afterward he did persuade Gene McCarthy to do so. He was committed to McCarthy as was I at that point, having voted for Bobby in Indiana. Both of us were there to listen. As I recall, the gifted speechwriter Richard Goodwin seemed to chair the group of wishful thinkers. Teddy was absolutely not available. He was far too grief-stricken.

Inside the convention hall, Indiana Governor Roger Branigan once again accosted me quite audibly and with as much sarcasm as he could muster—which was quite a bit—demanded, "Where's your McCarthy button? While I was staying with the President you were off voting for Kennedy." The governor's mind wandered as he mused, "I stayed with him, but for some reason people just don't seem to like him."

"Well, Governor," I said, " then I guess you'd say I stayed with the people." Indiana's chief executive snapped back, "You're going to be back with the people next January." I confess it was getting silly—but . . .

"Governor I've always tried to be with the people." It got sillier. "I mean without any shoes," said the chief executive. "Without any shoes?" It was not the best of the Branigan wit.

The people running the convention, the Humphrey people, submitted a platform plank on Vietnam. It was a pro-war one. A substitute was offered by the anti-war delegates and the Indiana delegation retired to a caucus room to discuss it. In speaking for the plank I invited the Hoosier delegates to consider the central unspoken phenomenon of the Democratic convention, the absence of the Democratic President:

> Cast your gaze back just four years. Remember the happy expectations of those exciting days and nights in Philadelphia, how the future seemed filled with curtailed crime, satisfactory schooling, waning

welfare because of an enhanced economy. With Lyndon Johnson, we were certain of success. Now, look at now. The gathering is grim. Optimism is scarce. And our Democratic President is even scarcer. His kingdom, his power and his glory are gone. Why? Because of Medicare? Does anyone here believe that? Because of aid to education? Does anyone here believe the overwhelming majority of the public doesn't like that? Or is it the war President Johnson promised America he wouldn't get us into? Everyone here knows the answer to that. By the time the leaves are falling in 1968, Hubert Humphrey will feel and his prospects will be a lot better if this convention equips him with this peace plank.

The minority plank was not adopted. When the Indiana delegation boarded the buses for the ride back to our hotel that night, however, the bright and thoughtful Bob McKinney, Indianapolis lawyer and a principal owner of three prominent Indiana businesses, went out of his way to compliment me on my remarks. At that time, in that place and under those unfortunate circumstances, his generous words were more comforting to me than he could have known. I thanked him.

The next day at the Indiana delegation hotel, I stepped into an elevator to see one of my most admired people, the immortal World War II army cartoonist, Bill Mauldin. I had met him years ago when he was in Indianapolis to campaign for Adlai Stevenson. I treasure the cartoon he did for me on the back of the event's printed program. And there he was on that elevator. I reminded him of the Indianapolis event and that I had suggested he run for Congress. He had seemed negative on the suggestion, but eventually tried it in New York to no avail. On the elevator, he asked what I was doing lately and I told him. We both laughed. Thank God for the comic relief. Speaking of which: when someone handed me one of those McCarthy buttons Governor Branigan was so worried about, the donor said something facetious about the Yippie Party candidate, Pigasus. That inspired me. Some of the Yippies *and* Pigasus had just been arrested and there was much merriment about their candidate among delegates to the convention. So the one who gave me the button and I scared up some transparent tape and printed on a round piece of paper: THE PIG. Thus, the pig button which I attached to my lapel. It played very well on elevators; it got what Woody Allen called "big laughs." No one could have guessed then that the joke would become a major issue in my fall campaign. But the opposition thought the matter most serious and sinister, as we shall see.

And so it was back home again in Indiana away "from the madding crowd" of the Chicago debacle. Well, almost away. My journalistic welcome home came in the form of two *Indianapolis Star/News* editorial cartoons. One had my face on a sheep with tags on the tail. One tail said—horror of horrors—"opposition to Vietnam War." The tags listed other atrocities I had committed in Chicago, including casting a vote for Gene McCarthy. By sleight of pen, they transmogrified Gene McCarthy into the infamous Joseph McCarthy whom they—not Gene Pulliam, Jr.—had supported. The tag referring to Gene McCarthy said *"McCarthyism."* The overall caption read, "Wagging His Tail Behind Him." They made my face even uglier than it *is*. On seeing the rendering, my father said, "Had I known it would turn out like this, I never would have got married"

In the other cartoon, I was depicted as Pinocchio, strings and all. In this cartoon, that awful Gene McCarthy was pulling those strings, which were labeled "get rid of J. Edgar Hoover," and "Segregationist William Fulbright," with whom Gene McCarthy and I agreed on the war, not civil rights. The caption on the second cartoon said, "String Along With Gene." I should—and do—repeat, in the mid 1970s, the *Indianapolis Star* and the *Indianapolis News* became entirely different, which is to say objective, newspapers in terms of news columns. The new *Indianapolis News* editorial cartoonist, Jerry Barnett, was not only one of the best in the nation, but one of the least biased. If it's funny, Jerry will hit it no matter who. When the Cold War essentially ended with the collapse of Soviet communism, Jerry did a cartoon which should be enshrined in the Smithsonian plus perpetuated by a Pulitzer. It showed communism in the form of an absolutely fleshless human skeleton lying flat on the ground with Cuba's commie Castro standing over it waving his arms in desperation. The caption has Castro imploring, "Get back, give it air."

In the 1968 campaign, candidate Richard Nixon proposed establishment of a United States Department of Crime. Since I served on the House Judiciary Committee at the time, I was asked at an Indianapolis news conference what I thought of the idea. Until the news conference, I hadn't heard of the proposal. It sounded like nothing more than a campaign gimmick. But I didn't want to say that publicly, so I said, "I think we already have one. It's called the Justice Department." Then, unwittingly putting my finger on a pathetic point of impending history, I added, "Unless he has something else in mind, I believe Justice can handle the chore." At the time it had not even so much as entered my mind that as president, Mr. Nixon himself would be caught up in criminal activity. So sad.

Crime. Crime was the national campaign of Richard Nixon. The situation was simple: Democrats were for it and Republicans were against it.

Eventually Richard Goodwin would write a speech for Senator Edmund S. Muskie to deliver to the nation. In that speech, Muskie said that it was traditional for Democrats and Republicans to fuss a bit around election time, but that lately there had been a departure from the tradition. One party, he said, had begun saying that the other party favored crime. Then he said the powerful Goodwin sentence: "It's a lie and everybody knows it's a lie." But much happened in the political arena before that speech on election eve, 1970.

In retrospect, the whole tactic seems not only bizarre, but ridiculously funny. The Nixon people drew up one-size-fits-all news releases for their congressional candidates nationwide. The only thing each candidate needed to do was fill in the blanks with the name of her or his opponent. But the one size didn't fit *all*. For example, one of the releases didn't fit me at all:

> For years, _____ opposed anti-crime legislation. But now, suddenly, _____ wants to put on a police uniform.

When the blanks were filled out in my congressional contest, the release came out this way:

> For years, Andy Jacobs opposed anti-crime legislation. But now, suddenly, Andy wants to put on a police uniform.

Very bad metaphor in my case. I had worn a police uniform for nearly four years. And not only that, but, by chance, I had recently received a letter of commendation from the Washington, D.C., chief of police because an intern, Chris Fager, and I had helped the police chase down armed robbers in the Capitol.

Long after Richard Nixon was gone from government, a Pat Robertson political front calling itself the Christian Coalition blundered in the same manner when it circularized the city of Indianapolis with a one-size-fits-all election campaign brochure. It listed perceived political sins which it applied to its enemies list. I had the honor of being included. My evaluation was mostly a result of social issues as viewed from the organization's curious brand of Christianity. The Gospel, according to the "religious wrong," was a Gospel not of Christian generosity, but of selfishness; not one of peace, but of war—especially war equipment profitable to certain government contractors. And their angry tones hardly reflected a Gospel of love.

One of the "Christian" items in the Coalition's brochure against me was the so-called Balanced Budget Amendment. Obviously not having the slightest notion of my position on the issue, the contrived Christians claimed I was opposed to the proposed amendment. That attack fit me as badly as the ill-fitting police uniform hanging in the earlier news release. Not only did I support the amendment, but I was the one who first proposed it back in 1976. I called it the Payment Book Amendment. It would have required not only a balanced budget, but payment, by installments, of the national debt. At the time, only two groups opposed my idea—the Democrats and the Republicans. It later became popular and new parentage sprang up.

Then there was the letter from a religious lady in Indianapolis. It came right to the point:

Dear Congressman Jacobs:
God does not want us in the UN. Now look, Andy, if you piss me off that's one thing. But if you piss off God, you'll really be in trouble.

Sweet.

In my research for this work, I have dug back into *Indianapolis Star* clippings from the late 1960s and early 1970s. It is said that as time passes we tend to repress or purge the negative from our conscious memories. I think that's true because even having been the target of slanted *Star* stories of that era, I am amazed at just how far they went. This from a news story in the *Star*:

A smiling and confident [opponent] kept a grim and edgy Congressman Andrew Jacobs, Jr. on the defensive for nearly all of a half-hour debate.

Later in the same story, the same Jacobs wasn't so "grim and edgy" after all:

Jacobs did an artful job of defending himself, verbally ducking, bobbing and weaving and counterpunching.

And now for the pig button. My opponent and I had several joint meetings with various organizations during the 1968 campaign. At one of the early ones, I was asked in all somber seriousness whether it was true that I wore a button that said "PIG" in Chicago. "Yes, I said, "you've found me out. I took a good look at all the Democratic presidential candidates in Chicago and discovered that Pigasus was the only one who had been martyred by arrest when he was taken into custody along with his hippie handlers. He, himself, was an innocent animal and therefore innocent of wrongdoing. So in keeping with my policy of always being for the *underhog*, I threw my considerable support his way. When the arrest was made, the ACLU protested that it was a violation of human rights to put the Yippies and a pig in the same paddy wagon. I liked the police response. It may have been the only rational statement in the whole dreary Chicago affair. The police spokesperson said, 'They came together, they go together.'"

Since it seemed that almost everybody at the meeting except the questioner was laughing uproariously, I assumed that the opposition wouldn't bring it up again. Not so. On the front page of the *Indianapolis Star* the next morning, there it was, a story whose headline read, "JACOBS ADMITS WEARING PIG BUTTON IN CHICAGO." And hard as it is to believe, that heinous and unconscionable act of mine became the major theme of the campaign against me that year—one *Star* story after another, day after day. I was embarrassed to hog-up so much space in the paper that people might think me a publicity hound.

James Grover Thurber wrote, "The far left began fighting humor long ago because they do not understand it and therefore fear it." Same goes for the far right.

Toward the end of the 1968 campaign, my opponent and I made a joint appearance before what was said to be the most staid of men's clubs in Indianapolis. By that time, everybody in town knew about the earthshaking PIG button issue, and I assumed that I was about to enter the lion's den of "Grouchy Old Men" where the rules of the club were the law of gravity. Wrong. A pleasant surprise awaited. The lunch meeting was unusual in that a paid professional speaker on the subject of political humor preceded our debate with a twenty minute talk. The guest speaker was a historian. Lincoln played prominently in his presentation. Lincoln, he said, took a lot of abuse from mossbacks because he, like Jesus, often chose to make his points with stories. And his stories were frequently humorous. In the most doubtful moments of the Civil War, Abe said, "If I could not laugh, I would die."

The members of the club were mostly elderly men, but they were very definitely not grumpy. Not only were they laughing, but along with that they were giving me knowing looks replete with winks of support. Though mostly members of his party, the gentlemen of that club turned out not to be a good audience for my opponent's anti-humor pitch that day. We had our discussion and somehow the PIG button just didn't come up. When the meeting ended, however, a large number of the members of that so-called mossback club came up to greet me and say how much they liked that other nemesis of the *Star*, my dad.

When the votes had been counted in the 1968 election, Richard Nixon had won, barely. Barely was good enough. My dad told a story about a little boy who made a purchase at a candy store. With furrowed brow he counted the change repeatedly until the proprietor asked, "Isn't it all there?"

"Well, yes," replied the boy. "But just barely." Richard Nixon's dream had come true. It turned out to be something of a nightmare for him and the rest of the country. But it did some very good things for a while.

His campaign had been very slick. For example, as he made the rounds, he called more than one place his second home state. His campaign ran a TV ad during the Indianapolis evening news. He said he considered Indiana a second home because his Millhouse progenitors lived in southern Indiana (true). But immediately following the news, on the same channel in a national, paid political telecast from Ohio, there was Nixon saying to a programmed and scripted audience that he considered Ohio a second home state. By the phenomenon of coaxial cable, within just a few minutes Hoosier voters saw him make both claims. Nixon was beginning to look plastic. Humphrey always seemed sincere even though a change in the political climate often brought about a change in his basic political positions. Nixon's Madison Avenue approach reminded one of American comedian Roger Price's line: "You can't fool all the people all the time, but if you can do it once, you're good for four years." With regard to the Vietnam War, that applied to Lyndon Johnson, too.

Despite the congressional map designed by Judge Cale Holder to be a gas chamber for me, I held my breath and was successful in my re-election bid in 1968. By chance—more likely God's sense of humor—Judge Holder and my dad encountered each other on a downtown sidewalk the very day after the election. Dad twinkled and asked the judge, "Does this mean Andy's in contempt?" Judge Holder roared with laughter. He and Dad were long-standing friends. And after all, what does anyone suppose a judge who had been Democratic State chairman would have done under the same circumstances?

I never felt the slightest animus toward Judge Holder. That was not the case with one of my Indiana Democratic colleagues who was quoted in the paper as saying some very shrill things about the judge after the St. Valentine's Day massacre was announced. But my colleague was playing with an empty hand and the judge knew it. The judge was quoted in the same story. To my colleague's desperately histrionic and ill-tempered statement, the judge simply said what might be expected of one who held all the aces: "Well, well." I, on the other hand might once again have publicly invoked the wisdom of Churchill to the judge: "You do your worst and we'll do our best." But I didn't say it; I was preoccupied with trying to figure out by what miracle "our best" had proved to be good enough.

Allard Lowenstein's efforts to "dump Johnson" had been generally viewed as windmill tilting. But now that the election was over, Al was considered more of a Jack the Giant Killer than a Don Quixote. And here is where I witnessed an historic moment at very close range—a couple of feet.

Lyndon Johnson never forgot anyone who did something for him or *against* him. Al Lowenstein certainly was in the latter category. And a few weeks before the inauguration of the thirty-seventh President of the United States, Lyndon Johnson went to the Capitol to bid farewell at a reception attended by senators and representatives and a few representatives-elect, including Allard K. Lowenstein of New York. Despite being busy dumping Johnson, Al had managed to get himself elected to Congress from Long Beach.

The reception was held in the Longworth House Office Building cafeteria. And it was crowded, so crowded that the President had to weave his way to the platform. Al and I were standing together when President Johnson, following his Secret Service blocking, found himself face to face with the initial and principal architect of his political demise. There was absolutely no way LBJ would not have known exactly whom he was facing. But he played poker, smiling exactly the same smile he had smiled to the less objectionable members in the room. In fact, neither man seemed embarrassed. I thought it remarkable.

As it turned out, dumping Johnson did not mean dumping the war. Al's efforts at that goal would continue for five more years. Just twelve years after that fateful cafeteria meeting, Al would have another fateful meeting, this one with one of his followers.

Now I had served twice as many terms in Congress as I had expected on election night 1964. And I was about to embark on yet another. But before I did, I was a guest of the Indianapolis League of Women Voters for discussion of the issues. During the preliminary pleasantries, a woman said, "Now that you've been re-elected, you must be moving up in seniority on the Judiciary Committee."

"That's true;" I said, "I've moved all the way from 'Hey' to 'Hey, you.'" In those days, the wheels of seniority ground very slowly. It was said that, during one period in the twentieth century, no one moved up even so much as one seat on the Ways and Means Committee for ten years.

Lee Hamilton and I, both Hoosiers, were freshmen together in the

Eighty-ninth Congress and became lifelong friends. But our styles were different. He and his wonderful wife, Nancy, were given to White House and embassy parties. I had no wife and had no taste for the formal Washington social life. When Edwin Newman wrote the novel *Sunday Punch*, the publisher flattered me by soliciting my comment for the dust jacket. Washington nightlife figured in the story. This is the blurb I sent:

> Ed Newman's new book affords a reader the opportunity to enjoy the absurdity of a Washington cocktail party without having to endure one.

Most of the White House parties probably were not absurd; there were opportunities to discuss legislative matters with colleagues. I just preferred other environments for such informal exchanges, say the House gymnasium, which Lee and I both used. In fact, Lee had been a star high school basketball player, winning Indiana's prestigious Trestor Award.

Lee's wife Nancy was wonderful in countless ways. She was one of the most pleasant people I ever knew. She was a gifted and celebrated portrait artist, eventually concentrating on the animal world, mostly people's pets. When my wife Kim's beloved Andy Dog—no direct relation to me—died, Nancy did a gorgeous painting of the dearly departed cocker spaniel. The picture is displayed prominently in our home. And the office Lee used on Capitol Hill had the look of an upscale art gallery, all of it Nancy's work.

During our early days in Congress, I occasionally baby sat the Hamilton children while Lee and Nancy donned their finery and sallied forth. And when I attended dinners at the Hamilton's, Tracy, Doug and Debbie would, with their smiles, urge me on with my not- altogether-reverent humor at the table.

The Hamilton kids gave me a book of disc-shaped lapel-stickers for Christmas, 1968. The gift was meant as a joke about my by-then-famous Chicago PIG button. Well, they were very young at the time and how were they to know that one of the stickers was a little more than a tad risque. It read, "Beware of Greeks Bearing Trojans." I hate to waste things, so I marked it "personal" and sent it to my friend Congressman John Brademas. On the chance you have not guessed it, John was of Greek descent—and at the time he was an active bachelor.

There was another Christmas present for me. I gave it to myself. Up until that time I had never, as an adult, taken a vacation and certainly not a junket at taxpayers' expense—unless you count that trip to Korea when I was eighteen and not allowed to eat en route. But it seemed to be S.O.P. for

Hoosiers who were elected to public offices to go to Florida after their elections. So I decided to follow suit just that once. I was tired and willing to spend the money for the four days in the sun—fresh orange juice, too. Stopping at one of the countless citrus stands near St. Petersburg, I received in change a rare item for the times, a Kennedy half-dollar. When I marveled at the ease with which I had just acquired one, the nice old man behind the counter said, "Well, I just take 'em from one Yankee and give 'em to another." Those four days in the sun left me, in the words of Steinbeck, "refreshed, renewed and ready to survive." So it was back to Washington to see how things would go with that first President's thirty-sixth successor.

chapter 6

FOUR MORE YEARS — OF WAR

ONCE IN THE WHITE HOUSE, President Nixon's crime proposals became modest compared to the one about a new Department of Crime. We heard no more about that. The administration's advocacy of preventive detention stirred the blood, however. The idea was authorization of judges to decide before trials who was dangerous and ought not be allowed bail. The general rule in most jurisdictions had been that all those charged with crimes were entitled to be released on bail pending their trials, unless the charge was first degree or premeditated murder. The argument for preventive detention was that it took a long time to get criminal cases to trial. During that long time, they argued, bad guys could go right on doing bad things. The proposal was before both the Judiciary Committee and the District of Columbia Committee, to be applied to federal criminal law and to the local District of Columbia criminal law.

As a member of both committees, I participated in all the hearings on the subject. How, I would ask, is a judge to decide without evidence which defendant will be dangerous if out on bail and which will not? "Is he supposed to follow the old Red Skelton routine, 'I've seen a lot of 'em in my time, and you just don't look right to me'?" The administration's answer was that "judges were experts about criminals and were therefore qualified to make such judgments."

"Fine," I'd say, "but if they're that good, why bother with a trial and waste time with something as boring as evidence? Just let the judge in a case take a good look and decide on the spot if a defendant is guilty. But judges usually see defendants at their best: best cloths, best behavior, and best assurances that they've been born yet again. Since the police are the officials who see suspects in their natural habitats, why not let the police decide who should be preventively jailed without bail or who's guilty of the crime charged by the police? Then we could take it all the way to our very own police state."

That's how the debate went and in the D.C. committee where President Nixon had the votes. When that bill was taken up on the floor of the House, super bright and super nice Congressman Abner Mikva and I offered a substitute which we called the "speedy trial" proposal. It provided that those charged with violent crimes would go to trial faster than those charged with minor, nonviolent crimes such as over-parking. This would be accomplished by using more courts for the violent crime charges and fewer courts for the minor, nonviolent crime charges.

When I spoke in support of the substitute, I was asked to yield to one of the preventive detention supporters. When I did, he asked, "What about the constitutional right to a speedy trial for those charged with misdemeanors?" That argument triggered some vehemence in me. "For God's sake," said I, "we have before us today the most radical departure from the time-tested and time-honored traditional principles of Anglo-Saxon jurisprudence ever, and the gentleman wishes to worry about how quickly a citizen gets to pay a parking ticket."

With the Republican-Southern Democratic coalition almost always in his corner, President Nixon usually held sway in the House. Our substitute failed and the President's plan prevailed that day.

Following my comments in the well, I took a seat in the back of the Chamber and heard a representative in the next row behind me badgering another member. The verbal attacker was, of course, the House bully, Wayne Hays of Ohio. My dad had been in the same freshman class with Hays during the Eighty-first Congress twenty years before. Dad said, "One thing you can say about Wayne: he never hits a man when he's up." True of most bullies. In this case, the man who was down was the great Allard Lowenstein whom Governor Nelson Rockefeller had just helped gerrymander so severely that Al's defeat in the next congressional election was a certainty. (Al's son, Frank, told his grade school classmates, "They've rearranged my father's seat.")

Al had said in a television interview that if the House Democratic Leadership continued to help gag anti-Vietnam representatives so that the latter could not make their arguments on the floor, those oppressed Democratic members might just withhold their votes in organizing the next House. Such a tactic would mean that the top Democrat in the House would not be the Speaker, but Minority Leader. Hays, certain of re-election himself, was doing what he could to make Al feel worse about his impending job loss. Hays said, "Y'know, Lowenstein, you can get a gang to throw bricks in the street, but you're not going to run this place. You're not going to be in the next Congress, anyway."

I don't know. Maybe it was my irritation over the preventive detention debate; maybe it was the outrage of Hays's accusing this Gandhi-like gentle peace advocate of a violent crime or maybe it was the cruel razing of a decent member of Congress about his pending exit, but something made the dike burst inside me.

I turned to Hays and said, "Who gave you the moral right to accuse an honorable member of this House of a violent crime?" Hays said, "Jacobs, you haven't won an argument since you came here." Sinking shamefully to his level, I heatedly said, "And you haven't made an intelligent argument since you came here."

To understand fully the rest of our exchange, which was becoming boisterous, you should know that Wayne Hays was not only a bully, but also a braggart. Only an hour before, I had sat at the same large lunch table with Hays and John Tunney, son of the boxer. There were several other representatives at that table, one of whom asked John the interesting question, "Did anyone ever make the mistake of not recognizing your father and picking a fistfight with him?"

"Well, yes," replied John in his elegant manner. "A football player did that and didn't realize his mistake until he woke up in the hospital the next day." Cute story, but of course Hays had to top it: "I was driving last weekend and a truck driver pulled over and dared me to fight. So I grabbed the tire tool and said, 'Come on, you son of a bitch.' He backed down." Sure, Wayne.

The next thing Hays said to me was, "Well, what are you gonna do about it?" I shouldn't be proud of this part of the story—it violates my principle of nonviolence. But I *am* proud of it for two reasons. First, I knew my words would not lead to violence for the simple reason that Wayne Hays only talked a good fight. As is the case with most bullies, he was a coward. And I didn't have the slightest intention of taking advantage of his puny pugilistic capability anyway; I just wanted to illustrate his phoniness. My reply: "I'll tell you what I'm going to do about it, you silly son of a bitch. Go down to your car and get your tire tool—I'll spot you that—and meet me in the gym in fifteen minutes." To which Hays said, "Ahhh," and walked away.

As I sat there thinking how unpleasant the world was at the moment, Al

Lowenstein slipped into the seat beside me and said, "Do you realize the effect you just had on that man?"

"Neither realize nor care," I replied. "Well," Al continued, "he just apologized to me."

"Fine," I said. " 'There'll be more rejoicing in Heaven if one sinner repenteth.' "

A few minutes later I had stepped off the floor to do a radio interview with a reporter and a tape recorder. As the recorder taped away, Wayne Hays approached and began to speak to me. I asked the reporter if she would turn off "the bubble machine." And Hays began again, "Y'know, Jacobs, Lowenstein and I can settle our differences amicably without your butting in—"

I interrupted with mock pugnaciousness, "Do you want to settle your differences with me amicably, Hays?" He asked for clarification, "What do you mean?"

"I mean just what I said. Do you want to settle your differences with me amicably?"

"Well, yeah," he said almost tentatively, whereupon, I thrust my hand forward and said, "Then put 'er there." This episode was reported in the book *Public Trust and Private Lust*, written by *Washington Post* staffers Marian Clark and Rudy Maxa. After describing the exchange between Hays and me in the Capitol hallway, the writers described Hays' response to my amicably extended hand:

> . . . and the meanest man in Congress put out his hand.

An exchange I had one day with a representative from Texas was also funny, but in a nice way. We were in the back of the House Chamber listening to a speech by a retired Marine. "Andy," said the Texan, "did you ever meet a Marine who wasn't an out-and-out braggart?"

"Well, maybe one or two," I quietly replied. Then he thought to ask the obvious question about whether I had served in the Corps. When I said, "I guess I did," my colleague told me, "You're the first Marine I ever met who wasn't an out-and-out braggart."

"Don't feel bad about it, Joe," I replied. "Now that I think about it, I believe you're the first Texan I ever met who wasn't an out-and-out braggart."

Of course, I had met many Texans who weren't the least bit braggadocios and Joe knew plenty of Marines who were modest too, including the kindly Representative James C. Corman from California, who fought at Iwo Jima. Moreover, my Texas friend can easily be forgiven for what he said that day on the spur of the moment; the Marine making the speech was definitely a pain in the, er, anatomy. Irving Leibowitz, the former editor of the *Indianapolis Times*, wrote the definition of a bore:

> One who was born in Texas, reared in California, played football for Notre Dame, served in the Marine Corps, and had an operation six months before.

A study in stereotyping, but funny and therefore very worthwhile.

Every year on Veterans Day, there is an outdoor ceremony in the midst of the Indianapolis downtown monuments which Joe Kraft called "a salute to Mars." I attended regularly and continued to do so after retiring from Congress. One year, the ambient temperature in Indianapolis dropped thirty degrees overnight between November 10 and 11. I didn't realize it as I walked into my home's attached garage and started out for the ceremony. Halfway there, I sensed that the weather wasn't altogether pleasant, but when I alighted from the car I knew I was in trouble. I was wearing a business suit with no overcoat to ward off the wind chill, which I later learned was about five degrees Fahrenheit.

When the seemingly endless ceremony ended, the commanding general of Fort Benjamin Harrison, General Stephen Woods, Jr., pointed to an Army colonel and said, "That's Colonel Smith and he just asked me how you could sit there for forty-five minutes, dressed as you are, without showing any signs of discomfort. And I told him, 'You have to remember Congressman Jacobs was a Marine.' And the colonel said, 'Yeah, dumb.'" Right, Colonel Smith, but I was also feeling plenty of discomfort.

A year or so later, I did better in an exchange with General Woods who was every inch the officer and gentleman. We both attended a meeting of the Ernie Pyle VFW Post and the general spoke just ahead of me. He explained to the crowd that Benjamin Harrison's grandfather was with our Revolutionary Army at Yorktown. With that, he turned to me and said, "By the way, Congressman Jacobs, there were no Marines at Yorktown." That was the end of the general's speech and I was next. When I went to the podium, I answered the general. "General Woods, I believe I can explain that. By the time the enemy is prepared to surrender, there is no need for Marines." There were no Marines at Yorktown and there were very few at the VFW post that night, either. For my trouble I received several good-natured boos. The Marine Corps, by the way, is one year older than our country.

While there was a great deal of sincerity and knowledge in the peace and environmental movements, there was a certain fad quality also. And the fad meant a certain amount of superficiality which produced inconsistency. Some so-called public peace demonstrations were anything but peaceful. Call them public hypocrisy. And when the first Earth Day came along during the Nixon administration, Capitol Hill staffers Edie Wilkie and her friend Debbie demanded of me what I was doing for Earth Day. I replied, "I'm not smoking." Both of them were. As it became clearer that sucking poison directly into one's lungs from a cigarette was far more dangerous, whiff for whiff than smoke from a factory—not to say that the factory smoke was just fine—they both stopped using the evil weed. I think refined sugar is another substance dangerous to human health. As that becomes clearer to the public, refined sugar, in the manner of tobacco, will become more and more controversial.

The story about the origin of the saying "Democrat" Party bears repeating. The name of the party is quite clear; it can be seen on any ballot as well as in the dictionary. The misnomer did not begin in ignorance. Ignorance accounts for its use in many cases today, but the misstatement was quite calculated and was begun back in the 1950s by Republican National Chairman Leonard Hall. Its meaning was meant to be demeaning. The name the Democrats gave their party sounded too good to Mr. Hall. He thought up the slur, but it was good ol' Joseph McCarthy who retailed it. And today it is right-wing dogma. But the oft repeated slur is also unconsciously used by many Democrats. This led my friend, Jim Beatty to say to our mutual friend, Tom Titsworth, "People who say 'Democrat Party' should be hung." To which Tom replied, "*Hanged.*" Sometimes it's hard to win. The correct name remains the Democratic Party. No one with standing has gone to Circuit Court to change it. As a member of the U.S. House, my dad dealt with the slur in his own inimitable manner. When a Republican friend would say Democrat Party during an exchange with Dad, the latter would speak of the *Publican* Party. Publicans were not the most admired in the Bible; they were tax collectors.

One of my best friends, who was also one of the dearest ladies of so-called Washington society, was Florence Mahoney. She was the somewhat adopted daughter of Governor James M. Cox of Ohio, founder of the vast Cox newspaper and television chain. Governor Cox was also the Democratic nominee for president in 1920. His running mate was a former secretary of the Navy named Franklin Delano Roosevelt. Warren Gamaliel Harding and John Calvin Coolidge won.

Florence's dinner parties were in marked contrast to the huge glittering affairs most often associated with Washington. They were small, serious, and cerebral. For reasons I have yet fully to understand, Florence often included me with the towering figures at her table. Shortly after Richard Nixon became president, I met Margaret Truman and her husband, Cliff Daniels, at Florence's home on Prospect Street in Georgetown. That evening I got an extra peek into American history. President Nixon had made a grand point of taking a grand piano from the White House to Independence, Missouri, where he presented it to former President Harry Truman. Truman was famous for his piano playing at the White House. But, though Nixon said the instrument was the very one Truman had played, apparently it wasn't.

Margaret told us that evening that after President Nixon left, her father, no Nixon fan, said, "It's that [Army language deleted] one from the third floor—always out of tune." Richard Nixon played the piano pretty well, too.

As the months and years of President Nixon's first term emptied into history, he continued to push the dragon of crime as a campaign issue, casting himself as St. George and the Democrats as knaves. I had introduced a bill to extend Federal Employees Compensation Act benefits to dependents of police and other public safety officers killed in the line of duty. My friend and coworker Louie Mahern obtained a special number for the bill. It was 714, the badge number of the famed and fictional Sergeant Friday.

The Nixon administration opposed the proposal, arguing that compensation for such survivors was a local matter. I reasoned that with travel and communication in our country what it is, a Georgia policeman could lose his life protecting a visiting New Yorker. Or a Hoosier criminal might kill a cop in California. In the case of criminal law enforcement and cooperation among departments, we were indeed "one nation under God." The bill lay dormant in the Judiciary Committee until the day after the particularly horrible murder of several New York police officers. The President seized the opportunity to have a White House news conference with several chiefs of police as his guests. The headline story the next morning quoted President Nixon as saying, "This incident should remind all of us what we owe to the nation's police officers."

The President's statement prompted me to have my own news conference. During my thirty congressional years I probably had five Washington news conferences; this was by far the most memorable. The gravamen of my message was summed up in two sentences: "I wish something would remind President Nixon's Justice Department that we owe a lot to our nation's police officers. Attorney General Mitchell is opposed to my bill to pay a part of what we owe to the surviving dependents of these martyred national heroes."

The *Washington Post* and, I think, the *New York Times* reported my lament, but there was nothing about it on the network television evening news. If fact, there was nothing about anything on the TV evening news that day except a diatribe and threat from the pit bull of the Nixon administration, Spiro Agnew. Or perhaps not a pit bull; in the manner of the snake who charms the bird from the tree, Agnew, with the facile pen of writer in White House residence Pat Buchanan, had so intimidated the three major networks that they surrendered their entire thirty-minute news programs to Agnew that evening. Agnew, in essence, used the simulcast monopoly to tell the nation why the networks just might be taken over by the government if they didn't shape up and tell the truth—as defined by the administration—about the administration. President Nixon echoed that philosophy when, during the Vietnam misadventure, he declared, "If the Congress wants to share responsibility, it must act responsibly."

The Agnew incident was hardly the networks' finest half hour. So far as I was concerned, it was tweak time. I tapped out a little news release on the Smith Corona manual typewriter given me by my father when I was in high school, made copies, and pinned them to bulletin boards in the various news galleries at the Capitol. According to the news release:

> Police officers and other public safety officers who lay their lives on the line in the line of duty should at least be assured that our country is not an ingrate when it comes to the needs of surviving dependents.
>
> Opposing federal help for those dependents, last night the administration managed to drown out my reminder about our obligation in this regard. It bullied the network news programs into abandoning their mission to give the nation the news. Instead, they gave Vice President Agnew the entire thirty minutes to make his socialistic suggestion that the government take over the private TV networks.
>
> Mr. Agnew is entitled to his opinion, which is bizarre enough to constitute news. But others had newsworthy things to say, also. And I believe I was one of them. Balanced news coverage requires airing more than one item. It should include the good news, the bad news and the Agnews.

The next day, some of the reporters who hang around the Speaker's Lobby approached me with the news that the vice president had been asked in South Carolina what he thought about my saying he'd made a socialistic suggestion. His answer was, "That'll be the day when Ted Agnew makes a socialistic suggestion." I was then asked what I thought about Mr. Agnew's reply and said, "If he doesn't want to be accused of making socialistic suggestions, he should stop making socialistic suggestions." In retrospect it seems comical, but less so at the time.

Just as the government had managed to fool the public about Vietnam, it was on the verge of doing the same about the so-called Liberal news media. The absurd assertion persisted well into the 1990s, with the right wing insisting that the "left wing" eastern press covered up private peccadilloes of prominent Democrats and rushed to print such embarrassments on the parts of Republicans.

The facts suggest otherwise. When Gary Hart was caught in a domestic indiscretion, the *Washington Post* reported it on page one and, in effect, helped blast him from his presidential front runner position. The *Post* certainly didn't hesitate to publish the peccadilloes of Bill Clinton. Does that mean that "liberal" paper was evenhanded? Hardly. The *Washington Post* had information that was worse about Senator Packwood—forcing himself on women—before voters went to the polls in Oregon to vote on his last re-election bid. The information was not published in the *Post* and the Senator went on to win by a slim margin. The *Post* had undenied information about an old extramarital affair of Bob Dole's just before the presidential election of 1996 and I think rightly decided not to publish it. Liberal press? Partial to the Democrats? Only if *God didn't make little green olives?*

The Nixon administration was riding high in those days before 1974, high enough actually to frighten the networks. Eventually, the White House got so cheeky that it produced what purported to be a valid executive order establishing national wage and price controls. It was a ridiculous effort to repeal the reality of inflation by political alchemy. The really frightening thing was that the public bought the price controls, so to speak. Here was another case for Secretary John Hay's amazement at "public acceptance of a concise impropriety." Perhaps needless to say, the unconstitutional controls had disastrous effects when they were lifted and the dam broke, releasing impounded demand which furiously flooded the economy with inflation.

Would the American public hold still for a monarchy? During the McCarthy era, a survey was taken among U.S. citizens about whether a certain unidentified document seemed like a good idea. A majority said it sounded subversive. The document was the first ten amendments to the U.S. Constitution, sometimes called the Bill of Rights.

The Agnew incident did advance my safety officer legislation somewhat. To this day we still do not have the full benefits of the Federal Employees Compensation Act for surviving dependents of officers killed in the line of duty, but the Nixon administration did go along with a federal lump sum payment to those family members. It remains the law, adjusted from time to time for inflation.

The National Aeronautics and Space Administration was also, you might say, riding high in those days, high in space and high on the hog of the federal budget. It was enormously profitable to the contractors who were in constant search of more and often redundant missions. When the repetitive Earth-orbiting manned shots began to look like a circus to many scientists at NASA, they resigned in protest, arguing logically that the far less expensive—and less profitable—*unmanned* deep space probes were much more scientifically probative.

Against this backdrop, I was one of the dinner guests in the Washington home of a good friend and congressional colleague one evening. Most of the people at the table were members of Congress and their spouses. It seemed social enough until the dishes were cleared and we were summoned to take seats in the living room.

There, in the manner of the unsuspecting captured audience of an Amway meeting, one of the guests, an official from NASA, began his pitch for appropriations. "We should colonize the Moon," he explained. He actually had the moxie plus corn to say, "If we can't find peace on Earth, maybe we can find it on the Moon." When the question period was announced, the other guests asked nothing critical; I did.

"In Fahrenheit," I said politely, "what is the variation of ambient temperature on the Moon during an average twenty-four-hour period?"

"Well," said the pitchman, "it's quite a bit."

"How much is quite a bit?" I continued. "Well, maybe a couple of hundred degrees." I thought it was more, but I let it go and asked another question as our hostess began to seethe, "What is the water supply on the moon?"

"Well, we think there may be traces of water in frozen form, but in any event, we could ship water from earth by tanker rockets." Glancing to my side, I remembered that among the guests were Congressman and Mrs. Bernie Sisk from the federally irrigated Yosemite area of California, so as most of the company began to feel uncomfortable and the lady of the house was about to throw me out, I propounded one more inquiry: "How would the cost of those tanker rockets compare with the cost of irrigating vast new areas of our western deserts?"

As our hostess began to eye the closet where my coat was hanging, the

Lord sent the cavalry in the person of Mrs. Sisk: "Well, I think this young man has a good point." Instead of ordering me out for being a troublemaker, the hostess suggested we all go into another room for coffee. The surprise home-style congressional hearing was adjourned, social life resumed, and I was even invited back for another dinner later, much later.

My faithful companion, my Great Dane C-Five, the one who, in the hallway, seemed to side with racist Representative Rarick, was a publicity hound. One way or another, he seemed to wind up on the front page of the style section of the *Washington Post* regularly. He just seemed to come by it naturally. One night when I had dictated the last reply letter and had returned the last phone call, C-Five and I left the office for the parking garage. Halfway to our car, I glanced at my shirt pocket schedule only to discover that I had overlooked a reception to which I was committed. It was a consumer advocates' gathering in the Rayburn House Office Building, under which was the garage in which we were parked. All I had to do was walk a few steps out of our way, put in an appearance, and go on. But what about C-Five? Well, why not? We entered the cavernous room to the delight of the two hundred or so participants. C-Five the celebrity was making a personal appearance.

One of those present was Virginia Knauer, White House special assistant for consumer affairs for the Nixon administration. She was also a canine fancier who owned a kennel in her home state of Pennsylvania. As she gravitated to C-Five and a *Washington Post* photographer snapped away, she did what professional dog people sometimes to do. She pulled upward on C-Five's uncropped ears. A few years before, President Johnson had brought down an avalanche of criticism by doing the same thing to his pet Beagle. So I said, "Mrs. Knauer, you are everyone's favorite administration official so let me refresh your memory. Lyndon got into trouble by pulling a dog's ears."

"Oh my goodness!" replied the pleasant lady, whereupon, I turned to the cameraman and asked if we could try the picture again. He smiled and said, "Surely." So the next day, there we were, Mrs. Knauer and I with C-Five between us, all smiles—maybe one of the smiles was actually a case of panting. I was quoted in the caption as saying that I brought the Great Dane to the consumer reception because " he is the biggest consumer I know." Mrs. Knauer was a bright and lovely lady. I believe Mrs. Nixon was the same.

chapter 7

FROM GLASS, A STONE'S THROW TO THE SENATE

ADLAI STEVENSON SAID that in politics, "You can't throw dirt without losing ground." An Indiana congressman learned that the hard way one election year. He was a candidate for the U.S. Senate seat held by a member of the opposite party. The congressman launched an early TV attack ad on the incumbent senator. The effort did not just backfire; it boomeranged.

The representative's campaign was robust with money, enough to hire an actor with an Asiatic countenance to play the part of a Vietcong soldier for the spot. The message was that somehow the senator had helped Communists kill American soldiers in Vietnam. That, of course, would mean the senator was a traitor. How so?

During his 1960 campaign, President Nixon had said he had a secret plan to end the Vietnam War. And critics said it was just oratory, that Nixon had no such plan. But he did; it was to grant U.S. trade concessions to Russia in return for Russia's ordering its Vietnamese clients to give up the south of their country. Of course the plan couldn't work; Russia had no such influence over the Vietnamese. But the plan was attempted. The congressman's ad attacked the senator for casting a congressional vote in favor of those Nixon-proposed trade concessions. The congressman was a member of Nixon's party and, therefore, was criticizing the senator for, at worst, being bipartisan.

The actor in the ad was dressed up to look like the Vietcong soldier, slowly turning a Russian rifle toward the camera as the announcer, in essence, said, "The senator voted to help the Russians kill our soldiers." As the announcer concluded, the communist soldier was pointing the Russian piece directly at the viewer. Pretty powerful stuff, except that . . .

The ad was especially ill-advised because the people who put it together were especially ill-informed; the Democratic incumbent senator had *not* voted for the bill. He couldn't have because he wasn't there. But *someone* had voted for the Republican administration's bill. And that someone, among many, many others, was the very Republican congressman who was running the attack ad against the senator.

This gave me an idea. My dad still had the Russian carbine I brought home for him from the Korean war. Jim Beatty and I borrowed it. We scarcely had two campaign nickels to rub together, but by digging deep we came up with enough to pay for one hour of video taping at a studio we knew would spy on us and report to the challenging congressman's campaign. It was the proverbial trollop-ploy.

We couldn't afford the actor, so we hung the carbine by a thin wire parallel to the camera lens. As one of our friends read our ad, Jim blew gently against the stock of the weapon causing it to turn slowly toward the camera. *Our* ad said, "Congressman (So-and-so) voted for a bill that liberalized trade with Russian. Russia is supplying arms to the Communists in Vietnam. Would it be fair to say Congressman (So-and-so) is helping the Russians kill our soldiers in Vietnam?" As the ad ended with that question, the Russian carbine was pointing directly at the viewer.

As expected, our ad was dutifully and immediately reported to the opposition party. The congressman's ad was seen no more. A very good result from our point of view, considering the fact that we did not have enough money to run our TV ad even once. The congressman's campaign was accustomed to plenty of money. It probably never occurred to them that we did not enjoy the same kind of treasury.

During one of my campaigns for re-election, the candidate with whom I competed went to Washington to attend his party's campaign training program. One of the instructors was a Republican representative who happened to be a good friend of mine—with good reason. I had defended his honor from a McCarthyism attack by a Democratic representative. The Republican had offered an amendment to strike a fat-laden slice of pork from military spending. The Democratic chairman of the Armed Services Committee had defended the profitable waste by attacking the Republican sponsor of the amendment. During the debate, the chairman said of the Republican congressman, "Apparently the gentleman doesn't care about his country." The minute I heard those words, I rushed to the Republican representative and asked if he had served in the military. He had. Good. I knew that the chairman was abnormally sensitive about not having served in the military himself. So I rose in the debate and was recognized to speak for five minutes, way more than I needed to say, "The sponsor of this amendment cares enough about his country to have served in our armed forces. I yield back the balance of my time."

It worked. Visibly angered, the chairman rose and apologized to the member he had so viciously attacked, adding, "I'm not apologizing because of anything the gentleman from Indiana said." As our friend Bob Dole would say, "Whatever."

At the Republican how-to-run-for-Congress session, my opponent asked his instructor if he knew anything that could be used against me in the fall campaign. To which the Republican instructor—my friend—replied, "Well, the worst thing I've been able to dig up on Jacobs so far is that he publicly defended my patriotism a few months ago." That fact was not used against me in that campaign, or any other.

One of the qualified joys of being a candidate is the expectation that you will go door-to-door and help your party register voters. On one such occasion when I was persuading people to participate in the process, a very attractive young woman approached me on the sidewalk and euphemistically said, "Are you looking for a date?" She obviously worked in a professional position. "No," I said, "but are you registered to vote?" On the spot she received her voter registration card. I didn't ask about her politics.

In that same campaign, there was a candidates night at a Catholic community center. Both the audience and the panel of candidates were unusually large, a hundred or more in the audience and about eight on the bipartisan panel. The Democratic and Republican candidates for various offices sat together at a table and passed a microphone down the line so that each of the eight could give his or her answer to each question from the audience. I was the last in line. When the inevitable question on pornography came up, my fellow candidates walked on eggshells. After all, this was a Catholic audience. About half way down the line to me, each candidate began denouncing *Playboy* magazine.

When the mike got to me, I said, "I have never bought a copy of that magazine. But when you're in Congress, the publisher sends you tear sheets of learned articles which appear in some editions. My only complaint is that when you turn those sheets over—all you find is text."

Ninety-nine percent of the crowd roared with laughter. Funny is funny, Catholic or not. The eggshells were the figment of the unimaginative imaginations of uptight candidates. It is true that I never bought the magazine. I've never cared for spectator sports.

Nineteen seventy was a Democratic year. A deep recession plagued the party that held the White House and the President was Richard Nixon. So, despite a vigorous and hardworking campaign by my opponent, I went back to Congress.

During the post-election interregnum before the Ninety-second Congress convened, a former member of Congress and close friend of mine, Jed Johnson, Jr., introduced me to the Reverend Fred Taylor, a minister at the Church of the Redeemer in Washington. Reverend Taylor had a suggestion and it was a good one. Junior Village, the vast District of Columbia orphanage, was dramatically less noble than supposed by wealthy families who had been widely admired for their generous gifts to the institution. My friends said there should be a congressional investigation and, since I served on the House District of Columbia Committee, I should hold the hearing. When I explained that the chairman of the committee and I were a long distance from close, they said, "So what? Just announce your hearing and do it by fiat." Well, I didn't know. But they did and they were right. I made the public announcement and the witnesses and news media came. For three days, it was the only political publicity game in an almost politically vacant town, making the front pages of the *Washington Post* and the *Washington Star*. And it was the lead story on the leading television stations.

Those who were abandoned at birth began their lives at a public hospital and lived there for six months. Thereafter they were, well . . . the best word is "inmates" at that cold and harsh institution some four hundred meters from the Potomac River. Witnesses testified that six-year-old children were marched military-style to their meals at mess halls. In the various barracks, children were even deprived of reliable parental figures because the custodians exchanged shifts and assignments. I believe it fair to say that the city was shocked. Within a very few years, the complex was abandoned.

The Church of the Redeemer had a better idea: group foster homes. The congregation had long since been operating their own. And they worked beautifully because there was a new twist. Not only did the church arrange for foster parents, usually widows, but also volunteer foster *uncles and aunts* who did what real aunts and uncles do. They took the kids on weekends to pleasant events such as the movies, the circus and playgrounds. Inevitably they took the children into their hearts.

The seventeen hundred kids who were liberated from Junior Village began much better lives in group homes. While naturally there were problems with the new system, the change was stunningly and positively dramatic. When enough time had passed for the 1970 group of little ones to become adults, one of them came to see me. He had become a talented and popular television reporter for a prominent Baltimore station. He thanked me. Made me a mite misty. It is a gift from God when you can contribute much by sacrificing little. Here's to my friend Jed Johnson, Jr., and the Reverend Fred Taylor. The former died in the early nineties, and the latter is still working hard at God's agenda as of this writing [1999].

When those of us who had toiled in that direction finally managed to pass a law that gave the American citizens in the District of Columbia the kind of representation the American citizens in Guam had, a nonvoting delegate in the U.S. House, a spirited campaign for the position ensued in Washington.

There were several candidates for the post, the three most prominent of whom were Cliff Alexander, Reverend Walter Fauntroy, and the fabulously colorful Julius Hobson. All three were of African descent. Most of the West-of-Rock-Creek-Park population—which was also most of the population of European descent in the District of Columbia—supported the very handsome Alexander. So did most of my coworkers in our Congressional office. I preferred to watch the campaign before choosing to whom I would send my modest contribution. Hobson was the firebrand whose performance was a joy to behold and initially I was inclined toward him.

Witness the TV debate among the contenders:

FAUNTROY: When Martin Luther King was here—
HOBSON (interrupting): What's he got to do with our contest?
FAUNTROY (trying to respond): Well, I was just saying, when Martin Luther King—
HOBSON (still interrupting): He's dead; let him rest.

Prior to the D.C. election, Fauntroy, lieutenant of the martyred Martin Luther King, joined Reverend Ralph David Abernathy in bringing a huge group to Congress to present a petition. The petition requested a national holiday to honor Dr. King. The several hundred petitioners had walked several miles to the Capitol, but Abernathy arrived in a chauffeured limousine. As they began to ascend the west steps of the Capitol, the petitioners were informed by the police that vice president Agnew had decided they couldn't.

At the top of the steps, I was part of the congressional delegation formed to receive the petition. It was a cold day for which I was insufficiently dressed. As I shivered with Senators Bayh of Indiana and Stevenson of Illinois, and two other representatives, negotiations were begun to see if the vice president would deign to change his mind. "I have an idea," I told my colleagues. "If Mohammed is not allowed to come to the mountain, let us, the mountain, go to Mohammed—at the foot of the steps."

"Can't do that, Andy. It's a matter of principle."

"No," I said. "It's a matter of temperature."

Eventually, the right of the People "to petition their government" was upheld. Dr. Abernathy and his post-limo followers mounted the steps along with the national press corps, including the TV networks. The crush of the crowd was welcome to me; it carried with it a warming trend.

As fishing-pole microphones were extended to where we stood at the center of the gathering, my colleagues, by turns, made their poetic speeches of acceptance and support. When they finished, I figured we could all repair to shelter. Not so. "It's your turn," Senator Bayh said to me. "I pass; let's go," I responded. "Andy, it would be an insult for you not to say something." Why argue? I turned to the reverend, whose nose was almost touching mine and said, "Dr. Abernathy, your petition is decent; it is reasonable and it surely ought to become law, but we'll try to get it passed anyway."

Abernathy obviously was baffled by the joke. He stared blankly at me. Not so, the fellow standing next to him. Fauntroy burst out in delightful laughter. I mailed a one hundred dollar check to his campaign the next day. My coworkers and I had chosen different candidates for D.C. delegate. Mine won.

The language of congressional floor proceedings is sometimes arcane. For example, since no one is allowed to say anything bad about another member on the record, strange terms of opprobrium have been invented, e.g., "I hold the gentleman in minimum high regard." Then there was the favorite of John J. Rooney from New York. When someone he didn't like was speaking and a murmur of conversation could be heard in the Chamber, Rooney would rise and say, "Mr. Speaker, I make a point of order that the House is not in order—*nobody is listening to the man.*" Then there were the exculpatory words of members when they callously imposed on the time and needs of their colleagues. The great, warm and wonderful Morris K. Udall of Arizona and I undertook the writing of *A Glossary of Congressional Cliches,* in which we gave English translations that explained what members *really* meant by some of the oft-heard banalities.

Two examples: "Mr. Speaker, I realize the hour is late." Translation: *My plane home isn't until tomorrow.*

"Mr. Speaker, I shall not use my entire five minutes." Translation (five minutes later): *Mr. Speaker, I ask unanimous consent to proceed for an additional five minutes.*

On the subject of strange communication, it's hard to beat the story about NBC's legal correspondent, Carl Stern. President Nixon had nominated two people in a row for a vacancy on the Supreme Court, both of whom Senator Birch Bayh opposed and both of whom were rejected by the U.S. Senate. When the second was rejected, some of us Northern Democrats on the Judiciary Committee were asked by Chairman Emanuel Celler to join him in signing a letter to the President endorsing Dick Poff of Virginia, a Republican member of the committee.

Dick was a brilliant and fully fair-minded legal scholar. There was one fly in his ointment, though; he had a bad civil rights voting record. But it was amply clear to those of us who knew him that he, in the manner of William Fulbright of Arkansas, was forced to that record by what Chairman Celler called the "political imperative" of his constituency. I, myself, had not the slightest doubt that Dick would be another Justice Hugo Black who, before his service on the Supreme Court, had been a member of the *Ku Klux Klan*. Black turned out to be one of the great civil rights Supreme Court Justices. Everybody knew that sooner or later, Nixon was going to get a Southern Republican Supreme Court Justice. So I welcomed the opportunity to endorse one I was sure we could count for decency, once released from that "political imperative." I signed the letter and NBC called on me for an interview.

Mr. Stern arrived with a crew and a camera with a huge lens. While the crew was setting up, Mr. Stern solemnly explained to me that "this interview is network." And I said, "Yes, I think I have that." But he pressed on. "This isn't local TV; you'll have to be concise."

"Right," I replied, "I promise to do my very, if humble, best." It was getting bizarre. Obviously, Mr. Stern had been spending a lot of time with senators accustomed to the unlimited debate rules the "upper body." Word discipline is the taken for granted in the U.S. House with its five-minute and one-minute rules. In those days, however, people like Mr. Stern seldom dealt with House members.

The crew was ready and the star—Stern, not I—was in place. Action: "Congressman Jacobs, why did you and nine other Northern Democrats endorse Southern Representative Richard Poff for the Supreme Court?" That was certainly a concise question. "We said we don't agree with his civil rights voting record," I answered. "But that we expect just the opposite from him on the Supreme bench. We said his legal acumen and scholarship are excellent and they are. Therefore we think he would be an excellent associate justice."

Mr. Stern was startled and I thought I saw an impish smile creep across the lips of the cameraman. With the cameras still rolling, Stern asked, "Is that it?" And I said, "I hope it was concise enough."

"Well," said the star as he used his hand to quaff his hair, "I wanted to get a two shot." That meant a good shot of himself for the viewers. So we did the same question and answer again . . . and again and again at least five times, each with a different camera angle on Mr. Stern. At the time there was a spaghetti sauce advertisement running frequently on TV. It showed a man taking a couple of big bites and exclaiming, "Mama mia, that's a good spaghetti sauce." The ad showed him doing it over and over at the director's direction, each time downing two huge gulps of the food. At last, they had the perfect *take* and the actor heaved a sigh. But the oven door fell open and, exasperated, the director said, "No, let's break for lunch." The actor looked ill. Cute ad. And it came in handy.

At last, Mr. Stern seemed happy with the way the camera was pointing at him so he asked the question once more and I blurted out, "Mama mia, that's a good spaghetti sauce." The crew broke up; Mr. Stern did not. He asked his question once more and, being completely bored with my oft-repeated answer, I said essentially the same with different words. That was the one they put on the air. His meticulous work with me finished, Stern said to no one in particular, "If I'm not at the White House in twenty minutes, it's going to be my fanny." At which I said, "Hold it; I think I understand the difference between network and local TV now. Back home I'm sure the local guys would have said, 'My ass.'" The network crew and I got along pretty well.

The Nixon administration, as all administrations, liked to make Supreme Court appointments that would shape the court in its own image. Eisenhower, to his later expressed regret, had appointed Earl Warren. Johnson had placed his close friend Abe Fortas on the high bench only to see him resign in disgrace. Bush would have to work hard to be proud of his Clarence Thomas appointment which I suspect he would not have made, had he known he was going to lose the '92 presidential election, anyway. Lincoln appointed to the Court his Secretary of the Treasury, Salmon P. Chase, who promptly participated in declaring unconstitutional federal issuance of the Greenback currency. As Lincoln's Secretary of the Treasury, the very same Chase had been the one who issued the paper money to pay for the Civil War.

Of course, in order for a president to make an appointment to the Court, there has to be a vacancy. And at one point the Nixon administration concocted a tawdry scheme of trumped-up charges to create one. The target was Associate Justice William O. Douglas, who, by the early 1970s, had served for decades. Franklin Roosevelt had appointed him.

Douglas had written a scholarly article which his literary agent had agreed to publish in various periodicals, one of which was a dirty magazine. All evidence indicated Douglas knew nothing about it in advance. The justice had also made a speech for some foundation that may or may not have had one shady contributor. There was no reason to suppose he knew anything about the organization's contributors. But these formed the flimsy basis for a dark innuendo of White House origin. The smear came in the form of a speech typed out by the President's people for delivery on the floor of the House by Nixon's best friend in Congress and eventual White House successor, Gerald R. Ford. It seemed to me that Jerry Ford was as innocent about the conspiracy as Douglas was of the bogus charges. Somehow the White House convinced Ford that, though on its face the speech made no actual allegation of an impeachable offense, there was good reason to deliver it. So Ford arranged for one hour to speak during Special Orders which take place after the real business of the House is concluded. Another hour was reserved for Ford's ally, Louis C. Wyman of New Hampshire.

There was much White House hype and dutiful news coverage about the impending attack on Douglas. And the more I read about it, the more I came to suspect the attackers were not sincere. For one thing, Ford's speech did not propose impeachment; it proposed a select committee to be created for the sole purpose of holding hearings around the country to determine *if* Douglas should be impeached by the House. They knew they didn't have any offense at all, let alone an impeachable one. It was clear to me that their scheme was to conduct a chautauqua and extensively trumpet the disingenuous suggestion that somehow the justice had done something wrong. They apparently thought that the harangue would hound the elderly jurist off the bench. Nice guys.

The plot against the justice offended my sense of justice and I decided to parry the White House thrust with a plan of my own. Any member of the House can file a resolution of impeachment. And if a resolution were already filed to impeach Douglas, there could hardly be any case for spending hundreds of thousands of taxpayers' dollars on an alleged effort to decide whether one should be filed. Filing an out-and-*out* impeachment resolution was obviously a countermove the White House had not thought of. So I did it, but not without a flourish that was bound to be fun.

When Jerry Ford's and Louie Wyman's Special Order came up, I was there and half way through Jerry's speech, I asked him to yield. He declined. Several minutes later, I asked again and he declined again. Someone made a point of order that a quorum was not present and during the forty-minute role call, I approached Jerry Ford in the well to remind him that not long before, during the Special Order on Vietnam, I yielded to him repeatedly, sometimes at mid-syllable. Yes, he said, he remembered and he would ask Representative Wyman to yield to me during the second hour which was, by then, at hand.

A representative need not have been recognized in floor debate in order to introduce a resolution of impeachment. She or he need only walk into the Chamber while a session is in progress and drop it into the proverbial hopper. The only reason I asked Ford and Wyman to yield time to me was to announce that I was about to introduce an impeachment resolution. Therefore, they need not trouble the House further with their speeches. Wyman yielded to me and this is what I said:

"The gentleman from Michigan has implied serious questions about Associate Justice William O. Douglas, questions to which I do not know the answers. But now that they have been publicly hinted, the public is entitled to answers. Therefore, if the gentleman from Michigan believes his strongly implied allegations, he has a duty to introduce a resolution of impeachment. Since the gentleman from Michigan declines to do so, I shall now introduce that resolution for him."

Wyman, shaken at the adverse turn of events, stammered out the utterly irrelevant assertion: "I did not yield for that purpose . . ."

I strolled over to the "hopper" and dropped in my resolution, thus bursting the belligerent trial-balloon. Two interesting things followed.

The next edition of the *Washington Post* reported that "Jacobs, a friend of William O. Douglas, introduced the resolution." I phoned the paper immediately to point out a substantial error. I asked the writer what made him think I was a friend of Douglas and he said he just assumed it. I assured him that he had assumed wrong. I had never even so much as met the justice and as it happened I strongly disagreed with his extreme interpretation of the First Amendment free speech provision. Under Douglas' view, a person could ruin another with libel and the victim would have no legal remedy. The *Post* ran a correction the next day. It is a sad commentary on our slow progress toward civilization that so many reporters automatically think there must be a selfish motive for anything anyone does. I think most people follow the Sermon on the Mount: "Blessed are they who thirst for justice." Even for an adversary.

The other thing that evolved from my adventure with the White House by way of Ford and Wyman was my chance encounter the following morning with Representative John B. Anderson of Illinois, whom I warmly admired. He handed me a memorandum signed by a staff worker in his office. It began by saying, "Andy Jacobs has pulled a coup on Jerry Ford." It was signed with a name I did not recognize at the time, but a name everyone came to recognize during the Reagan years, David Stockman. He and I became good friends and teamed up on some significant legislation when he became a member of Congress, himself.

I liked Jerry Ford because he seemed pleasant most of the time. But he could be unintentionally amusing, too. The White House speech repeated the name, "Justice Douglas" too many times for Ford. It became a tongue twister for him and before we knew it, Ford was miscuing by saying, "Dustless Jugless." Make your own jokes. Then there was that occasion on Lincoln Day, 1967, when Jerry told a banquet, "If Abraham Lincoln were alive today, he'd roll over in his grave." My favorite, though, occurred on the eve of the 1970 Congressional elections.

Democratic Speaker John McCormack entertained a motion to adjourn the House mid-afternoon several weeks before the fall election. The reason was reported in the *Washington Post* the following morning. As was traditional, albeit usually in the evening after Congress had adjourned for the day, President Nixon had held a one-by-one campaign picture-taking session with himself and Republican members of the House. But he couldn't get them all on just one day. So the same thing happened under the auspices of the same generous Democratic Speaker the next day. This time, though, that lovable rascal from Ohio, Charlie Vanik, was waiting. For sheer poker-faced, desert-dry wit, Charlie was an even better actor than Dan Flood of Pennsylvania. Vanik invariably wore a black suit and black bow tie at work, moving me once to say to the proprietor of the cloakroom lunch counter where Charlie was standing, "Ray, I knew you were doing well, but I didn't realize you had your own maître d'."

So here came the *Washington Post* predicting a unanimous consent request to adjourn at mid-afternoon for a second day in a row. By chance, that very week President Nixon had criticized the House for falling behind in its work. Charlie, tongue about to break through his cheek, reserved the right to object to the unanimous consent request and asked a question:

"Mr. Speaker, we have so much work to do, why in the world are we adjourning so early?"

Jerry Ford, the Republican Leader, took the bait and spoke up:

"Well, if the gentleman will yield, some Republican members are going to a White House reception given by the President *of the United States*."

Those last four words sounded as though they had been pushed through long-stemmed, pennanted trumpets.

Charlie inquired further:

"Well, let me see. Didn't we drop everything and adjourn early yesterday, too? What was that all about?"

Jerry rose to the occasion once more:

"Well, yesterday some Republican members went to the White House to attend a reception given by the President *of the United States*."

Same President, same United States, same trumpets. Now I asked Charlie to yield. He did and I addressed Jerry:

"Reception. Is it a reception or a campaign picture-taking session with the President—what my father calls the sheep dip?"

Ford was clearly shocked, even you might say flabbergasted. He stared at me in obvious disbelief, which puzzled everyone else present. After all, Charlie and I were just doing some good-natured teasing. I walked back to the office, still curious when the phone rang and I was told a wire-service reporter was on line two. I assumed he was just making sure how to spell my back-bencher name. As we chatted, I asked if he had spoken to Mr. Ford and he had. So I asked if he had any idea why Jerry looked so nonplussed when I kidded him about the *sheep dip*. "Oh," said the reporter, "that's easy. Mr. Ford thought you were saying something scatological. He didn't know what *sheep dip* means."

The next day on my way into the Capitol, I heard Paul Harvey's radio newscast; he reported the floor exchange between Jerry and me, adding, in the manner of his future "Rest of the Story" feature:

> Oh, for those of you who don't know what a *sheep dip* is: It's what they do to sheep in Montana . . . [the Paul Harvey pause] just before they're sheared.

Nineteen-seventy turned out to be just what Paul Harvey thought it would be, a bad year for Republican candidates; they got sheared. Things would be quite different just two years later.

chapter 8

MAPPED OUT

MUST ONE COMPROMISE to remain in public office? Sometimes, yes. But *must* one remain in public office? Good question.

Nineteen seventy-two was an especially memorable year in American history—mine, too.

I was given the choice that year between winning at a prohibitive moral price or just losing. So in a way, the correct way, there really wasn't much of a choice at all. In good conscience, I had to choose to lose.

At first blush, the matter seemed routine enough. The Nixon administration sent a request to Congress for sixty-five new federal judgeships. The request was referred to the House judiciary Committee of which I was a member. Then it was passed down to a Judiciary subcommittee of which I was not a member. The subcommittee had a caseload formula by which it judged the need for additional judges. Seventeen of the sixty-five requested fell short of the caseload mark of necessity and the subcommittee recommended that those seventeen be dropped.

One of the seventeen judgeships was a proposed trial court for the Southern District of Indiana. Up to that point, I hadn't even heard about the situation, but the subcommittee chairman approached me to say that the judgeship for Indiana was not warranted by need. On the other hand, he was willing to put it back into the bill if I wished since I was a member of the full Judiciary Committee. My answer was succinct; I had more taxpayers in my district than lawyers who wanted to be a federal judge. Fine, Indiana would, quite rightly, not gain the unnecessary judgeship. I gave it no further thought until the front page of the *Indianapolis Star* carried a story with the picture of an Indiana federal district judge, looking awesomely official, dressed in his black shroud.

According to the story, I, a former police officer, was soft on crime because I opposed a "desperately needed new Federal bench for Indiana." The story was zany, especially in a paper that claimed to be against government waste. Clearly the *desperately needed* new federal spending wasn't needed at all. And, for that matter, federal courts had next to nothing to do with the kind of crime implied in the story. Those courts took up rare kidnappings and occasional bank robberies as well as some so-called white collar crimes. But, by far, most of the administration of criminal justice was the responsibility of the states.

So what was going on? It didn't take long for me to find out. Congressman Bill Bray, my Republican colleague from Indiana who was like a father to me when I arrived in Congress, brought me a message from the Republican powers that were in Indiana. That message was succinct: Either get that new judge job for them or lose *my* Congressional job. They controlled the state legislature and it was time to draw the new Congressional map. *Gerrymander* was their weapon of choice. With the mandatory straight-party lever in Indianapolis, the lines of the district in which I lived could be drawn to cause certain defeat for me in a Republican presidential landslide year, which 1972 was shaping up to be. Kindly Bill Bray told me they weren't kidding. As a loving friend, he urged me to avoid the threatened political disaster for myself which, neither one of us realized at the time, would eventually prove to be one for him also.

"What in the world is all the fuss, Bill?" I asked. "Andy, they have a patronage problem in Indianapolis. They have a man they want to place." I smiled and remembered the speech vice presidential candidate Alben William Barkley had given at the 1948 Democratic National Convention. One of the GOP complaints about President Truman was that his administration was laced with waste in the form of *bureaucrats*. Then-Senator Barkley belted out this telling line with his delightful Kentucky accent:

"What is a *bureaucrat*? A *bureaucrat* is a Democrat who holds a job some Republican wants."

I didn't press our friendship by mentioning Barkley to Bill Bray. Other friends joined in beseeching me to cut the deal, but I told them I thought *pork* could be habit-forming, and after all, I had recently become a vegetarian anyway. I thought I was courageous; my mom said I was stubborn.

It was true; I had dropped meat from my diet the year before. And it was working wonders with some startling surprises.

I suppose most little children had problems with killing the live turkeys their parents often brought home for Thanksgivings when I was growing up. The birds would languish in backyard cages until their last appeals—voiced by the kids—were denied. But most of us got over it and went on to be carnivores. I did. In fact, I had a lot of trouble with the Pope each Friday when meat was *verboten* at our Catholic dinner table. We all heard the stories about how dinosaurs died out because they were not meat eaters, not knowing that many were meat eaters and not noticing that the likes of Clydesdales were still happily clopping along. We were told time and again that meat was indispensable to human health, the only adequate source of protein, by which was meant the right combination of amino acids. My favorite quotation on the subject was from writer Kin Hubbard's Abe Martin:

"Most vegetarians I ever seen looked enough like what they et to be classified as cannibals."

But in 1970 I changed my mind, partly because I began to listen to myself. As a metaphor in my speeches about government officials who sat in safety and comfort while arranging for tens of thousands of their constituents to be needlessly slaughtered on far-flung battlegrounds, my peroration was, "Many eat meat, but few go down to the slaughterhouse." And one day it dawned on me that the concept, taken literally, was troubling. Then I read a news story about the comedian Dick Gregory, who explained why he had become a vegetarian.

Gregory reported his wife and he had been on a freedom march in Mississippi when a so-called peace officer had thrown Ms. Gregory to the pavement and viciously kicked her in the solar plexus. Later, when Gregory was in a hotel in San Francisco, he "got to thinking. Did I fail to take action to defend my wife because I'm nonviolent or because I'm a coward? And if it wasn't because I'm a coward, then why do I participate in a system that brutalizes beings weaker than I?"

That pretty much did it for me. I was already somewhat spiritually worn out by our slow progress in ending our country's Vietnam foolishness and the torrent of attacks on my loyalty because I had the effrontery to call the emperor a streaker. And somehow I sensed the peace of a better conscience if I would stop my dietary and financial participation in the animal slaughter industry. So I did stop, cold turkey. For ninety days I found the change pretty rough, but then it felt as though I had slipped into a serene and effortless orbit. The craving was gone. There was not the slightest chance that I would ever eat meat, including fish and fowl, again. I did continue eating eggs and dairy products for a while. But within a few years I gave those items up as well, having learned that with a diet which excludes animals and animal products and includes green, leafy vegetables in general and broccoli in particular, it would be rather difficult not to get enough protein. But before I learned that, I believed the wives' tales about the indispensability of animal flesh for a healthful human diet. Therefore, at the outset, I expected that I would become anemic as a consequence of my new regimen. Not so. In fact, just the opposite of so. I got a very pleasant surprise.

Far from suffering diminution in my health, I experienced stunning improvement. A slight sinus condition that had bothered me from birth went away altogether. At eighteen, I had strained to do thirty-five consecutive push-ups in the Marine Corps; now at thirty-eight I was doing forty-five and going higher. Eventually, at the age of sixty, it was eighty-one and on a few occasions—about three of them—even a hundred and one.

Had I simply bothered to read some serious literature on the subject, I would have known in the first place that when the Nazis, by appropriation for their army, forced Norway into a vegetarian diet, the good health statistics in that country soared. In fact, the Norwegians are the leading researchers on the non-meat diet. One of their studies involved top athletes who were divided into control and experimental groups. The first ate the porterhouse steaks many of us had at football training tables. The second group followed the vegetarian diet. After a few months the two groups competed athletically. Of course I probably wouldn't be telling about it if the veggie group had not prevailed signally. They did. The control group had to spend a significant part of their energies trying to digest the steaks.

Look at the carnivores in the animal world and look at the vegetarians. The carnivores have the short intestines and vegetarians have long intestines. The reason is fairly obvious: In order to avoid the carcinogen meat often becomes as it lingers and decays, nature passes it quickly through the intestines of carnivores. Humans have long intestines in which meat lingers dangerously. The Japanese had essentially no cancer of the lower tract until we got back at them for Pearl Harbor by sending hamburgers to their country, following which they joined our culture in the cancer ward. We have something else in common with our vegetarian animal friends, mostly flat teeth. Our bodies know what we need, even if our minds continue the caveperson tradition. Think about this: People will pour down their throats the animal grease they will not pour down their kitchen sinks. Moreover, most of the food that will "stick to your ribs" will also stick to your intestines and arteries. Meat eating is a diet of death and not just for the animals.

In 1972, I received a postcard from someone in Gary, Indiana. He was not a constituent, but he was concise:

Dear Congressman Jacobs:
   You are an incompetent jerk.
   Sincerely,

My reply:

Dear Sir:
   Thank you for the kind compliment. Naturally I should dread being competent at being a jerk.
   Sincerely,
      P.S. Just in case you did not intend to compliment me, you, sir, are an incompetent name-caller.

One of the services expected of a congressional office is arranging White House tours for constituents. Sometimes they cannot be arranged because according to the White House tour office, the place is too crowded on a requested day. But there is an exception to the rejection. If the representative or senator will accompany the constituents, a tour will be granted anyway. Now, just how one more person on a tour would make the White House less crowded, I'm afraid I can't say.

In 1976, when they were competing for the Republican presidential nomination, future President Ronald Reagan accused then-President Gerald Ford of using the White House to entertain uncommitted convention delegates. It led to a well-publicized intramural fuss. In the middle of all that, my coworkers had me on a Ford White House tour. When our group finished entering the Green Room, the Secret Service guide said, "This is the Green Room; President Ford entertained the Prime Minister of Ireland here last week. Can anyone guess why?" I'm afraid I had to respond to the question with a question, "Was he an uncommitted delegate?" The difference between the Ford White House and the Nixon White House was underscored when the Secret Service agent broke up laughing; everyone else, too. Ford was not a Democrat, but "Happy Days (were there) Again."

Representative Morris K. Udall was among the wittiest members of Congress—ever. But he was so much in demand that it was not possible to get his actual participation in a 1972 Democratic Study Group assignment given to him, Representative James Symington, and me. That assignment was to write a gridiron satire for the first—and as it turned out, last—DSG Annual Gridiron Dinner. My acceptance was conditional. I would participate only if it would be a true gridiron, which meant that it must include both a Democratic and a Republican keynote speaker. And I had just the right Republican for the job, Representative Edward J. Derwinski of South Holland, Illinois. The DSG agreed; Ed was invited and accepted.

Now came the writing of the skits. Mo never did show. And Jim Symington mainly contributed the skill he had learned in his previous federal job as chief of protocol at the State Department; he wielded the blue pencil of censorship on the finished script. Listed among the credits published in the event's programs were the writers:

> **Roles Played by Writers**
> James .... major
> Andrew .... major
> Morris .... minor

The people who actually wrote the gridiron were my lifelong friend and coworker Louie Mahern, who later became an Indiana State Senator, and I. We set a basic ground rule: the show must be as irreverent as possible and none of the skits could exceed ninety seconds. It was a musical, rehearsed by the participating members of Congress roughly once—very roughly. And, of course, the skits were performed pretty roughly, too.

The show began with our friendly antagonists, Jim Symington the Democrat and Ed Derwinski the Republican. In a good-natured reference to long-before discredited McCarthyism smears against Democrats when Communist clubs were known as *cells,* Ed began by saying, "This is about as nice a cell meeting as I could imagine." By the time he finished, he had them rolling in the proverbial aisles. Then it was my turn to introduce the various skits. But before doing so, I had a word for Ed: "I've always heard that Republicans are not honest. And Ed you just proved it; you came in here and stole the show." Ed Derwinski was a delight.

Our first skit was about the two House nags or gadflies or, oh well, obstructionists. They were H. R. Gross of Iowa and Durward G. Hall, M.D., of Missouri. They were like the sundance twins, always sitting together during House sessions, taking turns raising dilatory objections that sometimes made the evenings late, indeed. You couldn't help liking them, but they were a handful. The skit made reference to our friend John V. Tunney, son of the boxer who, you may recall, critiqued the impromptu Birch Bayh "Indiana" art show for me. John's manner was elegant. As our congressional professional actors, Abner Mikva of Illinois and Tom Reese of Hollywood, danced out onto the stage dressed as H. R. Gross and Doc Hall, Doc addressed his sidekick thus: "H. R.—by the way, may I call you 'H'?—Well anyway, we're getting nowhere fast." Ab's H. R. replied, "Mr. Speaker, reserving the right to object, isn't that exactly where we want to get, Doc? Then the song began to the tune of "Side by Side":

> *Oh, we ain't got the class of John Tunney.*
>   *Maybe we're ragged and funny.*
> *But we'll gouge and we'll goad,*
>   *Blocking the road,*
> *Snide by snide.*

There was one skit on the emerging problem of Watergate. The trial of the actual burglars had just concluded with the Nixon administration's prosecutor's gratuitous assurance to the jury that that was it, no higher-ups involved. Our "Answer Man" skit starred Representative Jim Corman of California. A voice heard over the public address system said, "Why did the Nixon administration prosecutor say, 'I assure you that no higher-ups were involved in the burglary.'" The Answer Man's answer was, "He who prosecutes himself has a fool for a defendant." That pretty much summed up the case for the soon-to-be-enacted Independent Counsel, law which has not always worked so well, itself.

Our first foray into show business attracted no urgent telegrams from Hollywood. Louie decided we would not give up our daytime jobs. The politicians in Indianapolis, who wanted the pork of an unnecessary federal judgeship, had decided we would give up our daytime jobs. The gerrymander had already been put in place. At that point, with the Nixon landslide election of 1972 and the straight-party voting machine lever looming, it was hard to see any way for me to avoid defeat. But on election night, things did not go as well for the pork-barrel people as they had planned. That, however, would not happen for several months. In the meantime, there was more Congress in store.

On January 6, 1972, I received a letter from the mayor of Indianapolis, Richard G. Lugar. So did my coworker, Bud Myers—*the same form letter.* The first paragraph read:

> It is my pleasure to host a dinner on the evening of Monday, January 17, 1972, in honor of the Hoosiers in Washington, D.C. who have assisted the City of Indianapolis during the past year. I am especially

grateful for the support and aid you have given Indiana and Indianapolis during 1971.

It was nice of him.

That same year there was a bill before Congress to set national time zones. By its provisions, Indiana became something of a hybrid. Some argued that our state was being two-timed. And indeed it was. When the bill reached the House Rules Committee, I had the honor and mostly pleasure of being there. Representative William M. Colmer of Pascagoula, Mississippi, was the Chairman and Representative Ray J. Madden of Gary, Indiana, was next in line. They were not alike. Ray was a study in carefree living with loads of laughs. Bill wasn't. During the Rules Committee hearing on the time bill, Ray asked no question; instead, he went to the heart of the issue:

> Out in Indianapolis the other day, a fellow walked into the bus station and asked what time the bus left for Lafayette. "Ten o'clock," said the clerk. "And what time does it get there?" the visitor inquired. "Ten o'clock," came the answer. The stranger asked again, "What time did you say that bus leaves?"
>
> "Ten o'clock."
>
> "And what time did you say it gets to Lafayette?"
>
> "Ten o'clock," the clerk assured. Then the stranger walked away from the counter and the clerk called out to him, "Say, do you want to buy a ticket to Lafayette?"
>
> "No, I don't," replied the other, "but would you mind if I stayed around and watched that bus take off?"

The room roared, except for Bill Colmer, who buried his face in one of his massive hands as he rapped the gavel.

In 1982, the Indiana Democrats sponsored a dinner to honor the one hundredth anniversary of Franklin Roosevelt's birth. And who else but Ray was the right person to headline the event? I was given the privilege of introducing him and at the beginning of the meal I asked Ray how old he was. Quite clearly, he said, "Ninety-one." So in the introduction, I made a small joke about his large collection of years. But when Ray began his oration, he corrected me: "I don't know why Andy said I'm ninety-one; I'm eighty-nine." I found that puzzling until I later learned that he had taken an interest in the youngster seated next to him, a lady of about seventy. Not unlike others from time to time in politics, Ray decided to shave a couple of years. But he didn't do it for politics. It was a higher calling—nature's.

My proposed constitutional amendments averaged one per decade during my service in Congress. One dealt with the Sixth Amendment, one dealt with debt, and one dealt with the Fifth Amendment. In the case of the Fifth, my proposal consisted of four words. In the case of the Sixth, it consisted of two. The Fifth Amendment would have been changed to read that no person "shall be compelled in any criminal case to be a witness against himself, *except in open court.*" The Sixth would have been changed to read that, "In all criminal prosecutions, the accused shall enjoy the right to be informed of the nature and cause *and evidence* of the accusation."

That, of course, was heresy to most of the legal profession. But obviously I think it makes sense. The proposed change in the Sixth Amendment is uncomplicated. It simply would require prosecuting authorities to tell their defendants what they have on them, no tricks, no games. In the manner of the Equal Rights Amendment, case law and court rules in the administration of criminal justice have evolved in such a way as to make that part of my proposal *almost* unnecessary.

But my proposal regarding the Fifth Amendment would long remain controversial. We all know the principle by heart. Just as we automatically recognize and accept and often violate the maxim that a person "is innocent until proven guilty" ("until" is pretty much a presumption, itself. The maxim should be "is innocent *unless proved* guilty—better logic and better grammar). We can regurgitate by rote the rule that a defendant in a criminal case should not "be required to testify against himself." But defendants all over our country are required to testify against themselves all the time. To be sure, those defendants are subjects of civil actions, not criminal. But therein lies the nub of my reasoning which was my jurist father's reasoning as well.

As introduced in the first Congress, the Fifth Amendment proposal of the right of a defendant not to testify applied both to criminal and civil trials. But before Congress adopted the Fifth Amendment, and sent it along with the other nine for state ratification, the Fifth Amendment right not to testify was, itself, amended to exclude application to civil trials. Why? Because the evil against which the provision was proposed was the *Starr Chamber* in which, to borrow the phrase quoted earlier from *Captain from Castile,* "no one was too innocent to be proved guilty." The rack and the thumbscrew come to mind. The police had custody of, and complete control over the defendant in jail. Therefore the police had the physical ability, not the moral or even legal right, but the physical ability to force confessions. The First Congress cognized that such tactics could not be a threat in civil cases since the police would not have brought the charges and would not have civil defendants in custody. The defendants would simply go to court each day from their lodgings and therefore did not require the right not to testify in their own trials.

Had those representatives and senators thought further—there is no indication that they did—it might well have occurred to them that even in criminal cases the police do not have the cloistered control of defendants in open court that they have in their jails. The evil the Fifth Amendment was intended to prevent simply does not exist in open court. Just as plaintiffs in civil suits cannot apply thumbscrews to testifying defendants, prosecutors could not do so to defendants in open criminal courts. "Where were you on the night of October 5?" or "What is your name?" or even "Do you know where the body is buried?" are not unreasonable questions for any defendant in any open court. Of course, the general rules of evidence, including relevance, should continue to apply.

Since my "heresy" was referred to the Judiciary Committee, an all-lawyer committee at the time, it never even came up for a hearing in open committee. Perhaps, through public hearings, some future Congress will stop to think the matter through. Perhaps.

The months of 1972 rolled on into the presidential campaign summer as Richard Nixon and George McGovern received the Republican and Democratic nominations, respectively. Richard Nixon, the man who had talked America out of saying Red China and into the notion that wage and price controls would work and that he had the authority to impose them, had a commanding lead over McGovern. For a second time, Nixon even convinced the public that he had a plan for "peace with honor" in Vietnam. According to Nixon, it wasn't McGovern, but Nixon, who was the peace candidate. Nice trick. And, with that mandatory straight-party lever in Indianapolis and the computerized gerrymander against me, my prospects were not bright.

I can't think of a better person to be the beneficiary of the political punishment that was directed against me than Bill Hudnut. Ours was not a friendship that survived two Congressional election contests; we did not know each other before them. Our friendship, a close one, evolved from those two campaigns. Bill was utterly decent throughout the campaign of 1972, though honestly misinformed on one item. A few days before the election, Bill told students at the Indiana University School of Law in Indianapolis that he had "serious philosophical objection" to George McGovern's and my "positions favoring amnesty for Vietnam draft dodgers and deserters." He was right about McGovern's position, but badly mistaken about mine. I did not favor the war, nor amnesty for anyone who violated the law in connection with it. I was a former law enforcement officer; I favored following the law, all of the law. Still am and still do.

As has been said earlier in this work, I very much like and admire Senator Richard Lugar. But I must tell about an amusing event involving Dick when he was mayor of Indianapolis in 1972 and had handpicked Bill Hudnut in the spring to be the Republican nominee for Congress in Indianapolis.

A few days before the fall election, then-Mayor Lugar held a joint news conference with Bill to endorse him (again) for Congress. In that conference, Dick, with a tad of political hyperbole, said he could "think of no instance where Jacobs has represented the interests of the city." Somehow that reminded me of the nice D.C. dinner invitation Dick had sent me only a few months earlier, in which he wrote:

> I am especially grateful for the support and aid you have given Indiana and Indianapolis during 1971.

Could you have resisted the temptation to turn copies of that letter over to the news media a couple of hours after Dick's news conference? I couldn't.

That evening, the major television news programs carried Dick's campaign statement about my failure to do anything for Indianapolis. Then each anchor used the same transitional word before quoting from Dick's letter to me: "However." Pretty funny. The very next day, there was some dessert. Dick and I wound up side by side with silver shovels to help break ground for the new federal building a couple of blocks north of the old one. As each of us lifted a shovel full of dirt, I said to Dick, "Some of the news people here just asked me if I thought you really meant what you said in that letter to me. Guess what I told them?" Dick smiled a pleasant smile and asked, "What?"

"I told them that I thought you meant that just as much as you meant what you said yesterday." He smiled more broadly. Sometimes, in haste, politics can make people say things that they don't really mean.

The new federal building in Indianapolis evoked two more interesting stories. Up until the advent of uplink satellites and the Reagan administration repeal of the Fairness Doctrine for broadcasters, I was asked several times a week to do TV interviews in Washington for use by the three main stations in Indianapolis. I never declined, believing as I did that such interviews were part of my job, especially since I considered it a waste of literally tens of thousands of tax dollars per mailing to send out so-called congressional newsletters which were generally—there were exceptions—badly disguised campaign brochures.

My favorite interviewer was Carl Coleman, the stringer for Channel 6 in Indianapolis. One day when I was badly overscheduled already, he called and asked me to meet him in the Capitol Radio and TV gallery. It was a burden, but I dutifully went to the gallery. Carl was standing next to an easel with what appeared to be an artist's drawing of an office building, replete with little scrubs of trees and strolling ladies whose legs had no feet; they just withered to points touching pretty walkways.

The interview began with, "Congressman Jacobs, what do you think about the new federal building?" It was the first time Carl had ever failed to ask me about a legislative or foreign policy issue. I couldn't believe he called me all the way over to the Capitol for this. So I decided to be difficult. If there are two things TV interviewers don't like, they are long-winded and *short*-winded responses. The one wastes tape and the other is insufficiently dramatic. To tease Carl, I chose the second anathema. Pointing to the easel, I asked, "Is that it?" Grinning off camera at the suddenly reversed interview, he said yes. To which I responded, "It's okay by me." Actually, I thought it was ugly. Carl pressed our game of cat and mouse. "Well, what do you think about the design?" I said, "We must remember that the purpose of such a structure is to turn water and contain heat and air conditioning. And, if this one is put up in a workman-like manner, I suppose it will accomplish that." With a demeanor somewhere between waning amusement and slight exasperation, Carl tried again. "What do you think about its appearance?" The interview reversed once more. "You mean the aesthetics?" I inquired. "Yes," he allowed. "Well," said I with finality, "you should bear in mind that I'm a mere representative. If you want anything that cultured, you'll have to ask a senator." Evidently, Carl warmed to the idea because he did some more work on the "story."

My mother told me that when she saw the item on the news that evening, I was not the only member of Congress in the piece. Carl followed my suggestion; he did ask a senator, Vance Hartke of Indiana. In fact the very next image on the screen after I proposed a more esoteric source was Vance saying, "Magnificent edifice; it will change the entire skyline of Indianapolis." He was right; the A & W Root beer stand that stood there before was more attractive than the monstrosity that so savagely sullies the skyline of my hometown.

The second story concerns the architect's building material specifications which called for precast composition concrete and limestone chips to be used as siding. Just as its labor union had not modernized over the years, the southern Indiana limestone industry was somewhat stuck in a past era; it was still specializing in the old stone slabs. Even though the front end of the building resembles nothing so much as the back end of the saddest of tenements, it wouldn't have been quite so bad had the General Services Administration simply complied with the architect's specifications. But an Indiana member of Congress interceded for the limestone people. He persuaded the GSA to use the out-of-date slabs. When Senator Birch Bayh and I got wind of the shenanigans, we demanded that the architect's specifications be honored and the GSA officials told us they were pleased to have some congressional support for what they wanted to do in the first place, namely avoid a "concise impropriety." Having straightened things out, Birch and I went on to other duties. But the other member didn't; he doubled back and pled again for the change and when the building went up it had the bleak stone slab siding. Moral: schemers work long hours on their schemes and only seem to give up when you're looking.

In an absurd attempt to soften the assault on propriety, the GSA commissioned someone in New York to *paint* the stone siding. That was the coup de grace. Years later when the paint mercifully faded, the GSA proposed returning to the scene of the grime and doing the same terrible paint job all over. That's the focus of the second story. In 1996, I wrote the following letter to the acting administrator of the GSA, David Barram:

> Since you had nothing to do with the paint on this federal building, I shall write plainly about it. The paint job makes vandalism look graceful. Most Indianapolitans who have talked to me about it agree that it is an ugly reflection of the most unfortunate and extreme aspects of what some people alleged to be art in the '60s. It is grossly grotesque. By comparison, it makes psychedelic seem serene; it makes schlock seem gorgeous. When my eyes were first assaulted by it, I assumed it was an accident. No one—not even a seasoned vandal—could have done this atrocity on purpose. It looks as if a paint truck took that corner too fast. Through the years, as I have driven down Pennsylvania Street past [the building], my hand has instinctively turned the sun visor to my left.

The letter caused a stir, but not an immediate change. Indianapolis Channel 13 interviewed the proverbial people in the street on the subject. It was gratifying to learn that everyone in the survey seemed to agree with me. I met Al Hunt, the greatly gifted *Wall Street Journal* writer, for the first time in 1972 when he was part of the national press corps that accompanied Senator Ted Kennedy to Indianapolis to campaign for Senator George McGovern. When I ran into Al a couple of years later, he told me that while in Indianapolis, he was surprised by my demeanor in the face of all but certain gerrymandered defeat. It's true that I didn't view the matter as the end of the world. Political death, be not proud.

There was one aspect of election night, 1972 that surprised me—the closeness of the outcome. In the early evening, the Republican County Chairman said on TV, "We're in trouble in the Eleventh," which was the Indianapolis District at the time. The suburban Republican vote is usually reported to the public before the city Democratic vote comes in. And I was doing well enough in the suburbs to win the election even if the city voter turnout were at its absolute minimum. But it wasn't; it was substantially below that minimum. George McGovern lost that Eleventh District by seventy thousand votes. Matthew E. Welsh, who had served honorably and popularly as governor of Indiana four years before and, because of a constitutional provision, could not run again until 1972, lost the Eleventh by thirty-three thousand. I lost by forty-seven hundred. As it turned out, I could have won in spite of the gerrymander or I could have won in spite of the Nixon landslide, but I couldn't win in spite of both.

As I faced the cameras and a loving throng of sad supporters that night, I made my concession to Bill Hudnut in these words:

> When I spoke to my family by phone a few minutes ago, my youngest nephew, Greg, asked me if I were going to make my "confession" now. And I told him I didn't think I'd go quite that far.
>
> But the time has come for me to offer my congratulations to Bill Hudnut; and I do so, warmly. He is a decent person of whom Indianapolis will always be proud.
>
> As for me, shed no tears. It ill-behooves one whose cup runneth over to complain simply because there isn't still more.

The premise that there was not still more was not prophetic.

In going through my father's papers after tobacco killed him, I found this letter addressed to my four nephews:

> To Tommy, Marty, Danny & Greg
>
> My dear grandsons:
>
> It pained me to see your hurt over the defeat of your Uncle Andy. But this incident is useful in building your character, because all of us

must be tempered in some sorrow, else we are unable to cope with life's realities.

When your uncle said it ill behooves one whose cup runneth over, to cry because there is not more, he meant that, among other things, political preferment and the applause of the multitude were as nothing compared to the love of his loved ones for him and his love for them. His record is a proud one which brings only honor and pride to those who love him.

Every person I met today had the highest praise for him. This gladdens our heart, but most important is the power of the hurt in your hearts to remind you of the real values of life. The highest of these being love and honor.

I write you with deep love and respect. Each of you has brought me great joy and respect as did my children of the generation preceding yours.

Love, Grandpa

To my nephews, my father was "Geed." He wrote many letters to them and a particularly touching one to me toward the end of my year of living dangerously as a infantry Marine in Korean war combat. Here in part is what he wrote on my first post-teenage birthday:

My dear son:

Well, it was twenty years ago. I was just past twenty-six by two days. I thought I was quite mature. When Dr. Whitehead said, "It's a boy," I knew I was. You brought great promise into your mother's and my life. Sometimes I forgot how badly we wanted you, or rather at times it slipped my mind in all the fuss and bother of things. The pressure of keeping in sight of the Joneses and the frustration of not knowing whether we were rearing you properly, whether we were being too strict or not strict enough. And I recall with so much pleasure the many times you cuddled in my lap. And I wish that I could look back and say that I couldn't remember a time when I was ever unkind or unfair with you, but I can't. But I did always love you even when I was so human that I was somewhat inhuman.

The years went by so quickly and the war broke out. At first it did not occur to me that you were already in the Marine Reserves and might be called. I had not yet become reconciled to the fact that my little boy was a man, albeit a man of eighteen. When your outfit was called up, I was in Washington and you called me from six hundred miles away in Indianapolis. And I could tell from the tone of your voice (nothing you said) that you were alarmed and I recall how I wanted to take you in my arms, but you were so far away and I knew you were going much farther. Then it seemed that I was sure to lose you. Then came your leave to come home for Christmas and I saw you fly away and I thought that I might never see you again. I had no immediate worry for the two weeks we did not hear from you during your sad voyage across the Pacific.

Then came the battles and I heard from your battalion five days before we heard from you. I knew it had been cut to pieces, but I couldn't bear to tell your mother.

Then, here is a peculiar thing: when we heard from you after your first battle, I began to have hope for the first time. It seemed that I had had a baptism of fire myself. They say a combat infantryman can take it better after the first engagement. Well I was always anxious—still am a little—but I was able to be a bit less tense.

Well, son, I just sat down on your birthday and started to play on the keyboard of my little typewriter and reminisce about what we had together and perhaps what we missed, and to say that no one in the world ever wanted so much for someone else in the world to have a happy birthday and a happy life as I want for you. And no one in the world was ever more grateful that God spared what was so precious to him.

Love, Dad

Oh, my Papa . . .

chapter 9

INTERLUDE

IN EARLY JANUARY 1973 I picked up the ringing phone and heard the voice say, "Andy?"

"Yes, Bill," I answered. The caller said, "How did you know who I am?"

"Because," I said, "you're my congressman." It was United States Representative William H. Hudnut III, of Indiana's Eleventh District, not yet in office a whole week. He called me to see if I would sign some papers which would speed up the organization of the new congressional office and of course I would and did. We had a pleasant visit and he was off to perform the duties of the office. I was off—and in a financial position—to do pretty much what I wanted to do for the first time in eight years. In the paraphrase of Adlai Stevenson, "To the victor belongs the toils." And the thing I wanted to do was read. The congressional job required an enormous amount of reading, but not the sort over which I was smacking my lips now. I had plenty of time to read what I chose, mostly history and especially historical biographies—some physical science, too.

It was a dream come true. Beginning in the morning, I would read uninterrupted until hunger nudged me. Then I would have the two sandwiches that constituted my one meal a day and plunge back into the kingdom of letters until shadows fell across the room. At that point, it was time to go out and run a wide arc through the neighborhood. Most of the push-ups and weight lifting were for early in the morning, although I repeated about half the early routine after the running in the evening. I did teach one day a week at Indiana University-Purdue University Indianapolis (IUPUI). And I was technically "dabbling" in law at Jim Beatty's law firm where I was of *counsel*. I had some social life, such as dinner out with a ladyfriend on days when I skipped the two midday sandwiches. But most of the time it was reading *far from the madding crowd* and taking care of the Great Dane, C-Five, and his son, U-Two. Discipline with them was easy; I would say, "C-Five, sit," and to the other dog, "You, too."

The reason I was in a financially fortunate position was a case of "bread on the water." In 1968 my dad tried for months to rent or sell a building he owned in a dilapidated part of downtown Indianapolis. He thought the property would be developed someday, maybe ten or twenty years later. If and when that happened, the building would certainly jump in value. The property tax was very low at the time and Dad could easily take it in his fiscal stride, but the investment was getting on his nerves more each day and he wanted it off his hands. He offered it at the price he had paid a few years before, which wasn't much. But there were no takers. Believing that it was about time I did some investing for the future and believing that my dad needed some peace of mind, I bought it.

As soon as I became the owner of the building and it was no longer Dad's worry, he went right to work and within weeks found tenants for all the nearly one hundred linear feet of street-front store rooms. The income was more than enough to pay down the mortgage and it was time for me to indulge in the pleasure of replacing my two-year-old Oldsmobile with a spiffy new one. So I didn't; instead of payments on a new car, I kept the old car and doubled my payments on the building. By 1972, the mortgage was paid off and I had fee simple title. After taxes, insurance, and maintenance, the income was mine. But the situation got better.

Neil Alig was a principal stockholder and vice-president of Indiana National Bank. He and his friend Andy Steffen, pleasant and effective legislative vice president for the phone company, went to Washington once a year and threw an Indiana-oriented party. I got to know and like them both and even attended their parties without partaking in the repast. One evening in 1972 and in Washington, I received a call from Neil who said he was vacationing in Florida. Now, Neil and I were friends, but we were not calling-from-vacation friends. Therefore I assumed it somehow must be a business call, perhaps something about Neil's view on banking legislation. It wasn't about legislation.

Neil told me the bank would like to buy my building. *Hmmm*, I thought to myself, *what's up or, more likely, what—such as the value—is going up?* He didn't say what, if anything, was going up in the sense of a new building, but he did say the bank was prepared to double my money. That sounded very much like a first offer to me and this is where the movie *Giant* came in handy. In the scene where the wealthy landowner offers what looks like a good price to Jett Rink for a few acres of Texas land, Jett declines, saying, "I think I'll just gamble along with it."

Now, just as I had borrowed a line from the movie *Elmer Gantry* when I answered the lady who called the religious radio station, I borrowed from

Jett Rink's line: "No, Neil, I really don't want to sell my building; I think *I'll just gamble along with it.*" The matter did not end there. Neil said he thought he could persuade the bank to triple my money. By then, of course, I *knew* something was going up. So I said, "Neil, I really don't know much about downtown real estate. Tell you what, when you get home, why don't you talk to my dad about it?" There was a pause. Then Neil said, "Andy, don't do that to us." I told him I was afraid I had to. My dad was no pushover.

When Dad was summoned to represent me in the negotiation, it was the bank president who sat across the table from him. They quickly agreed on a long-term *net* lease based on *five* times what I had paid for the property. That meant the bank would pay all the property taxes and other expenses and I would get a monthly *net* rent check.

By chance, the bank president was President Nixon's Indiana campaign finance chairman. And one of the things presidents try to do is avoid inflation.

Without inflation, cost-of-living adjustments are not costly. Now that the rent for my ground had been decided, my father casually added, "We'll have to have periodic cost-of-living adjustments."

"No," said the president, "that just isn't done in long-term land leases."

"Well," said Dad, "it will have to be done in this one."

"All right," said the banker, who knew perfectly well that the bank could not put up its new "Gold Building"—it is literally gold colored—without my ground. "Andy will just have to keep his property and we'll keep our *money*."

"Fine with us," my dad said casually has he got up and walked toward the door. "Andy likes that building. He likes going upstairs and looking at those nineteenth-century hotel rooms. The beds, bureaus, and wash basins are still there. Might make a good movie location sometime."

My dad told me his hand didn't quite reach the doorknob before—as Dad expected—the bank president continued to negotiate. "Well, Andy [my dad], be reasonable." Dad returned to the table, sat down quietly and spoke so quietly as to sound confidential, "What's the matter? No faith in Nixon?" The bank president decided to demonstrate his faith in the President; a cost-of-living clause was included in the long-term rental contract. It was a nice stroke by Dad for me. It saved me from the ravages of inflation during the 1970s. *Oh, my Papa.* The deal not only benefited me financially, but, as we shall see, it was a godsend in 1981 when I participated in a U.S. House Ways and Means Committee hearing on President Reagan's first tax proposal.

In assessing my financial situation when I left Congress, Dad said, "Son, you're in a pear tree," adding, in his typically poetic way, "now you'll be on one of the lower limbs." Financial independence does not necessarily mean opulence. I was well off, not because I had so much, but because I wanted so little—I drove my 1966 Oldsmobile, the Red Rover for fourteen years and 240,000 miles. My next Olds was a 1980 Olds Omega which was still doing nicely twenty years later. We even had a twentieth birthday party for it. Friends brought some very imaginative gifts for the Red Rascal. I got the impression that Red's favorite was a decal from the production editor of the *Indianapolis Business Journal*, Tawn Parent, and her husband Steve Spicklemire. In shivering blue letters, it read "FEAR THIS." The secret to automobile longevity? Straight-weight oil, changed regularly. Multiple-viscosity oil gets very thin when the engine reaches operating temperatures—metal against metal wears out faster. Small wonder auto manufacturers recommend multiple-viscosity 10W40 or 50.

Two or three weeks after I officially became Bill Hudnut's constituent, a lady friend and I were having dinner at the Pleasant Pheasant Inn, whose owner, Milana Riggs, was a good friend. That evening, Milana was like the proverbial one-armed paper hanger: her dishwasher was absent and his work was piling up. The lady I was with readily agreed to my helping out while we awaited our meals, whereupon I donned the big rubber apron and attacked the dishes with scalding water. When waiters passed back and forth through the cafe doors, my noble effort could be seen by other patrons, leading one nice woman—according to Milana—to say to her friends, "I told you he couldn't do anything out of politics." Actually, I thought I did a good job on those dishes. Something even funnier happened at the Pleasant Pheasant a couple of years later.

At the time, I was dating the cousin of my friend and former congressional coworker, Bud Myers. She was of African descent. Joanie was, as lawyers say, "in words and figures," a very beautiful American Airlines flight attendant. Shortly after Joanie and I were seated at Milana's restaurant, a former Indiana Republican state party chairman and his wife were seated at the next table, only a couple of feet from us. I knew and liked him well. He and I were both Indianapolis lawyers. As the four of us conversed, I noticed that his wife had a strange expression on her face, hard to describe, but close to profoundly curious. She somewhat awkwardly began a line of questions addressed to Joanie. "Where are you from?" Joanie's answer: "Kentucky." I had not known that. "So am I; what part?" said the lawyer's wife. "Near Lexington," replied Joanie. "Same here. What town?" the examiner continued. I interrupted to say to my legal colleague, "One more answer and we'll have to file suit to quiet title to some real estate." The wife obviously was fishing for the superficiality of race. And she plodded on, "A lot of settlers in that part of the country intermarried with Indians." This, of course, was Joanie's cue to say she was not partly native American (I am). But she didn't. She simply said, "You're quite right." I'd give a gorgeous penny to have heard the after-dinner conversation between our friends as they drove home that night.

We met Paul Cantwell earlier; now we hear from him again, on the phone. Paul told me he had a problem and wanted some advice. By now, 1973, Paul was a city councilman and an adult student at IUPUI. At both places, he had managed to cause a stir. When the council voted on a proposal to have an opening prayer at each session, Paul cast the lone vote in opposition, saying to the news media, "It's a bunch of bull."

At IUPUI, the city councilman ran up a large number of parking tickets and arrived at his car one day just in time to see a campus police officer and a wrecker about to haul the vehicle away. That effort was thwarted when Paul jumped in his car and locked the doors.

Both incidents were duly and sensationally noted in the news. Typically, Paul seemed less embarrassed than flattered by the attention—until a local radio talk show host named David Letterman invited him to be a guest. Paul asked me what I thought he should say when his two sensations came up. Remembering Lincoln's probably apocryphal response to questions about General Grant's drinking, which was, "I'm going to find out what he drinks and send a case of it to each of my generals," I said to Paul, "On the prayer matter, tell them that the nuns at Saint Catherine's taught you that, according to the Book of Mathew, prayer is a very sacred and *private* thing. And you don't think it should be sullied by use as a sanctimonious political football.

"The incident at IUPUI is a little more complicated. You want to say that all you were doing was getting into the car to get the certificate of registration for the police officer. And when you got in, the automatic door locks jammed shut and you couldn't get out. You shudder to think of what would have happened if the car had veered off into White River; you probably would have drowned. In fact, the question reminds you to send a check to Ralph Nader."

Paul seemed happy at the prospect of saying those things and sadly disappointed when neither matter came up during the entire hour with Mr. Letterman.

In the summer of 1974, I was summoned once again by my friend Al Lowenstein to emcee the fund raiser for yet another of his attempts to go back to Congress. This time, however, the setting was rather more pleasant than that Manhattan artist's loft where I had come face to face with that latter-day Benedict Arnold, Alger Hiss. It was held in the home, nay, the castle, of Howard Samuelson, who, I was told, operated New York's off-track betting facilities. Situated on Long Island, the place was cavernous and the guests were resplendent. They included film actors and actresses and the owner of the *New Yorker* magazine. Kurt Vonnegut, Jr., was there, as well as assorted paragons of the peace and civil rights movements. And there was the beautiful and exquisitely talented Shana Alexander, noted writer and television sage. I enjoyed our conversation immensely. In fact, we chatted until the meeting was called to order and I was summoned to perform my master of ceremonies duties.

"I became aware of Al Lowenstein," I began, "by reading about him in the *Indianapolis Star*, where I got the distinct impression that he was a bomb thrower. But when I met him, I discovered that he was a veritable Spinoza, brilliant and pleasantly soft-spoken. When I heard Ron Dellems was coming to Congress, backed by the California Black Panthers, I was prepared to duck when I met him. Not necessary; polite and deferential, he was every inch a gentleman. Then I heard that Bella Abzug was disputatious and abrupt, but when I met her I discovered that she was disputatious and abrupt."

Despite the fact that in some ways Bella was beautiful and kind, what I said was true and the audience knew it was true. They laughed heartily.

When the formal part of the meeting was over, I returned to Ms. Alexander, who seemed to have had a turn of disposition. Indeed, she turned and walked away. No more enjoyable conversation. I confess I was puzzled and remained so for a couple of years. Then one day I picked up a copy of Shana Alexander's book, *The Talking Woman*. One of the early chapters was devoted to heartfelt adulation for Bella Abzug. At that moment, I mastered the meaning of that time-honored maxim, "Nobody ever lost an election because of a speech he didn't make." Actually, I was quite fond of Bella. She, along with Harry Truman, Barry Goldwater, and my dad, was like Popeye: "I yam what I yam."

After I left Congress to Bill Hudnut, I assumed I would never go back, just as I had assumed I would never go to Congress in the first place after losing my first try in 1962. Perhaps the possibility of another try, a rematch with Bill, did flicker in one of the remotest chambers of my mind. But the idea seemed unrealistic and not altogether desirable. The new drawing of the Eleventh District lines had turned it into what pundits called a Republican district. Moreover, Bill Hudnut was an extremely likeable person. He was clicking along very well as an incumbent. And as 1974 dawned, all bets would have to be on Bill. The person who first urged me to run again was the brilliant and soft-spoken Ted Boehm, who later served with distinction as a judge of the Indiana Supreme Court. It happened on a Washington Boulevard sidewalk just outside a meeting of the Senator Birch Bayh for Senator Committee. Ted gave several reasons why he thought I should run and he was persuasive. For several weeks thereafter, I considered the possibility as other friends urged me in that direction. I decided to try again.

The primary was a source of joy for me because my father was a fellow candidate, not for Congress—I would have lost—but for criminal court judge. We won our respective races and were on the Democratic ballot together in the fall. But in the spring our chances still were not convincing. True, there was the Watergate break-in, but most people, including me, still believed President Nixon was not involved in the scandal.

When the President resigned in August, prospects across the board seemed less bright for the GOP. But the Eleventh District of Indiana remained majority Republican. The factor that pushed things toward the Democrats was President Gerald Ford's pardon of his mentor, Richard Nixon, "for any crimes he might have committed."

My friend, the distinguished lawyer, Civil War historian, and author Alan Nolan, was kind enough to cut a tape to be used as a radio spot for me in the fall. His brother-in-law, Bill Fechtman, one of the best nose and throat surgeons anywhere, began referring to Al as having *dulcet tones.* Nevertheless, when Al had completed the recording, he said to me, "Now don't hesitate to tell me if this is less than what you want. I realize that for every light on Broadway, there are a thousand broken hearts." Somehow I don't quite believe it would have broken Al's heart if we had not bothered him in the first place; he was generous. The recording was beautiful; his tones *were* dulcet.

One of my friends in the advertising business, Sam Blandina, gave me an idea for a little TV ad in my campaign, little because it was short and also because it starred little people. One was the beautiful six-year-old red-haired daughter of Carlie and Don Anderson. The other was my youngest nephew, Gregory Welborn Landwerlen. In his case, it took some negotiation to get him on the set. This was the six-year-old nephew who had just talked my father out of a dollar and expressed his gratitude thus: "It's a pleasure to do business with you." Greg was a born salesman, later becoming very much in demand as a manager at various new car dealerships in Indianapolis. When I asked this six-year-old *personality plus* if he would help do the ad, his exact words to me were, "You mean I get so much each time it's shown? Well, we can talk about that later."

The ad was cute. It showed the children standing beside a chalkboard bearing the word, "gerrymander." The girl said, "*Gerrymander*: to divide into districts to give unfair advantage." The boy added, "That's what the politicians did to Andy Jacobs two years ago." The girl continued, "And the politicians won." The boy, with lower lip jutted forward and curled down in sadness, said, "Everybody else lost." Republican County Chairman Keith Bulen later told me that other Republicans had complained to him because he ran no ad in response. He said he told them, "The difference between Andy Jacobs and [name deleted] is that Andy Jacobs tells the truth." That Federal Judgeship patronage quest was important to him, but, in essence, Keith was frank enough to tell the truth about it.

There was one aspect of political campaigning which I did not enjoy in the least and did it only when I thought not doing so would hurt the feelings of loving friends and supporters. That aspect was what my dad called *the sheep dip*, standing at a shopping center or plant gate, mindlessly shaking one hand after another and mumbling something pleasant but essentially meaningless in terms of serious issues.

As mentioned earlier, I had an affection for the men and women of certain labor unions which were refreshing in their internal democratic practices. Prominent among them were the United Auto Workers officials— Dal Sells, Judy Pennington, Buford Holt, Elmer Blankenship, Ed Yates and Max Brydenthal to name only a few. Well, in the cold and rainy fall of 1974 some of them invited me to report at "o'dark-thirty" one morning to the plant gate at Chrysler's electrical plant in Indianapolis. With unhappy anticipation, I agreed and did appear at the appointed time and place. But the uniformed guard at the gate wasn't sure; he called the plant security chief who, in the absence of the plant manager, decided I should be ordered to leave. The brier patch into which the security chief tossed me was the dry warmth of the Waffle House restaurant directly across the street. There, enjoying pleasant conversation with the union fellows, I sipped what Kim has called my weird kind of "tea," just maple syrup in hot water. I couldn't help wondering if the union guys weren't just as happy as I to be in out of the cold rain.

There is a footnote to the plant gate incident. Several hours later, my campaign manager received a call from the plant manager who apologized for what he called the mistaken judgment of his security chief, adding that I was welcome anytime. Fortunately for me, there was no time left on my schedule that year. It wasn't that I did not enjoy visiting with the workers in settings where we *could* visit. I enjoyed that very much; it's just that waving a "high five" in the rain was a chore for me and likely an imposition on the person who was trying to punch in on time.

The first joint appearance Bill Hudnut and I made in the 1974 rematch was before a group which tended to favor my candidacy. During the meeting, Bill was peppered with accusatory questions about the Watergate scandal, a high stakes political burglary which involved the Nixon administration and eventually drove President Nixon from office. When the fourth question in a row was propounded to him, I touched his shoulder and asked if he would let me answer it. At that point he was more than willing to yield the floor. So I walked to the lectern and said, "In the early days of 1973 when Richard Nixon's kingdom, power, and glory were still absolutely intact, I saw Congressman Hudnut on television. He was asked if he thought White House personnel, who were dragging their feet, should be required to testify before the Senate Watergate Investigating Committee. His answer was a firm 'Yes, because if they don't, it will indicate they have something to hide.' I admired Congressman Hudnut for that answer then and I admire him for it now."

Years later, Bill's autobiography said that the Watergate scandal harmed his bid for re-election in 1974, adding that wherever he and I had a joint appearance, I used the tawdry affair against him. Precisely the reverse was true. I not only defended him from such absurd attacks in our first meeting together, but throughout the campaign.

Naturally I asked Bill about the stunningly untrue assertion and he told me that a woman at *Indiana University Press* had helped put the book together and obviously jumped to the conclusion that since many Democratic candidates were making such unfair charges against their Republican opponents, I must have done the same. I was reminded of the incident cited in William Somerset Maugham's autobiography, *The Summing Up*. He told of having dictated a manuscript and turning it over to an amanuensis with instructions to "make necessary corrections," which, of course, meant punctuation and the like. The work came back with cogent criticism—*of Somerset Maugham*—about style and meter. *Mad* magazine once ran the kind of silly "correction" an incompetent and envious high school English teacher would make of an essay written by a gifted student. The student *Mad*'s teacher assailed, however, was the Sixteenth President of The United States. The Gettysburg Address was torn gem from gem with marginal notes in red: "Too repetitious; bad parallelism, trite; 'four score,' too obscure, etc." Bill Hudnut had not caught the error before actual publication of his book.

Bill and I had a friendly debate on television just before election day 1974, shook hands and awaited history's respective summons and dismissal. No one would venture a guess as to which of us would receive which.

My friend Jim Beatty has always been the one to let me know by phone on election night whether the news for me is good or bad. On election night, 1974 his call was less than certain. The exact words were, "I can't put it in writing yet, but I think you have it." Hanging up, I continued to do my bachelor laundry Marine Corps style, by hand without a machine. Later that evening it became clear: Marion County was having one of its rare Democratic years. I was going back to Washington and Bill's political career was over—for *one* year, following which he would, for sixteen years, be the nationally known and, when it came to racial justice, courageous and celebrated Mayor of Indianapolis.

To quote again my friend Jim Beatty: "You never know on a given day whether you've won or lost in this life."

chapter 10

THE SECOND TIME: A LONG WAY AROUND

IN THE LATE 1960S a national magazine ran a story that analyzed tensions and strains surrounding the nonstop demands of congressional service. The piece ended with a "wistful" quotation from an anonymous member of the U.S. House: "If only there could be a sabbatical." That was the blessing in disguise in my case. A sabbatical means leaving and *coming back.* That rarely happens in the case of Congress for one of two reasons—three if you count dying in office. The first is that whoever takes your place is probably going to want to stay awhile and the second is that, if you do go back, you've lost whatever seniority you built up during previous service. You have to start the climb to greater authority all over again.

Reason number one applied in my case but, though he ran again, Bill Hudnut was hit by a political fate called Watergate. His loss had nothing to do with what he had done in office. Nonetheless, I did go back to Congress. As for the seniority loss, it applied to me, but as we shall see, not stringently.

As fate would have it, therefore, I did enjoy a rare congressional sabbatical. Jim Scheuer of New York and Abner Mikva of Illinois had the same good fortune. They lost their bids for re-election in 1972 and returned in 1975. There is an organization called "The Former Members of Congress." I suggested that Jim, Abner and I form a new club to be called The Former Former Members.

At the end of my "sabbatical," I made a public statement in Indianapolis. It included the Steinbeck quotation I mentioned earlier in this book:

Thomas Jefferson believed that elected officials should interrupt their

201

tenures from time to time and return to private life to refresh themselves for further public service.

I confess that my Jeffersonian sabbatical was not voluntary, but it happened all the same. And now I am, to paraphrase the words of Steinbeck, refreshed, renewed and ready to serve again.

Even though re-elected, I almost didn't serve again. Organization of the Ninety-fourth Congress occurred on the first Monday of December 1974. My trip to attend the preliminary meeting, therefore, was an official tax-paid one. A week or so after the election, I phoned TWA one evening to secure a reservation for the round trip. I would fly in on Sunday morning, get a good night's sleep, and attend the Monday meeting. The ticket agent told me that the Sunday morning flight was booked solid except for seats in first class. I hesitated because I was the author of thus-far unsuccessful legislation requiring members of Congress to fly coach unless seats there were unavailable, as they were in this case. So I went ahead and booked first class on that December Sunday morning flight.

Joking usually makes people feel better. Psychologists tell us, "He who laughs, lasts." And that's just what happened during my conversation with the ticket agent. It was a slow evening for both of us. So we struck up a friendly and humorous conversation. As we chatted, it occurred to me to ask, "By the way, do you have any coach seats on the night before?"

"Man," the agent said, "you could lie down sideways on that milk run."

"Well," I said. "It's the taxpayers' money and we're both taxpayers. How 'bout switching my reservation."

"Not a problem," he replied. That transaction was as fateful as any of the logic-defying deliverances that came my way during the eternal year of my Korean crucible.

When that December Saturday evening arrived, it brought significant snow to Indianapolis. My nephew Tom Landwerlen kindly drove me to the Indianapolis International Airport as snow piled up quickly on the pavement. I distinctly recall saying to him, "There's no need to risk our lives; just take it easy. If I miss this plane, there's probably a fair chance that I can still catch one in the morning. It'll cost more, but there's no reason to take chances."

Then an unusual thing happened; exactly at the intersection of the interstate outer loop and West Thirty-eighth Street, as a near blizzard continued behind us, there was no snow at all and the pavement was dry. It was amazing, as though the snow was walled off to our rear. Tom accelerated to the normal sixty miles per hour and we got to the plane just in time.

Mini cassette portable dictating machines were very new in those days, but I had already bought one and was using it on the flight to Washington to answer a stack of early congressional mail—Stevenson again: "To the victor belongs the toils." Among the letters was one from Galveston, Texas. Sue Brink, a friend from my previous Capitol Hill service, was planning to go back to Washington the following fall and wondered if she might work in our office. As I dictated the affirmative reply, my mind wandered for a moment to the previous first flight I had taken from private life to Washington and how apprehensive I was about flying. My dad had told me that on the new job, I'd just have to get over such thinking. And I believe I had by the time I came home in 1973. But now I had just the slightest tinge of the original feeling; planes were not completely immune to crashes. I had just dictated these words of encouragement to my friend, Sue: "You can count on the job in September." Then my mental excursion into the past prompted me to strike out the period and add, "as much as we can count on anything in this life."

The flight I decided not to take crashed into Weather Mountain the next morning, trying to land at Dulles International Airport. It had been diverted from Washington National because of a furious storm. Everyone on board, including three beloved friends of mine, perished in the pines, mud, rock, and jagged shreds of that disintegrated plane.

The black-box voice recorder revealed that, as the craft made its descent to land, the flight engineer glanced at the terrain chart and discovered the craft was below the prescribed elevation. His recorded voice said, "Hey, this dumb sheet [the nickname for the chart] says we're supposed to be at thirty-four hundred feet." The pilot frantically tried to pull up, but it was too late. Investigation revealed a misunderstanding between the pilot and the air traffic controller. When the controller said, "Cleared for landing," he meant no obstruction on the runway, but to the pilot it also meant normal descent.

The Monday morning *Washington Post* noted that two of my friends who had died worked, respectively, for Representative Barbara Jordan of Texas and Ron Dellems of California. Both members were of African descent. One had been my coworker in our congressional office when I left in 1973, a fact that was mentioned in the story as well. At the morning organizing meeting of the House, one of the remaining racist members approached me and, having read the story, asked, "Andy, your people in that crash—were they black?" Already numb and rubbery, I could not quite believe the man's insensitivity. How could anyone, even a person reared on racism, mention something so superficial at a time like that. I expressed no anger; I simply replied, "One of them was white, one yellow, and one both."

The husband, Jake Applewhite, was of European descent; the wife, Suzy Applewhite, was of Asian descent and their little four-year old boy, Bengy, was, of course, of both.

My friend Louie Mahern, who by then was an Indianapolis staffer for Senator Birch Bayh, had big ideas for me as I entered my new congressional incarnation; he thought I should be a candidate in the House Democratic Caucus for a seat on the Ways and Means Committee. My reply: "Come on, Lou, get real." His suggestion seemed far removed from reality. There were thirty-seven Democratic and Republican Members of that committee. Just about every member wanted a seat either there or on Appropriations, most prestigious. And I was a freshman representative all over again. Moreover, large states such as California, Texas, New York, Illinois, Florida, and Pennsylvania enjoyed multiple membership on Ways and Means. With thirty-seven seats and fifty states in the union and some states respectively having more than one seat, the chances for Indianapolis were imperceptible. Indeed, no Republican or Democratic representative from Indianapolis had ever before in the twentieth century been elected to the Ways and Means Committee. Add to this the fact that I had just lost my entire eight years of seniority and was hardly a favorite of the House leadership anyway, and you get some idea of the negative odds. Louie was dreaming. But his dream came true.

I *did* run for the seat in the Democratic caucus as did my friend Abner Mikva of Illinois and we both won. I've always suspected that the Democratic leaders did not oppose me because, during my two-year absence, they forgot what I was like, which was *like* independent.

I might have gone back to the Judiciary Committee where I was able to offend the Marion County Republican chairman enough to get myself gerrymandered out of Congress. But a freshman position on the Ways and Means Committee was generally viewed as more prestigious than my seniority on Judiciary would have been even if I had won the 1972 election. So, improbably, the cause of my loss of seniority during those two years out of Congress actually advanced me in some respects. The Lord works in strange ways, lots of blessings well disguised.

It seemed that the three puffs of white smoke had hardly risen from the smoke-filled caucus room where I was elected to Ways and Means, before the phone started ringing off the hook. Political action committees were calling to urge my acceptance of their contributions to my campaign committee. "What campaign?" I asked. "The election is over."

"Well," each said, "you can use the money to pay off your campaign debt."

"I don't have one," I'd reply. "Well, you could use it for your next campaign." They *really* wanted me to take that money. But I would decline again, saying marginally sincerely, "I don't know if I'll have a next campaign."

I had taken PAC contributions in the past without giving much thought to or getting much money from them, but this rush at me by almost every lobbyist in Washington was something new. It began to raise my consciousness. Obviously, it was an attempt to curry favor with a new member of the Ways and Means Committee. It was also obvious why; the Ways and Means Committee was increasingly the place to ripoff the public, the median of grab being tax loopholes which were easier to obscure than rigged government contracts to sell junk to the taxpayers. Tax loopholes steal from other taxpayers who must pay more themselves or see their children suffer greater national debt to make up for the influential people who get themselves out of paying their fair shares. It's difficult for six people to carry a piano, but it's especially difficult if two of the largest ones are riding on it.

For the next several weeks, I thought about PAC contributions almost constantly. By then, it was clear that I need only say one word in order to raise hundreds of thousands of dollars for a congressional campaign, and that word was "yes." But the connection between those contributions and a representative's committee assignment was no longer a matter of doubt in my mind. They were offered by every PAC because every PAC was interested in taxes one way or another. "But what about all that money knocking eagerly at your door?" a dark voice within me kept nagging. "You can have it for even less than the asking, just *the accepting*." But it wasn't just the accepting of money, it was the acceptance of the strings, ropes, and cables—attached to one's soul—that came with the money. Senator Bob Dole said it: "No (lobbyist) ever gave money to a congressional candidate's committee without expecting something in return." Something that belonged, not to the elected candidate, but to the constituency. The more I thought about the lobbyists' campaign money, the clearer it became that, attractive and legal as such money was, it was just plain wrong to accept anything of value from special pleaders at the national government.

My irrevocable decision was made one day just after I had cast a vote on the committee I judged to be in the public interest. I was headed to the Capitol in response to the bells announcing a floor vote. A lobbyist for an organization, which had made a two thousand dollar PAC contribution to my 1974 campaign, literally seized and started twisting my arm to reprove me for voting against his clients' interests. You could call it a post-vote twist.

In that precise instant, I made up my mind. Saul had been knocked from the horse to arise as Paul. Now, years after that lobby-paid dinner on that hungry night during my state legislature service and my waking the next day to swear off ever again accepting any personal gift from any lobbyist, it was clear to me that taking PAC campaign contributions was of the same cloth. I vowed never again to wear anything made of that cloth.

After a couple of elections without PACs, I was scheduled to meet with a lobbyist for a large international corporation. When he entered the congressional office, we shook hands, and he came out writing—a PAC check for five thousand dollars to my campaign committee. I was surprised because I thought that every lobbyist in town knew my policy on PACs. But he was not a lobbyist in town; he was based in Texas. So I politely explained that I did not accept such contributions and he politely put the check back into his inside coat pocket. And, without missing a beat, he politely proceeded to tell me how a recently passed federal tax law would unfairly sideswipe his company.

I listened carefully and said, "I think you're right. That was not the intent of the law. There'll be a *technical corrections bill* before Ways and Means in a few weeks and I'll offer an amendment to correct this situation. I doubt that there will be any opposition to it." Now it was the lobbyist's turn to be surprised, except that it was more like shocked. I don't believe his shoes touched the floor as he left. He obviously was having a hard time realizing that he could obtain simple justice from his government without crossing an official's palm with a substantial sum of silver.

It is wisely said that "who pays the fiddler calls the tune." If lobbyists pay the campaign fiddler, should anyone be surprised when they call the governmental tune? Why, at the close of the twentieth century, with general enlightenment about the horrible consequences of smoking tobacco, does anyone suppose the U.S. government continues to use the taxpayers' money to promote the production of the deadly weed?

For every Jessie Helms, there are ten or fifteen senators who do not come from tobacco states. In fact tobacco is a significant part of only a few states' economies. Why, then, would senators and representatives from regions which essentially do not grow tobacco cast votes to keep the tobacco subsidies going? Clearly, the answer is that there are cigarette packs and cigarette PACs (politcal action committees). The latter can grow anywhere. All that is needed is the sorted planting medium of soiled congressional representation.

Sometimes it's hard to say whether a particular PAC contribution is in the nature of bribery or extortion. There are cases where so-called powerful committee chairpeople—a contradiction in a democracy—have told lobbyists to pony up or be cut off from contact with the decision makers. The only reason the lobby money for members of Congress is not bribery or extortion is that Congress gets to say what bribery and extortion are. Where members of Congress have the authority to enact laws which inure to their own exclusive benefits, that which is legal is not necessarily right. Lobby money for congressional campaigns is wrong. And everybody who isn't in on it, knows it's wrong.

An old song says, "Nobody wins in a game of broken hearts"; some lobbies win at least temporarily at the game of PACs. But sooner or later, a bigger or more influential lobby comes along, as we shall see in the case of the American Medical Association and the petrochemical industry. If a special pleader has a case, as was the case with the lobbyist from Texas and his five thousand dollars, he or she should plead that case with civilized logic—unsweetened by cash, check, or money order.

Of course, in lieu of a good case, under existing law that should not exist, a lobbyist can always use cash, cash for the helpful members' campaigns which serve the members' deep personal desires to remain members. Too often, it works like this: In order to profit in the billions by polluting the taxpayers' air or saddling them with useless airplanes, the special pleader wants relevant regulations repealed, or unsavory appropriations passed. When successful, the organization, in turn, deducts a tiny portion of the loot, say two or three million dollars, and shares it in the form of campaign contributions with its special friends in Congress who were not overly scrupulous about the public trust. Let's look at it this way: What if it were legal for some wealthy person to pay local police officials to take away your property and give it to briber? It obviously is not legal to commit such an atrocity *directly*. But, in effect, on the doorstep of the twenty-first century, it remained legal to perpetrate that sort of outrage indirectly through the legislative process.

On closer examination, one must conclude that PACs don't so much buy elections as they buy elected officials. Most of the contributions go to influential incumbents who are all but certain to be reelected and don't need to spend much on their campaigns. But they like big campaign "war chests." The money can be used for TV ads necessary only for the egos of the incumbents. The cash also comes in handy for lavish non-election year fun parties in the name of vague campaigning for elections of the future. And never mind that the guests are personal friends of the incumbents who are certain to vote for the hosts anyway.

In essentially granting such organizations licenses to sack the public's lungs or pocketbooks or both, the miscreants in Congress echo a little-noticed and otherwise obsolete part of Article One, Section Eight of the U.S. Constitution, the authority to "grant Letters of Marque." That's what our Government did in early the days of our Republic. Letters of Marque were U.S. government conspiracies with pirates. Under the authority of our government, the cutthroats could sack foreign ships and pay to the United States Treasury a commission on the booty. The difference these days is that, instead of Letters of Marque to steal from foreigners, some faithless officials in our government, wittingly or unwittingly, help fiscal cutthroats make easy marks of our own citizens. And the white-collar cutthroats, in turn, pay the commissions, not to the U. S. Treasury, but to the officials in the form of free trips to the Caribbean to make dull speeches and in the form of campaign contributions.

Speaker Sam Rayburn, who was the mentor of Lyndon B. Johnson, one of the world's most notorious and acclaimed wheeler-dealers, was very much *not* a wheeler-dealer, himself. As was the case with my father and the kindly Congressman Bill Natcher of Kentucky, Rayburn, long before mid-century, refused money from any private interest while he served in Congress. We are told that on occasion, when he had been the guest speaker at a banquet and was offered a speaker's fee, he would angrily announce to all present, "I can't be bought!"

In 1972 a new law was enacted merely to restrict the amount of campaign spending so that one side could not drown out the other by lavish use of television. The measure was found unconstitutional by the Supreme Court which said the law violated the First Amendment freedom of speech provision. The legislation regulated no one's right to say whatever she or he chose, just how much could be spent to yell it louder and longer than anyone else. The law dealt with "conduct," not speech. In the case, *Buckley v. Valejo*, the court must have based its thinking on the familiar phrase, "money talks," and decided to pretend that *money* has the same First Amendment right to free speech that the Constitution, in reality, only gives to people. Indiana Governor Roger Branigan once told Earl Warren, "I took an oath to uphold whatever you have in your head." And Teddy Roosevelt had complained that whether a law was constitutional depended on "whether the fifth Justice comes down heads or tails."

In *Buckley*, the Court created a status it called "independent expenditures," which meant that a lavish Washington lobby, acting without talking directly to and coordinating with the opponent's campaign, could spend all it wishes to purge a member of Congress who cast votes for the public interest rather than for the lobby. The technique is not complicated.

The lobby, in essence, tells the member, "Sell out or we'll buy a ton of TV ads and tell your constituents that you sell out." In essence, the court handed down a Right to Buy decision. The subject of the court's ruling wasn't free speech, anyway. Free speech, in Jud Haggerty's phrase, means "thinking what you please and saying what you think," not a lobbyist-paid lopsided amplification of it. And that amplification was anything but *free* speech. It was very *expensive* speech. As we shall see, Representative Pete Stark and I were the first intended victims of a scorned, furious, and well-heeled Washington lobby which smacked its lips over this green light from the *gray brethren*.

Mad magazine had a feature called "Strangely Believe It," a spoof on Ripley's *Believe it or Not*. One edition told us, "Mrs. H. Q. had an odd array of pets: a rattle snake, a mongoose, and a rat. Oddly enough they got along very well and shared her equally." And so it is with the Valejo vultures who feast on the body politic.

The more I think about it, the firmer I believe that the British campaign system is the best. The taxpayers there buy blocks of television time and divide them equally among the candidates on the ballot. No money needs to change hands with the candidates' committees or the candidates. The latter simply report to the television stations and take their turns saying what, if anything, they stand for. The first to object to such a system in our country, of course, are the lobbies, followed closely by their congressional beneficiaries.

Here's how their argument goes: "Would you want to pay taxes for the dissemination of ideas with which you disagree?" My answer is, yes. Yes, yes, absolutely yes. I want to pay taxes for the opportunity to hear *all* the candidates, not just the ones who are cozy with lobbyists.

Then the defenders of the present corrupt system will fall back on name-calling jingoism, crying "more federal spending," which they "spend" all their working hours trying to promote for the benefits of their clients. I think it is fair to say that if the taxpayers put up three hundred million dollars every two years for the British system, they would save themselves two or three or even four times that amount in pork-barrel federal spending and pork-barrel federal tax loopholes.

Three hundred million dollars may be more than needed, anyway. My dad said that "the difference between a $30,000 congressional campaign and a $500,000 one is that, in the latter case, they'll find some way to waste $470,000." By the end of the twentieth century, it was not uncommon to see campaign spending in a single congressional district mounting up to several million dollars of influence buying. Consider this, too: Under the present system, the big campaign spender is likely to be the big government spender, because in both cases, she or he is spending *somebody else's* money. Again, "Who pays the fiddler calls the tune." If the public paid the fiddler, the public would come a lot closer to calling the government tune. Some things should not be for sale—our national parks, fully automatic machine guns and the souls of those we elect to serve *us*.

There is one other fall back position for the defenders of the corrupt lobbyist campaign finance system. *Disclosure*. If the source of the special interest money is disclosed, they argue, then each citizen will know about it and cast his or her vote accordingly on election day. What subterfuge.

What if it were legal for food processors to put cyanide in their products for public consumption as long as they made full public disclosure on the packages and in the back pages of newspapers? How many of us do you suppose would be left standing? It should be illegal to put cyanide in food and it should be illegal to put private money into public campaigns. In fact, it *is* illegal to put poison in food with or without disclosure. And it's already illegal for any private individual or organization to put money into the operation of a congressional office—the biggest rancher is not allowed to pay for the sheriff's gun except through the rancher's fair share of taxes. The sheriff should be no more beholden to one law-abiding citizen than to another. The same principle should apply to the selection of those we trust to make fair laws and proper expenditures from reasonable taxes. In a very real sense, the Medicare program did not first pass in 1965; it passed on election day 1964 when a majority of its supporters were elected to the Eighty-ninth Congress. Congressional nominations and elections are public institutions which should be paid for by the public, not bought by the highest bidders. When it comes to our government, "This land [should be] your land, this land [should be] my land." Under the corrupt system still in place at the dawn of the twenty-first century, that goal remained to be gained.

Even most of those who fancied themselves campaign finance reformers advocated only anemic steps in that direction. Under their proposals, the system of buying government favors was to remain in place. But lobbyists ought not be allowed to buy so much of the government. Few were proposing that lobbyists be allowed to buy none of it at all. Belgium philosopher Maurice Maeterlinck wrote:

> At the time of the Spanish Inquisition, the opinion of good sense and the good medium was certainly that people ought not to burn too

large a number of heretics; extreme and unreasonable opinion obviously demanded that they should burn none at all.

So the day may come when it will be just as outrageous for schemers to play jujitsu with our tax money unjustly to enrich themselves by paying commissions on their ill-gotten gains to the officials who sell us out, just as outrageous as to bribe Judges and police officers, or burn people at the steak because of the victims' religions.

"That's too idealistic," say the fainthearted reformers. "You can't get there from here. The Supreme Court has ruled that the First Amendment allows private interests legally to bribe [Congress gets to say what bribery is] members of Congress with campaign contributions. How can you get past that?" Well, it wouldn't take a people's armed revolution for the people to turn the government into one that is "of the people, by the people, and for the people." A simple constitutional amendment would do to explain to the Supreme Court that the First Amendment meant what it said in the first place. And if *the people* understood what the corrupt system costs *the people,* and demanded a constitutional amendment to stop the oppression, the theretofore defenders of the corruption would immediately switch positions and trample the theretofore fainthearted reformers to get credit for saving our country.

John B. Stoner, the sage 1950s head of the political science department at Indiana University, said it:

> Government is that means by which the strong will take what they would have taken anyway, and the weak can retire gracefully.

Which may be true. But in our nation, where each adult citizen has the vastly unexercised right to vote, "the strong" are those who understand the price they pay under the corrupt campaign system and go to the polls to send that system to the rubbish can in which it belongs and to which the Spanish Inquisition has long been consigned.

One more gasp from those who are in on the present outrage, "One way or another, legal or ill-legal, schemers will always be able to buy improper influence in Congress." Not so. Not even close to so. At present it is a prison-term felony to bribe a member of Congress by slipping her or him money to spruce up the office suite to which he or she in assigned. No matter how rich, just let someone try that. It would be, "Good evening, FBI, good morning, judge, and good evening, warden." *Of course,* white-collar felony laws can be enforced—much more easily than murder laws. And I don't hear anybody saying we should repeal murder laws simply because sometimes murderers aren't caught.

I should hasten to say that I do not condemn the members of Congress who accept PAC contributions as long as they are willing to cast votes to end the corrupt system in which they are bound up. I do disagree with those who say they can accept the lobbyists' money without being influenced by it. It is quite possible that many have convinced themselves, and therefore actually believe that they are not so influenced. But the subconscious mind is subtle; a person can be influenced almost without knowing it when the influence is brought about, not only by lobbyists' gifts in the past, but also and especially, by expectation of more such gifts in the future and fear that the money "narcotic" might be cut off.

Hydraulic exercise machines are supposed to emulate weightlifting, but they can help you fool yourself. The harder you push, the greater the simulated weight. Therefore, if you push with all your might and mane in the morning, you might well be pushing a hundred and fifty pounds. But if you push with all your might and mane at night after a long work day, you might think you're doing a hundred and fifty and actually be doing ninety-five pounds. The only way for the public to know and, for that matter, even the representative or senator to know for sure that lobby money for members of Congress is not an influence, is for there to be no lobby money for members of Congress.

The constitutional amendment and statute necessary to end this malignant and oppressive political practice should be adopted to end this lobby-money malignancy on the body politic. The cure is within the reach of the American people through the ballot box. We could cast our votes only for those candidates who will pass the amendment and statute to kill the corruption. If we as a nation ever do this, we shall be heeding the command of Isaiah to "undo the heavy burden and let the oppressed go free." After all, the "oppressed" are *we*.

By the time I attended my first meeting at the Ways and Means Committee, I had tried unsuccessfully for eight years to enact into law a very sensible suggestion given me by Marion County Circuit Court Judge John L. Niblack, a much admired friend of my dad. But now that I was a member of the committee, in a matter of minutes I got the judge's idea into a bill headed for certain enactment into law.

Judge Niblack told me the story of a young Gary, Indiana, steelworker who had fallen behind in his federal income tax obligation. The law allowed the Internal Revenue Service to take 100 percent of a delinquent's salary each week until the debt was settled. And that's exactly what the IRS was doing to the steelworker. Unable to feed his wife and children, he took a pistol and blew out his own brains. That would not have happened if the federal law had been like the Indiana law on garnishment. The Indiana law exempted enough of a garnishee's salary for him or her to meet minimal living expenses. I explained the matter to the committee—just as I had explained it many times before to the committee members when I, myself, was not on the committee. But this time the idea was adopted without even so much as taking a vote. The chairman simply asked if there was any objection, there wasn't, and my amendment was swiftly added to the bill. It has been federal law ever since. With regard to correcting a great wrong in the law, I was now in the right place, at the right time—at last.

C-Five, my beloved Great Dane who grew like a government contract, returned for a visit to Capitol Hill by popular demand in 1975. Three years before, he had bitten the hand of Congressman Jim Symington. C-Five never said why, but I had speculated at the time that it was a natural rivalry between two thoroughbreds. In consequence of his aggression, C-Five had been banished to the hinterland city of Indianapolis. During C-Five's exile in Indiana, people on Capitol Hill, especially the police, had missed him. As I resumed my commuting, C-Five remained in Indiana. But so many people in Washington wanted to know about him that my nephews—Tom, Mart, Dan and Greg—drove him to Washington in time for an office party in his honor one Friday after work. Our friend Al Hunt of the *Wall Street Journal* suggested that, in the manner of the recently resigned Richard Nixon, we should have a "photo opportunity" for the occasion. C-Five was such a publicity hound that no fewer than six television cameras attended.

When an uninvited guest arrived bearing the gift of cheese for C-Five, most eyes and all camera lenses were on the pair. It was the reunion I feared; Jim Symington had not been included on the guest list for his own safety. But he had faith in the cheese. Lo and behold, the mammoth accepted the favor, seemingly lovingly licking the fingers of the hand that fed him. This moved me, ham that I am, to turn to the bank of cameras and intone, "This is the millennium; if these two can compose their differences, there is hope in the Mideast." At that point I heard the most ferocious roar ever emitted outside a jungle or a zoo. The cheese aroma had wafted away. C-Five struck again. It was the same hand of the same man.

Former Representative and future lieutenant governor of Michigan Martha Griffiths put tongue in cheek and took pen in hand to send me a letter about the incident:

Dear Andy:

I represented my Michigan district in Congress for two decades. And never once was my picture on the front page of the *Detroit Free Press*. Yet, I picked up my paper this morning to find your picture there twice.

The best way to describe one of the pictures is the scene in the basement of the Dallas Police Station where Lee Harvey Oswald was killed by Jack Ruby. C-Five, whom I was firmly neck-tackling, had the expression of the fatally wounded Oswald. And Jim Symington, hands apprehensively lifted in front of his face, looked like the escorting detective with the Texas felt hat. The hand healed and C-Five moved to Indiana once more, but not before his furious picture appeared on the front page of the style section of the *Washington Post*, under the title, "Not Again, C-Five?" *The Miami Herald* ran an editorial cartoon depicting an angry-looking C-Five saying, "Politics had nothing to do with it. Didn't you ever meet a guy that just rubs you the wrong way?" Jim Symington was a prince about it. In fact, Jim Symington was a prince generally.

Among the stacks of mail that poured in following C-Five's indiscretion, was one from a Texan which read:

Dear Sir:
What this country needs least is damn politicians who take their damn dogs to the office [sic].
Sincerely,

My reply:

Dear Sir:
I believe you are in error.
What this country needs second least is damn politicians who take their damn dogs to their offices.
What this country needs least is you.
Arf,
P.S. Did you hear about the rich Texan who bought his dog a boy?

I liked that Texan; he threw in with me when he wrote the second time and said that when "Senator Lloyd Bentsen becomes President, we'll give you a job as speechwriter." Not a burning ambition of mine, but I appreciated the offer. Bentsen's presidency is still pending.

In the great American novelty called politics, watching the major parties swap sides on issues is choice sport.

For years the Republican Party championed the principle, if not the reality, of the balanced budget. Most Democrats scoffed at the Grand Old Party's fastidiousness on the subject. With the arrival of Reaganomics, however, Jack Kemp, a prominent member of the new Republican administration, informed the world that, "The GOP no longer worships at the altar of the balanced budget." And the Democrats began at least making vague noises of criticism about the mammoth borrowing the Reagan budget proposals ushered in.

The Democrats, under John F. Kennedy, introduced the lower tax rates on capital gains. Later, under Speaker Thomas Foley, the Democrats declared it to be a GOP plot to tilt the rates toward the rich.

In 1975, the congressional Democratic leadership proposed a huge tax cut, and the Republican president, Gerald R. Ford, strongly opposed it on the grounds that it would increase the national debt, thereby hurting the public more than helping it. I sided with the President and pointed out in my *minority views* attached to the Ways and Means Report that there was a national debt of six hundred billion dollars—it grew during ensuing years. I included the definition of "debt": "an obligation to repay." Government debt could also be defined as past budgets that either spent too much or taxed too little or a combination of both. The obligation, I urged, should be honored. The debt should be paid off and the compounding interest clock stopped before cutting the government's income. I added that elimination of special interest, pork-barrel spending would leave more of that income to pay the debt and end interest payments sooner. Then and only then should we make haste to give our country a real tax cut consisting of real, as distinguished from funny, money.

An *Indianapolis Star* editorial published December 10, 1975, under the title "Old-Fashioned Horse Sense," agreed with and commended me. By the early 1980s I had not changed my mind. I was still pressing for payment of the debt before tax cuts. But the GOP, and therefore the *Indianapolis Star* editorials, changed their minds. The Democratic leaders again made clucking sounds about changing their minds to embrace fiscal responsibility, but did a lot to help enact the tax cuts, anyway.

When the Democrats were the majority in Congress, they were all for the "previous question," a motion which barred debate and amendments to bills. I never cast my district's vote in favor of that autocratic tactic. And in those days, the Republicans in Congress complimented me highly for my fairness. But when the Republicans took over, they changed their minds and began using the "previous question" themselves, moving me facetiously to inquire of them why they stopped patting me on the back for opposing the oppression. At least they laughed. Members of both political parties seemed to be asking me if I didn't know that politics is a game of *who* is right, rather than *what* is right. I didn't; still don't.

My good and avuncular Hoosier friend and Republican colleague Bill Bray was defeated in 1974 in much the same way I was in 1972, by an opposition party landslide and a GOP gerrymander. The gerrymander that was directed against me had backfired just two years later. It gave Bill too many of my Democratic constituents and gave me too many of Bill's Republican constituents. All it took was a landslide for his party in 1972 to get me, and a landslide for my party in 1974 to get Bill. He therefore became a former high-ranking member of the Indiana delegation to Congress and dropped in to our Indianapolis congressional office occasionally to use the phone. I asked my coworkers not to treat Mr. Bray as though he were I, but to treat him with respect.

On a lovely summer's day in 1977, Bill called me. There was anxiety in his voice as he told me something stunningly hard to believe. His wife, the wonderful Esther Bray, had done the traditional honors when the keel for the new *USS Indianapolis* nuclear attack submarine was laid. Now, by tradition, it was time for her to bang the bottle against the bow at the launching of the vessel from General Electric's Electric Boat Division in Groton, Connecticut. But, Bill said, some Democratic members of the U.S. House had urged the new Democratic secretary of the navy to replace Esther with a Democratic woman.

It sounded too tacky to be true, but Bill assured me it was all too true. So I called the illustrious navy secretary, Gram Claytor, by chance, the commander of the first U.S. Navy ship to reach the sad site where the original *Indianapolis*, a navy cruiser, was sunk near the close of World War II. His ship picked up the survivors. Mr. Claytor was also celebrated for his success as president of Southern Railways. I told his assistant the nature of my call.

When Claytor picked up the phone, he hit the sound, well, gunning; "Congressman, I don't give a good [let's say] damn about politics. Since before John Paul Jones, the woman who has laid the keel has banged the bottle and commissions the ship. Besides, Congressman Bray served with great distinction as the Ranking Minority Member of the Armed Services Committee. And I'll be damned if I'll dishonor him and his lady." It was hard to believe that an old navy man would cuss so mildly.

I started to express my agreement, but the secretary continued to misunderstand my meaning and continued vehemently to lecture me: "I think this whole damn thing is pretty petty." As the salty World War II Navy hero drew a breath, I managed to wedge in, "Mr. Secretary, I agree with you. I only called to make sure Mrs. Bray would not be replaced."

"Oh," said the secretary, "that's different."

Mrs. Bray did slam the champagne for the shakedown cruise of the new *Indianapolis* and she led the celebration the following winter for the commissioning. By then, Claytor and I had become friends and he honored me with an invitation to be the speaker for the commissioning occasion. My speech from the deck of the ship—nuclear class submarines, unlike their "boat" predecessors, are called ships—was a great success because it lasted about forty-eight seconds; the wind chill off the ocean in Groton that day was somewhere around thirty-five degrees below zero Fahrenheit. Our good friend and dean of Hoosier broadcasters, Fred Heckman, was present. The American military never had a better friend than Fred, a World War II Navy veteran, himself.

Bill Bray always came by to see me whenever he was in Washington and he was always welcome. One day, however, he arrived when I had the proverbial burdens of a one-armed paper hanger—stacks of mail, stacks of phone calls, and other urgent demands. I hesitated. Of course, I would not ask my coworker to fib to Bill that I was not there, but I did think about stepping out into the reception area and telling him how covered-up I was. But I also thought about how kind he had always been to me, especially when I first went to Congress. So I asked him to come into the office I used. We talked for an hour and I'm glad we did because I never saw him again. Within the month he was gone forever.

In the early winter of the first year I was back in Congress, I was invited by the pretty and very smart Marlene Cimmons, writer for the *Los Angeles Times*, to participate in the first Washington Counter-Gridiron. It's amazing, but as late as 1975 female news reporters, though eligible for membership in the National Press Club, were not permitted to join that club's gridiron, an annual variety show of political satire.

So the women staged a gridiron of their own, replete with dozens of famous people who abhorred the stupidity of gender bias. For example, Tom Brokaw was the silver-tongued barker for the wheel of fortune. The well-known and eloquently outspoken *Washington Post* columnist Nicholas Von Hoffman and I were cast in "role reversal" roles—in the kissing booth. Instead of pretty women, they had the handsome Von Hoffman and the, well, me. Kisses that night were going for a dollar each and Nick had the first hour. When I went on duty, I put up my own sign next to the one designating the regular price. It was based on one of Frank Sinatra's hits and read:

> If somebody loves you, it's no good unless he loves you, all the way—
> *Ten Cents Extra.*

By and by, a famous woman walked up to my booth and ordered a kiss which I delivered as best I could. It was the facile Gloria Steinem. She said thank you and I couldn't have been more sincere when I said it was *my* pleasure, nor when I said, "That will be one dollar, please." In her lilting voice, she softly said, "I don't think so." That upset me because it meant either that one of my heroines was a deadbeat, or that my kiss failed its implied warranty. So after I got off duty and came face to face with Ms. Steinem in the swirls and eddies of the enormous crowd, I said to her, "Ms. Steinem, I am a lawyer and a former police officer. And I deem it my duty to tell you that what you did at the official kissing booth was larceny by trick." I paused because it occurred to me that technically I was the one whose assignment was to turn the trick. But I continued. "In essence, you stole that kiss and I insist that you give it back." Ms. Steinem's extensive vocabulary was not wasted on me as once again she said—I thought—with dreamy eyes, "I don't think so."

Now let's meet the honorable Millicent Findwick from New Jersey. Among all the new members of the House in 1975, Millicent would have to be listed as the most unusual. Born to landed gentry, she became a sales clerk in a department store during the Great Depression. Her genteel family still owned the real estate, but the rent stopped coming in when the economy collapsed. As the economy started coming back, so did the rents and Millicent was once again wealthy, wealthier really because she now knew how "both halves" lived. How could one be better prepared to represent all the constituents of a congressional district?

My first encounter with Millicent occurred when the new members and retreads posed for a group photograph on the east steps of the House. She stood out. Tall, slender, and beautiful were noticeable enough, but when she pulled out a pipe filled with tobacco, lit it, and began smoking, I realized the Ninety-fourth Congress was going to be unusually interesting.

Washington congressional offices are equipped with closed-circuit television signals from the respective chambers. It takes some practice, but it is possible for a representative to do office work and follow a floor debate simultaneously. The first time I heard Millicent speak, it was over the closed-circuit system. I thought I had accidentally touched a remote key that changed the channel to a daytime soap opera. Her diction and tones were so cultured as to sound precisely like those of a seasoned actress. And what she eventually said in her maiden speech made her sound like a seasoned debater. Her elegance misled one of the more primitive members. He walked right into Millicent's verbal knockout punch.

The measure under consideration was renewal of Public Law 480, the Food for Peace program. The specific amendment was to delete from the list of beneficiaries a small Third World country, controlled by a communist government. Millicent spoke against the amendment. In her peroration in favor of the aid, she said, "I think this is what the American people would want." My heart went out to Millicent. "This guy," I thought to myself, "is going to drop her with his traditional meat-ax jingoism." And, indeed, he did his best to do his worst. He asked Millicent if she would yield to him for a question. When she did, he snarled, "You mean you think the 'Mer'can [American] people would want to send food to a *communist* country?"

"Why couldn't someone have warned Millicent?" I sighed under my breath. But she didn't *need* any warning; she knew exactly what she was doing.

Her response was a symphony of both stump-speaking and theater: "I think the American people would want to help feed hungry children—all the more if those children were under the heel of Godless communism."

Point, set, match.

The Ninety-fourth Congress, which convened in January 1975, saw an end to bullying by Representative Wayne Hays of Ohio. My dad noted, "One thing you can say about Wayne; he never hits a man when he's *up*." This was the Congress of Hays's greatest success, and his most ignominious failure.

Hays had been given the job of collecting and distributing campaign contributions through the National Democratic Congressional Campaign Committee. As it became increasingly obvious that in 1974 the windfall of a Watergate landslide was coming to the aid of his party, his Democratic coffers began to bulge with undemocratic money from favor seekers. That meant Hays had a lot of money to pass out to those improbable Democratic congressional candidates who, under normal circumstances, would almost certainly lose in their respective districts, but this time almost certainly would win. Most of this group would-be Cinderellas who had never even been near the coach and six horses or the royal ball. They were politically uninitiated and—well, let's not say gullible—impressionable.

Hays knew that the campaign money he was in a position to give these novices, along with warm words of affection and encouragement, would buy him favor in the upcoming Congress. He figured correctly that, after their elections, most of the new members he had beneficially courted could be counted on to support his ambition to chair the House Administration Committee. It was a committee of petty pork which, among other things, passed out toilet paper to congressional offices. In that position, he again figured correctly, he could buy cooperation from his colleagues and sadistically compel hundreds of U.S. House employees to fear and obey him. Hays, the sound of whose name was generic, had a pathetic ego itch which he scratched by pushing weak people around. When he became chairman, he ordered the seats for elderly female elevator operators removed, not for the sake of efficiency, but just plain meanness.

During the 1974 Congressional campaign, a friend told me that Hays had said that, in the manner of the temptation at the top of the temple, he would send five thousand dollars to my campaign if I would call him and ask for it. He continued to live for several years because he did not hold his breath until I did; I didn't.

Having won his contest with New Jersey's Representative Frank Thomson—for whom I voted—to chair the House Administration Committee, Wayne was riding high in the Ninety-fourth Congress. He got married and arranged a lavish wedding reception for his bride and himself at the Capitol. With most of his colleagues—who wanted to keep their supplies of toilet paper coming—in attendance, it was something on the order of the wedding reception for Princess Diana and the latter-day Bonny Prince Charles, albeit with an impoverished person's Prince Charles who wasn't bonny in the least.

No sooner than the lavish occasion had finished, however, a sudden, cruel, and probably fair fate stepped in. A strange young woman named Ray reported that Hays had put her on the congressional payroll to accommodate his male appetites, adding that she couldn't even type or answer a phone. Of course, Hays' private life was not public business—until he stepped across the line and reached into the taxpayers' pockets for illicit use of federal employment. And he was caught and, gosh, exposed. "How are the mighty fallen?" Among other ways, this one.

Marian Clark and Rudy Maxa of the *Washington Post* were the Woodward and Bernstein of Wayne Hayes' political demise. Not only did they catch the bullying miscreant, they wrote a book about it.

Just as was the case in the Watergate scandal, the Hays scandal spawned an infestation of would-be imitator journalists all over Washington who pushed, scratched and mostly reached to find and expose a similar journalistic sensation. One cartoon captured the atmosphere perfectly. It showed a hairy-armed, portly, middle-aged man typing at a desk in Representative Bella Abzug's office. A news reporter, sticking his head around the corner, had just propounded a question. The captioned answer from the guy at the desk was, "Seventy-five words per minute and stop bothering me." Something similar happened in our office.

Following the 1974 election when I was still in Indianapolis and assembling a new staff with the help of already chosen staffers Winnie Burrell and Phyllis "Muffet" Coelho, a once and immediately future colleague called and asked me to hire a friend of his. He told me she was a Maryland suburban "housewife." He said she could type sixty words per minute. We needed such a worker. I trusted the congressman and asked Winnie and Muff to sign her up.

It would be a few more weeks before I would go to Washington myself. And something partly funny and mostly weird happened in the interim. Indianapolis friends who regularly traveled back and forth to Washington would wink, nudge and say to me in an insider tone of voice, "Hey, how 'bout that (*suburban housewife*) in the Washington office?" Not knowing, but sensing what they were talking about, I would ask and hear something like, "Yeah, really; you don't know." So I called Muff and asked, only to receive a similar comment: "Well, Andy! After all."

"Muff, speak plainly." She did. "Andy, the 'suburban housewife' is an ex-playboy bunny." Moral: A friend in need of finding work for an ex-lady friend is a friend, indeed—but to himself.

Well, the *housewife* was already hired and she did, in fact, work efficiently. So we all set sail on a new congressional term together. I was single, but not stupid. I was reared by my mother and, if anything, even more strictly by my father not to be boorish. There are certain rules of rectitude and one of them absolutely rules out office romances. Moreover, I was seeing another lady at the time and wouldn't have been interested, anyway. Never mind all that, though; an ambitious *Washington Star* newspaper reporter came by one day to interview my "suburban" coworker. According to Joe Roemer, another of my coworkers who sat next to the "housewife." the interview went like this: Reporter—"We have information that Jacobs has been hitting on you and . . ." According to Joe, the coworker interrupted to give this answer: "Him?" I was flattered—I think.

chapter 11

DOUBLE *DE*-FAULT

HAD UNITED STATES SENATOR R. Vance Hartke taken a couple of steps in the right direction and President Gerald R. Ford not taken just one in the wrong direction, it is more than just possible that they both would have won their bids for re-election in 1976.

In the case of Hartke, a Democrat, the Watergate windfall was still blowing in his direction during that two hundredth year of the Republic. In the case of Ford, a Republican, while it *was* a Democratic year, he had a Democratic opponent, Governor James Earl Carter, who took a wrong step, himself, right onto the pages of a sex-laced, soft porn publication. Moreover or more-under, Carter was maladroit generally in his campaign. Which is not to say Ford was facile; in one of his debates with Carter, he somehow managed to say that the Eastern European Soviet slave states weren't slave states. But that didn't even begin to offset the Carter blunder.

James Earl Carter was a holy man, deeply committed to public and shallow signs of sanctimonious religiosity. He wore his religion on his sleeve and tongue. So much so, that tracking polls in the campaign showed the public was getting tired of his unctuous utterances. He had put himself in the position of George Gobel's character who didn't drink beer and therefore "wore glasses with bloodshot eyes painted on the lenses, just so everybody would still think he was a good Joe."

So how could Carter lower the holy-water level? Why be a piker? Why blood-shot-eye novelty glasses? Why not go all the way to the bottom, so to speak? Yes, it would be an interview with *Playboy*, just the thing for a dignified presidential campaign. It probably cost the brilliant Virginia Dill

McCarty the Indiana attorney generalship for which she was running that year. During the *Playboy* interview, Carter confided to the thousands of people who read the rag and the tens of millions who followed the news, that holy men were human, too. He said he had "lusted in his heart" now and then for this and that lady. Surprise—it inspired a GOP bumper sticker, "In His Heart He Knows Your Wife." It hurt him a lot, but not quite enough to overcome the Democratic landslide, re-energized by the step President Ford soon took in the wrong direction.

When Ford pardoned Richard Nixon, he effectively dismissed himself from the White House. It seemed to me, though, that Ford would have received even fewer votes had Carter's campaign deigned to articulate the impropriety of the pardon. My friend Jim Beatty thought up an enormously effective thirty-second TV spot, which I would not have used in my own campaign, but was probably far above par as critical ads went. Jim's suggestion to Jimmy was not complicated and it was not a sleazy attack on Ford's private life nor a distortion of his legislative record. It simply contained three videotaped public utterances. One by Nixon and two by Ford, himself.

Beatty had located three short pieces of video tape which told the devastating tale, in fewer than thirty seconds. The first was the news clip of Nixon's choosing Ford to replace the felonious Vice President Spiro Agnew who, by plea bargain had resigned; the second was a sound bite and sight from the Senate hearing on the vice presidential replacement nomination. Ford was asked if, as president, he would be in a position to issue a pardon to Nixon. On the tape, Ford forswore the idea by saying, "The public would never stand for it." The third clip showed Ford as he actually read aloud and signed the pardon. It was the *old one two*—plus one more.

Devastating, except that the ad was never used. Jim asked me to call Carter's campaign manager, Griffin Bell, and convey the idea, which I did to no avail. After I explained the idea, Mr. Bell said this: "And you think this would help you in your district?" Here was a situation where I could explain it to him, but couldn't comprehend it for him—and the toll was running on the long-distance call. So I simply said, "Excuse the ring," and hung up. As Hoosier Kin Hubbard's Abe Martin would say, "You can lead a feller to [an idea], but you can't make him think."

Senator Vance Hartke's refusal to go through the newly instituted airport security system because he was a senator effectively canceled the fortuitous advantage dealt him by Watergate in 1976. The whole idea of metal detectors, which we all take in stride these days, was brand-new and a bit odd that year. But, as my father would say, most people preferred regulation to rigor mortis and patiently complied. It seems likely that Vance might have been thinking in terms of certain citizens who should be easily identified as not terrorists. But that is definitely not the way it looked in the news reports; it came off as a show of arrogance—a big shot, too important to be bothered. By the next day, the senator sensed the reverberations and resentful rumblings among the voters. He tried to flip a spin by saying that what he really meant was that no American citizen should be subjected to the electronic passageway. But it was too late; the irrevocable and indelible damage had been done in an instant. From then on, everything in Vance's campaign seemed to go wrong.

At the Chevrolet body plant gate in Indianapolis one morning, UAW official Buford Holt was helping the senator pass out his brochures to production workers as they reported for work. The production workers, who tended mostly to be Democrats, were throwing the brochures down on the pavement. After thirty minutes of that, Buford said, "Senator, I'm afraid it's not going so well." The senator's simple and self-assured answer: "They love me."

In the Democratic landslide of 1976, Republican Richard Lugar (pronounced "Loo-ger"—and mispronounced "Loo-gar" by none less than Nancy Reagan) had a landslide of his own. His statewide margin was a staggering 407,311 votes which was 59.5 percent. Dividing that margin by the eleven congressional districts Indiana had at the time, a U.S. House candidate would have needed a margin of 37,028 to equal Dick Lugar's percentage performance. In the Indianapolis Republican-majority Eleventh District, my margin was 41,895 or 60.8 percent. However, considering the fact that it was a strong Democratic year, Dick's success, or, more accurately, Hartke's failure, was more impressive.

Shortly before election day 1976, the highway people completed and dedicated the part of Indianapolis's innerloop that interchanges traffic on Interstate Highways 65 and 70. I was invited to sit on the bunting-bedecked platform. But, despite the ninety percent federal funding, I was pointedly not asked to speak to the huge crowd. Governor (and medical doctor) Otis Bowen knew nothing about the snub, and it may not be correct to call it a "snub," anyway. The term is probably too personal to fit the situation exactly. That close to an election, it was only natural for Republicans to deny a Democratic candidate for Congress what Teddy Roosevelt called "the bully pulpit."

Most of the crowd never heard my voice, but because of a momentary frustration over being squelched by my stage whisper, the chairman of the Highway Commission inadvertently told the entire crowd what I had to say.

Here's how it happened: Gaining enthusiastic momentum as he spoke, the chairman rhetorically asked, "And who do we have to thank for this wonderful facility?" Interrupting—or heckling—I answered his question: "The taxpayers!" In confusion, the chairman boomed out through the public address system, "Right, Andy, the taxpayers, but also the consulting engineer." The *net* moral of the story: No matter what your disadvantage, you never know when the other side will hit the net and fault.

Not long after traffic began to flow over the new facility, the design at one place in downtown Indianapolis proved deadly dangerous. The news people quickly dubbed it "Dead Man's Curve." The problem was a severe and partly obscure curve which hooked back at more than a right angle without sufficient warning. One after another, truckers were being killed because of their failure to perceive the full extent of the curve. The drivers would resume normal speed too soon and lose control as the curve continued beyond expectation.

I sent a letter to my friend Governor "Doc" Bowen, suggesting a series of chevron entry ramp signs along the highway curve to let people know the extent of it. Doc Bowen was a busy person who relied on the common sense of his appointees. So the letter was turned over to the highway commission *experts* for reply.

Now, you can always tell an expert, but you can't tell him much. In the manner of the Bill Mauldin cartoon where German small-arms fire was hitting all around the jeep carrying GIs, and the driver's saying, "I hate like hell to run [out of firing range] on a flat," the commission explained to me that regulations said chevron signs were for entry ramps and not for the highways themselves. Wonderful. Harry Chapin wrote and performed the song "Flowers are Red." It was about a little boy who was chastised by his nitwit preschool teacher for using imagination to draw pictures of violet leaves and orange skies, the teacher sternly chanting, "Flowers are red and green leaves are green. There's no reason to see them any other way than the way they always have been seen."

Exasperated, I decided that when obtuseness "is bliss, 'tis folly to be" otherwise. But very shortly after I received the obtuse letter, another trucker was killed at that Indianapolis death trap. Saddened and humbled by my failure to do so sooner, I telephoned Doc Bowen: "Doc, don't you think it's time for you to interject your common sense on this?" He did. He told me the chevron signs would be in place before nightfall. They were. And to the best of my knowledge, there has been no fatal accident on that site since. Doc Bowen was one of the most refreshing public officials I ever knew or ever knew about.

The big question in the spring and summer of 1976 was who would be the Republican nominee for president. Normally, it would be the incumbent Republican President, Gerald R. Ford. But there was another entrant in the intramural; he was the champion, nay—the passion was beyond all that—the *darling* of the far right, the handsome former movie actor and former California Governor Ronald Reagan.

His handlers had Governor Reagan take issue with President Ford's support for a new treaty with Panama which gave back the land on which the United States built the canal. Elementary Anglo-Saxon law holds that if I build an improvement on land you own, you own the improvement. Referring to the Canal Zone, California Republican United States Senator S. I. Hyakawa, a professor of English semantics, said, "We stole it fair and square."

There were genuine divisions in the Republican Party that year and they, too, probably contributed to Ford's failure in the fall election. The GOP presidential primaries got rough. The Ford people ran a radio ad about Reagan, whose foreign policy seemed—borrowing from the facile pen of columnist Joseph Kraft—"a salute to Mars":

> GOVERNOR REAGAN COULD NOT START A WAR—
> *PRESIDENT* REAGAN COULD START A WAR.

Reagan threw some heavy political punches also. For example, Reagan made an angry accusation that Ford was misusing the White House for entertaining uncommitted delegates to the upcoming Republican convention in Kansas City. This, Reagan insisted, was a shocking desecration of that hallowed place Lincoln, a pretty astute politician, himself, once called home. Later, both Bill Clinton and, for that matter, Reagan, himself, used the nation's First House to entertain campaign contributors. And, of course, there had been that Nixon White House campaign picture-taking business my dad called the "sheep dip." Getting politics out of the White House would be the rough equivalent of getting the gospel out of church. I found the Reagan charge against Ford much ado about not much. There was the incident in the White House Green Room where I answered the Secret Service guide's question about why anyone supposed President Ford entertained the Irish prime minister there. I asked if the prime minister was an uncommitted delegate.

President Ford, standing beside Archibald Leach, a rather better actor than Ronald Reagan, won the Republican party nomination in Kansas City. Leach was also known as Cary Grant. But Ford was badly wounded by his perfidy on the Nixon pardon and probably by the bad feelings some of Reagan's supporters harbored all the way into the fall.

In November, Carter's efforts were unsuccessful. Though trying mightily, he fell a little short of detaching himself from the 1976 Democratic landslide; he won.

chapter 12

THE MORAL EQUIVALENT

JAMES EARL CARTER BECAME President of The United States on January 20, 1977, and hit the ground shunning. At first, he seemed barely tolerant of the Congress, an attitude held by many of his non-congressional predecessors, but one they were generally better able to conceal.

Very early, he summoned several members of the House and Senate to tell them about the water projects he was going to terminate, apparently not grasping the fact that he could do no such thing without the cooperation of his guests. At one point, Senator Russell B. Long of Louisiana stood up. As chairman of the Senate Finance Committee, he needed no introduction to his colleagues, the news media or, really, even President Carter. But in mild, yet biting sarcasm, he said to Carter, "My name is Long. I am a member of the United States Senate." Carter, not dumb, reddened as the senator continued to explain the functions of the three coordinate branches of the United States government. Although I think President Carter was *right* on the money concerning those porky projects, his approach amounted to a very bad beginning.

At another congressional meeting with the President, House Speaker Tip O'Neill whispered to me, "He's not our kind of fellow, Andy." That was amusing to me because I'm afraid I wasn't exactly Tip's kind of fellow either, but much closer than Carter to being so. Tip liked my jokes and me; Carter neither.

If anything, Carter's congressional liaison aides did worse with the Congress than he, except for one. Valerie Pennson was the pretty and much more than pretty bright congressional liaison who did a lot to make up for the maladroit men who carried the President's messages to Capitol Hill. One of them was Hamilton Jordan, whose last name for some reason was pronounced "Jerden." Tip O'Neill occasionally said, Hamilton *Jerken.* It seemed to me that the White House press secretary, Jody Powell, was enormously capable. Many members of the Carter cabinet, such as Joe Califano, were high grade as well.

Mississippi Representative Jamie L. Whitten, as might be expected in those days, did not have a very good civil rights voting record in the House. And that was an issue in the Ninety-fifth Congress where his seniority on the House Appropriations Committee had brought him to the threshold of its chairmanship. Some of the Northern Democratic members announced they would cast caucus votes against his candidacy for the position, arguing that, while they liked him personally—he was most pleasant—and they realized he did not have much choice on civil rights bills if he were to stay in Congress during the 1950s and early 1960s, they thought it wrong for the party to seem to endorse his past votes on those critical matters.

Congressman Andy McGuire from New Jersey led the opposition but did not intend to speak at the organizing caucus. He said he thought his public statement of conscience was sufficient. But when the caucus took up the subject, an unexpected thing happened. Speaker Tip O'Neill of *Massachusetts* rose to speak in favor of Jamie's election to the coveted position. This caused Andy McGuire to change his mind and speak in opposition. His remarks were kind and respectful of Jamie as a friend, emphasizing that there was absolutely nothing personal in his position on the question.

As Andy spoke, I continued to marvel that Tip would go out of his way to make an unexpected endorsement of Jamie. After all, it was Tip who, as party whip at the time, had not so much as raised a whisper of protest when District of Columbia Committee chairman John McMillan disregarded my seniority and named the representative next behind me to chair the subcommittee it was my turn to chair. After both Tip and Andy had broken the expected silence prior to the secret vote on Jamie, I decided to say something myself and was recognized by the caucus chair to do so:

> Mr. Chairman, I have some information for new members who may not fully understand the seniority system. It will work against some and for others. For example, a few years ago I was in line to be Chairman of a subcommittee of the D.C. Committee. Despite my seniority, I was passed over by the full committee chairman because I

supported our party's national platform which favored home rule for the District of Columbia. Tip, the party whip, would do nothing to correct the obviously racial outrage. Having failed to support the seniority of a Member who worked to uphold citizens' right to vote, the whip, turned speaker, now argues to uphold the seniority of a member who cast votes in opposition to citizens' right to vote. But, as David Brinkley once said, "That's the way we do things in the *Free World*."

There were no more speeches. To the unschooled, it might have seemed that members were throwing away their votes, but only because secret votes in the caucus were cast by dropping small slips of paper into round metal wastebaskets.

I had not spoken directly against Jamie's candidacy, but apparently I had said enough for the caucus chairperson to name me as one of the anti-Jamie *tellers* to count the votes. We retired to the Speaker's Lobby to do so. When clerks dumped the ballots from the wastebaskets onto a large table, we began counting them. During the process, I felt a huge hand on my shoulder and looked up to see the smiling face of Tip O'Neill. And I said, "Tip, I have a love/hate relationship with you. And even though the love vastly exceeds the hate, the hate *is* genuine." It was true; you had to love Tip. But I thought that, in both instances, he went too far to keep the Southern racist element of our party in our party. Most of them were already switching to the southern Republican Party, anyway.

In the summer of 1977, I was interviewed by the *Indianapolis Magazine* and pledged not to run for any other office so long as I could hold the only Ways and Means Committee seat Indianapolis ever had in the twentieth century. It seemed like a reasonable pledge to me. I loved the House of Representatives and it was unlikely that any U.S. Representative from Indianapolis would be elected to the Committee again during the rest of the millennium. But in August, a Hoosier newspaper, the *Lebanon Reporter* ran this editorial:

> "I shall never run for senator, I shall never run for governor, period. This is not a prediction, it's a statement," Rep. Andrew Jacobs, Jr., D-Ind., said.
>
> The quote is from an interview in the August issue of *Indianapolis Magazine*. Jacobs was first elected to the House in 1964, was defeated for re-election by now Indianapolis Mayor William H. Hudnut III in 1972 and won back his seat two years later.

> "I'm saying I simply won't do it," Jacobs said. "If I ever change my mind, I want you to shove this magazine article under my nose and show me what I said back in 1977."
>
> "This holds true for all the reporters at the *Star*, all the reporters at the *News* and all the other newspeople at the local television and radio stations. I'm perfectly content in the House."
>
> We believe the statement above made by Rep. Jacobs is an unwarranted one. No public servant should close the door on future possibilities in which the people of his state might seek his service.
>
> Although this is a Republican newspaper, we believe Rep. Jacobs to be among the most truthful, independent and taxpayer-conscious officials in government today. We believe him to be a man of his word which makes it harder to take that he has restricted his political goals forever and forever.

Of course, I disagreed with the paper's disagreement with my pledge, but I was never more tenderly touched by a kind comment about me and said so in a letter to the editor. The *Lebanon Reporter*, by the way, was owned by Dan Quayle's wonderful grandmother to whom he paid public tribute in his 1988 nationally televised debate with his opponent for vice president, Senator Lloyd Bentsen of Texas.

I got to know pillar-in-the-Indianapolis-community Jim Morris in the same way I got to know Jim Beatty, by giving him a lift when he was waiting for public conveyance. Jim had worked with Dick Lugar at Indianapolis City Hall and now that Dick was Indiana's junior United States Senator, Jim was working with him in the Senate office. We took the same flight to Washington one day and, at the airport curb in D.C., I offered him a ride to Capitol Hill. Fortunately for the good of my fate, the traffic was heavy that morning just as it had been on that long trip up Massachusetts Avenue in Indianapolis a decade and a half before when I discovered the decent soul and brilliant mind of Jim Beatty.

Jim Morris, the Republican, and I, the Democrat, found much common ground while we inched toward the hollowed hill of American history. Over and over during the subsequent years during life's quiet moments of truth, as Jim Morris advanced to head the renowned Lilly Endowment and then the Indianapolis Water Company, I could see the civil saint he was. Jim Morris was one of the most religious people I ever knew or heard about, all the more so because of his positive response to the Book of Mathew, "Be not like the hypocrites who pray in public." Jim Morris did not wear his profound religion on his sleeve; he carried it much more deeply within and practiced its gospel of love, peace, and generosity quietly to the benefit of very many others.

United States Representative Jimmy Burke was different. He was from Boston, but he might as well have been one of Damon Runyon's New York characters. Jimmy *was* a character, and a fiery one. He was next in line to be Chairman of the House Ways and Means Committee in 1975 when I was elected to serve there. His preoccupation, some say *raison d'être*, was shoes. The shoe industry in Massachusetts had lost ground to foreign and, Jimmy said, "unfair," competition beginning with the second half of the twentieth century. Jimmy was in Washington to stop the onslaught. The unschooled ear couldn't always tell that Jimmy was referring to shoes during his histrionic outbursts, but it was usually a safe bet that he was. When the committee took up Jimmy Carter's remarkably ill-advised "energy" legislation, Representative Bill Green of Philadelphia, glancing from the corner of his eye at Jimmy, facetiously asked the top tax staffer, Larry Woodworth, whether the section on automobiles had anything to do with shoes. Larry, perfectly capable of some fun himself, promptly replied, "Brake shoes."

Once when Senator Ted Kennedy was testifying before Ways and Means in favor of one of his Senate-passed bills, Jimmy was asleep at the switch. The Senator had finished and was headed for the door when Jimmy realized he was missing an opportunity to praise his Senator for the Record. When Jimmy began doing so, Teddy's hand was on the door. The exchange went like this:

"Well, Mr. Chairman," Jimmy said. "I want to say that Senator Kennedy is one of the most hardworking members of—"

Teddy interrupted with his rich and very audible voice: "Just vote for the bill, Jimmy." It brought down the House—Ways and Means Committee, that is.

Then there was the time the newly elected United Auto Workers President Douglas Frazier testified before the Social Security Subcommittee, which Jimmy chaired. Mr. Frazier didn't know about Jimmy. When Jimmy took off on a convoluted flight of non sequiturs probably or at least maybe about shoes, the witness's eyes became heavy. I did catch one of Jimmy's phrases: "We are stranded on the beaches of hesitation," but I couldn't quite make out how it related. When Jimmy paused, the entire room was silent. Seated next to Jimmy, I deemed it my duty to hit the reset button on the committee hearing. So I said quite audibly, "Jimmy, that was beautiful." Everyone in the room roared, except Jimmy. He was oblivious to the mirth because he was flattered. As the testimony resumed, he leaned over to me and said, "You think you and the Kennedys are the only ones who are poetic."

J. J. "Jake" Pickle of Austin, Texas, LBJ's congressman and former staffer, was too large a hunk of history to fit into a couple of paragraphs. In fact, only a small part could be told in the normal-sized book *JAKE,* written by his daughter, Peggy, and himself (University of Texas Press, 1998). But it is fair to say that Jake was one of the most profound and wittiest people ever to serve in the United States Congress. He was also the loving, legislative antagonist of Jimmy Burke.

Jimmy had a solution to the approaching woes of Social Security and Jake liked it not even a little bit. When Jimmy wasn't talking about shoes, he was talking about his "One Third, One Third, One Third" plan, which would have required the employer to pay one third, the employee to pay one third, and the general Treasury of the United States government to pay the final third of the Social Security tax. Whenever Jake heard "One third," he wiped his right hand back along the hair on the right side of his head while shaking his head sadly. After several years of this highly qualified theater, I asked the performers to yield the Committee floor to me, whereupon I announced on the Record that the controversy had brought out the poet in me, to wit:

> *A man named Burke could amaze*
> > *When speaking of tax and who pays.*
> *A Caesar from Boston,*
> > *He showed Jake from Austin*
> *The gall to divide it three ways.*

If Doug Frazier was surprised by Jimmy Burke, President Carter was astounded. During a Ways and Means Committee meeting with Carter in the Cabinet Room, Carter made one of the most serious mistakes of his administration; he called on Jimmy Burke to speak. And speak Jimmy did—at length. When Jimmy paused, in the words of Lenny Bruce, "It was Mount Rushmore and an oil painting all rolled into one." Eyes glazed over, none more than those of the Thirty-seventh President.

By chance, Texas's Jake Pickle was seated directly across the table from Georgia's Jimmy. Jake brought the room back to consciousness with these words to Carter: "Welcome to the club, Mr. President."

Our committee met with Carter in the White House several times. On one occasion, we met just a few weeks before the midterm election of 1978. Jimmy Burke was never denied the opportunity to speak at such meetings even though he never seemed to have anything specific to say. He parenthetically had something quite clear to say, well, shout, at this gathering, "Mr. President, *you* don't have to run this year." I couldn't resist. So I said, "That's the best news he's had this morning." Everybody, even his faithful follower, Vice President Walter Mondale, laughed lustily. Everybody, that is, except President Carter. But then I always suspected that someone who smiled *all* the time would never laugh at anything funny, especially about himself.

Jimmy Burke left Congress shortly before his diabetes deprived us of his life. On his last congressional day there, which was that Congress's last day, too, Jimmy did what a showman is supposed to do; he left 'em laughing. That last day of the session was like a college commencement. Families of members filled the galleries wearing finery and the usual din of background noise on the floor was absent. One of the last House-Senate conference reports to be taken up was presented by the sometimes maladroit Ways and Means chairman, Al Ullman of Oregon. In such situations, the committee staff prepares canned answers for the chairperson to read in response to anticipated questions propounded on the Record by other members.

Anticipating what Jimmy Burke would say or do at any given moment was a daunting task which the staff was not quite up to on this occasion. Through the pervasive public address system, Jimmy asked his question. Al awkwardly read the prearranged reply, satisfied that he had satisfied Jimmy. But he hadn't. There was a pause, silence, "not a creature was stirring," and then the last words Jimmy Burke ever spoke on the record in Congress. No, not just "spoke." The rafters rang as he shouted in his high-pitched voice, "That's the *answer* you get!" A stand-up comedian should hope for the laughs that followed. It was a boiler factory of mirth. In his spontaneous and uncontrollable amusement, one man was almost injured. Speaker of The House Tip O'Neill lost his balance, fell backward, and landed on the Speaker's chair, barely missing one of the not too greatly padded arms. The curtain went down on one of the best acts that ever played Congress.

Jake Pickle stayed on until 1995, never to be forgotten. Kim, our sons, Andy and Bronco, and I visited his wife, Byrel. Yes, Byrel Pickle, and Jake in Austin after he retired. The citizens there all but burn candles to him. And why not? He was so special.

During his congressional days, Jake's one-liners became legend. The following are examples. "Now, Mr. Chairman, if you put this bill on the House floor, it'll be cut up more ways than a boarding house pie." Committee rules as well as ordinary courtesy required the author of an amendment to pass out copies before offering it. One day a member forgot to do so and began arguing for whatever the amendment was—no one else knew. Jake, betraying his Texas origin, made a point of order with these words: "Now, Mr. Chairman, you come out of chute one with this amendment." Then there was the time when the committee Democrats called time out and retired to their committee caucus for a frank discussion of the differences among them. Jake was the first to speak: "Now, Mr. Chairman, we're by ourselves now, so we can all lift our skirts a little." When Jake heard that Kim and I were about to be married, he stopped me on the sidewalk just outside the Capitol and said, "Andy, we hear you're getting married; we're all for it. It'll help." On Kim's and my first anniversary, Jake said to her via videotape, "Kim, being married has helped Andy . . . a little bit."

One of my dearest friends in and, later, out of Congress was Jim Shannon of Massachusetts. His IQ was almost as large as his heart. Both rivaled Mount Everest. He and I found a special mutual joy in the Jake jokes, which we called *Pickleisms*. We kept a running count in the manner of hand signals between pitcher and catcher. Sitting sometimes at opposite ends of the meetings, we would count on our fingers the Pickleisms we could agree, with a nod, were new. Following a meeting of the committee with the speaker in his office one morning where Jim Shannon and I had done some Pickleism signaling, one of Tip O'Neill's helpers told a coworker of mine that she was awed by the sophisticated strategy system Shannon and Jacobs used to coordinate their tactics in meetings. Er . . .

During an early 1976 dinner at my mother's and father's home, my father asked me what at first blush seemed like a facetious question: "When is the Federal Government going to pay off the national debt?" My answer was not imaginative, "Just not adding to it would be an accomplishment," I averred. The thought of actually paying off *six hundred* billion dollars—Yes, that's all it was that late in American history—was overwhelming at the time and I said so. "Well," said Dad, "when you were practicing law, what did you advise clients to do when they were over their heads in debt." Dad knew that, like him, I abhorred taking a client through bankruptcy and it dawned on me that he was suggesting something along the line of a composition of creditors and a schedule of manageable installment payments to retire the debt. Voila, the origin of the "Payment Book Amendment" to the U.S. Constitution which my father and I wrote and I sponsored in the U.S. House. I considered it our gift to Uncle Sam on his two hundredth birthday.

The amendment would have required the federal government to bring its accounts into balance by gradations over a three-year period and thereafter produce an annual surplus equal to 5 percent of the principal, thereby paying off the entire obligation by 1999. There was an escape valve.

In case of what a *three-fourths majority* of each House of Congress would call a national emergency, the government could borrow money, but only to the extent of 10 percent of the budget that year. The Government would have to pay back that 10 percent, separately, within three years.

When I introduced the measure, only two groups opposed it—the Democrats and the Republicans. But several members of both parties cosponsored it. The *Washington Post* editorial rooms went ballistic. Suddenly, editorials and columns in strong opposition to the idea blossomed both on the ed and op-ed pages. The thread of argument running through the stories was that "you shouldn't put a particular economic theory into the Constitution."

My response was, "What's so theoretical about a Constitution that requires the government to pay its current bills with current income?" But it was a long time before the *Washington Post* allowed me space, albeit out-of-the-way space, to tell my side. My argument was essentially this:

> For almost as many years as I am old, the federal government, regardless of party control, has indulged in the excess of unnecessary spending beyond its means, borrowing or printing the difference between revenues and outlays.
>
> Politicians like to say yes to as many spending demands from as many big campaign contributors as possible. And the opportunity to do so through deficits without having to ask for more taxes from the voters is the kind of big rock candy mountain that can produce landslides at the polls.
>
> Could a Constitutional amendment proscribing spending beyond income help remove that temptation?
>
> Most people recognize the need for protection from the weakness of human flesh. We wear goggles in factories and seat belts in cars. But what about the weakness of human nature? Knowing this weakness, Ulysses had himself lashed to the mast as his ship approached the sweetly whispered temptations from the Isle of the Sirens.
>
> Few seem immune to the human temptation to outspend their incomes. Senator Jesse Helms, whose conservative *rhetoric* is perpetual, somehow amassed an unprecedented $7 million for his recent North Carolina U.S. Senate campaign. He managed to spend it all and then some, the sum of the red ink being $180,000. If the *brightest and best* among us cannot summon the self-discipline to shun deficit, well maybe Ulysses knew what he was doing.

Money, in order to be worthy of the word, must represent goods and services produced. The dollars our government prints pursuant to real productivity are real dollars. However, when the government runs out of places to borrow these days, it still takes out of the economy the goods and services it wants and pays the bills by the addictive practice of printing unearned dollars. It sophisticates the process by seeming to sell bonds which it quietly and immediately buys back with "money" created out of thin air by the Federal Reserve. Economists call this "monetizing" the debt. It is anticipated that by 1979, $117 billion of an estimated $750 billion national debt will represent this latter-day alchemy. Alchemy never produced an ounce of gold. And government printing presses never produced a loaf of bread.

Fiat financing of government activities burdens the poor most. Since the individual income tax is based on the ability to pay, and since inflation applies to everyone at the same rate, inflation is rightly called the cruelest tax.

But it's worse than that, much worse. While federal deficits do not measure the length and breadth of American inflation, there is the economists' multiplier effect in reverse. When the government vampires the life's blood from the currency, people panic and struggle to stay abreast by grasping for more of the anemic dollars. And, in the manner of the wartime shopper who bought a huge supply of coffee "before the hoarders could get it," the wage earner and the shopkeeper demand more than enough to stay even as a hedge against further inflation which they, themselves, help bring about in a paper chase of expanding pandemonium.

Habitual government use of the printing press does not prime the pump, it sets off the wildfire.

We need a constitutional amendment forbidding red ink in government financing today for the same reason we needed the First Amendment forbidding government encroachment on our freedom to speak our minds. Sad experience had shown that day-to-day government could not be trusted without constitutional restraint when tempted to fatal excess.

So far as I can tell, most government officials are against my proposed amendment and most of the logic is for it. Why does the federal government spend more than it takes in? Because it can. Change that ability and you change the future of our country for the very much better.

A democracy is like a pony. Without restraint, a pony will eat himself to death; without constitutional restraint, a democracy will spend itself into decline and failure. That is what our Constitution is for, to protect us from our own self-destructive proclivities. "Let no debt remain outstanding." (Romans 13:8)

One day, one James Dale Davidson came by to see me. He had begun an organization called the National Taxpayers Union. He told me the organization liked my amendment and, for that matter, my voting record on fiscal matters. Thus began my happy association with an erudite friend and his organization which until some unfortunate changes in it, was very effective. One of his coworkers was Mark Hulbert. Mark was pure genius and all heart. The Taxpayers Union published a regular price-tag analysis of each representative's and senator's voting record. And, at first, unlike the ratings of financial special interest organizations, there was no bias about what was good spending and what was bad spending. "Liberal" rating organizations tended to oppose most military spending, even necessary military spending, while "conservative" rating groups tended to oppose most domestic spending, even including necessary education spending. And each side mainly reported votes on the other's priorities in the belief that spending on its own priorities was so holy as not to count. But, in its broad based, grass-roots days, the Taxpayers Union just reported each member's total spending domestic *and* military and told where all the chips fell for the taxpayers to pay.

The day the first report from the Taxpayers Union came out, copies spread rapidly in the House Chamber. One could see clusters of members gathered around their colleagues who had copies of this newly-arrived reality.

The cluster I was in consisted of a group of Ways and Means members, including the chairman, Al Ullman. I think Al was fond of me, but nervous about me, too. Chairpeople tend to be more relaxed with members of their respective parties who can be counted on to vote the party line, who make decisions according to *who* is right rather than *what* is right. The long-standing maxim was, "In order to get along, one must go along." Those, including me, who followed whichever drummer seemed to have the *right* beat on a given bill, obviously couldn't be automatically counted on by a Chairperson. And that meant rough sailing both for the Chairperson and the recalcitrant. *Maverick* was the nice name; troublemaker was more often heard in the cloistered corners of the halls of Congress.

As we looked at the ratings, we discovered that Chairman Al's was stunningly low, a "five." In fact, his score was the worst of the scores in our cluster. Looking perplexed, Al inquired about the rating of his fellow Oregonian, Les AuCoin. Les got 45 percent, which was above average. Al asked another in our group, "What did you get, Charlie?" Charlie's was above average as well. It was beginning to look as if Al had "gone along" much more than anyone else in the vicinity. When he asked me about my rating, I told him I didn't know and the fellow with the report read mine aloud: "Eighty-five." Al looked relieved as he said, "Well, that *must* be some nut group." Al was an organization man; he couldn't begin to understand someone who was otherwise.

It was hard to get Al Ullman to laugh at something funny. Being a *who* man, he had me down as one of the three or four committee members who liked jokes. So he was not only on his guard as to how I would cast my district's vote, but he was also on pins and needles as to when I was and when I was not kidding. Not having a sense of humor, he was forced to guess, and with remarkable frequency, he guessed wrong. If I said that I had read about a ghastly murder, Al would likely laugh. If I quoted from Indiana's super humorist Kin Hubbard, Al would nod sympathetically about the hilarious mythical plight of Hubbard's Abe Martin.

I set a goal for myself: Make Al laugh at something meant to be funny. One of the most delightful parts of life is that sometimes success comes when you aren't really trying. One boring day of repetitious lobbyist testimony—each earning his or her fee for saying exactly what all the others were saying about a greased tax loophole in the making—I wandered over to the press section of the huge committee chamber with a magic marker in hand. With it, I altered a sign hanging from the velvet cord which enclosed the fourth estate. The sign read, "Press Only." In order to elucidate, I added three words so that the sign read, "Press Only—Do Not Clean." Most of the reporters and members were so badly bored otherwise that they laughed in varying degrees of relief, but not Al, who seemed only curious.

As I returned to my chair to endure further torture from the witness table, an idea for a pantomime idled across my mind. In order to get over the velvet cord, it would be in order to unhook one end from the pedestal post, lower the cord and step over. The mime that came to mind was to unhook the cord, but *not* lower it. Instead, holding the cord exactly where it was when hooked, I swung each of my long legs over the normal barrier, making it pointless to have done the unhooking. Nobody, including me, gave much notice to the prank. Nobody, that is, except Al. He gave such a howl of laughter that the drone from the witness table was momentarily muted. Success! From then on, despite my continued fealty to my constituents rather than my fearless congressional leaders, Al was clearly more relaxed around me.

A U.S. Senate committee was kind enough to receive me one day as a witness in favor of the amendment to prohibit government borrowing. As was usually the case, only a few committee members were present. And as I testified, one more senator entered the chamber and took his seat. When the time came for me to answer questions from the committee members, the chairman asked some friendly ones and the next senator to question me was the late arrival. He said, "Who was this guy who was tied up in a boat?" For a moment I was stumped. My testimony was extemporaneous and I did not recall anything about "a guy tied up in a boat." Then it clicked and I asked for confirmation, "Do you mean my reference to *The Odyssey?*"

"No," said the senator, "you said something about tying a guy up in a boat." I was nonplused until I saw smiles creep across the lips of all the other Democratic and Republican senators. Then I believed what I thought I was hearing. I tried to be diplomatic. "Well, Senator, I believe I compared U.S. Constitutional restraints to the bonds Ulysses arranged for himself when his ship passed the Isle of the Sirens. He ordered his crew to lash him to the mast of his ship so that he would not succumb the fatal though deliciously whispered temptations."

Now comes the part for which I was not prepared. The senator asked, "Well, are you a Latin scholar?" I wasn't lashed to any kind of post, but I did manage to resist the temptation to get a laugh from those present and the C-Span audience. It crossed my mind but I did *not* say to the senator, "It's all Greek to me." Instead, I simply said, "No." The chairman, obviously stifling a guffaw, mercifully excused me from further participation.

The Constitution can be amended by two methods. The one most familiar to America begins with resolutions passed by a two-thirds vote in each House of Congress. The other and more obscure method is by initiation from two thirds of the several states. In either case, three fourths of the states must ratify in order for such a proposal to become a part of the Constitution.

After trying for a few years to pass my Payment Book balanced budget amendment in Congress, the Taxpayers Union and I decided to take it on the road. The Union would tell me when a given state legislature scheduled a hearing on my proposal and I would dig into my pocket and hope enough would be there to get me by air or auto to the hearing. In one case, it was the Montana State Senate. I had to be there on a Monday morning. When I called about air reservations for Sunday evening from Indianapolis to Helena, the price was quoted as over seven hundred dollars. But, in the manner of that fateful call concerning my first return trip to Washington in late 1974, the conversation between the ticket agent and me became social. At one point I expressed my distress at the price and the agent said, "Well, if you'd go Saturday instead of Sunday, it would only be three hundred dollars." I had only one question: "Does Helena have a Taco Bell?" Since the answer was yes, I filled my bag with mail to answer and other homework and headed for Helena on Saturday. You might even say I've been to Helena and back for the cause.

The trip to Helena was in the 1980s when President Reagan's PR people were trumpeting his support for a weaker version of my amendment. But we couldn't even get a presidential telegram of support to the majority Republicans in the Montana State Senate, let alone a personal appearance by President Reagan. This was all the more significant because, in a way, Montana was break point in our effort to line up enough states to move the proposal to the ratification process. It would not have been the last of the thirty-four states needed for referral, but it would have brought us to the same point reached through the same state initiative process in 1909. Congress had seen the handwriting on the wall then and, itself, passed the resolution for the Seventeenth Amendment requiring direct election of United States Senators. Had Montana fallen our way, it is nearly certain that Congress would have followed suit and passed our resolution on to the several states for ratification.

Why would the Reagan administration speak so much and do so little for the spending amendment? I think it not unfair to suppose that, having submitted one after another budget which called by quanta for the largest deficits in U.S. history, the Reagan administration felt compelled to preach, not act, against its own sin—in which a bipartisan majority in Congress participated out of greed in some cases and fear in others.

But, back in the 1970s, we who supported the idea of a constitutional bar to government borrowing, were optimistic; we were on a roll. One state after another, including my Indiana, was passing the resolution. Occasionally the effort was fun. For example, the Taxpayers Union asked me to accompany a right-wing college professor to Delaware to testify for my amendment. "Fine," I said, "so long as I don't have to pay his airfare. Politics makes strange bedfellows and I'm happy we agree on this one." As we sat together in one of the airports, the academician said he had heard about my vegetarian diet and asked what it included. When I mentioned peanut butter, he stopped me. Really, these were his exact words: "I thought you didn't eat animal products."

"That's right," I nonchalantly assured him. "Well," triumphed the wise man, "what about the butter?" I wondered if he also believed that all cottage cheese is made in cottages. I think I charitably told him he had me there. I thought it would be uncivil for me to ask if he believed the Empire State Building controlled foreign countries.

My trip to testify for the amendment before a committee of the Vermont Legislature gave me a chuckle. My testimony was scheduled very deep in a long line of witnesses. After waiting more than an hour and a half for my turn, I heard my name called and proceeded to the designated table. Just as I sat down, an attractive woman rose in the audience and announced that she would like to be heard before me. If I was to protect Indiana's reputation for chivalry, I certainly couldn't object. So she waxed these words:

"I just want the record to show that those of us who oppose this amendment don't have the kind of money the Taxpayers Union has. And we can't fly a member of Congress here to testify on our side. But there are plenty of members of Congress who oppose this amendment."

She had physically stood up and now physically sat down. But between those two exercises she had figuratively jumped to a conclusion, a wrong one.

Now it was my turn: "Mr. Chairman, it seems in order for me to state that I am here at my own personal and nondeductible expense. If members of Congress who oppose this amendment do not feel that strongly about it, that fact alone should enrich your Record. Perhaps I should add that I bought my ticket with my income tax refund from the State of Indiana whose Constitution forbids government borrowing."

As I left the statehouse, I was told that the pretty lady who took part of my turn was the lieutenant governor of Vermont. Why was I reminded of a pretty lady back at the Marine Corps base in San Diego who turned out to be a lieutenant and lectured me about not saluting?

Jerry Brown. Different. For a while after he became governor of California, the only thing I knew about him was that he chose not to use the excessive and luxurious governor's mansion with which Governor Ronald Reagan had saddled the taxpayers. But from that point, it was downhill.

I met him in New Hampshire in 1979. He was an unannounced candidate to compete with President Jimmy Carter in the following year's Democratic primaries. And he appropriated my Payment Book amendment as one of his campaign gimmicks. Both of us were in Concord to testify to the New Hampshire Legislature in support of the proposal.

However, the governor of New Hampshire was a Democrat and he opposed the amendment. One word from one of the governor's assistants at the statehouse door, and Brown, who had flown all the way across the continent to testify, backed down. The same assistant waylaid me at the same door and said, "You're not going to go in there and embarrass the governor by testifying for that amendment, are you?"

"Certainly not," I replied, "I'm going to testify for the amendment, but, assuming your governor is an intelligent person, I can't imagine that an honest and respectful disagreement between us could possibly embarrass him."

Later that evening, my New Hampshire allies and a friend from the Taxpayers Union took me to a little gathering which was also attended by Governor Brown. He was waxing, I think, superficially political to the group. He was extolling the amendment he had come to New Hampshire to testify about but didn't. When we were introduced, he shook hands athletically and said he felt strongly about the proposal. Uh-huh.

Back home again in California, Governor Brown reached me in Washington by phone one day. He said Allard Lowenstein suggested the call. Since I was serving on the Ways and Means Committee, I assumed Brown was calling about a tax problem involving his state and the federal government. But I was mistaken. Though he circled the point of his call several times, it was immediately obvious that he was calling to see if I would support him for President. Our conversation was published on the front pages of both the *Wall Street Journal* and *The Indianapolis Star*. The *Star* story was written by bright staff writer and my fellow Marine, Joe Gelarden:

Brown's Taking it Very Seriously "About the Presidential Thing..."

By R. Joseph Gelarden

When Democratic presidential candidate Jerry Brown called U.S. Representative Andrew Jacobs, Jr. (D-Ind.) this week, Brown was testing the presidential waters. Instead, he got his leg pulled.

Jacobs still isn't sure Brown got the joke.

According to Jacobs, his conversation last Wednesday went this way:

Brown: "Have you made any political decision about 1980?"

Jacobs: "Governor, this is beautiful. You mean you called all the way from California just to see if I'm going to run for re-election to Congress next year?"

Jacobs said he expected laughter. Instead, he said, he received Brown's straight assurance the Congress could hardly get along without him.

Then Brown tried again to find out if Jacobs would support his candidacy.

BROWN: "Have you made any decision about the presidential thing?"

JACOBS: "Well, I was in New Hampshire a while back. I believe you were there, yourself. Frankly, I had always thought of that state as the fabled Mecca of presidential politics where everyone is ten feet tall. But they turned out to be just ordinary folks, like Hoosiers. But running for President is pretty big casino for me. I really hadn't given much thought to it, although some of the New Hampshire residents did like what I said about the need for balancing the federal budget."

BROWN: [Silence, then . . .] "Whom would you favor between [President Jimmy] Carter and me?"

JACOBS: [with tongue now firmly planted in his cheek] "Do you mean assuming I don't get into it myself?"

BROWN: "Yes."

JACOBS: "Governor, I think I'll just lay in the weeds and let things develop."

BROWN: "Thank you."

Jacobs' final analysis of the conversation: "I was astounded with Brown. He didn't know I was kidding—no sense of humor at all."

Most of the mail I received as a consequence of the story expressed appreciation of the comic relief which validated Kin Hubbard's assertion through his mythical Abe Martin that, "Nothin' will take the starch out of a great man like meetin' a feller that don't think much of it." But one humorless missive from Tennessee expressed outrage over what was perceived to be my poor grammar:

Dear Sir:
What are you going to lay in the weeds, your secretary?
I'm sick and tired of politicians who can't speak the King's English correctly.

Sincerely,

England had a queen at the time. Thus, I answered the Tennessee fellow:

Dear Sir:
    I have a nodding acquaintance with the verb, "to lie" in both of its senses and its different tenses. In this case, however, I was quoting a well-known Hoosier political idiom which, I must say, is in better taste than your letter.

Sincerely,

    P.S. Apparently none of us uses flawless English. For example, my secretary is a "who," not a "what."

As the years went by and resistance to the Payment Book amendment became stronger, it occurred to me that there was no need for the provision that would allow the government to borrow if three-fourths of each House of Congress declared an "emergency." Why should the government borrow money in an emergency? It takes the goods and services from the economy at the same time it deals with the upheaval. If it really is a "national emergency," why shouldn't the entire nation make a simultaneous sacrifice through taxes to pay for coping with it? In many instances, that requirement alone might make the nation more skeptical about whether what the politicians call an emergency, really is an emergency.

Take the Carter administration's Energy Crisis. Carter called it "The moral equivalent of war." I'm still trying to figure that one out. Being out of gas just doesn't seem the equivalent of ripping people limb from bloody limb by hot lead and steel. On the other hand, if he meant that going to get a can of gas was no more moral than trying to kill people and destroy their property, the healthy mind would have to boggle. Impure and simple, war is not moral. And one cannot imagine any nonviolent thing so despicable and primitive as the *immoral* equivalent of war. Oh well, Washingtonese.

During my 1974 campaign to go back to Congress, I happened to be walking by a lady at a newspaper dispenser. The headline that day declared, "GAS MAY GO TO 75 CENTS PER GALLON." Not knowing me from Adam, she turned and said, "Once it hits a dollar, the energy crisis will vanish." And, of course, she was right.

We have one Henry Kissinger mainly to thank for the OPEC oil price hike. Kissinger had always been a Rockefeller retainer before all else. When he talked "our friend," the Shah of Iran into leading the price gouge against us, he couldn't have been more useful to the Rockefeller oil interests. OPEC's price increase was the excuse for Standard Oil and other domestic companies to raise their prices. And, of course, the Rockefellers desperately needed the money.

The Carter administration put on a full-court press to fight its equivalent war. It sent grandiose proposals for "energy" legislation to the Hill, most of which went to the House Ways and Means Committee. The administration insisted that nothing would do but that we add one more gas-guzzling limousine to the government's fleet by adding a new department to the President's cabinet. It became the Energy Department and supervised the multibillion tax-dollar Synfuels Corporation, the "moral equivalent" of a ripoff.

The administration had tax incentives in mind. It proposed tax credits for people who would put insulation in their attics. The fact that such a simple measure would cut a household's heating bill by up to one-third was judged an insufficient incentive. Why leave it at that when the government could get into the act and force the neighbors of the goof who hadn't insulated help pay for his or her insulation through the tax code? In an effort to bring my Ways and Means colleagues to their senses, I facetiously offered an amendment to grant tax credits to citizens who brushed their teeth. After all, I pointed out, "If a person brushes, it will prevent cavities which waste energy on dentists' drills." That mock nonsense did not pass; the nonsense offered earnestly by the administration *did*.

Though somewhat unrealistic, the administration came closer to the mark with proposed rules requiring automobile manufacturers to improve the gas mileage of their products. Such conservation is what put OPEC over its own barrel. But high gas-mileage Japanese imports probably had more to do with nudging Detroit toward efficiency than the new federal law. In any case, U.S. oil consumption went down, causing the price of the product to do the same. It was amusing in the early 1980s to hear President Reagan brag in a TV address, "And isn't it nice to be able to buy a gallon of gas for less than a dollar again?" He had strongly criticized Carter for the fuel efficiency law which had combined with imports to produce the better price. Because of his "bully pulpit," Reagan's speechwriters were able to bootleg the political best of both worlds, condemning the inconvenience of the candle and claiming credit for its light. By the spring of 2000, through the widespread us of so-called sports utility vehicles, America's voracious appetite for guzzling gas had returned along with a snicker and price boost from the same OPEC our government forced more than two hundred of our citizens in uniforms to die for. Natural gas and hydrogen, anybody? Clean air? Really put OPEC across its own barrels? And breathe "easy"?

One of the more interesting days at the Ways and Means Committee came when two proposals were taken up in tandem—one to give yet another tax loophole to the oil industry and one to let working parents of small children take tax credits for day care, one of the expenses of going to work and producing income. Naturally, the first passed. The second failed that day but, by dent of illustrative humor, passed twenty-four hours later. It came to be known as child day-care credit, and there is no more popular provision in the U.S. Internal Revenue Code.

A committee decision can be reconsidered and reversed on proper motion made within twenty-four hours by a member on the prevailing side the day before. Such a motion was made on the child-day care amendment the next day. When it was my turn to speak for the amendment, one of the main doors to the Ways and Means chamber was opened and three little kids dressed in costumes that looked like oil wells entered the inner sanctum. Some friends and I had concocted the outfits the night before and the models were the day-care children of two of my coworkers. In my comments about the previously failed amendment, I described how the decisions of the day before had further fattened fat cats and were uncaring about kittens. I said I thought that if kids looked more like oil wells, perhaps they would do better in the "Mean Ways Committee." A few of my colleagues were shocked and outraged at my irreverence, but most of them were amused and awakened.

I've never been very keen about using the tax code for social purposes—there are exceptions—but this provision was at least a hybrid. Its social implications are obvious, but there is something to be said for the proposition that day care for children of working parents is strongly in the nature of a business expense necessary to produce income subject to tax.

On other matters, I made the Johnny Carson monologue one night when I did not try to do so, and failed to make it one night when I did try.

The first incident involved the Delaney Clause of the federal Food and Drug law, named for Representative James J. Delaney of New York. Rumor had it that the FDA didn't much care for the provision and seized upon an essentially meaningless Canadian study of the effects of saccharin on laboratory rats as a means of discrediting the measure. The Canadian experiment alleged to show that saccharin would give rats cancer if you fed enough of it to the innocent rodents. But in order to produce the same result in a human, he or she would have to consume enough diet drinks to fill a railroad boxcar. Based on the Canadian test, the FDA made noises about outlawing saccharin in the U.S. Most thoughtful scientists sided against outlawing the product. So did I.

One of my coworkers, Pat Traub, had the sad habit of smoking at the time. In an automobile ride from the Indianapolis Airport to our downtown congressional office, I asked for a look at the warning label on his cigarette package. Then and there, I wrote the bill I introduced the following Tuesday to illustrate the absurdity of what the FDA was threatening to do. The bill would have required processors to place on the package of every product containing saccharin a label reading:

> **WARNING!**
> The Canadians have determined that saccharin is dangerous to your rat's health.

I was told Mr. Carson reported my bill in his warm-up monologue. It had been a long time since I had made my entry into show biz with the Batman idea. Nothing from *Variety* this time.

A few years later, I was asked to participate in a political fundraising roast of my friend and colleague, Hoosier Representative Floyd J. Fithian. On the night of the event, my nephew Tom Landwerlen, Jr., went with me to Lafayette for my participation in the show. I was tired, languid really. It was one of those times when thoughts or fragments of thoughts wander into and, just as quickly, out of one's mind. As I tried to think of something funny to say about the roastee, I would think to myself, "That'll work . . . but what was it? Great, it's gone." I was still grasping for some idea, any idea, as we pulled into the parking lot of the Holiday Inn where I had to take a turn roasting. The word "nap" came to mind. I should have taken one during the hour drive with Tom at the wheel. Now it was too late. As I struggled to my seat on the dais, I still didn't have a clue about what I might say. The other House members who had come from all over America were fresh, flashy, and funny. My achievement was staying awake, barely.

The horrible inevitable arrived; I heard my name called and felt my legs carrying me toward the guillotine-lectern. Though I don't drink, I felt like Jett Rink, who was dumbfounded when introduced to speak at the banquet in his honor in the film *Giant.* Except, that unlike Jett, I wasn't drunk, just zonked. Another in a long list of miracles, large and small, came my way. The Holy Ghost must have descended, because a gag tailor-made for Floyd landed firmly in my mind. Floyd was about as bright as anyone I ever knew; he had been a history professor at Purdue University. But there was that matter of his normal facial expression that looked the way I felt that evening. It masked his deep intellect and betrayed none of the heavy traffic behind his eyes. No doubt the Holy Ghost played a role, but my direct reference was both to a beer commercial that reminded people, "You only go around once," and to the occasional object of Johnny Carson's humor, his trombone-playing assistant bandleader, Tommy Newsom. Newsom, like Floyd, had an expressionless countenance.

With that in mind, I said, "I don't have to tell you that Floyd isn't exactly a ball of fire. He is not the Johnny Carson of Congress, more like your Tommy Newsom. Or putting it another way, Floyd's philosophy of life is, 'You only go around once, so why bother?'"

I mailed the joke to *The Tonight Show* writers. I thought it a natural, but I never heard anything from them. Once again, I was reminded of the comment of my friend, hero, celebrated Civil War author and attorney, Alan T. Nolan, "For every star on Broadway, there're a thousand broken hearts." That year the voters let me keep my daytime job, which sometimes extended through the night. By this time, I had served on the U.S. House Ways and Means Committee for three years; there would be nineteen more.

chapter 13

Rabbit Punch

During the second half of Jimmy Carter's presidency, he was chased by a swimming rabbit and collapsed while running in a marathon. This was poor PR. He also carried his own luggage when he emerged from Air Force One. Because of this and the tonal quality of his voice, he did not have what Hollywood would cast as the presidential image. Unfortunately for him, the candidate with whom he was destined to compete for re-election in 1980 had almost exactly what Hollywood would cast as the presidential image—and did cast many times in various other images.

The rabbit incident occurred when President Carter was fishing from a small boat. He reported that the rabbit swam toward the boat in a menacing manner. Since no one else in real life was ever attacked by a rabbit, the incident hit the headlines, something on the order of man bites dog. Apart from putting one in mind of the alleged attacks on U.S. vessels in the Indochina Gulf of Tonkin, there was a precedent in pretend life. In the film *Monty Python and the Holy Grail,* a cute little rabbit attacked and killed a few knights, but even then the incident was on dry land.

Carter had other bad luck. A fake oil shortage and a Henry Kissinger-inspired OPEC price gouge had set off an explosion of inflation that savaged the economy during Carter's watch.

One of the consequences of that inflation was magnification of a bad mistake made by Social Security actuaries when they drew the cost-of-living formula for annual adjustments in the benefits. Between 1972, when the adjustments were established, and 1977, the actuarial error had overstated inflation by 30 percent. Social Security "bonus baby" beneficiaries were being paid 30 percent more in *real dollars* than the correct amount to stay even in purchasing power. This economic calamity was compounded by a

10 percent decline in the purchasing power of those still working and paying the tax. The latter were getting 10 percent fewer beans on their tables as they paid the tax to put thirty percent more beans on the tables of retirees. Obviously, the Social Security error had to be corrected and corrected quickly.

As members of the Social Security Subcommittee, Bill Archer of Texas—a gentleman if there ever was one—and I advocated correcting the error in much the same way the Social Security Administration had always corrected accidental overpayment to an individual. In the individual case, the authorities quite logically took back the overpayments and paid the correct amount from then on.

Republican Bill and Democratic I proposed letting the bonus baby retirees *keep* the excess already erroneously given them, but, we said, at least stop making the overpayments in the future. We might as well have proposed a pay cut for Congress. Our colleagues looked at us as with unbelieving eyes. Didn't we realize the wrath that could be expected from the bonus babies, who had become accustomed to the overpayments? I think we did, but that wrath, we argued, would be dwarfed by the "third-rail" roar from subsequent retirees if they were paid the correct amount while their predecessors in retirement continued to be overpaid. The congressional "solution" became known as the "notch" or, in the parlance of presidential politics, the "Issue from Hell."

The notch adjustment meant that the bonus babies would go right on being overpaid while for five years each successive annual group of new retirees would be paid a little less than paid to the group before. This adjustment would continue until the benefits for those retiring in the sixth year would buy the same number of beans that could be bought by the same earnings record in the base year of 1972.

The retirees who followed the bonus babies, became loudly known as the "notch babies." Sometimes a retiree's next-door retiree neighbor, with a Social Security earnings and contribution record the same as her or his own, was receiving a significantly higher benefit. Whether the notch issue was from Hell or not, all hell broke loose.

A columnist for the lovelorn ingeniously trumpeted indignation over the asymmetry. Had she complained about the overpayment to the bonus babies, she would have been right on the money. But she didn't. Instead, she insisted that the notch babies were being underpaid. The reality, of course, was that those who had retired before the notch years were being overpaid. And for that matter, even retirees in the first few years of the notch years were being overpaid. There was no complication about the issue except the one born of the columnist's misperception and pettifogging by unworthy profit-seeking exploiters.

The complaints were strident and shrill. Organizations were formed to make money from the misunderstanding by collecting membership dues from naive retirees. One such organization paid Jimmy Roosevelt, eldest son of FDR, a substantial annual fee to front for it. The organization, by golly, was going to get justice for the abused notch babies, the average of whose Social Security taxes together with accumulated interest through the working years covered less than 20 percent of the corrected benefits they were receiving.

In fact, the whole idea of annual cost-of-living adjustments to Social Security benefits was not to liberalize those benefits, but to rein in Congress' feckless habit of increasing Social Security benefits each election year far beyond increases in the Consumer Price Index. As long as the ratio of workers to retirees was high, the political ploy worked just fine. The beneficiaries noticed their good fortune—and the incumbent candidate who arranged it—and the workers who paid for the excess did not notice. An old Broadway musical says, "If you can give a baby a locket from her daddy's pocket, son, you're a natural phenomenon at politics." But in the case of Social Security, it was just the other way around; the benefits for the daddy were paid for by the baby.

By 1972, the road ahead looked bleak. Congress and the presidents had been too generous; a real pinch was approaching. Congress, the presidents, and the country needed restraint from the profligacy that had been practiced in the past. Thus, the cost-of-living law which, in purchasing power, was passed to keep the benefits static—same number of beans through the years.

The Jimmy Roosevelt organization was one of the most interesting of those which sprang up to "champion" the misinformed notch babies, tagged "Notchers." Each of an enormous number of retirees sent ten dollars to the outfit. Its coffers were bulging by the mid-1980s when I was chairman of the Social Security Subcommittee. Senators and Representatives who knew better buckled under and cosponsored legislation not to stop the overpayments to the bonus babies, but to make the same overpayments to the notch babies. And never mind that such legislation would bankrupt the system in fairly rapid order.

In private conversations, the very members of Congress who sponsored the fiscally irresponsible legislation asked me to do what I could to avoid reporting their bills for full committee and House floor votes. Many of them even demanded that our subcommittee conduct a hearing on the tactics of the Roosevelt group, tactics which frightened the representatives and senators into sponsoring the irresponsible legislation. In other words, I was to be the lightning rod for the storm of protest from unenlightened retirees.

The Roosevelt group, which called itself, the Committee to Preserve Social Security, told its gullible dues-paying members that it was straining to save Social Security from the members of Congress who were trying to abolish it.

So we held the hearing. Brave senators and representatives who had declined to sponsor the irresponsible grab appeared before us to denounce in no uncertain terms the subject of the hearing who was sitting right there in the person of Jimmy Roosevelt, himself.

Whenever I chaired a congressional hearing, I disregarded the tradition of the chair's asking the first questions. Instead, I always called on each of the other members to inquire before me. My theory was that they would probably ask whatever I would have asked and we could save time by my not repeating those questions. But in the case of Jimmy, with whom I had served my first term in Congress, my colleagues had not pursued the line I had in mind, so I took my turn when they had finished. By that time, most of the witnesses had thoroughly excoriated poor—if you didn't count the easy annual fee—Jimmy.

I began with my old friend on a fairly light note. "Jimmy," I said, "what in the world have you been up to?" There was laughter including Jimmy's as he replied, "Well, Mr. Chairman, I'm just trying to be a good citizen." You couldn't help liking Jimmy Roosevelt; he had that delightful FDR personality. But I had a duty to perform and tried to go at it as illustratively as I could. Next, I asked, "Do you know of any member of Congress who is trying to abolish Social Security?" As I intended, that was an awkward question for the nominal head of an organization which was "crying wolf" about "members of Congress who [were] trying to abolish Social Security."

Jimmy wiggled, "Well, when our members write to my congressman, Bob Badham, he writes back." I closed in. "Is Bob trying to abolish Social Security?" Jimmy acknowledged that Bob wouldn't do such a thing. "Well," I pressed Jimmy, "which member of Congress would?" In essence, Jimmy said he couldn't really think of any. But he said his organization was standing firm and (therefore?) abolition was not happening. That prompted my final touch: "Does that mean that if your organization went to Indiana to protect us from polar bears, each of us should send you ten dollars?" Jimmy smiled. Polar bears have yet to be sighted in Indiana outside of zoos. Members of Congress who were trying to abolish Social Security had not been sighted either—even in zoos.

In time, the Roosevelt group became a much more responsible and, therefore, respected organization.

My good friend Congressman Bob Wise, who was every bit of what his name said, and whose wife, Sandy, was my very capable top coworker at the Social Security Subcommittee, invited me to speak to an organization of retirees in his Charleston, West Virginia congressional district. Upon my arrival, a young television reporter asked me some questions on camera. When I finished my talk to the retirees, they also propounded questions. It didn't take long for the notch controversy to come up. When it did, I said:

"When I arrived, I saw the bumper stickers on some of your cars; they read, 'We're spending our children's inheritance.' And I'm all for you on that. Most—not all—people who inherit a lot of money, turn out to be wimps. But in this situation, you're not asking to spend your children's inheritance. You're asking to spend their income. And that's not just wrong; it's downright unnatural."

At the end of the meeting, a refreshingly large number of retirees approached me to say they agreed. Some said that they thought the system should stop overpaying to bonus babies. I did, too.

Many members of Congress were guilty of tergiversation on the issue, reminding one once again of the Lord Chesterton observation that, "Sometimes it is easier to die for one's country than to tell her the truth." But there were heroes, too. They included Bill Archer, who never caved in. The same was true of Jake Pickle, who chaired the subcommittee before I and, in his friendly and self-effacing way, stood like a rock and didn't flinch. Jake was also one of the five Southerners who stood up and cast votes for the 1964 Civil Rights Law. Baseball Hall of Famer Jim Bunning, representative and later senator from Kentucky, stood tall and took the political punches for rejecting the unreasonable demand. Jim and I exchanged places, respectively, from ranking member and chairman of the subcommittee, to chairman and ranking member in 1995 when the Republican Party became the majority in Congress. Republican staff director Pete Singleton, USMC Ret., contributed mightily to our effort as did Kathryn Olson, Cathy Noe, and of course, super Sandy Wise.

Senator Pat Moynihan, who chaired the Senate Social Security Subcommittee, knew right from wrong and stood like steel against the bellicose demands on the notch. I was reminded of my father's quiet answer when asked what he could report about pressures felt by members of Congress: "Not much," he had said. "I heard about them, but I never felt them." And there was that observation by the Hoosier broadcaster, Elmer Davis: "This country was not created by cowards and it will not be maintained by them, either." The proposed raid on the trust fund was staved off—to the profound relief of most of the timid souls who cosponsored the assault.

In 1977 I was still pretty far down the seniority pecking order on the Ways and Means Committee, far enough that the chairman was most unlikely to ask me to preside over a full committee hearing in his absence. There were probably ten members between the chair and me. But at one hearing, I was surprised to notice that everyone ahead of me, including Chairman Ullman, was absent. Seconds later, the top staffer informed me the chairman wanted me to preside. Puzzled not a little, I accepted the gavel and called the next panel of witnesses, all but one of whom were the typical sort. The one proved to be a so-called cult survivalist, who, along with his ten or so followers occupying seats in the audience that day, insisted that the U.S. had no authority to tax them. They were from Pennsylvania, the state of the Whiskey Rebellion. He was the last on the panel to testify and he did not mince words: "Every member of Congress is a traitor who will be dealt with accordingly after the revolution."

And that was just for starters. More—a lot more—of the same followed.

By that time there were only two members of the committee present, the top Republican, Barber B. Conable, Jr., and I. Barber had no questions, so I proceeded with a rare reference to my military experience. I addressed the rugged individualist: "As a member of Congress with 10 percent combat disability, I find myself less than delighted with being called a traitor."

The witness shot back: "When we take over, we'll give you a fair trial."

The witness's followers became animated at that point. They all rose and clamorously advanced toward Barber and me. Barber, a former Marine himself, albeit an officer, urged me to summon the Capitol Police. But I remembered my own police work and the desk lieutenant who had also thrust me into a dangerous situation with the same lack of warning I got from Chairman Ullman. So once again I employed amateur psychology. To the leader of the revolutionaries, I said, "Now, Mr._____, surely when you take over, you'll want order and decorum in your tribunals."

It worked. No police. Their leader ordered his pack back to their seats. Evidently he thought it best to avoid a bad precedent.

When the Russians turned Afghanistan into their Vietnam, President Carter's response was to cut off Uncle Sam's nose to spite his farmers' fates. American wheat farmers and grain companies had hit a bonanza with the Russian wheat deal negotiated by the Nixon administration. Many of those farmers had borrowed heavily against expected profits from future sales. Carter canceled the deal and cut them short. The cancellation didn't hurt the Russians; they simply took their business to Argentina and Canada. But some of the American companies and very many of the American farmers, unable to service their debts, were plunged into bankruptcy. Some of the farmers had borrowed unnecessarily to buy luxury in the form of air-conditioned tractors with tape decks and other accoutrements. Other farmers were more cautious, even you might say, conservative; they survived Carter's foolish maneuver which, in effect, hit Russia right in the fist with our farmers' noses. Commenting on what he saw as reckless expenditures on the part of his peers, one farmer wrote to me, "It's not the high cost of living; it's the cost of living high."

In the case of one grain company, it was different. The fatal borrowing was a sensible investment, assuming the U.S. government could be counted on not to emulate the lemmings. When the Russian deal came along in the early 1970s, this company simply did not have enough railroad cars to get its grain to seaports. So it borrowed to buy enough cars to handle future crops efficiently and went under because Carter did emulate the lemmings. He not only hurt his countrymen, but also hurt himself by helping them decide to vote against his bid for re-election.

Carter's foreign policy was generally a naive and failed one with one prodigious exception: the settlement between Egypt and Israel. That was indelible plumage in his hat of, not only historic, but also scriptural proportions.

During the 1970s, the medical sector of the economy went wild with the flames of inflation, outstripping by far the staggering price increases everywhere else. The Carter administration had a proposal for controlling that medical inflation. The idea was to accept the American Hospital Association's own guidelines for annual price increases and, if hospitals failed to stay within those guidelines, the old governmental bromide would be imposed, namely more bureaucracy. The Department of Health and Human Services would help the hospitals run themselves—"I'm from the government and I'm here to help you." (Seldom welcome since the frontier days of the U.S. Cavalry)

The message was, "Raise your prices above your organization's own guidelines and we'll come down on you like a ton of regulations." To my naked eye, it looked like an only slightly modified case of the government price controls which were so disastrous under President Nixon. The theory here, though, was that the government bureaucracy would actually supervise the administration of private hospitals. To accept that idea, one would have to believe that government employees could manage hospitals better than the professionals who knew what they were doing. My father would have called it "the blind leading the nearsighted." Moreover, in those cases where the administrators were less than honest in their billings, they could be expected to run circles around the agents from Washington who wouldn't "know the territory."

The Carter proposal came to the Ways and Means Committee where I proposed a substitute which, at the behest of the administration, was rejected out of hand. Carter's expanded bureaucracy proposal passed the committee without the vote cast by me or a few other Democrats, as well as most of the Republicans.

When the bill was taken up by the House Rules Committee, there was a hearing at which the Ways and Means chairman made the traditional request for a *closed rule* to block floor amendments and allow the Ways and Means Committee to control the speaking opportunities in the debate on the floor of the House. The Rules Committee has the authority to recommend such a rule or modification thereof. And modifications were what my Ways and Means colleague Dick Gephardt and I sought that day.

Gephardt and I both asked the committee to recommend a rule that would make in order our respective substitutes for floor consideration. The committee granted our requests and the committee's recommendation was adopted by the House. But the substitutes were a long way from alike. Gephardt's could fairly be described as something less than a slap on the wrist. He proposed that if hospitals overstepped the association guidelines, the government would monitor and make public future hospital price increases. Since that was essentially what several publications were already doing, the effect of Dick's substitute was simply to kill the bill. And, while such a death would not advance the cause of a sound economy, at least it wouldn't make things worse, which the Carter proposal undoubtedly would have. In other words, having nothing was better than having Carter's proposal. And that's the way it all came out. For a few years the Gephardt *nothing* substitute was the law and the medical business continued to bite off more and more than its share of the economy year after year.

My substitute, though rejected during the Carter administration, later did, in essence, become the law of the land as we shall see. Instead of saddling the hospitals with more government bureaucracy if they failed their own guidelines, my proposal would have relieved them of *all* government bureaucracy. The government would simply stop doing Medicare business with any hospital that exceeded its private association's price guideline. In place of casting Uncle Sam as a meddler, my idea would have turned him into a prudent shopper. If the price at one hospital was too high, take the Medicare business elsewhere. *Competition.* Properly motivated by some old-fashioned incentive, the people who knew enormously more about running hospitals than government agents did could find effective ways to cut prices without reducing the quality which, under my substitute, Uncle Sam also had to take into account as he shopped.

Medicare got off on the wrong foot when it was enacted in 1965. It used a bad model, the infamous "cost-plus" method of procurement at the Pentagon.

Cost-plus was, in 1965, an oppressive atavism from World War II. In the early, dark, and frightening days of that struggle for freedom's survival, our country's effort was all-out. The heavy manufacturing industry must convert from things like cars to things like bombers immediately, if not sooner. Never mind the cost; in fact it had to be done "at all cost." And that's just about what happened. The deal with the companies was, "Tool up fast and whatever your costs, the government will pay you that cost, plus a fixed percent of it as your profit." Whoopee. In the entire history of the human race, never was there a stronger incentive, a more luscious invitation to waste.

Though an uninspiring substitute for public spirit at the time, at least there was an argument for cost-plus in those scary months following Pearl Harbor. Not so the cost-plus arrangement for Medicare payments to hospitals following the Johnson landslide of 1964. My proposal during the Carter administration would not have ended the error of cost-plus, but it would have taken a hefty whack at it. One member of the Carter administration understood and supported my idea. She was Esther Peterson, Carter's special assistant for consumer affairs. The administration didn't listen to her, either.

In the summer of 1978, I participated in another fund-raising roast, this one for my gentle, bright, and pleasant friend, Representative Dan Glickman from Wichita, Kansas. He later became U.S. Secretary of Agriculture. Wichita was heavily and humorously in the national news at the time. Its city council had passed a gay rights ordinance and the orange juice lady, Anita Byrant, had rushed there to get the voters to repeal it by referendum. They did so and a young councilman saw a political opportunity in it. He proposed an ordinance which would outlaw oral sex within the city limits of Wichita, Kansas. Mind you, his ordinance did not say *gay* oral sex, just oral sex. Naturally, I didn't take a public opinion poll in Wichita, but offhand I would guess that such an ordinance wouldn't be the way to get elected to anything. Our country's comedians, with Johnny Carson leading the way, had the proverbial field day with that one. So did I when I got to Wichita. Danny Glickman's wife, Rhoda, briefed the guest speakers before the show began. She told us the subjects she hoped we would avoid, saying, "Whatever you do, we can't have any jokes about oral sex. They would greatly offend the audience."

That genre had not occurred to me, but I was grateful for the suggestion. In the manner of my joke about *Playboy* in the Catholic parish meeting that night in 1970, I assumed this subject would play as well in Wichita as it did in Peoria when Johnny Carson used it on NBC.

Modesty forbids, or almost forbids, my revealing that by the middle 1970s, I wasn't altogether bad at doing impressions. I had President Carter's voice down pretty well when I was called to the dais that evening. Valerie Pennson, Carter's highly intelligent and just plain nice congressional liaison officer, was among the six or so roasters from Washington.

So when I mentioned Carter, she started paying close attention—she was two seats from me at the dais. Drawing on Carter's penchant for pious public pronouncements on the one hand and his famous *Playboy* interview on the other, I said we had a surprise guest, displayed a very toothy smile, and began my Carter shtick: "As you know, I've always admired your city for rejectin' the ways of Sodom and Gomorrah."

Ms. Glickman was mistaken. From the huge and well-informed audience came spontaneous laughter and several shrieks of delight. At this point I displayed even a toothier Carter smile:

"I think you went a little too far, though, when you tried to outlaw oral sex here in town. After all, I can't see anything wrong with just *talkin'* about sex—so long as you don't do it in front of a *Playboy* reporter."

Now several people were spilling beer as they leaned over in thunderous appreciation of the gag. Still using Carter's voice, I looked at his liaison lady and said, "Hi, Val."

I don't recall that Valerie laughed. If she didn't, she was the only one except me; that definitely would have been immodest. That was 1978. In 1998, I saw my gag in a *New Yorker* cartoon. Did they plagiarize? Of course not. They probably had never heard of me, let alone what I said on that rollicking evening west of the Mississippi. But it did take them twenty years longer than it took me to come up with it.

Among the most intelligent women in the United States Congress was Representative Helen Minor of New Jersey. One day in the late summer of 1978, Helen called me to report some shenanigans surrounding the Endangered Species Act which was scheduled for legislative extension sometime in the wee hours of the approaching nighttime. The problem, she said, involved the peregrine falcon, which not so mysteriously was dropped from the protection list in the bill reported by the Commerce Committee.

The bird clearly belonged on the list; nobody involved in the deletion could make reasonable argument otherwise. But there was an unreasonable reason for the change; Mideastern potentates were willing to buy the birds at half a million dollars per copy.

Helen asked me to speak in favor of her floor amendment to restore the protection. The night would be long because it was the last meeting of the Ninety-sixth Congress and there was much work to be done. She said she would call me a few minutes before she offered the amendment. That turned out to be about three o'clock in the morning. Having sneaked a short nap, I was still not completely awake when I stepped onto the floor. Helen had just been recognized and I heard her beautifully cultured voice explaining the case for extension of the bird's protection.

The chairman of the committee was my friend, the articulate John D. Dingell of Michigan. At least he was my friend up until that evening—later, too. John undertook a defense of the committee recommendation by explaining that being on the endangered list meant the peregrine falcon could not be moved around the country from aviary to aviary for the purpose of propagation. Therefore, he said, having the bird on the list was—I'll use my term—*counter*-reproductive.

When I spoke for Helen's amendment, I said that if it were not adopted, I would offer one that would keep the bird on the protection list, but allow it to be moved for the purpose stated by the committee chairman. There was an oft-repeated slogan used by those opposed to the Vietnam War—"make love, not war." For my peroration, I coined a paraphrase. "In other words," I added for the Record and edification of those present, all of whom knew perfectly well the motive for the recommended change, "make love, not money." In terms of laughs from *most* of the other members, I hit pay dirt myself.

The chairman didn't like it. As the debate continued, he walked into the well of the House and said to me, "You think that was funny, don't you?" To which I replied, "John, I'd honestly give it an 'eight' [out of ten]." My lighthearted reply clearly angered John all the more. The more he raised his voice and gestured with his long arms, the funnier the scene seemed to me. But, well, have you ever tried to suppress a cough during a sermon in church? What had happened years before, when I witnessed Chairman Celler quote from the Bible in his final stand against the Equal Rights Amendment, was happening to me again. My laughter was involuntary. I really didn't want to excite John more, but the more I heard, the more the laughter sputtered and spurted out of my mouth. John was not laughing; he was nowhere close to happy.

When the chairman strode away in something along the lines of a huff, I took a seat near the well and wrote out my amendment for the reading clerk. While I did so, a congressional page walked over to me and said, "Mr. Jacobs, I would never talk to another person the way that chairman just spoke to you." I said something to the effect that ordinarily the chairman was a pleasant person and the problem was probably partly the lateness of the hour. Then I heard a member ask John to yield the floor for a question; he declined. The other member proceeded to speak anyway. It was the duty of the presiding officer to rap for order and say, "The gentleman from Michigan declines to yield." The other member was clearly out of order. But the fellow in the chair, though not literally asleep, was definitely asleep at the switch. So John used the prescribed language to remind the chairman of the Committee of the *Whole* to do his duty. John said, "Mr. Chairman, I demand protection from the Chair." The offending member was called to order. And I was inspired to launch one more foray of fun. When I spoke for my amendment, I added at the end:

"A few minutes ago, I heard the gentleman from Michigan demand protection from the Chair. And the way that same gentleman approached me in the well just before that, flailing his arms and addressing me angrily, perhaps I need protection from the Chair. But I don't think so. Because if the gentleman from Michigan *ever* does that to me again, the gentleman from Michigan is going to find out what an *endangered species* really is."

Lots of laughs again from just about everyone but John. With few members in attendance, the committee bill prevailed. My amendment, just as Helen's, failed. Congress adjourned, and we went home to our respective districts to see if our constituents wanted us to represent them in the next Congress of the United States. When John and I came back after being re-elected, we pretty much fell all over each other apologizing. I was really fond of John, but the wee hours can do funny things to people.

There was an Indianapolis mayoral election in 1979 and one of the candidates showed up regularly at my town meetings with constituents. He was there to campaign to the crowd that came to talk about Congress, not city hall. Knowing who he was the first night he crashed our meeting and suspecting why he was there, I ignored his repeatedly raised hand all evening until I was sure the regular participants had finished their comments and questions. When I did call on him, he arose, walked to the front of the room, turned his back to me and said, "I am the Socialist-Labor Candidate for mayor." The reaction of an elderly lady in the front row was instantaneous and apparently involuntary. To the candidate's consternation, she burst out laughing, whereupon, I tapped him on the shoulder and politely said, "Obviously not one of your campaign staffers." The other forty people joined in the laughter. To the best of my recollection, the Socialist-Labor candidate did not win the 1979 Indianapolis mayoral election. I believe it was my good friend Bill Hudnut.

My dad had a good story about a farmer who was a socialist and tried to persuade his neighbor to become one, too. The neighbor said, "Do you mean that if you had two saddle horses, you'd give me one?"

"Yes," said the socialist. "And," asked the other, "if you had two milch cows, you'd give me one of them?"

"Certainly," declared the party member. "And," the neighbor inquired, "if you had two hogs, you'd give me one of them?" The socialist lowered his assertiveness and sheepishly said, "Now, you know I have two hogs." Incidents like that probably had something to do with the defeat of the Socialist-Labor candidate for mayor.

In 1979, one of God's noblemen, the pleasant, wise and scintillating Carl Dortch, ended his long tenure as president of the Indianapolis Chamber of Commerce.

Carl's retirement party was held in a vast tent on the grounds of the Indianapolis Museum of Art. I was privileged to be among those asked to speak. Having flown in from Washington that evening in a plane that was slightly late, I arrived at the party after the program had begun. My seatmate on the flight was Senator Birch Bayh who told me he had been invited, too, but had a prior commitment to fly on to Fort Wayne to participate in a conference at the Veterans Administration Hospital there.

The program at the party was imaginative; the speakers were scattered among the endless dinner tables and as each was called on by the master of ceremonies, each was handed a remote wireless microphone to speak her or his piece. Just before I was tapped, the emcee read congratulatory telegrams. But when he got to the one from Birch, he told the 99 percent Republican audience, "Here's one from Senator Bayh." And with that, instead of reading it, he made a pronounced gesture of wadding it and throwing it over his shoulder. It wasn't in the best taste, but it was done in fun and of course the audience roared. Then it was my turn.

After expressing my affection and profound admiration for Carl, I told a couple of jokes about the very small town where he was reared. "The town was *so small* . . ." Echoing the Johnny Carson *Tonight Show* routine, the audience chanted, "How small *was* it?" I told them. "It was so small that when someone pushed a toaster lever down, the street car stopped; it was so small that there was only one *Yellow Page* in the phone book; and it was so small that the cab driver asked *you* where to meet women." Then I added a note of apology for my having not arrived on time: "I flew in with Birch Bayh who had to press on to the VA Hospital in Fort Wayne. So I asked Birch if he'd like for me to deliver a message for him here. Birch said, 'Thanks, Andy, you don't have to do that, but could you let me know if they read my telegram?'"

There was a moment of silence at my slightly offbeat humor and then the place broke up with heavy-duty and sustained laughter. Nice people. They were not fellow Democrats. Much more important, they were fellow Americans.

chapter 14

LANDSLIDE

NINETEEN-EIGHTY WAS the last earthly year for a civil saint. Surely in God's eyes, spiritual, moral, and intellectual giant Allard K. Lowenstein ranks with Gandhi and King as being among the noblest of his noblemen. Al's words were soft-spoken, but they were powerfully compelling far beyond his physical presence.

The manner of Al's death was echoed by another tragic event that occurred eighteen years later on the afternoon of July 24, 1998. On that latter date, the world watched in horror and sorrow as television flashed the images of stretchers at the U.S. Capitol bearing two fatally wounded police officers, the dastardly deed having been provoked by insanity. A deranged man, said to have believed that the federal government had placed land mines around him and nuclear weapons around Helena, Montana, burst past a metal detector and fired a thirty-eight caliber pistol point-blank at two peace officers, both of whom died. One of the slain police officers had managed to return the fire and stop the assailant.

The same sort of person emptied a nine millimeter automatic pistol into the great heart of Al Lowenstein in New York on March 14, 1980. The assassin insisted that a dentist had installed radio equipment in his teeth at Al's behest.

Gifted *Washington Post* writer Richard Cohen said Al "mattered in Mississippi and he mattered in New York politics and he mattered in the U.S. Congress and in South Africa." All that was true. As a university professor, he had led one of the first freedom expeditions of Northern students into the old Confederacy. The students went south to help Americans of African descent in their attempts to vote. In 1968 Al was elected to the U.S. House from Long Beach, New York only to be gerrymandered out by Governor Nelson Rockefeller, after just one term. He was the only anti-apartheid person allowed by the South African apartheid regime to speak on government-run television there. They allowed it because Al was so different from other activists.

Al Lowenstein was not only a protester; he was a peacemaker as well. His message was one of reconciliation, of reminders that, though the two sides of a controversy were far apart, there was room for peaceful redemption of the oppressors who, after all, were for the most part humans with hearts that could be changed without violence—especially without violence. It had worked for Gandhi, King, Mandela, and, I presume to add, Jesus Christ himself.

Columnist Cohen could have mentioned other places where Al's stunning influence produced peaceful and positive results. Those places included Spain, Portugal, and Eritrea where he went to counsel underground movements that struggled for the freedom of democracy. Time and again he risked his life, which he consecrated to the cause of justice, often flying into clandestine airfields whose glide path instruments for landing were nothing more than flashlights. When those freedom movements succeeded in Spain and Portugal, it was Al who was in demand at the U.S. State Department because, unlike our official diplomats, Al knew the unwashed who had been freely chosen "by the people" to head the newly democratic governments. He served awhile as one of our ambassadors to the United Nations. One of his best books—there were many, all products of his prolific genius—was *Brutal Mandate,* a riveting expose of oppression in Namibia where once again he sailed in by stealth, risking his life to "undo the heavy burden" of a suffering people. Al was my friend and just about everybody else's, too.

He was not only a friend; with his puckish humor, he was a fun friend. On several occasions, a lady friend and I would go from Washington to New York for dinner and to see a Broadway show with Al and his wife, Jenny. Fictional Hoosier philosopher and non-grammarian Abe Martin tells us, "We're all pretty much the same when we git out of town." Trouble is that in the second half of twentieth century America, it became pretty hard to "git" out of town within Abe's meaning. So there we were in Manhattan on a lovely summer's evening, the four of us strolling along Broadway when I heard someone behind us say, "Congressman." I was reminded that we were in the presence of a big hunk of history. But even so, I was a little surprised that in that city with teeming millions of faceless faces, Al would be recognized; he wasn't. As the voice found its body, the woman was looking at me and adding, "Aren't you Congressman Jacobs?" She and her husband were in New York for dinner and a play. They had just flown in from Indianapolis.

Considering the way he lived, it was not altogether surprising that Al thought about his death and even planned his funeral. On Saturday, March 15, 1980, I received a call from Jenny, who told me Al had left word that he wanted me to speak at his funeral, which I agreed to do. The group he chose to speak was motley. There was Andrew Young, who at one time or another was almost everything in governmental service—U.S. Representative, Atlanta mayor, ambassador to the U.N. and close associate of Martin Luther King, Jr.—with his usual gentle eloquence. Others who spoke included Democratic Senator Ted Kennedy, Republican Representative Pete McCloskey and—brace yourself—conservative commentator William F. Buckley, Jr. It was inevitable that when Buckley and Al met, they would become friends despite their ideological differences. They admired each other's superior intellects and, more important, one another's intellectual honesty.

The funeral was held at Central Synagogue on Lexington Avenue at Fifty-fifth Street in Manhattan. The temple had seating capacity for about fifteen hundred, but that was not enough. Two thousand attended, the extra five hundred spilling over into the surrounding streets where the service was heard through a public address system.

Al wanted Peter Yarrow and Mary Travers, of the famous folk song trio, to sing along with musical storyteller Harry Chapin. All three were there and added beauty. There was a small controversy about one of the musical selections Al had requested. He wanted the mourners to hear his artist friends sing "Amazing Grace," which apparently was just fine with the young rabbis, but unthinkable to the older ones. The young clerics suggested that their leaders think about it, anyway, and when the seniors did, they thought it would be okay after all. A few weeks after the funeral, Harry Chapin himself was gone, killed in a surrealistic auto accident on a crowded New York freeway.

William Buckley said that, "In our time, Al Lowenstein was the original activist." Ted Kennedy said Al was "a one-man demonstration for civil rights" who carried his world, including clothes, in an old briefcase and therefore he was "a portable and powerful lobby for progressive principles." Pete McCloskey's powerful remarks were punctuated with the grief of a highly decorated Marine combat veteran who made it home only to lose one more close friend to gunfire.

When the rabbi nodded to me, I went to the microphone and stirred painful lament, admiration, and humor into the solemnity of that grief-stricken event:

> "The good die young." Lincoln, Gandhi, Evers, Kennedy, King and Kennedy again. And now Al. We are tempted to believe that the most dangerous thing on this earth to do is preach love and kindliness.
>
> Al was at war with war and his weapon was peace. Gerald Johnson wrote of the World War I pacifists, "They had no objection at all to fighting the police." But Al did have such objection. He believed deeply that any public demonstration for peace which, itself, was not peaceful was public hypocrisy. He practiced the promise of Lincoln that, "I shall do nothing out of malice; what I deal in is too *vast* for malice." Al knew that 'do as I say, not as I do' would never do for effective leadership. And his leadership was effective. He lost a lot of elections, but he won a lot of hearts and, in the process, helped in the effort to save our country's soul.
>
> When Al asked how you were, he really wanted to know. Each friend counted completely. Everyone here was Al's best friend. At one time or another in one way or another, everyone here was in that kitchen in Long Beach when Al did his impression of our former colleague Bob Pogue, who had a peculiar verbal mannerism: "Lowenstein, I don't want—aye—to hurt your—aye—feelings, but you—aye—have a reputation for—aye—bein' a *lib-rul*!"
>
> Al; what a paradox. Like a gentle tornado he would breeze into town, insist that you tell him your troubles, tell you about the troubles of others and what you ought to be doing about them, borrow your telephone—usually for long-distance toll calls—and be gone.
>
> One evening when I was low with flu, I saw Al in the House gymnasium. He wondered if I would like to go with him to Fred Graham's house for dinner. No, I wouldn't. I simply wanted a fast meal and an early bedtime. Al assured me that all this could be accomplished. We'd probably just eat out in the kitchen, have a few good words of conversation, and I could be home in bed by nine. Do I have to tell anybody here that when we arrived at the Graham home, a full court, black-tie dinner was in progress? Al never expected as much of others as he expected of himself. But he expected so much of himself that he could be damn hard on his friends.
>
> Politicians, not Al's constituents, decided Al would not go back to Congress; they gerrymandered him. He always wanted to go back because he thought he could serve his country better there. Once,

when he confided his disappointment, I mentioned the name Phil Hayes. Looking puzzled, Al asked, "Who's Phil Hayes?" And I said, "He's a Representative in Congress and he knows who you are." He didn't have to be in Congress to work his marvels. Politics "is the art of the possible." Al's was the art of making things possible. We shall never know how many deaths and corresponding broken hearts he averted by showing America the way away from war.

So thanks, Al, for being our good friend and our wise teacher.

Following the funeral, in a moment of sorrowful solitude, I searched for the essence of Al's effectiveness as a leader. And it came to me. Al had the gift of being able to *convince* people who differed that they need not fear one another and that, therefore, they need not hate one another and that, therefore, they need not harm one another. "Blessed are the peacemakers." There is such a severe shortage of them.

Among my most cherished treasures are the letters about my eulogy from Al's family. "To be beautiful and to be calm is the ideal of nature," the philosopher tells us. Such a person was Jenny Littlefield, Al's former wife. Her letter was almost as beautiful as she. Al's brother, Larry, proprietor of the Puffing Billy restaurant in Manhattan, sent words of comfort which he needed himself. And dear Dottie, Al's loving sister, showered her warmth with wonderful words. Her lifelong friend Barbara Dammann sent me a note of friendship from New York, adding at the end, "I might move to Indiana so I could vote for you, if I knew where it was." Al's close friendships with celebrated citizens were always a matter of modesty with him. But the facts came out at the funeral. There, I looked down into the faces of Jackie Kennedy, Lauren Bacall, countless other stars of life and one of my towering heroes, David Halberstam. I trust I do no violence to confidence by telling you the encouraging words he wrote to me from his hotel in Kansas City on March 20, 1980, a few days after the service:

Dear Andy:

This is just a brief note to tell you how much your remarks at Allard's service meant to me—they were wise and appropriate, catching not only strengths, but his flaws as well; this made him more human, allowing us to love him and miss him that much more. Thank you.

With appreciation, David Halberstam

Al was buried at Arlington. The evening before, Representative Doug

Walgren from Pennsylvania went to the cemetery to discuss arrangements with officials there. He was shown the site they had chosen and he told them it wouldn't do at all. Instead, he said, since Al was very close to the Kennedy family, Al should be buried close to President Kennedy and the Eternal Flame. Allard K. Lowenstein, American citizen extraordinaire, sleeps the big sleep immediately to the left of John F. Kennedy, just as Bobby Kennedy does immediately to the right. Arlington, our country's most distinguished immortal dorm.

The year 1980 brought not only a spectacular electoral success for the Republican Party, but also—and especially—an historic shift in the GOP's center of gravity. It was the year of fulfillment for the Goldwater Wing which had for so long wandered in the desert of U.S. politics.

Because of the landslide, Dan Quayle rode in and Birch Bayh rode out of the U.S. Senate. Sandburg tells us that Lincoln had expected to lose his bid for re-election in 1864. And since, in 1980, I was running for re-election in the same gerrymandered district where I had lost to the 1972 GOP Nixon landslide, I expected to lose again. The fact that Indianapolis was still using the straight-party voting lever was scarcely an encouragement to me as the storm clouds gathered over the Democrats' horizon that year.

Early in the year 1980, there was a cultural occasion in the House Ways and Means Committee chamber. Potted palms were brought in to surround an attraction that looked a lot like a puppet stage, including small velvet curtains. An expensive tax-paid tradition was being honored even as the taxpayers were not. The puppet show was actually a picture. A ten thousand dollar tax-paid painting of Chairman Al Ullman was to be unveiled that day. It rested on an easel behind the lush burgundy fabric.

I happened to be in the chamber checking some documents when the parade of props arrived. Among them, I noticed a stack of programs for the great event. As I perused one, I found an offset-printed picture of the painting. I do not ask you to take my word for this; if you ever get to Washington, you can go to that Ways and Means chamber where the large framed oil rendering hangs with all the others, and see for yourself. But I tell you now that it is grotesque, even scary. So much so that I was reminded of the novel *The Picture of Dorian Gray*, the story of a man who assigned his soul to the Devil, who in return arranged for his victim's age and sins to show up on a painting rather than the sinner's face.

Al Ullman was a sweet and innocent man. The image on the canvas reflects none of that. There is turbulent madness in the eyes and the human image appears against a dark and stormy background except for an explosion of garish light which frames the subject's head. I'm afraid the hellish work brought out something devilish in me. Even if you discount the humor in what I did, at the very least I struck a sympathetic blow for the taxpayers.

I took all fifty programs to my assigned seat on the Committee dais and went to work. There was no caption beneath the printed picture, so I supplied one in each copy. The caption I supplied simply inquired "The Picture of Dorian Who?"

My successful timing was a matter both of calculation and luck. When the guests filed in and took their seats with programs in hands, they busied themselves visiting with one another. And when the proceedings began they paid attention to the speakers, one of whom asked the "artist" to stand and bow.

Just before the shrouds were drawn aside, however, most of the audience tired of the embellished oratory and opened their programs. I don't think Hollywood could have choreographed it better. Exactly as the guests looked up from their programs to see the real work of dark art, at least three-fourths of them thundered with laughter. The important people who spoke had not so much as a clue about the cause of the outburst—until the dismissal when they discovered the addendum. Herewith I make my first public confession: I did it, guys.

There was another perk about which I was irked: the tax-paid slush funds for former presidents. I never objected to the Secret Service protection, although at this year 2000 writing, no former president, as such, has ever been the target of intended physical harm. Teddy Roosevelt was shot and slightly wounded in Cincinnati after he had served as president, but at the time he was running for president again and, in the darker historic parlance, was once again in the "big game" category. Former President Ronald Reagan was shoved when he stood at a microphone in California, but the *shover* clearly meant to do no harm to Reagan; he was just trying to get at the public address system. Nonetheless, I would err on the side of safety when it comes to funding the bodyguards for the ex-chief executives. But why the offices and staffs?

In all cases except Nixon's—he even paid for his own bodyguards—those offices would serve primarily as booking agencies for indecently lucrative speeches by the famous men who become ornamental trophies at well-heeled conventions. "The ex-presidency has become big business," my sage friend Jim Beatty said. Under the circumstances, I saw no reason why the taxpayers should cover the overhead of that big and enormously profitable business. So on May 14, 1980, I introduced the following bill:

The Former Presidents' Enough Is Enough and Taxpayers Relief Act of 1980

Be it enacted by the Senate and House of Representatives of the United States of America in Congress assembled, that the total annual Government expenditures for the care and feeding of any former President shall not exceed ten times the poverty level income of an urban family of four.

When I offered that bill in the form of an amendment to the appropriate appropriation bill on the House floor, it passed only to be killed in a House/Senate conference. But there was much sympathy for it both among the public and in the public press. Years later, the slush funds were shrunk, but a lot that shouldn't remain of those slush funds does remain. In a way, the burden on the taxpayers is growing. As the human life span lengthens, ex-presidents are beginning to pile up on us.

You will recall that in 1970 I was compelled by conscience to offend the powers that were and they gerrymandered me out of Congress. Now, in 1980, I again faced a choice between immoral appeasement and facing renewed efforts to railroad me out of office.

It was the stately old Union Station in Indianapolis. As a student at a Catholic military high school near Chicago, I had boarded trains many times in the Indianapolis station. And when I left with the Marines for war, it was on a troop train which sadly chugged out of the same place. But by the early 1970s, most of the facility had fallen to disuse and disrepair. The property was controlled by a bankruptcy court from which the Indianapolis city administration purchased an option to buy the dilapidated memory. The option was held long enough for the good sense of Mayor Lugar to study and reject a proposed $196,000 renovation project.

The proposal involved turning the property into a night spot for downtown entertainment. The city sold the option to a group of politically well-placed businesspeople who had so many stars in their eyes about making a financial killing that they failed to read the periodic journal on train station restoration. Had they done so, they would have discovered that, in the opinion of the publishers, some cities, such as St. Louis, were ideal for train station restoration. They would also have discovered that Indianapolis specifically was not among them. The long-term prospects were very poor because of the demography of Indianapolis. It seemed to me that there would be a few years of fad, followed by a return to the handier watering holes of suburbia. And that's what happened, but only after nearly twenty million federal-borrowed dollars were squandered on it. The failed project remains part of the national debt.

In addition to the five-thousand-dollar-cost of the option, the business syndicate paid about two hundred thousand dollars for the property. As the decade of the 1970s closed, the private syndicate began to realize what it easily could have learned from reading that train station journal several years before. There was no financial killing to be made. They were essentially in the position of the farmer who told friends he had bought hogs for four dollars each in the spring and sold them for four dollars each in the fall. To which his friends said, "You can't make money that way." The farmer agreed, "We found that out."

The difference was that we can assume the farmer had to suffer his loss. The train station syndicate was too well politically situated even to consider such a fate. No! Not when borrowing by the federal government in the name of the taxpayers was available. That's where duty called me. The syndicate wouldn't just settle for saddling the public with a bailout of their failed investment in the amount of the two hundred thousand dollar purchase price. They also wanted the taxpayers to put up another four hundred thousand dollars to cover the amounts the syndicate had subsequently poured down the money pit. In effect, the city administration said, "Anything you fellows say," and got the federal housing officials on the phone. "Yes, six hundred thousand dollars would do nicely for the city to buy the otherwise unsellable entity." Indiana Congressman Dave Evans joined in my request for a U.S. General Accounting Office appraisal. GAO came up with about three hundred and fifty thousand dollars as a value. Therefore, the federal housing folks used funds meant to help the solve the city's housing problems to write a check for the bailout, at the smaller figure Dave Evans and I had forced. And never mind that at the time, certain Indianapolis neighborhoods were sagging and needed the diverted funds. Holy cows get fed; regular cows get slaughtered.

While the city was maneuvering and manipulating federal funds for the bailout, I was asked to be the guest on an evening TV news show. The interviewer at one point asked, "Well, what are we going to do with the train station?" I gave the famous reply Tonto gave to the Lone Ranger when angry Indians were closing in: "What do you mean, 'we'? *We* don't own the failed project—unwise private investors do." I enjoyed her next question: "We don't?" She was not alone in being misled by the persistent propaganda. Of course, it wasn't long before "we" did own the turkey.

Once the city owned the white elephant, the officials had to come up with a yarn to justify the purchase/bailout. This was their official line: The building had once been a train station. On the theory that all cottage cheese is made in cottages, they'd just dub this restaurant, popcorn and beer entertainment debacle a "transportation center." That would convey to the U.S. Transportation Department the notion that it should make a multimillion-dollar federal grant, not to bolster the anemic public transit system in Indianapolis, but to make the bailout seem somehow to be in the general and unexplained transportation interests of the public. The less-fortunate citizens who spent time cleaning suburban homes could just continue to stand in freezing rain, singing, "Some day my bus will come."

My efforts to stop the scheme were, of course, in vain. The rails, you might say, had long since been greased. But I continued my opposition right up to the day the grant was made.

One day I picked up a copy of the *Indianapolis News* and saw this headline: "CITY OFFICIAL SEES NEW COMMERCIAL POTENTIAL IN UNION STATION." Next day, the same paper carried my response: "'UNION STATION HAS ALL THE COMMERCIAL POTENTIAL OF A DINOSAUR SADDLE': JACOBS." A few days after that I received two memorable letters. The first was from a well-to-do lady in Indianapolis. Written on embossed stationery with a fine hand, it was downright refreshing to a congressman facing likely defeat at the polls less than a year later. Her letter began, "Thank you for reminding me why I am so happy to have you as my representative." In an all-but-tear-stained reply, I thanked her.

The other letter came not from my Indianapolis district, but from the place of my parents' wedding, Greenfield, Indiana. The letter was from a man who reported in facetiously serious words, which is to say desert-dry wit, that, "I received a notice from a freight transfer company yesterday morning. There was a huge crate to be delivered to my home. When it arrived, I discovered a behemoth beast with an unbelievably long neck. Its skin was more like scales and, if anything, the tail was longer than the neck. So I was wondering if you have any idea where I might buy a saddle for it. Keep up the good work."

My message was beginning to get through to the public, but the rails were still greased—except for the PR arena. Therefore, the PR man for the syndicate crafted a letter which was published in the *Indianapolis Star*. In it he said that the city could succeed where private enterprise had failed because, unlike the private owners, the city would not have to pay property tax on the place. My response to the editor was published surprisingly quickly. Right, I said, "the city would not have to pay the property tax, the property taxpayers would. Every time one more parcel goes off the rolls, all the other property still in private hands is taxed more." Once again with haste, the *Star* published another letter from someone I did not know. He said that I had hit the nail on the head. The PR man used a few nails, himself, to put a dinosaur-size sign in his front yard promoting my opponent's candidacy the following fall.

In Jeremy Larner's screenplay *The Candidate*, a hapless, handsome young man is elected to the United States Senate. Bewildered by the good news on election night, he turns to his "handlers" and asks, "What do we do now?" I thought about that line when I read a May 22, 1980 story in the *Indianapolis Star*. The headline read:

CITY BECOMES UNION STATION OWNER; USES BEING STUDIED

Headlines told the story. By September 26, an *Indianapolis News* headline read:

UNION STATION COSTS CLIMB

And on and on. The enormously expensive government work was completed about halfway through the 1980s and the five year fad began. By the 1990s, Union Station was becoming the province of the pigeons once again. I dare say, I was vindicated. I really didn't need vindication with the general public. Even before the taxpayers were strapped under that *dinosaur saddle*, practically everyone who wasn't in on it saw it for what it was.

In 1986 there was an amusing incident in connection with the project. I picked up the phone one day in Washington and heard the voice of my Indianapolis City Hall antagonist, the official who honchoed the Union Station project. "You're not going to believe this," he said. "Try me," I said. "If I put my mind to it, I suppose I can be gullible."

"Well," said my friendly *enemy*—and he was friendly all along, no doubt not happy, but friendly—"if we don't get a transition rule on the tax bill before your committee, the Union Station project is dead." He meant the historic restoration tax credit which was about to be reduced in the 1986 tax act. The city contractors needed and had counted on every penny of the higher credit in order for the project to be viable. A transition rule meant the old law would apply despite the fact that actual expenditures would be made under the new law.

Under the Ways and Means Committee guidelines, in order to qualify for a transition rule a deal must have been made early enough to have reasonably relied on the provisions of the old law. Clearly that was the situation with the Union Station project. But qualifying didn't necessarily mean getting the transition tax treatment. And that's where I came in. As a member of the committee, I was at the table to plead the case. I had a question for my city hall caller: "How much of our money do you have in the project now?" Answer: "About twenty million."

"Well," I concluded, "if the taxpayers pay for a turkey, I suppose they should at least get the turkey." The transition rule was not in the usual technical gobbledygook of legalese; it simply said the old credit would apply to "any renovation to the Union Station in Indianapolis, Indiana." I did not break faith with my opposition to spending public money on the train station. Had the project fallen on its face in 1986, five years of revenue from it would not have been received for upkeep. In slight legalese, I helped mitigate the damage.

My service on Ways and Means enabled me to help Indianapolis many times. But not once did I advocate anything for back home that was not clearly in order. To do otherwise would have been at variance with what I had refused to in do the case of the unnecessary federal judgeship. But where I judged the request to be just, I worked hard to obtain results and usually did obtain them for my home town. Indianapolis was entitled to the tax help I was able to get for it, but had I not been at the Ways and Means table, justice for Indianapolis would have been a long way from assured. I was the only member of Congress from either party from Indianapolis to have been elected by colleagues to the House Ways and Means Committee in the entire twentieth century if you believe it ended at midnight, 12-31-99. It was more than probable that the same would be true if you believed that the century could not end until midnight, 12-31-00. Looked like the latter to me.

Of course, requests for beneficial tax provisions did not just come from Indianapolis. Wall Street was a regular communicant. One of the most brash of birds roosting on that wall was the E. F. Hutton Bond Brokerage. That group thought up a way to take legislatively unintended and enormously profitable advantage of municipal tax-free federal bonds. The scheme was simple; get local units of government to issue what Hutton called tax exempt mortgage bonds. Those who bought the bonds paid no federal tax and usually no state tax on the interest, making the bonds very attractive investments. The proceeds of the bonds would then be used for home mortgage loans at lower than market interest. But after Hutton, the bond opinion lawyers, and the holders of the bonds took their respective cuts, scarcely a third of the revenue lost to the U.S. Treasury was left to benefit of home buyers.

By the summer of 1979 the loophole was costing the treasury about

$2 billion dollars annually. About $700 million of those dollars went to subsidized home buyers and the rest, about $1.3 billion, was fluttering into the pockets of middlemen and women, largely including E. F. Hutton. This was an unintended social program with a *200 percent* administrative overhead. Compared to the vast Medicare program which had a *2—not* 200—percent administrative overhead, the mortgage bond rip-off smelled to high Heaven. And the news media got a bad whiff of it.

The onus was on the Ways and Means Committee to fumigate the matter. The schemers at the brokerage firm had a ubiquitous TV ad which everyone, including late-night TV comics, seemed to be quoting: "When E. F. Hutton talks, people listen." Problem: E. F. Hutton's campaign money *also talked* to those members of the Ways and Means Committee who received it in the form of PAC campaign contributions. Still, there was outrage in the land. So the committee knew it must either do something or *seem* to do something in the nature of reform. Comedians were beginning to get *rueful* laughs from taxpayers by referring to "E. F. Glutton."

The committee set about the task of weaving a foggy fig leaf. It would cap the tax expenditure at $1.5 billion a year, preserving the same ratio of ripoff in favor of the schemers and against everyone else. The split would be about five hundred million for a relatively small number of home buyers and a cool billion for the middle people. "The more things [would] change, the more they [would] remain the same."

The committee weavers protected their patrons' billion dollars and set new restrictions on just who could qualify to obtain mortgages from $500 million allowed to trickle down to the announced purpose of the program. Participants would have to be first-time home buyers. Yes, and they must have middle income or less—as if low-income people could buy homes, anyway. The legislative cobbling went on for several days and, to use the Hoosier idiom I used on Governor Jerry Brown, I "*lay* in the weeds," poised to break up the perfidious party.

In its June 12, 1979 editions, the *New York Times* ran an editorial entitled "The Lesser Mortgage Evil." The editorial laid out what had happened with regard to the mortgage bonds, severely criticizing the raid on the treasury. Then in paragraph five the editorial described what I did to frustrate E. F. Hutton's advocates in Congress:

> Enter Representative Jacobs. If the tax revenue has to be lost, why should all the benefit go arbitrarily to home buyers lucky enough to live in communities with tax-exempt bond programs? And why

provide a cut for the middlemen? He proposes instead a ten percent tax credit (with a four hundred dollar annual ceiling) to *all* middle- and lower-income buyers.

Compared with tax-exempt housing bonds, the Jacobs tax credit looks tolerable. It would cost no more; the ten percent credit also would drain $1.5 billion annually from the Treasury. Yet many more homeowners would benefit because none of the money would be lost in transit and all would be apportioned fairly.

In the committee it happened a bit more dramatically. I had sought recognition to introduce my substitute the first day of our deliberations, and was told by Chairman Al Ullman that my proposal would not be in order until the end of the regular amendment process. But by that time, several days later, he and certainly all of the E. F. Hutton advocates—on and off the committee—had completely forgotten my announced substitute. Therefore, though I did nothing to bring it about, I very definitely enjoyed the element of surprise. If you could have seen the faces of the interested lobbyists and their counterparts on the Committee when they realized what I was proposing, you would better understand why I so savored the moment. If you could have seen the looks on the same faces when Committee members who were not in on the slick plan began to show interest in my idea, you would better understand why all those expensive suits and Gucci shoes in the audience began to squirm and shuffle.

You should understand that when we met that day, most members, including the chairman, assumed we would only go through the formality of a final vote on whether to report the bill to the House with the changes thus far adopted as the Committee's recommendations. But just as the chairman was about to put that question, I raised my hand and reminded him that I had a substitute pending.

Poor Chairman Al Ullman seemed bewildered; clearly he had forgotten. But one of his staff assistants whispered into his ear a confirmation of what I said. Warily, the chairman said I was recognized for five minutes, more than enough time to describe my substitute. Copies of my substitute had been distributed to the membership, but my colleagues didn't seem to be picking it up, depending instead on my non-legalese description:

> Mr. Chairman, now that we have spent several days determining the kind of a home buyer and the kind of home that can qualify for benefit under this bill, let us now decide how much of the one and a

half billion dollars will be devoted to the stated beneficiaries and therefore how many American homebuyers will be helped. My substitute would put none of the one and a half billion in the pockets of middle-people; instead it would put *all* of it in the hands of the people who buy the homes to live in.

I then described the direct distribution through the percentage tax credit. And, as if the proposal itself were not enough to raise beads of perspiration on the brows of our elegantly dressed onlookers, when the hands of members flew up to express agreement with my proposal, the lobbyists and their very good friends on the committee were just plain and, from my point of view, delightfully flabbergasted.

Bear in mind, thirty minutes would have been plenty of time for the committee to discus my idea and hold a roll call vote on it. Perhaps another ten minutes would have been required formally to report the bill from the Committee. And I had finished my brief presentation long before lunchtime. But the advocates needed a "time-out" to huddle and call a new play. They needed to find some way to answer the unanswerable logic of my proposal. The cat was out of the bag. One of the committee members—my good friend, the country and western songwriter and singer Ken Holland from South Carolina, who was a dead ringer in appearance and voice for the country and western immortal Roger Miller—wrote a verse on the spot and handed it to me:

> *The gentleman from Indianny*
> > *Gave the moneychangers a boot in the fanny.*
> *The route that he went*
> > *Saves 66 percent*
> *For he was a blind hog, not a nanny.*

The bill was not reported that morning, nor was there a vote on my proposal. The chairman announced that further consideration of the legislation would be postponed indefinitely, or in "Congressese"—"pending the call of the Chair." Weeks later, we took up the bill again. I have no way of knowing how many dinners, weekend junkets, and other *gratuities* had worked their wondrous and wicked ways in the interim, but when consideration of my substitute was resumed, the proposal was watered down—not killed. The final product allowed a given municipality a choice; it could further enrich the middle-people or allow its citizens—subjects?— to receive all the money through the individual tax credits. E. F. Hutton began to "talk" locally and apparently some state and local governments listened. Eventually the company, its name and slogan merged into another corporation.

When the time came to start my campaign for re-election in 1980, some of my friends urged me to suspend my policy of not accepting lobbyist PAC money. They plied me with the same logic I heard when I would not relent on the unnecessary and therefore wasteful federal judgeship demanded by certain Indiana politicians before the 1972 election. The price had been my job in Washington; I was, of course, ejected by the computerized gerrymander. This time I gave essentially the same answer as then: true, a Reagan landslide looked likely and my chances against it seemed bleak, but one does not cave in on principles merely once; it's habit-forming. Even once is enough to prove that my policy against PACs wasn't one of principle after all. I like what Robert Bolt wrote in his play, *A Man for All Seasons*:

> When a [person] takes an oath, he is holding himself in his own hands like water. If he spreads his fingers then, he need never hope to find himself again.

So I embarked upon the forbidding journey of my campaign for re-election unburdened by special interest obligations. Also unburdened by a heavy pocketbook.

On April 27, 1980, the *Indianapolis Star* ran an editorial entitled "Keeping Score." It began with:

> After researching the "spending" votes of Hoosier members of Congress, the National Taxpayers Union named Democrat Andrew Jacobs, Jr. the "thriftiest" . . . spender of the Indiana Congressmen."

The editorial concluded:

> Hoosiers who believe that the federal government has spent too much money might well remember the names of these legislators and their scores. It might come in handy some day when Hoosiers go to the polls.

The Taxpayers Union was still maintained by grass-roots donations in those days. Many members of Congress tended to take sides between domestic and military spending, looking the other way when it came to waste of the side chosen and finding nothing but waste on the other side of the accounts. My habit of standing in the middle and shooting both ways at waste usually gave me high marks from organizations that based their ratings on the *total* federal tab. But most of them did not; they followed the path of the Congress, itself. Thus, some organizations were connected with military contractors and naturally found no waste in military spending. Other organizations sided with domestic spending advocates and didn't report waste in that area.

The beauty of the original Taxpayers Union was that it didn't take sides. Spending was spending and waste was waste, domestic or military, and the total amount for which a member cast votes quite logically determined how much of a spender she or he was. In time, the beauty of the organization faded as it received more and more of its funding from sources close to the "military industrial complex." In the process of that transmogrification, the Taxpayers Union scored my spending votes as less frugal, even though those votes remained the same.

The Dan Quayle who was elected to the U.S. Senate in the Reagan landslide was the son of Gene S. Pulliam's sister. During the campaign, people noticed a similarity in appearance between Dan and the actor Robert Redford. To most people it was an interesting coincidence, to some it was amusing, and no one took it seriously, except the actor.

Mr. Redford was a Democrat who supported Quayle's incumbent opponent, Birch Bayh. And, lo and behold, here came a telegram to Indianapolis from California. It was addressed to Dan Quayle and signed by the Hollywood heartthrob, himself. He was angry and I was puzzled. As nearly as I could tell, the actor was demanding that Dan Quayle stop looking like him. Bizarre? Quite. After the election, I saw Dan in the House gym one morning and he wondered if I had a suggestion for an answer he could send to the actor. "Well," I said to Dan, "let me take a cold shower and think about it." This is what I came up with:

Dear Mr. Redford:
    So far as I know, no one has said that I look like you. They all say I look the way you did when you were my age.
                          Sincerely, DQ (not Dairy Queen)

I have a habit, good or bad, of giving nicknames to people I especially like. For example the brilliant top Democratic tax lawyer on the Ways and Means Committee staff is Janice Mays; to me she was Amazing Janice. My sobriquet for the delightful representative John B. Anderson was John

Christian Anderson. Actually, they shared each other's positive qualities. Janice and another staffer, Beth Vance, as well as my office coworker Joe Roemer, gave me invaluable help on the mortgage bond matter.

A few weeks before New Years Day 1980, I received a letter from the Indianapolis Division manager of a huge manufacturing conglomerate. For me, it was Clint Eastwood's make-my-day and Richard Nixon's I'm-glad-you-asked-that-question, all rolled into one. Here in part is what it said:

Dear Congressman Jacobs:

We are very concerned about the growing number of employees on the government payroll.

Will you please inform me how many employees you had on your staff when you first took office and how many employees you have today? Also, if not confidential, please provide a comparison of the amount of your total payroll at the beginning with that of today.

Thank you for any information you can give us to pass along to our employees.

Sincerely yours,

I don't believe it was a friendly letter or even an impartial one. The part about passing the information along to the employees looked like an intended threat. I doubt very seriously that the manager bothered to "pass along" the answers I sent him:

Dear [Manager]:

During my first term in Congress, the authorized personnel for our congressional office numbered 11 and that's how many we had. Today, the law authorizes 22.

. . . our present contingent is 9. On January 1, the number of full-time workers will be 8.

I believe that in 1965 the [staff] payroll was something on the order of $120,000. And at the end of this month it will stand at $187,000. The Consumer Price Index increase from 1965 to now has been approximately 220 percent. Thus, in current dollars, our payroll has gone down $77,000.

At present, the Congressional salary is $60,000; I am accepting $44,600 of it.

I enclose . . . an article from the *Indianapolis Star* relating to the [overall accounts] of [this] congressional office.

Sincerely,

Our overall congressional office accounts were the second-lowest in the nation. My hero, Bill Natcher of Kentucky, beat us, but district office space in his rural district was less expensive than that of Indianapolis. In any case, I do not think my answer was the one for which the plant manager had hoped—or that he voted for me. In fact, I never heard from him again, but it was fun.

In the fall, the contest for Congress began in earnest. The opposition charged that I was untruthful in my statement that I did not accept campaign money from lobbyists. An erroneous entry on the records of the Federal Elections Commission was the culprit. Here's how the *Indianapolis Star*'s Sunday feature "Behind Closed Doors" described it:

> Message from the Andy Jacobs Jr. for Congress Committee to [his opponent] Campaign Committee. Thanks!
>
> For his past three campaigns for the 11th District Congressional seat, Jacobs has placed an ad in the *Star* asking for donations to his campaign, noting that his opponents always outspend him because they accept "special interest" contributions.
>
> When the 1980 version was published recently, Jacobs' 1980 opponent charged, through a news release, that Jacobs too accepted "special interest" contributions.
>
> What [the opponent] had done, though, was fall into the same trap Common Cause, the so-called citizens lobby in Washington, had more than a year ago.
>
> The National Real Estate Political Action Committee had mailed a check to an Indiana operative to be donated to Jacobs' '78 campaign. Jacobs, his campaign and several members of his Congressional staff were asked by the operative to accept the check and all refused. The check was never cashed by anyone, but the donation still appeared on the committee's contribution reports.
>
> Common Cause apologized to Jacobs when he pointed out their error.
>
> However, the error [of Jacobs' opponent] and publicity on [the opponent's] charge and the Jacobs response doubled the amount of money Jacobs raised through the advertisement.
>
> One Jacobs campaign spokesman said as many people attached newspaper accounts of the teapot tempest as attached the advertisement.
>
> Because of the bulge in Jacobs' campaign coffers, no apology from his opponent will be necessary. The money will do nicely, thank you.

Despite that "bulge" in my 1980 campaign treasury, I was outspent by the opposition *ten to one,* a ratio which paled by comparison with the ratio that would occur between the greater spending on my opponent's campaign and the spending on mine six years later.

Dud campaign ammunition for my opponents from Washington was not always unintentional. Read this item from the Sunday *Star*'s "Behind Closed Doors" column of August 13, 1978:

> The Republican National Campaign Committee is sending out a series of news releases blasting Democratic congressmen and calling them "the other side."
>
> Last week the *Star* received one such release chiding Rep. Andrew Jacobs, Jr. (D-Ind.) for his vote in opposition to federal funding for a nuclear-powered super aircraft carrier for the Navy.
>
> The RNC ought to look into its files before launching the press releases because there is a little problem with this one.
>
> One of their bright lights, Senator Richard G. Lugar (R-Ind.), is on record as opposing the nuclear carrier because it is too expensive.

A big part of the 1980 campaign was the Reagan handlers' untrue claim of U.S. military weakness in the face of Russian "superiority." In truth, we were light years ahead of the Russians in the dark art. The Kennedy campaign of 1960 had made the same erroneous claim, perhaps with less of a profit-making motive.

The Reagan people, starting with General Electric, were military industry people. "Trouble in River City" was the way *Music Man* sold band instruments. And trouble in the U.S. *holster* was the way to sell junk at jewelry prices to taxpayers through the Pentagon. The B-1 bomber was an example. It was advertised to make supersonic seem slow and never achieved its promised velocity. Its cost was prohibitively in the billions. The same amount would buy many cruise missiles, which were not just more effective in terms of reaching a target. Unmanned, they were also lifesavers for American military personnel. Less profitable for military contractors, though. My opposition to the B-1 was a large part of the campaign against me. Eventually, the plane fell of its own weight and took an enormous number of tax dollars with it.

By 1980 the *Indianapolis Star* and *News* had changed. As mentioned earlier, it had become a *newspaper,* rather than a tract in its news columns. Eugene Pulliam, the younger, had seen to that. The editorial pages remained the same, but, to some degree, other views began to appear on the op-ed pages. And even on the editorial pages, moderate views were sometimes expressed. One editorial in the *Indianapolis News* flabbergasted just about everybody, including me. It endorsed me for re-election. It was entitled "The Different Congressman," and commended my fiscal record, adding:

> For his courage in battling the Washington tide, Andy Jacobs, Jr. deserves another term in Congress.

"Battling the Washington tide" had moved some *Washington Post* writers to dub me "quirky and eccentric," an appellation which was picked up in the *Washington Post* review of my book, *The 1600 Hundred Killers*. In that volume I had the audacity to point out that presidential wars—with no declaration from the Congress as required by Article One, Section Nine, Clause Eleven of the Constitution—are illegal. The Constitution assigns to the Congress the *exclusive* authority to decide if, where, and when we go to war. A president has no role in the process, not even a signature, before the decision is made. After that, as Commander in Chief a president has the duty to conduct the war. A president can go before the Congress and request a declaration, as happened immediately following the most recent military attack against us by a foreign power; that was in 1940. During the second half of the twentieth century the Constitution in this regard was regularly violated, with the exception of the Eisenhower years.

Whether it helped or hurt, the 1980 *Indianapolis News* editorial was heartwarming to me and I called *News* editor, Harvey—yes—Jacobs, to thank him. He was most pleasant and reported that he had said to his publisher, Gene Pulliam, "If you can endorse your nephew—Dan Quayle—I guess I ought to be able to endorse my 'cousin.'" I assumed he only referred to the coincidence of our names—my dad had nicknamed the editor, "cousin Harvey"—but on the occasion of Harvey's sad and untimely death, his son told me there was reason to believe that we were distant relatives. That's fine with me; nicer people never lived.

One of the complaints about me from the opposition in 1980 was that I had been in Congress for fourteen years and had not become a committee chairman or even a subcommittee chairman yet. This was untrue on its face inasmuch as I had served as the chairman of the District of Columbia Subcommittee on the Judiciary before I was gerrymandered out in 1972. As for the Ways and Means Committee on which I had served for six years, the likely chairman after the 1980 election was Dan Rostenkowski of Illinois; he had served there for nearly two decades. And, in the unlikely event that I survived the Reagan landslide, I would probably become a subcommittee chairman despite those tender six years.

When news reporters asked me about the charge, I gave the above account and said, "When I was gerrymandered out by my opponent's party in 1972 after serving for eight years, I lost all my seniority and had to start up the ladder all over again when I went back to the House in '75. To be criticized for the handicap of the interrupted service which they brought about is like someone's shooting a person in the leg and criticizing him or her for limping."

One morning in mid-October, I received a call from the dean of Hoosier broadcasters, my much admired friend Fred Heckman. And I really mean, *morning*; it was a few minutes before six. Fred and I first met when I was a deputy sheriff in my law school days. On this day, he told me that Senator Frank Church of Idaho had just announced that there was a battalion of Russian soldiers on Castro's commie Cuban island. Church wasn't wrong; that battalion was in Cuba, but it was well known to anyone with a memory to have been there for twenty years. Frank Church was running for re-election in 1980 and the Cuba "revelation" reminded me of a story I heard the senator tell one evening a decade before in the home of my friend Representative Jim Corman.

On that occasion, Senator Church had told us that when he ran for re-election in 1962, he asked the Kennedy White House to give him some tidbit he could announce about the Cuban missile crisis. He figured it would impress voters in Idaho. After waiting several days, the senator had received the tidbit in the form of a technical hint of the approaching Russian "blink." That was the buzzword for Russia's backing down in its historic confrontation with the United States. Put plainly, the tidbit was Senator Church's campaign gimmick. Now, in 1980, he was doing it again. He was a very nice, intelligent, and likeable man and the ploy was really pretty innocent, but when my friend Fred asked for my opinion of the senator's lame revelation, I couldn't resist. After telling Fred's audiotape the reality of the situation, I added, "I think we're witnessing a separation between Church and statesmanship."

I never willingly declined a joint appearance with an opponent, but beginning with the 1980 election, nearly every time there was a joint appearance I faced two opponents from the same party, my opponent and the opponent of my neighboring rural congressman, Democrat Dave Evans. Organizations began combining the two districts for the discussions. But Dave usually declined and that left me with two critics who were allotted two-thirds of the time. Since generally—and specifically in 1980—the two made non-stop attacks on me and my time-honored policy was to make none—no matter how juicy—on them, the allocation of time was hardly fair. In tennis, if it's two to one, the one gets to play doubles court while the two must keep it inside the singles lines. Obviously, this was not tennis; "love" seemed not to figure in any way.

Moreover, in a one-on-one debate, even equal time isn't quite fair if only one side does all the attacking. It takes more time to mend a shattered window than to throw a stone through it.

So there I was in those two-to-one appearances, with two attackers going after me for thirty minutes and with fifteen minutes for me to remember the worst of the rapid-fire criticisms and give understandable answers. At one meeting of downtown business and professional women, I began my response by asking the audience if they would think it only fair for me to be given sufficient time to answer the torrent of attacks I had just sustained. Most nodded "yes." None shook "no." I had just made it through five major attacks and was about to answer the sixth, when the chairwoman of the meeting rose and said through the microphone, "I'm sorry, but we have to go on to questions from the audience." I doubt that she was sorry. She was not being sporting for a very understandable reason; she was a partisan of my opponent's party. She smiled artificially sweetly at me and I turned to the audience and said, "Doesn't anyone want to know if I favor loafers on Welfare?"

The chairwoman smiled more saccharinly and triumphantly asked for the first question from the assembled group. An attractive woman in her early thirties was recognized and said, "My question is for Congressman Jacobs: Do you favor loafers on Welfare?" The questioner smiled, too, but her smile was genuine, not nasty. She obviously enjoyed breaking up the rigged gig.

I explained about the legislation involved and its additional features that had nothing to do with "Workfare" and were odious in the extreme. I also explained that the State of Indiana was already authorized to implement Workfare, but hadn't because administering it cost more than the taxpayers got back. The appropriate disposition of actual loafers—people who were employable—on Welfare was to dump them off.

After the meeting, I thanked the woman who had asked the question. She told me that she, as were most members of the organization, was a Republican, adding, "Most Republicans believe in fairness." To which I agreed and still do for the simple reason that most people believe in fairness.

After that three-ring circus, the biased organizations tried another tack;

they arranged for me to be the middle speaker so that I would have no opportunity to answer the attacks from my second critic unless someone in the audience would bring them up. That happened rarely. But one time, Dave Evans's opponent seemed not to realize that I was to be recognized to answer whatever attack he might make upon me. So he let go with an indictment of me for casting a vote for a bill which I had in fact opposed.

There was a look of surprise on his face when I was called upon to respond. I began by saying, "[Dave's opponent], you are confused." Before I could continue, he interrupted by calling out, "That's what my wife says." This drew hearty laughs from the mostly male audience who laughed even harder when I quietly rejoined, "Who would know better?"

During the campaign a service club called to say that my opponent had been its guest that day for lunch. The spokeswoman said that some pretty strident attacks had been made on me and that the club members would like to hear my side the following week. I agreed to be there. When the members had finished their lunches, I was handed a list of the charges made against me the week before and was asked to read aloud each attack and give my response. So I proceeded with the first, "During his fourteen years in Congress, Jacobs has never even introduced a bill." Of course it wasn't true, but before I could draw a breath to say so, a man at the table called out, "Good!"

"Okay," I said, " let's go on to the second one."

Everybody in the room knew the opponent's assertion was absurd, and the play between the fellow in the audience and me brought down the house—or room.

In early October a friend told me the results of an Indianapolis Republican poll on my contest for re-election. They showed me up by about seven thousand votes. Compared to the prospect of once again being swept away in a GOP presidential landslide, the tip was more than welcome.

The actual election margin was 26,261 which gave me 57 percent of the vote. Indianapolis GOP polls were known to be accurate. Why the additional twenty thousand votes came my way, I suppose we'll never know. But the gain was concomitant with a few weeks of pretty angry attacks against me in paid-political television ads. A lot of people don't like that sort of thing.

On election day, 1980, Ronald W. Reagan, who had played just about everything else in the movies, was elected in a landslide to the real role of president of the United States.

chapter 15

"ENTER, STAGE RIGHT"

THE FIRST TIME I SAW RONALD REAGAN in person, he was walking down the center aisle to make his first address to a joint meeting of the House and Senate. The floor guests included foreign diplomats, the U.S. Joint Chiefs of Staff, the U.S. Supreme Court Justices and his designated cabinet members.

No question about it; he was resplendent in his tailored suit and beautifully coiffured hair together with that famous boyish smile that could melt any heart including mine. During the eight years that followed, I never changed my mind about liking him personally. But I certainly had my disagreements.

At the inaugural ball, the President and Mrs. Reagan, who was said to be wearing a twenty thousand dollar dress, looked more like royalty than most of the world's real monarchs. Of course, both of the Reagans were professional actors.

Addressing the dancers, the President told a cruel joke at the expense of the absent poor. One of his insensitive writers had placed it in his hand. You may recall that one evening when Calvin Coolidge was strolling with a friend along Pennsylvania Avenue past the White House, the friend facetiously asked, "Who lives there?" The President said, "Nobody; they just come and go." Nothing cruel about that White House joke. For Silent Cal, it was pretty funny. But the Reagan joke bespoke his handlers' attitude of condescension, even contempt, toward the poor—including not only the lazy—it's pretty hard not to feel resentment about them—but also those who were poor through no fault of their own.

Herblock summed it up in a 1964 cartoon about Barry Goldwater when the latter was still reciting the simplistic philosophy of the far right.

The cartoon showed a stern Goldwater staring down at a mother and her kids huddled in the doorway of an abandoned building in a blighted neighborhood. Goldwater lectured her, "If you had any incentive, you'd get out and inherit a department store"—which Goldwater, himself, had actually managed to do. And there was the story about a Hollywood school in which children were asked to write essays about poor people, with one of the kids writing, "Once there was a very poor family. The father was poor, the mother was poor, the children were poor, the maid was poor, the cook was poor, the chauffeur was poor, and the gardener was poor." The view of the poor from the country club is frequently unfocused.

As the First Couple took their leave from that opulent evening of the 1981 Inaugural Ball, the President announced to the radiant and mostly wealthy gathering, "We're living in public housing now." The audience roared with no apparent thought of "there, but for the grace of God, go I"— in rat-infested filth, violent crime, and despair. Ronald Reagan was not a cruel man. He was kind, but limited, perhaps "not too tightly wrapped." His remark was not a slip, it was a script.

His PR people nicknamed him the Great Communicator. The Great Communicator; at the very least it had a Lincolnesque sound to it. But it applied only to utterances he read from cards and TelePrompTers. And for such sight-reading, he had an astonishing talent. With a script in front of him, even one he was seeing for the first time, he was like a beautifully streamlined diesel locomotive gliding gracefully and powerfully across America. But take the track away and he was in elocution trouble.

When Reagan's secretary of the interior, who was an adversary of the interior's environment, lamented the moderating advice some administration officials and especially the First Lady were giving the President, the secretary was widely quoted as saying, "Let Reagan be Reagan." This prompted a cartoon by my nephew Martin Landwerlen. It depicted a bewildered Reagan at a lectern as his interior secretary snatched the scripted speech away. The caption, of course, had the secretary saying, "Let Reagan be Reagan."

My Republican friends were quick to tell me, "You have to admit he's a great communicator." And I was quick to answer, "You're right. Every time he speaks extemporaneously, it takes fewer than three days for his staff to clear up what he meant." Many of them smiled their agreement.

One morning in January 1981, I received a call from the newly elected chairman of the House Ways and Means Committee, Danny Rostenkowski. There was urgency in his voice as he told me that the chairman of the House Rules Committee, Dick Bolling of Missouri, had just proposed that I be stripped of my seniority and transferred from Ways and Means to the District of Columbia Committee. "No kidding," I said rhetorically, "well what do you know about that?" Danny knew a lot about it.

According to Bolling, I'd had the temerity to cast my district's vote against his motion for the *previous question* when, in the organizing session of the new Congress, he offered the Democratic proposed rules for the upcoming sessions. The *previous question* simply meant no amendments or even comments could be offered by the then-minority Republicans. I did cast the vote against the motion, but I was hard-pressed to see how that involved temerity; it just seemed like fairness to me. What would have been wrong with considering Republican-proposed changes? Some of them might be good ideas.

Dick Bolling was a Democrat who was also something of an autocrat. He believed in party discipline, which pretty much translated into party bosses. And that meant never mind what the individual representative thought and, least of all, what her or his constituents thought. Once in Washington, toe the party line—even when it changes its mind and heads in the opposite direction from time to time. Let there be party discipline and let the real bosses, the citizens of each congressional district, show some respect for the party bosses. "Here, sir, the people [*don't*] rule." And after all, as Bolling's thinking apparently went, this was a vote on the rules of the *club* House, not the *people's* House. That philosophy was always wrong, but by 1981 it was beginning to be anachronistic in terms of the public's enhanced perception—and so was Chairman Bolling. He had entered Congress with my dad in 1949 and they had been friends. And unlike the defender of congressional limousines, Chet Holifield, who was also my dad's friend, Dick Bolling had been quite friendly toward me during our service together up until this point.

Bolling's motion had been made in the Democratic Steering and Policy Committee of the House Democratic caucus. There were thirty-four other Democrats on that leadership panel. One of them was my friend, Danny Rostenkowski. In our phone conversation, he suggested that I repair to the committee and explain my vote. "Danny," I said, "I'll explain the way I cast that vote to any one of my employers any time, but they don't live in Washington and Dick Bolling isn't one of them." Danny came from the Chicago machine of Boss Dick Daley, but, despite his rough exterior, he was a pussy cat, which is to say big-hearted. No doubt I was speaking Greek to him, but he was nice about it. "Well, Andy I'm not trying to tell you what to do, I just don't want to lose a good member of the committee."

"I understand, Danny, and I am grateful for your concern, but I keep remembering what Gary Cooper said in *Friendly Persuasion*, 'A man isn't worth a hill of beans if he doesn't live up to his own conscience.'"

The question was not put to a vote in the caucus committee for two or three days, during which the news media had a field day speculating about my fate, indeed the fate of my interpretation of democracy. David Broder had written a book entitled *The Party's Over*, in which he lamented the passing of party discipline. He held that voters could better fix responsibility if each party spoke with one tongue and voted with one policy. Others, including me, believe that every vote counts in Congress as well as among those whose Congress it is. Each district was entitled to choose a U.S. Representative according to the blend of views presented by each candidate in that district. Those blends seldom would fit some Washington mold. To toe the line with party leaders necessarily would mean *not* to toe the line with the sovereign, the constituency. What was called political courage often was closer to pseudo-elite insubordination to the American people.

Somewhat scripturally, on the third day the committee rose to the challenge and made its decision about me. The vote was thirty-four to one Bolling; my seniority would remain intact; I would stay on Ways and Means. For the second time I would become a subcommittee chairperson. But this time it would not be on the glorified city council of the District of Columbia. I was about to become chairman of the Health [Medicare] Sub-Committee of Ways and Means. With me in that position, certain lobbyists were even more willing to share their money with my campaign committee. Thanks, but no thanks.

When news reporters asked for my reaction to the leadership committee's decision, I said, "Evidently they thought it over and decided that democratic principles do not violate Democratic principles."

While I basked in editorial praise for independence, my nephew, Gregory Landwerlen, master manager of an automobile dealership, sneaked one of his dealer advertising plates onto the front bumper of my then-new Oldsmobile Omega. The plate read, "Demo for Sale." Very funny; well, a lot funnier than it would have been had it been true.

It is customary in Congress and no more than ordinary courtesy for a member to notify a targeted colleague before an attack such as the one Bolling launched against me. No such notice was given in this case. A few days later, I ran into Dick Bolling and he greeted me by saying, "How's my independent friend?" To which I replied, "Still waiting for the courtesy of a notice from you." It would be accurate to say that his smile was somewhere between sardonic and cynical. Somehow, though, I still liked him personally. He could be pleasant at times and was.

About a week later, there was a formal meeting of the House Democratic caucus with then-Majority Leader Jim Wright of Texas leading the discussion about caucus rules. On the record I asked Jim to yield and he did. So I propounded this question:

"Is there any rule of this caucus that requires a member to cast a vote in favor of any motion for the *previous question*?"

Jim Wright was in an awkward position; the chairman of the House Rules Committee was sitting directly across from him and Jim needed Dick's cooperation to move legislation. On the other hand, there was the *truth*: no such rule. So Jim attempted a soft landing: "Well, serving on the Ways and Means Committee is a great privilege granted to very few by this caucus." I liked Jim Wright too much to grind the point into the ground, so I simply said, "Serving as Majority Leader is also a great privilege granted by this caucus, but would the gentleman from Texas agree that neither position should be put in jeopardy for violation of a caucus rule *that does not exist?*" Jim said, "That sounds like a fair observation to me."

Only one Democrat had joined me in casting a vote against Bolling's motion for the *previous question* on the first day of that Ninety-seventh Congress. He was Representative Buddy Roemer of Louisiana. Bolling demanded that Roemer's seniority be stripped, also. But Buddy wouldn't have lost much even if Bolling's motion had been successful. Buddy was a freshman and his seniority could be measured in hours, whereas mine ran to years.

As the new administration set sail, I received a critical letter from home:

Dear Congressman Jacobs:

This is the first time you've had the opportunity of voting on a measure which has as its goal the balancing of the federal budget and you've voted against it! . . . I think you should reconsider your position. You say you want fiscal responsibility in government. Yet when it comes to taking the necessary measures to accomplish this goal, you become an obstructionist.

We don't understand.

Respectfully yours,

My reply:

Dear _____:

Since so far in this Congress the U.S. House has taken only one vote on a fiscal proposal, and since that proposal was President

Reagan's request for an increase in the national debt, I don't understand either.

Sincerely,

Why do so many people go by the "who" of an issue, rather than the "what"? The President's debt increase requests would continue and the increments would grow to undreamed of, nay, *un-nightmared of* proportions. A lot of people in Congress who knew better were frightened enough of the Reagan "who" to go along with his requests for enormous increases in federal spending while supporting tax bills that went in the opposite direction, ballooning the national debt to prodigious heights, eventually tripling it by the early 1990s. The federal watchword of the period seemed to echo a familiar contemporary TV pitch, "Send no money; you'll be billed later." With compounded interest.

In a much publicized trip to Boston, the new President visited an Irish pub and bellied up to the bar with several of the fellows from the old sod. He also made a speech to a business gathering in which, in essence, he said he knew he might be criticized for the suggestion, but he thought the corporate income tax should be repealed. CBS News called me for a comment. Roger Mudd reported the story about the President's radical thought, saying, "Representative Andrew Jacobs, Jr., a Democrat from Indiana and a member of the House Ways and Means Committee, was asked for his reaction. He asked whether the President made the suggestion before or after he visited that bar. The answer, Mr. Jacobs, is *after.*"

The traditional political advice to members of Congress was, "Vote for all the appropriations and against all the taxes." Such behavior had always been considered cowardly and irresponsible. It did not betray strength of character. But with the arrival of Hollywood writers in the White House, all that changed. Suddenly, increasing federal spending—which the first four Reagan-submitted and congressionally approved budgets did to the cumulative tune of one thousand times a billion dollars, while cutting taxes by $750 billion—mostly for very high incomes—was somehow dubbed by the writers as not only virtuous, but even courageous. My father, who usually said things exactly right and refreshingly succinctly, said, "Prudence has become un-American." The lovable Jack Kemp had been quarterback for the Buffalo Bills. Now he was the quintessential and quixotic quarterback for the movie's "Gipper." Defining the "Reaganomics" of the "Reagan Revolution" for history, Jack said, "The GOP no longer worships at the altar of the balanced budget." Jack wasn't wrong.

It has been generally thought that the Reagan administration and its willing bipartisan congressional helpers whammed up federal spending only on the military, space, and foreign aid programs. But that is not true. The administration's farm program cost six—yes, *six*—times as much as the farm program of the previous administration. It should surprise no one that most of the subsidies went not to fabled and picturesque "small family farms," but rather to wealthy farm conglomerates. Every time President Reagan made a speech about fiscal responsibility, I thought about one of Jud Haggerty's favorite sayings: "The louder he protested his honesty, the faster we counted the silver."

It was the Reagan Revolution, time to reorder our priorities by ending the "welfare state." The "welfare queen"—it always seemed to be the same one; I believe she lived in Chicago—was going out of business. Actually the law didn't have to be changed to get the queen in question; her rip-off was already a crime. She had been caught and punished or she would never have come to the administration's attention. But she was reason enough to go after people who were actually down on their luck, with a vengeance—while catering to people up on their luck with unctuous reverence. A TV comedian said that "in this revolution, everybody will have to give up something; the poor will have to give up eating and the rich will have to give up paying taxes."

Of course, to paraphrase Edison's words, good luck often involves effort and bad luck, just the opposite. But a lot of people who are down on their luck work full and backbreaking time with little to show for it on payday. A lot of people who are up on their luck have the native talent or just a good tip on the market to show handsome profits.

The first Reagan budget was reckless. It was reckless because it was cobbled together with blind ideological fervor during a frantic night in the White House basement. The President's handlers were amazed when they learned how many Democratic members of Congress feared Reagan's popularity in the polls. Before realizing the extent to which members of the Democratic Party were willing to fall on their philosophical swords, the administration had only hoped for a few amendments to boost military spending and perhaps take a pickle or two out of the school lunch program. When it dawned on them that they could pass anything they wanted during those early months of 1981, it was too late for a carefully considered list.

On that fateful night before congressional action, the White House budget, in the form of a *reconciliation substitute*, was slapped together so fast that the right hand didn't know what the far right hand was doing. In fact, fifteen hours later, the House of Representatives enacted a young woman's phone number, which had been written on the margin of the document. It was assumed that a romance had emerged in the wee hours of maneuvering.

Reckless. So reckless that most of those in Congress who voted for the sweeping measure did not have a clue about the bulk of its contents. In fairness, I'd have to say that the Democratic budget had its own serious flaws; I cast the Indianapolis vote against both.

Referring to the pig-in-a-poke administration budget, our friend Representative Ed Jenkins of Georgia, held his family Bible high and declared, "This is the only document I'll take on faith." But one congressman with a very Biblical name did take the document on faith and shortly afterward testified before the Ways and Means Committee in favor of repealing part of it. Representative Gerald Solomon of New York testified that he had no idea the administration's proposal included the feature he was against. Finally, it was my turn to speak:

"Mr. Chairman: This illustrates how dangerous it is summarily to pass whatever a popular President sends to Capitol Hill. I mean, if even someone with the wisdom of Solomon can be fooled by such a procedure, what chance does an ordinary member of Congress have to cast an un-regrettable vote in the absence of scrutiny by the committee system?"

The one who laughed loudest was Congressman Solomon, who later became a good friend of mine. Of course, the fact that he was a Marine helped. Eventually he became chairman of the House Rules Committee.

The Reagan White House was dazzled by an economic theory called the Laffer Curve, which was also known as supply-side economics. It was the tingle of wishful thinking from Tinsel Town. It was push-ups without pain and a doughnut diet all rolled into one. Pay less, get more; eat more, weigh less. The old syndicated cartoon *Grin and Bear It* summed up the political shell game of economics powerfully. There was Senator Snort orating to a summer picnic crowd in which a little girl was tugging on her mother's dress and saying, "I didn't think grown-ups believed in Santa Claus."

Supply side was the product of a facile phrasemonger. It wasn't *supply* side at all; it was sumptuous *consumption* side. The theory was that if taxes were substantially cut for people who could afford to invest in the stock market, they would. But they didn't. Instead, they bought luxuries. In fact, after the Congress and president had passed President Reagan's tax cut (Reagan's tax cut in more ways than one; his own personal income tax was reduced by twenty-five thousand dollars per year) and after the big White House champagne celebration of its passage, President Reagan's handlers put him on TV to lecture the beneficiaries of the bill about their obligation to invest in the market and their failure to do so. But there wasn't a word in the new tax law obligating them to invest so much as a penny in anything.

So why was the Laffer Curve so laughable? Why didn't the big guys who suddenly found themselves with a lot more money left in their hands rush to the market and produce *capital formation?* Maybe no one can say for sure, but history has some hefty hints. Supply side economics was actually Keynesian economics with a new name. Both added down to deficit financing. The President promised that reducing government revenues would so stimulate the economy as actually to increase government revenues and balance the federal budget by 1984. We'd borrow our way to prosperity. Never worked before and didn't work this time. Government revenues did increase during the Reagan years, but that was because of several tax *increases* signed by the President and because of a growing work force that not only paid additional taxes, but received additional governmental services. In any case, under Reaganomics, the gap between government spending and government revenues expanded vastly. The administration's tax cut did not stimulate investment and, therefore, did not stimulate the economy.

Investors need faith in the economy for the courage to invest. No such faith can be inspired in knowledgeable investors by a government that borrows its people into gargantuan debt to pay current expenses. The administration's assurances that economic reality can be repealed, and that taxes can be cut while government squanders ever more, simply rang hollow to gifted economic counselors.

In the early days of our republic, Alexander Hamilton insisted that the government pay the overdue bills for the Revolutionary War. Those bills were mostly in the form of paper money called "continentals" that had been issued as payment to soldiers and suppliers. But the continentals, to use a common phrase of years gone by, "weren't worth a continental." That is until Hamilton persuaded the fledgling government to make them good, partly with the Excise Act of 1791. That's what the Whisky Rebellion was about, although it didn't turn out to be much of a rebellion by the time George Washington and his soldiers got to western Pennsylvania.

Honoring the continentals had meant a tax increase. As soon as it was implemented, our economy and investment in it soared. Wise business people want, indeed, need stable and fiscally responsible government policies. They have more faith in a government that deals in reality than one filled with those phrasemongers whose task it is to fog over cause and effect. Math has its old-fashioned facts and no new math can change them. Two and two are surely four. Two minus four leaves you with two less than nothing. And all the "brilliant idiots" in the world, all the scams for easy earning, all the thin air of the emperor's newest tonsorial style, cannot change that. At the close of the twentieth century, the United States government lacked nearly six thousand times a billion dollars of having even one penny. To be sure, it had some non-liquid assets, but on balance, the government's accounts were out of balance; its net worth was crimson.

The government that meets facts straight on and pays its bills instead of blowing dreamy smoke through mirrors into people's eyes is the government investors can trust.

Wealth comes from work, including the work necessary to develop natural resources. And work usually comes from the desire for wealth, or at least enough of it to meet the cost of living. It is possible for some to live off other's work and wealth, but intrinsic wealth is wrought by work. No form of alchemy ever did or ever will produce wealth. Each of its latter-day forensic forms tends to appeal to what George Orwell called "The voice of the belly protesting against the soul."

The ultimate in government sponsored-something for nothing is the lottery. My father called it a first cousin to stealing, the motives being the same: gain without work. The rare lottery winner steals from the suckers who eagerly dump their money into his lucky lap. And of course *the house*, the government, always wins. Anyone who has stood behind an obviously poor person at the bulletproof booth of a gas station and noted the five dollars' worth of gas and the ten dollars' "worth" of Lotto tickets, can testify that the taxation called government lottery is cruelly regressive.

Democratic Keynesian economics and Republican Reaganomics were the same. They meant eat now, pay later. But later never came in either case, just more eating and more borrowing until the eating was "ashes in the mouth" and the throat of the body politic was choked with debt. These threadbare theories were the exact reverse of the prudent advice given to pharaoh by Joseph; build a surplus now as the sun shines, so you can eat later on a rainy day.

Whatever the economic name conjured by the phrasemongers to mask their political alchemy, it is a consistent subterfuge which assaults the dignity of truth and invites indolence in individuals and, therefore, combines to cause national decline.

The prudent government that tells the people the economic truth appeals to what is best in us and inspires the prudence that produces honest work, which, in turn, blends into a national ethic. That is the real wealth of a nation.

The enormous 1981 tax cut for people at the top preceded immediately the worst recession since the Great Depression. Then, some time in late 1983, the economy began to revive and investment picked up. Was the tax cut finally generating the results promised by the administration? Did it, in fact, produce even greater government revenue? Or was there another factor? You bet there was. Contrary to propagandized public opinion, it was the Reagan-signed 1982 tax *increase* which, in real dollars, remains the largest tax hike since World War II. It was that tax increase which preceded the recovery. Intelligent businesspeople saw a glimmer of light as the government seemed to be sobering up to fiscal responsibility by getting some revenue to pay more of its bills, even if not all of them. Unprecedented deficits continued, but at least there was a signal that the government had not lost all its wits.

Like the Reagan tax increase in 1982, the Reagan tax cut of 1981 was the largest since World War II. Phased in over three years, it cut the top marginal income tax rate for individuals from 74 percent to 50 percent. And, especially in the case of certain military manufacturing corporations, one of which had once employed the President, it cut federal income tax to zero for a three-year period. During those salad months, General Electric wound up paying less federal income tax on a cumulative profit in the billions than the average single, low-income mother of three. She paid about three thousand dollars in income tax, not counting Social Security taxes, and GE paid a grand total of *nothing*.

The administration tax proposal could not be passed by Republican members alone in that Democratic Congress. It needed some Democrats. Since I had a painfully earned reputation for independence, I was on the White House potential *friends* list.

The first to call me was my former congressional colleague and friend, President Reagan's vice president. The phone rang at about seven in morning on an early spring day. "Andy, it's George Bush."

"George, congratulations." He understood that I meant his election.

From the vice president: "The President needs your vote on the third year of his tax plan." An old expression crossed my mind: *People in Hell need ice water*. But I didn't say it. Instead I said, "Well, George, you convinced me with that speech you made in Texas."

The speech in Texas was one given by George Bush during the contest for the 1980 Republican presidential nomination when George, himself, was competing with Reagan for the party nod. Brainy Jane Bryant Quinn had already opined that Reaganomics neither added up to budget surplus, nor subtracted down to reduced government spending. In his famous speech, Bush had summed up Reaganomics succinctly and pithily. George said Reagan's fiscal proposals were "Voodoo Economics." That was what I reminded him about at a few minutes after seven that fresh spring morning. But the vice president had an answer.

"Those words were taken out of context, Andy." I had a question: "What is the context now, George? Getting to be vice president?" The conversation ended on a friendly note, but I had made no secret of my opposition to much, but not all, of the Reagan tax proposal. I agreed that the top marginal individual income tax rate had too much altitude. But the administration's ideas about amortization of capital investment amounted to *expensing*. That meant deducting in one year the entire cost of a piece of long-lived capital equipment. That was the principal provision by which corporations like General Electric avoided paying any tax at all on enormous economic profits.

The administration's tax cut was to be phased in over three years. As advertised, it would bring down inflation, interest rates, unemployment, and federal deficit spending. You'd have to stick a lot of pins in a lot of Caribbean dolls to do—or even believe all that. These thoughts were much on my mind when the phone on my desk rang at the respectable hour of ten a few mornings after I spoke with the vice president.

It was the new Secretary of the Treasury, Donald Regan, an amiable former Marine who was point man on behalf of the administration's economic program in testimony before the Ways and Means Committee. The secretary's quest was the same as the vice president's and my answer was the same as before. But this time I had a suggestion. I asked, "What are you going to do about the God-awful deficits you'll get?"

"Congressman, we know a way to do this without inflation."

"Of course you do," I replied. "Instead of printing the money to cover the deficit, you'll borrow it. And that will probably crowd the money markets and cause recession." Then I added my suggestion:

"Mr. Secretary, have you considered, as a part of your tax plan, an annual discontinuation clause based on the progress or lack thereof toward your economic goals?"

"How would that work?" the secretary asked. "Well, rather than lock in the whole three years, why don't you make the cut for each of the two succeeding years contingent on whether interest rates, unemployment, inflation, and deficits actually fall? If not—and I'm afraid I don't think they will—the next phase or phases of the cut would automatically not take place. In other words, each year's cut would be contingent on whether the rosy prediction blossoms or only grows thorns."

The secretary seemed genuinely interested; "Do you have anything in writing on that?" he asked. "There's really not much that I could add to what I just said," I replied, "and if you're recording this, you could just get someone in your department to type it up." I was just kidding; but when he denied that a tape was rolling and denied it again, I couldn't help being curious. I never heard any more from him about it and assumed that, unlike him, the White House handlers weren't as interested in the economy as they were in the tax cuts for their highest-income, well-heeled friends. My proposal was adopted in the Ways and Means Committee anyway, but the administration recruited enough Democratic representatives to reject the Committee report and substitute for it the administration's very own plan.

During the next couple of years, employment and the economy came tumbling down. Congressionally-complied-with administration spending and the deficit went tumbling *up*. Reagan's fault? Yes, partly. But the fault of many Democrats, too. Bipartisan baloney.

chapter 16

HARD TIMES

ON JANUARY 7, 1982, the President of the United States dined with two United States senators. Those senators were Strom Thurmond and Jesse Helms. The next day, the U.S. Treasury Department announced that it would reinstate theretofore suspended tax exemptions for Bob Jones University and Goldsboro (so-called) Christian Schools. The exemptions had been denied because federal law prohibited federal financial benefits for racially segregated institutions and the two schools were very much that. They had brought suit in federal court for reinstatement of the tax breaks, arguing essentially that federal tax exemptions are not federal financial benefits. Prior to the Reagan administration, the Civil Rights Division of the Justice Department had filed an answer in opposition to the plaintiffs' lawsuit. Now, in the Reagan administration, the Civil Rights Division switched sides, arguing for the exemptions. The administration's January action appeared to be an extralegal favor for Thurmond and Helms. And, I am convinced, it was a favor from a non-racist and non-comprehending President. In any case, the White House handlers obviously thought the action, if not pleasing, at least would be acceptable to its principal constituency, the Republican suburbanites. *Au contraire.*

The administration was blindsided by its own maneuver. Just as had been the case with Congresswoman Martha Griffiths's proposal to exterminate rats, White House tracking polls showed the suburbanites were outraged by the administration's bow to racism. This move was too obvious and shameful for mainstream Republicans. Theirs was the party of Lincoln and maybe they had gone along with the subtle racism of Nixon's "Southern Strategy," but this was blatant and the polls showed they were having none of it.

The administration had to think fast. How could they get back to center court on this one? Send in the PR people, of course. Here's what they came up with. It was a variation on a theme that comedian Flip Wilson made famous, "The devil made me do it." Only in this case, they insisted, it was *the law* that made them do it. They argued that they had no choice but to restore the exemptions, because the exemptions had been taken away by an earlier administration—the Nixon administration—simply by a regulation that had no basis in law.

The problem for the administration was that in order to argue that the IRS regulation was not authorized by law, they had to deny the obvious. They had to make the ludicrous assertion that a tax exemption is not a *financial benefit*. And that was just the assertion they made. Thin and transparent as it was, it was the only PR fig leaf they could think up. "Honest, folks, we're with you;" they insisted, "we don't think those awful, racist schools should have tax exemptions, either. It's just that even though the law prohibits financial benefits for segregated schools, the law won't let us take the tax exemptions away because they are not financial benefits. But"—the good news from the administration—"we're sending a proposal to Congress for a new law right away, a law that will allow us to do what we really wanted to do in the first place, deny the tax breaks to these racist schools."

Very good, except that, of course, the PR assertion was simply not true. But the administration was in a tough spot; and it had to carry out its charade. So up to the Capitol went the administration's sapper team of Treasury and Justice Department officials to testify before the Ways and Means Committee in favor of their sham bill. If not a fun day, it was a funny one—well, it was both.

Some said that every Washington tax lawyer took the day off to attend the hearing and see just how good the administration would be at pretending we didn't already have a law against granting those exemptions.

The leading actor at the witness table was a deputy attorney general whose name was Edward Schmultz. Sounded about right for a show biz administration. In President Reagan's movie-actor days, "schmaltz" meant high cinematic achievement. The sapper team also included the head of the Civil Rights Division of the Justice Department, one William Bradford Reynolds, who spent a lot of time helping the administration switch sides in the struggle for civil rights. Treasury was represented by a non-ideologue named R. T. McNamar. He seemed pretty nice.

Mind you, their contrived cause at the Ways and Means hearing that day was to enact what they insisted was a badly needed law, badly needed to get themselves out of their PR jam—not needed at all to support an Internal Revenue regulation denying exemptions to racist institutions. This is where the charade got really funny. In the manner of the little boy who faked this note from his mother to his teacher: "Johnny was absent yesterday because *I tore my pants,*" once in the heat of exchanges with committee members, the administration people forgot their ploy and reverted to type, arguing for, not against, granting the exemptions. Instead of saying clearly that they wanted a law that would let them deny the exemptions, they seemed to be saying the exemptions were okay because they did not *financially* benefit the racist schools.

As I awaited my turn to question the administration witnesses, I enjoyed the showbiz that was being conducted by the Schmultz performers. The audience in the committee chamber seemed to be enjoying it, too. And they didn't even have to buy tickets.

By the time I was recognized by the chairperson to ask questions, it was pretty clear that the sapper team had forgotten their PR scheme and were arguing against their own ploy. To the naked ear, they sounded very much as if their decision to grant the exemptions was based on what they *wanted* to do, not what they thought the law required them to do.

I set out to make the obvious even more obvious. My first question was directed to Mr. Reynolds, the frail, blond, and bespectacled "civil rights" man from Justice. "Why do you want to deny tax exemptions to Bob Jones University and Goldsboro Christian Schools?"

The man was clearly confused. He answered my question by saying he didn't understand my question. That was very likely the truth. The man had just spent forty minutes arguing that the schools should have the exemptions because the exemptions weren't financial benefits, and here I was asking why *he* thought the exemptions should not be allowed.

When Reynolds said he didn't understand my question, I looked at Chairman Rostenkowski and said, "Parliamentary inquiry, Mr. Chairman. Why are we here?" Back came the chairperson's reply: "The committee is conducting a hearing on the administration bill to deny tax exemptions to segregated schools."

"Oh," I said in clearly mock surprise. "Well, does the witness understand my question now?" I said to Reynolds. The poor guy had the look of "gadzooks!"

"Well," said the embarrassed witness, doing a 180 degree turn on a dime. "We think it's wrong to give those exemptions to such schools."

I pursued the matter. "But they have teachers' salaries and light bills to pay; why would you want to hamper their ability to do so?"

"We just don't think the federal government should give such schools benefits." He said it, the thing he had spent forty minutes saying a tax exemption *was not*. Now it was time for me to do a George Carlin. So on the fifth word of my final question, I leaned into the microphone, dropped my voice half an octave and rasped it out: "Would that be a 'financial' benefit?" Not only did I make my point and expose the administration's crocodile tears, but I also got belly laughs from most of the three hundred people in the room, the three hundred who were not at the witness table. The latter did not find it amusing.

How would you like to have had a little mouse in the chauffeured limousine that carried the administration witnesses back to the administration after the hearing? I had one in that car. Maybe "mole" would be a better word. "Deep Throat" might be better still. In any case, during that trip from Capitol Hill, the Justice Department man whose name sounded like *schmaltz* said, "Broadhead from Michigan is mean; and that Jacobs from Indiana is snide." Broadhead was Bill Broadhead and he was not mean, but his questions were not easy, either. As for the description of my own conduct, I would have preferred humorous, but it would be hard for me to deny the word the administration's show biz man used. How about, *justifiable chide-a-snide*?

The administration's sapper team had been sent on a *mission impossible*. The best it could hope to accomplish was a charade of pettifogging. The facts and the law were against their contrived position. It took no great talent on the part of people like Bill Broadhead, Charlie Rangel of New York and me to win the debate. We were dealt the better hand. But it was the administration, itself, that had done the dealing. Despite the Reagan Justice Department's unprecedented alliance with the racists, the Supreme Court on May 24, 1983, by a vote of eight to one, made it clear that despite the administration's switching sides, the law, itself, would not switch sides. The suspensions stood and a lot of Reagan supporters had reason to wonder what he stood *for* when it came to race in America. Told of the public perception that he had rapport with racists, he was said to be both surprised and outraged. I sincerely doubt that Ronald Reagan was a racist—or that he had a clue as to why anyone would think he was. I believe he was sincerely "surprised and outraged."

Despite the rapidly rising debt and deeply declining economy, the administration continued to present Ronald Reagan in his *Music Man* role: "trouble in River City," and the river was the Potomac. Profitable sales to the taxpayers by military contractors must be maintained at any cost. Following a year of controversy over whether the administration was squandering the taxpayers' money on junk at jewelry prices in the name of military necessity, the *Southside Challenger*, a Greenwood, Indiana, newspaper ran a January 5, 1983, article entitled, Russia superior, says Reagan, In "Model A Ford Age," says Andy Jacobs, based on CIA report. Written by reporter Becky Whitney, the story said, in part:

> The question of who has military arms superiority, the U.S. or the Soviet Union, is already answered in the mind of U.S. Rep. Andrew Jacobs, Jr. (D-IN).
>
> He doesn't agree with President Reagan, who recently claimed that "in virtually every measure of military power the Soviet enjoys a decided advantage," as reported by the *Washington Post*. Jacobs said, based on a CIA study made in April '82, that the military strength of Soviets is in the "Model A Ford age."
>
> ... The CIA report confirms his charges. In the four major arms areas—missiles, aircraft, Navy and battlefield tactical weapons—the CIA reports that the US is significantly ahead.
>
> Congressional funding of the MX nuclear missiles is a ridiculous expenditure, Jacobs feels. He said in a press conference, "The MX missile isn't needed. Any land-based missile is obsolete—a radar-guided bow and arrow that's easy to detect."

The story of the MX is a story of scandal. Simply put, it was the highly effective state-of the-dark-art Trident submarine missile, hauled up onto dry land like a fish out of water.

The reason the Trident missile put us light years ahead of the Soviets was that it moved about far below the surface of the ocean and could not be detected by Soviet technology. I strongly supported appropriations for it. But the dry-land scam was easy enough to detect; once tooled up to produce the missile for its all-important role in our defense system, the contractor wanted to sell more of the missiles than our Trident subs could use. So the name was changed to MX and President Reagan was programmed to push its sales. In fact, the whole thing was so obvious that some key members of the President's own party on Capitol Hill backed away, suggesting the avoidance of embarrassment for the President by appropriating just enough to buy a few.

The administration tried to overcome the obvious fact that missiles in the deep had rendered land-based ones obsolete because the latter were detectable by an adversary and our new technology of missiles in the deep, was not.

Well, the administration suggested, the MX could be put on railroad cars and pulled around the country. But that didn't wash because they could still be seen.

There were more zany basing plans than warheads on a MIRVed missile. But the advocates were desperate; there was a lot of money to be made. The administration basing idea I found most amusing was called Dense Pack. There would be so many missiles based in one spot that some would survive a preemptive strike against them. The beauty of that one was that it carried its own logic for buying even more of the turkeys. The preemptive strike which destroyed that sales pitch comprised six well aimed words from a wag in Congress: "They tried that at Pearl Harbor." Congress approved a few of the duds—and urged the White House to find something else from which its friends could make money. The White House was running out of ideas, though. It had to settle for seats, six hundred dollar toilet seats.

W. Henson Moore was an intelligent and likable representative from Louisiana and, when he joined the Ways and Means Committee, we became good friends. Earlier, however, there was an incident on the floor of the House that might have caused friction between us had he been a lesser person. We all have our linguistic blind spots. Until a good editor gets hold of this manuscript, some of mine no doubt will lurk in it. Henson took his turn at the pitfall one day during House consideration of a appropriation to subsidize National Public Broadcasting. The night before, the organization had held a reception for members of Congress in one of the cavernous rooms on one of the subterranean levels of the Rayburn office building. There was a buffet fit for, well, officials who would decide the next day how much of a subsidy Public Broadcasting would get.

Henson Moore was offended by this attempt to "sweeten the judgment" of public officials. I believe he was right. But Moore drafted his amendment to the appropriation in haste, to wit:

No funds appropriated by this act shall be used for entertainment.

As Moore used his five minutes quite rightly and extemporaneously eloquently to argue against the event on the night before, I could feel some devilment creeping up my spine. So I sought and obtained recognition to participate in the debate:

"Mr. Speaker, I confess that with some of its stuffy British plays, public broadcasting doesn't manage to entertain me, but I don't think we should make it against the law for it to try."

Moore asked me to yield, which I was happy to do. And he said, "My amendment would prohibit the kind of bash these people threw last night."

To which I responded: "It would no doubt do that. But the gentleman's amendment does not restrict the word 'entertainment' to meals for wheels."

"But that is what I mean," said Moore.

I again: "As Hubert Humphrey says, 'They don't know what you mean; they just know what you say.'"

At that point, kindly and wise Representative Charley Bennett, World War II combat infantry veteran from Florida, strolled over to Moore with a scrap of paper which he handed to his new colleague while whispering something in his ear. Moore asked unanimous consent to amend the amendment which then passed, the vote I cast for Indianapolis being in the affirmative. Moore smiled a touche.

A similar, yet subtler, incident took place during committee consideration of the Social Security bailout legislation of 1983. Social Security was in immediate danger of defaulting to some extent on its obligations that year because the deep recession had diminished revenues from the Social Security tax.

The solution was obvious from the start of the crisis and this crisis was not contrived. Both sides of the Social Security equation had to give up something; The benefits had to be reduced and the tax had to be raised. And since Social Security had been called "the third rail in American politics"— touch it and you die politically—neither of the major political parties would touch the solution without the complicity of the other. Therefore, as the Ninety-eighth Congress started up in 1983, entitlements took center stage.

Congress and the President couldn't dodge this one. So the Ways and Means Committee voted to recommend for House passage the "Blair House" plan for bailing out Social Security. The proposal was developed in that historic structure across Pennsylvania Avenue from the White House, by Bob Dole, Tip O'Neill, and the President's handlers. Pursuant to their proposal, the Social Security tax would rise by increments over the next few years so as not only to meet current benefit obligations, but also to build up a substantial surplus to help pay the expected jump in payments as baby boomers began to retire after the first half of the second decade of the approaching twenty-first century.

On the other side of the ledger benefits would be reduced by introducing means testing. For the first time, retirees' benefits would be based partly on need, meaning that the better off you were otherwise, the more your benefits would be reduced, but not below the amount you had paid-in and the interest earned by that amount over the years. Relative to benefits received, that amount was small in the average case. How small is small? At the time of the legislation and for more than a decade to come, about eighty percent of the average Social Security retiree's benefits, in essence, were and would be public assistance.

As usual, doing the deed of benefit reduction directly, by reducing the checks to the better-off retirees, was too simple and straightforward for Congress and the President. So the bipartisan agreement provided a convoluted formula to reduce the benefits for the better-off retirees—without seeming to have done so. But in obscuring the politically dreaded phrase, "means testing" for Social Security, the wise men brought upon themselves another ta boo, a new income tax. Every retiree would continue to receive the same amount as before, but in some cases, some of it—the amount depending on how much other income the retiree had—would be taken back by the Social Security Administration through the federal income tax. Yes, taken back by Social Security, because the income tax collected on the retirement benefits would *not* go into the general treasury. Instead, it would go right back into the Social Security Old Age and Survivors Trust Fund.

A retiree could choose one or the other of two formulas to determine how much, if any, of the Social Security retirement benefit would be taxed. The first formula went like this: Count one half a retired couple's Social Security benefits, add to that all their additional income—earned and unearned, taxed and tax free—and if that total exceeded thirty two thousand dollars, then fifty percent of the Social Security benefits must be included in adjusted gross income, and federal income tax, at whatever rate applied to the couple, would have to be paid on that one half of the benefits. It really wasn't very unreasonable when you considered that more than 80 percent of the average benefit was a windfall in terms of what had been paid-in. The new law was simply taxation of a part of that windfall.

The second formula was designed for the couple whose income, counting half of the Social Security benefit, exceeded thirty-two thousand dollars by not much. In such a case, the couple would pay income tax on less than half the Social Security benefit. They would simply divide by two the amount by which their formula income exceeded thirty-two thousand dollars, and pay income tax on the part of their Social Security benefits which equaled what they got when they divided by two the income that exceeded thirty-two thousand. Thus, if a couple's formula income exceeded thirty-two thousand dollars by only one dollar, the amount of their Social Security benefit subject to federal income tax would be the princely sum of fifty cents.

I give you the foregoing details because, ten years later, in 1993, a so-called think tank near the waters of the Potomac either did not, or pretended it did not, understand what these means-testing formulas, signed into law by President Reagan, meant.

When the new Social Security law went into effect, I began receiving letters of complaint from retirees who were well known to be wealthy. In fact, I received only one letter from a retiree that expressed agreement with the means-test benefit reduction. The writer of that letter said, "It's about time you did this. I paid-in so little compared to what I'm getting out in benefits, I almost feel like wearing a mask to take it." And that letter wasn't even from a constituent of mine. He was a constituent of my colleague, Danny Burton in the district next to mine. The writer was my father. "Oh my papa."

The agreement hammered out at Blair House had a tedious balance to it, and the political parties agreed none would steal a march on another by amending it in the legislative process. That was fine for the leaders, but they had no tool but persuasion, plus intimidation in some cases, to bring about compliance from rank and file members of Congress.

Bill Thomas of California was in his third congressional term that year and, I thought, still a tad callow. He rapidly evolved into one of the wisest and most reasonable members, a man with keenly topical humor whom I liked and admired greatly. But when the Ways and Means Subcommittee on Social Security took up the bailout legislation, Thomas, as a new member there, had a stack of amendments. The party leaders had made their deals; he hadn't.

The party ratio on the subcommittee was seven Democrats, of whom I was one, and four Republicans, of whom Thomas was one. Obviously it would have been more awkward for his fellow Republicans to cast votes against his amendments than for the Democrats to do so and, therefore, keep the grand agreement intact. That's what happened on his amendment's roll call votes, one after another.

Our friend, smart-as-a-whip and funny-as-a-crutch Jake Pickle, chaired the subcommittee. Time and again, one heard Jake say, "The clerk will call the roll." And each time it came out seven to four against—until Jake repeated the directive for the fourth time. Before the clerk could begin droning out the names of the members, Thomas blurted out, "I bet you ten dollars it will be seven to four, Jake." Once again, I felt that old devilment creeping up, this time ten dollars' worth.

The next voice I heard was the clerk's. Since I was, by then, the first Democrat down from Jake, it was my name she called first. And I said,

"Pass." My abstention meant the vote would come out *six* to four, still preserving the bipartisan and essentially sensible agreement among our fearless leaders, but making Thomas lose his bet. To show you how fast the gifted mind of Bill Thomas worked, grasping the meaning of the moment before any of the others, he jumped up from his seat, *ran* to Chairman Pickle and handed over the cash. Jake seemed ten dollars better off. But for Thomas, not all hope was lost.

Before a chairperson asks the clerk to announce the result of a vote, each member has the opportunity to change how she or he is recorded. At that point I said, "How am I recorded, Mr. Chairman?" From the corner of my eye, I could see something like a searching hope in Thomas's eyes. He seemed to perceive a reprieve from his lost wager. Maybe, he might have hoped, Jacobs was a "go-along" Democrat—he did not yet know me—afraid to be recorded against the wishes of mighty leaders. So I paused for Thomas to entertain the optimistic possibility. Then I exacerbated the suspense, "Mr. Chairman, off pass," ah, would I say, "on No?"—thus restoring the ten dollars to its former owner? 'Fraid not. I continued, "on present," meaning that the one vote remained un-cast. In announcing that Thomas's amendment had lost, six to four, Jake was also announcing that Thomas, himself, had lost by the same margin. In subsequent years, Bill Thomas won a lot of thoughtful proposals which enriched the legislative process. We became friends.

The bill passed the House intact, but the Senate version varied enough from it to necessitate a House/Senate conference of which I was a member. It was my responsibility to argue for a House provision which seemed acceptable to all the senators except one. He was dead set against it and, being from the deep South, he shouted out his disgust in accents that were beautiful. But I had the better part of the argument according to all the other senators. This only frustrated and raised the decibels of the Senate dissenter. If I do say so, a few well chosen and quiet words from me during the exchange gave the senator pause. And he did pause long enough for me to say with a smile, "Tell us a hound dog story." Even he grinned at that. The provision stayed in the bill. A funny thing happened as my opposite number was histrionically haranguing the conference. A senator from Kansas named Dole—Bob Dole—reached his good hand behind the orating senator, opening and closing his pointer finger and thumb as well as his lips, sending me the silent signal of mock "jabberwocky." Bob Dole was one of my very favorite officials; he saw life in Technicolor.

By the early 1980s, the deadly narcotic tobacco had become a hot issue. The companies that pushed the drug were circling their wagons as more and more of their victims tried to escape the smoky and addictive dungeon. The government became a player on *both* sides. On the surgeon general's side of Uncle Sam's mouth, the message was, "don't smoke tobacco." On the Department of Agriculture's side, the message was "subsidize it."

Members of Congress took sides, too, and a lot of them also took money from the tobacco pushers. It was a schizophrenic three ring congressional circus. In one ring were the reformers—including me—who decried the obvious. In the second ring were the companies' congressional friends who denied the obvious. In the third ring were those who tried to stay out of it by quietly accepting the tobacco money for their election campaigns and hoping their votes for the subsidies and against measures to keep the cancer sticks away from kids, wouldn't be mentioned by their election opponents. In the case of opponents who accepted tobacco PAC contributions, the hope was not in vain. Without addicting kids, the tobacco companies would go out of business in a generation. Survival of the industry, if not its victims, depended on how often it could nick a teen with nicotine.

The second ring in the controversy included such holier-than-thou moralists as Senator Jesse Helms of South Carolina, who correctly railed against the cocaine that Columbia produced in quanta, but insisted on U.S. government subsidies for tobacco which his state of North Carolina produced in quanta. I have often wondered what Jesse would be telling us if tobacco had been the cash crop in Colombia and cocaine had been the cash crop in the Carolinas. Just a thought.

The Reagan administration, just as the Democratic and Republican ones before it, also had a split tongue on tobacco. The secretary of Health and Human Services, my friend and the former Hoosier governor, Otis Bowen, had a proposal on tobacco the White House didn't like. Between 1952 and the early 1980s, the Consumer Price Index had risen four hundred percent. But the federal cigarette tax, couched not in percentage, but in pennies—eight of them per pack in 1952—had been adjusted for only half the 400 percent accumulated inflation. The tax in the early eighties was sixteen pennies per pack. It was a sad commentary on our civilization that, in effect, the cigarette tax in the 1980s was half what it was in the early 1950s before the Surgeon General's report on the deadly danger of the wicked weed.

Doc Bowen presented efficacious studies showing teenage smoking dropping off when cigarette prices rose. Moreover, smokers were a disproportionate burden on the Medicare system. Stressing both phenomena, Bowen proposed that the federal cigarette tax be brought back to its 1952 level, in *real* copper pennies adjusted for inflation. He further proposed that the sixteen cents from the adjustment be deposited in the Medicare Trust Fund as a smoker-paid *user's fee* to cover the disproportionately higher claims on the system by smokers.

The White House announced its opposition to the noble proposal, arguing that the tobacco tax was *regressive* and was therefore unfair to ordinary citizens. I'm afraid that once again we were treated to crocodile tears. This was the administration that licked its lips over regressive taxes to replace the progressive income tax. The combination of President Reagan's mammoth 1981 income tax cut for high rollers and his mammoth 1982 excise tax increase with its disproportionate burden for on low rollers was, to a considerable extent, a tax shift from the country's well-off to the country's not-so-well-off citizens.

So the battle lines were drawn. It was another Ways and Means hearing that threw sparks. One of the witnesses was our former congressional colleague Horace Robinson Kornegay of North Carolina. Tall, handsome and friendly, Kornegay had become head of the Tobacco Institute, the voice of the smoke-filled industry. When my turn came, I said, "Horace, I don't know of anybody I like more and agree with less than you. Now, since you and President Reagan don't like President Reagan's secretary's proposal, what would you think about taking a page from the life insurance industry and putting a suicide clause in the Medicare Program? If you attempt suicide by smoking, you lose your Medicare coverage."

No, the Southern gentleman didn't cotton to that idea.

I continued: "This issue has brought out the poet in me. I have written a verse entitled "Friendship." It goes like this:

> *There was a young man named Jess,*
> > *Whose tobacco was causing a mess.*
> *So he told his friend Ron,*
> > *"You I depend on*
> *To make sure the tax is less."*

Jess, of course, was Senator Jesse Helms. But the poetic joke fell short; most of the knowledgeable people in the room laughed, but I didn't get even a smile from Kornegay. I wasn't being facetious when I told him I liked him; I did. But the battle continued for the hearts, lungs and right minds of people.

When the time came in the committee for me to offer Doc's idea as an amendment to a bill, staff people told me I had the votes. But, reminiscent of the struggle over E. F. Hutton's get-richer scheme involving mortgage bonds, the chairman told me my amendment would not be in order until several hours later. What a difference several hours make. Tobacco lobbyists descended on the committee like a combination of locusts and vultures. One tobacco state congressman, not a member of the committee, showed up with peanuts for the late evening palates of the officials who would decide the question. *Peanuts.* I don't think anyone would sell out for those, but the cigarette pack PAC contributions, well, that was a different matter. The votes that were there at five P.M. had gone up in blue smoke by nine. The amendment failed signally.

When my birthday rolled around in 1984, I learned once again that my mother had a faster wit than I. She had a nice party for me with family and friends. When it was finished and I was at the door to leave, I paraphrased one of my favorite movie lines from the Jack Lemmon film, *Operation Mad Ball*: "I'd be money ahead if I'd never been born." To which my mother quietly—and quickly—said, "So would we." You just didn't play the dozens with her. *Oh, my mama.*

About the same time, my frugal father surprised me. Whenever I was in doubt about a personal purchase, his advice was uniform: "Don't." For several years, I had hankered for a certain vintage car, often pulling over to the curb to sigh a bit when I saw one. Then I heard about one of the coveted cars said to be virtually unused. It was for sale in Lafayette, Indiana, about an hour's drive from Indianapolis. On investigation, I was convinced that the oldest story about a used car was true about this one. It literally had been purchased new by a man who immediately passed away and his widow had left it undisturbed for years—in a heated garage. The price tag was commensurate with car's sparkling condition and I called my dad and asked what he thought. For a moment I wasn't sure I had dialed the right number.

The voice sounded like Dad's, but the words didn't: "Son, you've lived a Spartan life for years. If you really want it, you should buy it." I felt a chill. Was this the same man who had taken a look at the fancy car I had bought upon finishing law school and said, "That car was made for a gold-plated idiot"? Yes it was, but that had been many years before and there were some differences now. For one thing, I had saved considerably more than enough to buy this car. So I went to Lafayette and tried it out. What a joy, but I told the owner that I would have to think it over overnight and that I would call the next day to let him know one way or the other. It turned out to be "the other" when I called him the next morning. One of the Abe Martin-like sayings I had made up was, "If a person skips buying something she or he wants, he or she will be able to buy something she or he really wants." My own words haunted me and I didn't buy the *jewel*. My next call was to my dad: "Dad, you've heard of post purchase depression?" He had. "Well, I think I'm experiencing post refusal euphoria." I could sense a smile at the other end. *Oh, my Papa.*

In 1980, Hoosiers lost a seat in the U.S. House. The 1980 decennial census showed we had lost that seat by a few thousand citizens. Eleven U.S. Representatives had been sent to the U.S. House in 1980 and they all were candidates for reelection in 1982. Clearly, one of them would not be a member in 1983. The state was redivided into ten congressional districts for the 1982 election and the incumbent whose district most nearly disintegrated was my Democratic friend Representative David Evans.

Evans was first elected over Republican Congressman Bill Bray in the Sixth District in 1974 partly because of the Democratic landslide and partly because Bill Bray's own party took so many Republican voters out of his Sixth District and put them into my Eleventh District in that 1972 gerrymander which was aimed squarely at me. As the incumbent who campaigned tirelessly, Evans won the next three elections in the weakened former GOP stronghold.

When the Legislature redrew the Indiana congressional map for 1982, this time with 10 districts, the Sixth District was taken to the political "chop shop" and used as parts for the new districts. One of those parts was southwestern Indianapolis, which included territory taken from my Eleventh District in previous redistrictings. Now it was back in the exclusively Indianapolis Tenth District. The Indianapolis District was always given the highest number among Hoosier districts. When Indiana had twelve congressional districts, Indianapolis was the Twelfth.

In 1982, I already represented about 56 percent of the newly drawn Indianapolis District, while Dave Evans, who lived in a town south of Indianapolis, represented about 33 percent of it. The remaining ten percent was then represented by Republican Bud Hillis, whose pre-1983 district, because of the contorted gerrymander of 1972, ran from Thirty-eighth Street in Indianapolis all the way north some 75 miles through Logansport, Indiana. That 10 percent had been removed from my pre-1973 District because it had too many Democrats in it for my own *bad*. Not only had I represented that area before, but it was the part of town in which I grew up.

At first, Evans talked about running for the next Congress in the southern Indiana Eighth District where he grew up and the incumbent was a Republican. But eventually he settled on the Indianapolis District, continuing to live in his Bargersville home south of Indianapolis, but registering to vote from the address of a cousin on the east side of Indianapolis.

Although it was well-know that I had never had a legal residence anywhere but Indianapolis, I was not at the time living within the newly drawn Tenth District. For years, I had lived at the Essex House, a downtown apartment building which was in the heart of the new Indianapolis District, but I had recently moved in with my mother and father who lived about thirteen blocks north of the new line. In a way, it had been worse than that in 1972 when the gerrymander left my parents—not me—out of the Eleventh District by *two* blocks. Seeing the new map in the paper at the time, my mother said to me, "This means I won't be able to vote for you." And I replied, "That's true, Mother, but it also means you won't be able to vote against me." She was always ambivalent about my being away in that fast-track city on the Potomac. *Oh, my Mama.*

For a while, it was like playing hopscotch. No sooner did I settle in one part of Indianapolis than the Congressional District would be redrawn necessitating my moving a few blocks to stay in it. Republican State Representative Charlie Bosma, chairman of the committee that drew the new map for 1982, presented the drawing at a news conference. When he got to the Tenth District, he essentially said what the GOP county chairman, wise and friendly John Sweezy, had said a few weeks before. They had decided to "stop wasting Republicans on Andy." The district Charlie announced for Indianapolis was majority Democratic and he said that "Andy will move a few blocks to stay in it." Charlie was a part of one of the finest and most respected families of Indianapolis. By chance, they had been close neighbors of ours on the southeast side when I was a small child. And by further coincidence, Charlie had been my friendly, gracious, and unsuccessful Republican opponent in 1978.

Charlie was right; I moved back to my Essex House Apartment, harboring my long-standing wish for a house on a large lot. I found that large lot because of the new congressional map. One evening after work in Indianapolis, my friend and top coworker Loretta Raikes and I picked up a map of the new district and drove along its borders to learn them better. One of the lines on the north side was Sixty-fourth Street. As we tooled along west on Sixty-fourth, we passed the Lienert Gym Camp, owned by Walter and Mary Lienert. Soft-spoken and courtly, Walter Lienert was one of the world's finest gymnasts and conducted classes on that graceful sport. The camp consisted of many acres just six miles north of downtown Indianapolis and about three miles south of Indianapolis' northern border, north of which the city's bedroom neighborhoods continued for miles. Sixth-fourth Street was deeply inside the city.

The city of Indianapolis, in the manner of New York's Central Park, had simply grown around the remarkable area through which we were driving. Many of the real estate parcels there were very large. Just across the street south of Lienerts' was a thirty-three-acre horse farm, the Grandview Stables, owned by Art and Sally Renahan. The urban island farm was home to them and about seventy beautiful thoroughbred horses. I don't recall ever seeing Art or Sally when he or she was not smiling. Art looked and sounded remarkably like another horseman, Roy Rogers.

As Loretta and I continued west, we crossed a bridge. There, on the south side of the street, I saw three things of interest—three acres of ground, a log cabin and a "for sale" sign. It looked like my dream come true. The place was barely, but definitely, inside the congressional district. So I called my real estate "hit man" Ed Mahern, brother of my former coworker Louie Mahern, who was by then an Indiana State senator. (Ed later became an Indiana State representative himself.) Ed looked up the property in the Indianapolis Multiple Listings and told me it included *six* acres. "Something's wrong," I told him. "The lot I saw couldn't have been more than three acres."

"Well," said Ed, "let's just go take a look tomorrow."

The property was indeed six acres. The bridge Loretta and I had crossed passed over Crooked Creek and the place for sale was on *both* sides of the watercourse, extending on the east all the way to the line fence of the horse farm. The lot was magnificent; the cabin was not. Scarcely winterized, it had been the summer retreat for revered Marion County Probate Court Judge Joe Wood, a dear friend of my father's. In fact, Judge Wood's whole family were friends of my siblings and mine as well.

My friend Jim Beatty, a prestigious real estate lawyer, wasn't very keen about my buying the place, calling it "bulldozer bait." But he was thinking only of the structure. Not being a yard enthusiast, he discounted the rolling topography, which included woods, creek, and that beautiful view of those thoroughbred horses munching their bluegrass each morning. The cabin? Well, it was a "mechanic's special" with a mere 912 square feet that included two small bedrooms, an abbreviated Pullman-like kitchen and a 12-by-38-foot everything-else room which was exactly half the house.

The purchase price was fifty thousand 1981 dollars. Times were hard, interest rates were above twenty percent and the real estate market tended to be a buyer's one. Since I had been looking and saving—not buying the vintage car helped—for the likes of the Wood property for a long time, I was able to pay cash and move in. My plan called for a lot of work to be done over a lot of years, some of it hired and much of it with my own hands and those of three of my nephews.

Eight years later the log cabin had disappeared into a very large home, replete with solar and geothermal energy. There were large decks and patios. In addition to the original two-car garage that became an attached workshop, we had added a two-stall carport and a new three-car garage with a winterized and summerized room attached. I had exclusive use of the workshop until Kim's and my two sons became five and seven. The whole layout was a homemade home, improved gradually as savings and free time were accumulated—no mortgage. It had a name: "The Fun Farm." Some said two letters were missing from the middle word. It was also a work farm, but to my family and me it was worth it. Kim turned it into a garden spot. One of her many gardens, the vegetable one, bore the name, "Garden of Eatin'."

A decade after Indiana lost that 11th congressional district, and Dave Evans and I had competed in the Indianapolis primary, a new map was drawn. In the process, I was asked by Bill Schreiber, one of the participants in the process, what request I had with respect to the geographical lines. I had only one: leave The Fun Farm in it. They did. In fact, they moved the northern border several blocks north of Sixty-fourth Street. When the mapmakers finished their work, our Tenth District was an island inside Danny Burton's Sixth District. I was quoted in the news as saying, "Danny finally has me surrounded; I might as well give up."

Back in 1981, I was not the only reason the Republican mapmakers produced a Tenth District that brightened prospects for Democrats. State GOP Chairman Bruce Melchert undertook the pleasant task of drawing *for himself* a super safe Republican Sixth congressional district, essentially in suburban Indianapolis. Bruce very definitely did not want to "waste Republican voters on" me. The lyrics from the old song, "You Were Meant For Me," included these words: "Nature patterned you/and when she was done/you were all the sweet things/rolled into one." When Bruce "was done" patterning his district, it had "the sweet smell of [GOP] success." Some said that the new Republican district, now designated the Sixth, had the aroma of the second-strongest Republican district in the United States. But alas, the best laid districting plans can go astray—*astray,* spelled D-A-N-N-Y B-U-R-T-O-N, who exercised his right as a Republican to enter the Sixth District primary *and won.*

During that primary season which, because of the high stakes in both "safe" districts, lasted for a full year—from the spring of 1981 to the spring of 1982. Danny and I met from time to time along what is politically, poetically, called "the campaign trail." Then it was that our warm friendship began to evolve.

The contest between Dave Evans and me was a *contrast* between us as well. From the Indianapolis congressional office, I sent no unsolicited mail at taxpayers' expense. Dave Evans did. In fact, Congress had managed several years before to slip a loophole into the franking (tax-paid mail from members of Congress) law. Every ten years, an incumbent could send mass-mailed "reports" to citizens outside the district he or she was elected to represent. It was a gimmick for incumbents. They could use official tax-paid mail for campaigning to people they were *not* elected to represent, but would like to represent in the next Congresses. The only condition was that the new district be contiguous to any part of the old district where such a representative had actually been elected.

In our contest, then, Dave sent government-paid mail to my Eleventh District constituents, in one case actually telling them he was "elected to serve you and I intend to continue doing just that." He also sent a map on which he labeled his Sixth District office "your Indianapolis *District Office*." He even sent government-paid color picture books of the U.S. Capitol with tax-paid postage to the precinct committeepeople who would be voting in the Tenth District Democratic Slating (endorsing candidates) Convention. But, even though Dave had always entered the convention for its endorsement in the Indianapolis part of his old Sixth District, he stopped courting the Indianapolis Democratic slating convention delegates with such mailings when he concluded he could not win a majority of their votes.

Because of another *contrast* between Dave and me, I did not have enough campaign funds to send out a non government mass mailing to assure my Eleventh District constituents that I had not, by some mysterious turn of events, suddenly ceased being the representative they had, in 1980, elected to represent them in the U.S. House. The second contrast between Dave and me was that I accepted no lobby money and Dave did.

These two contrasts alone made the Tenth District Democratic contest rare, two incumbents competing, one sending no congressional "junk mail" and accepting no lobby campaign money and the other doing both with gusto. It was a classic, right down the alley of *Common Cause,* the organization which pushed for an end to lobby money in campaigns and for an end to the use of congressional office facilities, such as official mail, for campaign purposes. Therefore, my friend Jim Beatty wrote to the organization suggesting that their news magazine do a story on this race. He never even so much as received the courtesy of a reply. In 1992 a similar contest between two incumbents occurred in Illinois. One of them, Congressman Glenn Poshard of Marion, accepted no PAC money in his contest and won.

The lobbyist groups were for Dave and that included the AFL-CIO, the bankers, and on and on. Jim Beatty said he was happy to see them all in the same corner. The realtors—not counting Ed Mahern—were for Dave. But I was pleasantly surprised by some stunning help I did get from Hollywood. It was in the person of an American icon. My very good friend Jim Corman, former representative from California, was a friend of the movie star Gregory Peck. He sent a letter to Mr. Peck asking for an audio recording I could use in my primary campaign. Jim enclosed a few flattering articles describing my record in office. Back came a letter from Mr. Peck in which he said he would record the message for use in my campaign. Mr. Peck added, "Andy Jacobs sounds like my friend Judge (Frank) Johnson of Alabama." Judge Johnson was a Titan in the struggle to honor the civil rights of an oppressed segregated segment of United States citizens in the South. Presently, we had a beautiful radio spot. The great Gregory Peck had come to Indianapolis by magnetic tape—on my side. I can hear his dulcet tones:

> Andy Jacobs, the congressman who never took a junket, the congressman who never took the full Congressional salary or used the franking system for thinly veiled political mail, the congressman with the second-lowest office expenses in the country, may never be a congressman's congressman, but he is a *people's* congressman. And that's what counts.

Mr. Peck's help counted, too. We used the tape for radio announcements in both the primary and the fall elections. On election day in November, a man at my polling place announced slightly brusquely to me, "It's your fault that I'm here. My wife heard Gregory Peck on the radio and said we had to vote." I apologized—just a little bit.

In the fall, Ways and Means Committee Chairman Danny Rostenkowski came to Indianapolis to campaign on my behalf. While he probably thought it odd that I declined PAC lobby contributions, he agreed to be the headliner at a small donation reception held for me in the beautiful North Meridian Street home of good friend and fellow lawyer Bob Shula and his wife. When asked by a news reporter why the chairman would "come to Indianapolis on behalf of Jacobs when another Democratic congressman was in the contest," Danny promptly replied, "He's my friend." And, despite the fact that Danny could never talk me out of my decisions regarding votes, he was right; I was his friend and *remained so* when he got into some trouble over what had been lawful—but in my opinion improper—perks when he first came to Congress in 1959. These perks were among the few that were subsequently outlawed—by popular *demand*. Old-timers like Danny—and there were many others, most of whom were never charged—were in the habit of participating in those perks of the past and, to a considerable extent, unwittingly continued to do so after the law was changed.

Danny lived life to the fullest. A "hale fellow, well met," he worked hard and played the same way. His favorite watering hole in Washington was a restaurant in Georgetown called Morton's of Chicago. He would often gather ten or twenty friends for dinner there. Apparently I was invited several times to join them, but since my coworkers regularly declined dinner invitations for me, it wasn't until Danny himself approached me one day in the House Chamber that I found out about it. Still preferring evenings in the office for answering the mail, I got the feeling that my not accepting his invitation hurt his feelings. So I went that very evening.

Later, I was quoted in a *Washington Post* magazine article:

> Eighteen of us were seated at a long narrow table with Danny at the head of it. Suddenly a stevedore appeared, pushing a cart laden with the bodies of slain animals. He asked each guest which of the deceased he or she wanted to eat and how its remains should be further desecrated by fire. When Danny looked up and saw the mortician approach me with a question no vegetarian should be asked, he called lustily to the establishment's agent:
>
> "He's my friend; bring 'im lots of vegetables."

Danny had a big heart, was both kind and loyal to his staff, and he had a candor that could be disarming. Once when he attended a class reunion at the high school from which he had graduated, he was stopped for driving with a tad too much beer in his blood. On the golf course the next day, some reporters caught up with him and one asked, "Did you have too much to drink last night, Mr. Chairman?" Danny didn't weasel; in his rough-hewn voice, he said, "I had *enough*." No denial, no further publicity. Then there was the eventual and inevitable unveiling of the chairman's painted portrait with the usual festive setting at the committee chamber. Cameras rolled and flashed, speeches hurled encomiums, and the vice president of the United States was introduced. George Bush and Danny had become fast friends those many years before when they sat as back-benchers on Ways and Means. The vice president reminisced about those youthful days. Then it was Danny's turn to respond to the wonderful things he had just heard.

When he got to the veep, he sent the several hundred listeners into convulsions by saying, "George, when we occupied the last seats here, I never dreamed that one day I'd be chairman of this committee. And who the hell ever thought you'd be vice president?"

There was another very good thing about Danny; he was fair. The contrast between the way his predecessor presided at meetings of the Ways and Means Committee and the way Danny did it was dramatic. The predecessor was a nice man who meant to be fair, but sometimes was too confused to pull it off. He could not call on members in the order in which they sought recognition for the simple reason that he could not remember the order in which they sought recognition. And those members gauche enough to interrupt a member who had the floor were not called to order. After one particularly vexing example of this, I wrote a letter to that previous chairman, "Your performance rewards the rude and punishes the polite." No reply, probably because he couldn't think of what to say; he would not have failed to respond out of anger; he just wasn't that sort of person.

Danny, on the other hand, was the picture of precise procedure and fairness. If the last member in seniority had her or his hand up first, that Member would be recognized first. If an attractive proposal came from that lowly member, Danny made sure no one else, including himself, stole the idea to get credit. I was happy when Danny's legal problems were behind him.

In an *Indianapolis News* story about our 1982 primary, a retired city policeman whom I knew when I was on the sheriff's force, was quoted as saying, "They say Jacobs is a gentle Marine. Who needs a gentle Marine?" It reminded me of something I often said of the Corps: "When I think of Marines, I think of strength without brutality and pride without arrogance."

Some words from Shakespeare's *Henry the Fifth* came to mind also: "In peace, nothing so becomes a man as modest stillness and humility . . ."

The ex-cop's attitude probably didn't make much difference in my primary, anyway. He was a Republican and the contest at hand was in a Democratic primary.

There was other newspaper coverage. Even if the Common Cause publication didn't have any interest in a real-life contest between its professed principles and the system it claimed to abhor, another Washington journal did. The *Washington Post* sent a reporter to nose up a campaign story in Indianapolis. His report referred to me as an "eccentric," evidently because technically, "insane" means different from the majority. And my non-PAC policy really did make me different from most other members of Congress who reached out for as much lobby money as they could get. A few years later, it was said that the same reporter quit the *Post* to join an organization that shared my eccentricity about the inherent corruption in which foxy lobbyists give more than chicken feed to their fine-feathered friends in Congress.

I had a lot of help, though, from precinct committeepeople. Louise Marr had once been my constituent, but now was Dave's. Nonetheless, Louise and I had been warm friends for so long that she went out of her way to help me. And there were others, many others.

Dr. Zhivago's General Strelnikov told the good doctor, "The private life is dead in the Soviet Union." And so it was for me during that year, stretching from spring to spring, in which every time that otherwise would have been free time, was intense campaigning time. It was a year of living publicly. As the long months drew to a close and the May 1982 primary day was at hand, my friend Bill Schreiber designed and, with the help of volunteers, conducted an opinion poll to see how I was doing. The result was stunning.

Up until then, I really had no idea who might win. Theoretically, the fact that Indianapolis was my hometown gave me some advantage. And Indianapolis City-County Council members Susan Williams, Rozelle Boyd and future council member Mary Moriarity Adams were among the prominent Democrats in my corner. On the other hand, Indianapolis was *not* Bill Hudnut's hometown and he had won our first contest. Of course when Bill ran for Congress, he did actually live in Indianapolis and had lived there for some time. All the other factors seemed to favor Dave. He had the PAC money, he used the franking system to flood the district with that "thinly veiled political mail," and the lobby interests, including labor—the UAW was kind enough to dissent and be neutral—were squarely in Dave's corner. Washington political handicappers figured Dave had it hands down because campaign money is the only index to political success in their perverse universe. The pollster for one Indianapolis radio station assured his client that it was Dave by a landslide. Dave himself was saying it would be very close. Bill Schreiber's poll surprised me by saying otherwise—otherwise to the tune of 64 percent.

A few days later I saw a story about Bill's poll in the *Indianapolis Star*. The story reported the result and quoted what Dave thought about it:

> Andy is running scared. Releasing a favorable-sounding poll just before an election is the oldest political trick in the book.

Dave went on to refer to Bill Schreiber and Jim Beatty, both former

Marion County Democratic chairmen, as "political hacks." This moved my objective dad to murmur, "A little shrill." I didn't know if the poll was accurate, although Bill's usually were, but I was quite sure it was not a "political trick." In any case, we would all soon know, but not as soon as we all had supposed.

My friends had a plan for me on primary day. They insisted that I not drive around from polling place to polling place to campaign on a hit-or-miss basis. Instead, they urged me to stand in one place from six in the morning when the polls opened to six in the evening when they closed. That one place was where two precincts voted, the two most heavily Democratic precincts in Indianapolis.

Even now it's hard to believe those twelve hours finally went by. Though infinitely physically safer, those hours reminded me of an eternity my fellow Marines and I spent on a mountain top in North Korea trying to attract enemy fire for the edification of our battalion commander. There was a large clock at the entrance to the polling place and at times it seemed as though the hands were actually going backward. They certainly weren't going forward very fast. I stood in the same place all the while. Not having had any food or beverage, I had no need of the men's room. And as I endured, I thought of my father's words those many years before when he saw me writing an endless stack of postcards to plead my case to precinct committeepeople: "It's a hell of a way to make a living." Those cards and the friendships I had with so many of those precinct officials were working wonders for me on the endless primary day of 1982.

I shook hands and baby-sat not only babies, but dogs and one cat entrusted to my care, as voters entered unencumbered to exercise their freedom to vote. When six P.M. somehow arrived, I thanked the poll workers and with stiff legs made it to my car. And I managed to sit down behind the wheel. I savored the sitting for a while before inserting and turning the key. It was reasonable to expect that, within the hour, sophisticated super computers at the *Indianapolis Star* would break the suspense; we would know how the contest had come out. Either way, I would be expected to submit to television interviews and worn out as I was, I did not have the wit to do that very well. The solution, of course, was a quick nap at the Fun Farm.

At home, I lay down on a sofa for some sleep, which, because of my curiosity, did not come with rushing speed. Thoughts coursed through and collided in my mind. For the first time ever, I had agreed to an exact time for a post-vote interview at a television station. It was Channel 6 at eight. Since Jim Beatty would have phoned the results to me by shortly after seven,

I shouldn't have any trouble keeping that commitment; I could leave the Fun Farm as late as a quarter till eight and make it. It was only six-thirty as I nodded off for what I hoped would be a fifteen-minute nap. "Hope springs eternal."

Within three minutes, the silence was shattered by the telephone. Languidly I hauled myself up and trudged the few feet to answer. It couldn't have been Jim Beatty already and it wasn't; it was a California friend who was driving through Indianapolis on her way to Washington. Just called to say hello and knew nothing of the political contest of the century which was unfolding in Indiana that very evening. At that moment, she and I were in two different worlds. I said nothing about the primary in the hope that the conversation could be abbreviated. It was as I wished her well on her journey. She had already told me that she hadn't enough time for dinner. Though somewhat hungry, neither did I.

Forget the nap; now my only hope was a good shower, clean clothes, and a sandwich, all of which helped. But suddenly it was seven-fifteen and no call from Jim. I did have a call from my lawyer nephew Tom Landwerlen, Jr., who reported that in the precinct he worked for me, I had *only lost* by eight votes. That was not exactly what I needed to hear at that point, but neither was it devastating inasmuch as that precinct was in the part of the new district which Dave Evans currently represented. My losing margin there was fairly small probably partly because I had represented the same people several years before. Still, it was my only report since the polls had closed, and it was not, by its semantics, uplifting.

I reached the finger-drumming stage at about seven-thirty. Fifteen minutes until departure for the TV station and still no word from Jim. Nor did I receive a call from him during the next fifteen minutes.

As I reached for the bedroom doorknob, I glanced back at the digital clock, realizing that for the first time on an election night, I would be reporting for an interview without knowing whether I had won or lost. Not a soothing situation.

The red numbers on the clock popped up to seven forty-five and suddenly their silent message was shattered by the ringing phone. Could it be? Yes, at the last possible second, it was the traditional call from Jim. In what sounded like a downbeat tone, Jim said, "Have you heard?" I asked what I considered to be a very logical question: "Have I heard what?"

"Well," said Jim, in his characteristically low-key inflection. "You've won—and big—64 percent."

There wasn't time for me to ask why the result of the contest took so long to determine. I arrived at Channel 6 exactly at the appointed hour, prepared to receive the usual congratulations. As I entered the building, however, I encountered neither smiles nor sympathy. It was simply like one more day of the campaign. Entering the studio, I saw two anchor desks. One with popular restaurant critic and delightful wit Reid Duffy, and the other manned by the top Channel 6 TV news anchor, Howard Caldwell. The scene was surrealistic; no big smiles and way-to-go's. Just business as usual with the big tote board behind Howard. But the tote board had no totals.

Did I get a nap after all? Was I just dreaming Jim Beatty's call? Told that my interview would not take place for a few more minutes, I found a phone and the phone found Jim. He was at Democratic County Headquarters where Bill Schreiber and he had counted every vote phoned in by the precinct committeepeople from all the precincts. And yes, it came out 64 percent for me. "Why," I asked, "didn't you call me when you had enough to make a statistical inference?"

"Too busy counting," he said. "Jim, there's something weird at Channel 6; they don't know the results. What's going on?"

"Well," said Jim, "that's something else you haven't heard. Hardly anyone else knows the results, either. The *Star* computer has broken down."

That said it all. The *Indianapolis Star*'s computerized election returns were so fast and so accurate that other news organizations, from the national wire services to the last little mimeograph weekly newsletter and one-lung radio station, had discarded their own vote-counting methods and subscribed to the *Star*'s service. The computer glitch meant that so far as the Indianapolis primary results were concerned, there was a blackout. The *Hare* had sprained his ankle and, by eight-thirty P.M., only the Beatty and Schreiber *Tortoise* team had managed to plod across the finish line.

As I sat with Reid Duffy, awaiting the pointed finger of the producer and the red light of the camera, I was among the very few who *knew*. The finger pointed our way, the red light blinked, and Reid said to me, "It looks like a long night, right?" My evasive answer was, "Well, it certainly has been a long day." The studio monitor flashed on and there was my opponent, Dave, standing in front of his expensive headquarters, surrounded by chicken-eating and beverage-drinking supporters. Reid addressed his next question to Dave, who obviously did not yet even have a clue about the results. Reid asked Dave how it was going and Dave said it was too close to call, that the returns coming into his headquarters were seesawing back and forth.

I faced a dilemma; should I tell what I knew and seem boastful, or give another non-answer to the inevitable question to follow? Follow it did from

Reid: "When do you suppose we'll know who won?" I glanced over to the completely civilized and handsome Howard Caldwell and, with our fortunate radio spot in mind, said this: "I don't think we'll ever know for sure until the Gregory Peck of Indianapolis, Howard Caldwell, tells us." My mother said that on her screen Howard looked embarrassed at the flattery.

I called her and my dad from the station to break the good news. My nephews, Tom, Mart, Dan, and Greg, having caught up with me at the station, then drove me to greet my supporters who were gathered at the home of Louie Mahern in the Woodruff Place neighborhood. We had to park two blocks away and the walk to Louie's, mostly in total darkness until I was blinded by a portable floodlight. It was a crew from one of the TV stations. I couldn't see which or who, but the question I was asked showed that news of my good fortune had finally reached the newspeople. "What does this prove?" the reporter asked. "It proves that Bill Schreiber is a whale of a pollster and pretty good at counting, too," I said. A few more steps and another camera. This time the question was, "What do you think the people are telling you?" My answer: "I'm not sure what they're telling me, but I know what I'm telling them; thank you, thank you very much."

Not once during my thirty years in the Congress of the United States was I so presumptuous as to think that I or anyone else could fully deserve the honor of serving there. To be sure, that honor has been sullied by some from time to time, but honor it was and honor it remains. Without Congress and the courts, as friend and former Representative Phil Sharp said, "We would have either dictatorship, in which the government shoots the people, or anarchy, in which the people shoot each other."

Following our contest, Dave Evans sent me a nice telegram:

Dear Andy,
    Too bad one of us had to lose. Worse yet, it was me.
    Congratulations and good luck in November.

Dave's campaign was markedly different from mine, but his was not unusual. The PAC and franking tools he chose were legal and most members of Congress use those tarnished tools. After all it was Congress that fashioned them in the first place. But, as mentioned before, when legislators pass laws that do themselves favors, that which is legal is not necessarily right. As for Dave and me, we remained friends.

My Republican fall opponent was about as able and as nice a person as Indianapolis ever produced. Mike Carroll was not only a skilled city government administrator—deputy mayor in two Indianapolis city administrations—he was just plain nice, a pleasant person to be with.

Some of his campaign literature was a little rough, but it wasn't really his. It was boilerplate GOP organization material, including the line, "In sixteen years, what has Andy Jacobs done for you? *Nothing!*" That just wasn't the sort of thing Mike would have said or thought.

One interesting GOP handbill came to the attention of one of my friends. It said:

>REWARD
>$100
>For information leading to the determination of one park, project or program, bridge, building or bill providing a service to the good of the city and/or the people of Indianapolis which is the direct result of the [16] years that Andy Jacobs, Jr., has been Congressman in the U.S. House of Representatives, Washington, D.C. In twenty-five words or less write to:
>
>Jacobs Record
>Box 44167
>Indianapolis, IN 46204

My friend applied for the reward. She reported to "Jacobs Record" that, "He arranged for acreage at Fort Harrison to be ceded to the city for a park and for a federal housing project near White River." Of course there was much more, but the offer's restriction to twenty-five words apparently was designed to prevent telling about it. My friend directed that the reward be sent to the Jacobs for Congress Committee. It wasn't, nor did she so much as receive an answer. You don't suppose the handbill was just rhetoric, do you? It was odd rhetoric for the GOP, its pitch normally being against federal aid projects "that could be handled better on the local level without sending the money to Washington in the first place." In Indianapolis, however, the city that for so many years said no to federal aid, the GOP city administrations lapped it up and liked it. And I have letters and public statements from three Republican mayors in a row commending me for the help I gave to obtain it—when I thought it proper. You will recall I didn't think it proper in the case of the old train station.

The result of the fall election was stunning. I won two to one, or rather the votes I received were two to one. Because of what was generally called the Reagan recession, 1982 was a bad year for the Republican Party. Fate had dealt Mike a poor hand. He worked his heart out, wasn't much responsible for the rougher campaign attacks, and was quoted in the paper the next day as saying, "Andy is a tough competitor. We were friends before this election and we're good friends now." Amen.

Not nearly enough years later, Mike left us forever. He outdid me in giving something to our city; he gave his life. Still hard at work to improve the community, Mike and three other civic leaders were killed in the line of civic duty. As its commissioners, they were planning the new Indiana White River State Park. The small plane in which they were headed to Ohio to study a similar park collided with another plane and fell to earth where our friends were killed on impact. As they sleep the big sleep, a memorial sculpture for Mike, banker Frank McKinney, Jr., builder Bob Welch, and businessman John Weliever will grace forever the gentle slopes of Mike's beautiful dream come true, the White River State Park in downtown Indianapolis.

A few days before the Ninety-eighth Congress convened in January 1983, the realtors came to see me in the Indianapolis congressional office. Their national organization had a project to urge on Congress a balanced federal budget. They thought reform of the entitlements was an important step in that direction. The president of the local organization asked me what I thought about it. I had some tongue-in-cheek fun telling him:

"Let me explain to you why it is so difficult to reform the entitlements. Members of Congress know that voting more benefits for retirees will be appreciated by the retirees and hardly noticed by the workers whose taxes pay for the favors. But even when a benefit is so excessive that most members agree that there *should* be reform, they fear that if they perform the reform, their election opponents will attack them, stirring up retirees to take revenge at the polls."

One of my guests asked, "Why can't they show a little backbone and do the right thing?"

"Some do," I answered. "But all the others see the consequences. For example, for years the benefits for U.S. civil service retirees were adjusted for inflation *twice* a year, while the adjustments for Social Security retirees were made once a year. And, unlike Social Security, the civil service retirement costs beyond contributions do affect the unbalanced part of the federal budget. So there was a vote in the House a year or so ago to cut the civil service retirement benefit cost-of-living adjustments back to once a year. That, of course, cut federal spending significantly. I cast the Indianapolis vote for the reform.

"My next election contest was this year's primary with Dave Evans, to whom your organization gave a substantial campaign contribution which helped him send computerized letters, strongly critical of the vote I cast, directly and exclusively to the civil service retirees in the Tenth District."

The president of the local organization made a statement: "We could just as well have supported you, but I met Dave when I sold him and his wife their home in Bargersville."

"Oh, I'm not complaining," I replied. "If the coincidence of a casual acquaintanceship is more important to you than the issue of the excessive Civil Service Retirement entitlements about which your organization is concerned, that's your business, not mine. I only give an example with which you are familiar, to answer the question about why so many members of Congress are afraid to do what obviously needs to be done. They see the punishment meted out to reformers by organizations like yours and lose their appetites for reform. But please don't misunderstand; I don't complain; I just explain."

The realtors laughed and nodded their understanding. That is, all of them except the president; he understood, but did not laugh. The realtors were treated grossly unfairly by a tax bill a few years later, and it was I who worked to right the wrong after having voted against it in the first place. The situation was similar to the one concerning the five thousand dollar offer to me of a campaign contribution from the big corporation that had been unjustly hurt by another tax law. You will recall that I shocked the lobbyist by rejecting the money and then offering the successful amendment that redressed the grievance. That private interest did not have to "sweeten an official's judgment" just to get justice. And, of course, the Realtors had done just the opposite in my case.

At Christmastime 1982, I was one of the speakers at an Eastside lunch meeting where my friend State Representative Charlie Bosma also was on the program. Charlie spoke first and said this to me: "Andy, you have a good district. Don't forget it was a Republican gift." The folks chuckled. When I spoke, referring to the yearlong contest for the Democratic nomination in the new district, I said to Charlie, "I'm grateful, but you'll confess it took me a year to unwrap that gift." Not long enough after that, Charlie died and, because of that, Indianapolis died a little bit, too.

chapter 17

REFORM

As THE 1983 SOCIAL SECURITY bailout law was gliding toward certain approval in the Ways and Means Committee, the Reagan administration made a suggestion. It was a good one. Why not take care of the festering problem of Medicare along with the Social Security Old Age and Survivors program? Sounded good to me and that was good for the administration because I was the chairman of the Ways and Means Subcommittee on the vast Medicare program.

The Health and Human Services Department of the Reagan administration had some wonderful people serving as officials. One day, some of them came to call on me in my capacity as chairman of the subcommittee. They told me their idea with apparent apprehension; they didn't know much about me and from their earnest and detailed explanation, which bordered on salesmanship, I could tell that they knew nothing of my effort during the Carter administration to pass a Medicare reform similar to, but not as good as the one they were bringing to me on this occasion. I was delighted with this development, but, just for brief fun, kept a poker face.

When the deputy and under secretaries—I never did understand the difference—finished their pitch in favor of the Harvard brainchild which came variously to be called Prospective Payments and Diagnostically Related Groups, DRGs for short, I sat silently both for a moment and for fun. I knew that when I spoke, their looks of anxiety would brighten into smiles of delight. And that's what happened when I quietly said, "I'm with you. Your proposal is great."

Both my Carter-era substitute and the Reagan proposal were grounded in the concept of Uncle Sam as a prudent shopper, the market working its wonders on a perplexing, public problem. DRGs meant, for example, that in the Medicare program, Uncle Sam would pay a hospital a certain amount to set a broken bone which "fell"—so to speak—into a diagnostically related group. If the hospital could do the job for the offered price and make money, then it would stay in business; if it couldn't, then it wouldn't. No more cost-plus gimmickry which invited wholesale inefficiency and fraud. From time to time, Uncle Sam's offered prices would be adjusted for inflation.

The administration's proposal was not universally acclaimed. For example, the American Medical Association came out flatfooted against it. The proposal applied to Medicare Part A, which dealt with hospitals, not physicians. The latter came under Medicare Part B, but I suspected the AMA figured the Part A proposal was only one of two shoes to be attracted by the gravity of the situation.

Nevertheless, with the cooperation of Congressman Henry Waxman of California who chaired the Health Subcommittee of what was then the House Commerce Committee, I managed to steer the entire new program into an entirely new title of the Social Security Reform bill. Together they stood, because very few members of Congress would vote against saving Social Security once the combined bill came to a floor vote. Ways and Means Chairman Danny Rostenkowski supported the Medicare title enthusiastically. In fact, Danny had a lot of good laws to his lasting credit. In candor, I have to say the misnamed and much *mis*-advertised and ballyhooed '86 tax "reform" was not one of them.

Our Medicare Subcommittee conducted hearings on the prospective payment proposal under the procedures I had developed for expediting the process. Scheduled witnesses had always been sent instructions in advance about the rules governing their appearances before the panel. Fifty typed copies of their statements had to be filed a couple of days before the hearings and oral reading of each statement could not exceed five minutes—it usually did. My addition to the tradition read:

> The five-minute rule will be strictly enforced—at mid-syllable if necessary. Each witness will be allowed two "finallys" and one "in conclusion." A Susan B. Anthony silver dollar will be awarded the witness with the briefest testimony and a Kennedy half dollar will be given to the runner-up.

It worked. On one occasion, the president of an enormous international conglomerate made a very brief statement and then said, "I believe I'll win the dollar, Mr. Chairman; my statement took thirty-three seconds." God knows what that man's income was, but it's safe to assume that he was not desperate for another dollar. Never underestimate the power of trinkets or the spirit of competition. By the way, Bella Abzug, the "plain speaking" representative from New York, was not happy with the vote I cast against striking the Susan B. Anthony silver dollar in the first place. I told her it was not male chauvinism that motivated my miscreant behavior, adding that, "I'd cast a vote to change the name of the Washington Monument to yours, but the coin they plan looks too much like a quarter and I think it would cause havoc at the cash register. Besides, when it comes to naming a coin for a woman, why pick a woman with a last name that was male? And come to think of it, how much do you flatter a woman by placing her name on something that looks like the proverbial coin of the oldest profession?" Contrary to common perception, Bella was not without humor; she did smile at my last point.

A year or so after enactment of the DRGs, *Newsweek* credited the reform with already having saved billions of tax dollars. The story was kind enough to credit me with the accomplishment, but of course credit should also go to many others, including all the subcommittee members in general and Representative Bill Gradison in particular as well as staff members capable Cathy Noe, wise Sandy Wise, proficient Paul Rettig, and devoted Dan McGinn. By the early 1990s, the reform had saved billions more. All in less than a month's work involving long days of long and enervating hours. I was happy to find something of significance on which I could agree with the Reagan administration. I wasn't too crazy about its various, reckless, and unconstitutional wars.

As we approached the presidential election of 1984, U.S. interest rates remained astronomically high, in large part because of historically high borrowing by the federal government. The government was hogging up the country's savings and bringing pressure badly to bear on our money markets. There were other factors; the Federal Reserve had used high interest rates in its attempt to wring inflation from the economy, but the Fed had eased up during the wrenching recession of 1982.

High interest rates are no way to get re-elected, and President Reagan's handlers knew it. The rates must come down. But how? To them, reducing their priority federal spending or increasing taxes to cover the huge jump in outlays simply were not options. The big agriculture conglomerates had to be fed pitchforks full of federal subsidy dollars and contractors had to make money from the likes of MX and Star Wars, which I called "Lab Scam." And there was little left in lunch buckets, following cuts already made in the school lunch program.

The administration had worked too hard cutting upper income taxes to commit the sacrilege of recouping any part of those cuts, just for the frivolous reason of reducing the crushing deficits. The ordinary citizens, the ones who cast the most votes, wouldn't be happy with another Reagan-signed hike in regressive excise taxes like the one in '82, the highest hike of any kind of tax in the entire second half of the twentieth century. What in Heaven's name could they do to bring down the interest rates and at the same time keep the borrow-and-spend party going?

Someone in the White House had a bad idea, but one that would work very well for them. The reasoning went this way: Interest rates are high because of the pressure federal borrowing puts on American money markets. We have to take that pressure off U.S. money markets without stopping the borrowing which is indispensable to our program. So let's start borrowing a lot more on foreign money markets. Someone else probably said we were already borrowing as much as we could on those markets; how could we get those investors to buy more of our bonds than they are already buying?

"Simple," said the schemer. "We'll just pay higher interest to the foreign nationals than we pay to our own citizens."

"But," asks the unconvinced administration official, "wouldn't our citizens get upset about that? Is that any way to win an election?" There was an answer: "They won't get upset about it if they don't know about it. They won't notice it if we hike the rates for foreigners in an obscure way. As it stands now, the 30 percent withholding on income to foreign nationals from U.S. portfolio investments means they have to pay our federal tax on that income. All we need to do is repeal that withholding provision and we, in effect, have repealed the tax. Since foreigners will no longer pay us income tax on the interest we pay them on our bonds, they will, in effect, get a higher interest rate than Americans who are taxed on the interest income from our bonds. Too complicated for our people to notice."

The scheme effectively to pay higher interest rates to foreigners meant even greater addition to our national debt, but "everybody's business is nobody's business," and to the schemers, the election was the most important business. How could they save the country if they did not save their administration for another four years?

While they were at it, they added one more layer of subterfuge to the hoax. To avoid highlighting tax-free interest paid to foreign nationals on U.S. government bonds, they would repeal federal income tax on *all* U.S. portfolio investments, public and private.

The dirty deed was done quietly in conference between the House and Senate on an unrelated tax bill. Most members of Congress didn't know the grand political plan was bootlegged into the bill by use of a very few obscure words. I was one of them. When I caught on, I did what I could to tell the public that in one more case, the emperor's clothes were missing. But to no avail. The news media either didn't get it or didn't *want* to get it.

One of the news people to whom I wrote about the historic hoax was the financial editor of the *Washington Post*, the very gifted Hobart Rowan. Two weeks later, I was in Indianapolis where he reached me by phone at our "Fun Farm." After explaining that he had been in Tokyo when my letter arrived, he said he was fascinated by what I wrote. After we talked for twenty minutes, he was convinced. I was convinced, too, convinced that I would soon see an expose in Washington's largest newspaper. I didn't. Either he changed his mind—highly unlikely, considering the enthusiasm he showed in our conversation—or his story was killed somewhere up the line.

After President Reagan was re-elected, some of his treasury officials were sniffing around the Ways and Means Committee with an eye toward restoring the tax on income to foreigners from *private* U.S. portfolio investments. But they were told by the committee staff that it would be unwise to call people's attention to the matter. It would only help me sound the alarm. Fifteen years later, most Americans still knew nothing about that "concise impropriety."

There is wide misunderstanding about another aspect of the economics of the federal government. Over and over some members of Congress, who surely know better, have asserted that the government takes Social Security tax revenues and spends them on other things. The disingenuous word there is "takes." The government *borrows* money from the surpluses in the trust funds and spends it on other things. When it does so, it has a legally enforceable obligation to pay back the borrowed principal with accumulated interest to Social Security. Those bonds have the same obligations as any other bond the U.S. government sells. To underscore this, when I became chairman of the Social Security Subcommittee, I introduced successful legislation that required the regular government to issue the actual bond certificates to the Social Security Administration, whose safes in Parkersburg, West Virginia, now contain those bonds.

Only once in history has the Federal Funds Budget—the actual budget not counting the earmarked tax trust funds—just plain taken money from the Social Security Trust Fund for general government functions. That once ironically was when the hero of the group making the incorrect accusation was pretending to close down the federal government in a dispute with Congress over spending and taxing priorities. The technical name for the maneuver was "disinvestment." Getting wind of it, Congress passed a measure requiring the Reagan administration to pay the money back together with interest at the rate prevailing at the time of the taking. The cat was out of the bag, and the White House signed the measure into law.

During the process of passing the restoration legislation, the House passed a different approach from that of the Senate. So there was a House-Senate conference in which I had the responsibility to present the House position. Presenting the argument for the Senate was the lovable Daniel Patrick Moynihan of New York—born in Tulsa. He spoke first and, when he finished, the chairman of the conference called on me. I read the exact legalese of the Senate provision, looked up and said, "Can anybody here tell me what that means?" Of course, to the naked untrained ear, it was gobbledygook. But the senator took up the challenge, asking, "Will the gentleman yield?"

"Certainly," I said. "It means," said the senator with typical animation, "that *the administration can't use the people's Social Security money to buy missiles!*" My response: "Write it down that way and we'll accept it." It was probably a poor beginning to what turned out to be a very good working relationship between us.

With interest rates falling—albeit at the unconscionable cost of one more addition to the national debt because of the higher U.S. government bond interest paid the foreign nationals—and with Hollywood script writing soaring to inspirational heights, President Reagan coasted toward re-election in 1984. By now, he was known as the "Teflon President," an appellation coined by Rocky Mountain Representative Pat Schroeder of Colorado. Responsibility for mistakes and other unfortunate administration behavior just wouldn't stick to the President. One day CNN came to our office to interview me. I had no idea what the questions would be and was astounded to learn what they were.

With the big camera grinding away, the reporter asked me, "Do you think President Reagan can tell a joke well?" For an instant, I thought I had misheard the question and said, "What?" When the reporter repeated the inquiry, I did my best to stumble through an answer, wondering why CNN didn't have better things to do with its time—I did.

"Well," I replied, "he's a trained actor, but I've seen him boot a few jokes. In the main, though, I'd say he does pretty well."

There was another question. "How do you suppose the President so easily escapes responsibility for his mistakes?"

"Oh, that's an easy one," I responded. "It's because of his boyish smile, the twinkle in his eye. People look at that countenance and say, 'Don't tell me he'd send a couple of hundred Marines to their unnecessary deaths in

Lebanon or get some Americans unnecessarily killed by faking up an American war a few days later in Grenada. That's like saying he would arrange for his former employer General Electric to sell nuclear technology to Communist China. Cut it out; stop being partisan.'"

Somewhat surprised by my answer, the reporter said, "You really think it's just his smile?"

"Well," I said. "Let me put it this way: Did you ever see Idi Amin on television when he wasn't smiling?" Amin was a very bad dictator. That really stirred the reporter who said, "You're not comparing the President of the United States with Idi Amin, are you?"

"Certainly not," I assured him, "just their styles."

With the approach of one more Reagan landslide, other contests were going on in Indiana. I could scarcely overlook the one in the Tenth Congressional District since, after all, I was in it. The Republican nominee was a handsome and friendly young man, on leave from his job as aide to one of our United States Senators. His campaign managers made the campaign somewhat comical in one respect. Apparently they did not know about my policy of ignoring the conventional wisdom that incumbents should not give publicity to their opponents by making joint appearances with them. That probably is wise political advice, but in terms of civics, it is very poor advice indeed. If the opponent's managers had simply and directly asked me to the meetings they wanted me to share with the GOP candidate, and, if I were in Indianapolis on such occasions, I would have participated. Not knowing this, they devised stealthy ploys to trick me into such joint appearances, once even using a public schoolteacher who invited me to an official visit at his school. When I arrived, there was my opponent sitting on the stage waiting to share the speaking occasion. Since I would have agreed, anyway, I found the subterfuge amusing.

My campaign chairman, attorney Gary Taylor, being one of the brightest stars in God's human constellation, knew when the bogus requests came in and, smiling to himself, always agreed to them. By Labor Day, my opponent and I were scheduled to have about twenty joint appearances before the election. To those, one more was added, this one *legit*.

The Indianapolis League of Women Voters planned a big one, a debate on U.S. foreign policy to be held at the Children's Museum of Indianapolis and covered by live television. That, of course, meant a lot of publicity for both of us. Nothing boring about that; I looked forward to saying a few words about the unconstitutional presidential wars that plagued post World War II America. But the event never happened. My opponent called the league and canceled twenty-four hours before the appointed time. By that time, he and his managers had changed their minds about joint appearances with me in general and this one in particular. We had already met for three or four of the meetings into which I had been "tricked." Now, apparently, they wanted to trick their way out of them. Pretty tricky.

One of those meetings occurred in the evening at a public school auditorium. The audience numbered perhaps fifty. To one of the posed questions my opponent gave a very long answer that sounded convoluted and made a lot of the audience forget exactly what the question was. When the moderator turned to me, I answered the question with one word: "No."

At that point, the moderator refreshed memories by repeating the question, "Do you favor federal farm commodity subsidies?" Again, modesty *almost* forbids; the crowd registered mirthful appreciation.

The opponent stopped showing up at the meetings his managers had labored so furtively to bring about. The opposition implemented a modified policy; my opponent would show up for a planned meeting, but he would arrive and leave before I arrived at the scheduled time. On one such occasion, at the All Souls Unitarian Church in Indianapolis, there was a dinner before the actual meeting and my opponent had been there for the meal and done some smiling and handshaking. He was not there when I arrived shortly before the meeting began.

As I visited with some friends at one of the tables, the pretty, former wife of a lawyer I knew, approached and said, "You're really in trouble this time; your opponent was here and his remarks were brilliant." I agreed that the earlier visitor was a very nice fellow, and she proceeded to her table. Not a whole minute later, another woman approached and pointed to an elderly lady three tables over. The much younger woman said to me, "When your opponent spoke a few minutes ago, that nice old lady turned to me and said, "That poor young man; he hasn't any idea what he's talking about." Something on the order of bad news/good news. I, of course, found more encouragement in the latter.

At about mid-October an organization to whom my opponent had spoken invited me to do the same. Lo and behold, the same former wife of the lawyer was in that audience. I liked the meeting a lot because the members were investors, quite conversant with tax law. It turned out to be more like a nonpolitical seminar for more than a half hour. Then the woman from the previous marriage held up her hand. When I nodded, she asked a question that was just a bit out of sync with the mood of the meeting: "Why should we vote for you?" Not only could I see, but I could actually feel the noiseless groans among the rest of the audience. I looked at the lady for a silent moment and gave the reply the others seemed to appreciate, "Oh . . . I don't know. What's the next question?" Big laughs.

The financial interests groups weren't often in my corner when it came to elections. There were exceptions where the groups and I freely—without financial sweeteners—agreed on matters of importance to them, legislative policies I viewed as no more than fair. Not only did I not accept campaign contributions from their PACs, I also refused contributions from the personal funds of anyone directly involved in the companies.

One company, which had been at the forefront of Dave Evans's primary campaign two years before, probably stepped across the line in its efforts to help my fall election opponent in 1984. With much fanfare, it gave him a job and announced that he was beginning a new career in the company's field. That seemed strange on its face since he was a candidate for a more than full-time job in the Congress. Even so, there would not have been the slightest legal problem, had it really been a job. But there was reason to believe it wasn't. Only a day or two after the launching of the "career," my opponent was quoted in the paper as saying he would be campaigning "full time" right up to election day. There certainly was no suggestion that his duties at the company in question would be performed at night when the company did no business. The "career" clearly was a field of daytime work. The arrangement smacked of an illegal corporate campaign contribution. If, as it strongly appeared, the job was a no-show ghost employment and the salary was deducted on the company's federal income tax form, there would be a serious question about tax evasion.

During the campaign I said nothing about the suspicious matter to anyone, except my close advisers Gary Taylor, Jim Beatty, Julia Carson, Jim Maley, Loretta Raikes, Marge Landwerlen, and Jim Seidensticker. But after the election, I did send word to the company in question that I did not want them to get into trouble and that they would do well to check with their lawyers before stepping out onto barely frozen water in the future. Perhaps needless to say, after the election, the "career" was quickly discarded, and my erstwhile opponent went off the payroll, or perhaps the paid role, and moved away from Indiana. The company in question indicated their gratitude for my advice. Actually, I came to like the main political mover and shaker in the firm.

An amusing thing happened on election night 1984. WIBC radio presented its traditional format of one Republican and one Democrat as guest commentators during coverage of the returns. The idea, of course, was that the listeners would hear both sides give their respective interpretations of the trends. But this time it was different. In effect, there were two people giving the Republican view and no one speaking up for the Democrats. One of the guests was a nominal Democrat; in fact, he was a former state Democratic chairman, but as a practical matter, though still registered as a member of the party, he was a former Democrat.

The news media seemed always to get the Tenth District election returns from heavily Republican precincts first. Most news people understood this and drew no hasty conclusions early in the evenings. Election night 1984 was no exception so far as the professionals at WIBC were concerned, but the "Democrat" announced very early that my candidacy was in serious trouble and that whatever the outcome, it would be very close. When a trend in the national returns showed President Reagan winning, the same guest commentator said that the Democrats would just have to start making their policies more like Reagan's. Later in the evening, with the trend clearly going heavily my way, he continued to say my race was nip and tuck, adding at one point that, "Andy's just going to have to start raising more money." That was really funny; my committee had tried "to raise more money" by twice asking this very same "Democrat," himself, for a modest donation—to no avail.

When the doubtful Democrat was state chairman, another funny thing happened. He had been invited and declined to be a *roastee* at the annual Indianapolis Press Gridiron Dinner. But he was only playing with them; he did show up for the show. But, based on the state chairman's reply to the invitation, the roastmaster, Dave McGee of Indianapolis Channel 6, prepared an "empty chair" spoof. So there was Dave with his prepared put-on about the chairman's chickening out and, at the last moment, there was the chairman sitting in that "empty" chair. I was seated next to the podium and whispered to Dave, "Read exactly what you you've written. I have a good ending for you." I assume that from Dave's point of view it was any port in a storm, so he trusted me. By tradition, when the roastmaster finishes skewering, he or she will say a line or two of praise for the "victim." As Dave read his jokes about the absent chairman who was not absent, those jokes seemed to be on Dave McGee, himself. But I handed him the napkin on which I had scribbled the proposed punch line at which he smiled and which he read: "Chairman [so and so], a man who, no matter where he is, has no presence."

Now the crowd was laughing *with* Dave.

Because of our defector's comments election night on the radio, many people actually thought I had barely squeaked through to win the '84 election. A few days after the returns were fully reported, my erstwhile opponent and I attended the wedding of a mutual friend who, when he addressed the reception guests, said, "and Andy almost lost." Reality check:

Ronald Reagan's big win which, in the opinion of our former state chairman, necessitated a change in the basic philosophy of Democrats, was 60 percent to 40 percent. My "squeaker," which our former state chairman said necessitated a change in my low budget campaigns, was 60 percent to 40 percent. Moreover, just as I ran behind my opponent in the heavily Republican precincts of the Tenth District, President Reagan ran behind me in the whole of the Tenth District. He lost the district 51 to 48 percent. But at sixty-forty nationwide, on the following January 20, President Reagan was sworn in for the second time.

When Republicans were sworn into the presidency, it was my practice to send our Tenth District congressional allotment of inaugural tickets to the Marion County Republican Chairman, John Sweezy. It was not unreasonable to assume that more Hoosier Republicans than Democrats would be interested in attending. John was always most gracious in his acceptance. I liked him. He was efficient, effective and, more important, fair.

The other Indiana congressional race that merits mention was the one held in the Evansville Eighth District, where my friend and fellow Democrat Francis X. McCloskey was the incumbent. That race was so close and the returns so disputed that it was thrown into the U.S. House for final determination under Article I, Section 5, of the U.S. Constitution:

> Each House shall be the Judge of the Elections, Returns and qualifications of its own members.

At principal issue was an ancient and completely nutty Indiana statute which provided that, if there were any error, no matter how inconsequential, in a precinct vote tally sheet, none of the votes cast in that precinct that day would be counted as part of the overall election returns. In other words, if just one of the several election day precinct officials missed initialing just one page of a tally report after initialing all the others and signing the certification of the totals, and if the officials of both parties agreed explicitly that the numbers on the tally were correct, even though you may have been disabled in combat as a member of America's armed services, your right to have your vote counted in that precinct was dead for that election. Did I write that the law was nutty? Please forgive the understatement.

Using that statute to throw out votes of precincts which went for McCloskey, the Republican Indiana secretary of state certified the Republican challenger in the Eighth District as having been elected. McCloskey challenged that certification in the U.S. House and a commission of ostensibly two Democrats and one Republican was impaneled to study the returns and make a recommendation to the full House. However, shades of the WIBC commentators on election night, in the case of most of the votes in the panel's deliberations it was more like two Republicans and one Democrat. In fact, one of the nominal Democrats was a somewhat former Republican.

During the debate, which preceded the appointment of the recount commission, a Democratic member from Texas, oddly arguing in favor of applying the crazy Indiana statute to the obvious disadvantage of McCloskey, cited the 1969 Supreme Court holding in *Powell v. McCormack*. He seemed to be going out of his way by using a flawed argument to side with the Republican candidate. This was understandable later, but not at the time; the Republican White House of Ronald Reagan had already privately told the "Democratic" Texan that he was going to be a Republican-appointed federal judge, for life. My father called such appointments "Political Heaven."

The about-to-be Texas federal judge badly misstated the holding in the *Powell* case. So I asked him to yield the floor to me, which he graciously did. And I said, "I believe the gentleman has misstated the holding in *Powell v. McCormack.*" The Texan said what all lawyers will always say in such situations: "Well, has the gentleman read the opinion?" I had an answer: "I wrote a book about it." And I had, twelve years before—*The Powell Affair: Freedom Minus One.*

On two key recount commission votes, the former Republican, then-Democratic, member sided with the full-fledged Republican member. One vote was to ignore the clear House precedent with regard to counting votes in precincts where there were more votes than *people*. The precedent provided for "proportional reduction," which meant that if there were ten too many votes and candidate "A" got sixty votes to candidate "B's" forty, six votes would be subtracted from the total of "A" and four would be subtracted from the total of "B," or a net gain of two votes for "B." McCloskey turned out to be "B" in the preponderance of those irregular precinct returns and the Democrat from California voted with the Republican from California to trash the precedent and leave ten obviously illegal votes in the tally.

The other key vote in forming the recommendation of the commission involved absentee ballots that had been declared illegal at the county and precinct levels by the officials of *both* parties. There were two categories of such absentee ballots, those declared illegal at county clerk offices and never sent to the precincts, and those overlooked by the county clerk offices and erroneously forwarded to the precincts where both sides agreed that they were illegal. The second category was put to a vote in the recount commission first and, again, the Democrat voted with the Republican to count the illegal ballots. But when the first category was taken up, the illegality, having been declared by elected officials, was too clear to be ignored. The "Democrat" from California cast the deciding vote to keep those illegal ballots where they belonged, out of the totals. In the end, the commission, using its constitutional authority to overrule the Indiana statute that savaged citizens' right to vote, found that McCloskey had won by *four* votes. Had the commission not counted the ballots both the Republican and Democratic officials at the precinct declared to be illegal, McCloskey would have won by seven votes. If the House precedent on excess votes in several precincts been honored, McCloskey would have won by even more.

Throughout it all, an ambitious Republican representative from Georgia advanced his name by insisting from the very start and then night after night in House *special orders,* that the majority Democrats were going to "steal" the election in Indiana's Eighth District. It was a clever tactic; if it frightened enough Democrats into voting to seat the Republican, that was an accomplishment. And if it turned out that the Democrat was the actual winner—the nonpartisan U.S. General Accounting Office did the actual counting—the Georgian could say, "See, I told you the Democrats would steal it." On another occasion, the same congressman attempted a major hoax and got caught. As I quoted from my cousin, Delmer Claise, in this volume, I hate to put a name on a bad story. But here I make a slight exception: the Georgian's initials were Newt Gingrich.

The other hoax happened one night as the future Speaker of the House was again speaking during House "special orders," which are carried on television by C-Span but are not a part of the official business of the House. The tricky solon pretended there were Democrats present in the House chamber while making outlandish accusations against the Democratic Party. As he did so, he would pause from accusation to accusation to ask if any Democrat would deny the allegation. Of course, there was no Democrat present to respond. But the C-Span audience had no way of knowing that because the cameras were, by tradition, constantly trained on the member who was speaking in the well during special orders. It was one thing to allow representatives to pretend there was a full House audience hanging on their pears of wisdom long after everyone else had gone home for the night. But to use the tradition to fake a consent from the opposition party that the opposition was despicable, was itself, several levels below despicable.

Thus, the subterfuge on this occasion led the national audience to believe that, under the doctrine of *qui tacet consentire* (silence gives assent), the Democrats were agreeing to the wild and farfetched charges against them. The ploy, which might have made Senator Joseph McCarthy blush for shame, worked for a while. But Speaker Tip O'Neill was watching that night from his home and later said he'd had enough. So he phoned the Capitol and directed the camera people to pan the Chamber periodically to show the C-Span audience that, in fact, no Democrat was present for the diatribe. Of course, the faker on the House floor had no idea that his hoax was being exposed nationally as he spoke.

Instead of being embarrassed and apologetic the next day, the perpetrator of the nocturnal nonsense in the U.S. House was indignant at the sneaky thing Speaker O'Neill had done. There's no reason to believe that brass beyond belief is doomed to failure. The congressman who was in the well that evening, of course, eventually became Speaker, himself, and went right on with his outlandish fakery. For example, in an interview with NBC's Tom Brokaw, he said that a young mother in South Carolina who murdered her own children did so somehow because of the Democrats. At her trial, it was disclosed that, as a teenager, she had been repeatedly statutorily raped by her stepfather who was not only an official of the so-called Christian Coalition, but also happened to be a former *Republican* county chairman. Obviously, that didn't mean the Republican Party was at all to blame for the heart-wrenching murders. But it sure as Heaven didn't mean the Democrats were to blame, either. If President Reagan was the Teflon President, this fellow Gingrich was surely the Tabloid Speaker.

At one point, a special order on the Indiana election controversy lasted all night and well into the next day. By chance that next day was the one on which I had arranged for Martin Luther King, Jr.'s magnificent minister for civil rights in Indiana, Reverend Andrew Brown, to be the guest chaplain and give the opening prayer for the House. Andrew flew to Washington to do the prayerful honors, but as House Chaplain Jim Ford regretfully pointed out, because the next calendar day was the same *legislative* day as the calendar day before, there could be no opening prayer. The House had not adjourned. Jim Ford suggested that Andrew and I meet him in the House gallery to watch some of the spectacle responsible for the problem. There was nobody nicer than Jim Ford and nobody with much more courage. He had traveled from the U.S. to the United Kingdom on a one-man sailboat.

As we sat watching the torrent of trashing words, I got an idea. Surely God did not mean for Andrew to travel all that way from Indianapolis without gracing the House with his special words. I wondered if . . .

A few minutes later, I stood on the House floor and asked the designated below-the-belt hitter to yield to me. He did so after saying, "I see the Democrat leadership has sent a senior member of their party to answer us." Then he yielded to me.

"I think the *Democratic* leadership knows me better than the gentleman in the well does," I said. "They know it would be a hot day in heaven before I could be sent anywhere by anybody but my constituents. I'm here on my own hook to point out for the record that because of this extended special order, God will not specifically hear from the House today. There can be no opening prayer. I thank the gentleman for yielding so that C-Span watchers can understand why God is being left out of our proceedings today."

It worked. All I had to do was roll that "holy hand grenade" (*In Search of the Holy Grail*) into the game, sit down, and watch the show. The fellows on the floor were generally beholden to the "religious wrong," and when I suggested that their grandstanding was sideswiping heaven, they went into a perceptible panic. From the member in the well: "No, er, we have to have an opening prayer." From another of the participating attackers: "Parliamentary inquiry, Mr. Speaker. Isn't there some way we can work this out?" There was; it was agreed that the congressional sapper team would yield the floor for a few seconds so that the House could recess long enough for a prayer. Thus, Andrew Brown became the only guest chaplain in history to give the second opening prayer on the same legislative day.

Andrew Brown was so special. When he died, I was given the privilege of speaking at his funeral which was held at Saint John's Baptist Church, from which he had done so much to free both the oppressed and the oppressors from the mutual prison of racial arrogance. He had served his country as a soldier in World War II and suffered the same old segregation when he came marching home.

Andrew's coffin was three feet from the pulpit where he had preached so much love and understanding in that mammoth struggle to cast off the silly ignorance about race in a potentially shining society. Now I stood in that pulpit to speak my words of farewell to and love for him.

Pointing first to the pulpit and then to the casket, I said, "What a short distance from here to there. But what a long journey, a journey through depression and oppression, war and ingratitude and oppression again as he trudged further toward salvation of our society's soul. Now that he has left us, what do we have? You know what we have; we have each other. And we have the memory of him and his wondrous words together with the knowledge that he is in a better place where the car you drive and the skin you wear have nothing to do with what you are."

Andrew's prayer in the U.S. House was, as usual, beautiful. Then it was back to the House histrionics. In his steady "special orders" drone of accusations that Democrats were plotting to "steal" the election in Indiana, Representative Gingrich badly misquoted an historic parliamentary case. It was the John Wilkes matter in the British House of Commons. According to a magazine reporter who was present, an assistant told the congressman about his error and asked the strange solon if he would like to correct the *Congressional Record*. According to the reporter, the congressman told the staffer to forget about it. This was at variance with the famous words of his party's immortal giant, Abraham Lincoln:

> If I have ever made an assertion not warranted by fact and it is pointed out to me, I shall withdraw it cheerfully.

On the day of the fateful House vote officially to declare who had won in the Eighth District of Indiana, several Republican House members sported lapel pins which said, "Thou Shalt Not Steal." By chance it was the very day I told the House about the term I coined to describe the chicken hawks, war hawks, who roosted there. The term was "war wimp"—"one who is all too willing to send others, but never gets around to going himself." Saying that only took a few seconds of my minute, so I added this:

"I note that some Republican members are wearing buttons saying 'THOU SHALT NOT STEAL,' an implied accusation that honorable members of this House are criminals. The Lord God gave more than just one commandment. Another of them is, 'THOU SHALT NOT BEAR FALSE WITNESS AGAINST THY NEIGHBOR.'"

I saw it with my own eyes: most of the members who were wearing them removed their buttons then and there. I suspect they had been coerced into putting them on in the first place. In all the years I was in Congress, I easily found things to like in all my Republican and all my Democratic colleagues, except for one Democrat and one Republican. Again, I won't mention their names, but their initials were Wayne Hays (D-Ohio) and Newt Gingrich (R-Georgia). Bipartisan barbarism.

The debate on the Frank McCloskey seating question seemed to last forever and I was a major participant. When, at six o'clock, it concluded and I walked back to our congressional office, I was wrung out and hungry. I ate only one meal a day, usually around one in the afternoon, so I was five hours overdue for that. But the seating ordeal was finished and now it was "Miller Time." I could relax and eat. Or so I thought.

The phone rang. It was my coworker David Wildes, who said the C-Span cable network had just called to say they wanted me on the call-in program which had just started at six. "Isn't the request a little late?" I asked.

"Of course," said David, "but [the Democratic congressman who sided with the Republican on the Commission] was supposed to be there and he chickened out. It's a one-hour program, so you could be there for forty minutes of it." In frustration I said, "David, I'm languid, rumpled, and crumpled. I don't think I have the wit for it."

"Well, Andy, it's either you or no one. Gingrich was on the program last night, making all kinds of wild charges and this is the chance for a Democratic response."

The C-Span studio was fewer than five blocks away and I was seated in that studio by six-twenty. The program was, as they say, in progress. My first caller unpleasantly said, "You've got a nerve showing your face after stealing that election." To which I replied, "That's a serious accusation; have you any facts to back it up?" *Bang!* The caller slammed down the phone. The next two calls were roughly—very roughly—the same and the host said, "They don't seem to have any facts. Why don't you tell your side?" So I did:

"I don't think there are any facts to indicate what these three people have said. But if anybody knows anything about this controversy that I don't know, I'd be glad to listen. Growing tired of the false accusation that my party was stealing the election, I buckled down and studied the matter pretty closely. Therefore, I'm handicapped by knowing facts. The recount commission *was* unfair—to the winner. It bent over backward to give some illegal absentee votes and some other invalid votes to the Republican candidate. But the Democrat still won by four votes.

"Now, the commission, acting under the plenary authority of Article I, Section 5, of the Constitution, did set aside the crazy law that probably unconstitutionally disenfranchised law-abiding Americans where the most minor of errors of form occurred in reporting what both Republicans and Democrats agreed were correct vote tallies in a precinct. But God, in her infinite humor, arranged for exactly the same kind of case to come before *Indiana* House of Representatives this year. The only difference was the reversal of party roles. Republicans control the Indiana House and in the disputed election to that body, it was the Republican who was declared the winner after the same nutty law was disregarded under the same kind of constitutional authority. Well, there was one other difference: the Indiana House Democrats didn't recklessly accuse the majority Republicans of stealing the election."

Four calls later, a man asked, "Did I hear you say 'her' when you said 'God'?" That call I had not anticipated, but, as my tongue ambled over toward my cheek, this is what I said:

"I don't know. I've never been quite sure that gender plays a role in Heaven—they don't seem to give birth to babies there. So, not knowing for sure, I say 'his' or 'her' every other time, and I forget which time this was."

By now, according to my mother, I was bobbing up and down on the screen. The camera people were all women and they were laughing pretty hard as the caller continued:

"Five thousand years of the Bible says 'his.'"

"I know that," I responded. "But we have to remember that the Bible was written by men. And I'm sure they meant to get it right. But just as subconscious subjectivity can creep into the writing of the most objective newspaper reporter, it could be that the male writers jumped to the conclusion that God is male. I'm just not sure. The Old Testament is rather long and I confess I haven't been all the way through it. But the New Testament is not so long. I've read it and I think my friends in the Christian Coalition may be mistaken in their view that Jesus is a Republican. I can find no instance in which He rode into Jerusalem on an elephant.

That last line was the one I wrote for Jim Seidensticker to use at the Young Democrats convention back in 1962. For some reason, there were no more calls about the election. What was left of the program became something of a religious hour. A few days later when the fundamentalist mail began to pour in, I received this information: "If you had ever had a personal relationship with God, you would know God is a man." My reply: "If I'd ever had a personal relationship with God, I'd hope to God that God was not a man." In my serious view, every child of God has a personal relationship with God. What's more personal than being created?

A few months after Frank McCloskey was seated in the U.S. House, the *Indianapolis News* ran an editorial on the subject of the notoriously weird Indiana statute that denied innocent citizens the right to have their votes counted. It said, in part:

> In most elections, the margin of victory is such that ballots invalidated because of handling errors do not matter. But, in close elections, the validity of each ballot assumes paramount importance.
>
> Witness the recent Indiana 8th District congressional race, which ultimately hinged on which votes were counted or discarded. In that race, the U.S. House of Representatives, which conducted the recount under its own rules, gave priority to the intent of the voters, rather than to technical requirements of the election laws . . .
>
> It is a sin when a qualified voter does not go to the polls to cast a ballot. And it is a greater sin when the vote tally is manipulated by

fraud. But, the greatest sin of all may be when those who do go to the polls are disenfranchised by the carelessness, sloppiness or ignorance of those entrusted with the ballots.

Several years after the publication of that editorial, fraud, in the form of vote buying, *was* found in the Eighth District election of 1984. But those charged and convicted were *not* buying votes for McCloskey; they were buying votes for his Republican opponent. The future Speaker from Georgia who, night after night on *C-Span*, had falsely accused Francis X. McCloskey and his supporters of criminal fraud, must have told his staffer once again to forget about correcting the *Record*.

The story about the federal crime convictions was published in the *Indianapolis News* on June 13, 1990:

> A four-year probe of vote-buying in a rural Indiana county ended Friday when U.S. District Judge Gene E. Brooks sentenced former Rockport Mayor [name deleted for this book] to 60 days in prison.
>
> As chairman of the Spencer County Republican Party, [the former mayor] directed what many consider a traditional Spencer County practice of buying votes with dollars and whiskey.
>
> Each election year, at least for the period 1982–1986 that was investigated, the [former mayor] and others raised thousands of dollars that were funneled to "drivers."
>
> The drivers would round up voters on election day, paying them $25 to $50 for their vote or buying them liquor.
>
> The [former mayor], 70, was only one of 17 persons to be convicted in the vote-buying scheme. Others included two Republican Party county treasurers, a county commissioner and a township trustee.
>
> In 1984, Spencer County vote-buying nearly changed the outcome of the 8th District congressional race. State officials initially declared the Republican . . . the winner by 34 votes, but the House refused to seat him.
>
> A federal recount declared Democrat Francis X. McCloskey the winner by four votes.

I placed the article in the *Congressional Record* along with this comment of my own: "Mr. Speaker: There are a lot of people who owe Mr. McCloskey and his party an apology. But don't hold your breath until the apology is made."

If anyone, even someone long-winded with huge lungs, did hold his or her breath waiting for that apology, that person died a long time ago.

In those early days of 1985 there was madness in the air. According to *Rocky Mountain News* columnist Charles Roos, the representative from Georgia and his henchpeople "likened McCloskey and his Democratic supporters to Nazis, Communists and Marcus Junius Brutus."

In the 1986 election President Reagan campaigned for several GOP Senate candidates, but only one GOP House candidate. In a rematch with Frank McCloskey in Indiana's Eighth District, that Republican candidate was the same one who had run in 1984. When the President arrived in Evansville, he urged the voters to "take back what is yours." They did take what was theirs, but they did not take it "back"; they already had it. Francis X. McCloskey was re-elected with a 13,312-vote margin. As late as 1998, *Washington Post* columnist David Broder was still implying that McCloskey's opponent was unfairly counted out in the U.S. House action of 1985. I doubt that the columnist did it out of malice. More likely, it was ignorance.

Please do not even begin to think I am suggesting that either party is essentially dishonest or that either is without its bad apples. Trusted officials of both major parties have been convicted for fraud at the polls. But as a rule of thumb, it's a good idea to watch closely the unctuous official who proclaims his own honesty while insisting his adversary should be listed as a "criminal." In either party, it's usually the grandstander and not his or her target who ought to be investigated. Or in Jud Haggerty's favorite words, "The louder he protested his honesty, the faster we counted the silver."

When the new Congress had convened in January 1985, Doug McDaniel, Washington correspondent for the *Indianapolis Star*, nephew of Eugene S. Pulliam, cousin of Dan Quayle, and prince of a fellow, filed a story about the opening day ceremony. In it he described what each member of the Indiana delegation to the House was doing while the invocation and flowery oratory were waxing. When he got to me, he wrote, "Andy Jacobs peeked during the prayer." I was single at the time, but I wasn't checking out the gallery for pretty ladies. I just wanted to see if God was listening. She probably was.

(*Above*) I helped hold up my end of the ribbon at opening ceremonies at Black Expo, July 9, 1977. Ribbon-cutting honors went to then-Mayor Bill Hudnut (*in light-colored suit*). Yours truly is fourth from the left.

(*Left*) Bill Hudnut and I at Black Expo, 1977.

Meeting the press with James Davis, chairman of the National Taxpayers Union (*center*), and Indiana Republican Senator Dick Lugar (*right*) as we explored the possibility of a balanced federal budget in February 1979. (AP Laserphoto)

Schmoozing with "Goodtime Charlie" Wilson of Texas and *Mission Impossible* star Greg Morris in 1975. (Ankers Capitol Photographers)

In 1970, I had the pleasure of holding court on the Capitol steps with the Supremes—the singers, not the justices—and New York Representative Al Lowenstein (*second from right*) and Ohio Representative Louis Stokes (*right*). (Democratic National Committee photo)

chapter 18

BIG MONEY —
Ask Not to do Much for Your Country

MY LAWYER FRIEND JUD HAGGERTY said he "had a client who made big money. That was the trouble; it was about a quarter of an inch too big." 1986 was the year in which I personally had some brushes with big money; and it was the year in which those who had enjoyed the big-money tax cut of 1981 came back for more. Only this time they were squeamish about calling the cut a cut. So they picked a nicer name: "The Tax Reform and Simplification Act of 1986." But underneath the camouflage crafted by the phrasemongers, the mother lode was a tax cut—again mainly at the top. To paraphrase the words of my friend the late Hoosier attorney general Jack Dillon, no matter what the reform, some people always come up with checks clinched in their teeth. Call it coincidental—on purpose—economics. According to Ronald Reagan and Steve Forbes, the economy would prosper and we'd all feel better if they paid less in taxes.

The federal income tax returns of President and Mrs. Reagan told the story graphically. The 1986 act cut their personal income tax almost twice as much as the 1981 act which they admitted was a tax cut. Their 1981 law knocked twenty-five thousand dollars a year off their own federal income tax, but the 1986 "Reform and Simplification" Act reduced their personal income tax by another forty-nine thousand, to a total tax reduction of seventy-four thousand dollars per year. All this was included in the Reagan budgets, passed by a cowed Congress, which called for more than tripling the national debt. The really high rollers respectively enjoyed literally millions in personal income tax cuts.

The propaganda for the pseudo-reform legislation claimed that the new law would close loopholes for the rich and, in return, it would cut the tax rates on their returns. But the "loopholes" that were closed to pay for the second round of top-bracket rate cuts hardly involved the rich. Repeal of deductions for interest on consumer loans and deductions for sales taxes were the mules that drove the rate cuts at the top. Obviously, very-high-income citizens don't do much, if any, borrowing to purchase consumer goods and sales taxes do not gobble large percentages of their personal budgets. Those "loopholes" were, in reality, the traditional deduction staples of middle- and lower-income citizens. And there was a loophole within the closing of those "loopholes" in the cases of homeowners.

Under the 1986 act, if you had a mortgage on a home, no matter how expensive the home or how high the mortgage, you could deduct both the interest on that mortgage, and if a new car struck your fancy, you could take out a second mortgage on the home, use the proceeds to buy the car, and deduct that interest as well. What about the renter? Nothing. If she or he takes out a chattel mortgage to buy a car, no deduction.

The Reagan personal tax returns did tell the story in noteworthy numbers, but conservative writer Kevin Phillips told the same story in withering words:

> What Reagan has really done with tax reform is put two Mercedes in front of every house in Darien. Eventually, people will realize it.

Ronald Reagan said that the Earned Income Tax Credit for the working poor was the best welfare program our country ever had. In a way, he was right. But that garden of welfare reform went untended during the first few years of his administration. Weeds of inflation were killing the flowers of incentive. The program was like the negative income tax advocated by President Nixon, except that a citizen had to have income from a job to benefit from the credit Reagan's speeches praised. The intent of the credit was to subtract from the progressive income tax of a working poor person—someone who might be working hard eight hours a day, but not being paid much for it—an amount equal to the regressive Social Security tax deducted from that person's low wages. It was designed to be both a help and an incentive for welfare clients to go to work. But the program, not adjusted for inflation, was so eroded by inflation that by 1986, poor working people had actually suffered a substantial tax *increase*. Adjustment was long overdue and in 1986 it was a perfect teaser to deodorize the administration's new round of tax cuts for the highest incomes. So it was placed in the bill. Poor working people didn't get a tax cut in the 1986 act; they were just brought back to where they were at the beginning of the decade when their taxes started going up and the taxes of high-income citizens started going down.

Halfway through the deliberations of the Ways and Means Committee on the Reagan tax proposal, they stopped calling it "simplification." The bill was not just falling short of simplifying the code. Because of the contortions employed to obscure the actual goal of the legislation—one more tax break at the top—the legislation was making the tax code more complicated by the hour. Loopholes for the high rollers were going to stay in the bill, but they had to be obscured for PR purposes and that contributed to the complications. For example, the oil barons certainly weren't going be troubled by losing their loopholes; Senator Lloyd Bentsen of Texas saw to that. Where there was some tightening up of deductions such as the ones for business entertainment, the new method for calculating those deductions made businesspeople jump through hoops to do the calculations.

In the end, the "reformers" had so egregiously exacerbated the complications already in the code that they had to come up with at least something, *anything,* in their bill they could call "simplification." The best they could do was the rate chart. Anyone who has ever filled out a 1040 tax return form knows that by the time one gets to the rate charts, its "Miller Time." It's scarcely more complicated than looking up a number in the phone book; and, since the numbers are in order in both cases, it doesn't make much difference how large the phone book or the rate chart is.

Nevertheless, the PR spin, put out by the advocates, said the number of brackets had been reduced and therefore the new law simplified the code. But even that ploy was doomed to disproof, because whereas the highest number of calculations per bracket before was three, in one of the new brackets, the number of calculations was *seven*.

Several years later, CBS wondered how many, if any, of the Ways and Means members filled out their own federal tax returns. There were two of us, my friend Bill Archer, Republican of Texas, and I, Democrat of Indiana. So CBS correspondent Bob Schieffer went down to Washington and interviewed Bill and me. One of the questions he asked me was, "Don't you find it complicated?" My answer was, "I didn't—until they simplified it in 1986."

One should remember that, no matter how much taxable income an individual has, he or she pays exactly the same rates on the first parts of that income as the people whose respective total taxable incomes equal the sum of those various parts. The top bracket rate applies only to the part of a high income which falls into that top bracket.

The 1981 act had cut the top, or "marginal" tax rate, for people at the top, from 74 percent to 50 percent. In 1986 the real goal of the Reagan "reformers" was to hammer that ceiling all the way down to 28 percent. All the rest was finding ways to pay for the cut without taking away loopholes for the most favored of their high-income friends. As they fed into their computers the data with which they hoped to feed their highly financed friends, the machine continued to cough back demands for repeal of more and more deductions generally perceived to be justified, even noble. The deduction for couples who adopted crippled children was jettisoned. At one of the hearings, I asked the United States Secretary of the Treasury James Baker about that callousness. The exchange was published in the *Washington Post* column of gentle and brilliant Coleman McCarthy:

> Jacobs asked Baker about the administration's plan to drop the $1,500-a-year exemption given to parents who adopt handicapped or other children with special needs.
>
> "Why," Jacobs wondered, "has the administration found the tax code a suitable place to give exemptions to oil, coal and fuel corporations for the discovery of energy, but not a place to support the adoption of handicapped children? Do you believe it should be that way?" Jacobs asked Baker.
>
> "*Yes sir*, I do," answered the secretary. Jacobs reports that "a collective gasp" was heard from many of the three hundred people at the hearings.

The exchange was strange; James Baker of Texas was Reagan's secretary of the treasury, but he was well known actually to be Vice President Bush's man. In 1988 Baker was at Bush's side when the president-elect declared that one of his first orders of business was going to be restoration of the very same tax break to help helpless kids.

One by one, more and more tax breaks for ordinary citizens were bludgeoned The credit for grass-roots, small contributions to election campaigns bit the dust. As the computers demanded more and more to pay for the tax-cut cake for the country club crowd, things got more and more desperate. A nun's rosary beads wouldn't have been safe that last night of jiggling the figures. Having run out of small fry to bleed, they reluctantly turned their greedy gaze toward one, and only one, big fry: the real estate industry. There were some inexcusable features in the real estate sections of the 1981 tax law. These were provisions that mindlessly and harmfully distorted the market, producing a staggering surplus of the likes of gambling casinos—some say one casino would be too many. But closing the real loopholes was insufficient to finish financing reduction of the top rate to 28 percent. So they whacked the realtors quite unfairly in the area of reasonable deductions for passive losses, whereupon the administration's goal of a top rate of 28 percent was met. A few years later, other outraged members of the committee and I managed to restore those deductions.

The White House had originally gone after the life insurance industry a little bit. The Administration had proposed taxation of "inside build-up" on whole life policies. This meant that if you had such a policy, you would have to pay tax each year on the increasing value, or inside build-up without having cashed the policy. During the initial sparring in the Ways and Means Committee, I compared the White House proposal with taxing homeowners each year on the increased nominal values of their real estate, even if they had not sold it and realized a gain.

When the Ways and Means Committee held briefing meetings for other House members to solicit floor support for House passage of the rich Rube Goldberg tax cut, the venerable Charlie Bennett of Jacksonville, Florida—the one who had come to the aid of our friend Henson Moore during floor consideration of Public Broadcasting appropriations—made a penetrating declaration: "You fellows are letting the rich con you."

There was some criticism of me from the editorial rooms of the *Indianapolis Star* in connection with the "reform" proposal. On September 23, 1985, which was during the preliminary sparring over the President's new round for the rich, the *Star* published this editorial entitled "Tax Plans":

> It is not clear whether Rep. Andrew Jacobs, Jr. likes the present federal income tax system. What he is at pains to make clear with a recent statement is that the President's plan does not meet his high standards. It's a giveaway to the rich, he declares.
>
> In the same breath he confirms that the administration puts high priority on ending deductions for state and local taxes—that is, the existing big break for the wealthy especially in states with high graduated taxes.
>
> Is Jacobs trying to get in the corner of Mario Cuomo and the numerous New York millionaires? Why doesn't he tell us what the tax system should be, not what it should not be? After all, Congress invited the Treasury Department to go out on a limb.

Because of pressure from those millionaires, the Reagan administration soon dropped the repeal of the deductions for state and local income and property taxes, pushing all the harder for repealing the deductions for sales taxes.

The *Star* had run another editorial on taxes just seventeen days before the one about me. Published on September 6, 1985, under the title, "Block the Grab," the opinion piece said in fair part:

> There is a way for workers to torpedo the proposal that they pay federal income taxes on fringe benefits such as health insurance provided them by their employer. It is irksome that the federal government, instead of restraining its habit of ever-increasing spending keeps trying to balance the budget by eroding the benefits of the workforce.

Sensing in the final paragraph of the editorial about me an invitation for me to respond, I sent this letter to the editor:

> Your September 23 editorial, *Tax Plans* says, "It is not clear whether Rep. Andrew Jacobs, Jr. likes the present tax system." It is difficult to imagine how my position could be more clear: I voted against it. I believe historians will record the 1981 proposal, which is basically the present tax system, as having ushered in a national orgy on borrowed money.
>
> When I voiced the same opposition to a proposed tax cut by Democrats in 1975, the *Star's* December 10, 1975, editorial was kind enough to call my position "old-fashioned horse sense."
>
> Old-fashioned horse sense told me that cutting our income in 1981, when we were already in the red, was foolhardy and would not, by some arcane alchemy, "balance the budget by 1984" as President Reagan claimed. Even less perception was required at the time to see the foolishness of cutting already-inadequate income while planning to spend even more—a trillion dollars more in Mr. Reagan's first term than in Jimmy Carter's term. And that trillion dollars is just about the amount added to the national debt since Mr. Reagan took office.
>
> Nor is it correct to say that Congress crammed the bloated spending down the administration's throat. Contrary to general perception, during the first Reagan term, Congress approved one percent less overall spending than Mr. Reagan asked for. The record shows that I opposed much of the spending plans of both the President and the Congress. But the money has been borrowed and spent and the interest on the debt is running wild.
>
> In your editorial of September 6, "Block the Grab," you quite rightly denounced the proposal to tax fringe benefits and identified the source of that proposal as "the federal government." But it was not

some faceless bureaucrat in Washington who issued that proposal; it was none other than Ronald Wilson Reagan, himself.

America needs changes in the present tax law, but those currently proposed would correct few of the 1981 law's many wrongs and compound the most egregious wrong [the 1981 28 percent cut in the top rate] by providing still more unconscionably disproportionate tax cuts for those with the very highest incomes.

Mr. Reagan's May 28, 1985, proposal included restoration of the marriage penalty on two-earner couples, reduction of the child-care break for low-income working women, new taxation of unemployment and disability compensation, plus repeal of the one-time $1,500 tax reduction for couples who will adopt crippled children. His proposal in the real estate area would undoubtedly drastically raise rents for practically everybody and the proposal regarding inside build-up of life insurance policies is so illogical as to be explained only by a desperate search for tax increases to make up for the new breaks for individuals at the top. Some reform!

In fairness I must point out that I have both agreed and disagreed with this administration. I was chief House sponsor of the new law, proposed by the administration, which has made a revolutionary change in the method of paying hospitals under the Medicare program. I led the effort in the House because I thought the administration was right.

But in this attempt to erode still further the time-honored principle of ability-to-pay as a basis for federal taxation, I believe the administration is wrong. When young men have been drafted for war, with its suffering and death, they have been sent forth on the basis of their physical and mental abilities to pay. Surely a patriot would apply the same principle when the rest of the citizenry is called upon to make a much safer contribution to their country in the form of taxes. Will Rogers said it: "It's a great country, but you can't live in it for nothin'."

The *Star* published almost all of my letter, but not quite. The paragraph about its unwitting condemnation of President Reagan over his proposal to tax fringe benefits was omitted. It would be pretty hard to argue that the deletion was necessary because of space limitations. In place of the missing paragraph, The *Star* ran a picture of me. I'm hard pressed to remember ever before or ever since seeing a letter to an editor published with a picture of the writer. In a way, though, I can't much blame the editors. As I said in my letter, I think the paper was quite right in opposing the proposed tax on the fringe benefits. And it had to be embarrassing and a little disappointing to them to learn that the man they strongly supported was fooling around with their employer-paid health insurance. The Pulliam press was enormously generous with its employees.

You will recall that because I was on the committee, I was able to preserve for Indianapolis the historic monument preservation tax credit that saved the unfortunate train station boondoggle from being even worse. I managed to get a couple of other "transition rules" for Indianapolis projects which clearly deserved them, but probably would not have received them without their representative in the room where the decisions were being made. In effect, a transition rule means that the provision in an existing law that is to be repealed remains applicable to certain projects which were well on their way when the change was first seriously proposed. That is what made even funnier a cartoon done by one of the masters, Charles Werner at the *Star*. The toon took me to task for obtaining transition rules for Indianapolis and then casting the Indianapolis vote against the bill. He obviously did not understand that defeat of the bill would have had the same effect for the Indianapolis projects as the transition rules; the old law would have remained in effect until congressional changes could be passed, changes one might hope that were fair as most people perceive fairness.

The 1986 Reagan tax cut for the top incomes along with its window-dressing cancellation of the painful tax hike on the working poor, did become law. The act was not completely without merit, but it was mostly without merit. Repeal of real loopholes for high rollers did not happen and probably won't until public finance of election campaign communication takes the U.S. government off the auction block and places it where Alexander Hamilton acknowledged it belongs, in the hands of the people.

My next brush with big money in 1986 came in the form of a lawsuit—against me. It was filed in Washington by a TV household holy man. One Friday morning when I was washing some dishes at the Fun Farm, the Associated Press in Washington called and asked if I knew that Pat Robertson had just filed a $35 million libel suit against me. "No," I said, "you have the honor of being the first to tell me."

"Have you a comment?" the reporter inquired.

"Well, my dad says that the trouble with suing someone for libel is that he's liable to prove it. Thanks for the call." My dad's pithy observation was in the cute-quotations-of-the-week section in the next *Newsweek*. It was also prophetic. When I hung up, I stepped to the picture window and looked out at the woods, the creek, and beyond all that, those handsome horses next door. And *mostly* in jest, I recalled an old Western movie line: "Sure am going to miss this place."

It all started when Robertson announced that he would enter the Republican presidential primaries in 1988. His platform seemed typical for the religious wrong: a truculent foreign policy and rank selfishness for a domestic policy. I really hadn't known anything about him until a few years before when, on my way through the channels to the TV news, I saw a warmly smiling face telling people about God. My first impression was that, yes, like the other TV "profits," he had turned the Lord into a money-maker, but I remember thinking that he seemed different—better. The voice was friendly and engaging. And even though what he was saying wasn't particularly profound, at least it did not seem like mindless rote. One of the things he said was, "When I was fighting in Korea, I wasn't able to be in business." That, of course, pricked up my ears, but I skipped on to more contemporary and specific news.

The next time I heard about Robertson it was from my friend, fellow Marine and Republican colleague in the U.S. House, Pete McCloskey. He told an amusing story about a rowdy, hard-drinking fellow Marine lieutenant who was on the Korea-bound ship with Pete. Pete said the young lieutenant was the son of a United States senator from Virginia, Willis Robertson. The younger Robertson, Pete said, bragged all the way to Kobe, Japan, that his senator-father was going to get him out of combat and that his listeners would just have to fight the reds without him. And sure enough, when they got to Kobe, a Marine personnel officer came aboard and took Pat Robertson and Robertson's best friend, another Marine named Ed Ganes, together with four other Marines—who later decided they had been decoys to obscure the scheme—off the ship and stationed them in Otsu, Japan.

Ganes was the son of the chancellor of William and Mary College. Both Ganes and Robertson were part of the Virginia aristocracy. The conversation between Pete and me was brief and amusing because Pete said Robertson was by then a TV preacher, preaching a sermon quite different from the Lord's view about peacemakers as expressed in the Sermon on the Mount. The TV holy hustler was a "kill-a-commie-for-Christ" man, Pete said, but he hadn't been a "kill-a-commie- (and maybe get killed himself) for-his-country" man when duty called. At the time, I had little interest in the vicariously brave words of a TV money-making missionary. His silly pitch probably resonated with people accustomed to writing checks to keep the commies out from under their beds. It was their business and his *business*, but it was none of mine.

When the holy video voice decided it was time to skip God and try his hand at presidential politics, his war policy and contrasting war record seemed appropriate for public discussion. Sounded war wimpish to me. I was pretty sure, but not completely sure, that Pete had told me about that Fifth Replacement Draft which included Robertson and Pete. So I wrote a letter of inquiry to Pete. The answer was, "Dear Andy: no, I did not tell you that story."

As I read the letter, the nagging and impatient bells rang for a vote on the House floor. Ordinarily, I would have finished the short letter and tossed it into the wastebasket. But in my haste to cast the vote, I left the missive on my (I owned it) desk. When I returned, I finished reading the letter and made a discovery; the letter wasn't from Pete McCloskey, nor had my letter been sent to Pete McCloskey. Mine had inadvertently been sent to another colleague, my good Hoosier friend First District Representative Pete Visclosky. My original letter was dispatched again, this time accurately addressed and answered by Pete McCloskey.

Pete's answer took six pages. In addition to what Pete had told me before, he added that another Marine officer had told him the Marines who went to Otsu had eventually made it to Korea and that all, *save* the Senator's son, had actually gone into combat. Robertson, instead, was assigned to First Marine Division Headquarters so far to the rear as to be much safer than the average U.S. city. Pete wrote that one of the "decoys," a Marine named John Gerhart had told him Robertson became the Division Headquarters' liquor officer. Pete added that he assumed Robertson had official duties, also.

I don't know exactly why, but some of my most interesting calls those days reached me when I was at home in Indianapolis. The one from columnist Robert Novak was no exception. He asked if it were true that I had received a letter about Robertson from Pete McCloskey. When I affirmed, he asked if he could have a copy and I said, "I don't know. I'll have to check with Pete." Pete said okay and the next day Bob Novak had a photocopy. The day after that, all Heaven broke loose. News of the letter and its contents began in the Evans/Novak syndicated column and from there spread like wildfire through the wire services and into the major TV networks as well as the nation's newspapers large and small.

Robertson was in a bad spot; he knew the truth of it, but in the manner of Senator Joseph R. McCarthy of Wisconsin, he figured he had to file a libel case at least to pettifog the reality until the key Republican primaries were over. Actually he filed two suits, one against Pete as the originator of the alleged libel and the other, not against the *New York Times*, the

Washington Post nor any of the other major papers that carried the story, nor CBS and the other major TV networks, but against me as the publisher of the alleged libel. It took no genius to figure out that the giant corporations were left out because Robertson's lawyers wanted to avoid deep pockets on the defendants' side of the case. As Pete put it, Robertson's people assumed that, with his castle, stables, and Christian cash machine, Robertson could romp over us and we would quickly become exhausted financially.

Robertson didn't know about our secret weapon, my dad. Robertson claimed to have personal conversations with God, one in which he talked the Almighty into changing the deadly course of a hurricane. During one of those conversations, he should have asked God if, in creating my father, He had created one of the best libel lawyers in America; God had. At the time my dad was eighty years old, but the scent of legal contest perked him up. Who says Robertson couldn't work miracles?

Dad's legal defense work for Pete and me was *pro bono* and, through my long-standing friend Senator John Culver, the stellar help of Washington lawyer George Lehner was recruited. George was compensated, appropriately enough, partly by contributions from by-then-inactive Marines who somehow preferred war hero McCloskey over war wimp Robertson.

Pete also had a home owner's insurance policy which he thought covered him as a defendant in a libel case. At first, the insurance company thought otherwise. But after submitting to a deposition, in which Pete was represented by his old Marine friend, boot camp honor man and later attorney Clayton R. Janssen, the company contributed to the defense of the case Robertson filed against Pete. The only personal expense I had was for half of the depositions. That came to about fifteen thousand dollars, which I hated to lose. But I quoted to myself, "Our lives, our fortunes, and our sacred honor." Not only did our revelation help George Bush win the nomination, but it helped the country avoid Robertson. Besides, I was in the habit of saving and I had the cash.

When the depositions began, things came our way quickly. Marine lieutenants who were on that Fifth Draft ship and who were now successful business and professional people backed up Pete's story—except for one aspect, the liquor officer part. John Gerhart testified that Pete was mistaken; John had not told him that Robertson was a liquor officer. Gerhart added that Pete was honorable and heroic—Navy Cross for valor in battle—and that no doubt someone had told him about the liquor officer matter, but it was not he, Gerhart.

Of course, being mistakenly described as a liquor officer was not libel *per se* anyway. And there were no apparent circumstances in these cases that would make it libel *per quad*, which means a false statement which is harmful to another person because of a peculiar circumstance pertaining to that other person. A textbook example of libel *per quad* would be a nephew left money in the uncle's will on the condition that he remain a teetotaler. The publication of a false assertion that the nephew was a merely social drinker, though not libelous under other circumstances, could be a libel per quad against the nephew.

Though never alleging facts to establish libel per quad, Robertson's lawyers avoided discussion of the real issue in the case by harping on the liquor officer story. Because of an investigative report published by the *Richmond* (Virginia) *News-Leader*, which nailed down that real issue in our favor, Robertson's lawyers needed a diversion from it.

The *News-Leader* reported proof that Pete had the story of political influence right. The reporter examined the late Senator Robertson's papers in the archives at William and Mary College. And, sure enough, there were letters from the senator to general Lemuel Shepherd, commander of the Fleet Marine Force in the Pacific during the Korean War. One letter from the senator to the general thanked the latter for arranging that Pat "wouldn't have to go into combat until he had more training." That would be *more training* than the other Marines would get. Since Robertson never did any "fighting in Korea," apparently he never got enough "more training." Another letter from the senator assured the parents of Pat Robertson's friend, Ed Ganes, that they needn't worry, because Pat and Ed were going to "an interesting and historic place in Japan." The English translation of the interesting place, Otsu, by the way, is "demon disguised as priest." Who says God doesn't have a sense of humor?

So the Robertson lawyers went to work on the liquor officer "issue." When they took my deposition, an apparently humorless lawyer asked, "Don't you think it's disgraceful to be a liquor officer?" My answer was, "I hope not. One of my nephews is a bartender. They repealed Prohibition here a while back." The lawyer also produced another letter Pete had sent to me. In it, he suggested I file the letter under "officers and other forms of low life." Pete and Pat were officers; I was enlisted. The lawyer, without laughter, asked me a direct question: "Do you consider officers low life?"

"No," I said. "If anything, I would consider them high life." Now his put-away Perry Mason shot: "Then how do you account for what Mr. McCloskey wrote to you about officers?"

"Well, I don't really remember the letter, but I assume he was engaging in some self-deprecatory humor." The court reporter liked that answer; she laughed. The lawyer did not.

As the months rolled by and my savings rolled out, my dad's observation about the trouble of suing for libel was validated. Things were clicking along for the defendants. In my case, we made a motion for summary judgment. Technically, I had "published" the alleged libel just by giving a copy of the letter to Bob Novak. So the issue under the landmark case of *New York Times v. Sullivan* was whether I knew the assertion to be false or had reckless disregard for whether it was. Obviously neither factor was a part of the incident and the motion was granted.

The same day I won my case, Pat Robertson, as a candidate for president, was making a talk at the National Press Club. When he stepped out into the hall afterward, some reporters gathered around and told him he had lost the case against me. And, according to the resourceful reporter from the *News-Leader*, Robertson said, "Andy Jacobs has found a new way to lie, congressional immunity."

"But," said one of the reporters, "the case was not decided on congressional immunity; the decision was on the merits." What happened next according to the *News-Leader* reporter made me think maybe my first impression of Robertson had not been entirely wrong; maybe there was something good in Robertson. The reporter told me that Robertson turned to his PR man and quietly said, "How am I going to get my foot out of my mouth this time?"

Summary judgment was not granted at that point in the case against Pete. Although not libelous on its face, the liquor officer part left air space for further litigation, that is, until I received a call from New Orleans, Louisiana. It was from a retired professor of English, but he wasn't calling to correct anyone's grammar. He was calling because he was a former Marine officer stationed with Pat Robertson, not on the troop ship, nor at Otsu, but right there at First Division Headquarters where he was Robertson's tent mate.

In his deposition, the Marine turned professor said that not only was Pat Robertson the unofficial liquor officer, but also that Robertson was pleased to call himself the liquor officer. The professor further testified that Robertson had the enviable assignment of flying to Japan periodically as a courier of codes. While on these cushy missions, Robertson would pick up liquor and fetch it back to thirsty Marines at the division headquarters officers club.

When a person files a libel suit, he or she is subject to wide examination about past activities related to reputation. So the professor was asked about Robertson's general behavior back at division. That's when he gave evidence far more damaging than the holy man's—nay, I believe Robertson claimed to use God to heal a few people, so let's say the *medicine man's*—involvement with liquor.

The professor testified that young Korean women worked at the division headquarters, usually as domestics, cleaning tents. He said that many of them were prostitutes. But others were not and the one who cleaned the quarters the professor had shared with Robertson was a nineteen-year-old woman who wanted nothing to do with prostitution. That's the one, the witness said, that Pat Robertson hit on. He went on to say that the young woman was terrified when Robertson would chase her outside the tent and "pinch her." She was terrified, he said, because other Koreans who saw the spectacle might think she was a prostitute. As the professor explained, "Prostitutes were dead meat with other Koreans" when the Americans moved on. But apparently, as far as Robertson was concerned, that was *her* problem.

A few days after the New Orleans deposition, Robertson moved to dismiss his case against Pete. He had agreed to a trial date of March 8, 1988, for the obvious reason that it was Super Tuesday, a grand-slam day when many states held their presidential primaries. By the time the big day arrived, the campaigning would be over for a while; plenty of time for him to participate in the trial of the case he, himself, had filed. Naturally, his stated excuse for backing out of his sham lawsuit did not involve the put-away testimony against him in New Orleans—a mere coincidence. No, he suddenly discovered he just wouldn't have time to pursue his case. The case had been filed, it was said, on the advice of ultra-Conservative activist, Paul Weyrich—whom, by the way, I later found to be a pleasant fellow. The theory was to fog over the facts during primaries. It was reminiscent of a sham libel suit filed by "smearsmith" Joseph McCarthy of McCarthyism infamy. That libel suit was against Senator William Benton of Connecticut. McCarthy's excuse for backing out of his lawsuit was that nobody believed what Senator Benton said anyway. I was a student at Indiana University at the time and signed a nationwide "I believe Benton" petition.

Robertson had a little more trouble getting out of than getting into the trouble he caused the court and the taxpayers with his insincere suit. The case was dismissed "with prejudice." That meant Pete won the case. Moreover, Robertson was ordered to pay all the costs. My dad said that Robertson was a "deputy God, uninhibited by truth." When asked by the news media to comment on the dismissal of the case against him, Pete said of Robertson, "He's chickening out now just as he did thirty-seven years ago."

In an editorial, the *Chicago Tribune* said:

Somehow it just doesn't seem fair that under the American system of justice someone can bring suit against another person, causing the defendant great legal expense over a couple of years, and then seek dismissal of the action and walk away without dropping a dime on the other guy's lawyers.

But that's what the former reverend and sometime Republican presidential candidate Pat Robertson seems to have brought off in his altercation over honesty and honor with Pete McCloskey, the one-time California GOP congressman.

As you must have heard by now, much-decorated ex-Marine McCloskey had accused not-so-decorated ex-Marine Robertson of having his daddy, the senator from Virginia, pull strings to get him off a troop ship during the dangerous early days of combat on that peninsula. Not-so-decorated ex-Marine Robertson, who spent a few extra months in training in Japan before being assigned to a headquarters post in Korea, cried libel and sued much-decorated ex-Marine McCloskey.

The trial was to have started on Super Tuesday, but Mr. Robertson asked that his suit be dismissed, pleading that the time needed for court room participation would force him to dismantle his presidential campaign. The judge granted dismissal "with prejudice" upon Mr. Robertson's acceptance of an order to pay court costs. Legally that left Mr. McCloskey the victor.

But because Mr. McCloskey had sought $400,000 for attorneys' fees, which was not granted by the judge, Robertson found cause to crow that the judge "gave me what I considered the real victory."

Mr. McCloskey's lawyers have said they will consider a countersuit to recover their claimed legal fees. And Mr. McCloskey has talked of setting up a legal defense fund to pay them off. But that's not how it ought to work. Pete McCloskey shouldn't have to go out and take up a collection to pay lawyers who were defending him from charges in a suit that Pat Robertson called off. You know, there ought to be a law.

Pete's defense fund, mostly contributions from those magnanimous Marines, did pay a large portion of the fees of the other legal work, but not my father's. Pete asked Dad to accept a substantial compensation, but no, Dad said he "was happy to do it for Andy and Pete."

There are a couple of postscripts to the story. After Robertson's rear had been saved by being stationed in the rear, through his dad's influence, the old senator faced a tough re-election campaign. By then, Pat Robertson was already making a mark—and a buck—in commercial religion and the senator asked his holy son to help in that campaign. Lord, no! The younger Robertson couldn't possibly participate in politics; his life was committed to the Almighty—dollar. The elder Robertson, like King Lear, found out "how sharper than a serpent's tooth it is to have a thankless child." The senator was defeated. Later, when the younger Robertson decided he wanted to get into politics himself, well, that was different. Before the cock crowed very much, his Godly commitment for life expediently ended. The lure of Caesar had one-upped God. In a TV interview, the holy manipulator even denied he had ever been a TV evangelist. No, he had been a broadcaster, a businessman all along. He was telling the truth that time—all the way to the bank. Amen. For good measure, during his presidential campaign, Robertson officially cast off the cloth; he resigned his preachership.

During his campaign, Robertson was compelled to cast off some other things, too—a few of his earlier public statements. He took "combat" out of his biography (years later slipping it back in), and he acknowledged backdating his wedding day, the actual date giving his first child only ten weeks of gestation—there was no marriage for several months after discovery of the pregnancy. And, no, he wasn't actually a lawyer, but he had gone to law school. A *Washington Post* article by T. R. Reid published on October 8, 1987, included the following:

> "I have never had this kind of precision demanded of me before," Robertson said in an interview yesterday, noting that his statements were not challenged during his religious career the way they have been since he entered politics. "I would ask a little mercy . . ."

That was, by coincidence, just what that young Korean woman had asked of him decades before. And it was at least puzzling just how someone who was never an evangelist, just a broadcast businessman, could have experienced anything during his religious career. Maybe a miracle.

In an Indianapolis TV interview by Channel 13 stalwart John Kofodimos, I was asked about Robertson's view that there is disparity between scrutiny in religion and scrutiny in politics. "I do not share Mr. Robertson's opinion that politics demands more honesty than does true religion, considering that one of the latter's basic tenants is, 'Thou shalt not lie.'"

These latter-day, televised Elmer Gantrys who grow wealthy from their contrived crosses of gold tend to give religion a bad name. Such people are in marked and stark contrast to the real ministers of the Gospel, people like Andrew Brown, Russ Blowers, Bill Munshower, Jim Armstrong, Jim Ford, Tom Brown, T. Garrott Benjamin, Joe Bottorff, Dick Hamilton, Paul Landwerlen, Boniface Hardin, and thousands of others who live out their lives in the modest manner of their Lord, modest demeanors, modest possessions and modest material desires. In their ordinary clothes and their ordinary cars, they are the real heroes among the real Christian "soldiers." For, as the immortal Robert Bolt wrote:

> If we lived in a state where virtue were profitable, common sense would make us good and greed would make us saintly. But since we see that anger, avarice, pride and stupidity commonly profit far beyond charity, modesty, justice and thought, perhaps we must stand fast a little—even at risk of being heroes.

In fairness, I should add that Billy Graham and Robert Schuller seem to be exceptions to the TV ministry-for-money crowd. Despite the enormous incomes of their respective operations, they, themselves, seem to exercise personal restraints that give hints of modesty in their creature comforts.

When the Robertson case was over and he had legally lost, he did some PR damage repair by spin-editing Pete McCloskey's videotaped deposition so as to make it look as though Pete had lost. He then put his cut and paste job on his reconstituted "religious" TV show. Following his failed foray into politics, he had somehow slipped back into some kind of churchly cloth. Oh, well.

A few years later, I walked into the House gym and ran right into a dripping wet, completely undressed President of the United States surrounded by several guys who appeared to be blind and hard of hearing. The forty-first President thanked me for a vote I had cast that pleased him. I replied that he owed me no thanks for exercising my best legislative judgment, adding, "On the other hand, Mr. President, you may owe Pete McCloskey and me something for putting things straight about one of the Republicans with whom you competed in the spring of 1986." The President smiled; his blind guys with hearing aids didn't.

My friend Doug McDaniel, the Washington correspondent for the *Indianapolis Star,* the one who caught me peeking during the prayer, called me one day and apologized right off the bat. It wasn't his idea, but his editors wanted him to conduct a survey of the Indiana delegation to

Congress on the subject of marijuana. Specifically, he had been asked to inquire about whether any of us had ever smoked it. I assured Doug that I had no problem with the question. He was kind enough and had a sense of humor enough to quote me precisely thus:

"No, I have not; but I have so many friends who have that I'm almost embarrassed to admit it."

It was quite true. In the first place, I never had the slightest interest in it. And in the second place, I assumed that sooner or later the question would be asked. On reflection, I'm not sure I was never at a party where someone was smoking the stupid stuff in another room and that I never got a whiff of it as it wafted down some staircase. If I did, of course, that would make me different from President Clinton who once smoked it but didn't inhale. I may have inhaled it, but I never smoked it. In any case, I thought the Senate's rejection of one of President Reagan's nominees for the Supreme Court simply because the man had blown a little pot when he was in college was nuts.

On the same subject, one day as I was riding the trolley from the Rayburn Office Building to cast a vote in the Capitol, I found myself seated across from Charlie Rangel of New York. Among other honors Charlie had earned, he was the chairman of the House Narcotics Committee. To Charlie's right sat a plain-cloths officer from the Drug Enforcement Agency. Between me and one of the strangest, or at least most absentminded—delightful too—members of Congress sat a younger narcotics officer. The one seated next to Charlie, who looked like a clone of J. Edgar Hoover—old-style felt hat and all—was buttering up the chairman:

"Mr. Chairman, we've eradicated 31 percent of the marijuana in Colombia. And you probably heard we only eradicated 19 percent of the marijuana in Hawaii, but we actually got 26 percent."

Now, that struck me as ridiculous. How could this guy know what percent of marijuana he eradicated in those places, given that he could not possibly have known the total? So, naturally—for me—I decided to have some fun. Looking over at the other member seated second from my right, I said, "Joe?"

"Uh, yes?"

"You got a joint?"

So help me, our slightly vague colleague actually felt his pockets and replied, "Uh, no," whereupon the old narc said to the chairman, "Oh, this guy must be kidding."

"No," I said, "just give me some pot and a match, and I'll eradicate some for you right here." Somehow, by now, the broad-brimmed braggart was sure that what I said was in jest. But the name he selected to claim comprehension was a tad dated. He said to Charlie, "This guy's a regular (not David Letterman nor Eddie Murphy, but) Milton Berle." Everything may have been up to date in Kansas City, but I wasn't so sure about things at the DEA.

A Texas professor of economics named Dick Armey enlisted in the U.S. House in 1985 and ten years later was the majority leader. At first Dick was, in my dad's word, a bit shrill. If Russia was the evil empire, Washington was the sinful city. Dick would have no more to do with it than duty required. He said he wouldn't even have an apartment there; he'd sleep nights in the House gym.

Well, I didn't sleep in the gym, but years before Dick arrived, I had bought an eight-foot sofa and had slept nights on it in our Washington congressional office. It worked out just fine. I had already developed the habit of going to the House gym each morning, working out, showering, and enjoying brief, but delightful visits with my witty friend Dennis Fogle, who was the athletic director. So when I began sleeping on my sofa in the office, it wasn't much of an adjustment. In fact, I liked it. If I should wake up in the middle of the night, I'd simply walk a few feet to the desk and get some more of the perpetual mail answered. On snowy days, the commute was a beaut. I didn't try to hide my accommodations—they were mentioned in a *People* magazine article—but neither did I stress them. Most people were unaware of my Rayburn "hotel" accommodations.

Two funny Indianapolis radio disc jockeys certainly didn't know where in D.C. I spread my blanket in those days. The morning the wire services moved the story about Dick Armey's gymnastic sleeping arrangements in Washington, Indianapolis radio station WFBQ comedians Bob and Tom had a comment: "And you thought Andy Jacobs was close with a dollar." My friend Jim Beatty was listening on his way to work that morning and said he almost ran off the road laughing.

Dick stopped me on the House floor one day to see if I would be his Democratic cosponsor of a bill to end a federal government outrage that began in the Great Depression. The U.S. government had named a few peanut barons around the country, mostly in Georgia, as peanut gatekeepers for human palates. You could win the Indiana State Fair with the spiffiest, tastiest, and safest peanuts in the world and, without permission from one of the barons, you couldn't sell them for human consumption, only for feeding live stock. Of course, we didn't get much support from the Georgia delegation, but we were gaining in other areas until 1995 when Dick became Republican majority leader. He bailed out, it was said—by one of his staffers—because he had a Georgia problem. Hmmm.

Most people think foreign aid helps hungry people in other countries and once in a while, to a very small extent, it actually does. But like farm commodity subsidies, all the do-good advertising is reflected only in the tip of the iceberg. Most of the money finds its way by short route to large financial interests—with influence to match—in the United States. The International Monetary Fund is a good example. President Carter asked Congress for an extra five-billion-dollar U.S. contribution to the IMF and President Reagan, not to be outdone, asked for another eight billion. Not a penny of that money put even one bean on the table of a hungry home anywhere, but it put a lot of bread in the accounts of a few New York banking institutions. It worked this way: the big New York banks lent enormous sums to third world countries, confident of two things: first, that those countries were not likely ever to be able to pay the money back and, second, that our government would bailout the banks and charge the gift to U.S. taxpayers.

So the big banks had very little risk in making those third world loans, but they pretended they did and charged commensurately high risk interest payments which, in effect, the International Monetary Fund often wound up paying, too. Thus, the banks would never need to have their principal back, just the interest on it so long as Uncle Sucker stayed viable as a republic. It was the same as owning an office building with only one tenant who could keep on paying the rent, but not buy the place. Not only were the big New York banks guaranteed the interest payments by the biggest endorser on earth, but, pretending that there was a substantial risk involved, the banks could charge some of the highest interest rates in the earth. Sweet. But not for U.S. taxpayers.

I do not believe it extravagant to say that I was among the leaders of the opposition to the two successive administrations' bipartisan requests for the cumulative twelve- billion-dollar increase in our donations to the IMF. In those days, the Taxpayers Union was still a grass-roots organization and it, mostly in the person of my friend Mark Hulbert, helped and inspired me enormously in my efforts to stop the giveaway.

The Carter administration got its IMF wish by a solid House and Senate vote. However, since it involved a case of coming back to the (red-ink) well for a second time in a short period, we almost won our effort against the Reagan requested additional eight billion dollars. But, as the House vote glided toward completion and we were slightly ahead, I knew we'd lose. Slightly ahead just won't do it when that much money and that much influence are involved. The floor leaders of both parties start making deals and twisting arms. When the Reagan request cleared the hurdle by about five votes, I walked up to the majority leader and said, "Until a few minutes ago, I don't believe I ever saw a Rockefeller sweat." He may have smiled—slightly.

During consideration of the Carter administration five billion dollars request for the IMF, I offered an amendment limiting salaries at the IMF to a level no greater than the congressional salary which, at the time, was sixty thousand dollars per annum. My proposal was strongly opposed by the managers of the bill. As I was making my case, one of them asked me to yield, which I curiously and happily did. Somewhat vehemently he said, "You can't get a good man [man, that is, not person] for less than a hundred thousand dollars." To which I replied, "We got you." The amendment failed. After all, the folks at IMF wrote the checks to the banks. And the lobbyists wouldn't want those checks tearstained.

The high rollers were constantly banging away on the people's piggy bank. One day during debate on an appropriation for the ill-fated Space Station whose overruns were gobbling U.S. Treasury checks like potato chips, I stepped onto the floor to support our valiant Hoosier treasury watchdog, Representative Tim Roemer, in his effort to bring the boondoggle to a taxpayer-friendly finish. At that point, a representative—of somebody—was saying that "for every dollar we spend on the Space Program, we get back seven." When he yielded to me, I said, "That's great; how much would we have to borrow and spend on it in order to pay off the national debt?" The claim was ridiculously extravagant, but since there was big money involved, Tim's decent amendment was defeated. What difference do facts make when there is money to be made *from* the taxpayers, *by* the contractors and, by way of campaign contributions, *for* the representatives who play ball. "Here, sir, *some* people rule." If we had public finance of campaigns, as the British do, *the people would* rule.

There were several congressional scandals during my time there, but most of them were legal; they shouldn't have been, but they were. Some, however, were not even legal. One of the latter was called Abscam—from which I made the parody Labscam, to describe the Star Wars spending hoax. FBI agents set up video cameras in a motel room and dressed-up one of their number to look like a prosperous Arab, headdress and all. They then invited congressmen out to take cash bribes for helping the poor rich foreigner get a friend into our country.

Though tragically pathetic, some of the fellows caught in the dragnet did give funny performances. Right there on the big screen we saw and heard one of the dishonorables approached the "Arab" and said, "Money talks and bullshit walks." In time he walked right into a federal prison, later becoming both an ex-congressman and an ex-con. Another, known to be sanctimonious in protesting his superior honesty—"The louder he protested his honesty, the faster we counted the silver"—was seen stuffing the fifty thousand cash dollars into all the pockets he could find in his clothes and asking his soon-to-be captors, "How do I look?" He looked better than several months later when he, too, wore the drab garb of a federal prison.

The Abscam case that puzzles me to this day was the successful prosecution of a friend of mine from New Jersey. I never saw the videotape of him, but the *Washington Post* reported that he clearly told the sting operators he didn't want their money after bragging about his influence and saying that he could get the Arab's friend in the country if he wanted to. According to what I understood, the stingers poured him more and more whisky, which he was well known for savoring, until, quite drunk, he accepted the money. I just don't know and never asked him how the government made the case against him. But he was convicted and sent to the minimum security facility at Lexington, Kentucky, where once a month I drove from Indianapolis to visit him.

Though a former police officer who more than once worked with the FBI, I still had a lot to learn about the federal prison system. I believe just one visit would give potential white-collar criminals second thoughts. The furniture in the visiting room was circa 1950s, tubular steel and plastic chairs and sofas with pedestal ashtrays arrayed everywhere. The floors might have been vinyl covered, but then again it could have been linoleum. When I visited my friend, the room was teeming with inmates and their families.

By 1986 the American Medical Association had become unhappy with me. As mentioned earlier, I had already offended them a little bit by piloting the Reagan administration's hospital prospective payment proposal through the House. But that was more like a storm warning for the AMA, the dropping of the first foreboding shoe. The second shoe dropped right through the ceiling onto their heads, albeit lightly so.

In 1984 the Reagan administration called on me again in my capacity as chairman of the Medicare subcommittee. This time it concerned part B, the physician section of the program. According to the officials at the Department of Health and Human Services, in the manner of the Social Security "Notch" fuss, the Medicare formula for cost-of-living adjustments to physician payments had a glitch which, in ten years' time, was paying the doctors *80* percent more than the actually accumulated inflation.

The administration, in effect, asked if I thought we should let the taxpayers play some catch-up ball by freezing the level of payments for fifteen months. Sounded good to me, but I thought we should also prohibit increases the level of private fees a physician could charge her or his patient in a Medicare case, so that a doctor could not, in effect, nullify the freeze at the unreasonable expense of the Medicare patient. The administration said the AMA had already said doctors would not charge more on the private side during the fifteen months. In truth, the AMA was embarrassed by the overpayments and did not object much to the freeze on the government payments. It was the freeze on the private charges they abhorred, despite what they had said publicly about it.

After much machination, including negotiation with my old friend Dave Stockman, who, as budget director, represented the administration, the fifteen-month freeze on the level of both the part of the doctor's fee paid by Medicare and the part paid by the patient was passed by Congress and signed by President Reagan. All Hell broke loose. The AMA filed a lawsuit to have the new law declared invalid because of my part of it, the freeze on the level of the private charges in Medicare cases. But the freeze was based on the physician's participation in the Medicare program. It did not apply to doctors' billings to strictly private patients. So the law was perfectly constitutional as found by a federal court in fairly rapid order.

The Association of American Retired Persons held a news conference to celebrate the new law a day or so after its passage. I was invited to participate, as were a few of my House and Senate colleagues. Before I was called on for remarks, my colleagues, by turns, had praised the AMA—whose representative was sitting in the front row among the newspeople—for its support of the wonderful legislation against which they had just filed the lawsuit.

Facts compelled me to take exception. I said that if the AMA had helped put the legislation into effect, it chose a strange way to do so inasmuch as it had just filed a lawsuit to kill it. My colleagues fingered their collars and glanced at the ceiling. The AMA had either the first, or second-richest PAC in Washington and the probability that each of my friends had received generous contributions from it was at least strong.

In a way, the fact that the AMA had filed the suit wasn't so interesting as where the group had filed it. The nominal defendant was the Secretary of Health and Human Services, the pleasant Peggy Heckler. She worked in Washington and lived in Massachusetts, but the suit was filed—brace yourself—in Indianapolis, Indiana. Gee, what a coincidence—my hometown. As if that weren't enough, the AMA got my mother's politician-doctor, the one who misdiagnosed my father's fatal smoking-related cancer, to be their Indianapolis plaintiff. It was really funny. When the AMA held its news conference in Indianapolis, the first question was, "Why in the world Indianapolis?" Well, said the spokesperson, the AMA just couldn't find a doctor to be a plaintiff anywhere else. It wasn't much of an explanation, but the spokesperson certainly wasn't going to give the real one.

I got a nice letter from a western United States physician in which he said he wished he could give me my next proctology exam. When I wrote back, I turned the other cheek by suggesting, "As long as you're down there, why not kiss it?" Pretty hard to believe the AMA couldn't have talked him into being a plaintiff in its case.

The next time I heard from the AMA, it was another 1986 case of big money. About $350,000 big. The AMA was the first huge Washington lobby to cram its money through the loophole placed in the federal campaign spending law by the Supreme Court. Incensed at my work on the fee freeze, the AMA PAC people announced an "independent expenditure" campaign for my opponent in Indiana's Tenth District. The AMA would show other members of Congress that it was unwise to give any sass to the organization. It was just my luck that my opponent was an Amway man who used that group's peculiar methods to raise a half million dollars for his campaign. That made about four fifths of a million dollars arrayed against my re-election effort. Concerned, my small contributors sent more than usual to a total of $40,000 that year. We spent $33,000 of it and held the $7,000 surplus for the next election when we would ask the contributors to send less than usual.

I'm happy and grateful to be able to say that the Indiana Medical Society refused to participate in the effort to punish me politically. There wasn't much reason for the AMA to do so. With the exception of the payment issues, we had agreed on just about everything. Indeed, the AMA had agreed in principle with my private fee provision in their public pronouncement prior to its enactment.

Moreover, I asked the AMA's advice constantly in discharging my duties as chairman of the Health Subcommittee. By 1986 I no longer chaired that subcommittee anyway. My successor, Representative Pete Stark, was no favorite of the AMA, either. Pete was sweet, but sometimes he could be abrasive. So while it was at it, the AMA also went after Pete in the '86 election. But in the case of his "safe" Democratic district, they spent only a quarter of a million dollars and gave up early.

It is said that money can't buy happiness; it also couldn't buy elections in Pete's case and mine. In fact, PACs aren't usually as interested in buying elections as buying souls. They generally try to give the money to candidates who are likely to win anyway, but are happy to have all they can get to pour into campaigns for more than good measure. Remember my dad's words: "The difference between a $50,000 congressional campaign and a $500,000 one, is that, in the latter case, they'll find some way to waste $450,000." An enormous part of the one-third of a million dollars the AMA spent against me was paid to "consultants." One could only wonder just whose cousins those consultants were.

At the very beginning of the AMA effort, something amusing happened. The doctor who headed the PAC, a Michigan man named Berglund, announced to the world over network television that Pete Stark had saddled the country with the heinous hospital and physician legislation. Andy Jacobs, on the other hand, is rude and inaccessible, the physician explained. The doctor didn't know the territory; he got Pete and me mixed up. Pete didn't preside over the prospective payments nor the physician freeze legislation. And none of the AMA lobbyists would say I was "rude and inaccessible." They would and did say just the opposite about me. I'm sure the good Michigan doctor meant well, but his transposition was the only thing from the AMA that harmed me somewhat. I had to explain that rudeness matter to my mother.

CBS caught me for an interview about the AMA's attempt to purge me. The interviewer was the super smart and very nice Leslie Stahl. *What was it all about?* she asked just before the CBS backlight fell over on me. When the crew righted the equipment, Leslie repeated the question. And, glancing back to make sure about the light, this is what I said:

"I think the AMA considers Pete and me obstacles between it and the U.S. Treasury and, like tonsils, they think we have to come out. That's the bad news; the good news is that doctors aren't taking tonsils out much any more.

"When the administration asked me to help stop the overpayments from Medicare to physicians, I said, 'What's to stop a physician from charging more on the private side of a Medicare patient's pocket to make up for your freeze?'

" 'Not to worry,' said the assistant secretary. 'The AMA has adopted a resolution on that very point. The physicians won't do it.'

" 'Fine,' I said. 'Let's write it down in the statute.' "

At that point, the ham in me came to the fore. I turned away from Leslie, looked directly into the camera, and said to the viewers:

"Friends, hell hath no fury like a New Year's resolution taken seriously. A dozen years ago, when I was first elected by my colleagues to a seat on the Ways and Means Committee, I had scarcely sat down in it before I got a call from the AMA wanting to cross my campaign palm with silver certificates. Since by then I did not take PAC money from anyone, I declined and got a funny look. They're spending seventy times the amount they offered then to get rid of me now. So I have sadly concluded that, when it comes to the AMA, you are either in their stable or in their sights."

It was nice seeing Leslie again and it was nice supposing that I might have got a few laughs.

The AMA assault actually helped me in my campaign for re-election in 1986, albeit unintentionally. And because, in addition to the fact that I was opposed by a big-money Amway opponent, there was another negative coincidence which militated against my aspiration, the AMA help couldn't have come at a better time. I suppose I should have been greatly grateful. And I was, not so much for their counterproductive effort to purge me, as for all the informed advice they had given me at the Ways and Means Committee. Besides, I admired their unrelenting efforts against the use of the deadly narcotic tobacco and their early condemnation of the uncivilized so-called sport of prizefighting.

The local political problem that sideswiped me was that the Democratic county chairperson and all but one of the central committee officers had so deeply offended many Democratic voters in the central city that those voters decided not to be voters that year. The defection took its toll, probably defeating our popular Democratic Sheriff, Jim Wells, who was a candidate for county clerk. In other words, there was a serious erosion of the Democratic base vote in Marion County that year. And there is good reason to believe that the gauche AMA gouge at me almost made up for all the erosion of the party's base in my case.

It seemed everywhere I went—the hardware store, the grocery, offices— good Republicans would say, "I never voted for you before and I'll probably never vote for you again, but if *they're* against you, you must be doing something right." By the day after election, we learned that those good Republican crossover votes had replaced almost all the Democratic ones that had stayed home. Despite the absent Democrats, my margin was only slightly lower than normal. The AMA announced that it had shown that other members would cross the organization at those members' own peril in the future. And in the cases of members less well known in their districts, the AMA, despite its unpopularity at the time, was probably right. Which makes all the clearer the case for the British system of exclusive public finance for campaigns. "Who pays [or scares] the fiddler, calls the tune."

chapter 19

STATE OF VICE PRESIDENTS

IN 1982 I WAS THE GUEST SPEAKER at a Democratic dinner in northern Indiana. And I was greatly impressed by the chairwoman of the event. For some reason, I didn't quite catch her name, but I did understand that she was a professor of business administration at Valparaiso University and a city councilwoman as well. When she spoke, she did so beautifully articulately.

Four years later I was told I had an appointment to meet with A lady named Jill Long who was running for the Democratic nomination in a congressional district north of Indianapolis. As she and I sat and talked, it slowly dawned on me that she was the councilwoman who had so impressed me at the dinner meeting those few years before. Nonetheless, I had to tell her I didn't think she had much of a chance for the House nomination because of the popularity of her primary opponent. But I had another idea and asked, "Why don't you run for United States Senator?" She thought I was kidding; I wasn't. I suggested that if she ran for and lost the House nomination, she'd have made little impression on the party. If, on the other hand, she were the Senate nominee—at the moment that seemed quite possible to me—she would likely be defeated by Senator Dan Quayle in the fall. *But* she would have become well known as the one who carried the party's banner and, therefore, would have a considerable amount of good will to run for some other office in the future.

My friend and former coworker Louie Mahern had been the odds-on favorite for the Democratic Senate nomination that year, but he fell ill and dropped out of politics to recuperate. The Democratic state chairman had appointed a search committee to find a good candidate to take Louie's place. As a member of that committee, I thought Jill should be the candidate. She had some competitors, the front-runner of whom bragged his way out of the running when he appeared before the committee. When Jill spoke, she dazzled the group and after two ballots became the choice of the fifty-member committee.

The committee's recommendation was accepted by the primary voters and Jill was off and running in the fall. The long odds against her were lengthened further when the *bad*-old-boy network of curmudgeons in her own party criticized her both privately and publicly for "not being political enough," which is to say that she wouldn't make political hack attacks against Dan Quayle. Of course, in many of the good old boys' eyes, she had committed the ultimate offense of being female and presuming to run for office in the first place. In essence, they denounced her decency. On one occasion she was taken to task for truthfully answering a question in a southern Indiana news conference.

At an Indianapolis meeting of Democratic moguls whose purpose was to denounce Jill's exemplary campaign, a fellow Democrat who supported tobacco subsidies to keep the producers of it politically happy, stridently told Jill that it was stupid for her to state opposition to tobacco subsidies in that part of the state. Shame on Jill for giving an honest answer about the cancer crop. She quietly asked if her attacker thought she should have lied when the reporter asked the direct question. The attacker reddened, not, I thought, from chagrin, but from anger. One of her fellow Democratic candidates on the state ticket was nobly supportive and that was not forgotten by Jill and her friends. That fellow candidate was elected secretary of state in '86 and progressed from there. Two years later, Evan Bayh was elected governor of Indiana and served for eight years. He left office enormously popular and headed for his dad's old U.S. Senate seat, to which he was elected on November 3, 1998.

Jill Long was not without loyal supporters in her campaign for the Senate. Our literary friend Patty Welch provided lodging for Jill during the campaign in Patty's beautiful Indianapolis home. Pat Ulen, Jim Beatty, Jim Seidensticker, Virginia Dill McCarty, Gary Taylor, Kay Kelly, Loretta Raikes, and many others around the state cared more about Jill's principles than her prospects and were squarely in her corner as hardworking supporters.

Jill lost the election and won a lot of hearts. In 1988 she easily won the Democratic nomination for the U.S. House seat of the district around Fort Wayne, Indiana, losing in the fall to Representative Dan Coats who had succeeded Dan Quayle when Dan moved on to the Senate in 1981. However, in 1989, when Dan Quayle became vice president, Dan Coats was appointed senator and a special election was held in the Fort Wayne congressional district. A Republican candidate for Congress in that district, under normal circumstances, would have the advantage. But when the special election was held, the circumstances were not normal. The Republican city administration had angered some suburban Republican voters by annexing their neighborhood into the city. The angry Republicans took it out on their party's candidate in the special election. Jill won and went to Washington, eventually marrying a bright and handsome airline pilot and later becoming assistant secretary of agriculture. She remained a bright and inspirational light on the political landscape of America.

When I first entered Congress, I got a suggestion from my friend Bill Warren, whose lovely wife, Wilma, headed our Indianapolis congressional office in those days. Bill asked me to introduce a bill to change the national anthem from "The Star Spangled Banner" to "America the Beautiful." I didn't have much sympathy for the idea, but did as I was asked, introducing the bill "by request." Through the years, it was reintroduced with my other idealistic and therefore unlikely-to-pass legislation. You might say I ran it up the flag pole to see if anyone would salute it. Hardly anybody in Congress did. But somewhere along the way, I began thinking and reading more deeply about the proposal. One Sunday on David Brinkley's "intellectual ghetto" TV program, all three of the fussing fellows—David, George Will, and Sam Donaldson—found something on which to agree implicitly: The national anthem should be "America the Beautiful." James J. Kilpatrick wrote a whole column in favor of the change, in which he said, "The song [current anthem] is unsingable. Yes, the sopranos of the Mormon Tabernacle Choir can make it, but [most others] trying to reach the land of the free will collapse along the way."

My cosponsors for the change added up to two Republicans, Vin Webber of Minnesota and Mike DeWine of Ohio. But the effort was beginning to pick up steam with the public. CBS correspondent Charles Kuralt did a lengthy story on it. Later, Larry Smith, the very bright and friendly editor of *Parade* magazine, asked me to do an article on the subject. The magazine had taken a survey of its readers about whether they thought the anthem should be changed and most said yes. Singer Ray Charles and a host of other entertainers, including some U.S. military bandmasters, supported the idea. So did the master maestro Eric Kunzel, who conducted the orchestra at the U.S. Capitol Fourth of July celebrations. I wrote for *Parade*:

> Should the United States Congress designate "America the Beautiful" as our new national anthem?
>
> Millions of my fellow Americans and I think so and here's why.

"America the Beautiful" celebrates our power and ability to live and work in peace, the beauty that is our land and the possibilities inherent in our people.

The message of "The Star Spangled Banner" is war, almost a celebration of it. But martial matters do not measure the length and breadth of our national being—not by a long shot.

I do not suggest that we scrap "The Star Spangled Banner." I think we should keep it as a suitable and stirring sound for military, football and other paramilitary occasions.

"The Star Spangled Banner" was written in 1814, but it was not officially adopted as the national anthem until signed into law by Herbert Hoover in 1931. Before that, "Yankee Doodle" was in vogue. Ulysses S. Grant said, "I have two favorite songs. One of them is 'Yankee Doodle' and the other one ain't."

Not generally known is the fact that the third verse of Francis Scott Key's poem spews hatred for our long-since friends, the British, to wit: "Their blood has wash'd out their foul footsteps' pollution . . ."

The music of "The Star Spangled Banner" is not American. It was written in eighteenth century England by John Stafford Smith as a sex and drinking song. The music to "America the Beautiful," on the other hand, was conceived on a loftier plane and on American soil. It was composed by the American musician Samuel Augustus Ward in 1882. Its strains flow evenly and suggest the inner peace of a self-confident people. "America the Beautiful" is not about an American war; it is about America.

The words, written in 1893 by our fellow citizen Katharine Lee Bates, contain no hatred of others. Rather, they celebrate "a patriot dream that sees beyond the years" and emphasize a people's love for the strength and beauty of their land. The phrases scattered throughout the hymn suggest brotherhood and sisterhood, the glory of the land, and pride in accomplishment: "O beautiful for pilgrim feet/Whose stern, impassioned stress/A thoroughfare for freedom beat/Across the wilderness!"

Those favoring making "America the Beautiful" our everyday anthem include Eric Kunzel, who conducts concerts at the U.S. Capitol, Danny Thomas and Representative Vin Webber, a representative from Minnesota. Russell V. McConnell, a retired bandmaster of the U.S. Army, declares, "Amen and hallelujah."

"Our present national anthem," McConnell explains, "is so complicated that bandmasters were taught it as a separate art form unrelated to any other music played by Army bands."

The Rev. Robert Schuller, whose program from the Crystal Cathedral is regularly seen across the nation, has said: "The message in 'America The Beautiful' so far outdistances the limited human values that are found in 'The Star Spangled Banner' that thoughtful people who make decisions on substance more than on emotional tradition would welcome the change." Amen and hallelujah.

Others disagree. California Republican Rep. Bob Dornan, a former Air Force pilot, says: "I personally love fireworks. And the 'rocket's red glare' grabs me more than 'above the fruited plain.'" In addition, William Schaefer, the Democratic Governor of Maryland and former Mayor of Baltimore where "The Star Spangled Banner" was written, asserts: "It is that special piece of music that is the symbol of everything for which the U.S.A. stands."

We know the first verses to both songs. But few of us will ever master the singing of "The Star Spangled Banner," Retired Brandeis music professor Caldwell Titcomb says it "covers a span of a twelfth, which is an octave plus a perfect fifth."

Still, "The Star Spangled Banner" can do wondrously chilling things to our innermost feelings. When I hear "The Star Spangled Banner," I snap to attention and present arms. "O'er the land of the free and the home of the brave." I love that line even if I can't sing it. "America the Beautiful," however, would send a more positive message to others at a time when enlightenment seems to be spreading its peaceful and liberating dividends across the globe.

In a sense, "America the Beautiful" is already our national anthem. At the official service for the fallen *Challenger* astronauts, our pride and our sorrow were best expressed through "America the Beautiful," which was played that day. The rededication of The Statue of Liberty was laced and graced with "America the Beautiful." As a nation, we are coming of age.

We have never been soft as a people and the change I suggest would not make us so. "America the Beautiful" does not lack suitable tribute to heroes who have physically defended our country: "O beautiful for heroes *proved/* in liberating strife/Who more than self the country loved/And mercy more than life." Heroism is proved not so much by inflicting pain as enduring it.

Passion is important in life, but to be steadfast is crucial. "America the Beautiful" is not boisterous. Neither is true patriotism, which is an abiding thing, calm and steady on stormy seas as well as in the safety of the harbor. This is one of the things most beautiful about America, and that's something to sing about.

In 1984 Indianapolis and Baltimore had a tiff. The Baltimore Colts left Baltimore in the middle of the night and ended up in Indianapolis, where they underwent a name change to the Indianapolis Colts. Baltimore Mayor William Schaefer was not happy. Later, when the *Parade* article appeared, he was sadder—or angrier still. He was quoted in the *Baltimore Sun:*
"First they steal our Colts; now they want to steal our anthem."
He was an unusually colorful and lovable man.

Federal Catastrophic Health Insurance was an idea whose time came and mostly went during the Reagan years. The administration said the supplemental insurance for Medicare beneficiaries would be signed into law if it came out cost-free to the government. To make that happen, the drafters provided a sliding scale of premium rates depending on the respective incomes of the participants. This meant that the better-off Medicare beneficiaries would pay more than an equal share in order to subsidize their less-well-off cohorts. That was bad medicine, because, in effect, the subsidies were welfare which is usually financed by all taxpayers, not just those who happen to be the same age as the welfare clients. The program got off the ground, but crashed a few months from the runway. Most of the law was quickly repealed. The main survivor of that crash was a financial provision to lighten the burden on an elderly person whose spouse requires long-term care. That part of the law permitted the spouse to keep the couple's home and still qualify for public assistance to pay for the sick partner's nursing home care.

As the ill-fated legislation was being initially considered by the Ways and Means Committee, there were features that brought to Washington high officials of the Eli Lilly company. They asked if I would offer amendments in the Committee to strike three of the bill's provisions. First, they wanted to get rid of the provision for a National Formulary. "I'm with you on that one," I said. That provision meant that the United States government, rather than your doctor, would decide the correct medicine for your condition. The flaw there speaks for itself.

The next feature they thought America could nicely do without applied to the way physicians wrote prescriptions. Under common medical practice, if a doctor does not want a generic substitute drug for her or his patient, the doctor need only put a check mark in a box with the preprinted words, "Fill as prescribed." Naturally, that is of interest to the producers of brand names. The feature Lilly wanted dropped would require doctors to write out the words traditionally preprinted for them to check. I had no problem with that Lilly request either. The person who gets through eight or so years of medical training is not likely to be such a ninny as not to understand what it means to check a box next to such plain language. Besides, who can read the notorious handwriting of doctors, anyway?

It was the executives' third request that I couldn't gargle. What would I think, one of them inquired, about striking the provision that would require participating pharmacies to post price comparisons between brand and generic drugs. "Let me get this straight," I said, "in the age of glasnost in the Soviet Union, are you asking me to oppose letting people know what things will cost? Is that what you're asking me to do?" They smiled as one of them said, "We didn't think it would hurt to ask." To which I replied, "You were right. It didn't hurt to ask. But I'm afraid it's also not going to hurt for me to say 'no.'"

My amendments were successful in the committee, moving the *Washington Post* to refer to me as "the congressman from Eli Lilly." In the same story, however, I was quoted as saying, "The chairman of the board at Lilly's contributed one thousand dollars to my opponent in the most recent election and I expect him to do it again." The second part of my statement was poetry. While such a contribution in the future was a possibility, I really didn't expect it. My opponent in 1986 was said to have been a next-door neighbor to the board chairman.

When Dan Rostenkowski was our committee chairman, war hero and wonderful Sam Gibbons was the next member down on the Democratic side. Danny was always laudatory of the staff workers, but Sam sometimes could grow impatient with a slow or confusing answer from them when he asked a technical question. One day in a committee meeting to mark up a controversial bill, Sam said a few intemperate words to the staffers.

Because the bill pitted two giant financial interests against each other, there was already tension among most of the members, not including me; I didn't accept campaign contributions from either side. Responding to Sam's chastisement, Danny slammed his huge fist on the table and thundered, "Damn it, we have the best staff on Capitol Hill. They stay up late at night doing our research after we go home. And I'm not going to stand for bashing them." To which Sam, seated in cramped quarters next to Danny, replied, "Well, then you'd better just keep seated, Mr. Chairman, because I'm going to call them as I see them."

The Reagan administration people present were frozen in shock. The rest of the people in the room weren't doing much better. In the words of comedian Lenny Bruce, the whole room was an oil painting. It was as if a person had slapped his or her spouse in the middle of a dinner party. Since timing is said to be everything, to myself I counted to four and then blurted out in mock vehemence, "I *hate* the staff!" That broke the ice rather nicely. Laughter, even from the two temporary antagonists, did abound. I turned to my sister-like friend, senior staffer Janice Mays, and added an old high school line, "But with a passion." She probably groaned.

There came a day when an authentic comedian came to Washington to accept some organization's declaration that he was the "Comedian of the Century." And of course, that comedian was Bob Hope. You may have to work hard to believe this, but I was a witness; it actually occurred. Someone on the Ways and Means Committee proposed making many, many-times-multimillionaire Mr. Hope income tax free. Reason? Because he was a national treasure. Of course, if such a proposal passed, he wouldn't be much of a national treasure to the national treasury.

Clearly, Mr. Hope knew nothing about the idiotic idea. Your credulity is about to be taxed even more: Some members of the Committee took it seriously and started mumbling "hay-now" approvals—for about fifteen minutes. When I put up my hand and was recognized, I said, "I don't think you fellows understand what 'Comedian of the Century' means. It means most of his jokes are that old."

If I didn't love Bob Hope for any other reason—and I did—I would have loved him for his kindness to the husband of another sister-like friend of mine, my secretary, Phyllis Coelho. Phyllis and I had worked together since I left law school. Her husband was Tony Coelho. As a young man, Tony had studied to be a Jesuit priest, but was tossed out of the monastery after a severe tractor accident at the monastery injured his head and brought on epilepsy. Someone told Mr. Hope about Tony and Mr. Hope gave him a job in the Hope home. For a few years, Tony met some of Hollywood's heaviest-hitters and eventually became a member of Congress, rising rapidly in the ranks of leadership. Moreover, I was only joking about Bob Hope's jokes. But it did bring the committee to its senses.

At about the same time, a combination of government officials and private citizens organized to build a memorial in Washington to Americans who were Korean War veterans. The sculptor was Frank C. Gaylord II, future husband of colossal Judy Collins. The motif was in the manner of the Vietnam War Memorial—in sorrow, not glory. The effort began with a big organizing dinner, one of the few such events I ever attended in Washington. Entertainment for the function included none less than Rosemary Clooney and Bob Hope, whose material that night was very definitely not old. He reported that his friend Phyllis Diller had undergone several face lifts, but had no nips and tucks taken in the rest of her body. "Or to put it another way," the supremely gifted comedian said. "The other night a peeping Tom threw up on her window."

The dinner had the tint of show biz. At one point, the orchestra played a medley of military songs recognizing each branch of the service. It was time to single out the guests of honor, members of Congress who served in Korea. When the Marine Corps Hymn was played, three young Marines approached my table and presented me with a necktie. The design of the small superfluous garment was a combination of the United Nations and the Korean flags. As the young Marines marched on, I'm afraid I looked the gift tie in its design and mouthed the following: "This is the ugliest tie, and quite possibly the ugliest thing I have ever seen." Bad move. I knew no one at the table. The man sitting directly across from me said, "My company makes those ties." Oops. My res gestae was this: "I'll wear it tomorrow."

Unfortunately, I had to chair a hearing the next day and therefore explain to those present why I was wearing the odious item. In essentially no time at all, I saw one of his staffers hand a sack to Congressman—and later Senator—Hank Brown of Colorado, the ranking Republican on the subcommittee and a good friend of mine. Hank, in turn, handed the sack to me. In it was a tie to rival my dinner acquisition. Hank explained for the record, "Two birthdays ago my aunt gave me this tie. Until today, I thought it was the ugliest tie in the world. Since the chairman has shown he has the strength to wear that thing, I'm sure he can make good use of this one."

By and by, I received a small package by mail. It had been sent by the dinner companion, David Strongin, who had so magnificently nailed me on the occasion of my faux pas about his company's product. This time, his company, an Incline Village, Nevada, firm whose name was "Ties of Honor," did better—much better. It was another tie, a tie that was as beautiful to my eyes as its predecessor had been ugly. The new arrival was a civilian tie in the colors of the Marine Corps. There was an accompanying message from my friend, who turned out to be the company's owner:

Dear Congressman Jacobs:
  Marines have notoriously bad sartorial taste. But, perhaps this one will suit your fancy.
              Sincerely, David Strongin

It did. So much so that I haven't worn any other kind since. Every couple of years, I order a duplicate for replacement. In the case of the first one, I sent the following reply:

Dear Mr. Strongin:
   I love the tie, the second one, that is. But I can't wear it unless you cash my enclosed check for fifteen dollars.
                                       Sincerely, Andy Jacobs

   The check covered only half the price and I sent the rest later when I learned of my error. Inasmuch as I had been buying my ties at a drugstore for five dollars each, I had assumed that fifteen dollars would easily cover the new tie. Having initially, albeit unintentionally, been bilked out of half his price, Mr. Strongin had written back:

Dear Congressman Jacobs:
   Wear the tie. We've cashed the check. We're all going off to Hawaii for vacation. Would you believe stand-up lunch at 7-11?
                                       Sincerely, David Strongin

   The Korean War Memorial was dedicated a few years later. My wife, Kim, went to Washington with me to participate in the ceremony which began at the White House and then moved to the memorial site on the Mall. But, something happened that was reminiscent of the incident with Reverend Andrew Brown, who had gone all the way to Washington to deliver the opening prayer, only to hear that he couldn't because of that weird special order. The same Gingrich who had organized the special order was, by now, Speaker of the House. And he did something weird again. He announced that spouses would not be permitted to join members—even members who fought in Korean combat—in the congressional section at the ceremony. When that word came down, both Republican and Democratic House members expressed their disagreement to me. One member, Duke Cunningham, a Republican from California and combat flying ace in the Vietnam War, graciously offered to give Kim his seat at the morning service, saying to me, "I know you would do the same for me if it were the Vietnam Memorial dedication." It was wonderfully noble of Duke and I told him I was touched by it, but I was so offended by the Speaker's announcement that Kim and I both skipped the event. Instead, we had a long lunch together.
   The American Broadcasting Company pulled off a stinging journalistic coup in the Caribbean during the late 1980s. ABC dressed its camera people up to look like tourists, equipped them with the newly popular video-8 camcorders carried by tourists. In their disarming disguises, the ABC camera experts captured in living color members of the House Ways and

Means Committee frolicking with lobbyists in the sand and sea of Barbados—expenses paid, of course, by the lobbyists. When the expose was telecast to the nation on an ABC news magazine, a pan shot of the Ways and Means Committee members at work was included. Members in business suits were seated and looking serious.

As the camera caught me, I was reading an amendment with impressive concentration. Had my campaign committee been able to afford it, I'd have been pleased to have made a TV spot of that shot. But, to show you how the eye can fool the mind, the morning after the show was shown, Representative Bill Nelson of Florida approached me in the House gym to say, "Andy, I didn't know you were on that trip to Barbados."

"You don't have to know that, Bill," I said, "because I wasn't. You need to master the difference between a suit and a swim suit." Nice guy—only U.S. representative to have traveled in space, although a few of our other colleagues tended to be a little spacey, themselves.

There was a hearing one day at our committee on a bill to

> Amend Title 31, United States Code, to increase both citizen participation in and funding for the war on drugs by directing the secretary of the treasury to issue drug war bonds.

The idea was to resurrect the old World War II national spirit of unity to fight the common foe. A bit fanciful and in the genre of "all cottage cheese is made in cottages." The author of the bill was the first witness. He testified that perhaps in addition to the Drug War Bonds, there could be Drug War Savings Stamps for schoolchildren to buy and get into the fight, themselves, just as happened in the war against Hitler. Children could learn the value of fighting drugs.

When my turn came, I asked my colleague, a very nice member from out West, what about teaching the children the good, sound business value of not borrowing money for current expenses. "No," the witness said. "We need to teach kids the importance of fighting drugs."

"Fine," said I. "But why not teach them the importance of fighting drugs *and* the importance of staying out of debt? What's the theory here, 'You load sixteen kilos and what do you get, another day older and deeper in debt'?" My paraphrasing the old song "Sixteen Tons," recorded by entertainer Tennessee Ernie Ford garnered big laughs. Just as my time ran out, the witness took an inexpensive shot when he said to me, "Welcome to the War on Drugs." That was boilerplate campaign oratory to suggest one's opponent was "soft on drugs." As a former police officer, I had been on the front line in the "War against Drugs" before my colleague ever entered politics. But I didn't blame him for being irritated; the bill was his baby and I had just diminished what little chance it had for passage. Besides, I liked him personally. So I just skipped the squelch about my law enforcement background.

One—well, not just one—silly drug measure did pass Congress. This one was in the form of an obscure amendment noticed by almost no one. It required all members of the House to file annual statements of "drug policies" in their respective offices. Drugs! The political villain of the times. Communism had been the fad villain for decades, but now with the cold war in history's rear view mirror, it was drugs. It was a time of anti-druggier than thou, especially if thou happened to be an opponent.

Bill Mauldin did a cartoon in the early post-World War II period of a husband and wife reading different parts of a newspaper in their living room, the wife saying to the husband, "Here's a triple ax murder on page forty-seven. No veterans involved." Veterans were the national preoccupation then.

But now it was drugs. Most politicians made their common pitch to the public: "I'll protect your kids from drugs, whereas my opponent is soft on Communism, er, drugs." It got so nutty and extreme that those politicians who got to Congress started a bidding war on who could think up the most unreasonable punishment even for a kid who did a little bit of pot. Thus, the politicians, who pledged to protect constituents' kids from drugs, passed laws that filled up federal prisons with kids who only dabbled or experimented with joints and were bound to get over it anyway, just as some of those same politicians had when they grew up or, should I say, got older.

Most members knew nothing about filing copies of their respective office "drug policies" with the House Clerk until the day we all received notice to do so. Shortly afterward, this editorial, entitled "The Right Drug Policy," appeared in the Capitol Hill newspaper, *Roll Call*:

> Some 60 congressional offices have filed "drug policy" statements with the office of the Clerk of the House. Most of these statements are redundant and inane. Rep. _____, for example, requires his employees to affix their signatures to this bit of prose: "I agree that I will not and/or do not use in Rep. _____'s office controlled substances. I acknowledge that violation may result in my immediate dismissal."
>
> Talk about stating the obvious! Perhaps members should have employees sign statements saying they won't murder their colleagues

while on congressional property, won't kidnap pages, or steal money from the Longworth Cafeteria cash register.

Rep. Andy Jacobs (D-Ind) has the right idea. On Tuesday, he sent Clerk Donnald K. Anderson this letter:

Dear Donn:
The following is the policy with regard to drugs in the office of the Tenth District of Indiana:
The law-abiding citizens who work in this congressional office declare that they abide by the law, including the part on drugs.
Sincerely, Andy Jacobs, Jr.
P.S. The theory of our free society is that a person is innocent unless proved guilty, not that a person is guilty unless proved innocent.

Jacobs is exactly right. Bravo.

I don't think I ever got around to thanking *Roll Call* for the compliment. So here goes: Thanks, *Roll Call,* for the encouragement. It meant a lot to me. "When ignorance is bliss . . ." being even a little bit wise can be lonely.

Drugs! The passport to political success. In the words of comedian Jimmy Durante, "Everybody wants to get in on the act." Even Mrs. Reagan offered an arrow from her anti-drug quiver. It was a slogan: "Just say 'no,'" Though much ridiculed, it may have had some efficacy with suburban high school kids—probably none at all with the poor kids who were the most vulnerable. For them, in all likelihood, it had all the impact President Ford's *Win* buttons (whip inflation now) had on their target. As mentioned before, the view of the slums from the country club is often unfocused.

Drugs weren't the only commodity of political interest in the 1980s. I was scheduled to participate in a call-in program at a small Indianapolis radio station one Saturday. I assumed it would be like all the others, an electronic town meeting to cover a variety of subjects. Not so. There was only one subject—guns. The host was a gun enthusiast, the two other guests were gun enthusiasts, and participating by phone from suburban Washington, D.C., was the national spokeswoman for the National Rifle Association.

The NRA didn't like the Brady Law. On the other hand, I had supported it. I pointed out that the Brady Law, which required a waiting period to buy a pistol, had been on the books in Indiana for decades ranging back before my police days. But the Indiana statute was tougher. The Brady Law allowed an exception to the waiting and the Indiana law did not. The exception allowed immediate purchase if a police official certified to the dealer that the purchaser was under some sort of death threat. The waiting period was for the very reasonable reason of giving the police a chance to find out if the putative purchaser was a felon, underage or a mental case. With computer refinement, the period was later reduced drastically.

Actually, we didn't have a lot to disagree about on the radio program. The subject of the NRA's silly stand against banning pot metal "Saturday Night Special" pistols and the organization's opposition to outlawing ammunition that could pierce police bulletproof vests never came up. But there was one amusing moment. A self-described gunslinger called in and began the litany of love for lethal weapons. Suddenly, his voice fell silent. There was much speculation about that in the studio. The host suggested that the engineer had pushed a wrong button. One of the guests thought aloud that the caller might have accidentally pushed the wrong button on his phone. Then came my suggestion: "Maybe he shot himself." The more reasonable of the other two studio guests laughed out loud. Even the others smiled. I have no idea about the reaction of the "Pistol Packing Mama" on the Potomac. It would be six more years before I would get crossways with the D.C. pistol people again.

In 1988, Indiana once again validated its appellation, *Home of Vice Presidents*. This time it was my friend and former House colleague, Senator Dan Quayle.

By all accounts, the offer from then-Vice President George Bush was a surprise to Dan. When it came, it must have been overwhelming.

In his famous first national news conference upon being tapped for the GOP vice presidential nomination, Dan handled himself beautifully on the most serious point raised. What about his joining the National Guard stateside haven when facing the possibility of being drafted to go to Vietnam?

"When I did that," he answered. "I had no idea that I'd be where I am today."

Perfect! Very few American hearts would not be melted by such candor, such humanity. Then James Baker put some brilliant-idiot PR consultants on the case and they went to work with their transparent phony damage control. And that's when and how Quayle's PR troubles started.

For the next few days, the phones of the Indiana delegation to Congress rang off their hooks. Mine was no exception. The national press was on the scent. My first call was from Mike Royko. He all but sternly hung up on me when I wouldn't assist his planned column thesis that Dan came under the meaning of my term, "war wimp." Dan was not "all too willing to send others." *Newsweek* called; wasn't Quayle dense? My reply was in the negative. I said, "He's no genius, but neither am I." They had what they wanted, using the first part of the sentence and dropping the second to make it seem as if I were criticizing Dan. In a CNN interview, I was asked if I considered Dan a little slow. "Absolutely not," I replied.

"Danny Quayle is plenty bright," I continued. "But anyone can be disoriented. One day you're a quiet Hoosier senator and the next day you're staring into a mega-gang of microphones, cameras and note pads, hearing questions all the way from the square root of three-point-three to the kind of tree you would you be if you were a tree. Remember what happened to Ted Kennedy in the Roger Mudd interview of 1980? He got a question that so threw him off stride that he was disoriented for the next month of his campaign for the Democratic presidential nomination. I've known Dan Quayle for quite a while, and his discourse in extempory conversation is about the same as anyone else's."

The Saturday morning after Dan was nominated, the phone rang at our Fun Farm. I answered it in the workshop. "Andy?" the caller asked.

"Yes. Dan? Is that you?" It was. So I asked what I considered to be a logical question: "Don't you have something better to do today than call me? I know I do; I'm trying to build a wagon."

"Well," Dan said. "I just want you to know that you are one of the very few elected federal officials who have stood up for me the past few days."

"Well, thank you," I said, "I just try to give uncomplicated answers to the questions. Officially, I hope we beat your brains out, but unofficially, if you win, I'll be very happy for you." He did and I was.

About a month before Dan Quayle was nominated for vice president, Indianapolis NBC affiliate Channel 13 anchor Kimberly S. Hood and I exchanged wedding vows and, in a hail of bird seed, drove from the church in a yellow Volkswagen bug convertible accompanied by Friend, the mammoth fawn Great Dane (thirty-nine inches at the shoulder) and Annie, the little cocker spaniel.

In a sense, Kim's and my courtship had begun a year before at an amusing and fateful news conference. I had made my bimonthly blood donation at the Indiana Regional Blood Center in Indianapolis. At the time, the center's public information officer was my longtime friend, Andy Murphy. (A decade later, she would be a well-received author of a book exposing some of the flaws in the blood business, and my literary agent.) On that day in 1987, Andy told me that blood donations had fallen dramatically because of the AIDS scare, whereupon I suggested that I might be able to round up some other elected officials and hold a news conference at the blood bank to reassure the public that, while there had been some accidents with people who received blood, there had been none with people who gave blood.

A few days later, Indianapolis Mayor Bill Hudnut, Indiana Secretary of State Evan Bayh, Indiana Congressman Dan Burton, and I participated in a news conference in the basement of the blood center. As I glanced at the people behind the bright lights, I saw an anchorwoman from Channel 13—pretty smart, pretty popular, and pretty pretty Kim Hood.

When each of us had made his and my pitch for blood donations and several questions from the newspeople had been answered, Danny Burton, who is nothing if not exhuberant, suddenly said, "Let's all prove our sincerity by going upstairs and giving blood right now." With the cameras rolling, the microphones gobbling sound bites, and pencils coming to the points on pads, Andy Murphy blurted out, "Well, Andy can't give blood!"

Had I not taken the trouble to clear that up on the spot, there may never have been a wedding involving Kim and me. Deadpan, I looked at Andy, who was standing among the cameras, and asked, "Would you mind saying *why* 'Andy can't give blood'?" She smiled sheepishly and said, "Oh. Well, he just donated a few days ago." I said a sincere "Thank you."

My sartorial habits fell far short of *Vogue* magazine standards, especially in those casual bachelor days. Since I always did my laundry by hand, I also always used "wash 'n' wear" shirts. In their early incarnation, such shirts did not often come out looking ironed. Through the years, they improved and through the years, I repeated the same joke I made up about them. Whenever the subject came up, I would allow that my shirt was "wash and stare." And nobody ever got the joke—until I met Kim, the master seamstress who, as one of her many avocations, *designed* and *made* wedding dresses. On our first date, I almost unconsciously muttered that my shirt was "wash and stare." She broke up and I broke out—in a cold sweat. I fell in love on the spot. Thank God we had been friends first.

I wrote a verse for Kim during our courtship:

> *From God came the gift we call Kim,*
>   *So caring, so witty, so prim,*
> *The one the wise choose*
>   *To bring them the news,*
> *My joy is to be*
>   *Her own him.*

In late January 1989 I accompanied Kim to an NBC gala at the

National Theater in Washington. NBC gave its award for the year's best affiliate. The network had asked the new president, George Bush, to make the presentation, but unable to make it, he asked his newly minted vice president to do the honors. So, there on stage, stood Dan and Marilyn Quayle awaiting the honoree as he made his way to the lectern. Dan then read the framed certificate, handed it to the local TV man, shook hands, and yielded the microphone to the winner. There was the usual expression of gratitude which began with these words, "I want to thank the vice president and Mrs. Bush . . . er . . ." Before he could untangle the faux pas and with the audience laughing it up, Dan Quayle gently took the microphone and said to the hundreds of news people, "I'd like to see what you guys would have done to me if I'd made that gaff." The laughter intensified. Dan was bright, witty and obviously completely spontaneous. And I was vindicated.

Though both of us had been married before, Kim and I became parents for the first time when she was older than the average mother biologically and I was just plain older than the average—operation late start. For a while it seemed as though there might be no "start" at all. On the advice of our good friends former Indianapolis Methodist Hospital president Frank Lloyd and his super friend, "super nurse" Judy Barrett, we went to the fertility clinic at their hospital. We went through the usual tests, including follicles, eggs, sperm count, and interior passageways.

When I was summoned to give a specimen, I was handed a key which was attached to a flat piece of wood. On the wood were the letters "JOR." I was then directed to that room and told there was a television set for my use. It was about noon and I was puzzled as to why they thought I would want to watch the news at a such an embarrassing moment. Later, I discovered just how obtuse I had been. The TV was hooked up to a VCR, and dirty movies were available. As I said in an earlier chapter, I never cared for spectator sports, anyway.

We went to the clinic once a week—it was rather like going to the dentist—and waiting for the word on my sperm count was liking sweating out a bar exam. The day for the sperm count report finally arrived. When we went to the clinic, some tests were administered to Kim; eggs and follicles doing fine. Now we stood in the hall with the nurse, who read to us from her clipboard. We learned about a lot of things, *not* including the sperm.

Trying to sound as casual as possible, I said, "Oh, and the sperm?" No, it hadn't come back yet. Not even so much as a "probably be here next week." I was left dangling. The following week, Kim had some more tests and again we found ourselves standing in the same hall with the same nurse who read from the same clipboard. But this time I heard her say, "And the sperm count . . ." Through the bone and flesh of my head to my teeth and eventually my ears, I heard myself weakly say, "Yes?" The nurse continued, "Oh, it's on the high side." Right answer. But with everything okay in both of us, well, what was the trouble?

We were told it was time for a procedure that was invasive, but very little so. Kim must undergo a laparascopy to discover whether—and repair of if—she had a common malady called endometriosis. The scars from it somehow impede the uterus' ability to conceive. It was our more than good fortune that Dr. Earle U. Robinson, Jr., a protege of Dr. Lloyd, had recently returned from Germany where he had completed a course in the surgery.

The first try after the operation was devastatingly unsuccessful. The second try, well, both of us knew Kim was late, but we were too superstitious to mention it to each other.

While we were crossing our fingers and praying, I went to North Central High School one morning to participate in a mock trial. The defendant was capital punishment. One group of students defended its use and another was opposed. The leader of the opposition was a pretty bright and pretty young woman who was president of the Young Republicans. She had invited me to be a witness against capital punishment. When I arrived that morning, my recruiter met me at the door and apologized. For what I wondered aloud. She explained that her opposite number, a young man in his senior year, was crushing in his cross-examination and that she had not known it when she invited me. "Well, that's all right," I told her. "Anything for the cause."

Presently I was undergoing the withering cross-examination. The put-away question was, "Are you a father?" My answer: "I don't know." The two hundred or so students and faculty members in attendance burst into laughter, but I raised my hands and waived them horizontally, saying, "No, that's not it." They all knew I had been a young single Marine in a foreign war. I continued, "My wife doesn't think I know it, but she went to the clinic this morning to see if we're expecting." Now the crowd began to applaud. I signaled for them not to do that, either, saying the ancient Chinese disavowal, "Bad rice; don't push our luck."

That evening, I watched Kim give the news on Channel 13. That's when I knew we were pregnant. Any time a TV news anchor reports a horrible automobile crash with a smile on her face, you know she's had some good news, too. About a week later, Kim asked if we could trade cars for the day. "Okay by me," I said. "No," said Kim. "On second thought, let's not.

Your Christmas present is in my trunk." To which, glancing at her waist, I said, "It surely is." Our cousin, Marsha Miller, gave us encouraging counsel as we approached the land of parental responsibility.

Having knocked at the door of parenthood with no answer for such a long time, we were ecstatic over the promise of the problems and joys of it as they headed our way. My dad said of child-rearing, "It's a burden, but a pleasant burden." Immersed in euphoria, Kim and I went to the annual White House Christmas party a few days after learning about our expanding family. I'm afraid we more than mentioned it to everyone would listen at the gala gathering. And since parenthood was old hat to most of them, I'm sure we bored or, at least, amused most of our friends there. They suspected we had not invented the miracle.

The conversations continued from the foyer to the West Room, through the Green Room and finally into the East Room, where the orchestra was just beginning its last medley. Our first dance was the last dance. "Dreamy" is corny, and so we had been all evening. And the moment was, in certifiable fact, dreamy for us—for about ten seconds.

Like a shark lurking for a tourist to take a dip, it was "Good Time" Charlie Wilson, U.S. Representative of Lufkin, Texas. Charlie would only be flattered to be called a ladies' man. But he was out of sync with the tradition for people of that proclivity. He was a strong supporter of Women's Liberation. And right there in the lovely East Room of the people's mansion, Charlie liberated a woman by tapping me on the shoulder to "cut in." As I understand it, under the edicts laid down by Emily Post or some such social supervisor, when Charlie began dancing with Kim, I was supposed to dance with Charlie's date, who stood, cigarette in hand and wearing a dress whose upper part consisted of breeze-sensitive feathers. She awaited my pleasure; I declined. Instead of dancing with Charlie's date who, some said, was "Miss Outer Space" or "Miss Universe," I asked a nearby photographer if he'd like to get a good shot. He would. Explaining the situation to him, I said that I was about to cut back in in my inimitable fashion. I still have the picture. As it was snapped, I tapped Charlie on the shoulder with my left hand and as he turned, I swung a fake roundhouse right to the head of this charming and benign Casanova. He laughed—that's in the picture, too. And several of the surrounding couples—who knew Charlie—applauded as an expectant couple was reunited.

The birth of our little Andy was via caesarian section which, because of its relatively antiseptic nature, is also part of our home movies. You can see and hear it; when the nurse took the new arrival to the scales, she said, "Oh my goodness, eleven pounds, five ounces." Anyone can catch those words from the video. So far, only I seem to have been able to discern the reply of our huge newcomer; I think he looked right up at the pretty nurse and said, "What are you doing tonight?" I could be mistaken.

Kim, the mother of the marvelous monster, was five feet, four inches tall and not stocky. In the paper the next day, I was quoted as saying: "The [Indianapolis] *Colts* will never lose again."

In another news story, I said, "Of all the miracles of life, the most awesome is the beginning of it." Another Andy had joined the ranks of God's children on Earth. His brother Steven "Bronco" weighed only ten pounds at birth, but he was premature. Steve gave us a scare. A few months into the pregnancy, the result of one of Kim's blood tests was ambiguous. It suggested the possibility of Down's syndrome. Our doctor, Bill Stone, suggested and we rejected an amniocentesis. We said we wouldn't abort anyway. Then he told us that there were other good medical and psychological reasons for the procedure and we agreed. We were told that the results would reach us in two weeks which seemed more like two centuries. And by chance, the report was due on election day, 1990. Perhaps needless to say, during that period, thoughts about the election results paled by comparison with those about the results of the amniocentesis.

On the Friday afternoon before election and amnio day, we went to Dr. Stone for a routine examination and he expressed surprise at our having been told the big test result would be back so soon. He said that it was usually more like three weeks. Swell! Shades of the sperm test. Then, when we arrived at the Fun Farm, the phone was ringing and I picked it up to hear, "May I speak to Mrs. Jacobs?" Kim took the call and said, "I see. Thank you, " Then she hung up, turned to me and said, "It's a normal boy." To which I replied, "Ber [as in Kim-*ber*-ly], I'd trust you to the ends of the earth, but if that kid's normal, I'd like to know who the father is." He did not have Down's, but, I'm happy to say, neither was he normal. For example, we subscribe to the considered view that to "spare the rod" is to spare the teaching that violence is an appropriate punishment for minor perceived infractions as long as the punisher is bigger than the punished. Our view, in line with medical science, is more like bear the rod, roil the child. But each of us lost it once. In Kim's case, Bronco's four-year-old rear end was on the receiving end. As the light swat connected, he looked up at his mother and intoned, "Hitting me is not going to solve anything." You have to give it to Kim for self-control; she stifled the erupting laugh.

By the time he was seven, Bronco knew what to expect when he asked for something he knew he was not likely to receive. The conversation would go this way: "Dad, I want a horse." Response from Dad: "People in Hell want ice water." One evening, when Kim was attending yet another civic meeting and the boys had practiced their music, done their homework, and even cleaned their room, I took them to Taco Bell for a sumptuous dinner. Upon arrival, Bronco announced, "Dad, I want a Godzilla cup." Certain of my conversation stopper, I asked, "What do people in Hell want?" He had an answer: "Ice water. And I'll take mine in a Godzilla cup." He didn't get the cup, but he did get the laughs and the satisfaction of totally squelching his progenitor.

Our nineteen-month-older son, Andy, was no slouch either. As was the case with his bother, his intellect was frightening. On Christmas mornings when I would undertake the "some-assembly-required" task of merging parts into toys, Andy was always ahead of me. "No, Dad, that goes there." My humiliation wasn't completely wasted, however. Kim, whose consummate talents seemed endless—in contracts with Indianapolis Channel 13, she and all the other on-the-air employees were designated by the term, "talent"—was a very good cartoonist whose work was published in the *Saturday Evening Post*. My Christmas morning predicament inspired her. Her next cartoon pictured the typical Christmas scene with toy parts scattered on the floor and the father hopelessly in over his head. On the side of the box in which the toy parts had been packed were the words, "Some intelligence required." It's comforting for one to know that he can be an inspiration to his wife.

One more on Andy: While working at my desk at home one evening, I heard a sound behind me and asked, "Bronco?" Then I heard Andy's voice announce, "No, it's an alien life form." Remembering the bedlam both boys constantly made of my workshop, I repeated one of Bryant Gumble's favorite lines, "You got that right."

If you display a bumper sticker that says, "WE ARE THE PROUD PARENTS OF AN HONOR STUDENT AT [such-and-such] HIGH," you might be happier if you skipped this paragraph. I personally believe such braggadocio to be inappropriate. Some kids find it easier to get top grades than others who work just as hard, maybe harder. And if you want to say a word or two about your child's gifts, you might mention the matter quietly to God in something closer to a thanksgiving mode. The kid who is physically handicapped probably isn't going to run "the hundred" as fast as a kid whom nature has not limited. But that's not something for the latter to brag about; it is something about which to walk humbly with her or his God about. It was in this spirit that I composed and had printed our own bumper sticker: "WE ARE THE PROUD PARENTS OF A 'TRUSTY' AT THE COUNTY JAIL." Honor among peers.

When flattering lobbyists expressed awe at our sons' pictures, which hung all over the walls of the reception room in the Washington congressional office, my response was uniform: "Our children are special for one reason; they're children." What child is not?

When I arrived at the Indianapolis airport one Thursday night a few years after our boys' births, one of those blinding TV cameras caught me and I was told that Governor Evan Bayh and his wife, Susan, had just become the parents of twin boys. I was asked if I had any advice for them. "Yes," I said, "I do. As long as the boys are tearing down the governor's residence, do not waste money on pediatricians; your sons are in perfectly normal health."

When our boys were five and three, respectively, they, Kim and I flew to Washington for some special occasion. On the same flight was Sue Ann Gilroy, who then was a staffer for Senator Richard Lugar. A very beautiful and brainy wife and mother, Sue Ann later became Indiana secretary of state and, along the way, was the Republican nominee for mayor of Indianapolis.

Having a car at the Washington airport, we offered Sue Ann a ride to Capitol Hill. When I brought the car around, Kim asked Sue Ann to ride in the front seat so that Kim could corral our boys in the back. As I was about to pull away from the curb, I heard Kim express surprise at how warm it was in Washington. She said she was going to take off her coat. To me, that meant squirm out of the coat in the back seat. To Kim, it meant step out onto the curb and remove the outer garment without squirming. Acting on my interpretation, I pressed the accelerator and the car glided away—with the right rear door flapping. It was then that I heard the dulcet, cultured, and professional voice of the beautiful Kim Hood Jacobs, beckoning me back.

I had picked up about twelve yards on the play. As we tooled along on the Fourteenth Street bridge over the Potomac, with my wife as a witness, I said to Sue Ann, "The next time we run off together, I promise not to bring the kids."

Congressman Sam Gibbons and I at a 1984 House Ways and Means Committee hearing. Staffer Sandy Wise sits behind me.

(*From left*) Senator Birch Bayh and I with Julia Carson and Carson's pastor, Johnathan Bailey.

With Chancellor Gerald Bepko at Indiana University-Purdue University Indianapolis when I received an honorary Doctor of Law degree from IU. (IUPUI Publications photo)

My beloved beautiful bride, and our terrific boys, Andy (*left*) and Steven "Bronco."

chapter 20

THE SIX-PACK

W. C. FIELDS WROTE A BOOK, *Fields for President,* a chapter of which was entitled "How to Beat the Federal Income Tax and What to See and Do at Alcatraz" (then a federal prison).

At about the time Uncle Sam decided to start poking his nose into other countries' disputes and make the world "safe for democracy," the Sixteenth Amendment to our Constitution was adopted. In part it provided

> The Congress shall have power to lay and collect taxes on income, from whatever source derived.

One of the "sources from which it is derived" is the sale of something you own for a greater price than you paid for it. That's called capital gains. If a person buys a painting from a struggling and unknown artist who suddenly becomes known, the original buyer can make some easy and real money by selling the work for more than he or she paid. Easy money. At the other end of the scale is the situation described by old friend Abe Martin:

> The feller who works the hardest for his money is the feller who marries it.

Somewhere between those extremes, but closer to the plight of the "feller" with the wealthy wife, is the person who digs dirt to make a ditch. His work is obviously harder than the work of the person who hit paydirt with the picture. And, on average, the citizen with the shovel contributes more to the economy. My mother likes to tell the story about two people digging in the ground, each asked what he was doing. The first said, "I'm digging a ditch; the second replying, "I'm building a cathedral."

Nonetheless, President John F. Kennedy strongly supported the idea of lower federal income tax rates on capital gains than on income from work. And, one way or another, the rate differential remained in the tax code until its repeal in 1986. Some, including the Kennedy administration, said that the rate differential stimulates investment. But the Reagan administration spent a lot of public money trying and failing to prove the theory. That doesn't mean the theory is wrong, but it probably means that it is not significantly right. Moreover, purchases of corporate stocks and bonds that are not new-issues do not expand the economy; they merely swap the ownership of it. Economists call it churning.

For most people, gain from the sale of a principal residence became essentially tax free in the mid 1990s. President Clinton signed into law a renewed lower rate on gains from other capital transactions.

My view has always been that, except in the case of gain from the sale of one's home, a real capital gain—one in inflation adjusted dollars—should be taxed at the same rate as would be applied to other income. And the word "gain" was the key to my membership in what the *Washington Post* was pleased to dub, "the Gang of Six." We were Democratic members of the Ways and Means Committee who worked with President George Bush and the ranking minority member—later chairman—of the Ways and Means Committee, Bill Archer, to produce House passage of a capital gains measure.

While I believed that capital gains should be taxed the same as other income, I also believed that those gains should be real rather than inflationary fluff.

Take the case of the elderly widow who sells the business she and her husband began fifty years earlier. She will receive an enormously greater number of nominal dollars than were invested in the first place. But what will those dollars buy now compared to what they would buy back then? The part of them that will buy more now, quite rightly, I think, should be taxed and taxed at the widow's ordinary rate. But the part that is not actual gain, in fairness, should not be taxed at all.

From the day I was elected to the Ways and Means Committee, I tried to persuade my Democratic colleagues to help change the Internal Revenue Code so that only real gains would be taxed, but taxed at ordinary rates. Most of those colleagues were not interested, one arguing a befuddled logic that as the property inflates in nominal dollars, the owner can borrow more on it. But "more" did not mean borrowing more in purchasing power.

Clearly, it is not right to tax gain that does not exist. But there was an even more basic reason for my advocacy: proper use of the English language.

Pure and simple, "gain" means advancement. Inflation means spinning the wheels in place.

In 1990 I found myself in a position rarely enjoyed by just one member of Congress. I was the only member of the Ways and Means Committee not committed one way or the other on President Bush's proposal for a new system of reduced income tax rates on capital gains. The vote I would cast would be the deciding one. My neutrality was compelled by the respective positions of the two sides. I couldn't cast the vote with the Bush administration's proposal because I did not favor a reduced tax rate on actual capital gain. On the other hand, I could not support the new position of my Democratic Party on capital gains because it did not include indexing the basis, meaning, where applicable, purchase price plus inflation, minus depreciation deductions already taken. Real gain would equal the difference between that calculated basis and the sale price if the sales price is the greater of the two. For decades, the Democratic leadership had no problem with the rate differential. Now, Democratic Speaker Tom Foley's hostility for the party's traditional position on the issue was, well, strident. At the time, Tom was being accused of irresolution as a leader. The capital gains issue seems to have been what he used to show he was tough after all.

The "hung juror" usually gets a lot of attention and, back at the Ways and Means Committee, I was no exception. I preferred to find some consensus with my own party and asked once again if the leaders could support indexing the capital bases of assets. No dice. A few days later, Democratic Representative Ed Jenkins of Georgia called me. He told me that he and the ranking Republican on Ways and Means, future chairman and perfect gentleman Bill Archer of Texas, had been discussing a coalition consisting of five of the committee Democrats, including Ed, and all of the Committee Republicans to put across the Bush administration's proposal to reduce capital gains tax rates. But that coalition was one short of a majority on the committee. If I sided with them, the coalition would win in the committee and, therefore, in all likelihood, in the House. Ed asked if I could join them.

Eddie Jenkins was one of my favorite people on Ways and Means. First of all, he was pleasant; beyond that, he had a terrific sense of humor. So it was not awkward for me to speak candidly. I said, "no" and then explained my position on capital gains. "Any possibility for a compromise?" he wondered. "Now you're talking," I told Eddie. "Let's talk." We reached an agreement. The administration would get two years and two years only of its reduced rates after which I would get my basis-indexing at ordinary rates— permanently. The other four Democrats in the coalition were young, handsome, friendly and bright Mike Andrews of Texas; smart as a whip and delightfully witty Beryl Anthony, Jr. of Arkansas; and the bright, shining Ronnie Flippo of Alabama. In other words, I was the only Northerner among the six of us. We got to know one another pretty well over the next several weeks because of our frequent meetings. Not only did we get to know one another, I got to know a lot about hound dawgs and grits.

So, according to the *Washington Post*, the Gang of Six was born. The name, of course, was a play on the post-Mao Chinese dissidents. When asked by the *Washington Post* for my reaction, I said, "If we're the Gang of Six, there must be some thoughts of Chairman Mao around here somewhere."

Chairman Dan Rostenkowski was realistic about the inevitable outcome of the coalition's compromise agreement in the committee. He never so much as spoke to me on the subject. He knew I had given my word to the camp I had joined with the compromise agreement. In his Chicago world of politics, one's word to others was inviolable. It would not even have entered his mind to attempt turning back the clock and reopening negotiations between my Democratic colleagues and me. To Danny, a commitment was a commitment and that was it. But Speaker Foley wasn't from Chicago.

A few days before the committee vote on capital gains, the committee Democrats held a caucus meeting in the chairman's rooms at the Capitol. The regular Ways and Means Chamber was in the Longworth House Office Building. We were there to discuss other tax matters, or so I thought. Suddenly, the huge door swung open and "Fee Fi Fo Fum," in walked the speaker of the House, followed by the majority leader, Dick Gephardt, a former member of Ways and Means.

Dan Rostenkowski stood up and moved away from his chair at the head of the huge conference table, whereupon the speaker sat down—in the chairman's chair—and spoke. He said the Democrats "had not been ungenerous with upper-income people" in the 1986 tax law. He got that right; you will recall that President and Mrs. Reagan got a cut of forty-nine thousand dollars per annum from that "Reform and Simplification Act."

But, the Speaker said, the Democratic Party position was against changes in the taxation of capital gains. I couldn't help wondering who the Democratic Party was. There certainly had been no vote on the subject of capital gains in the House Democratic caucus. Could it be that the "Democratic Party" was in the person of Tom Foley, who was interested in taking a strong stand against something, especially something the Republican President favored?

When Tom Foley finished, Jake Pickle of Texas, one of the six "gangsters," was the first to respond and his response was a classic. I believe my close friend, Congressman Jim Shannon, and I agreed it was the best Pickleism we ever heard: Jake looked at the Speaker and said, "Now, Mr. Speaker, you come in here six weeks after we made our commitment. That's like standing outside the maternity ward and having your mother tell you, 'You shouldn't have kissed that girl.'"

I'll give Tom Foley credit; he laughed just as hard as all the others—very hard.

When the bill was debated on the floor, more than one Democrat insisted that it was un-Democratic to support the capital gains provision. So when I spoke, I answered the assertion:

"Up until a year or so ago, I never heard a Democratic leader complain about John F. Kennedy's capital gains position. I am reminded of the year 1964 when the Speaker and I were first elected to Congress. The Democratic Party was, you might say, *dead*-set against whamming up the Vietnam War. That was what wild Barry Goldwater would do. Within six months after the election, only a few of us Democrats were left supporting the party's platform against escalation. Our fearless leader had done an about-face while we marched on toward peace. Someone at the time said, 'They told me if I voted for Goldwater, the war in Vietnam would escalate. I voted for Goldwater, and sure enough, the war in Vietnam escalated.' Couldn't my Democratic colleagues at least be kind enough to agree that the Democratic Party position on this matter is a matter of opinion? Or should we simply rely on the revelation of Will Rogers, 'I belong to no organized political party; I'm a Democrat.' Let's hear it for that *big tent*."

I found no joy in the social aspect of my disagreement with Tom Foley on this issue. But at times like that, I would recall the words of the old spiritual, "I have to live with my truth, whether you like it or not." I was always happy when I could be with my party leaders, but I had two other categories of leadership before them, my constituents and the logic I proposed to my constituents before a majority of them elected me.

Tom Foley's accusation that on capital gains—that the President was catering to very-high-income citizens at the expense of middle and low-income citizens—took a toll. The President's standing in the polls began falling significantly. For our country's good, it was a bad time for that to happen. The President had recently announced that the economic sanctions he managed to obtain against Iraq over its invasion of Kuwait, would take about a year to work. But with his poll numbers plummeting, the President reversed his policy of reliance on the sanctions and initiated Desert Storm in which, one right-wing commentator said, "We rented our military to the Saudis." We paid a lot of the rent ourselves, in silver certificates and *death* certificates.

At about that time, I was invited to speak at a touching cultural event in Indianapolis. I don't think anyone was ever wiser or nicer than Mildred Compton, retiring curator of the Children's Museum of Indianapolis. The attendance at her retirement gathering was huge and, it seemed, for the most part well-to-do. Two public officials spoke before I was called on. They were the good governor of Indiana, dapper and friendly Bob Orr; and the tall, witty, and gracious mayor of Indianapolis, Bill Hudnut.

The governor gave Millie the highest honor the State of Indiana can bestow, a framed document called Sagamore of the Wabash. I was beginning to feel uneasy because I couldn't think of any such honor I could present to Millie. When Bill Hudnut presented the retiring curator the official proclamation of "Millie Compton Day" in Indianapolis, I felt like a kid who didn't have a gift at a friend's birthday party. As I looked around at the radiant throng in their finery and remembered that the museum was a favorite charity of the "upper four hundred" in Indianapolis, I knew exactly what to say:

"Dearest Millie, because of the nature of the office in which I serve, I can't declare you a Sagamore of the Wabash and I can't turn today into Millie Compton Day. In fact, I can't give you anything but love—and a few tax deductions for your patrons."

There was an amused and, I sensed, appreciative smile of acknowledgment from the assemblage. I had found some Scarlet Ribbons.

The Indiana delegation to Congress could be quite bipartisan when clear interests peculiar to the state were at stake. For example, in the early 1990s, Chrysler made noises about closing its Indianapolis electrical plant and buying a new kind of engine starters from Japan rather than making them in America. In order for Chrysler to make those new starters, itself, the company would have to do what it always had done in the cases of its new models, retool. But maybe it would be cheaper, in more ways than one, just to outsource way out in the Pacific. Thus began a series of meetings in Washington between Chrysler officials and the Indiana delegation to Congress.

Congress had passed a law making Uncle Sam an endorser on a loan to bail Chrysler out of its darkest hour in the 1970s. And the bailout worked beautifully. The patient recovered and paid back the loan with interest. Wanting not to seem ungrateful, the Chrysler people obviously wished us to think that they were still considering keeping the Indianapolis plant open.

So we all met and met until, at the final meeting, the Chrysler officials told us they had decided to go ahead and deal with Japan. There was a trend in those days for executives to appear in their companies' respective television commercials. Chrysler's boss, Lee A. Iacocca, was one of them. He was pretty good at it. With a nice smile and down- to-earth delivery, he gave a feel-good patriotic message—motherhood, apple pie and the flag. His company made American-made cars. The slogan was "Born In America." When the spokesman for Chrysler announced to the congressional delegation the final company decision, I said that I had just one request. He asked what it was and I told him: "Would you please take that 'Born in America' ad off the air?" The response was equivocal.

When Social Security was born in America during the 1930s, it set out certain qualifications for receiving retirement benefits. One must have paid Social Security taxes for at least ten of her or his working years, one must have attained the age of sixty-five for full benefits, and one must be retired. That sounds clear enough; the tax and age requirements are a matter of math. But how does one define retired? The law does that with a so-called retirement test. That is not a completely mathematical matter. First there are the concepts of "earned" and "unearned" income. The latter means income from investments, interest and rent, for examples. "Earned income," under the law, means being paid for active work—not being retired.

The retirement test essentially defines the difference between "full time" work and "part time" work. If a sixty-five-year-old person *earns* less than a given amount, which changes upward through the years theoretically on account of inflation, she or he is entitled to full retirement benefits from Social Security. For every three dollars earned above the retirement test, the Social Security retirement benefit is reduced by one dollar. In the mid-1990s, the retirement test was about twelve thousand dollars per year. That meant that if a sixty-five-year-old participant in the system, whose full retirement benefit was twelve thousand dollars per year, had an earned annual income of forty-eight thousand, his or her benefit would be reduced to zero. In other words, under the law, that person would not have been retired. By year 2000, the retirement test was seventeen thousand dollars.

The sixty-five-year-olds who were not eligible for retirement benefits because they were not retired had to be doing pretty well on their earned income. But not well enough to suit the editorial writers at the *Wall Street Journal*. On June 4, 1990, they published this:

STALKING ROSTY
The last time Ways and Means Chairman Dan Rostenkowski tried to

block a tax cut for the elderly—the catastrophic health-care tax repeal—a group of seniors besieged him outside his car in Chicago until he fled in his car.

Now Rosty's committee has become the main obstacle to repeal of the most unfair laws in the U.S. tax code, the earnings limit for Social Security recipients. Illinois Representative Dennis Hastert has 226 cosponsors to repeal this tax on people over 65. A House majority is 218. Yet Rosty, abetted by Subcommittee Chairman Andy Jacobs of Indiana, won't even let the bill come to the House floor for debate. Maybe Congress should consult the Supreme Soviet for a lesson in Democracy.

The earnings limit amounts to a surtax on the working elderly. For every $3 earned by a retiree over a certain limit, he or she loses $1 in Social Security benefits. The limit in 1990 is $9,390 for seniors between age 65 and 69; it's $6,840 age 62 to 66 [who lose one dollar in benefits for every two dollars earned above the limit]. The special tax expires at age 70.

This means in practice that retirees face an outrageously high marginal tax rate. A man in the 15 percent federal tax bracket who works at McDonald's can face a marginal rate of 55 percent. Since the earnings-limit tax also cuts his wife's Social Security benefits [even if she doesn't work], the marginal rate for the couple can reach 105 percent. And this doesn't count state and local taxes. The couple ends up paying the government for the privilege of working. As that Soviet emigre says, what a country!

It gets worse. The tax only applies to "earned" income, the sort that comes from working for a wage or salary. If income derives from interest or dividends, no Social Security benefit is lost. So the rich elderly can have a lower marginal tax rate than the average working stiff. Democrats used to care about such matters of 'equity,' but nowadays they'd rather be tax collectors for the welfare state.

Rosty and his comrades [Yes, Joseph McCarthy seemed to live on in those editorial rooms] are petrified that repeal might "cost" the Treasury revenue. In the static computer models of the Congressional Budget Office, repeal would "cost" $3.6 billion the first year, and $26.2 billion over five years. This assumes repeal wouldn't change anyone's behavior. Former Treasury economists Aldona and Gary Robbins, who do consider behavior, have estimated that enough would happily work more and the federal government would gain revenue. Not surprisingly, labor participation rates among the lowest are right around the income levels worst hit by the earnings-limit tax.

The earnings limit is an artifact of the Depression era, when the U.S. wanted seniors to retire so scarce jobs would be open for younger people. But many parts of the U.S. now have a labor shortage. The skills and experience are one of our most unused assets, and will become even more valuable as the Baby Boom generation retires. The punitive tax of the earnings limit sends the message to seniors that their country doesn't want them to work, or that they are fools if they do. It's time for another run at Dan Rostenkowski's limousine.

The car in which Dan Rostenkowski was riding to withdraw from the unruly Chicago group was an old Chevy. Moreover, the "man" working at McDonald's at the time was getting about ten thousand dollars a year and, therefore, would lose very little of his Social Security benefits. But he was of little concern to them, anyway. He served as a transparent decoy. Their tears were crocodile ones. Had they really been interested in him and those who had slightly higher earned incomes, they would have advocated raising the retirement test some, not repealing it altogether. The same writers and their followers constantly advocated "doing something about the entitlements," by which they meant curbing benefits for those who needed them and fast-laning benefits for those who did not. Their concern about the McDonald's worker, therefore, was that he was getting too much from Social Security.

Repealing the retirement test altogether meant brand-new benefits—some said golf cart money—for lawyers, businessmen, doctors and others who at age sixty-five could easily go right on earning six-digit incomes or more. By no stretch of a rational imagination could such people be considered "retired." The $26 billion cited in the editorial as the cost of the radical change they advocated would come about because of suddenly paying benefits to people who had already figured that a hundred thousand dollars a year or more in earned income was preferable to twenty thousand dollars in Social Security benefits.

As the Social Security system evolved politically over the decades, a very large part of the benefits paid to retirees greatly exceeded what they had paid in and what that amount had earned in interest. In other words, the freebee part of Social Security benefits was public assistance, sometimes called welfare. It would be a hot day in Heaven before the *Wall Street Journal* would argue that welfare benefits should be paid to low-income people working full-time barely above the poverty level.

The *Journal* editorial named me as an abettor in blocking floor action on the benefit grab for the high-income people. And that sounded pretty bad if you didn't know that a great number of the cosponsors had quietly asked me not to report the bill. So I sent a letter to the editor and it was published on June 28, 1990, under the title, "Social Security Lotto: Win Without a Ticket":

> The headline on your June 4 editorial was "Stalking Rosty." In nostalgic reminiscence, President Bush might suggest another headline: "Voodoo Too."
>
> In the editorial you advocate the ultimate liberalization of a federal retirement program by paying retirement benefits to seniors under seventy who are not retired. These are people who never paid a nickel into Social Security without the condition that they meet the act's definition of retirement before they receive retirement benefits.
>
> How do you get the $26 billion to pay for this giveaway? The same place they got the $750 billion to pay for the mainly upper-bracket income tax cut and the trillion-dollar net spending increase during the first Reagan term: Simply dust off the "laughable" curve, rosy up the assumptions and "just say no" to reality.
>
> Reality and the Social Security actuaries say that substantial liberalization of the retirement test in the past have produced no significant increases in tax receipts from earnings of Social Security retirees. Reality has also falsified the rosy assumption that as a result of the Kemp-Roth-Laffer alchemy of 1981, harder work and greater income tax collections would balance the budget by 1984.
>
> You suggest that obeying long-established law that denies retirement benefits to seniors who are not retired amounts to an unjust taxation of those seniors. Here we apparently need a primer on the difference between the apples of government taxes and the oranges of government benefits. The government collects the former and pays out the latter. The seniors who fail the retirement test do not have something taken away from them by taxation. They simply are not given something that is not owed them. If a car dealership won't give you a car you never paid for, it is not taxing you $10,000.
>
> Contrary to calculated myth, there is nothing in the Social Security law that prohibits a senior citizen from working full time. There is and always has been something in the Social Security law that prohibits a senior citizen from working full time and pretending to be retired.
>
> The retirement test is, in essence, the definition of part-time work. Not only is that test indexed for wage inflation, but the federal

government has recently liberalized that test in real dollars and is about to do so again with my full support and that of Chairman Dan Rostenkowski, whose "limousine," by the way, is as much fantasy as the rest of your editorial.

But to repeal the retirement requirement altogether would mean that those senior professional and business people who have already chosen continued six-figure incomes instead of, say, $12,000 Social Security benefits, would hit a big Social Security lotto—without even having purchased a ticket. Whoopee.

Rep. Andrew Jacobs, Jr., Chairman
House Ways and Means
Sub-Committee on Social Security

History will record that in the late winter of the year 2000, Congress caved in. Because of strange machinations in the Republican presidential primaries, members of both parties in Congress weren't sure how the fall election would evolve. In politics, uncertainty often produces especially desperate government spending. So the already hard-pressed Social Security trust fund was tapped for an unjust election-year gift to mostly well-off voters between the ages of sixty-four and seventy. The House voted to repeal the retirement test—unanimously. Full retirement benefits began to be paid to people who were not retired.

In the House debate, the same old specious arguments were made. Senior citizens should be allowed to work. No federal law had prevented them from doing so. Senior citizens who worked at McDonald's shouldn't be penalized. They weren't. The retirement test in 2000 was seventeen thousand dollars per year. Only managers were paid more than that at McDonald's. The trust funds would get it all back from the windfall recipients in the additional Social Security taxes they would pay and the extra credits they now would not be paid after age seventy. I wont bore you with the details, but, *balderdash*! Most of the recipients of the taxpayers' forced new generosity were already working as much as they would and therefore would pay no more in Social Security Taxes. Net loss to the trust fund by 2010: $23 billion. Whoopee again. Both parties voted for the giveaway; only one party would win the election.

Those of us who stood at the barricades to resist this lavish and unworthy raid on the Social Security retirement trust fund—Sandy Wise, Cathy Noe, Jake Pickle, Kathryn Olson, Danny Rostenkowski, (amazing) Janice Mays, and others—did manage to hold off the assault for a couple of decades, saving tens of billions of dollars for the huge and approaching obligations to the baby boomers when they would retire. And there is some satisfaction in that. "We few, we happy few. We band of brothers [and sisters]." Shakespeare's Henry V.

In the fall election of 1990, the so-called *Christian Coalition* was at it again. The group passed out generic anti-Democratic Party handbills in Indianapolis accusing me of all sorts of terrible things. The accusation on the leaflets that amused me most was the one that said I opposed a balanced budget amendment to the U.S. Constitution; I had started the movement for it in 1976. The same holy hucksters sent a mass mailing to Indiana Tenth District voters in 1998. The form letters said, in part, "Call Rep. Julia Carson today and urge *him* to vote for the Religious Freedom Amendment" (emphasis added). Far right though they were, they just couldn't seem to get it right.

If you have ever loved a pet, you will probably understand the following; if you haven't, you might not. We have a pet cemetery at the Fun Farm, replete with marble headstones which the American Granite and Marble Company of Indianapolis cuts and beautifully engraves for us. On one stone are the words, "Our Beloved Bergen." She was the daughter of C-Five, the Great Dane. Another reads, "Andy Dog. That was Kim's cocker spaniel who died young from a pancreatic disorder. Now it was Friend's turn. He was the largest Great Dane I had ever seen or heard of. His health problem was common among Danes—except, of course, for Marmaduke, who lives on and on—arthritis in the hips. At 4:30 P.M. on a summer day, I helped Friend up and sent him on his way around the corner of the house to do his business. After five minutes, which made him overdue, I looked down the hillside and saw him on all fours, leaning—you might say tilted—against a large lilac bush and the deep piano chords began to thunder in my ears. Life for Friend could not go on. "Beware of giving your heart to a dog," Kipling admonishes. But many of us do. Friend died from friendly fire, a lethal shot of instantly fatal poison administered at the Fun Farm by our veterinary friends, Bob McCune and his wife, Priscilla. His headstone reads, "Friend Forever."

Had the anti-arthritis drug Rimadyl been available at the time, Friend probably could have gone on for two more years. We were able to use it to prolong the life of our next Fun Farm Great Dane, a harlequin named Morgan, whom we adopted from the Humane Society of Indianapolis. She had been egregiously abused, taken away from her criminal owners by the police and delivered to the shelter. After thirty days without adoption, she had only three days left to live. That's when Jeff Pigeon told his WIBC radio audience about her and the impending death. Our close friend Paul Raikes heard the announcement and passed along the information to us through his wife, my sister-like friend and coworker in the congressional office, Loretta Raikes. Morgan was in such horrible condition that we adopted her just so she could die in a loving home. She was three when she joined us and stayed with us for seven healthy years when a massive stroke ended the joy she brought. I dare say she had formed a better opinion of humans by then. Only a few weeks before Morgan's death, we had lost our cocker spaniel, Annie, to a pancreatic disorder (the same illness that had taken the life of Kim's cocker, Andy). Morgan's headstone read, "Mild-Mannered Morgan—She added love." On the headstone of Annie, whose name evolved into "Annie Banana Boat" and then just "Boat," one can find these words: "Annie Boat—She paddled her own canoe." She was an independent pet.

A few years before the deaths of Morgan and Annie, we lost another orphan dog who had wandered into our lives when she was nearly hit by a car on a heavily traveled road. Named Lady, because that's what the little white-furred beauty was, she lived with us for four years before she died of heart failure. Her headstone read, "Our Fair Lady." And we wrote a poem about her:

> *She named herself,*
>   *The way she'd behave,*
> *So sweet, so gentle,*
>   *Yet very brave.*
> *Just a dog?*
>   *Yes . . . well maybe.*
> *But can we live*
>   *Without our Lady?*

My fall opponent in 1990 was Butler University economics Professor Janos Horvath, a Hungarian by birth and rearing who had been an envoy from his native land to the U.S. during a very short respite from communist and Russian domination in Hungary. To say Janos was a scholar and a gentleman would be an understatement. We competed once more in 1992. Both times fate fell my way. But that did not mean Janos was never elected to be a national legislator. In 1998 he was elected to the Parliament of his mother country. In Hungary, the "heavy burden" had been undone and "the oppressed" were free. And Janos was home.

chapter 21

THE GOVERNORS

SURPRISINGLY, EARLY IN 1992 NBC aired a debate among candidates for the Democratic presidential nomination. Three of the participants acted in a mature and civilized manner—Governor Douglas Wilder, Governor Bill Clinton, and host Tom Brokaw. The others performed in varying degrees of childishness. The one who just missed being in the first category was Senator Bob Kerrey of Nebraska. His only offense was braggadocio about his Medal of Honor war record.

Wilder and Clinton reminded me of words from Kipling's "If": "If you can keep your head while all about you are losing theirs." The two governors were refreshingly civil and cerebral. Later, when George Bush and Bill Clinton were the respective nominees of the Republican and Democratic parties, some altitude was lost. The following are excerpts from an *Indianapolis News* editorial entitled "Truth Takes a Holiday," published on August 26, 1992:

> The silly season has begun.
> Otherwise known as the campaign year, the silly season kicks off when the Republicans and Democrats finish their conventions and begin devoting themselves to rhetorical excess . . .
> Thus, this week Democratic presidential nominee Bill Clinton has been traveling about the country telling audiences that President George Bush went everywhere in the world during his first term "except America."
> The line is designed to be a shot at the President's supposed lack of domestic accomplishments. The fact that it is grossly exaggerated is

beyond question. During Bush's term, Congress passed and the President signed a child care bill, a bill for Americans with disabilities, civil rights legislation and many other significant domestic measures.

It is the silly season.

Ditto for President Bush's claim that, as governor of Arkansas, Clinton raised taxes 128 times in 12 years. In arriving at that number, the President and his researchers counted as a tax increase every time a license bureau stayed open longer hours (they can collect more money that way), one-dollar court fees imposed on convicted criminals and other such minor adjustments. As columnist Michael Kinsley and others have noted, if the same standards were applied to the President's tenure in the White House, it could be argued the he has raised "taxes" 133 times in only four years. . . .

It is the silly season.

In their defense, both President Bush and Governor Clinton—and many other candidates this year—doubtless will argue that they are only observing the rules of the political game as it is now played. They would say that a candidate must oversimplify, bend and distort an opponent's positions and record beyond any semblance of reality, if he or she expects to have a chance of winning.

In response, we simply offer two names: Richard Lugar and Andy Jacobs, Jr.

Lugar and Jacobs are living, breathing rebuttals to the argument that a political candidate has to compromise standards of truthfulness and fairness in order to be successful.

Not coincidentally, each of them is generally returned to office by an overwhelming majority of the vote.

Modesty "almost forbade" my including the latter part of that editorial in this work. But I didn't want to shortchange Dick Lugar, er . . . ah . . .

On September 23, 1992, my campaign treasurer, Alberta M. Snyder, sent this short letter to our contributors:

This is not a request for a contribution to Andy's fall campaign.

Because of your past generosity and that of others, we believe we have sufficient funds on hand to conduct our effort through November 3.

We write simply to thank you for your help. Especially in this age of cynicism about anyone in government, your continued confidence in Andy's congressional service is enormously encouraging.

Exactly thirty days later, the *Indianapolis News* ran a story by Washington correspondent David Haase, a part of which said:

> Rarely does a candidate lose the money election and win the November election. Only one Hoosier race repeatedly defies this pattern.
>
> In the 10th District, which lies entirely within Marion County, challengers often outspend Democratic Rep. Andrew Jacobs, Jr., but none has outpolled him since 1972 when Bill Hudnut won a single term in Congress.
>
> In this cycle, Jacobs has spent $8,346 compared with the $46,049 shelled out by [his opponent].

What is the secret to spending so little on campaigns? Simple. Though I would have enjoyed seeing TV ads singing my praises, I would not have enjoyed serving in Congress with lobbyists as financial backers; I'd have preferred to do some other line of work. There was one other secret, the one revealed at Bunker Hill: "Don't shoot 'til you see the whites of their eyes." We aired our radio ads on the weekend and Monday just before the election—when people were paying attention. "Waste not . . ."

Of the seven U.S. presidents with whom I served, my two favorites were now competing. Though both Bush and Clinton had their warts, Clinton's were of greater interest to right wing voyeurs. I liked both presidential candidates personally. They were most pleasant conversationalists in relaxed moments. The other five presidents had their good and bad aspects, but they seemed too limited either by slow intellect or emotional instability.

Now one or the other would be in the White House after January 20, 1993.

In a weak moment, George Bush let a couple of congressmen talk him into suggesting Bill Clinton was somehow working with Soviet secret police when, in a public demonstration, he correctly said his country was making a mistake in Vietnam. It really was a weak moment. The real George Bush, the one who said he was "going back to the real world" after his White House service, just wasn't like that.

On economic issues, the Clinton administration would be different; it would discontinue the quite bipartisan con game with the American people, the political game that said to the voters, pay less, get more and send no money; you'll be billed later. It was time for reality and some relatively modest personal checks made out to Uncle Sam from those at the top whose taxes had been twice slashed during the 1980s. Despite all the partisan screams of injustice and ponderous pseudo-scholarly predictions of national economic collapse because of it, the 1993 repeal of a small part of the Reagan-era tax cuts for the topmost, proved to be a significant part of a miracle cure for the ailing economy. As Lazarus, the economy sprang to a life of better health than we had enjoyed during those decades of deceit from the pens of those phrasemongers described earlier in this book. It had been a very long time since the government had gone beyond slogans about fiscal responsibility, and actually practiced more than a modicum of it.

The President proposed about $246 billion in tax increases and about the same amount in spending cuts over a five-year period. Critics immediately dubbed the tax increase the largest in history, but in real dollars adjusted for inflation it was not. In 1993 dollars it was about $58 billion lower than the regressive tax hike President Reagan signed into law in 1982—304 billion in *1993* dollars. And neither of those two was the largest in history; Reagan's was just the largest since World War II.

U.S. Representative Marjorie Margolies-Mezvinsky was a genuine American hero. It was she who cast the deciding vote for Clinton's sensible and bonanza-bound economic measure. Because of her political courage, she lost the next election. There is no greater love than to lay down one's "life for a friend." It is also lavish love to lay down one's political life for her country. Marjorie did just that. She told *political* death to "be not proud" and the American people prospered from her sacrifice.

The Clinton economic plan had a tax cut of its own in the form of an increase in the earned income tax credit for the working poor. In the Tenth District of Indiana, the President's entire plan as adopted meant tax hikes for twelve hundred families with top incomes and tax cuts for thirty-five hundred families with bottom incomes.

Taxes were changed mainly in three ways: a nickel more on a gallon of gas, the price of which was falling at the time; a widespread income tax cut for the working poor and an income tax increase by gradations on those with incomes of $185,000 or more per annum, the same citizens who received the heavy end of the two big tax cuts in the previous decade. Even in the last category, the changes were hardly draconian.

In terms of U.S. Treasury receipts, under the 1993 tax act, a couple with an income of two hundred thousand dollars paid eighteen dollars more per week and still paid twenty thousand dollars a year less than would have been the case had the two cuts of the 1980s not happened. The couple with a million dollars in annual income paid a thousand dollars more per week under the 1993 Act, but still paid about half what they would be paying without their big tax cuts during the Reagan years.

There was another apparent tax increase, but as already described in this work, it was really a further *benefit* reduction for the better-off among Social Security retirees. You will recall that proceeds from the income tax on Social Security retirement benefits are not income to the U.S. Treasury, but instead go right back into the Social Trust Fund from whence the taxed benefits came. The thinking of a think tank in Washington was confused about this matter when it issued a news release declaring that, in 1993, for the first time, nontaxable interest income from municipal bonds would be taxed.

The things that confused the "thinkers" were the two alternate formulas for determining how much, if any, of a Social Security retiree's benefits must be included as income subject to federal tax. That formula, in essence, was a means test, a determination as to how well-off, how much income—earned, unearned, taxed, or not taxed—a retiree had. Therefore, citizens must state on their federal income tax returns, not only what taxable incomes they have, but also, in a separate and non-taxing part of the return, how much nontaxable income there is. The latter figure is *not* added to the taxable income. It is there only to help determine how many beans a given retiree can put on the dinner table and, therefore how large a part of the Social Security benefit would be taxed.

Despite the demonstrable fact that the reported municipal bond interest is not added into taxable income on the 1040 tax return, the "thinkers" somehow managed to say they thought it was. Theoretically, they tried to have it both ways, that the-tax free interest was being taxed and that the larger part of the Social Security benefit was being taxed, too. But there was only one additional tax and even "thinker" thinking could not rationally argue that it could be counted twice. There was even a federal court decision which included this obvious truth. Moreover, the formula was not new in the 1993 act which President Clinton signed into law. The basic formula was enacted ten years before in the 1983 Social Security Act which President Reagan signed into law.

It was one more in the series of hoaxes about Social Security. Its predecessors were theft of the Social Security funds by the regular government (only true for a couple of days during the Reagan administration), the notch disinformation, and that most Americans paid more in Social Security taxes than in income taxes. The third claim would be true only if you counted the Social Security taxes an employer pays on each employee. And the only way to say the employer's tax is actually the employee's tax being paid by the employer, is to argue that if the employer were relieved of that tax, he or she would inevitably raise the worker's wage by the same amount. Some might, but, let's face it, most wouldn't; they would look on the change as a tax cut for them.

Before the 1993 Act, 50 percent was the maximum part of a Social Security retirement benefit on which federal income tax could be levied. The only thing that was changed about taxation of Social Security retirement benefits in 1993 was that ceiling. It was raised to 85 percent—the portion the average retiree had not paid for during his or her working years—only for retirees who had very high incomes. A very small percent of retirees had enough income to make 85 percent of their Social Security benefits taxable. The overwhelming majority of retirees' benefits weren't subject to any federal income tax at all. The change meant that a relatively few retirees would pay their respective income tax rates on the entire freebee portion of what they received from Social Security.

In 1994 I had been a voice in the wilderness for more than a decade with regard to garnishment of federal employees' salaries for legitimate, which is to say court-determined, debt. Because of "sovereign immunity," deadbeat federal employees—a small percent of all federal employees—could thumb their noses at creditors. Uncle Sam was deemed different from other employers and would not, as the others do, cooperate with the courts in the collection of just debts.

Through the years, the federal government did agree to garnish wages for child support and debts owed the government, itself. But otherwise, federal employees could avoid payment from their wages of even *tort* judgments. There was an automobile accident case in California in which a federal employee had recklessly crippled a woman for life. But he never had to pay a penny of the court-determined damages to her because his wage could not be garnished. A federal employee in Virginia bilked a lady out of the thousands of dollars she had paid him to remodel her kitchen. She wasted her money getting a judgment; his wages could not be garnished. Neither of those employees had other property of value from which the judgments could be satisfied.

There were congressional hearings during the Reagan and Bush years and the administrations testified against my bill to turn Uncle Sam into a decent employer who, like other employers, would accept court-ordered garnishments. The Clinton administration sent officials to testify against my proposal, also, but there was a difference; eventually the President did sign it into law.

One witness from the Defense Department argued that some of the military personnel were as young as eighteen and were away from home for the first time. They sometimes were swindled by town merchants and ought not be subjected to garnishment. My reply was, "Determination of whether a person has been swindled is the function of the courts. No one gets garnished unless a court has determined a legitimate debt. And as for whether an eighteen-year-old should be held responsible for the debt he or she runs up, bear in mind that kids younger than eighteen—the usual dividing line between juveniles and adults—have been tried as adults for crimes." It was a pleasure to work with Senator Larry Craig of Idaho and, eventually, with President Clinton to achieve this simple correction. "The wheels of justice grind slowly," more than a decade in this case.

In the 1992 election campaign I made two pledges. But, because of the multiple content of the 1994 firearms bill, it was impossible for me to keep my word on both. I had pledged to cast the vote against outlawing domestic manufacture of about nineteen designs of semiautomatic "rifles"—in the Marine Corps they are pieces—the ones of which the Bush administration had banned importation. I also pledged to support outlawing manufacture of ammunition magazines whose capacities exceeded ten rounds. I didn't think keeping those semiautomatics legal was as important as making those magazines illegal and said so during that campaign. I just didn't see any reason for distinguishing the pieces in question from the other five hundred styles of semis not contested by gun control advocates. When lobbied by Senator Dianne Feinstein and Attorney General Janet Reno to support the ban on the weapons, themselves, I said that because of my combat service in the Marines and my time as a police officer, I had at least a nodding acquaintance with gas-operated semiautomatic weapons. And I was convinced that, no matter how fearsome looking, none of them could be fired any faster than another by the same finger.

When the bill came to the floor for debate and disposition, there were the two issues wrapped into one bill, one part outlawing manufacture of the pieces and another outlawing manufacture of the oversized magazines. But very little mention was made of the magazines during the press release artillery duel leading up to the actual floor battle. And the floor debate was concentrated on the semis. So when I went to the floor to cast my district's vote on the question of whether the bill would pass, I had all but forgotten the ammunition magazine feature. Accordingly, I inserted the voting card and pressed the red button for "nay."

The southwest corner of the House Chamber was my usual roosting place during floor debates, which were so often so redundant as to be boring. Pleasant conversation during such otherwise unedifying moments relieved the pain. Pleasant conversation was what I got from the regulars in that spot, Bill Young and Mike Bilirakis of Florida, Joe McDade of Pennsylvania, and Jim Traficant of Ohio, as well as my close friend Pete Visclosky of Indiana. Three of us were Democrats, but that southwest corner was on the Republican side of the proverbial aisle. On those occasions when duty required me to participate in the floor proceedings, I would gravitate toward the southeast corner on the Democratic side where the Pennsylvania Democrats Paul McHale, Paul Kanjorski, Jack Murtha, Bob Borski and Bill Coyne gathered. Both groups were scintillating anesthetics to some of the more brutally boring of redundant floor speeches.

On the evening when I cast the "nay" vote against the firearms bill, I slipped into my usual spot nestled among the Floridians, Republican Pennsylvanians and my Democratic buckeye and Hoosier buddies. As we visited, their voices, indeed the steady din of informal noise in the chamber, became distant and then muted to my consciousness. The big electronic scoreboard that shows the totals of "yeas and nays" showed the vote was dead even. That meant, at that point without the Speaker's breaking the tie—there was talk that he might not—the bill would fail. It also meant that there were five more minutes in which votes could be changed by those who had cast them. And somehow it meant that my other and competing pledge came to mind, the one about the ammunition magazines. This was a controversial bill; members had taken their stands and were not likely to switch their votes. Vote switches usually occurred on obscure bills where members might have cast votes and then learned of objectionable provisions. That was not likely in the case of the firearms bill. So far as observers could tell, it had lost by one vote.

It dawned on me that I was suddenly in a position to take a short walk and change history. I considered the size of those ammunition magazines of paramount importance to public safety. I had argued in 1992 that limiting ammunition magazines to ten rounds could harm no one, but under ghastly circumstances could save the lives of many. This was true, I said, because on those rare but all too real occasions when maniacs would go after crowds with semis, if they had to reload, children would have a chance to scurry to safety. I was vindicated later when such a maniac did open fire in a Long Island, New York, commuter train and did stop to reload. While reloading, he was subdued by some brave and quick-thinking passengers.

Now there were about three minutes remaining to change votes. My friends might have thought it strange for me to arise in the middle of a good story and walk away. Then I was standing in the well of the House with a green preprinted card in my hand which I handed to a clerk, who, in turn, passed it up to the reading clerk who announced, "Mr. Jacobs—off 'no' on 'aye.'" The bill passed and all hell broke loose from East Coast out into the Pacific, past Hawaii, all the way to Guam.

Representative Joe Kennedy of Massachusetts burst through the door from the Speaker's lobby and told me the bells were ringing on the Associated Press machine. The World was being told that *I* made the firearms bill pass. As I managed a nod of acknowledgment to Joe, I shrugged to myself, "big deal." Bigger than I thought. In our congressional office, the phones were ringing off the proverbial hooks. They were tied up for forty-eight hours. There were calls from as far away, yes, as Guam. Most of our own constituents couldn't get through. Someone else, right there in Washington couldn't get through, either, the President of the United States. White House operators did manage to reach one of my coworkers in Indianapolis and asked her to have me call the White House, if the Indianapolis office heard from me. It might have been simpler just to call one of my Rayburn Building neighbors and ask that the message be relayed.

Most of the calls were from members of the National Rifle Association. Their attitudes ranged from upset to angry to outraged to furious to maniacal to regular run-of-the-mill nutty. One hoped I would rot in Hell. Now, to me, rotting means sitting on a sofa, eating chocolates, and staring at what my dad called the gawk box, sometimes called TV. Though not healthful, it really didn't sound so bad. I didn't want to burn in Hell, but rotting, well that was another thing.

When I received word of the President's call, I returned it and heard his voice say my name and thank me for casting the vote as I ultimately did. I told him that I had done so as a matter of my best legislative judgment and that I thought it was a favor to the whole country and only as a citizen did he owe me any thanks, adding that I was happy we agreed, but only on the magazine part of the bill. The President said that perhaps the administration should have placed more emphasis on that aspect. I hate to take up a busy person's time, but I did say, initially in Hoosierese, "Mr. President, as long as I have you on the phone, I'm going to tell you why you're in a special Pantheon of mine, heretofore occupied by only three other U.S. presidents—Adams, the elder, Lincoln, and Truman. I believe that extremists have maligned the four of you more than they have any of our other presidents. When Truman was in the White House and my dad was in Congress, Dad said, 'They thought they had Truman in '48. And ever since, they've been going around like a mad dog whose victim escaped.'" He thanked me for the encouragement and I thanked him for the call.

Next morning in the *Washington Post,* the principal sponsor of the firearms legislation, Representative—later Senator—Charlie Schumer of New York was quoted as saying in reference to me, "We left him alone. Andy makes his own decisions and colleagues don't talk him out of them." I took it as a very nice and intended compliment.

The following Saturday, the *Post* ran a feature story about me. The byline was Jason Vest, a young and greatly gifted writer just in from Indiana University. I was quoted as saying, a tad facetiously, "I looked up at the tote board and saw the tie. Then a Cajun voice that would have been familiar to anyone in the White House, came to me saying, 'It's the magazines, stupid.'" The voice I joked about was that of the President's PR man, James Carville, who, during the 1992 presidential campaign, was said to have posted signs in the Clinton headquarters telling workers, "It's the economy, stupid." I assume the message was meant to steer them away from sideshows such as the candidate's sex life and the silly suggestion that, as a kid, he had worked for the KGB.

The funniest interview I did in connection with the firearms vote was with a *Time* magazine reporter. He asked me if I thought I would have cast the vote for the bill if I were running for reelection that year of 1994. My answer was, "That's not a particularly difficult question to answer inasmuch as I am running for re-election this year." A lot of Democrats with long tenures were retiring at the time. I'll give this to the classy guy from *Time*: even though the joke was pretty much on him, he laughed a genuine laugh.

The mail was much like the angry calls in the same varying degrees of denunciation from the critics except that, whereas those critics dominated the phone lines immediately after the vote, they sent a minority of letters. One I enjoyed a lot was from a man in Alabama:

Dear Sir:
I am going to send a check for $1,000 to the campaign of whomever has the privilege of running against you this fall.

He went on to explain just how stupid it was for me to cast the vote as I did. In response, I wrote:

Dear Mr. _____,
First, I believe we have a grammar problem. The pronoun you needed in your first sentence was "whoever," not "whomever."

Back came his reply:

Dear Sir:
You have a grammar problem. My preposition was "to" and the object of that preposition was "whomever."

So I wrote again:

Dear Mr. _____,

Wrong again.

My worst nightmare has come true. I shall have to explain your grammar problem to you in detail. "To," as you say, is your preposition, but the object of that preposition is the objective phrase, "whomever [sic] has the privilege of running against you this fall." The objective phrase takes the subjective pronoun.

Another letter from Alabama:

Dear Sir:

My worst nightmare has come true; you are right. I looked it up. Still hoping you will be unemployed come November (but enjoying our correspondence in the meantime).

Sincerely,

Later, when I decided to retire from Congress, I wrote to the fellow in Alabama once again, saying that he might be one of the happiest to learn of my decision. In his reply, he said that out of curiosity he had looked up my record and thought I ought not retire. All of which brings to mind the Lincoln quotation:

Do I not destroy my enemy when I make him my friend?

chapter 22

The Mirror

Two scandals in the U.S. House came to light just before the 1992 election. One involved the members' bank and the other the House post office. But, under the sage maxim of Senator Vance Hartke that "when the politicians and newspeople are up to here in it, the general public is just getting the soles of their shoes wet," they didn't sink in with the public until the 1994 election. In that year, they sank in deeply enough to sink the Democratic ship which had organized the U.S. House for forty years.

Speaker Tom Foley had, in effect, been the CEO at the time the corruption was discovered, but there was nothing corrupt about Foley, just negligent. He wasn't minding the store which was the housekeeping of the House. This is not to say that he didn't care about corruption; it is to say that he placed too much faith in the rectitude of others and did not look over their shoulders. "While the cat's away, the mice will play."

Part of the bank scandal wasn't very scandalous after all. It involved a mistake made by several succeeding House sergeants at arms. Traditionally, the sergeants-at-arms office ran the House bank and the House payroll. The law on representatives' salaries required that they be paid in monthly installments at "the end" of each month. Under the statute, payday was the same for House staff and other employees. But without explanation, somewhere along the way, the pay of members was delayed until the first day of the following month. The error was repeated from that day forward. A large number of "bad" checks written by representatives to pay end-of-the-month bills, were, in fact and in law, good checks written on the assumption that the law was being followed with the direct deposits of their salaries to their sergeant at arms bank accounts.

I had always assumed that if a bank said one thing and my checkbook said another, the bank was right. Not so the U.S. House bank. I was told by the bank that over a three-year period, I had written two bad checks. But when I checked, they were both good. The first one was written during the month and the bank had not posted a prior deposit that much more than covered the draft. I had the properly dated deposit receipt as a subsequent audit confirmed. The second check was for the bulk of the part of my salary I didn't send back to the U.S. Treasury. I deposited that amount in the Indianapolis bank account of our family on the last day of each month when, by law, my salary was supposed to have been credited to my sergeant-at-arms account. But, of course, the law was being violated each month by one day.

Nevertheless, there was real scandal. When I first entered Congress, the money allowances for congressional office supplies and postage stamps were, under law, part of the congressional salary. Whatever was not expended from those accounts for official business could be cashed by members as part of their taxable incomes. That never smelled quite right to me and I never did it. In my view, it fell into the category of legal, but not right. In fact, when Bill Hudnut was kind enough to take up my congressional burdens in 1973, I was told by a House post office official that I had several thousand dollars in my stamp allowance and I could take it as taxable income. Big-time legal; big-time wrong. I declined.

I was at a loss to see why there was a stamp allowance in the first place. All official mail from a congressional office was carried under the franking system. Long before the 1990s, the personal income aspect of the stamp allowance had been outlawed. But the stamp allowance for each office had been retained. That was an open invitation for shenanigans because stamps are so easily convertible into cash. That was apparently part of the House post office scandal.

In the case of the House bank, there was some actual abuse. A few members did use the loose practices there intentionally to write bad checks in large amounts as a form of interest-free loans. This was ironic. Since the only money in the House bank belonged to the members, I used to joke to the member just ahead of me in line at a teller's cage, "Leave some for me." As it turned out, even as we spoke, in some cases, life was imitating my not-so-artful joke. I also enjoyed telling tellers the joke about a John D. Rockefeller check which was returned, marked "insufficient funds, not yours—ours." Life was again looking like art.

Nineteen ninety-four was the mirror image of 1974 with reverse roles for the political characters. In 1974 it was the Watergate scandal that embarrassed Republicans all over the country, and in great numbers they stayed home on election day. The Democrats had a landslide, but not many more votes than they usually got. It was just that, because of the stay-at-homes, a lot of votes were subtracted from the Republican column.

In 1994 Republican candidates didn't get many more votes than usual, but they had a landslide because Democrats, embarrassed by their party's scandals in the U.S. House, stayed home on election day. There was one difference between Watergate and Bankgate, though. Bankgate was bipartisan, which is to say, major bad check writers included Republicans as well as well as Democrats. But, despite the fact that there were many perfectly innocent Democrats—just as there had been many perfectly innocent Republicans at the time of Watergate—the Democratic Party had the reins of House administration and therefore, quite rightly, had the major responsibility for the outrage.

Had I not run ahead of the Democratic ticket in the Tenth Congressional District, I would have lost the 1994 election. My party lost the district 55 to 45 percent; I won 53 to 47 percent. Obviously, I had Republican and independent voters to thank. And I certainly did thank them. They had given me their votes for years and I was always grateful. In 1994 they saved the (election) day for me, so I am all the more grateful.

It is said that the more things change, the more they remain the same. It was true of the 1994 change of party guard in the U.S. House. The pork barrel continued to roll, albeit with different beneficiaries. Official travel frequent flyer airline tickets, paid for by the taxpayers, continued to be converted to the private use of members who chose to misuse them with impunity. The rule allowing such blatant wrong was specifically retained, one new leader saying it was a "Mickey Mouse issue." I, on the other hand, smelled a rat.

The new Speaker made much of discontinuing delivery of ice to congressional offices each business day—we had declined it in our office all along—but he prevailed upon the tax-supported Smithsonian Institution and an unnamed private entity to spend thousands of dollars to sculpt a frighteningly realistic replica of a Tyrannosaurus Rex head and turn it over to him for display in the office assigned to him.

The coldest of the right wing became all the more vocal in those days. At a national Republican gathering in Indianapolis, most Indiana Republicans were shocked by a bumper sticker some members of the extremist wing passed out. It read: "Feed the homeless to the hungry." The joke about public housing someone wrote out for President Reagan to tell at his first inaugural ball was insensitive, even mean. But this harebrained handicraft could only have been conceived in the cranial cauldron of vile and vicious venom. By comparison, Marie Antoinette was kind. These purveyors claimed to be Christians, and better Christians than the rest. "In as much as ye have done it unto one of the least of these my brethren, ye have done it unto me." (Mathew 25:40) And even "if your enemy is hungry, feed him; if he is thirsty, give him something to drink." (Romans 12:20; Proverbs 25:21) To invoke once again my father's words, "They were Christians; they'd ostracize you for doubting the divinity of Christ and persecute you for following his teachings."

There was a wide misperception about the freshmen Republican representatives who helped make up the new majority in the U.S. House. Sloppy thinking saw them all stereotypically as mean and selfish. That was probably true of a few, but a very few. As in Richard Nixon's 1962 story about the contract to deliver a hundred thousand frogs each week, the obnoxious ones were the few who made the most noise. Most of those new members were quiet-spoken and kind people who understood that their differences of opinion with others were just that and not matters of good and evil. Good examples were John Ensign of Nevada and Dave McIntosh of Indiana, hardworking and sensitive members, who used reason rather than doctrine in making their decisions.

Moreover, on the Ways and Means Committee, the new chairman and the new chairman of my Social Security Subcommittee were good and admired friends of mine. Both, by chance, had successively been the top Republicans on the subcommittee when I chaired it. Not only were we good friends, but far more often than not—the "not" applied to one significant issue only—we agreed on important policy matters.

When the first meeting of the Social Security Subcommittee in the new Congress convened, Baseball Hall of Famer Jim Bunning of Kentucky, who had been the most recent ranking minority member when I chaired the subcommittee, was the chairman and I was the ranking minority member. We had changed places and worked together just as we had before. In opening statements, I mentioned a letter my dad had sent me when I was in combat. He wrote that, during the early part of World War II, General Patton was General Bradley's commanding officer. Later, it was the other way around. But there was no loss of dignity either way. Apart from their personal friendship, they shared a common goal and worked together to achieve it. I added that Jim Bunning was an admired friend and that we differed on one issue and agreed on practically all the others. Both of us said on the Record that day that we would work together in the future just as we had in the past, in friendship and in the line of duty.

I especially liked Jim Bunning because of his political courage, which usually means standing up to pressure groups such as the charlatans of the Social Security notch controversy. Another issue on which Jim and I stood shoulder to shoulder was a proposal by two members of his party to put pictures on Social Security cards as tools in the effort to catch illegal immigrants. We agreed that the idea was a masterpiece of superficial logic since such cards were so easy to obtain under assumed names. During the floor debate, Jim pointed out that the cost of the proposal would be about six billion dollars and would accomplish very little. When it was my turn, I said that all an illegal immigrant needed to do to get a Social Security card was produce a birth certificate, which was easy to fake. At that point, one of the proponents asked me to yield, which I did. He said, "Well, we could put pictures on birth certificates."

As I continued my statement, I said in response: "There go another six billion. These days, citizens get Social Security cards at a very early age. Just think about that. Some people look different at twenty-five from the way they looked just after birth, so there's another bunch of billions. Or take Mrs. Clinton; she might have to change her Social Security card each time she changes her hair."

There was a lot of society page space devoted to the fact that the First Lady often changed her hairstyle in those days.

The new chairman of the full committee was Bill Archer of Texas. I never knew anyone of greater civility, scholarship, or intellectual honesty. In addition to the notch matter and capital gains taxes, we had worked closely together on other issues including Medical Savings Accounts which became controversial principally because of public statements by one of Bill's fellow Texans, a member of the United States Senate. As was the case with Jim Bunning, Bill Archer and I agreed on all but one of the salient issues concerning Social Security. And, as was the case with Jim Bunning, Bill and I had several differences on several issues not related to Social Security. But Bill Archer was one of my warmest friends.

When the full Ways and Means Committee held its first hearing with Bill as chairman, he had to remind me of a little-noticed House rule which I had overlooked and mildly violated. But what I did was fun.

The fact that "the more things change, the more they remain the same" doesn't mean that the names of things remain the same. For example, in the civic sin called spin, for years the Democratic Congress, with the asinine assistance of phrasemongers, predicted good things on the basis of "econometric models" when it wanted to borrow or print some more money to do some more wasteful spending. The Republican majority didn't want to plagiarize when it came to subterfuge. So the new leaders made up their own pretty names for pretty bad stuff. Whether a given budget is considered in balance depends on the outlook for future economic activity and, therefore, tax revenue levels. When the majority—either party majority—wants to spend some more of the public's money to the benefit of campaign contributors, it simply assumes a rosy economic outlook and declares the budget in balance or at least no further out of balance than the previous budget.

In the case of the new Republican majority, the phrase for budget subterfuge was "dynamic scoring." It had nothing to do with college dating; it simply meant that, in budget calculations, the various components would be scored according to an agreed-upon fantasy, rather like the Reagan administration's prediction of a balanced budget by 1984 as a result of increased spending and reduced taxes for high rolling citizens.

When it was my turn to speak at that first hearing with Bill in the chair, I looked directly into the *C-Span* camera and said, "Mr. Chairman, I have a public service to perform. Attention, C-Span junkies. I know you've been puzzled by the new budget term, 'dynamic scoring.' And I am happy to report that the definition of it has just been discovered in the old movie *My Little Chickadee*. In that film, Mae West made this new term as clear as it ever will be made. She said, 'One and one's two. Two and two's four. Four and four's *ten*—if you know how to work it.'"

Big laughs from practically every member of the committee, Republican and Democrat alike. Stifling his smile, the chairman said, "The gentleman is admonished that House rules prohibit addressing the C-Span audience directly." To which I replied, "In that case, I withdraw the statement, incorporate it by reference and direct it to just anyone." Bill's smile crept back as I yielded "back the balance of my time."

There was an almost universal refusal to distinguish between the words, *debt* and *deficit*. Debt is what one owes; deficit is what one adds to what one owes. Yet, with the national debt approaching six thousand billion dollars and absolutely no effort in sight to pay down any of the principal, a Catholic priest named John McLaughlin, who had flipped his collar around to layman, announced in a raised and apocalyptic voice on television, "*Debt-free by 2002*." He, of course, meant deficit-free, but seemed oblivious to his blunder.

The spin was dizzying enough to bring about credence in most of the news media which blindly reported that already in 1998, the federal budget produced a surplus. Both Republicans and Democrats claimed credit for the rapidly falling annual deficit beginning midway through the twentieth century's final decade. Republicans pretended they had cut the pork, which they hadn't—just shifted it to *their* contributors—and Democrats claimed to have made a valiant effort in the same direction and did their best to direct largess to their contributors. But the improvement in the accounts had little to do with reduced spending and almost everything to do with a whirlwind of stepped-up economic activity and the enormous upsurge it produced in government revenues which was partly a consequence of the 1993 revenue act that indicated some fiscal responsibility to replace decades of something-for-nothing politics.

Exactly what the Laffer Curve said would happen—and didn't—after taxes were drastically cut in the upper income brackets, did happen after taxes were *raised* a bit in the upper-income brackets. Confidence that the government was starting to be prudent and stop claiming that the invisible hand of political alchemy could allow more spending with less taxation, inspired investment in the economy and the economy flourished. But, even though dramatic, the flourish had not been so great as actually to produce a surplus by 1998—not without misrepresenting the actual amount of income to the actual, or Federal Funds budget.

In order to explain the chicanery, I wrote this in a regular column I did for the *Indianapolis Business Journal*. It was published on June 15, 1998, a year and a half after I left Congress:

> There's no telling how much human effort goes into denying the obvious—pay less, get more: eat more, weigh less.
>
> In the final decade of the eighteenth century, when France was chain-smoking its revolutionary governments, each outdid the other in printing what nineteenth-century economist Andrew White called "fiat currency." And it became a death penalty crime for the French to use any other unit of exchange—gold, for example.
>
> What happened was what will always happen. Farmers would not bring their produce to market as the flames of inflation ravaged the economy. The public began to see through this paper alchemy and therefore government officials knew they must either quit watering down the economic soup, or seem to. So they made a grand display of smashing printing presses on the front steps of a government building even as other presses in the basement continued to gush out the bogus bills.
>
> It took forty years for the French economy to recover.
>
> Now, here we are two centuries later being told by both major political parties that the federal government is producing a surplus in

its annual budgets. By its own rosy calculations, it is doing no such thing.

If a balanced budget means anything, it means not borrowing money. Do these contemporary bipartisan budgets require no more borrowing? In the word of my Marine infantry skipper, "negatory."

The government has been borrowing billions every year from the American public, foreign nationals (to whom it pays higher interest rates than it pays to its own citizens) and from the federal *trust* funds, including the vast ones that make up the three parts of Social Security.

Read the small print in these budgets and you will know, as the White House and Congress already know, that the government plans to stop borrowing from the American public and from foreign nationals, but it plans to go right on borrowing from the trust funds. And never mind that the continued borrowing from Social Security takes place on the eve of that day of reckoning when the mountains of money already borrowed from Social Security must be paid back with interest to cover checks for retiring baby boomers.

Some will say the borrowing from trust funds is simply borrowing by one government entity from another and that such borrowing doesn't count. Which, of course, means that, in order to make the budget seem balanced, officials count Social Security receipts as though they were income to general government accounts, technically called the Federal Funds Budget.

But in the same breath, if not the same side of the mouth, the same officials will tell you the government does not violate the trust funds by directly appropriating the earmarked taxes for regular government purposes.

They are right the second time. It was my privilege to be the author and sponsor of a law that requires the U.S. Treasury to issue specific bonds reflecting the legal obligation to repay, with interest, money borrowed from Social Security. I also cosponsored the law that *prohibits* the federal government from pretending Social Security taxes are income to the Federal Funds Budget.

Sad to say, the wondrous world of no federal borrowing three years before 2001 is another kind of *Space Odyssey* itself. Call it a ledger legerdemain.

The pious suggestion that the newfound surplus *might* be used to help the Social Security system amounts to a suggestion that what already belongs to Social Security might be given to Social Security. An old Broadway musical included this lyric: "If you can give a baby a locket from her daddy's pocket, Son, you're a natural phenomenon at politics." That was back in 1949 and people are still buying the same sleight of tongue.

Thus it has always been and always will be as long as people are willing to believe what they want to hear, however farfetched. Fooling oneself might be the cruelest joke, but it is usually the most expensive one, too.

For years, writers have uniformly tapped the third-party payer system as responsible for the explosion in medical costs. The most intense surge in those prices came with the advent of Medicare. It was the same economic principle that had long applied to automobile body repairs. In repair shops across the nation, as guys with clipboards rubbed dust off dented fenders and began scribbling, they would casually ask, "Is this an insurance job?" And if it was, the price would automatically go up to meet the capacity of the deep pocket. As long as the insurance was paying, the automobile owner had little financial incentive to shop for the best price and therefore stimulate competition.

On the other hand, without health insurance, perhaps the best shopped-for price would still make it either out of reach or most difficult for the average person to pay. How could a worker get the bills paid by a third party and at the same time have inducement to shop for the best price? My friend Pat Rooney, a Golden Rule insurance company executive, had a very good answer. Let the employer have the option, under the Internal Revenue Code, of either deducting premiums for employee health insurance, or, in lieu of deducting the premiums on regular health insurance, deducting payments into respective individual employee accounts from which employees could pay their own medical bills directly.

The second option would be subject to two conditions. First, after all the bills for a year were paid from an employee's account, the remaining money would become the taxable and disposable income of that employee when she or he reached retirement age. Second, the employer must also furnish high-end deductible catastrophic health insurance for such an employee. Premiums for such catastrophic insurance are low because the risk is lower for high-figure claims. There would be a gap between the annual deposit made by the employer into the medical savings account and the beginning of coverage by the catastrophic insurance. And that gap would be in the nature of a deductible on normal health insurance. But instead of the employee's having to pay the deductible before her or his account began paying bills, he or she would only have to pay a deductible if the bills exceeded the amount in the medical savings account at a given time. In other words, with the medical account, an employee had the equivalent of a "first dollar" payment system—no deductible to be met for the first few hundred dollars, only after the account has been spent in cases where it is.

The beauty of the second option was that it provided the best of both worlds: money to pay the employee's medical bills would be supplied by the employer and the employee would have strong incentive to shop for the best price. Collectively, millions of employees would naturally stimulate competition for their health care dollars. That, in turn, would drive market prices down, not just for them, but for all consumers, including Uncle Sam in the Medicare and Medicaid programs. Where there was a year-end surplus in the account, it would carry over to help pay future medical bills—in which case the interest earned would be taxable just as in a regular bank savings account. When the employee retired and became eligible for Medicare, the balance in the medical savings account would be hers or his to spend as desired.

On the other hand, if the employee had the bad fortune to incur medical expenses higher than the balance in his or her medical savings account, the catastrophic insurance would cover to the stratosphere after a one or two thousand dollar deductible.

We didn't have to depend on theory; even without the income tax deduction, the Forbes organization was using medical savings accounts (MSA) with its employees. And it was working wonders. One employee was told by her doctor that she needed an eight-thousand-dollar operation. As she explained it, the eight thousand would wipe out the balance in her MSA, and take her into her deductible for the catastrophic coverage. So she did some shopping. The next doctor told her that the first doctor's price was in the red zone of rip-off. The price with doctor number two would be four thousand. The employee said she felt as though she was on a roll, so she sought out a third opinion. On the third try, she must have been charmed by Diogenes' lighting system. The third opinion, validated by both time and subsequent examinations, was that she didn't need the operation at all—at any price.

I first introduced a bill containing the MSA idea when George Bush was in the White House and Democrats were the nominal majority in Congress. A lot of Democrats and Republicans on the Ways and Means Committee were for the proposal; they easily made up a majority.

In consequence of my once again being the deciding vote on the committee with regard to reporting a larger health proposal for floor consideration, I was able to barter the MSA's into the reported House bill during the first two years of the first Clinton administration. But the larger bill, which I, myself, could not support for actual House passage, failed and the MSAs along with it.

The idea enjoyed bipartisan congressional popularity well into the Clinton administration. But Democratic supporters began to peal off in droves as Senator Phil Gramm of Texas began stressing the medical savings accounts every time he made angry verbal attacks against President Clinton. Mainly one senator had managed to transmogrify the matter from a what-made-sense to a who-was-right issue.

Eventually the MSA plan was incorporated as a limited pilot project in a new tax law, but in such a way as to trip it before it got out of the starting gate and guarantee a bad result. Part of the congressional sabotage was a requirement that the catastrophic insurance have a deductible of at least three thousand dollars. That was meant to and did discourage employees from choosing the plan. The three thousand was, in effect, a frightening leap from the security of the MSAs to the catastrophic protection. Experience had shown that a two thousand dollar deductible was about what the average employee considered reasonable.

As this sleeper-sabotage provision was discovered, there were strong signs that the reformers were waking up and moving legislation to rectify the matter. To mix metaphors, the congressional wheels of common sense grind slower than the flow of molasses at the first of the year.

President Clinton's secretary of labor was Harvard Professor Robert B. Reich and he was a good one. That is to say he had common sense when it came to correcting goofy regulations written by talismanic theorists down the line in his department. The case of the Indianapolis Paul Smith Plumbing company is an excellent example. Someone wrote a Labor Department regulation that was the envy of the Mad Hatter. If an installation and repair company let its employees take company trucks home at night so as to drive shorter distances directly to wherever the their respective work sites were the next business day, the ridiculous regulation required the employer to pay wages at the time-and-a-half rate for the employees' travel to and from work. And never mind that, in practice, the arrangement meant couples could get by with one car, rather than two.

Mr. Smith wrote to me about the absurdity; I wrote to Secretary Reich and by return mail Secretary Reich gave me the happy news that the regulation was history. The moral: it's possible—perhaps not easy—to rub elbows at Harvard without losing common sense.

Time, as I see it, has two functions; the first is to coordinate human activities and the second is to go by. And it refuses to go by without taking us with it. By November 1995 time was speeding up and I was slowing down—literally. My legs had sustained a lot of wear and tear early in life. One leg was broken and not properly cared for during my brief and undistinguished high school football career. And I had climbed far too many mountains far too fast on forced marches in the Far East as a teenage Marine infantryman in the Korean War.

By 1994 climbing stairs was more or less against my doctor's orders. Yet, seemingly every other day, the long escalator at the U.S. Capitol designed to convey representatives from the Rayburn Office Building tunnel toward the House floor was out of order. It was either climb fast enough to be on time or fail to do one's duty to cast constituents' congressional votes. My general health and life expectancy were far above average and my colleagues noticed nothing of the sheer pain it became for me to do the climbing. But I noticed; and I was tiring of these latter-day, escalator-failure forced marches. Moreover, on a flight to Washington, I looked up from a report I was reading, blinked at the forward bulkhead and, for an instant, literally did not know whether I was coming or going—whether it was Thursday evening or Tuesday morning. Those trips had been essentially weekly for a third of a century. Moreover, our sons, Andy and Bronco, were six and four years old and in need of a father for more than just parts of weeks. Kim and I talked about the possibility of winding up my work in Washington. We decided the time had come.

Rumors about my possible retirement circulated in Indianapolis. A lot of people flattered me by asking that I run again. I remembered what Harry Truman was said to have said to his attorney general, J. Howard McGrath, in 1951, when the latter urged the President to run for re-election: "This is a man-killing job; you wouldn't want them to carry me out of here feet first, would you?" One crisp day in September, Kim, the boys, and I were stopped by an elderly lady in a store. She looked at me and said, "Please run again." My answer was in the Truman style and it was a put-away, or so I thought. Glancing at Kim and then back to our stranger/friend, I asked triumphantly, "Would you want this woman to be a single mom?" The nice elderly lady's answer was an emphatic, "Yes!" I could only weakly reply, "Well, I shot my best shot."

The retirement news conference was planned to be in our home at the Fun Farm on November 18, 1995, well after the expected adjournment date for the first session of the One Hundred Fourth Congress. But what happened was reminiscent of the appointment I'd made with the TV station for eight P.M. on primary night, 1982.

Humans always hope we'll be in fine fettle for the few unusually important moments of our lives. But something about fate always seems somehow to deny us the ability to be our physical and mental best when those moments at last arrive. And so it was on the day I announced that I would step down.

Congress had not adjourned by the November date. Indeed, it was in session deep into the night before. I got to Indianapolis barely in time to shower and dress for the occasion. In addition to a large contingent of newspeople, some 150 of our warm and loving friends, Republicans and Democrats alike, attended the occasion. With a third of a century as a prelude, it was a dramatic moment when I walked into our great room to face the cameras. But I didn't and couldn't feel very dramatic; I was zonked, languid, wiped-out.

I had always been amused at members of Congress who held news conferences to announce what everybody already presumed, that they would be running for re-election. What news was there in something people already knew? The only reason for a news conference, I would say in those days, would be an announcement by the incumbent that she or he would not run again. By that reasoning, it was at last reasonable for me to have a news conference that day. But it became unreasonable the day before when the *Indianapolis Star* banner headline said I would announce my retirement in about nineteen hours.

Knowing that I would be physically worn out at 3:30 P.M. the next day and that my announcement would not be news anyway, I asked close friends to call the meeting off. They asked me to go ahead with it in order to answer questions including the inevitable one about whom, if anyone, I would support to be my successor. The answer to that particular one wouldn't be news, either. It was well-known in political circles that I would support Indianapolis Center Township Trustee Julia Carson, who was like a sister to me and had been since my earliest days in Congress when she was my coworker there. Still, all those friends had been invited; so on with the party. And even if I would be sluggish by the next afternoon, why not have some fun with it?

Since everybody assumed I would announce my retirement, I thought the conference would be more interesting if I seemed not to do so—at first. This was my sleepy statement to the assemblage:

> In 1992 and again in 1994, rumor had it that I was about to retire from Congress. On those occasions I paraphrased the words of Mark Twain: "Rumors of my retirement are greatly exaggerated." Now, once

again I mimic Mark. Rumors of my retirement next year are "greatly exaggerated."

Despite persistent and printed rumors to the contrary, I shall not retire from Congress in 1996. [appropriate pause] It will be *1997*. As prescribed by the Constitution and in the words of Thomas Jefferson, on Jan. 3, 1997 at twelve noon, I shall "go forth to accept a promotion from servant to [employer]."

On that January 3, God willing, I shall have intermittently been in government service for thirty-seven years, two as a teenage combat infantry Marine in the Korean War, three as a Marion County deputy sheriff, two as a member of the Indiana General Assembly, and thirty years as a member of the Congress.

To my severest critics, thirty minutes of my congressional service would probably be too much. But surely, even to my loving friends and supporters, thirty years are enough.

I am well aware of the fact that I would not have served even so much as thirty minutes were it not for the help of such people as Jim Beatty, Mary Berry, Jud Haggerty, Loretta Raikes, Jim Seidensticker, Gary Taylor, Jim Maley and an overwhelming number of other Democrats. I know also that I have been helped by a substantial number of Republicans and independents as well. To all these people who have been so wonderful to me, I say simply, but sincerely, thank you—thank you very much.

Mary Beth Schneider, the enormously talented and scintillating political editor and writer for the *Indianapolis Star*, asked, "When did you decide to retire?" In fun—she and her husband were two of my favorite people—I replied, "Just as soon as I read it in the *Indianapolis Star*. I figured that if the *Star* said it, it must be true."

"Why did you decide to leave Congress?" another newsperson asked. I quoted from the song, "Some Enchanted Evening": "'Fools give you reasons; wise men never try.'"

About a week later, the *Washington Post* ran a story about reasons for retirements from Congress. Each retiring member, except for me, was quoted for about a paragraph. Some said it wasn't fun anymore. It didn't seem that way to me. The civility had vanished, according to others. It seemed about the same through the years to me. There were always fifteen to twenty unpleasant members of the House and perhaps by the mid 1990s there were five or ten more, but the overwhelming majorities in both parties were decent and polite people from my point of view. Other reasons were cited. I was the last to be quoted. After all those ponderous and, I guess, apocalyptic reasons, the *Post* had me saying, "'Fools give you reasons; wise men never try.'" The arrangement in the story was not my doing and I was somewhat embarrassed—amused, too.

The same kind of journalistic juxtaposition happened earlier in the Indianapolis paper *Nuvo News Weekly* in connection with a city hall decision to rename the Hoosier Dome, home of the Indianapolis Colts. For about ten million dollars, the city agreed to call it the RCA Dome. Some citizens were unsympathetic. As a taxpayer, I thought it was a pretty good deal. *Nuvo* went to press with long quotations from a number of outraged people, ending the story with one from me: "A sports dome by any other name would smell as athletic."

My super sister in spirit, Julia Carson, won the Tenth District Democratic nomination for Congress in 1996. In November she was elected to be United States Representative Julia Carson and, yes, Kim and I smiled along with thousands of Julia's other admirers.

As my last days in Congress rushed to join the past, there were many requests by journalists for interviews. The Capitol Hill newspaper *Roll Call* asked the same question of each retiring Member, "What will you miss most and what will you miss least about Congress?" My published reply was:

> I shall miss most those rare moments when childish, partisan posturing is laid aside and sensible solutions to *real* problems are sought with civility. I shall miss least all the rest of the time.

The last statement I made in the well of the House was repeated on Public Television's *Washington Week In Review.* Having attended a farewell breakfast for retiring congressional Marines, hosted by the commandant of the Marine Corps, the dynamic General Charles C. Krulak, I decided it was time for my swan song to the U.S. House:

> Mr. Speaker, as I take my leave following thirty years in the House, I have two pieces of advice. First, get to know each other and you will like each other; there is a lot to like in each member of this institution. Second, say a prayer and do what you can for those unfortunate children of God who are addicted to tobacco and other deadly drugs. They will die before their time, or wish they could.

My good, wise, and funny friend, Congressman Jim Traficant of Ohio told me toward the end of my last session that he could not be in

Washington to keep a commitment to speak to a visiting group from his district. He wondered if there was any chance that I could fill in for him. I could and agreed to do so. The gathering was scheduled for a weekday at six in the evening and he had booked the cavernous Ways and Means Chamber for it. When I walked in the door that evening, I was blinded by floodlights mounted on TV cameras. And, just as I was supposed to be, I was surprised. It was a surprise party in recognition of my retirement. It was not small. Nearly three hundred people attended, friends ranging all the way back to my grade school days. My three best friends had drifted into Washington without giving the slightest advanced hint. They were Kim, Andy, and Bronco.

I don't believe the old TV show *This Is Your Life* ever had so many participants. Such distinguished citizens as my friends Senator Richard Lugar and Congressman John Myers said kind and generous things from the podium. One friend, Robby Nichols, came all the way from Sweden. Leading citizens such as Bob and Skip McKinney, Jim Morris, Buford Holt, and Jim and Joyce Brower traveled from Indiana. Staff people who had scattered to the far points of the compass were in that overwhelming, kaleidoscopic smile of faces. At one point in the proceedings, Kim narrated a style show in which the models—Andy and Bronco and their cute little cousins, Emma and Jake Landwerlen, paraded across the long, lower, curved table at which members of the committee sat for official business. What did they model? My relaxed wardrobe for days at the Fun Farm, which is to say some pretty ratty rags. Bronco was the exception. For him, Kim had dug out my old Marine Corps dress blues. At the sight of that, I said a swift and silent prayer that he and his cohorts would be spared the insane scourge of war.

The style show did not inspire awe, but it got endless and lusty laughter—pretty much at my expense. I always tended not to spend a lot on clothes and to wear them, well, with no expiration date. But when I spoke, I did make this reference to the not-quite-Paris review:

> One of the imponderables is: "Do the clothes make the man or does the man make the clothes?" I know how wretched most of these clothes must look to you, but once I don them, you have no idea how magnificent they look.

There was laughter and then a hundred different conversations. But, as was the case with the final passage of the firearms legislation, the sounds of that animated room shut down to "sounds of silence" in my ears. A third of a century had come and gone—quickly. Now it was over. And as I watched all those wonderful people moving about and thought about all the ones who were not there, but as those present, had always "been there" for me, I recalled the night I lost the election of 1972. I had asked that there be no tears for me, adding that "it ill-behooves one whose cup runneth over to complain simply because there is not still more." But there was still more, twenty-two years more, during which my constituents continued to give me the historic and precious privilege of serving in the highest councils of our Republic. My cup had not just barely overflowed; gallons had passed through it. And I knew that all those loving friends together with all those decent adversaries, many of whom became loving friends, were the nectar that flowed beyond the brim. My heartfelt gratitude runneth over.

Epilogue

KNOWING WHAT I KNEW THEN

NOTHING ELSE SO SYMBOLIZES leaving an office job as cleaning out one's desk. That was not necessary in my case because it really was *my desk*. I had bought it in Indianapolis during my two years as a private citizen in the early 1970s. When I went back to Washington in 1975, I brought the desk with me. Now, on the eve of 1997, I was leaving Washington again. Without opening the drawers, I just loaded the desk, my sofa, and other personal items into a U-Haul trailer van and headed home.

My poor little four-cylinder 1980 Oldsmobile Omega did its best to creep to the peaks of the Appalachians and keep up with the speed limit across the flatlands of Ohio. The "little engine that could" was passed on steep grades by heavily laden semitrailer-trucks. The good news was that my *rig* never actually went backward as it approached the crests of those mountains; the sobering news was that its speed fell to as low as twenty-one miles per hour before whizzing down another side of the mountain range roller coaster.

Once west enough to relax and enjoy the glaciated area of Interstate 70, I made up a parody of the song identified with one of the states through which I had just passed. The song's words, "Country road, take me home to the place I belong, West Virginia . . ." were written by three people: John Denver, Patty Nivert, and Bill Danoff. My parody, which seemed apropos to the moment, almost wrote itself: "Interstate, take me home to the place I belong, Indianapolis . . ."

Congressman Dan Burton and I participated in a weekly radio program on WIBC, Indianapolis, each Monday morning at nine. WIBC's wise and witty talents Terry Stacy and Steve Simpson were also part of the program. It was unofficially called *The Dan and Andy Show* and it was conducted in

Epilogue: Knowing What I Knew Then   443

the manner in which all discussions should be, with civility and good humor. When we disagreed, we did so in serious and polite demeanor, occasionally with the spicy seasoning of fun. On that final trip with the trailer, I got to Columbus just in time to join our program by pay phone, which I found in the lobby of a motel.

The program's first brief discussion was about my in-progress U-Haul adventure in moving. Then we moved on to whatever was the burning issue of the day. Next came the call-ins, the first from a lady who said, "I just think it's terrible the way the Democrats distort the Republican message." I was the first to respond: "Ma'am, I suspect that has been the lament of every political party since the dawn of organized society."

"Well," she said. "If the Republicans could just go on the radio and deliver their message for just an hour without being interrupted, people would all vote Republican."

"Well," I responded. "It's strange that you would pick WIBC to air your complaint. Rush Limbaugh is on here every afternoon for much more than one hour lecturing about the extended splendid qualities of the Republicans and the strictly icky essence of Democrats, uninterrupted and unfettered by the inconvenience of a spokesperson for the other side."

At that point, Steve Simpson said, "Well, Andy, we regard Rush as entertainment." To which I responded, "Yes, if you look at it right, I suppose you could call it entertainment." Now my friend Danny Burton weighed in: "Andy, are you saying Rush has no substance?"

"Certainly not," I replied. "I've seen him on television. He has lots of substance." Shortly before that exchange, Al Franken came out with a book entitled, *Rush Limbaugh is a Big, Fat Idiot*. Later, Limbaugh went on a successful diet. It is said that he became thin and handsome. At this writing, to the best of my knowledge, Franken has not yet written the sequel, *Rush Limbaugh is an Emaciated Moron*.

When my nephew, scholar and master carpenter Dan Landwerlen and I set the forms for the concrete slab of the new three-car garage at the Fun Farm, he had an idea that eventually proved invaluable to the writing of this volume. He suggested that we extend the west form and add a twelve-by-fifteen-foot room. The room sat unfinished for several years before I wired, insulated, and drywalled it. On the day I arrived at the Fun Farm from Washington with the U-Haul trailer, the room off the garage became the equivalent of an impoverished person's presidential library except that, in this case, it was something more like the scale model of our Washington congressional office. There were the same pictures, same sofa, and same desk, all transferred from Washington to Indianapolis roughly along the route of the old National Road. It was an office where I could work away from the downtown law office of my nephew Tom Landwerlen and his partner, Bob Rothkoph, where I became *of counsel*. Indeed, that little room dubbed the Sacrosanct—off limits to the unsupervised and therefore destructive adventures of our young sons, Andy and Bronco—was the place where I wrote this.

On those likely occasions when one of our young sons made off with a stapler or tape dispenser from the large worktable, I remembered to reach into a drawer of that erstwhile Capitol Hill desk and find replacements. Old friend and former fellow worker David Wildes could no longer place on that desk those mountains of mail for me to climb by writing. He was six hundred miles from Indianapolis, but I kept the room locked anyway.

The question most often asked me in public was, "How do you like retirement?" My answer became boilerplate: "I look forward to it; I sometimes wish I could go back to work and get some rest." When people think you have nothing to do, they ask you to do more than you can do. Such things pile up quickly. I lost count of the number of charitable boards on which I found myself. During my first year away from Congress, I gave questionable counsel to the law office, taught at three different universities, and served on the boards of those charities and the board of Bob McKinney's First Indiana Bank, one of the few remaining homegrown banks in Indianapolis. The speaking engagements seemed more numerous than they were when I was in office. And then there was that minor matter of the two minor sons in Kim's and my care. Andy and Bronco, having gone to preschool for four years, which brings to mind subbasements, were in the early years of their Washington Township public school careers at Crooked Creek Elementary.

At the end of his first day in the first grade at Crooked Creek, Bronco announced to his teacher, Mrs. Pat Sanders, "This is the best school I've been to yet." He had been to one other, the Orchard School, for his early childhood program. Orchard was excellent and so was Crooked Creek, but Bronco was a politician.

By and by, there came word that a bill was working its way through Congress to give a name to the main Indianapolis Post Office, mine. I confess I was touched—embarrassed, too. The chief sponsor was my erstwhile opponent and very good friend, Danny Burton. The bill was cosponsored by all the other members of the Indiana House delegation. Then came the nice ceremony beside the building at Illinois and South streets. Congresswoman Julia Carson and Congressman Burton both spoke, along with postal officials. Then I was called on to speak to the guests, who

Epilogue: Knowing What I Knew Then 🏛 445

included Kim, Andy, and Bronco; my sisters, Wanda and Marge; the latter's husband Tom, and many of my nieces and nephews as well as very many of my other dear friends.

Before beginning my remarks, I asked Kim to join me at the podium where I planted something just this side of an X-rated kiss. Finishing that pleasure, I settled into the solemn character of the occasion—or seemed to. I said to the assemblage, "This is a dream come true—playing *post office* at the post office."

Another cosponsor and the floor manager of the House bill was Congressman John H. McHugh of New York. I told my friends at the dedication that during my final term in office, John had been kind enough to help me with an idea I had about mailboxes. If a citizen bought a large enough box, why couldn't she or he receive in it the daily newspaper to which she or he subscribed? The law would have to be changed to make such common sense possible and the postmaster general opposed the proposal, arguing the "sanctity of the mailbox." To which I replied, "I'm all for the sanctity of the mailbox, but whose sanctity is it, that of the citizen who bought and paid for it, or the postmaster's?" The bill was still pending when I left office. I also said to the group at the assemblage, "A few days ago, I wrote to Congressman McHugh, 'Kid, I like your style; if you can't give a guy a mailbox, give 'im a post office.'" Then there was something serious to say:

> On his deathbed, my father said, "How could people call themselves *conservatives* and call for the dismantling of the two civic institutions most responsible for the success, prosperity and general well-being of our country?" He referred first to our American universal education system, which is mainly to say the public school system and, second, to the Postal Service. What would our work force be in the early twenty-first century, if, as in the dark ages, only those from well-financed families had been educated? As for Ben Franklin's American universal postal system which enables efficient written communication throughout our vast nation, I am still awed by the fact that on a cold and snowy night you can drop a piece of paper into a steel box on a lonely corner in New York and for a few cents have it delivered a few days later to your Aunt Emma in Muleshoe, Texas. These are institutions well worth *conserving*.

As all of us streamed out of the post office, my nephew Dan Landwerlen pointed catercorner across the street to something else that was an institution in Indianapolis, the Landwerlen Leather Company, his grandfather's long-standing family business. "Two corners to go," he remarked with his delightfully puckish smile.

Lyndon Baines Johnson said that even a blind hog will pick up an acorn now and then. And, although the hog is among the ten most intelligent lower animals on earth—the dog is not—I presume that my intellectual capacity has enabled me to pick up a few philosophical nuggets during those thirty years of my congressional service.

I have observed an elitist disposition, not suitable to a democracy, on the part of some people I have known in public life. Whether members of this minority, yet influential group, of public officials called themselves Conservatives or Liberals, many of them shared a common attitude about the public, an attitude best expressed by the bandit leader in the play *The Magnificent Seven*: "If God had not wanted them sheared, he would not have made them sheep." Sheared, that is, or slaughtered in the case of unnecessary war, trumped up and trumpeted by unworthy politicians seeking self-aggrandizement. My dad used to speak of drawing room officials who were "for the people so long as they didn't have to get acquainted with them."

As time goes by, those who had the arrogance to visit inhumanity upon their fellow humans have usually, but not always, been relegated to history's balcony for buffoons. Adlai Stevenson said, "It is better to fail in a cause that will ultimately succeed than to succeed in a cause that will ultimately fail."

Despite some frightening signs, there is still cause for faith in the future. Heed these wise words of Hoosier broadcaster Elmer Davis: "This country was not created by cowards and it will not be maintained by them, either."

Out of the crowds that have included cowards, heroes have also emerged, heroes who understood my mother's maxim that "Courage is fear that has said its prayers." One of the stories about Illinois Governor John Peter Altgeld is well known. He commuted the death sentences of anarchists who had been convicted, by insufficient evidence, of the Chicago Hay Market murders. In the bargain, Governor Altgeld was vilified and, as happened to John Adams, the elder, was not even welcome at his successor's inauguration. Since Paul Harvey was an Illinoisian, too, let us borrow his phrase and tell "the rest of the story."

In those days, the railroad industry was king, king enough to have got a biased bill through the Illinois Legislature. But that bill, whose purpose was further to enrich the railroads at the consumers' unfair expense, could not become law without Governor Altgeld's signature. According to the late and splendid Senator Paul Douglas, Governor Altgeld was offered an

Epilogue: Knowing What I Knew Then 447

enormous bribe to sign the bill. With seriously failing health, no wealth and the ingratitude, indeed the hatred, of most of his fellow Illinoisans, whose freedom he had so courageously advanced, the governor hesitated. The would-be bribers handed him the key to a safety deposit box that contained several hundred thousand dollars and suggested he think it over during the weekend.

Something foreboding happened; the governor took the key and the happy miscreants withdrew. After all, look what the governor had to gain; and what did he have to lose? Did he owe an ungrateful public anything? Officially yes—he was elected to do his duties honestly right up to the finish. Unofficially and emotionally, the answer most would give was essentially no. But he did owe something to one person, himself. He owed himself respect, which is to say a clear conscience. The bill was on his desk Monday morning and the bad guys were among those present when he quietly returned the key and killed the bill by veto. He died in 1902 at the age of fifty-five, having lived out the rest of his life in physical wretchedness, but spiritual peace.

Kipling explains that quality of soul over sustenance:

> Force your heart and nerve and sinew to serve your turn long after they are gone. And so hold on when there is nothing in you, except the will that says to them, "hold on."

It would have been so easy for that martyred public servant to secure a sumptuous life in his declining years, but because of his "heart and nerve and sinew," he was able to "hold on" to his decency forever. With some people, when it's easy to steal, it's hard not to. We call that, "temptation." Some of the officials I've known who surrendered to such temptation and took bribes did so partly because they chose life-styles beyond their legitimate means—home dinner parties with catering cooks and white-jacketed waiters at Washington prices. Such social climbers piled up terrifying and hopeless debt with only one thing left to hock, their souls. Very few seemed to have the fortitude to reform, to jump off the "Hell-bound Train" and choose the good life as Kin Hubbard's Smiths did:

> Th' Smith family who dropped out of sight six weeks ago wuz discovered yesterday livin' within its means.

It is said that a person is rich not according to what she or he has, but according to what he or she can do without. We are the slaves of others only to the extent that we find indispensable the things only they can let us have. The key to the contented life is constant reexamination of what material things we perceive to be indispensable. Our Tenth District congressional office almost always came in first or second among the most frugal in the nation. Yet, each time we looked again, we found new ways to eliminate wasting the taxpayers' money. While there is no such thing as perfection in this life, there can be continual progress toward it and the splendid contentment rectitude brings.

When I entered Congress, there were dreams to be clothed with reality. Some of them were, and they have long since become part of our proud American institutional heritage. Others remain on the agenda, goals for other officials to advance.

"The world is very different now," said John F. Kennedy on that snowy January day in long-ago 1961. He said it when VCRs, microchips, family camcorders, word processors that type what the human voice says, and the Internet were unperceived by most of the world's population. The world will always be very different at any given *now*. And depending on which way you point your view, it can either be expected to be different for the worse or the better in the broad and swift sweep of time. For the pessimist, that "thin veneer of civilization" my dad talked about, is getting thinner. For the optimist, it is, on balance, thickening.

The only thing that takes less time than you thought is life. Which is to say that nothing goes past so fast as the past. The life of my congressional service took a long time, yet, in a way, less time than I had anticipated. Is there a happy ending to all this? No. And there isn't a sad one, either, because there isn't any ending at all. The philosopher tells us that the most descriptive thing about life is that it goes on. It goes on with or without us. For some, life is always the hopeless and therefore unenjoyable calm before the storm; for others, including me, life is the hope-filled storm before the thoroughly enjoyable calm. As we weather the storms and celebrate the calms of our future, may Almighty God grant us the wisdom and the love "to live together in peace as good neighbors."

Andy Jacobs, Jr.
Major Legislative Achievements

- Helped write the 1965 Voting Rights Act
- Led House debate that helped get U.S. out of Vietnam
- Sponsored law that allowed Smithsonian to acquire J. K. Lilly gold coin collection
- Only U.S. Representative from Indianapolis in the twentieth century to have been elected by colleagues to the U.S. House Ways and Means Committee
- Nationally praised as being one of the top two most frugal members of Congress
- Credited with securing House passage of revolutionary cost-saving prospective payment reform in Medicare
- Elected by colleagues both as chairman of the Medicare Subcommittee and later, the Social Security Subcommittee
- Chief sponsor of law to stop overpayments to physicians under Medicare, resulting in the American Medical Association's spending one third of a million dollars in 1996 to defeat Jacobs (effort failed)
- Chief House sponsor of historic change of Social Security Administration into an independent agency
- Chief sponsor of law requiring U.S. government to issue actual bonds to Social Security for money borrowed
- Chief sponsor of law against mail solicitations which pretend to be official documents of the U.S. government
- Chief House sponsor of law forbidding Social Security disability benefits to prison felons
- Chief House sponsor of law to correct "nanny tax" fiasco
- Chief sponsor of law that repealed withholding tax on savings accounts—opposed by chairman of Ways and Means Committee and President Reagan
- Originated law to pay U.S. death benefits to dependents of safety officers killed in the line of duty

- Authored law to prohibit the IRS from taking 100 percent of a paycheck for delinquent taxes
- Chief sponsor of law restoring Social Security benefits to independent insurance agents
- Chief sponsor of law allowing volunteer fire departments to issue tax-free bonds for the purchase of real estate and equipment
- Chief sponsor of law ending age-old immunity of federal employees from court process to collect just debts owed by them
- Chief sponsor of law establishing Father's Day as a legal holiday
- In 1976 began the movement for a so-called balanced budget amendment to the U.S. Constitution to forbid federal government borrowing and to require repayment of the national debt by installments (The Payment Book Amendment)
- Made the speech in the U.S. credited with blocking a huge sales tax boost on groceries in the District of Columbia.
- Praised by three Indianapolis Republican Mayors for effectively protecting Indianapolis interests in Washington.

Index

Abernathy, Rev. Ralph David, 167–168
Abernethy, Thomas G., 125, 126, 127
Abzug, Bella, 196, 332
Adams
  Brock, 132
  Mary Moriarity, 322
Agnew, Spiro, 97, 159–160, 223
Alexander, Shana, 196
Alig, Neil, 192
Allen
  Buddy, 72
  George E., xxviii
Altgeld, John Peter, 446–447
"America the Beautiful.", 380–383
Anderson
  John B., 172, 280
  William R., 129–130
Andrews, Mike, 404
Anthony, Beryl, Jr., 404
Applewhite
  Jake, 204
  Suzy, 204
Archer, Bill, 251, 254, 354, 402, 403, 429, 430
Armey, Dick, 370–371
AuCoin, Les, 239
Ayres, George "Dutch", 41–42, 55, 69, 80, 81

Badham, Bob, 253
Bailey, Johnathan, 400
Baker
  Bobby, 85
  Howard, xxiv
  James, 355, 391
Baker v. Carr, 89–90
Barkley, Alben W., 176
Barnett, Jerry, 144
Barram, David, 187
Barrett, Judy, 394
Barton
  John, 131
  Marian, 41
  Patrick J., 31, 41
Bates, Katharine Lee, 381
Bay of Pigs, xiii
Bayh
  Birch E., xiii, xvi, 35, 36, 56, 57, 59, 64, 65, 66, 68–69, 85, 107, 118, 131, 167, 168, 169, 180, 187, 204, 262–263, 269, 400
  Evan, 393, 399
  Marvella, 128
  Susan, 399
Bayt, Phil, 30, 42, 76–77, 79–81
Beatty, James W., xx, 30, 66–68, 69, 70, 76, 80, 81, 87, 91, 113, 117, 121, 131, 157, 164, 191, 200, 223, 231, 270, 316, 318, 322, 324, 338, 370, 379, 438
Bell
  Griffin, 223
  M. Walter, 31, 89
Bennett, Charles, xv, 307, 356
Benton, William, 365
Bentsen, Lloyd, 54, 214, 231, 354
Bepko, Gerald, 400
Berry, Mary, 438
Bilirakis, Mike, 420
Blandina, Sam, 197
Blankenship, Elmer, 198
Bob Jones University, 301, 303
Boehm, Ted, 197
Bolling, Dick, 289–290
Borski, Bob, 421
Bosma, Charles, 315, 329
Boswell, Charles, 56–58, 59, 76
Bowen, Otis, 47, 224, 225, 311
Boyd, Rozelle, 322
Brademas, John, xv
Bradshaw, Jack, 54, 56
Brady Law, 390
Branigan, Roger, 85, 116–118, 137–138, 142, 143, 208
Bray
  Bill, xv, 132, 176, 216, 314
  Esther, 216, 217
Breskow, Shell, 120
Brink, Sue, 203
Brinkley, David, 380
Broadhead, Bill, 304
Broder, David, 291, 349
Brokaw, Tom, 217, 343, 414
Brooks
  Bill, 38
  Gene E., 348
Brower, Jim & Joyce, 440
Brown
  Rev. Andrew, 343–345
  H. Rap, 133
  Hank, 386
  Jerry, 242–244
Broyhill, Joel T., 126
Bruce
  Donald C., xx, 59, 61–62, 62–63
  Lenny, xxiv
Brydenthal, Max, 113, 198
Buchanan, Pat, 159
Buckley v. Valejo, 62, 208
Buckley, William F., Jr., 266
Bulen, Keith, xxxii, 198
Bunning, Jim, 254, 428–429, 429
Burke, Jimmy, 232–234
Burkert, Don, 25
Burrell, Winnie, 221
Burton, Dan, xiv, 309, 317, 393, 442, 443, 444
Bush, George, 298–299, 320, 362, 391, 394, 403, 415, 416
Butler, Phyllis. *See* Coelho, Phyllis "Muffet."
Buxton, Lealand, 35–37
Byrant, Anita, 258

C-Five, 162, 191, 213–214, 412
Caldwell, Howard, 325, 326
Califano, Joe, 229
Campaign, Jamison, xxi–xxii
Cantwell, Paul, 92, 94, 195
Capehart, Homer E., xiii, 59, 64, 65
Carroll, Mike, xiv, 326, 328
Carson, Julia M., xxxvii, xxxvii–xxxviii, 68, 93, 338, 400, 412, 437, 439, 444
Carter, James E., 222, 228, 233, 246, 250, 255–256, 371
Carville, James, 423

451

Celler, Emanuel, 1, 108, 119, 122–123, 169, 260
Chandler, Harry, xix
Chase, Salmon P., 170
Chicago Tribune, xix, 6
Children's Museum of Indianapolis, 406
Christian Anti-Communist Crusade, 15
Christian Coalition, 145–146
Church, Frank, 285
Cimmons, Marlene, 217
Claise, Delmer, 342
Clark, Marian, 155, 220
Claytor, Gram, 216–217
Clinton
 Hillary, 84
 William J., xv, xviii, xxviii, 8, 402, 414, 416–417, 420
Clooney, Rosemary, 385
Coats, Dan, 379
Coelho
 Phyllis "Muffet", 39, 69, 75, 93, 221, 385
 Tony, 385
Cohen, Richard, 264, 265
Cole, Ben, xix, 62
Coleman, Carl, 186
Colmer, William M., 182
Columbia Journalism Review, 138
Compton, Mildred, 406
Conable, Barber B., Jr., 255
Conrad, Mary Lou, 64
Conyers, John, Jr., 106
Cooley, Wester, 32
Coolidge, J. Calvin, 157, 288
Corman, James C., xv, 128, 155, 181, 319
Cox, James M., 157
Coyne, Bill, 421
Craig, Larry, 420
Cunningham
 Duke, 387
 James F., 69

Dalmbert, Bob, 46–47
Daly, George, 73
Daniels, Cliff, 158
Davidson, James Dale, 238
Davis
 Elmer, 105, 254
 James, 350
Dean, John, xviii
Delaney, James J., 247

Dellems, Ron, 64, 196, 203
Denny, George, 73
Denton, Winfield K., 116–117
Derwinski, Ed, 180
Detroit Free Press, 214
Dewey, Thomas E., 3–4, 6, 55
DeWine, Mike, 380
Dick, Bess, 122
Dillon, Jack, xxii, 30, 120, 121, 352
Dingell, John D., 260–261
Dirksen, Everett McKinley, xvii, 95
Dole, Robert, xxiv, 160, 307, 310
Donaldson, Sam, 380
Dornan, Bob, 382
Dortch, Carl, 262–263
Douglas
 Helen Gahagan, xxix, 10
 William O., 171, 172
Dozier, William, 104
Duffy, Reid, 325
Dukakis, Michael, xv

E. F. Hutton Bond Brokerage, 275–277, 278–287
Edwards, Frank, 4–5, 37, 76
Eisenhower, Dwight D., xxvii, xxviii, 12, 14
Elliott, Bob, 19
Endangered Species Act, 259
Ensign, John, 428
Equal Rights Amendment, 122
Espy, Mike, 110
Evans
 David, 272, 285, 314, 317, 318, 322, 324, 325, 326, 338
 Lane, xv
Evers, Medgar, 133

Fager, Chris, 145
Fairchild, Frank, 73
Fairness Doctrine, xvi
Fauntroy, Rev. Walter, 167
Fechtman, Bill, 197
Feeney, Al, 3
Feinstein, Dianne, 420
Findwick, Millicent, 218–219
Fithian, Floyd J., 248–249
Flippo, Ronnie, 404
Flood, Daniel J., 114–115
Foley, Thomas, 215, 404–406, 425

Fontroy, Walter, 127
Ford
 Gerald R., 171, 173, 179, 215, 222, 223, 226
 Harold, 110
 Jim, 343
Fort Wayne Journal-Gazette, xxxvi
Fortas, Abe, 128, 170
Franken, Al, 443
Franzene, Dick, 93
Frazier, Douglas, 232
Fulbright, William, 144
Fulton, Dick, 135

Ganes, Ed, 360, 363
Gasaway, Bessie, 79
Gaylord, Frank C. II, 385
Gelarden, Joe, 243
Gephardt, Dick, 257, 404
Gerhart, John, 362
Gibbons, Sam, 384, 400
Gilroy, Sue Ann, 399
Gingrich, Newt, 342–343, 345, 348
Glickman, Dan & Rhoda, 258
Goldsboro Christian Schools, 301, 303
Goldwater, Barry, 82, 85, 86, 88, 89, 288, 405
Goodwin, Richard, 142, 145
Graham, Fred, 267
Grant, Ulysses S., xii
Green, Bill, 232
Grider, George W., 129
Griffiths, Martha, 122, 123–124, 213, 301
Gross, H. R., 95, 180
Gude, Gilbert, 125, 126
Guider, Cliff, 72

Haggerty, Jud, xvi, xxiii, 35, 56, 58–59, 67, 68, 69, 80, 93, 131, 294, 349, 352, 438
Halberstam, David, 268
Hall
 Durward G., 180
 Leonard, 30, 157
Hamilton
 Alexander, 296
 Lee, xv, 34, 132, 149, 150
 Nancy, 150
Handley, Harold W., 38
Hardin, Percy, 31
Harding, Warren G., 157

Index

Hart
  Gary, 160
  Jane, xxv
  Phil, xxv
Hartke, R. Vance, 186, 222, 223, 425
Harvey, Paul, 174
Hatcher, Richard, 120–121
Hathaway, Bill, xxiv, xxxvi
Hay, John, 160
Hayes, Phil, 268
Hays, Wayne, 153–155, 219–221, 345
Heckler, Peggy, 374
Heckman, Fred, 217, 285
Helms, Jesse, 236, 301, 311
Hillis, Bud, xv
Hiss, Alger, xxiii, 196
Hobson, Julius, 167
Hogan, Larry, 129–130
Holder
  Cale, 137, 148
  Neil, 38
Holifield, Chet, 290
Holt, Buford, 198, 224, 440
Holtzman, Elizabeth, 123
Hoover, J. Edgar, 127–128, 128, 129, 130, 144
Hope, Bob, 385
Horton
  Frank, 125
  Willie, xv
Horvath, Janos, xiv, 413
Hudnut, William H. III, xiv, xxx, xxxiii, xxxvii, 184–185, 188, 191, 196, 199–200, 230, 262, 350, 393, 406
Hulbert, Mark, 238, 371
Humphrey, Hubert H., 131, 135, 141
Hunt
  Al, 187, 213
  Lester, 54–55
Hutchinson, William L. "Big Bill", 8

Iacocca, Lee, 407
Indianapolis Business Journal, 194, 431
Indianapolis News, xvii, xxvi, 2, 54, 112, 144, 283, 284, 347
Indianapolis Star, xvii, xix, xx, xxiii, xxv, xxviii, xxxi, 2, 42, 54, 55, 57, 59, 76–77, 79, 96, 113, 138–139, 144, 146, 147, 215, 274, 282, 283, 325, 356–358, 438
Indianapolis Times, 2, 15, 55, 59, 87

Jackson, Jesse, 54
Jacobs
  Andrew III, 75, 396–397, 398, 400, 444
  Andrew, Sr., xii–xiii, xvii, xix, xxx, 1, 3, 4, 8–11, 13, 15, 16, 27–28, 29, 43–44, 48–49, 50, 55, 56, 66, 71, 73, 77, 90, 96, 116, 153, 188–190, 192, 193–194, 235, 262, 313–314, 362
  Elizabeth, 71
  Harvey, 284
  Joyce, 73
  Karl, 3, 71
  Katherine, 71
  Kim Hood, 4, 68, 392–397, 399, 400, 440, 445
  Maud, 71
  Mike, 71
  Steven, 81, 397–398, 400, 444
  Wanda, 445
Janssen, Clayton R., 362
Jenkins, Ed, 295, 403
Jenner, William E., 14
Jiang Zemin, 8
John Birch Society, xiii, 54, 60, 62
Johnson
  Charlie, 87
  Jed, Jr., 132, 166, 167
  Lyndon Baines, xxi, xxii, 68, 75, 81, 83, 84–85, 91, 99, 105–106, 117, 137, 143, 149, 208
Jones, Bill, 51
Jordan
  Barbara, 203
  Hamilton, 229
Junior Village, 166

Kanjorski, Paul, 421
Keating, Thomas R., xxxv
Kelly, Kay, 379
Kemp, Jack, xxxii, 215, 293

Kennedy
  Edward "Ted", 142, 188, 232, 266
  John F., xiii, 8, 41, 49–50, 66, 68, 82, 133, 135, 215, 269, 402, 448
    assassinated, 74–75
  Joseph, 421
  Robert F., 133, 137, 138–139, 142, 269
  Rose, 50
Kerrey, Bob, 414
Kiker, Douglas, 105
Kilpatrick, James J., 380
King, Martin Luther, Jr., 133, 167, 266
Kintzele, Henry J. "Bud", Jr., 40
Kirwan, Michael J., 108–109
Kissinger, Henry, 245, 250
Knauer, Virginia, 162
Kofodimos, John, 367
Kornegay, Horace R., 312
Kraft, Joseph, 156, 226
Krulak, Gen. Charles C., 439
Kunzel, Eric, 380, 381
Kuralt, Charles, 380

Laffer Curve, 295, 296, 431
Landrum-Griffin Law, 41
Landwerlen
  Dan, 68, 104, 132, 188, 213, 326, 443, 445
  Greg, 68, 188, 197, 213, 291, 326
  Marjorie Jacobs, 68, 338, 445
  Martin, xxvi, 68, 104, 132, 188, 213, 289, 326
  Tom, Jr., 68, 104, 132, 188, 202, 213, 248, 324, 326, 444
  Tom, Sr., 445
Law, Merit, 38
Lebanon Reporter, 230–231
Lee, J. Bracken, xxv
Lehner, George, 362
Leibowitz, Irving, 55, 66
Lesinski, John, 8
Lewis, John, 105
Lienert, Walter & Mary, 315
Lincoln, Abraham, xxxix, 1, 89
Liuzzo, Viola, 105
Lloyd
  Daisy, 87
  Frank, 113, 394

Long
 Jill, xv, xxxvi, 7, 378–380
 Russell B., 228
Los Angeles Times, xix
Louisville Courier Journal, 58
Lowenstein, Allard K., xxiii, 142, 149, 153, 154, 195–196, 243, 264–269, 351
Luce, Henry R., xix, xxvii
Lugar, Richard G., xiv, 181, 185, 224, 350, 415, 440
Lyst, Jerry, 80

Madden, Ray J., 141, 182
Maddox, Lester, 140
Maehling, Walter, 44
Maeterlinck, Maurice, 210
Mahern
 Ed, 316
 Louis, 139, 141, 158, 180, 181, 204, 326, 378
Mahoney, Florence, 157
Maines, Charlie, 58
Maley, Jim, 338, 438
Mannweiler, David, xxxv
Margolies-Mezvinsky, Marjorie, 417
Marr, Louise, 322
Marshall, George C., 14
Martel, Arlene, 100, 103
Maugham, Somerset, 199
Mauldin, Bill, 12, 143, 389
Maxa, Rudy, 155, 220
Mays, Janice, 280, 385, 411
McCarthy
 Coleman, 355
 Eugene, 137, 138, 141, 142, 144
 Joseph, xxxvi, 7, 16, 30, 144, 365
McCarty, Virginia Dill, 222, 379
McCloskey
 Frank, xv, 340, 341–342, 345, 347, 348, 349
 Pete, xv, 266, 360–362, 363, 365–366, 368
McConnell, Russell V., 381
McCormack, John W., xxxiii, 114, 118, 173
McCormick, Robert R., xix
McCune, Bob & Priscilla, 412
McDade, Joe, 110, 420
McDaniel, Doug, 349, 368

McDonald, Larry, 63
McGee, Dave, 339
McGeever, Pat & Rachel, 113
McGinn, Dan, 332
McGovern, George, 140, 184, 188
McGrath, J. Howard, 436
McGuire, Andy, 229
McHale, Paul, 421
McHugh, John H., 445
McIntosh, Dave, 428
McKinney
 Frank, Jr., 328
 Robert, 143, 440, 444
 Skip, 440
McMillan, John L., 125–126, 127, 229
McNamar, R. T., 302
Mead, Bob, 88
Meany, George, 5
Melchert, Bruce, 317
Merchenson, Clint, xxi, xxii
Miami Herald, 214
Mikva, Abner, 116, 153, 181, 201, 204
Miller
 Bill, 85
 Marsha, 396
Minor, Helen, 259–260
Mondale, Walter, 234
Moore, Henson, 356
Morris
 Greg, 351
 Jim, 231, 440
Moynihan, Pat, 254, 335
Mudd, Roger, 293
Mullin, Owen, xxviii
Murphy, Andy, 393
Murrow, Edward R., 13, 60
Murtha, Jack, 421
Muskie, Edmund S., 145
Myers
 Bud, 87, 93, 139, 181, 194
 John, xv, 440

Natcher, Bill, 208, 282
National Rifle Association, 422
National Taxpayers Union, 238, 242, 243, 279–280
Nature, Bill, xv
Nelson, Bill, 388
New York Times, 94, 159, 276
New York Times v. Sullivan, xxx, 364

Newman, Edwin, 150
Niblack, John L., 212
Nichols, Robby, 440
Nixon, Richard M., xxx, 13, 50, 66, 144–145, 148, 152, 153, 158, 163, 184, 197, 199, 223
Noe, Cathy, 254, 332, 411
Nolan, Alan T., 197, 249
Novak, Robert, 361, 364

O'Bannon, Frank, 84
O'Brien
 Jack, 118
 Larry, 88, 135
O'Hara, Barratt, 116
Olson, Kathryn, 254, 411
O'Neal, Robert A., 17, 43
O'Neill, Tip, 228, 229, 230, 307, 343
Operation Head Start, 99
Orr, Robert, 406

Pantzer, Kurt, 113
Parent, Tawn, 194
Parker, Crawford, 37–38
Peak, Betty, xxxix
Peck, Gregory, 319
Pegler, Westbrook, 8–9
Pennington, Judy, 198
Pennson, Valerie, 228, 259
Peterson
 Bart, xxxviii
 Esther, 258
Pfau, Vic, 82
Phillips, Kevin, 353
Pickle
 Byrel, 234
 J. J. "Jake", 233, 234–235, 254, 309, 405, 411
Pigeon, Jeff, 412
Poff, Dick, 169
Poshard, Glenn, xv, 318
Powell
 Adam Clayton, 118–120
 Jody, 229
Powell v. McCormack, 119, 341
Proxmire, William, xxxv
Pulliam
 Eugene C., xvii, xviii–xix, xxi, xxiii, 42, 55, 76, 77, 79, 88
 Eugene S., xix, xx, xxxv, 283

INDEX 455

Quayle
　Dan, xvi, 7, 54, 65, 269, 280, 349, 378, 379, 391–392, 394
　Marilyn, 394
Quinn, Jane Bryant, 298

Raikes
　Loretta, 68, 93, 315, 338, 379, 413, 438
　Paul, 412
Rangel, Charlie, 304, 369
Ransom, William, 73
Rarick, John, 63–64
Rayburn, Sam, 208
Reagan
　Nancy, 224, 288, 352
　Ronald, xv, xviii, 4, 5, 47, 103, 179, 226–227, 241, 246, 287, 288–289, 293, 295, 304, 334, 335, 352, 353, 358, 371
Reese, Tom, 132, 181
Regan, Donald, 299–300
Regula, Ralph, xv
Reich, Robert B., 435
Reid, T. R., 367
Renahan, Art & Sally, 316
Reno, Janet, 420
Reston, James "Scotty", xxxv, 83
Rettig, Paul, 332
Reuther, Walter, 32
Riggs, Milana, 194
Robertson, Pat, 49, 145
　libel suit, 359–368
Robinson, Dr. Earle U., Jr., 395
Rockefeller, Nelson, 153
Roemer
　Buddy, 292
　Joe, 221, 281
　Tim, xv
Rooney
　John J., 168
　Pat, 433
Roos, Charles, 349
Roosevelt
　Franklin D., 53, 92, 157, 171
　Roosevelt
　James, 252, 253–254
Rostenkowski, Dan, 284, 289, 290, 303, 319–321, 331, 384, 404, 407–409, 411
Rothkoph, Bob, 444

Roush, Ed, xv
Rousselot, John, 63
Rowan, Hobart, 334
Royko, Mike, 391

Salb, Richard, 78
Samuelson, Howard, 196
Sanders, Pat, 444
Scanlon, Mike, xx
Schaefer, William, 382, 383
Scheuer, Jim, 201
Schieffer, Bob, 354
Schmultz, Edward, 302
Schneider, Mary Beth, 438
Schreiber, Bill, 317, 322, 325
Schricker, Henry, 38
Schroeder, Pat, 335
Schuller, Rev. Robert, 382
Schumer, Charlie, 422
Schwarz, Dr. Fred, 15
Seidensticker
　James P., Jr., 2, 46, 49, 50, 51, 52, 53–54, 56, 68, 76, 80, 86, 121, 338, 347, 379, 438
　James P., Sr., 79
Seigel, Charley, 127
Sells, Dallas, 40, 198
SerVaas, Beurt, xv
Severeid, Eric, 50
Sexton, Larry, 30–31, 81
Shannon, Jim, 235, 405
Sharp, Phil, xv, 326
Shellabarger, Samuel, xxviii
Shonaker, Chet, 79
Shula, Bob, 319
Silberman, Charles, 99
Silver, Greg, 113
Simpson, Steve, 442, 443
Singleton, Pete, 254
Sisk, Bernie, 161
Slinger, Jimmy, 79
Smaltz, Donald, 110
Smith
　Asa J., 28–30
　Larry, 380
　Margaret Chase, xxxvi
　Marie, 78
　Maude, 17
　Neal, xv
Smothers, Tommy, 132
Snyder, Alberta M., 415
Solomon, Gerald, 295
Sorenson, Ted, xii
Spencer, Herb, xxxiii
Spicklemire, Steve, 194
Stacy, Terry, 442

Stahl, Leslie, 376
"Star Spangled Banner", 380, 381, 382
Stark, Pete, 376
Staten, Bob, 80
Steffen, Andy, 192
Steinem, Gloria, 218
Stephenson, D. C., 29
Stern, Carl, 169–170
Stevenson, Adlai E., xii, xv, xvii, 12, 13, 56, 163
Stivers, Vic, 121
Stockman, David, 173, 374
Stokes, Louis, 351
Stoner, John B., 211
Strange, Wanda Jacobs, 71
Strongin, David, 386
Sweezy, John, 28, 315, 340
Symington, Jim, 180, 213–214

Tabbert, Don, xiv, xxii, xxxiii, 83, 87, 88
Taylor
　Rev. Fred, 166, 167
　Gary, 336, 338, 379, 438
Thatcher, Margaret, 104
Thickston, Walt, 25
Thomas
　Bill, 309, 310
　Clarence, 170
　Danny, 381
Thomson, Frank, 220
Thurmond, Strom, 107, 301
Tippit, J. D., 74
Titcomb, Caldwell, 382
Titsworth, Tom, 30, 157
Tobin, Dan, 55
Traficant, Jim, xv, 420, 439
Traub, Pat, 247
Travers, Mary, 266
Truman
　Harry S, xvii, xxiv, xxvii, 3–4, 5, 6–7, 11, 158, 436
　Margaret, 158
Tuck, Bill, 106–107
Tunney, John, 118, 154, 180
Tyler, Gary, 61

U-Two, 191
Udall, Morris K., xxxiii, 168, 179–180
Ulen, Pat, 379
Ullman, Al, 234, 238–240, 255, 269–270, 277

USS *Indianapolis*, 216

Valente, Jack, 85
Van Deering, Lionel, 132
Vance, Beth, 281
Vanik, Charlie, 173
Vaughn, Robert, 121
Vest, Jason, 423
Visclosky, Pete, xv, 361, 420
Von Hoffman, Nicholas, 217
Vonnegut, Kurt, Jr., 196

Walgren, Doug, 268
Wall Street Journal, xxviii, 407, 409
Wallace, George, xxvi, 79
Walsh, Lawrence, xviii
Warren
  Bill, 380
  Earl, 170, 208
  Wilma, 93, 380
Washington Post, 5, 7, 16, 92, 134, 159, 160, 172, 173, 236, 321, 404, 422, 438
Washington Star, 7
Watergate, xxvi, 197, 199
Waxman, Henry, 331
Webber, Vin, 380, 381
Weiland, Mary Ellen, 53
Welch
  Bob, 328
  Ginny, 81
  Patty, 70, 113, 379
Weliever, John, 328
Wells, James, 26, 377
Welsh, Matthew E., 51, 57, 79, 80, 188
Werner, Charles, 359
Weyrich, Paul, 365
Whitney, Becky, 305
Whitten, Jamie L., 229–230
Wiggins, Chuck, 120
Wilder, Douglas, 414
Wildes, David, 345–346, 444
Will, George, 104, 380
Williams, Susan, 322
Wilson
  Charles "Goodtime Charlie", 351, 396
  John V., 43, 65, 66
Wise
  Robert, 254
  Sandy, 254, 332, 400, 411
Woods, Gen. Stephen, Jr., 156
Woodworth, Larry, 232

Wright, Jim, 292
Wyman, Louis C., 171–172

Yarrow, Peter, 266
Yates
  Ed, 198
  Sid, 114
Young
  Andrew, 266
  Bill, 420

Zazas
  George, 54, 55–56, 66–67
  Sylvia, 113